The Book of Job

The Book of Job

A History of Interpretation and a Commentary

Stephen J. Vicchio

FOREWORD BY
Edward L. Greenstein

WIPF & STOCK · Eugene, Oregon

THE BOOK OF JOB
A History of Interpretation and a Commentary

Copyright © 2020 Stephen J. Vicchio. All rights reserved. Except for brief quotations in critical publications or reviews, no part of this book may be reproduced in any manner without prior written permission from the publisher. Write: Permissions, Wipf and Stock Publishers, 199 W. 8th Ave., Suite 3, Eugene, OR 97401.

Wipf & Stock
An Imprint of Wipf and Stock Publishers
199 W. 8th Ave., Suite 3
Eugene, OR 97401

www.wipfandstock.com

PAPERBACK ISBN: 978-1-7252-5725-2
HARDCOVER ISBN: 978-1-7252-5726-9
EBOOK ISBN: 978-1-7252-5727-6

Manufactured in the U.S.A.   03/03/22

This book is dedicated to the memory of my former Hebrew teacher, Professor William F. Albright.

Contents

Foreword by Edward L. Greenstein | ix
Preface | xi
Abbreviations | xvi

Part I: The History of Interpreting the Book of Job | 1
Part II: The Book of Job Commentary | 46
Hapax Legomena in the Book of Job | 298
Aramaisms in the Book of Job | 304

Endnotes | 308
Index of Foreign Words | 389
Appendix A: Theological Responses of the Principal Characters | 397
Appendix B: The Book of Job as a Law Case | 399
Bibliography | 403
Index | 415

Foreword

MY FAVORITE TEXTUAL FORMAT is that of the Rabbinic Bible—*Miqra'ot Gedolot*. In this late medieval or early modern work, the text of the Hebrew Bible is surrounded on the page by the standard Aramaic translation (the Targum), the commentary of Rashi (R. Solomon Itzhaki, 11th-century France), and, in larger editions, a host of additional classic medieval commentaries, such as those of Abraham Ibn Ezra (12th-century Spain and Europe), Ramban (R. Moshe ben Maimon, 13th-century Spain and Israel), and others. The impression is created that the interpreters are contending with each other in seeking to draw out or provide the most helpful and relevant meaning of a word, phrase, verse, or passage. The student or reader is at first glance given notice that there is no single or definitive meaning of the text. Even the greatest of exegetes propose conflicting interpretations.

The book of Job has been interpreted by many scores of commentators over the centuries; and even in our day, when we are aware of so much that has been done before us, there is no sign of Job commentary slowing down or letting up. But even among this large and growing crowd of Job interpretations, Stephen Vicchio's commentary stands out. Most commentaries acknowledge some predecessors, sometimes referring to and polemicizing with them in the course of suggesting their own understandings. Vicchio seems to know and use far more commentaries than anyone else. For example, he cites many of the church fathers' readings, as well as numerous medieval Jewish commentaries, from Saadia Gaon (10th-century Babylonia), who is widely known, to R. David Altschuler (18th-century Europe), who is not. The English-language commentaries he cites, from the nineteenth and early twentieth centuries, include many that, I dare say, are unfamiliar to most contemporary Job scholars. Vicchio is actually a world expert on the history of Joban interpretation. His uniquely informative three volumes, *Job in the Ancient World*, *Job in the Medieval World*, and *Job in the Modern World* (2006), are by far the most comprehensive survey that has ever been made. A precis of those invaluable works forms the bulk of the introduction to his commentary.

But Vicchio advances the interpretation of Job dialectically, through the juxtaposition of diverse, as well as overlapping, commentarial remarks. His approach is not text-driven—seeking to work out his own best take on the meaning of a term or a passage; or hermeneutic-driven—seeking to apply a favored interpretative approach; but rather exegesis-driven—seeking to lay out the interpretative options and express his own tendencies mainly through the voice of an earlier exegete, whether early or late. This is not to say that Vicchio displays no independent philological judgment;

but rather that he often sees the merit in more than one suggestion, and he shares that respect for diverse approaches with his readers. In this regard his work, although formatted in a single stream, has something of the effect of the Rabbinic Bible mentioned at the outset. One comes to realize that there may be some sense in this view, but also in that view. One may conclude that one cannot decide with any degree of confidence in the validity of this interpretation, or of that.

In this way, Vicchio's commentary, whether he intended it or not, exudes something of the postmodern spirit, of the times in which we live. For one thing, his presentation of a variety of potentially valid interpretations goes hand in glove with contemporary notions of indeterminacy and the hermeneutics of suspicion. For another, his writing is highly quotational, reminding one of the intertextual truism that our words are in the large part a quotation or recombination of our predecessors' formulations.

And yet, Vicchio's commentary on Job is, on the whole, fairly traditional and classic in its reliance on earlier efforts. It is within those somewhat conventional bounds that this interpreter interweaves the history of the book's interpretation and the exegesis that he presents and proposes. For example, in grappling with the Satan's gnomic expression "skin for skin" (Job 2:4), Vicchio cites a nineteenth-century commentator to the effect that this apparent proverb is perplexing; but he goes on to invoke one interpretation favored by both Gregory the Great and Saadia Gaon, and another "most compelling" one by the twentieth-century European and Israeli scholar N. H. Tur-Sinai: the skin of the heart is protected by outer skin—the Satan wants to affect Job's soul. For this reader, even if the last-mentioned interpretation is less than convincing, I am sure that, with Vicchio, the meaning is not certainly one or the other.

Another arena of commentarial debate involves the nature of the two larger-than-life beasts that the Deity trots out to exhibit his grandeur and prowess, the Behemoth and the Leviathan. Are they purely animal—hippopotamus and crocodile—as some commentators aver? Are they mythological creatures, harking back to the time of creation, as others have maintained? Or are they symbolic, figures of the Satan and the Order of Chaos, as yet others have proposed? Vicchio allows for the diversity of opinion but appears inclined to the latter two positions, by illustrating the representations of the mythological sea monster from third-millennium BCE cylinder seals from Mesopotamia up through twenty-first-century CE art. Similarly, he traces the treatment of the Leviathan in literature and other areas of culture from classical rabbinic aggada (legend) through modern science fiction.

All in all, Vicchio's commentary on Job is both classic, in citing the classics, and current, in engaging in and even adopting some generally held critical positions—such as the belatedness of the Elihu speeches and the challenges of the transmitted text. It is a work whose wealth of information should be mined, and whose broad exegetical perspective should be emulated.

Edward L. Greenstein

Professor Emeritus of Biblical Studies, Bar-Ilan University, Israel

Author of *Job: A New Translation* (Yale University Press, 2019)

Preface

THIS WORK HAS BEEN in the making for over fifty years. My interest in the book of Job goes back to my days in high school in the 1960s. At that time, I met my dear friend Professor William F. Albright of Johns Hopkins University. It was from Bill Albright that I learned my first Hebrew, in his study at home, in the few years before his death in 1971. Dr. Albright insisted that I call him "Bill," though by all accounts he was the most gifted and accomplished scholar Johns Hopkins has ever had.

After my undergraduate years at the University of Maryland, Bill Albright wrote a letter of introduction to the famous book of Job scholar Marvin Pope of the Yale Divinity School. Bill said in the letter that you should "take care of my friend, Stephen. He is enthusiastic to work with you." In my years at Yale, I worked closely with Mr. Pope. And he helped to secure me a fellowship at Oxford University for an MPhil degree at Hereford College, and then a PhD at St. Mary's College, at Saint Andrew's University, in Fife, Scotland.

Back in my Yale days, I told Mr. Pope that I wished to write a history of how the book of Job has been interpreted over time, from the ancient world to the present. At the time, Mr. Pope told me to give up the idea, for "no one can know as much as you would need to complete such a project. For one thing, it would require the mastering of more than a dozen languages." I must confess, I ignored Pope's advice and by the mid-1990s, I had begun to pull together three manuscripts on "Job in the Ancient World," "Job in the Medieval World," and "Job in the Modern World," which were published by Wipf and Stock in 2006.

After completing the three manuscripts, I sent a draft of them to Mr. Pope, who had since retired at YDS. He wrote me back a few weeks later, suggested that I come see him in his house in Connecticut. A few weeks later, I did so, and he apologized for telling me all those years before that I should abandon the project. Pope was enthusiastic of the history, and he told me that he was not well. Indeed, he died on June 21, 1997—just six months later.

So, this work—an essay on the history of the interpretation of the book of Job, and a commentary—has been in the making since 1965. Along the way, I have been helped by a variety of my teachers, colleagues, and other scholars. These are too many to mention, so I will only point to the teachers. These include: John Titchner and Tom Benson, in my undergraduate years. Marvin Pope and Dean McBride, at Yale. Dr. James Barr, at Oxford; and Peter Coxon, Bill Shaw, and George Hall, at Saint Andrews.

Before moving to the essay on the book of Job, the reception history of the book, and the commentary itself, however, we will first make some preliminary remarks about the "problem of evil" and styles, or motifs, by which the figure of Job has been understood over the years. We also will make some heuristic observations that will aid us in the remainder of this work.

Some Preliminary Remarks

First of all, in the Judeo-Christian tradition, from the ancient Jews to the present, at least nine basic responses to the problem of evil have been put forward to explain Job's suffering.

The problem of evil asks the simple question, "If God is all-good, all-knowing, and all-powerful, then why is there so much evil and suffering in the world?" These nine views that respond to this question may be summarized this way:

1. Retributive Justice.
2. The Influence of Demonic Forces.
3. The Free Will Defense.
4. Original Sin Theory.
5. The Contrast View.
6. The Test Perspective.
7. The Moral Qualities Theory.
8. The Divine Plan Perspective.
9. The Deprivation of the Good Theory.[1]

The first of these theories says that the reason that Job suffers is because he, or his family, has done something wrong. This is a fairly common response in the Old Testament, and it is put forth many times in the book of Job, such as at 1:5, where Job makes sacrifices for his sons, "in case they may have sinned in their hearts." Bildad also argues for retributive justice when he suggests that Job's children may be the cause of his suffering in ch. 8. The retributive justice theory also can be seen at: 4:7; 8:3; 11:20; 13:26; 20:5; 22:16; 24:22; 31:3; 35:7–8; 36:13–14; and 38:15.

The second position argues that Job's suffering is the product of the Satan or his minions. This view often has been expressed in a number of thinkers in the history of Judaism, Christianity, and Islam, but it has been employed much more often in Christianity and Islam than in Judaism. Among these scholars are Augustine, Gregory, and Thomas Aquinas. In the Qur'an as well, we find passages attributing Ayyub's, the Arabic name for Job, suffering to *Iblis* or *Shaytan*, the two words in

---

1. Vicchio, 1:3–4.

Islam to express the demonic. The two appearances of the Satan in the book of Job, in chs. 1 and 2, also have been interpreted as a version of the influence of demonic forces theory.

The advocates of the free will defense suggest that Job's suffering is caused by his own, free choices. Again, the free will defense regularly has been employed as an answer to why Job suffers. It may be found in the sermons of John Calvin, for example, as well as countless other Jewish, Christian, and Muslim writers. The Old Testament idea of the two *yetzerim*, or "imaginations," or "inclinations," the *yetzer ha-ra* and the *yetzer ha-tov*, is also a version of this third theory.

The fourth view, held by Augustine and Thomas Aquinas, for example, says that the sin of Adam and Eve in the garden of Eden has been inherited by all humans after them, and this original sin is the source of Job's troubles. This fourth theory is most fully developed in Augustine, but it also can be found in Gregory, Albert the Great, Thomas Aquinas, Martin Luther, John Calvin, and many others. Original sin theory is much more prevalent in Christian thinkers than in Judaism or Islam. In Job, several passages have been interpreted as arguing for original sin theory, including 14:1; 15:14; and 25:4.

The contrast view suggests that we have to have evil in order to understand, or to know, the good. When this theory is alluded to in the book of Job, it most often comes in the context of discussing light versus darkness. Among these passages are: 12:25; 17:12; 18:6 and 18; 24:13–14; 22:11; 24:13–14 and 17; 30:26; and 38:19–20, among many other places, where this theory has been employed. In all of these, *owr*, or "light," is associated with God and goodness, while *choshek*, or "dark," is associated with evil.

The test perspective says that God uses evil and suffering to test the moral characters of people. Some have interpreted the Prologue of Job with this sixth theory. Other places in Job where this theory has been alluded to are: 7:18; 9:32; 22:30; 34:3.

The moral qualities theory suggests that certain moral virtues like fortitude and courage, for examples, can only be developed by experiencing evil and suffering. Some of the places in Job where this theory has been found by interpreters include: 5:19–20 and 27; 11:7–11; 22:29–30; 33:16; 36:10 and 15.

The divine plan perspective argues that although evil and suffering may not make sense in the present time, in the long view, we will see that God has a divine plan, by which all "will work out for the good." This theory often has been the interpretation of God's speeches from the whirlwind in chs. 38 to 41. It also may be alluded to at Job 37:14–20 and 21–24. At 42:2, Job uses the word *'esa*, or "plan," in answering Yahweh's voice from the whirlwind. This verse, then, also may be interpreted with the divine plan theory.

Finally, the deprivation of the good theory says that evil is not something positive but rather it is a negation or absence of the good. This view is first seen in the Stoics, and then in Augustine, Gregory, Albert, and Thomas Aquinas, as well as in a number of modern Christian philosophers, like John Hick and Alvin Plantinga, for examples. This ninth theory, however, does not appear in the book of Job, but, as we shall see, all eight of these other approaches show up in the course of this work.

A second heuristic device that may aid us in interpreting views on the biblical book of Job is the many styles, motifs, or kinds of Jobs that have been seen in the receptive history of the book. The following list may be of some help:

1. The Patient Job.
2. The Angry or Iconoclastic Job.
3. The *Jobus Christi* View, or Job as Christ Figure.
4. The Job of the Resurrection.
5. The Job as Warrior or Wrestler.
6. The Penitent Job.
7. The Existentialist Job.[2]

Again, each of these seven "kinds of Jobs" show up in the course of the history of scholarship on the book. The Patient Job, of course, is the Job of the prologue and epilogue, the Job in the prose of the book. Interestingly enough, however, the classical Hebrew term for "patience," *erek*, does no appear in the book of Job, nor the root from which it comes, *arak*, that means one who is long-suffering.

The Angry or Iconoclastic Job is the Job of the dialogue, the poetic portions of the text. This is the sometimes brusque and combative figure of the poetic portion of the text, in chs. 4 to 37. The *Jobus Christi* view is self-explanatory. Some exegetes say the most important aspect of the Man from Uz and his book is his affinity to the life, death, and resurrection of Jesus Christ. Indeed, many Christian interpreters over the centuries have maintained that Job is a "Christ-figure." This perspective is not found in Judaism, nor in Islamic scholars.

The image of the "Job of the Resurrection" are those scholars and exegetes who suggest the central way to understand Job is as a Jewish patriarch who professes an undying belief in the resurrection of the body. The principal text in the book where this motif of Job can be seen is 19:25–27, the *Goel* passage. Another verse where survival after death has been the primary interpretation is 14:14.

The "Job as Warrior or Wrestler," which is often tied to the Patient Job Perspective, says that Job is a kind of warrior or wrestler dedicated to helping the cause of God. Many of the early church fathers often employed this image of the Man from Uz and his book. The first Christian scholar to hold this view was Clement of Rome.

The advocates of the "Penitent Job" suggest that the central passage of the biblical book is Job's response to God's voice from the whirlwind. These advocates point out that the tenor of Job 40:3–5 and 42:5–6 is one of penitence and reconciliation—and

---

2. Vicchio, 1:4.

this is the most important attribute of the patriarch. Finally, the "Existentialist Job" is the lonely, isolated Job of ch. 3. This is the Job who believes that the central understanding of the Divine by Job is that "God is Silent," or he is a "Distant God." Many thinkers in the first several decades of the twentieth century, mostly in Europe, as we shall see, have seen the image of Job this way.

Throughout the course of the introduction to this work, the receptive history of the book of Job, and the commentary that follows, we will continually make references to these nine responses to the issues of theodicy and the problem of evil, as well as these seven different motifs, or kinds of Jobs that appear in the history of interpreting the Man from Uz and his book.

Abbreviations

AJSLL	*American Journal of Semitic Languages and Literatures*
BA	*Biblical Archeology*
Bib	*Biblica*
CBQ	*Catholic Bible Quarterly*
HUCA	*Hebrew Union College Annual*
IDB	*Interpreter's Dictionary of the Bible*
Intp.	*Interpretation*
JBL	*Journal of Biblical Literature*
JJS	*Journal of Jewish Studies*
JNES	*Journal of Near-Eastern Studies*
JPS	Jewish Publication Society
JQR	*Jewish Quarterly Review*
JSOR	*Journal of the Society of Oriental Research*
JSOT	*Journal for the Study of the Old Testament*
JSS	*Journal of Semitic Studies*
JTS	*Journal of Theological Studies*
KJV	King James Version
LXX	Septuagint
MT	Masoretic Text
NAB	New American Bible
NEB	New English Bible
NIV	New International Version
Or.	*Orientalia*
REB	Revised English Bible
RSV	Revised Standard Version
NRSV	New Revised Standard Version
VT	*Vetus Testamentum*
VTSup.	*Vetus Testamentum* Supplement
ZAW	*Zeitschrift für die Alttestamentliche Wissenschaft*

Part I: The History of Interpreting the Book of Job

THE PURPOSE OF THIS first part is to explore how the biblical book of Job has been interpreted over the centuries in Judaism, Christianity, and Islam. We will begin this introduction by looking at the earliest Jewish sources where the book of Job is discussed, or is the object of interpretation. This will be followed by a discussion of the earliest Christian sources on the book of Job, and then the most important ancient Islamic understandings of the Prophet *Ayyub*, or Job in Islam.

We have divided the following receptive history into three periods. The premodern, to 1500; the early modern, 1500 to 1800; and the modern 1800 to the present. We will begin with the premodern period.

Premodern Views of the Book of Job to 1500

The earliest Jewish reference to the book of Job comes in the Greek Septuagint version of the ancient text. Several general conclusions can be made about the LXX's version of Job. First, it was completed in the third or second century BCE, in the city of Alexandria. Second, the editors of the LXX Job were Jewish scholars. Third, the Septuagint version of the book of Job is 20 percent shorter than the Masoretic Text.

Fourth, there are a number of elements in the Greek text that are not found in the Hebrew text. Job is identified as sitting on a "dung heap" in the LXX; Job and his friends are identified as royalty in the Greek text. Job is identified with the figure of Jobab, a patriarch in Genesis in the LXX version; Job is infected with "worms" in the Greek text; and finally, Job is seen as a champion of resurrection in the Septuagint text of the book of Job.

This final difference can be seen in the Greek text's treatment of the *Goel* passage at 19:25–27, at 14:14, and at the end of the book at the epilogue of 42:7–17. In the Masoretic Text of 14:14, the verse is rendered in the interrogatory. "If a man dies, shall he live again?" In the LXX, the same line is translated in the declaratory—"If a man dies, he shall live again." In the MT, the book of Job ends this way: "And Job died an old man and full of days." The LXX, however, adds this to the end of 42:17:

> And it is written that he will rise again with those whom the Lord has raised up. This man is explained from the Syriac book as living in the land of Ausis on the border of Edom and Arabia; formerly his name was Jobab.[1]

The simplest explanation of Job being identified with Jobab is that the names are similar, and that the Jobab of Gen 10:29 and 36:33 and 1 Chr 1:23 lived in the patriarchal age. The references to Edom and Arabia are most likely the origins of the belief among some ancient Jewish scholars that Job was not an Israelite. Indeed, many rabbis in the Talmud believed the Man from Uz was not a Jew.[2]

There are a number of other theological differences between the Hebrew text and the Job of the LXX. The Greek text tends to tone down the most vitriolic speeches of Job. The Greek Job is also considerably less anthropomorphic than the Hebrew Job. We also have indicated that the LXX indicates a strong belief in resurrection of the body, something not found in the MT.

A second collection of ancient Jewish views of the book of Job are references to the patriarch found in the Jewish Apocrypha. Among these are the book of Tobit; Sirach, Aristeas's *Life of Job*, and the Testament of Job. The book of Sirach is a third- or second-century BCE text that mentions the figure of Job at 49:9. The text tells us:

> For God also mentioned Job, who had held fast to the ways of Justice.[3]

The book of Tobit is a romantic, apocryphal tale set in the time of the Jews' captivity. The major reason the book of Tobit is important for our purposes is that it contains a number of affinities to the biblical book of Job. Among these are the righteousness of the central characters; a lack of confidence on physicians; the cursing of the wives; and the fact that both wives work outside the home. As far as we know, Saint Jerome was the first scholar to point out these parallels of the book of Tobit to Job.[4]

The Testament of Job is an anonymous text that is roughly the same size as the book of Romans. The book purports to contain the last testament of Job, also called Jobab in the book. There are a number of features of the Testament of Job that are important for our purposes. First, Job is described as a king of Egypt (28:8). Second, Satan is described as a demonic figure. Third, in the Testament, Job's wife is given a name, Sitidos, and she offers a lament in ch. 24 that looks much like Job 2:9. But in the Testament, the wife laments the death of her children, something that does not occur in the MT.

In the Testament of Job, we also find strong beliefs in both immortality of the soul and resurrection of the body. Again, two things not found in the Masoretic Text. Like the book of Job, in ch. 43 of the Testament of Job, Job declares that his three friends have "speaken falsely against Job," and that they can be saved through Job's intercession, much like the MT's 42:7–8.

Above all, the most significant thing about the Testament of Job is that theologically it is much closer to the Septuagint version of Job than to the Hebrew original. For this reason, it may be that the work originally came from Greek-speaking Alexandrian Jews.

A final Jewish apocryphal work that is important for our purposes is Aristeas's "Life of Job." The book is written in Greek and identifies Job, as the LXX does, with the figure of Jobab in Genesis and 1 Chronicles. Like the LXX, Aristeas refers to Job and his friends as "kings." But there are also some interesting differences in Aristeas's Job. For one thing, Job's sores are healed at the end of the fragment from "The Life of Job." For another thing, the central attribute of Job in the Aristeas text is not patience. Rather, it is courage. Thus, Aristeas assents to the Job militant motif.

Finally, another collection of perspectives among the ancient Jews is what the Talmud and the Midrash have to say about the Man from Uz. After the Babylonian captivity, the people of Judah had lost their political and economic independence, as well as the one place that Josiah had proclaimed that sacrifices only could be performed—in the temple at Jerusalem.[5]

The written Hebrew Bible had come into its final form around the year 400 BCE. But new context where the law applied, or needed explanation, now began to arise. The major effect of this fact is that two additional bodies of literature arose in ancient Judaism—the Talmud and the Midrash. The former consisted of the Mishnah, a summary of oral law, from the fifth to the second century BCE, and the Gemara, a collection of materials that illuminated the Talmud.[6]

In the two versions of the Talmud—the Palestinian and the Babylonian Talmuds—rabbis began to comment on the Hebrew Bible, in both theological and exegetical ways. Most of the references we find in the Talmud on the figure of Job are about four central questions about the patriarch. First, when did he live? Second, was Job a Jew or a Gentile? Third, was he a patient or an angry figure? And finally, what was the cause of Job's suffering?[7]

There are a variety of answers to these four questions developed in the Talmud. Some rabbis believed that Job was as old as any patriarch in the Bible.[8] Others that he lived much later in the history of Judaism.[9] The rabbis also disagreed over the issue of whether Job was or was not a Jew. Some rabbis believed Job was to be characterized by his patience and courage, while other scholars of the Talmud saw Job as an angry figure.[10] Indeed, some say his mouth "should be filled with dirt."

Both versions of the Talmud also suggest a number of opinions about the origins of Job's suffering. Some say it was God;[11] others that it was Satan;[12] and still others that it was his testy personality.[13] Additionally, the Talmud makes comments about Job's wealth; and whether Job was forgiven by God, as well as whether he believed in survival after death.[14]

Still other Jewish views of the figure of Job can be found in texts discovered among the Dead Sea Scrolls, as well as the Targumim that began to appear in other languages, including Greek, Aramaic, and Syriac, like the Peshitta, for example. In fact, some of the rabbis of the Talmud believed that the book of Job was originally written in Aramaic and then translated into Hebrew.[15]

The very earliest of Christian sources in regard to the book of Job are from the first century CE. The first of these is the Epistle of James, ch. 5, vv. 11 and 12. There Saint James remarks:

> You have heard of the steadfastness of Job, and you have seen the purposes of the Lord, and how the Lord is compassionate and merciful.[16]

It should be clear from this verse in the Epistle of James that from the very beginning of the church, the patriarch Job was seen as a man of patience and steadfastness. A second first-century text that mentions the figure of Job is Clement of Rome's first letter to the Corinthians, composed at the end of the first century. In this letter, Clement quoted directly from both 1:1 and 14:4–5 of the Masoretic Text and the Septuagint. The first of these passages is about Job's moral character—that he is blameless and upright. And the second passage—the one from ch. 14, is taken by Clement to be a proof text for original sin.[17]

In his first letter, Clement also quotes Job 38:11 to discuss the Lord's sovereignty over all creation. And throughout the letter, the first-century scholar makes a number of plays for the early Christian to be humble and patient in the face of suffering, much like the figure of Job.[18]

What is significant about these mentions of Job by Clement, of course, is the patriarch's steadfastness, patience, and humility; and these were the earliest understandings of Job in the earliest Christian church.[19] They are indications of the Patient Job. A third early Christian text that mentions the Man from Uz is a text known as the "Apocalypse of Paul," most likely written sometime between the second and fourth century CE.

The text in question purports to have been written by Paul of Tarsus in the first century CE. In the text, while Paul travels the heavens, he meets a variety of patriarchs and saints, mostly from the Old Testament. These include: Isaiah, Jeremiah, Ezekiel, Amos, Micah, Zechariah, Moses, and Job.[20]

When speaking to Paul, Job tells him that he suffered from a disease for thirty years; that he was tempted by Satan; and that he never ceased to sing the praises of the Lord. The Job of the apocalypse also indicates his belief in the resurrection of the body—something not found in the Masoretic Text of the book of Job. Thus, the Apocalypse appears to employ the Patient Job and the Job of the Resurrection images.

The first four or five centuries of the church also saw the first large commentaries on the book of Job, in both the Eastern and the Western Churches. Among these early theological treatments of the book of Job in the Christian tradition were the following: Polycarp of Smyrna (1st and 2nd c.); Clement of Alexandria (2nd and 3rd c.); Justin Martyr (2nd c.); Theophilus of Antioch (2nd c.); and a host of church fathers like Cyprian of Carthage (3rd c.); Tertullian (3rd c.); and many other of the church fathers in the fourth century.[21]

Among these fourth-century Christian scholars who wrote about the figure of Job were the following: Acacius of Caesarea; Amphilochius of Iconium; Anthony the Great; Gregory of Nyssa; Gregory of Elvira; John Chrysostom; Methodius of Olympus;

Peter of Alexandria; Theodore of Heraclea; Theodore of Mopsuestia; and Victorinus of Petovium. Each of these fourth-century church fathers either wrote commentaries on the book of Job, wrote about them in their sermons and hymns, or otherwise discussed the Man from Uz one way or another.[22]

The Arabic name for the Prophet Job is "Ayyub." The earliest references to Ayyub in Islam come in al-Qur'an, where there are four main references to Job. These come at: surah 4:163; 6:84; 21:83–84; and 38:41–44. In the first of these, Prophet Ayyub appears among a list of a number of other Old Testament worthies, including Ibrahim (Abraham), Ismail (Ishmael), Ishaq, or Isaac, Jacob, Jesus, Jonah, Aaron, Sulayman, or Solomon, and Daud, or David. In the view of al-Qur'an, Ayyub is on a moral par with the same kind of revelation of these other Hebrew Bible and New Testament figures.[23]

The second reference to Prophet Ayyub in al-Qur'an, which comes at surah 6:84, again places the prophet in the companionship of other Old Testament figures. This time the list includes: Isaac, Jacob, Noah, or Nuh, David, Sulayman, Yusuf, or Joseph, Musa, or Moses, and Aaron. Allah has revealed himself to Ayyub the same way he has to these other prophets, or *Nabiim*, in Arabic.[24]

At surah 21, the third mention of Ayyub in al-Qur'an, the Arabic text in translation tells us this:

> And remember Ayyub when he cried to his Lord. Truly, distress has seized me, but Thou art the Most Merciful of those who are merciful. So we listened to him. We removed the distress that was on him, and we restored his people to him, and we doubled their number—as a grace from Ourselves, and a commemoration, for all who will serve Us.[25]

Here the premium is on patience and fortitude. This text also points to several elements of the Job of the Old Testament. Among these are that Job experienced much distress; that Ayyub's family was taken away from him; and that those family members were restored double.[26]

The final reference to Prophet Ayyub in al-Qur'an comes at surah 38:41–44. The text in translation advises us to: "Commemorate Our servant Ayyub. Behold, he cried to his Lord, 'The Evil One has afflicted me with distress and suffering.'"[27] This section of the Muslim Holy Book goes on where Allah instructs Ayyub to "strike the ground," and a cool, refreshing stream appears at the spot. The text again mentions Ayyub's double restoration, and that the prophet's most important attributes are patience and "constancy."[28] Many images of Prophet Ayyub in Islamic art show the figure accompanied by the Angel Jibril (Gabriel). Usually, the two stand in the stream that appeared when the prophet struck the ground as commanded by Allah.[29]

Ayyub appeals to Allah, and God conceives of Ayyub's suffering as a kind of test that the prophet passed with flying colors; but the source of Ayyub's suffering is not God, nor Ayyub's friends. Rather, it is Iblis, or Shaytan, the Arabic words for the devil. Thus, one of the answers that Islam employs to discuss the cause or meaning of Ayyub's suffering is what we have called the "test theodicy." That is, that Allah sometimes uses evil and suffering to "test" the character of believing Muslims.[30]

The following conclusions may be made about these earliest sources on the Prophet Ayyub in the Islamic faith. First, the emphases on the most important attributes of Prophet Ayyub in Islam are on patience and fortitude. Second, Ayyub experiences serious "distress" in his life. Third, the cause of that distress is Iblis or Shaytan. And finally, one way to understand Ayyub's suffering is that Allah brought these troubles to Ayyub as a test of the prophet's moral character.[31]

In addition to these direct references to Prophet Ayyub in al-Qur'an, there are also other examples in the Holy Book where al-Qur'an seems to be quoting directly from the Hebrew text, such at al-Qur'an's 9:19 and Job 16:19, or the ephemeral descriptions of a spider web that appear at al-Qur'an's 29:40 and Job 36:9. There are also certain linguistic, Semitic language similarities or roots that link Hebrew, Aramaic, Syriac, and Arabic words.

One good example of this latter phenomenon in the Qur'an is surah 63, where the Arabic of the surah looks very much like phrases uttered by Job in the Hebrew Bible. Other scholars point out that the writers of the book of Job and Muhammad in the construction of al-Qur'an knew about scientific theories on embryology. Specifically, both Job 10:10 and al-Qur'an, at 22:5, 23:13–15, and 39:6, all point to very modern theories about the embryo. Other scholars, however, suggest both texts are plagiarizing Aristotle's *Generations of the Animals*.[32]

At any rate, this brings us to the second section of this history of the reception of the book of Job—Job in the medieval period. As we shall see, there are a number of significant commentators on the biblical book, in Judaism and Christianity, as well as in the Islamic faith.

The Image of Job in the Medieval Period

There were a variety of Jewish commentaries on the book of Job in the medieval period, from the tenth to the fourteenth centuries. Although there are more than a dozen of such commentaries in that period, five stand out above the others. These were completed by Saadiah Gaon (882–942); Rashi (1040–1105); Joseph Kara (1065–1135); Moses Maimonides (1135–1204); and Gersonides (1288–1344).

The commentary of Saadiah on the book of Job was completed sometime in the late ninth century. Saadiah was born in Upper Egypt in 862, and died in the city of Sura, one hundred miles south of Baghdad. For the final sixty years of his life, from 882 until 942, Saadiah lived in Sura. The school of exegesis at Sura was primarily concerned with today what we might call the "historical-critical method." In fact, Saadiah relied far more on the philosopher Aristotle than he did on the comments on Job made by rabbis in the two versions of the Talmud.

Saadiah was best known for his Arabic translations of the Torah, the Psalms, and the Song of Songs; and he wrote an extensive commentary on the book of Job called *The Book of Theodicy*, published by Yale University Press, and translated from Arabic and edited by L. E. Goodman.[33]

In the introduction to his commentary on the book of Job, Saadiah makes two pronouncements about the origin of the Man from Uz and his book. First, Saadiah believed that the book of Job was written by Moses. One of the reasons he held that view is that it is clearly "one of the oldest books of the Tanach."[34] Saadiah's other observation about the beginnings of the book of Job is that the Egyptian philosopher thought it was written during the period of the patriarchs, around the "time of the Jews flight from Egypt."[35]

Saadiah employed a number of theological responses to the problem of theodicy in his commentary. Again, in the introduction of his commentary, Saadiah speaks of three separate responses. He calls these: discipline and instruction; purgation and punishment; and trial and testing.[36] In the first of these views, Saadiah suggests that God brings evil and suffering to human beings for the "purposes of discipline and instruction."[37] What he means by this view is that God brings evil and suffering to believers for the purpose of developing certain moral characteristics, like fortitude and patience.[38] Earlier, we called this the moral qualities perspective.

The second of Saadiah's responses, the purgation and punishment view, is a version of what we have called retributive justice. In this view, Saadiah believes that suffering comes to those who have sinned and whose lives need to be "purged and punished."[39] The third of Saadiah's responses, the trial and testing perspective, is a version of what we have called the "test theodicy." This view relates that God at times uses evil and suffering to "test" the moral characters of certain believers, or simply to improve their moral characters.[40]

In the introduction to his commentary, Saadiah also mentions at least four other theological responses to the problem of theodicy. He mentions what we have called the divine plan point of view, in his commentary on Job 38:1ff., God's first speech from the whirlwind, for example. In fact, throughout his commentary, he often returns to this perspective.[41]

Saadiah also regularly refers to the free will defense in his commentary on the book of Job, often in the context of his descriptions of the ancient Hebrew theory of the two *yetzerim*, or inclinations or imaginations. Saadiah clearly believed that God placed in the souls of human beings two separate inclinations or imaginations—the *yetzer ha ra* and the *yetzer tov*, or the evil imagination and the good imagination.[42]

In his commentary, when Saadiah refers to the Satan figure, he calls him the "Adversary," but he refuses to conclude that the figure is a demonic force responsible for Job's suffering.[43] In his commentary on 1:6, however, Saadiah suggests that Satan is a "human being, and not a devil or an angel."[44] In regard to his commentary on Job 15:14, Saadiah refuses to assent to a theory of collective sin. Although Saadiah was much aware of the Christian view of original sin, his translation refused to indicate such a view. Thus, he translates the verse in question this way:

> What is man that he should be pure?
>
> The offering of a woman that she should be righteous.[45]

In his commentary of Job 1:1, Saadiah forcefully argues against the view that Job has sinned. In fact, he translates *tam ve-yashar* of the line as "blameless and upright," and he sees these as moral categories, or, as Saadiah says, "as moral a man as one can be."[46] Saadiah also points out that there is no reason to believe that the book introduces a form of Dualism.[47] In regard to Job 2:7, Saadiah suggests that, ultimately, it is God who is responsible for Job's sores.

In fact, in regard to 2:9, Saadiah does not agree with the Christian view that Job's wife is often seen as a "handmaid of the devil," as Augustine and many others have claimed.[48] Saadiah also does not find a belief in resurrection of the body at Job 19:25–27. What he does find is that either "God is Job's *Goel*, or that Job is a witness to himself."[49] In Saadiah's view, then, the *Goel* is not a Vindicator to be found in this life, or the next. In fact, when it comes to survival after death, Saadiah is perfectly willing to let the text speaks for itself. In that regard, the Egyptian philosopher finds survival in his commentary at 7:21 and 14:12.[50] Although it is clear that Saadiah believed that God is capable of raising the dead from the grave, he thinks the "sought and not be found," may refer to resurrection.

Although Saadiah makes frequent references to Midrashic understandings of Job, for the most part he eschews allegory and sticks instead to the *perash*, or the literal understanding of the biblical text. Above all, Saadiah was a philosopher and he brought the notion of God's providence as the foundation for all that he has to say about the book of Job, as well as the Man from Uz himself.

Rabbi Shlomo Yitahaqi, or the acronym, Rashi, was born in Troyes around the year 1040. He was identified with the School of Mainz, that was begun by Rabbi Judah of Metz (960–1040.) This center became a central school of Talmud and Mishnah study in the period, and often concentrated on the *derash*, or allegorical understanding of the Hebrew Bible.

Rashi's comments on the book of Job come in connection to his general commentary on the Scriptures, as part of his analysis of the *Kethuvim*, or Writings. In his introduction to his remarks on Job, Rashi compares Job to Abraham. Like him, Rashi saw Job as a pious and holy man; but Rashi sees Job, nevertheless, as a flawed man. The source of the flaw was not hubris, in Rashi's view, but a lack of intellectual capacity. In this regard, Rashi believed that Job needed to be educated to attain the most lofty brand of holiness. In fact, Rashi believes that Job 33:12 is precisely the kind of instruction that Job needs. He translates the verse this way:

> Behold, in this you are not right. I will answer you that God is greater than man.[51]

Rashi makes another reference to this instruction of Job that is necessary in his view with his translation of Job 34:36. For that verse, Rashi gives us this:

> Would that Job were tried or tested to the end because he answers like a wicked man.[52]

Thus, Rashi appears to be endorsing both the moral qualities view and the test theodicy in his comments on the Man from Uz and his book. The former, in regard to Job 33:12; the latter at 34:36.

In reference to the God of the book of Job, Rashi mentions a third example of this instruction of Job. It comes in this translation of Job 36:15:

> He delivers the afflicted by their affliction, and He opens their ears by adversity.[53]

Rashi's commentary on Job 5:2 that speaks of "Job being tested" is a fourth example of the need for Job to be educated in the proper ways of the Lord. Indeed, he endorses here what we have called the "test theodicy," as well.

From these comments, it is clear that in regard to the biblical book of Job, Rashi endorses both the test theodicy and the moral qualities view. At times Rashi also endorses the divine plan perspective, such as in his commentary of God's first speech from the whirlwind in ch. 38. Rashi also appears to endorse the contrast view in regard to the many mentions of darkness and light in the book of Job, such as at 10:22, 12:22, and 30:26, for examples.

From all of this we may conclude that Rashi very much favored the more teleological understandings of evil and suffering, while also trying to combine the *Perash* and the *Derash* brands of interpretation. Nevertheless, Rashi provides what at times are rather odd translations of passages in the book of Job. At 3:2, for example, Rashi renders the line this way:

> May the day in which I was to be born be lost.[54]

Rashi renders the two attributes applied to Job at 1:1 as "sincere and upright." And he does the same in God's dialogue with the Satan at 1:8 and 2:3.[55] Job's wife's speech at 2:9 Rashi translates as, "Do you still maintain your sincerity?" And Rashi's narrator answers that question this way: "And Job did not sin with his lips."[56]

Rashi calls the *bene ha Elohim*, the "Angels of God."[57] He translates the patriarch's profession of faith at 1:22 this way:

> Despite all of this Job did not sin, nor did he utter unseemliness to God.[58]

Rashi translates the *Mokiah* of 9:33 as "Arbiter." The *Edh* of 16:19 as "Witness." Rashi calls the *Goel* at 19:25–26, his "Redeemer."[59] He renders 42:6 this way: "Therefore,

I despise my life and I will be consoled on dust and ashes."[60] Rashi translates the end of 42:17 this way: "Then Job died, being old and sated with days."[61] Rashi renders Job 14:10 this way:

> But a man may die and he was wicked. He perishes and then where is he?[62]

Rashi renders Bildad's suggestion about Job's sons at 8:4 this way:

> If your children have sinned against him, he sent them among in the hands of their transgressions.[63]

Rashi saw the line as a conditional, while the MT is in the declaratory. One final element of some significance in Rashi's commentary on the book of Job is that in order to soften the patriarch's more vitriolic speeches, he often attempts to tone down those speeches. At 13:15, for example, Job says,

> Behold, he will not slay me; I have no hope; yet I will defend my ways to his face.[64]

Rashi's commentary on 13:15 softens the message this way;

> I shall not separate myself from Him, and shall always believe in Him. Therefore, there is no rebellion in my words.[65]

In his commentaries on Job 9:22 and 13:21, he again also attempts to soften the messages of these verses—9:22 suggests that God "destroys the wicked and righteous alike."[66]

Rashi's version is softer: "It is all one. He destroys both the innocent and the wicked."[67] He adds an introduction and reverses the order of the nouns. At 13:21, to cite another example, the MT has Job asking God to "withdraw His hand from my face, so that he might not terrify me." Rashi tones down the line. He gives this rendering of 13:21:

> Distance our compulsion from me, let your face not terrify me.[68]

Rabbi Joseph Kara, the third of our medieval Jewish commentators who wrote a commentary on the book of Job, was born in Troyes in 1065, and spent the rest of his life there with the exception of studying for a short time in the city of Worms. Kara died in the city of Troyes, in northern France, in 1135. Kara first studied under his father's brother, a man named Mendhim Ben Helbo. One of Rabbi Joseph's companions was Samuel Ben Meir (1085–1158), also known as Rashbam, who was also the grandson of Rashi.

For the most part, Kara quotes directly from Rashi's commentary when discussing or writing about the book of Job. Kara gave similar renderings to Rashi at Job 19:26, the *Goel* passage, and at 42:5–6. He also agreed with Rashi that although Job was a good man, he was not a perfect one. Also, like Rashi, Kara thought that Job's character required moral education.

But Kara suggests that Job's use of his *yetzer ha ra* may have been responsible for his flaws in character. Thus Kara seems to assent to the moral qualities view and the free will defense, as well.

Like Rashi, Kara also believed that the speeches of Elihu, and elsewhere in the text, show how that moral education is to continue. Kara says of Job 33:24, for example, that "God reproves Job for his own good."[69] Another big difference between the comments of Job by Rashi and Joseph Kara is that the latter frequently condemns Christian uses of the Hebrew text of Job.

Also, like the commentary of Rashi on the book of Job, Rabbi Joseph Kara also tends to soften the more vitriolic speeches of Job in the book. Kara softens, for examples, 7:20, 9:20, and 12:4. In the first of these, Job asks in Kara's commentary, "Why have you made me your mark? Why have I become a burden to you?"[70] Kara makes it much more explicit that Job is speaking to God in the verse.

Kara translates Job 9:20 this way:

> Although I am innocent, my own mouth would condemn me; although I am blameless, He would still prove me perverse.[71]

In the fourth verse of ch. 12, Kara employs the noun for "laughingstock" twice, though again he uses the word *tam*, or "blameless" in the same line. Like Rashi's commentary, for the most part Rabbi Joseph Kara tends toward the literal-historical sense of the text. And like Rashi, he does periodically refer to the Mishnaic, more allegorical understandings of the text. He spends time in his introduction to his commentary on the book of Job discussing whether Job was a Jew and whether his book was written by Moses. Kara answers in the negative to both of those queries.[72]

Moses Maimonides, also called the Rambam in Jewish history, was born in Cordoba, Spain, in 1135. His family frequently moved during his childhood and he eventually settled in Egypt. The Rambam was trained as a physician, as well as a biblical exegete. In fact, he became the court physician for Sultan Saladin. He also became one of the leaders of the Jewish community in twelfth-century Egypt. Maimonides died on December 13, 1204, in Cairo. After a funeral of several days, his body was transported to Tiberius, in the Holy Land, where it still rests today.

Although the Rambam did not write a lengthy commentary of the book of Job, he did complete extensive remarks on the book in the third part, chs. 22 and 23 of his *Guide for the Perplexed*.[73] In his introduction to the book of the Man from Uz, in ch. 22 of the *Guide*, the Rambam suggests that Job was a fictional character, "written for the purpose of discussing the Providence of God."[74]

Maimonides translated the *tam va yashar* of Job 1:1 as "sincere and upright."[75] He relates that "Job was perfectly just, but not necessarily wise." He adds, "Job was afflicted by his misfortune, but he committed no sin."[76] The moral characteristic that the Rambam believed Job was missing was humility.[77] Or, in Aristotle's terms, Job suffers from a lack of development of the intellectual virtues, like wisdom and humility, for examples.

In his remarks on Job, Maimonides calls the Satan the "Adversary." And he identifies the Satan with the *yetzer ha ra*, or the evil imagination. Because of this flaw in Job's character, the Rambam suggests that the evil imagination is counteracted by the *yetzer tov*, or the good imagination that is personified in the "Angel of Reconciliation" at Job 33:23. In tandem with this angel, Maimonides believed, were the theological views of Job's fourth friend, Elihu. Indeed, the Elihu figure is also seen by the Rambam as a personification or reification of the *yetzer tov*, as well. In fact, both the angel and Elihu were/are figures of correction and reconciliation in the eyes of Maimonides.

The Rambam also saw the figures of Eliphaz and Bildad to be believers in the retributive justice theory; and he also says that Zophar held a theological view that the Divine Will has control over all things in the heavens and on earth.[78] Maimonides suggests in the *Guide* that Elihu's understanding of God's providence "far surpassed the other friends, as well as Job himself."[79]

The Rambam says this about Elihu's "new idea":

> But after due consideration we see clearly the new idea introduced by Elihu. . . . The new idea, which is peculiar to Elihu and has not been mentioned by the others, is contained in his metaphor of the angel's intercession.[80]

Maimonides goes on to say that what he means by this is that Elihu turns the Job debate from looking backward and assenting to retributive justice, to then looking forward and establishing belief in the test theodicy, the moral qualities view, and, above all, to the divine plan theory. In fact, the Rambam believed that the speeches of Elihu are a preliminary to the speeches from Yahweh in chs. 38–41.[81]

At several places in his comments on the book of Job, Maimonides calls the story of Job an "allegory."[82] About Job 42:6, the Rambam renders the line, "Therefore, I abhor myself and repent concerning the dust and ashes."[83] Throughout his comments on Job and his book, Maimonides professes belief in immortality of the soul. Though, interestingly enough, he does not believe that Job 19:25–27 has anything to do with resurrection of the body.[84] The Rambam translates the *bene ha Elohim* as the "angels of the Lord." And he renders Job 28:28 this way:

> The fear of the Lord is wisdom and shunning evil is understanding.[85]

From this analysis of the two chapters on Job in the *Guide for the Perplexed*, we may have the following conclusions. First, Maimonides is familiar with the ancient rabbis' views of the Man from Uz, and at times quotes directly from them. Second, he identifies the Satan with the *yetzer ha ra*. Third, the Rambam frequently employs other passages from the Hebrew Bible as proof texts for his views on Job. He quotes Num 22:32, to cite one example, as proof that the Satan is a demonic influence on Job.[86]

Fourth, like Saadiah and Rashi before him, Maimonides relies more on the historical-literal understanding of the text than the allegorical or symbolic views. Finally, Moses Maimonides is indebted to the philosophy of Aristotle far more than most Jewish philosophers, before him or since. In fact, the works of the Rambam was one of the major sources of Thomas Aquinas's five arguments for God's existence.[87]

Antti Laato, professor at Abo University in Finland, in the introduction of his work *Theodicy in the World of the Bible*, suggests about Job's suffering:

> Maimonides is unwilling to follow Saadiah's "simplistic" retributive model for the interpretation of suffering; but he argues that suffering can be seen from an exoteric and an esoteric view point.[88]

Laato goes on to say that the exoteric view is "the traditional Jewish solution."[89]

Presumably, by this he means retributive justice. "From an exoteric viewpoint, however, mankind cannot understand the ways of God, and, therefore, the mistake of Job was that He imagined God to be like humans."[90]

Professor Laato adds:

> Only at the end of the story Job realized that God is strikingly different and that man cannot understand God's thoughts and ways.[91]

Laato's view of Job and his book is very much like the analysis we have suggested earlier in this chapter. The exoteric view is backward-looking and posits a belief in retributive justice; but the esoteric understanding of Job is forward-looking and can be found in the words of Elihu and God's speeches from the whirlwind. In terms of the language of moral theory, the exoteric view is deontological, while the esoteric understanding is teleological in character. This brings us to the work of one final medieval Jewish thinker who wrote extensively on the book of Job, the figure of Gersonides.

Levi Ben Gershom (1288–1344), also called Gersonides and Ralbag, was a Jewish medieval exegete who spent most of his academic career in Orange and Avignon, France. Gersonides was born in Bagnols, and like Moses Maimonides, he was trained as a biblical scholar and a physician. Also, like Maimonides, Gersonides was a great follower of the philosophy of Aristotle. In 1342, the work of Gersonides was so respected by Christian scholars that Pope Clement VI arranged to have many of Gersonides's scientific treatises translated into Latin.[92] In the seventeenth century, Baruch Spinoza quotes from the work of Gersonides many times, particularly in relationship to the Dutch philosopher's views on miracles.

Few of Gersonides's letters are extant, and his contemporaries say very little about the life of Gersonides. Hence, we know very little about the philosopher's life. One account suggests he married a distant cousin and practiced moneylending; but these claims cannot be verified by any other sources.[93] The *Milhamot Ha-Shem*, which was completed in 1329, is Gersonides's major philosophical work. It took a dozen years to complete.[94] He also wrote a number of scientific treatises, including the *Sefer Ma'aseh Hoshev*, or the "Works of a Counter," and the *Bacullus Jacobi*, or "Jacob's Ladder," a work that contains a method for measuring the size of stars above the horizon.[95] In fact, because of his early work in astronomy, one of the craters of the moon is named "Rabbi Levi" in his name.[96]

Gersonides also completed a work on Aristotle's logic that he called "On Valid Syllogisms," completed in 1319.[97] Because of this treatise, Gersonides is known as the "Father of Modal Logic." The work was translated from Hebrew into Latin, but Gersonides's name did not appear on the title page. The major sources then for Gersonides's understanding of the book of Job were the following: Aristotle's philosophy, Maimonides's *Guide for the Perplexed*, as well as other earlier medieval Jewish commentators like Saadiah, Rashi, and Rabbi Joseph Kara.

By far, Gersonides's greatest contribution to Jewish scholarship was his biblical commentaries. He completed his *Sefer ha-Iyyov*, or book of Job commentary, in 1325. It proved to be one of his most popular works among scholars. Indeed, his commentary of Job was one of the first early Hebrew books printed in Hebrew, in Ferrara in 1477.[98] His Job commentary, in a lot of ways, is a companion piece to book IV of Gersonides's *Milhamot*, a work that is chiefly concerned with the providence of God and the issue of theodicy.

In the introduction to Gersonides's commentary of Job, contemporary scholar Abraham Lassen gives a general introduction to the commentary. Lassen informs us:

> The class of commentaries to which Gersonides's commentary on Job belongs is that of philosophical exegesis. The Book of Job deals primarily with the problem of injustice in the world, namely why the wicked prosper and the righteous suffer.[99]

In the same introduction, Lassen points out that nearly three-quarters of the *Milhamoth* is devoted to the issue of innocent suffering.[100] And the methods of exegesis that Gersonides employs, for the most part, are those of Aristotle. He does, however, say that he takes a three-level approach to any biblical text. The first of these is the historical-literal understanding of the text; this is followed by what he calls the "General Reading" of the text. Finally, at the deepest level of interpretation, Gersonides finds the philosophical sense of the text, primarily in terms of Aristotle.

Gersonides's first level of interpretation is primarily philological and historical; the second level also provides an interpretation of the text using tools from Aristotle; but the deepest level of the text provides allegorical and symbolic meanings, what the medieval Jewish philosophers called the *Derash*.

Gersonides begins his commentary on the book of Job by providing a paraphrase of Job 1:1–6. He points out that these verses do not ascribe wisdom to the Man from Uz. Like Maimonides, Gersonides sees the flaw in the figure of Job to be connected to what Aristotle calls the "intellectual virtues." These are primarily virtues connected to teaching and learning; and for Gersonides, this is what Job lacked.

Gersonides suggests that the proper translation of *tam va yashar* of Job 1:1 should be "perfect and upright," but he points out that the text does not ascribe to Job the adjective of wisdom. In his view, Job knew a great deal about the sciences, but suffered for a lack of the intellectual virtues. In commenting on Job 1:6, Gersonides identifies the Satan as "the one from whom comes all imaginary evils that originate in external causes, the Satan."[101]

Gersonides goes on to say that the purpose of the Satan is "to cause people to deviate from the path and the will of God."[102] Gersonides saw the Satan as a demonic force, but not as a part of the divine plan. Gersonides does not include a translation, nor a commentary, for Job 19:25, 27, and 28. Nor does he make any comments about the nature of the *Goel* in 19:25–26. In fact, he says nothing about the verse being connected to resurrection of the body. Gersonides does observe, however, that in ch. 14 of Job, at vv. 12–14, the patriarch believes that "resurrection is a possibility for human beings at the end of time."[103]

Gersonides says that Job makes these comments in ch. 14 "in order to refute the opinions of his friends who attempted to prove he is suffering for his rebellious acts or words."[104] About the Elihu chapters, Gersonides says that the fourth friend is angry with the other friends because they claim to be as righteous as God. Elihu, at least for Gersonides, says that the cause of Job's suffering is that he says words against God.[105]

Still, like many of the other medieval Jewish interpreters of the book, Gersonides believed that Elihu is an advocate for the test theodicy, the moral qualities approach, and the divine plan theory. In fact, Gersonides sees the speeches of the fourth friend to be a precursor to the speeches of Yahweh, beginning in ch. 38. Gersonides renders Job 42:5–6 this way:

> Before I heard of your Providence by hearsay,
>
> But now my eyes have seen You.
>
> Therefore, I reject my former opinion, and I am comforted
>
> With the pains that have stricken me.[106]

Gersonides supplies "my former opinion" as the direct object of 42:6, and he says nothing of the *afar va efer*, or "dust and ashes." He translates the verb of 42:6b, *niham*, as "comfort," but he says nothing about Job being comforted in dust and ashes. What he does say, according to Gersonides, is that he is comforted about the "pains that have stricken him."[107] Whether this means that Job is content that he is mortal, or some other interpretation, is not entirely clear.

In the period of the Christian church from the form of the New Testament in the first century to the time of Jerome and Augustine in the fifth century, there are a variety of scholars, hymns, and texts that mention the patriarch Job and his book. Among these early Christian thinkers are: Polycarp of Smyrna (ca. 69–155); Justin Martyr (ca. 100–165); Clement of Alexandria (ca. 150–215); Tertullian of Carthage (155–225);

Origen of Alexandria (ca. 185–260); Lactantius (ca. 260–330); Anthony the Great (ca. 251–356); John Cassian (360–432); Cyril of Alexandria (375–444); Didymus the Blind (313–398); Ephrem the Syrian (ca. 306–380); Gregory of Nyssa (335–394); John Chrysostom (349–407); Theodore of Mopsuestia (ca. 350–428); and fourth-century poet Prudentius (348–405).[108]

Of these Christian thinkers and texts, the most significant for our purposes are: Tertullian's work "On Patience," particularly ch. 14; Cyprian's "God and Patience"; John Chrysostom's "The Power of Man to Resist the Devil"; Theodore of Mopsuestia's "Homilies"; and Prudentius's poem the "Psychomachia." In this latter work, Prudentius describes the fight between the allegorical Patience and her defeat of Ire, or Rage.[109]

If we date the beginning of the Dark Ages with the fall of Rome in the fifth century, then Saints Jerome and Augustine are our first two commentators on the book of Job in the Christian Middle Ages. The former saint's comments come mostly in his Latin translation of the book. The latter, in a number of his works, where the Bishop of Hippo alludes to the Man from Uz and his book. Among these works are his *On the Forgiveness of Sins and Baptism* and in book XX of the *City of God*.[110]

Saint Jerome completed two separate translations of the book of Job, one from the Septuagint around 389, and the other from the Hebrew text, completed in the spring of 406. He tells us twice in his preface to his translation how difficult he found the book to render into Latin. In fact, he tells us he persuaded some Jewish scholars to teach him to read the book in Hebrew.[111]

Despite the fact that he studied the Hebrew language, he nevertheless makes a number of misreadings that a more experienced hand and mind in the language would not make. In some places he simply mistakes the meaning of the Hebrew (6:15 and 25; 11:3; 13:9; 19:27; and 24:5–8, for examples); in another seven instances, he misreads sentence divisions (12:19; 13:13; 19:25; 22:24–25; 26:2; 33:7; and 39:28). In another six verses, Jerome, or his copyist, made transcribing errors (7:2; 8:16; 16:15; 17:19; 19:24; and 30:12).[112]

In a much larger number of examples, Jerome prefers the Septuagint reading to that of the Hebrew text. Among the most important of these are at: 2:10; 3:12–13; 7:1 and 21; 8:5–7; 10:2; 14:17; 19:25–27; 33:21; 35:14; 38:3; and 41:14. Many of these preferences for the Greek text have to do with theological issues. For example, in the Hebrew version of Job 14:14, the text asks a rhetorical question, "If a man dies, shall he live again?" The Septuagint, as well as Jerome, translates the line from an interrogatory to a declarative statement:

> If a man dies, he shall live again.[113]

The editors of the Septuagint took a similar approach to the end of Job 42:17, where the Greek text adds several lines to imply that Job believed in resurrection of the body—something not found in the original Hebrew text. Jerome, at the end of the book, follows the LXX, over and against the MT. In Jerome's rendering of Job 1:1, he translates *tam va yashar* as "simple and upright," perhaps in an attempt to show that, because of the doctrine of original sin, no man is "blameless and upright," as the Hebrew has it.

In many other smaller ways, Jerome deviates from the Hebrew text. He gives Latin equivalents to the names of Job's comforters; He does not insist, as the Greek text does, that the friends are "kings." Jerome keeps the Hebrew sense of Job 9:22, "All is one, I say, he consumes both the innocent and the pious," but the translators of the Septuagint could not bring themselves to the same conclusion.[114]

Saint Augustine makes many comments on the book of Job in the two works mentioned above—*On the Forgiveness of Sins and Baptism* and in the *City of God*. In the former work, the Bishop of Hippo employs Job 9:2–3; 1:22; 34:34; 42:5–6; 1:8; and 1:21 to argue for the doctrine of original sin.[115] He does the same thing in the *City of God*, using Job 1:2; 14:4; 15:14; 34:30; and 38:7. Of these comments, 14:4 is the central one. Augustine agrees with Jerome that the proper definition of the line should be this:

> Who can bring a clean thing out of an unclean thing? There is not one.[116]

Similarly, Augustine thought the proper rendering of Job 15:14 should be, "What is man that he should be clean? Or he that is born of a woman, that he can be righteous."[117] In book I, 23–24 of the *City of God*, Augustine compares Job to Cato, the Younger. The latter committed suicide, while the former refused to do so.[118] The Bishop of Hippo identifies Job's wife with Eve's actions in the garden of Eden. In fact, Augustine calls her a *Diablo Aduitrix*, or a Handmaid of the Devil.[119]

Saint Augustine correctly identifies the theological points of view of Eliphaz, Bildad, and Zophar to be retributive justice; but he points out that the understanding of the fourth friend of Job, Elihu, is quite different from the views of the other three. In fact, he ties this conclusion to the close of the book, where God tells Eliphaz that he, and his two friends, have not "spoken the truth, as Job has done." Augustine points out that Elihu is nowhere to be found.[120] Much of what Augustine says about the Man from Uz and his book may also have come from his teacher, Saint Ambrose, Bishop of Milan, who wrote a work called *Job and David*.[121]

In this text, Ambrose presents Job as an exemplar of patience. Ambrose also saw Job's wife as an agent of the devil, as Augustine did. Ambrose also detects resurrection of the body at Job 14:7–11; and original sin at 14:4 and 15:14.[122]

The period from Augustine until the fourteenth century saw two major commentaries on the book of Job—that of Gregory the Great and Thomas Aquinas. We move next to an exploration of these two Christian scholars, and what they have to say about the Man from Uz and his book.

Pope Gregory the Great, a member of the Anaci family, was born in Rome in 540. His father was a wealthy lawyer and Roman administrator. In the year of Gregory's ascension to the papacy, Rome was struck with a violent flood and a bout of plague that followed. Altogether, Gregory was pope from 590 until 604, the year of his death.

During his time as pope, Gregory also suffered from ill health, mostly digestive and heart problems, so he often saw himself as a Job figure much like Jesus.

Gregory began the work on his *Moralia in Job* in the year 579, and it was not completed until 595, after he had been pope for five years. In the preface to his Job commentary, Gregory vows to bring out "the allegorical meanings of the letter of the story . . . and also to give the moral meanings of the text."[123] Gregory tells us that "this kind of project had never been conducted in the Church before."[124] Thus, his conclusion about his method is this:

> I desired to lay open the deep mysteries in the Book of Job, so far as the truth could inspire me with the power of doing so.[125]

Gregory also indicates in several of his letters that he has other personal reasons for completing the commentary. In a letter to Leander, the Bishop of Seville, for example, Gregory refers to the suffering that has been brought to his personal life, and desires more thoroughly to understand the place of that suffering in the providence of God. Thus, in his four-volume commentary on the book of Job, Gregory takes each verse of the book and renders the literal, moral, and allegorical understandings of the text, though at times it is difficult to keep the three separate. In fact, Lawrence Besserman, commenting on Gregory's historical and moral understandings of Job 3:3, tells us this:

> Without checking back to see which is which, most readers, I think, would be hard put to say which of the latter two passages is the historical, or literal interpretation of Job 3:3, and which is the moral, or non-literal one.[126]

In the preface to his first volume of the *Moralia*, Gregory speaks to the question of whether Job was a Gentile or a Jew. His answer is that Job "is a Just Pagan, and he is set side by side with the lives of the Just Israelites."[127] Although Pope Gregory did not know Hebrew, he nevertheless, relied on three sources for his understanding of the book of Job—the Septuagint, the Vulgate, and earlier church fathers who had commented on the book.

In his *Moralia*, Gregory finds Job 14:4 as a proof text for original sin, as he does 25:4. Like Augustine, Gregory also sees Job's wife at 2:9 as a *diablo aduitrix*, or a "helper of the Devil."[128] He calls the first three comforters "stupid, mean-spirited men," and he offers fanciful meanings for their names. Eliphaz means "contempt for God." Bildad, "old and alone." And Sophar, as he calls him, means "with dwindling prospects."[129]

Gregory finds proof for resurrection of the body at Job 1:5; 14:14; and 19:25–27, the *Goel* passage. Gregory finds that Job sitting on his dung heap at 2:8 to be a "sign of the Incarnation." In fact, throughout his commentary, Gregory sees the patriarch as a *Jobus Christi*, or Christ figure. Gregory also in several places in his commentary of Job displays a blatant anti-Semitism, such as at 4:4 and 38:14. In the former, Gregory says that the punishment of Job's children is "actually symbolic punishment of the Jews."[130]

At 38:14, Gregory relates that in Egypt the Jews were abandoned to the ways of the Gentiles; but when he brought them forth to the promised land, he gives them a "Seal" for the "preservation of His mysteries."[131] In many other places in his commentary on Job, Gregory also displays an anti-Semitic stance, though he was decidedly against the idea of "forced conversion" in regard to the Jews.[132]

The period from the death of Gregory the Great in the early seventh century to the birth of Thomas Aquinas in the early thirteenth century saw a collection of nearly two dozen Christian thinkers who made voluminous comments on the Man from Uz and his book. Among these exegetes were the following:

1. Paterius (6th and 7th c.), disciple of Gregory.
2. Andreas (7th-c. monk who collected earlier comments on the book).
3. Fructuosus (d. 665) a Gothic general and abbot of Dumium.
4. Maximus the Confessor (ca. 580–662), Palestinian-born theologian and scholar.
5. Adamnan (ca. 624–704.), abbot in Iona, Ireland, and author of *The Holy Sites*.
6. Lathcen (d. 661.), French exegete.
7. John of Damascus (650–750), Arab monastic theologian.
8. Theophanes (775–845), bishop of Nicaea and writer of hymns.
9. John the Elder (8th c.), Syriac writer in the Church of the East.
10. Cynewulf's "Ascension" (late 8th c.) mentions Job throughout the poem.
11. Cassia (ca. 805–867), poet and hymnographer; founded convent in Constantinople.
12. Photius (ca. 820–891), Byzantine churchman.
13. Arethas of Caesarea (ca. 860–940), Byzantine scholar and archbishop of Caesarea.
14. Walafred of Strabo (808–849), Benedictine abbot and theologian.
15. The "Phoenix" (9th-c. anonymous poem that mentions Job several times).
16. Ishodad of Merv (mid-9th c.), Syrian bishop of Hedatta.
17. Eynsham's "Homily on Job" (10th c.).
18. Symeon the New Theologian (ca. 949–1022), Byzantine Christian monk.
19. Theophyllact of Ohrid (ca. 1050–1108), Byzantine archbishop of Ohrid.
20. Bar Hebraeus (1226–1286), Syrian bishop and interpreter.[133]

Many of these items are little more than commentaries of Gregory's *Moralia*. Of these texts, the most significant are those of: Lathcen, John of Damascus, Walafred of Strabo, the poem the "Phoenix," and the commentary of Syrian bishop Ishodad of

Merv. Indeed, Ishodad made commentaries on many books of the Old Testament, including Job, as well as all of the New Testament.[134] Additionally, the Venerable Bede, Albert of Metz, John the Abbot, and Odo of Cluny, a learned tenth-century Frankish monk, also completed a commentary on Gregory's *Moralia*.[135]

Two centuries later, in the late twelfth century, Peter Riga wrote a poem called "Liber Iob," or "The Life of Job." Riga (1140–1209) was a Latin poet and canon of the Rheims Cathedral. His *Liber Iob* is written in six hundred lines of hexametric poetry, in much of the same spirit as Odo of Cluny two centuries before him. The most striking elements of Riga's poem are his emphasis on the Patient Job, a promise of survival after death, Job's wife as an agent of the devil, and Job as a *Jobus Christi* figure; but another significant element of Riga's poem on Job are the many passages he adduces from Gregory and Odo to prove the moral culpability of the Jews. In fact, in Riga's six-hundred-line poem on the Man from Uz, he finds over two dozen passages that allude to God's condemnation of the Jews for not accepting the Messiah.[136]

Like Gregory, one of the passages where Peter Riga finds anti-Semitism is his comments on Job 1:5, where Riga sees both an allusion to the sacrifice of Jesus, as well as the Jews' failure to recognize and worship the Messiah.[137] Peter Riga also finds beliefs in immortality of the soul and resurrection of the body at Job 10:1; 14:14; 19:25–27; and 42:17, among other Jobean passages. This brings us to the most significant Christian commentary of the book of Job in the High Middle Ages, the commentary by Thomas Aquinas, the subject matter of the next part of this history.

Thomas Aquinas (1225–1274) was born to royal parents on both sides in a town called Roccasecca, not far from Naples. He was a student of both the Benedictines and the Dominicans, and eventually studied with Albert the Great at the University of Paris in 1245.

Later they moved together to Cologne, from 1248 until 1252. In 1252, Thomas returned to Paris, where he taught philosophy and theology until 1259. From that time until 1268, Thomas was an adviser to the papal court in Rome. In 1269, he returned to Paris for the third time. He remained there until 1272, when he returned to his native Naples. He died two years later.[138]

Thomas Aquinas's most famous works are his two summas. The *Summa Theologica* (1265–1272) and the *Summa Contra Gentiles* (1260.) Thomas also wrote a number of other treatises that range on topics from the nature of truth and evil, to the eternality of the world and the nature of being. In addition, Thomas also wrote a number of biblical commentaries, including works on the Psalms, the Gospels, and the book of Job.[139]

The method of Thomas Aquinas's exegesis is decidedly on the side of the literal-historical perspective. In the introduction to his commentary on the book of Job, Thomas tells us this:

> Our intent is to expound the book according to the letter, for the Blessed Gregory has opened its mystical meanings (*mysteria*).[140]

Although Thomas was primarily interested in expounding the literal meaning of Job, and although the literal level of the text says nothing about Job suffering from original sin, Job's wife as an agent of the devil, and belief in immortality and resurrection, Thomas finds these doctrines and beliefs throughout the book in his analysis. It is important to remember, however, that Thomas did not know Hebrew, so he worked primarily from the text of the Vulgate.

In his commentary on Job 1:1–5, Thomas makes a distinction between two kinds of *puritas*, or purity. He calls these *puritas innocentis* and *puritas poenitentis*. The former refers to those who have not departed from God's plan. The latter are those who have departed, but who have genuinely repented. In Thomas's view, Job is an example of *puritas innocentis*. Thus, he renders 1:1 as "without guile and upright."[141]

In his commentary on Job 2:9, Thomas finds Job's wife very much the same way as Augustine and Gregory did. Thomas tells us about Job's spouse:

> She proceeds to works of perverse suggestion, saying Bless, that is Curse, . . . curse to gain prosperity . . . as if to say, Consider yourself dead, since nothing is left to you who insists in integrity.[142]

For Thomas, the real motivator of Job's wife, however, is something we have seen many times before:

> Not only through his wife was the Devil trying to upset Blessed Job's soul, but also through his friends, who, although they came to console him, nevertheless proceeded to words of rebuke.[143]

In regard to the Satan and the *Bene ha Elohim*, or "Sons of God" in the Prologue of Job, Thomas makes distinction between good angels and bad angels. "Good angels are related to the judgment of God . . . this is different than those things done by the wicked angels."[144]

Thomas says that Satan's purpose "is to lead Job to impatience and blasphemy."[145] Thomas finds belief in immortality at 7:16 and 14:14; resurrection at 19:25–27 and 42:17; and original sin at 14:4; 15:14; and 25:4.[146]

Thomas argues that if Job has a weakness, it is in relation to what Aristotle calls the intellectual virtues, particularly in regard to humility. Like the Jewish medieval exegetes on the book of Job, Thomas thinks that Job lacks an "intellectual humility." Thomas also believes that the ten children restored to Job in the Epilogue are the same set of children he lost in the Prologue.[147]

Between the time of Thomas Aquinas in the thirteenth century and the Reformation, beginning in the sixteenth century, there are two other significant treatments of the Man from Uz in the Christian tradition. These come from Thomas à

Kempis (1380–1471) and the philological and exegetical work of Nicholas of Lyra (1270–1349), Franciscan commentator at the University of Paris.

The source of Thomas à Kempis's comments on the book of Job is his *Imitatio Christi*, or "Imitation of Christ." Most contemporary scholars date the work sometime between 1390 and 1440. The work is constructed in five sections. Those sections are divided this way:

- Section 1. "Hints for Spiritual Living."
- Section 2: "Emphasize Spiritual Rather Than Material Things."
- Sections 3 and 4: "Affirmations of a Christ-Centered Life."
- Section 5: "The Importance of the Eucharist."[148]

Chapters 13 and 14 of the *Imitatio Christi* are the most important for our purposes. The former chapter discusses "The Uses of Adversity." The chapter also offers us a model for dealing with adversity—the Man from Uz. About Job 7:1, Thomas à Kempis reminds us, "The life of a man upon the Earth is a trial," an obvious reference to what we have called the "test theodicy."

In the same chapter, Thomas à Kempis refers to the Prologue of Job, "where the Devil finds occasions to deceive, for he never sleeps, but goes about looking for those he might devour," a version of the demonic forces view. In regard to Job 14:4, the fifteenth-century writer suggests that Job believes in original sin. Thomas à Kempis relates about the verse:

> There is no man wholly free of temptations so long as he lives because we have the root temptation within ourselves, in that we are born in concupiscence.[149]

Nevertheless, à Kempis sees Job as a model for "resistance to temptation." About holy men like Job he relates:

> For through them we are humbled, purified, and instructed. All saints have passed through much tribulation and temptation, and have been purified by them.[150]

In these two short chapters of the *Imitatio Christi*, Thomas à Kempis employs Job and his book to explicate his views on the Christian ability to withstand suffering and temptation. In the process, he employs the influences of demonic forces theory, the test theodicy, and the moral qualities perspective, all in a space of twenty pages.

In the period between Thomas Aquinas and the Reformation, the most significant commentator on the book of Job is the French Franciscan Nicholas of Lyra, who was born in Normandy in 1270 and died in Paris in 1349. Nicholas's best-known exegetical work, and the one by which he became famous, is his *Commentary of Universal Holy Scripture*, a fifty-volume commentary on the entire Bible, including a lengthy commentary on the book of Job.[151]

For the most part, Nicholas tends toward the literal-historical understanding of the text; but he makes a distinction between what he calls the "Prophetic Literal" and the "Divine Literal."[152] Additionally, Nicholas believed that the allegorical or mystical brand of exegesis had been "choking the literal sense."[153] A few centuries later, Martin Luther agreed with Nicholas. Speaking of Lyra, the German reformer tells us this about his predecessor in this couplet:

Si Lyra non lyrasset / If Lyra had not piped

Lutherus non satasset. / Luther would not have danced.[154]

One important difference between the commentaries on Job of Thomas Aquinas and Nicholas of Lyra is that the latter had a basic understanding of the ancient Hebrew language. In fact, Lyra says, "The Latin Vulgate cannot compare to the Hebrew Truth."[155] In fact, Nicholas's knowledge of Hebrew led the French scholar to several startling conclusions about the book of Job, often at odds with the history of Christian interpretation of the book.

Among these conclusions are the following: the Satan works for God, and everything he does is with God's permission; that the Hebrew text of Job 19:25–27 is so corrupted, it is beyond understanding; that the terms *tam va yashar* should be translated as "morally blameless and upright"; that the Masoretic Text shows little interest in survival after death, either immortality or resurrection; and that the book of Job features a man who is patient in the beginning and end, but angry in the dialogue.[156]

Nicholas also showed an impressive command of the early Judaic materials about the book of Job, particularly from the Talmud and the Mishnah. He broke away, for example, from more than a thousand years of Christian interpretation of Job that said the patriarch was the grandson of Esau. Nicholas argues instead, along with rabbis from the Babylonian Talmud, that Job came from the line of Nahor, Abraham's brother.[157]

At any rate, the influence of Nicholas of Lyra's exegetical talents was felt immediately in biblical scholarship in general, and on the book of Job, in particular. Luther called Lyra, "A fine soul, a great Hebraist, and a true Christian."[158] Indeed, if there is a father of the historical-critical method in modern Christian exegesis, it is Nicholas of Lyra. This brings us to understandings of the figure of Job in medieval Islamic scholarship, our next topic of this history.

The earliest medieval Muslim sources on Prophet Ayyub are two Yemeni Jews who converted to Islam, Ka'b Al-Ahbar and Wahb Ibn Munabbih. The former is the earliest authority on South Arabian Folklore. The latter (654–744) served as a judge for many years in the early eighth century. They are important for our purposes because the pair offer a description of Prophet Ayyub. According to the two Yemeni scholars, Ayyub was a "tall man with a large head, and crisp hair, beautiful eyes, and a short neck, with long limbs."¹⁵⁹ An early follower of the Prophet Muhammad, Ibn Ishaaq tells us that Prophet Ayyub "was from the area of Edom, south of Palestine."¹⁶⁰

There is much confusion in the Islamic tradition about Ayyub's family. Al-Thabani, who died in 1035, in his *Stories of the Prophets*, refers to Ayyub's wife as "Rahma," the daughter of Ephraim.¹⁶¹ Others call her Dinah, Leah, and Mahkir, the daughters of Manassas or Jacob.¹⁶²

Still other Muslim traditions identify Ayyub's wife as "Dina," most likely a variant of Dinah, as Ayyub's second wife. This tradition says that "she bore 26 news sons to the prophet Ayyub."¹⁶³

Al-Tabari (839–923), Persian scholar and historian, tells us that "the most loved and holy men of Allah are able to withstand many tortures, like those of Prophet Ayyub."¹⁶⁴ Persian scholar Al-Zamakhshari (1075–1144), a member of the Muta'zalite School of Qur'anic exegesis, wrote an Arabic paraphrase of Prophet Ayyub. In that paraphrase, Ayyub says to his wife:

> I am ashamed before Allah to call upon Him when the length of my tribulations has not reached that of my belongings.¹⁶⁵

In the twelfth century, scholar Ibn Asakir, anecdotal historian, suggests that at the resurrection of the dead, Prophet Ayyub will be held up "as a role model to others."¹⁶⁶ Asakir believed the source of Ayyub's great patience, or *Sabir* in Arabic, was his foreknowledge that all of his goods and family would eventually be restored by Allah. This is a tradition that may have its roots in the *Testament of Job*.¹⁶⁷ Ibn Asakir also believed that Ayyub's home was in the city of Damascus.¹⁶⁸ Palestinian judge and historian Mugir Ed-Din Hambeli (1456–1522) was also of the opinion that Ayyub was from Damascus.¹⁶⁹ This is a very old tradition in Islam going back to the medieval period.

Medieval Arab geographer Al-Maqdisi (945–991) thought that Prophet Ayyub sat on his dung heap for "seven years, seven months, seven weeks, seven days, seven hours, and seven seconds," while fourteenth-century exegete Ibn Kathir believed that "Ayyub's suffering last eighteen years."¹⁷⁰ Thirteenth-century commentator Al-Baydawi held many views of Prophet Ayyub that cannot be distinguished from Christian understandings at the same time. Indeed, about the Qur'an's 21:83, one of the Arabic passages that mentions Ayyub we have introduced earlier in this study, Al-Baydawi tells us:

> We ought to be patient like Ayyub was patient, for we will be rewarded the way that prophet Ayyub was rewarded.¹⁷¹

Al-Baydawi suggests that Ayyub's reward consists not just in double recompense and a long life, but also in eternal life in paradise, or *Jannah*, in Arabic; but al-Baydawi implies that the form of survival after death will be immortality of the soul, or *Nafs*, or *momin*, in Arabic.¹⁷²

PART I: THE HISTORY OF INTERPRETING THE BOOK OF JOB

Mohammad Ali, Egyptian medieval scholar, suggests that Ayyub's suffering is meant to remind us of Allah's later prophet Muhammad. Indeed, Ali turns Ayyub into a "Muhammad figure," rather than a Christ figure.[173]

In medieval Islam from the seventh to the fifteenth centuries, the following conclusions may be made about the Prophet Ayyub:

1. He was known for his patience.
2. His suffering lasted many years.
3. Ayyub was seen as a model for how to deal with adversity.
4. He came from the area near Damascus, or possibly Edom.
5. There is some confusion about the wife of Ayyub, particularly her name.
6. There is some confusion about how many sons with which Ayyub was compensated. Some say fourteen; others as many as twenty-six.[174]

This brings us to an analysis of the figure of Job in Jewish scholarship in the early modern period, the fifteenth through the seventeenth centuries—the subject matter of the next section of this history of interpretation.

Early Modern Readings of the Book of Job (1500 to 1800)

The fifteenth through seventeenth centuries saw the development of six major Jewish commentaries on the book of Job. These were those of the following scholars:

1. Simeon Duran (1361–1444)
2. Joseph Albo (1380–1444)
3. Isaac Abravanel (1437–1508)
4. Abraham Farissol (1437–1575)
5. Leon Judah de' Sommi (1525–1590)
6. Abraham Yagel (1525–1590)[175]

Of these Jewish commentaries the most important one is that of Rabbi Simeon Duran, who was born on the island of Majorca. As a young man, he studied philosophy, astronomy, mathematics, and medicine, first in Palma, and later in Algiers, where he died.[176] Duran mostly was known for his commentaries on the Talmud and the Bible, including his treatise called the *Ohev Mishpat*, his commentary of the book of Job.[177]

Duran's work was written in two parts. The first part is an introduction to the biblical book of Job. It mostly relates to Moses Maimonides's, and other Jewish scholars', use of Aristotle's philosophy. The second part of the *Ohev Mishpat* is a lengthy commentary on the book. The *Ohev Mishpat* was originally published in Venice in 1589. Later, a second edition was published in Amsterdam from 1724 until 1727.[178]

For the most part, Duran's commentary on Job is a series of glosses on the comments of Maimonides and other scholars on the book; Duran does, however, make a number of genuinely original comments about the book. He suggests, for example, that the book of Job should be afforded the same authority as the five books of the Torah. In fact, in several places in his commentary, he says, "The Book of Job is Torah."[179]

Another original idea of Simeon Duran about the book of Job can be found in his commentary on Job 26:5–7. The Hebrew of these verses looks something like this:

1. The shades below tremble, the waters and their dwellers.

2. Sheol is naked before God, and Abaddon has no covering.

3. He stretches out the north over the void, and hangs the earth upon nothing.[180]

Duran makes a number of observations in his commentary on these verses. Among these is the view that he believes that the earth described here is round and is suspended in the air. Indeed, Duran makes a number of comments about cosmology in his commentary on the book of Job, including Job 22:14; 28:24; 37:17–18; 38:4, 12, and 31; 39:1 and 19. The Hebrew of the first of these texts speaks of God walking on the *Hug*, or "vault," of heaven.[181] This is most likely a reference to the Old Testament idea that the world rests on pillars that are connected by the *Hug*. Rabbi Simeon Duran gives Amos 9:6; Isa 40:21; and Prov 8:27 as parallel texts concerning the *Hug*. In the first of these passages, as Duran points out, it speaks of "the *Hug*, or vault, upon the Earth."[182] Duran suggests that Isa 40:21 should be rendered this way:

Have you not known? Have you not heard?

Has it not been told to you from the beginning?

Have you not understood from the foundations of the Earth?[183]

By this Duran tells us the text means the *Hug*, and the pillars that hold it up; but, as we indicated earlier, Duran believes the earth is round, and it is suspended in space. Duran also gives an original interpretation to the tenth verse of Job 28. The Masoretic Text gives us this for the verse:

He cuts out channels in the rocks, and his eyes see every precious thing.[184]

Duran believes the "precious things" are "silver and gold." But he points out that just two verses later in ch. 28, the "Hymn to Wisdom" begins and continues to v. 28; and that may be exactly what the text means by "precious things." That is, human knowledge of *Hokmah*, or Wisdom.[185]

The exegetical work of fifteenth-century scholar Joseph Albo on the book of Job also contains a number of original ideas on the Man from Uz and his book. In his commentary of ch. 3, for example, Albo suggests that there are two basic views for understanding human life, what he calls the "Philosopher's View" and the "Astronomer's View." In the former view, Albo informs us, the earth and the planets exist in an entirely sublunary existence. In the latter view, the astronomer's view, life is determined by the movement of the stars, or a kind of stellar determinism or astrology.[186]

Indeed, Rabbi Albo believes that Job is an advocate of the astronomer's view. He thinks that Job cursing the day of his birth, and in the rest of ch. 3 of the book, give ample evidence of this position.[187]

Another original conclusion that Rabbi Joseph Albo makes about the book of Job is that the patriarch rejects the idea of reincarnation, or *Gilgul* in Hebrew. He says about the idea, "It is not necessary to come again."[188] Another original idea that Albo has about the book of Job is that the major response the patriarch makes to why Job is suffering is what we have labeled the free will defense. Indeed, Albo finds this position in many of Job's speeches in the book, particularly at 1:1–5 and 42:5–6, or where Albo discusses the two *yetzerim* theory.[189]

Rabbi Albo does not find much, however, with regard to Job's belief in survival after death. He does not, for example, give the interpretation of immortality for the "tree passage" at Job 14:7–13. Nor does he give resurrection of the body as an explanation for Job 19:25–27.

In fact, in Albo's view there is little in the book to suggest belief in immortality, resurrection, or transmigration of the soul.[190]

Rabbi Isaac Abravanel, fifteenth-century Portuguese rabbi, also wrote an extensive commentary on the book of Job. Like Duran and Rabbi Albo, Abranavel also develops a number of original ideas about the Man from Uz and his friends. Perhaps the most interesting of these is Rabbi Isaac's view of Eliphaz, Bildad, and Zophar. While most Jewish commentators on the book identify the theological view of the three friends to be retributive justice, Isaac Abravanel takes a much more positive view of the first three friends of Job—much more so than the other medieval Jewish interpreters in the fifteenth to seventeenth centuries.

For example, Rabbi Abravanel suggests that the activities of Bildad, Eliphaz, and Zophar develop in three stages in their relationships to Job. First, Rabbi Isaac tells us, the friends tore their robes when they saw Job's disfigurement. Then they threw dust and ashes into the air, to signify mourning. Second, the friends sat silently for seven days and did not utter a word. Finally, Abravanel tells us, "the three friends offer words of advice and consolation."[191]

Throughout Isaac Abravanel's commentary on the book of Job, he continues to take a much more positive view of Eliphaz, Bildad, and Zophar—much more so than other medieval Jewish exegetes. Rabbi Abraham Farissol was born in Avignon, France. When he was seventeen years old, his family moved to Farrar, Italy. Farissol's commentary on the book of Job was written around the year 1470. It was first published in a Rabbinic Bible, the Bomberg Bible, in 1517. It was subsequently published a second time in Amsterdam in 1721, in what was known as the Buxtorf Bible.[192] Rabbi Farissol only completed two commentaries of books of the Hebrew Bible—*Qoheleth*, or Ecclesiastes, and the book of Job.[193]

Farissol's commentary on the book of Job is important for a number of reasons. One of them is that in an addition of the commentary from 1524, America was mentioned for the first time in a Hebrew book. Much of Farissol's commentary on Job is taken up with what he sees as inaccurate Christian understandings of the Man from Uz and his book. For example, Farissol completely rejects the idea that the *Goel* passage at Job 19:25–27 is nothing more than what Christians see as an indication of the resurrection of Jesus.[194] Rabbi Farissol does point out, however, that the Masoretic Text's version of the three verses "is beyond our ability to interpret it, for it is corrupted beyond repair."[195]

Rabbi Farissol arrives at similar conclusions about Christian understandings of a number of other passages in Job that they believe indicate either immortality of the soul or resurrection of the body; and chief among these passages are Job 14:7–13; 33:4; and 34:14.[196] Another polemic to be found against Christian understandings of the book of Job by Rabbi Farissol is what amounts to a sustained attack that something like the Christian doctrine of original sin is to be found in the Hebrew book.

More specifically, although Christian scholars have found original sin in passages of Job like 5:7; 14:4; and 25:4, Farissol argues quite convincingly that none of these three passages have anything to do with the Christian understanding of original sin. Other passages that Farissol points to that Christian scholars believe indicate original sin include: Job 4:17; 9:2; 14:1; 15:14; and 22:2. Farissol also maintains that Christian scholars find immortality at Job 34:14 and resurrection at 7:4, in addition to 19:25–27; but he finds none of these to be persuasive arguments.[197] Farissol also suggests these views are also a product of Christian scholars' ignorance of classical Hebrew.

Along the way, in his commentary of the book of Job, Abraham Farissol points out that the Elihu chapters of chs. 32–37 have a much larger variety of names for the Divine than the earlier dialogue. Farissol also sees the Elihu chapters as a precursor for the God speeches that follow the fourth friend. We know that Farissol was familiar with Christian texts like Gregory the Great and Thomas Aquinas on Job, and even sixteenth-century Spanish exegetes like Lopez Ayala and Juan de Pineda.[198]

In his commentary on the book of Job, Abraham Farissol also points to a number of peculiarities in the Masoretic Text of the book. Among these are the many *hen*, or "behold," and *'im*, or "if," clauses of ch. 31; the variety of Hebrew words for "trap," "rope," "net," etc., in ch. 18; and the five different words for "lion" in ch. 5.[199]

Other theological elements of Rabbi Farissol's commentary on the Man from Uz and his book are what he sees as the Hebrew Bible's "Book of Deeds," at Job 14:5, and Job's belief that he comes to believe that God is hidden, as exemplified in chs. 23 and 24. The "Book of Deeds" in ancient Judaism was a view that all that happens on earth occurs because of a book on which God has written the affairs of all humans and other creatures.[200] Rabbi Farissol gives Lam 2:17; Eccl 3:1–8; Isa 14:24; and Jer 10:23 as parallel texts to Job 15:5.[201]

The idea of a Book of Deeds is much stronger in Islam than in Judaism or Christianity. In Islam, it is known as the "Preserved Tablet," or *Al-Lawh Al-Mafooz*. A number of passages in al-Qur'an speaks of the Preserved Tablet, such as surah 10:26; 18:16; 22:70; 42:48; and 57:22. In most of these, humans are completely subordinate to the "Decrees of Allah." Although Italian playwright, actor, and poet Leone Judah de Sommi (1525–1590) did not write a commentary on the book of Job, he nevertheless did make three observations about the Man from Uz and his book that have had some historical importance in the history of the reception of Job. First, Sommi believes that Job was the first drama written in the world, much older than the Greeks.[202]

Second, Leone Judah de Sommi thought, as many rabbis of the Talmud did, that the book of Job was written by Moses. In fact, like earlier medieval Jewish scholars, Sommi believed that the book of Job had the status of the Torah.[203] Finally, Rabbi de Sommi was the first Jewish scholar to argue that Job's theological position was much closer to Agnosticism than it was to Theism. Many Jewish scholars, particularly in the twentieth century, made the same argument. Thus, Leon de Sommi appears to have assented to the "Existentialist Job" motif.

Rabbi Abraham Yagel (1525–1590), Italian, Jewish catechist, philosopher, and Cabalist, also completed a commentary on the book of Job. Rabbi Yagel only wrote eight commentaries in all, one each on the books of the Torah, Psalms, Proverbs, and Job. The only extant edition of Yagel's commentary on the book of Job was published in Warsaw in 1857.[204]

For the most part, Yagel's commentary on the book of Job is a series of glosses on rabbinic views of the patriarch, as well as on Maimonides's views and other medieval commentaries, like Rashi, Abranavel, and Rabbi Farissol.[205] Nevertheless, Rabbi Yagel still makes some original observations about the Man from Uz and his book. Among those are: God rebukes Job for neglecting the study of nature; that the book of Job has a "happy ending"; and that Job should best be presented as a "novella," rather than as a book of the Bible.[206]

In addition to these works on Job by Jewish scholars in the fifteenth to seventeenth centuries, a number of other Jewish writers also wrote about the figure, including seventeenth-century Dutch philosopher Baruch Spinoza (1632–1677), who received an Orthodox education in his youth, but it was not long before he began to call into question many aspects of the faith—including the existence of angels, immortality of the soul, miracles, as well as the interpretation of Scripture.

Fearing retaliation from the Christian authorities in regard to Spinoza, the Jewish community of Amsterdam excommunicated Spinoza from the synagogue, in July of 1656. A decade later, the philosopher began working on his three-volume *Ethics*, and his most important exegetical and theological work, called the *Tractatus Theologico-Philosophicus*. This latter work was published anonymously and with an imprint on the title page from Hamburg, rather than Amsterdam.[207]

In his introduction to the *Tractaus*, Spinoza sketches out the purpose of the book. It is intended to show, he tell us, that "not only is liberty to philosophize compatible with devout piety, and with peace of the state, and that to take away that liberty is to destroy public peace and even piety itself."[208] In the same introduction, Spinoza observes that "the biggest mistake is for people to use philosophy to answer questions about the Bible."[209]

Spinoza believed that Christian scholars were often the principals who made this mistake; and chief among these Christians were those who used Greek philosophy in speaking about Scripture. For the Dutch philosopher, one of the chief offenders was Robert Burton and his *Anatomy of Melancholy*. Indeed, Spinoza argues against the Renaissance thinker's propensity to see the book of Job as a Renaissance text, disguised in ancient, philosophical clothing.

Later in the *Tractatus*, Spinoza gives us three exegetical rules for reading and understanding Scripture. These are the following:

1. It is important to understand the nature and properties of the language in which it was written.

2. One should organize the content by subject, lumping together what is about the same topic.

3. One must understand the time and place of the writing of a work. Who wrote it? For what purpose? And for whom?[210]

Using these exegetical rules, Spinoza makes some startling conclusions about the Bible. The Torah could not have been written by Moses; that the writers of Scripture were no wiser than his beginning students; that miracles are natural events to be explained with natural laws; and that, above all, the moral content of Scripture is the most important aspect of the text.[211]

Spinoza also applies his methodology specifically to the Man from Uz and his book in chapters 7 and 10 of the *Tractatus*. In chapter 7, Spinoza refers to Ibn Ezra's view of the origin of the book of Job. Spinoza writes:

> Aben Ezra affirms in his commentary that the book of Job was translated into Hebrew out of another language, and that its obscurity arises from this fact.[212]

Spinoza repeats this claim in chapter 10 of the *Tractatus*, though he does not reveal what language he thought the book was originally in. Spinoza was fully aware of the issues that ancient and medieval Jewish commentators had raised about Job and his book. Whether, for examples, Job was a Jew and whether he was a historical figure. But the Dutch philosopher does not answer these questions. Rather he gives the following critique about the book:

> I myself must leave these matters undecided, but I conjecture that Job was a Gentile, and a man of very stable character, who at first prospered, then was assailed with terrible calamities, and finally was restored to great happiness.[213]

One final conclusion that Spinoza makes about the Man from Uz and his book is about the author of the text. Spinoza observes that it is less likely that a wretchedly ill man, lying among his ashes, wrote the book, "than a man reflecting at ease in his study."[214] Nevertheless, Spinoza ends his discussion of the book of Job by observing, "But these are mere conjectures without any solid foundation."[215] This brings us to Christian interpretations of the book of Job in the same period, the fifteenth to seventeenth centuries.

In the Christian tradition prior to the Reformation, in the fifteenth century a number of late medieval English literary works appeared with Job's motifs. These include an early fifteenth-century *Pety Job: Lessons of the Dirge*; an anonymous fifteenth-century Middle English paraphrase of the book called *The Life of Job*; and an anonymous fifteenth-century Middle French poem, "The Patience of Job." In addition, Chaucer, in his *Canterbury Tales*, also makes several references to the Man from Uz and his book.[216]

What all these late medieval Christian works on the book of Job have in common is that the Job being discussed, paraphrased, depicted, or turned into a drama is the saintly, patient Job of the prose Prologue and the Epilogue. The Job of the poetry, the angry or iconoclastic Job, is nowhere to be found in these fifteenth-century texts. The *Jobus Christi* image, that Job is a Christ-figure, and the Job as warrior/wrestler motif, are also both very prominent in these texts.

In the sixteenth century, the primary materials on the book of Job in the Christian tradition are major commentaries on the book, particularly in Spanish, and the Man from Uz and his book in the Reformation. Chief among Reformation thinkers who wrote extensively on the book of Job are Martin Luther, John Calvin, and Theodore Beza.

The sixteenth century saw six major literary works patterned on the book of Job. These are:

1. *L'Hystore de Job* (anonymous 16th-c. French text).
2. Robert Green's 1594 *The Historie of Job*.
3. Ralph Radcliffe's *Job's Afflictions* (ca. 1550).
4. Hans Sach's *Der Hiob*, German work (1546).
5. J. Narhausr's *Historia Jobs* (1546).
6. Phillip Desportes's *Poesis Chrestiennes* (1598), a collection of French poems on Job and other patriarchs of the Old Testament.[217]

The sixteenth century also saw the development of many musical compositions on the book of Job, usually motets. Among the European composers who completed motets on the book of Job were the following: Joachim Burck, William Byrd, Orlando di Lasso, Claudin De Sermisy, Georg Telemann, and at least a dozen other European composers in the sixteenth and seventeenth centuries who wrote motets with Jobean themes at their centers.[218]

The Reformation of the sixteenth century also saw a number of Christian scholars who completed translations, sermons, or other genres of literature with the Man from Uz and his book as the subject matter of these genres. Martin Luther, for example, translated the book of Job from the original Hebrew to German; John Calvin completed 159 sermons on the book of Job; and Theodore Beza wrote a commentary on the book of Job.[219]

Luther's understanding of exegesis was based on two principles. First, he eschews the allegorical method of interpretation. And second, he insists on the primacy of books that "preach Christ." As Luther tells us: "This is the touchstone by which all books are to be judged. When one sees whether they urged Christ or not."[220]

Luther, in a letter to his friend, George Spalatin on February 23, 1524, wrote about the difficulties of translating the book of Job. He informs his friend:

> The translation of Job gives us immense trouble on account of its exalted language, which seems to suffer even more, under our attempt to translate it, than Job did under the consolation of his friends, and seems to prefer to lie among the ashes.[221]

Presumably, what Luther meant by this remark is that the Hebrew version of the book of Job is among the most difficult Hebrew of the Old Testament. In translating the *tam*, or "blameless" of 1:1, he renders it *fromme*, or "pious." When introducing the Satan for the first time at 1:6, Luther uses the definite article *Der*; but Luther suggests *Der Satan* is *unter ihnen*, or "under them," rather than *betokh*, or "among" the sons of God. Perhaps this suggest that *Der Satan* has a lower status than the other angels in the mind of Luther.[222]

Luther's account of Job's wife at 2:9 is also quite different from the Hebrew text. In Luther's German, Job's wife says, "*Sage Gott und stirb*," or "Say God and die." Luther did not employ either the common High German word for "bless," which is *beglucken*, nor did he choose the most common word for curse, *verfluchen*.[223] Luther also makes some subtle adjustments to the language of chs. 7 and 14 of Job. He renders *ruah* ("spirit") and *nefesh* ("soul"), as *die Seele* and *Der Geist*, suggesting a body-soul dualism not found in the Hebrew.[224]

Luther employs the noun *Erloser* to translate the *Goel* in 19:25–27; the remaining of v. 26 is just as confusing for Luther as it is in the Hebrew original. Luther uses the German verb *erheben*, "to lift up," suggesting that Job will rise from the grave at *der letzte*, or "the last." Luther uses the verb *selbst*, or "perceive," rather than the traditional "see," at the end of v. 26.[225]

Luther also makes some subtle adjustments to the speeches of Elihu in chs. 32–37. Luther gives the fourth friend to look much more teleological than the other three friends. In fact, the German exegete suggests that Elihu argues for what we have called the "Moral Qualities View, as well as the Divine Plan Perspective."[226] At 38:1, rather than a whirlwind, Luther suggests that God speaks from a *Wettersstrum*, or a "tempest."[227]

Luther's account of 42:5–6 is also a departure from the Hebrew text. In Luther's rendering of these verses, v. 5 is a word-for-word translation, but he gives us this for 42:6:

> *Darum spreche ich mich schuldig und Busse und Asche.*[228]

This may be rendered in English:

> Thus, I am guilty myself, and repent in dust and ashes.[229]

In general, Martin Luther's German translation of the book of Job, which was completed in 1524, is a much more faithful rendering of the Hebrew original than any other translation before it, including the Septuagint and the Vulgate. In his preface to the book, Luther tells us that the purpose of the book of Job is this:

> The Book of Job deals with the question of whether misfortune comes from God even to the righteous. . . . Job stands firm and contends that God torments even the righteous without cause.[230]

Luther suggests that when Job speaks to God, he "speaks wrongly, but that in contending against his friends about his innocence before his suffering came, Job has spoken the truth."[231] In the end, Luther says this about the book of Job's conclusion:

> So the book carries this story ultimately to this conclusion: God alone is righteous, and yet no man is more righteous than another in the mind of God.[232]

In Luther's account, this is true because of the doctrine of original sin. Indeed, Luther finds *peccatum originale* in the book of Job at 4:17; 5:7; and 25:4, among other places.[233]

By the year 1553, reformer John Calvin had written over seven hundred sermons, but very little about the book of Job. From 1554 to 1556, however, he undertook a massive project of preaching on the Man from Uz and his book. In fact, altogether in those years, he completed 159 sermons on the book. Susan Shreiner correctly identifies the tenor of these sermons of Calvin on Job. She relates:

> Calvin too sees the story of Job as a book about the nature of Providence and History. He also portrays Job as one who insists on defending the doctrine of resurrection, and thereby extending divine justice to the last day.[234]

In the first of his sermons on Job, Calvin informs us that "Job's virtue is more than angelic, but he persists in hope until his final vindication."[235] Thus, Calvin employs the resurrected Job motif. Calvin also clearly sees Satan as a demonic figure. About the figure he observes:

> When the Devil lights the fire, he also pumps the bellows, that is to say, he finds men who are his own to prick us continuously and to lengthen their illnesses.[236]

Throughout his sermons on Job, Calvin maintains that the patriarch endorses retributive justice, but he renders 1:1 as "possessing integrity," rather than "blameless." He says "no one can possess perfection in this life." In a way, then, Calvin refuses to grant a basic presupposition of the book—that Job is "blameless and upright." Needless to say, Calvin, like Luther, did not render *tam va yashar* this way because of their doctrine of original sin.

It is curious, however, that Calvin does not use Job 19:25–27 as an Old Testament reference to Jesus and his resurrection. In fact, Calvin warns the reader not to take the *Goel* "out of context."[237] In his sermons on Job, Calvin also has positive things to say about Elihu and his speeches. In fact, he sees the fourth friend as having the best theological observations in the book, other than the God speeches.[238]

In the end of his sermons on the book of Job, Calvin falls back on his overriding theological principle of the sovereignty of God, and a concomitant view of divine plan theory that he finds in Elihu and the God speeches. Again, Susan Schreiner gives us a neat summary of Calvin's 159 sermons on Job. She relates:

> Calvin stood in a long line of exegetes who used the story of Job to confront the issue of suffering and providence.[239]

Theodore Beza (1519–1605), friend and biographer of Calvin, also became the head of the Geneva government after his mentor's death. Beza is important in the history of interpreting the book of Job in the Christian tradition for three important reasons. First, Beza translates the Hebrew *tam* of Job 1:1 the same way that Calvin did, "as possessing integrity."[240] Thus, like his mentor, Beza was unwilling to accept a fundamental presupposition of the Hebrew text—that Job was "blameless and upright." And like Calvin, Beza uses this translation because of his doctrine of original sin.

Second, Theodore Beza appropriated a very old tradition about the book of Job that goes all the way back to the fifth century and Theodore of Mopsuestia—to wit, that the book of Job was modeled on Greek tragedy.[241] This same claim was made by Horace Kallenin in the early twentieth century in his book entitled *The Book of Job as a Greek Tragedy*, published in 1918.[242]

Beza makes the same claim about the Man from Uz and his book, with the figure of Job being a classic tragic figure whose tragic flaw is *hubris*.[243]

The third and final reason that Theodore Beza is significant in terms of the history of interpreting the book of Job in the Christian tradition is that Beza invented a new genre, the paraphrase, for Europeans who wished to write about Job in the sixteenth and seventeenth centuries.

In those two centuries, particularly in English, French, and German, the following scholars constructed paraphrases of the book of Job:

1. Theodore Beza, *A Paraphrase of the Book of Job.*
2. George Sandy, *Paraphrase of Job.*
3. Helie le Cordier, *Paraphrase of Job.*
4. Henry Oxenden, *Jobus Triumphans.*
5. Richard Blackmore, *Paraphrase on the Book of Job.*
6. Frederick Spannheim, *Historia Jobi.*
7. Francis Quarles, *Job Militant.*[244]

Each of these seven works reduces the size of the biblical book by about a third. Each also primarily sees the Man from Uz from the Patient Job and the Job Militant points of view. There are also a host of other literary works based on the book of Job that were produced in Europe in the seventeenth century. Among these thinkers were Pedro Calderon, John Dryden, Felipe Godinez, and Daniel Defoe and Jonathan Swift's mentions of Job in their major works.[245] Oliver Goldsmith's *Vicar of Wakefield* also portrays the Vicar as a Job figure who suffers much, while suffering from overweening pride.[246] Thus, Goldsmith employed the *Jobus Christi* motif.

This brings us to modern views of Prophet Ayyub in the Islamic tradition, the topic of the next section of this receptive history.

In the modern period of Islamic history, from the fifteenth century to the present, there are very few references among scholars to Prophet Ayyub. Instead of philosophical and exegetical comments on Ayyub, what we do see in Islamic history are references to the prophet in Islamic art and among non-Muslim scholars in the Middle East. One of the most interesting fifteenth-century depictions of Prophet Ayyub in Islamic art is an illustrated manuscript owned by the Chester Beatty Library in Dublin.[247]

In the image, a healed Ayyub is accompanied by the Angel Jibril, who presents the prophet with a rose. The legend of the piece, which is written in Farsi, says, "Ayyub healed with the aid of these waters, and he died at the age of 93."[248] Several other Muslim sources also mention this age of Ayyub at his demise. It bears no relation to the extra 140 years Job is given in the Hebrew text at Job 42:17. At any rate, the image includes a stream that runs around Ayyub's feet. The healing stream appears to be the source of why the prophet's sores are healed.

Another sixteenth-century Islamic image of Prophet Ayyub is owned by the New York Public Library. The text is known as "The Legends of the Prophets" and was constructed by Quisas al-Anbya.

Again, Job is shown standing in a spring that flows around his feet. Again, Ayyub's sores appear to have been healed by the spring.[249] In this image, as well, Prophet Ayyub is accompanied by the Angel Jibril.

Among the modern, non-Muslim commentators on Prophet Ayyub, three non-Muslim European scholars may be mentioned. The first of these is British Orientalist and part-time solicitor George Sale (1697–1736). Sale completed the first major translation of al-Qur'an from Arabic to English, which he published in 1734. Sale makes a number of comments on Prophet Ayyub in his "Notes and Preliminary Discourses," at the beginning of his translation.[250] Sale also commented on Prophet Ayyub in Islam with regard to the four major passages of the Muslim Holy Book, where Job is mentioned. One of these comes in his commentary on the Qur'an's 21:83. Sale remarks:

> His wife, however, whom some call Rama, the daughter of Ephraim, the son of Joseph, and the others, Makhir, the daughter of Manasses, attended him with great patience, supporting him by what she earned with her labor. But then the Devil appeared to her one day, and after reminding her of their past prosperity, promised her that if she would worship him, he would restore all that they had lost; whereupon, she asks her husband's consent, who was so angry at the proposal, that he swore, if he were to recover, then he would give his wife one hundred lashes.[251]

George Sale also speaks of other modern Islamic views of Prophet Ayyub when he writes in the context of a Qur'anic passage on Job:

> Allah sent Jibril, and taking Ayyub by the hand, he raised him up; and at the same time a fountain sprang up at his feet, of which, having drunk from it, the worms fell off his body; and washing therein he recovered his former health and beauty; that God then restored all to him double; his wife also became young and handsome again and bearing him 26 sons; and that Ayyub, to satisfy his oath, was directed by God to strike her one blow with a palm branch having one hundred leaves.[252]

Two other non-Muslim nineteenth-century European scholars also mention Prophet Ayyub in their writings. The first is French archeologist Charles Clermont-Ganneau (1846–1923). The other is German scholar J. G. Weitzstein (1815–1905), Orientalist and Prussian diplomat.[253] At the end of the nineteenth century, the former traveled to Syria, where he found a monastery near Damascus that was called the "Monastery of Ayyub." The French scholar also saw what was called "Ayyub's tomb," as well as a rock on which he tread.[254]

Johan G. Weitzstein, as well, was taken to an area in Syria, near the city of Dennaba, where he was shown various items associated with the life of Prophet Ayyub, including his petrified worms. Earlier, Muslim scholar Mugir ed Din Hanbeli (1456–1522) also associated the life of Prophet Ayyub with areas near Damascus and elsewhere in Syria. Two other Muslim scholars who associate Damascus with the biblical Land of Uz are fourteenth-century historian and Arab geographer Abufelda and Jakut El-Hamawi (1179–1229), who was born in Constantinople but became an encyclopedist of Islam.[255]

What all modern accounts of Prophet Ayyub have in common in the Islamic tradition are five principal things. These may be summarized this way:

1. Ayyub is a prophet from Allah.
2. He is known for his humility and patience.
3. With Allah's permission, Shaytan became the agent of the dissolution of Ayyub's family and property.
4. Shaytan may have acted through Ayyub's wife, Rahma.
5. Ayyub's life is restored doubly in the end.[256]

This brings us to Enlightenment and nineteenth-century Jewish images of Job, the topic for the next section of this receptive history.

Modern Readings of the Book of Job (1800 to Present)

The Enlightenment era saw the development of a number of Jewish commentaries on the book of Job. Among these, the most significant were:

1. Moses Mendelssohn (1729–1786), *Book of Job*, commentary, 1777.
2. Aaron Halle-Wolfssohn (1754–1835; German Jew and student of Maimonides), *Commentary on the Book of Job*; great representative of Jewish Enlightenment (Prague, 1791; Vienna, 1806).
3. Euchel Isaac Abraham (1756–1804), *Book of Job*.
4. Israel Ben Abraham of Lissa (1766–1829), *Sefer Iyyov* (Berlin, 1802).
5. David Ottensosser (1784–1858), commentary, 1808 (Furth, 1805).

Mendelssohn's commentary was published in 1777. This work is important for a number of reasons, including the fact that it was completed in the eighteenth-century Enlightenment spirit of Deism and the new Rationalism. In his commentary on Job, Mendelssohn regularly quotes from Kant's essay on theodicy, as well as Spinoza and Maimonides's comments on the biblical book.

THE BOOK OF JOB

Another reason that Mendelssohn's commentary on Job is significant is that for the first time in Jewish literature, we see a scholar who employs the historical-critical and form-critical understandings of the Man from Uz and his book.

Mendelssohn in his commentary, for example, speaks of the fact that in the prose portions of Job, we find the name *Yahweh* to refer to God, but rarely in the poetic portion, where there is a much broader use of names for the Divine.[257] Mendelssohn also points out in his commentary that the Hebrew of Job 19:25–27 is much too corrupt to make proper sense.[258] Above all, however, Mendelssohn finds support in the book of Job for his most fundamental philosophical doctrines, like immortality of the soul and the divine plan response to the problem of evil.[259]

Mendelssohn's views on Job also can be found in the work of his student, German Jew Aaron Hale-Wolfssohn, whose commentary on Job was published first in Prague in 1791, and then in Vienna in 1806. Like his mentor, the overarching theological view of Job is the divine plan theory, like many Christian exegetes from the same period.[260]

Rabbi Euchel Isaac Abraham completed a German translation and commentary on the book of Job, published in Berlin in 1802. This commentary relies on Rashi, Maimonides, Spinoza, and Moses Mendelssohn in explicating the book of Job. Abraham's commentary on Job is also included in a Hebrew text known as the *Sefer Ne'emanah Firyah*, an early nineteenth-century work that includes the comments on Job from a number of Jewish scholars of the day.[261]

Another of these Hebrew scholars in the *Sefer Ne'emanah* was the comments of Rabbi David Ottensosser, who completed his commentary on the Man from Uz and his book in 1808, after publishing his classic commentary on Isaiah a year earlier. Altogether, Ottensosser completed Hebrew Bible commentaries on only eight books. In addition to Job and Isaiah, Ottensosser also completed lengthy commentaries on Ezekiel; Samuel; Daniel; Ezra; Nehemiah; and Chronicles.[262]

In addition to these six Jewish commentaries in the Enlightenment period, the Mendelssohn family also produced one other work centered on *Sefer Iyyov*. This is a cantata on Job called the "*Hiob Cantata*," completed by Fanny Mendelssohn (1805–1847) in 1831. The cantata was written for "Chorus and Orchestra," with contrapuntal voices inspired by lines from the biblical book of Job. Fanny was the older sister of Felix Mendelssohn. Altogether, she composed some 460 pieces of classical music in her lifetime.[263]

Like the eighteenth century, the nineteenth century also saw the development of more than half a dozen Jewish commentaries on the book of Job. Among these were the following:

1. Israel Schwarz, *Tikwat Enosh* (Berlin, 1860).

2. Meir Loeb Ben Jehiel Michael, *Job* (1870).

3. Rabbi Isaac Wiernikowsky, *Das Buch Hiob* (Breslau, 1897).

4. Abraham Geiger, *Hiob* (Frankfurt, 1866).

5. David Cassel, *Iyyov* (Vilna, 1849 and 1866).

6. Frederich Hitzig, *Das Buch Hiob* (Leipzig, 1874).

7. Benjamin Szold, *Sefer Iyyov* (Baltimore, 1866).[264]

The most significant element of these late nineteenth-century Jewish commentaries on the Man from Uz and his book is how deeply these commentators employed the nineteenth-century biblical techniques first used by Julius Wellhausen earlier in the century. Indeed, each of these seven Jewish scholars relied heavily on Moses Maimonides and Halle-Wolfssohn's commentaries that also depended on Enlightenment ideas, as well as comments by Baruch Spinoza and Immanuel Kant on the book of Job.

This brings us to an analysis of Christian images of the book of Job in the eighteenth and nineteenth centuries, the central concern of the next section of this receptive history of the biblical book of Job.

With the exception of the twentieth century, the nineteenth century saw more Christian references and uses of the Man from Uz than any other time. The Romantic movement, for example, in the West, saw many poets and writers who employed the book of Job. Among these Romantic writers were: the German poet J. G. Herder, in his *The Spirit of Hebrew Poetry*; J. W. Goethe's appropriation in the opening scene of Job in part 1 of his *Faust*; in France, Francois-Rene Chateaubriand saw the figure of Job as a central figure in the development of French Romanticism; Victor Hugo, in the *Hunchback of Notre Dame*, also portrayed the figure of Job as a Romantic hero.[265]

Another Frenchman, Alphonse de Lamartine (1790–1869), also completed a lengthy essay on the Man from Uz and his book. In fact, Lamartine saw the book of Job "as the height of poetic achievement."[266]

Several of the English Romantics also had several uses of Job in their scholarly work. Thomas Carlyle, Samuel Coleridge, Lord Byron, Alexander Pope, and Michael Joseph Lebensohn all appropriated the figure of Job in their literary works.[267]

Romantic art in the nineteenth century also produced a number of images of the book of Job, including: Alexander G. Decamps's oil painting of *Job and His Wife*; a sculpted piece by Flemish artist Francois Nermeylen, entitled *Job Dejected*; and Oskar Kokoschka's three-act drama, also just called *Job*.[268]

Perhaps the most significant of the British Romantics who dealt with the book of Job is William Blake, who completed a series of lithographs on the book of Job, produced and published in 1825. His *Illustrations of the Book of Job* was the final of his works he called his "Prophetic Works," the other two being his "Gates of Paradise," and "Blair's Grove." Blake's twenty-two illustrations of the book of Job, by far, are the best of these three works.[269]

Other literary figures who incorporated passages of the book of Job in their work include: Fyodor Dostoyevsky in his *Brothers Karamazov*, and Herman Melville in his classic *Moby Dick*, published in 1851.²⁷⁰ Among nineteenth-century philosophers: George Hegel, Soren Kierkegaard, and Ernest Bloch, whose essay *Atheism and Christianity* gives an interesting analysis of the book of Job. John Henry Newman, James Froude, Arthur Peake, Josiah Royce, and American philosopher William James all gave philosophical readings of the book.²⁷¹

In addition to the genres discussed above, the nineteenth-century Christian churches also produced several dozen Christian commentaries on the book of Job. Among the most noteworthy of these nineteenth-century commentaries were those by:

1. J. R. Scharer (1810).
2. H. Ewald (1830).
3. D. Umbreit (1837).
4. L. Hirzel (1839).
5. B. Welte (1849).
6. K. Schottmann (1851).
7. C. A. Berkholz (1859).
8. Franz Delitzsch (1864).
9. A. Dillmann (1869).
10. E. O. Merx (1871).
11. F. Hitzig (1874).
12. J. G. Hoffmann (1891).
13. C. Siegfried (1894).
14. G. Bickel (1894).
15. K. Budde (1895).
16. B. Duhm (1897).²⁷²

Among nineteenth-century French Christian commentaries on the book of Job, the most important are: Ernest Renan's 1863 commentary, *Le Livre de Job*; A. M. Le Hir's *Book of Job*, published in 1873; Abbe H. Lesetre's commentary, finished and published in 1886; and Alfred Loisy's *Book of Job*, first published in Paris in the late 1880s.²⁷³ Each of these twenty or so commentaries on Job, in their own ways, made original observations about the biblical Man from Uz and his book. This brings us to some observations about the interpretation of the book of Job in the contemporary period, the twentieth century to the present.

PART I: THE HISTORY OF INTERPRETING THE BOOK OF JOB

Job in Contemporary Times: Twentieth Century to the Present

From the beginning of the twentieth century to the present age, we have seen a far greater spectrum of scholarly views and uses of the biblical book of Job than any previous age. Among dialectical philosophers, for example, Martin Buber, Paul Tillich, Karl Jaspers, Margarete Susman, and Peter Wessel Zapffe all have given dialectical philosophical accounts, usually Existentialist accounts, of the Man from Uz and his book.[274]

Of these figures, the views of Susman and Zapffe are the most interesting. Susman, in her book *The Book of Job and the History of the Jewish People*, finds that the "silence of God, is the most important aspect of Job's encounter with the Divine."[275] Peter Wessel Zapffe, in his *The Tragic Life*, sees Job as a classic tragic hero; but he also sees Job as "uncovering God's most genuine nature of being a benighted tyrant." Above all, Zapffe sees Job as the "first of the Existentialists."[276] In fact, both Susman and Zapffe may be seen as employing the existentialist Job motif.

The first few decades of the twentieth century also saw the development of some of the most important commentaries on the biblical book of Job. Among these are the following:

1. F. Prat (1903).
2. Edmee Delebecque (1914).
3. F. G. Vigouroux (1915).
4. E. Dhorme (1926).
5. M. Bigot, "Job," in *Catholic Dictionary* (1925).
6. A. Guillaume's "Job," in the *New Commentary on Holy Scripture* (1928).

Of these French commentaries, by far the best of them is that by Dhorme, who makes a number of form-critical and historical-critical remarks on the book. For example, Dhorme's work on the relation of Job to other ancient Near Eastern mythologies and texts on innocent suffering is extraordinary. Dhorme was also a fine linguist and made a number of original observations about the philology of the book of Job.[277]

Among English commentaries on the book of Job in the early twentieth century, the following are significant:

1. A. B. Davidson (1903).
2. Arthur Peake (1904).
3. S. R. Driver (1908).
4. W. R. Harper (1908).
5. G. A. Barton (1911).
6. E. C. S. Gibson (1918).

7. C. J. Ball (1922).

8. M. Buttenwieser (1922).

9. A. H. Mumford (1922).

10. Horace Kallen (1918).[278]

Each of these early twentieth-century commentators of the book of Job made striking and original conclusions about the book. Horace Kallen's *Book of Job as a Greek Tragedy*, published in 1918, revised the view of Theodore Beza in 1587, who also maintained that the biblical Job was written as a Greek tragedy. But unlike Beza, Kallen believed Job was modeled after the dramas of Euripides.[279]

The early twentieth century also saw the development of a number of philosophical essays that included discussions of the Man from Uz and his book. Rudolf Otto discusses Job in his 1917 *Idea of the Holy*. Hayim Greenberg, in his collection of essays called *The Inner Eye*, published in 1940, highlights the theme of the silence of God in two essays in the book.[280] Gilbert Murray (1866–1957), British classical scholar, likens Job to the dramas of Aeschylus;[281] and Gilbert Chesterton, English novelist and literary critic, provided an introduction to a new edition of the book of Job, published in 1916. Among other things, Chesterton finds Job battling against what he calls "two great enemies of society—pessimism and optimism."[282]

British exegete H. Wheeler Robinson devoted a substantial portion of his *The Religious Ideas of the Old Testament*, published in 1913, to the problem of innocent suffering or theodicy. In fact, Robinson sketches out five different responses to the problem—all of which he finds unsatisfactory alone. Among these views are retributive justice after the grave and what we have called the divine plan answer.[283]

Another important treatment in the period on the book of Job comes from C. A. Row's discussion of Job in his *Future Retribution*. Row's book is important for a number of reasons. One of those is that he sees both the Patient Job and the Angry Job. He also finds the views of Elihu to be more theologically sophisticated than those of the other three friends of Job. He also sees the overall question about Job as being how evil and suffering work as part of the providence of God.[284]

Among twentieth-century literary works patterned on the book of Job, one of the most interesting is Archibald MacLeish's drama *J.B.* One of the most interesting aspects of the play is McLeish's decision to present Bildad, Eliphaz, and Zophar as a born-again preacher, a Marxist sociologist, and a Freudian psychoanalyst, three forms of twentieth-century Determinism in European culture.[285]

Altogether, the years of the twentieth century have produced a staggering number of literary depictions and adaptations of the book of Job. An incomplete list includes: thirty-five plays in ten languages; over fifty poems in a variety of languages, as well; more than two dozen novels and an equal number of pieces of short fiction. In the first few decades of the century, for example, German literature completed plays inspired by the book of Job by Fritze Weege, a 1926 miracle play, and by Bartholamaeus Ponholzer (1927); Rudolphe Borchardt (1905); Oskar Kokoschka's *Hiob*, published in 1917; and a novel called *Der Blummenhiob*, by Hans Kyser (1909).[286]

Karl Wolfskehl's 1946 book of poems is called *Hiob*.[287] Berthold Wulf's drama *Hiob* was published in Zurich in 1971; and many writers have written about the parallel structures and plots between the book of Job and Franz Kafka's *The Trial*.[288] The first half of the twentieth century also saw the appearance of many French dramas modeled on the book of Job. Among these French plays are works by:

1. Emile Baumann (1922).

2. J. Debout (1932).

3. Edouard Ned (1933).[289]

In other European languages that produced dramas about Job are Swedish playwright Karin Maria Boye's *The Seven Deadly Sins* (1941); Victo Spitzer's Yiddish drama, *Iyyov*, completed in 1925; H. Leivick's *Iyov*, another Yiddish verse drama, published in 1953; H. de Bruin's Dutch epic poem *Job* (1944); and two Italian plays, Giovanni Batista Angioletti's 1955 drama, *Giobbe*, and Giovanni Limentani's *Le Grande Seduto*, written and produced in 1979.[290]

British and American writers in the twentieth century also made substantial uses of the Man from Uz and his book in their literary efforts. Among the twentieth-century English novels that employed themes in the book of Job are: H. G. Wells's *The Only Fire* (1919); Joseph Roth's *Job: The Story of a Simple Man* (1931); Muriel Sparks's *The Only Problem* (1984); and, most recently, Jean Shaw's *Job's Wife*, published in 1990, and Beverly Brodsky's 1986 novel, *The Story of Job*.[291]

The twentieth century also saw the development of fourteen English dramas inspired by the book of Job. The most dramatically interesting of these are Thornton Wilder's three-minute drama, *Hast Thou Considered My Servant Job?* (1928); Robert Frost's *Masque of Reason* (1945); I. A. Richards's 1971 verse-drama *Job's Comforting*; and, of course, Mac Leish's *J.B.*, discussed earlier.[292]

The twentieth century also saw a number of essays and collections of essays devoted to themes in the book of Job. These include a collection entitled *Critical Perspectives on the Book of Job*, a number of essays written by Martin Buber and others on the biblical book.[293] Alan A. Berger has edited a collection of essays written by second-generation survivors of the Holocaust.[294] Nahum Glatzer also edited a collection of twentieth-century essays on the book of Job called *Dimensions of Job*, published in 1986; and Ralph Hone's *Voice from the Whirlwind* is another anthology, produced in 1960, that contains historical essays on the biblical book. Hone's book includes selections from: Calvin, Francis Bacon, Blake, John Henry Newman, and biblical scholar Morris Jastrow, among many others.[295]

In more contemporary times, other twentieth-century essays on the book of Job have been produced by: Judith Baskin; Michael Fishbane; Langdon Gilkey; Rene Girard; Gustavo Gutierrez; C. S. Rodd; Norman Habel; John Hartley; Robert Gordis; James Barr; and David J. A. Clines. In fact, Clines has constructed the most comprehensive bibliography on the book of Job, in his 1989 Word Biblical Commentary, published by Thomas Nelson.[296]

One new image of the biblical book of Job that began to appear in the post-Holocaust era is what may properly be called the "Existentialist Job," a view of the Man from Uz and his book of an isolated and worrisome patriarch who worries, above all, about the silence of God toward him. British scholar David C. Tollerton's book *The Book of Job in Post-Holocaust Thought*, published by Sheffield Press in 2012, gives a lengthy treatment of the Existentialist Job. This Existentialist Job also has been seen in contemporary literature in drama, poetry, the novel, and short fiction. Earlier, we have said that Margaret Susman and Peter Zapffe have employed this motif in their work. Marshall H. Lewis also has recently produced a work that ties the psychological insights of Viktor Frankl to the interpretation of the book of Job.[297]

Book of Job in the Twenty-First Century

Since the turn of the millennium, an astounding number of works have been produced with Job and his book as the subject matter. Major commentaries have been produced by Rabbi Moshe Eisemann; C. L. Seow; David Clines; and see also the studies and recent annotated translation of Edward L. Greenstein. A plethora of essays, articles, and small books on the Man from Uz and his book also have been produced in the twenty-first century.

Among these essays and articles, some of the most significant are the following:

- Yair Hoffman, *Blemished Perfection* (1996).
- Richard Rohr, *Job and the Mystery of Suffering* (1998).
- Raymond Scheindlin, *The Book of Job* (1999).
- Samuel Terrien, *Job: Poet of Existence* (2004).
- Robert Eisen, *The Book of Job in Medieval Jewish Philosophy* (2004).
- Stephen Vicchio, *The Book of Job: A History of Interpretation* (2006).
- David J. A. Clines, *Job: 21 to 37* (2006).
- Irving Greenberg, *Theology after the Shoah* (2006).
- Ray C. Stedman, *Let God Be God* (2007).
- Francis Andersen, *Job* (1976/2008).
- Carol Newsom, *The Book of Job: A Contest of Moral Imagination* (2009).

PART I: THE HISTORY OF INTERPRETING THE BOOK OF JOB

- Robert Alter, *The Wisdom Books* (2010).
- John Gray, *The Book of Job* (2010).
- James Crenshaw, *Reading Job* (2011).
- Kathleen M. O'Connor, *Job: New Collegeville Bible Commentary* (2012).
- David C. Tollerton, *The Book of Job in Post-Holocaust Thought* (2012).
- Mark Larrimore, *The Book of Job: A Biography* (2013).
- C. L. Seow, *Job 1–21* (2013).
- Katharine Dell, *Reading Job Intertextually* (2013).
- Duane A. Garrett, *Shepherd's Notes: Job* (2017).
- Eric Ortlund, *Job: A 12-Week Study* (2017).
- Lisa Harper, *Job: Bible Study Book* (2018).
- Edward L. Greenstein, *A New Translation of Job* (2019).
- Jim Szana, *Origins and Suffering* (2019).

Each of these twenty or so works have made substantial contributions to the literature of the book of Job. Clines and Seow offer the most extensive bibliographies; Hoffman, Greenstein, and Robert Alter all contribute significant insights about the philology of the book. Gray, Newsom, O'Connor, Stedman, Seow, Clines, and Harper are all significant commentaries. Seow and Clines, along with Vicchio, provide the best bibliographies on the book of Job.

Edward Greenstein, in 2019, has produced an astoundingly accurate translation of the book of Job, published by Yale University Press. He gives a much better translation, for example, of Job 42:5–6 than most traditional Jewish and Christian interpreters of those verses.

Yair Hoffman's book *Blemished Perfection* provides deep reflections on the philology of the book. Newsom and Alter's works on Job are very significant and helpful for scholars. Jim Szana's text makes a number of interesting observations about the issues of the problem of evil and theodicy, as well as the book of Job.

The works by Larrimore, Vicchio, Greenberg, and Eisen are significant for their historical observations about the history of interpreting Job, while Rohr, Dell, Garrett, and Ortlund are all good general works on the Man from Uz and his book. Andersen's fine 1976 commentary was reissued in 2008 by the InterVarsity Press. James Crenshaw's 2011 book offers insightful comments on the Man from Uz and his book.

Both Tollerton and Greenberg view the book of Job in the context of the post-Shoah era. Kathleen O'Connor's commentary was produced for the Collegeville Bible Series. Duane Garret's work is a short commentary of notes for preachers on the book of Job; and John Gray's commentary on the book, produced in 2010, is also a useful, small work on Job.

This brings us to the end of our essay on the history of interpreting the book of Job. We move next to the second part of this study—a commentary on the biblical book, followed by a bibliography, the notes, and a number of appendices.

Part II: The Book of Job Commentary

The Prologue: Chapters 1 and 2

The Meaning of the Name "Job" (1:1)

THE MEANING OF JOB's name in Hebrew has been debated for many centuries. One possibility is that the name *Iyyov* was derived from a verb meaning "hostility," and the noun form *oyev*, or "enemy." If this is the correct etymology of the name, then the name would be quite ironic, for Job would mean "enemy of God."

Another way the Hebrew root for Job's name can be understood is in connection with an Arabic root *'yb*, that means "repent" or "return." This again would be an ironic sense of the name, for Job spends most of the book insisting that he does not need to repent. Curiously enough, immediately after God's speeches from the whirlwind, Job turns right around and repents at 42:5–6, a version of the Job repentant motif.

The name Job, or its cognates, has been found in several archeological inscriptions beginning about 2000 BCE. A number of well-to-do Canaanite men had the name Job. Thus, there is no reason to believe that the author made up the name. Many biblical characters—particularly those from the patriarchal age—are introduced with full genealogy, though no mention is made of Job's clan or tribe.

The name "Job," then, is attested outside of ancient Israel. Dhorme says the name "belongs to the West Semitic group of names, as confirmed by the uninflected form A-ia-ab."[298]

The transformation of *Aiab* into *Ayob*, and then on to the Arabic *Ayyub* and the Hebrew *Iyyov*, is a series of short jumps, indeed. A certain *Ayab* is mentioned in the fourteenth-century BCE Tell el-Amarna Letters. He is referred to as the "Prince of Ashtartu in Bashan." W. F. Albright discusses this name in an essay for the *Bulletin of the American Schools of Oriental Research*.[299] The name Job occurs as *A-ja-ab* in another of the Amarna Letters, as well as another text among the Egyptian Execration Texts from around 2000 BCE.[300]

In addition to the name Job appearing in ancient Semitic inscriptions, the name also appears at Ezek 14:14 and 20, where the name is mentioned together with Noah and Dan'el (not the biblical Daniel), another ancient Near Eastern worthy of some moral character.

The name is pronounced *Hiob*, in German; *Yaop* or *Yawp* in Dutch; *Giobbe*, in Italian; *Ayyub*, in Arabic; *Iob* in Greek and Latin; *Iyyov*, in modern Hebrew; and *Job* in

French and English. There is no evidence that the name was regularly used until the modern era, beginning with the Reformation.

The name Job was adopted by many seventeenth-century English Puritans. The name fell into disuse in the late nineteenth century. The name Jobina is the female form of the name. In English, the male name Jobe is sometimes used. It is pronounced the same way as Job. In more modern times, the name Job has come to mean one who has suffered unjustly. Thus, there has arisen the phrase, "the patience of Job," to describe the patriarch's character.

Various historical and modern scholars have posited views about the meaning of the name Job. Hitchcock's dictionary of the Bible says the name Job means "persecuted." *Easton's Bible Dictionary* says the same thing. The *International Standard Bible Encyclopedia* conjectures that the name Job means either "object of enmity," or "he who returns."[301]

Terrien suggests the name *Iyyov* is connected to the Hebrew *ayabh*, "to be hostile," or "to be an enemy."[302] Ewald believes the name *Iyyov* was derived from the Arabic *'awab* that means "one who turns to God."[303] Robert Gordis understands the name *Iyyov* as a passive participle of *'ayab*, meaning "one who is hated or persecuted."[304] G. Fohrer, in *Gensenius Hebrew Grammar*, also connects the name to the root of the word *oyev*, or enemy as Christ-figure.[305] Gregory the Great thinks the name *Iob* means "mourner," or "grieving," after the Latin *dolens*.[306]

The Land of Uz (1:1)

The Hebrew Bible, and the book of Job specifically, give us ten pieces of information regarding the land of Uz. We learn about the location of the Land of Uz that:

1. Job was the greatest of all the "men of the East."
2. It was a land of plentiful pastures, according to Job 1:3.
3. Portions of it are land suitable for plowed crops (Job 1:14).
4. It was near the desert or wilderness (Job 1:19).
5. A number of kings and their peoples lived nearby (Jer 25:20).
6. It was in proximity to the Temanites, the Shuhites, the Naamathites (Job 2:11), and the Buzites (Job 32:2), and to Dedan (Jer 25:23).
7. There was a colony near Edom called "the daughters of Edom in the land of Uz" (Lam 4:21).
8. It was in raiding distance of the Sabeans and the Chaldeans (Job 1:15, 17).
9. The Septuagint tells us, "It was on the borders of Idumea [Edom] and Arabia."

The name Uz is mentioned several times in the Hebrew Bible. At Gen 10:23, Uz is a son of Aram, a direct descendant of Shem. Uz is sometimes identified with the kingdom of Edom, an area in modern-day southwestern Jordan or southern Israel. Lamentations 4:21 tells us, "Rejoice and be glad, oh daughter of Edom, that dwells in the Land of Uz."[307]

Other locations proposed for Uz include: southern Arabia, especially Dhofar. The city of Bashan in southern Syria; elsewhere in Arabia, east of Petra, near or in the Wadi as-Sirhan and southeast of Damascus, in the Arabian Desert, West of the Euphrates, in the Persian city of Persepolis; northern Mesopotamia; the district of Hauran in Syria; in Bethenije, near the city of Damascus; in present-day Edh-Dhuneiben, or Dennaba, near Damascus; at Scheikh Sad, where "Job's stone can be found"; the city of Kanawat, where "Job's summer home" is said to have been; in Basra, Iraq, there is a tomb said to be "Ayyub's tomb," and even another site in modern-day Uzbekistan.[308]

The most recent opinion about the location of the Land of Uz comes from G. Frederick Owen, who wrote an article on the "Land of Uz" for the *Zondervan Pictorial Encyclopedia of the Bible*, published by Zondervan in 1975. Owen suggests that Uz is to be found in the Wadi Sirhan, southeast of Jebel ed Druz, fifty miles east of the city of Amman. Much of this area is still vast, flat, pastureland, well suited for the raising of cattle, sheep, goats, asses, and camel.[309]

The *Wall Scroll*, a document from the Dead Sea Scrolls, suggests that Uz is "somewhere beyond the Euphrates, possibly near Aram." At column II, v. 11, the scroll mentions:

> They shall fight against the rest of the sons of Aramea: Uz, Hul, Togar, and Mesha, who are beyond the Euphrates.[310]

In modern scholarship two separate locations have been identified for the Land of Uz. One of these suggests that Uz is near the ancient kingdom of Edom, south of the Dead Sea. We shall call this the "southern view." The other theory maintains that Uz was northeast of Palestine, near the city of Damascus, in Syria. This second view we will call the "northern view."

Evidence for the southern view include Lam 4:21 and Jer 25:20–21 that associates Uz with Philistia, Edom, and Moab. The Septuagint also supports the southern view, when it associates Job with the Jobab of Gen 36:33. B. Moritz also held the southern view of the location of Uz.[311] Gregory the Great also supports the southern view in the preface to his *Moralia*, saying that "Job sprung from the stock of Esau."[312]

There is also a good bit of evidence that supports the northern, Syrian theory for Uz. The genealogies at Gen 10:23 and 1 Chr 1:17 both suggest the northern view. Another Uz, or the same one, is said to be the oldest son of Nahor, the Aramean brother of Abraham (Gen 20:20–21). The Geneva Bible and John Wesley also support the northern view.

The reference to Job being of the "Children of the East" could possibly mean east of the Jordan River, if the author lived in Palestine. Josephus's *Antiquities* suggests that Job's home was near Damascus,[313] and most Arabic and Islamic sources are advocates of the position that Job's Land of Uz was somewhere near Damascus.[314] Other modern scholars who maintain the northern view include P. Dhorme and his essay "Le Pays de Job,"[315] and Friedrich Delitzsch, in his "Land of Uz," who sketches out both the southern and northern theories as supportable understandings of Job's home.

Tur-Sinai attempts to reconcile the two theories by arguing that Job initially settled on the borders of Edom, and then later moved to an area near Damascus.[316] Marvin Pope, however, thinks it is impossible to make the two theories consistent.[317] Dhorme settles on a place "on the borders of Edom and Arabia," saying "we cannot legitimately argue from tradition in order to adopt a different location from that which is suggested by the OT texts" (Jer 25:20 and Lam 4:21).[318]

One way to settle the issue of the location of the Land of Uz is simply to say that in the same way that Job is an Everyman, and that he suffers from the "disease of diseases," Job should also be considered a resident of the "place of all places." That is to say, that the patriarch Job resided in any location where human beings have suffered in intolerable ways since the beginning of humankind. In this sense, Job is a resident of Everyplace.

Tam va Yashar: Blameless and Upright (1:1)

The Hebrew expression *tam va yashar* to describe Job at 1:1 has been understood in various ways over the centuries. The word *yashar* is also employed at Job 4:7; 6:24; and 33:27. In general, *yashar* has a moral understanding, comparable to the contemporary English expression "going straight." The word *tam* also has a moral sense in classical Hebrew. It stood to signify the opposite of "guilty," or to be without moral culpability. The word *tam* is also employed at Job 2:3; 9:20; and 9:21, two times. Bildad employs the word at 8:6.

The words *tam* and *yashar* are also used throughout Wisdom Literature. The latter, at Ps 7:10; 11:2 and 7; and 49:14, for examples. *Yashar* can also be found at Prov 14:11; 15:8; and 16:17, for examples. In the book of Job, the narrator uses *yashar* at 1:1. God employs the adjective of Job at 1:8 and 2:3; and Job uses it to describe himself at 17:8.

Clement of Alexandria render 1:1 as "upright and innocent."[319] The Vulgate has it "*simplex* and *rectus*."[320] Saadiah Gaon has "blameless and upright,"[321] while Luther renders them "blameless and pious."[322] Pope prefers "blameless and upright."[323] Dhorme, "perfect and upright,"[324] as does Gersonides.[325] Both Terrien and Gibson have "blameless and upright."[326] Rashi renders 1:1 as "sincere and upright."[327] John Wesley as "perfect and upright,"[328] as does the Geneva Bible.[329]

David Clines renders 1:1 as "blameless and upright,"[330] as do Bruce Zuckerman, C. S. Rodd and Norman Habel.[331] Raymond Scheindlin, in his 1998 commentary, prefers "innocent and upright."[332] Solomon Freehof has them as "whole-hearted and upright," while Edwin Good renders these terms as "a man of perfect integrity."[333]

Adam Clarke has them as "perfect and upright,"[334] while John Wilcox, Diane Bergant, and H. H. Rowley all prefer "blameless and upright."[335]

Gregory the Great renders the two terms as "simple and upright," after the fashion of the Vulgate.[336] Thomas Aquinas, in his commentary on Job, prefers "perfect and upright," but he adds the note, "without guile and upright."[337] Driver and Gray have the two Hebrew terms in question as "perfect and upright."[338]

What all these renderings have in common is the understanding that *tam* and *yashar* are moral terms. The Hebrew suggests that Job is of a moral character only reserved for the most holy of the ancient patriarchs. Comparable moral terms are only used in the Hebrew Bible for Noah and Abraham. See Gen 6:8–9 and 17:1, for examples.

Bene ha Elohim, Sons of God (1:6 and 2:1)

The Hebrew expression *bene ha Elohim* literally means "the sons of God." The word *ben* is used in the Hebrew Bible not only to describe the family of a person, but also his intimate relations. Various nicknames use the word *ben*, like "son of strength," "son of wickedness." In another context, all human beings are sons of God, or children of God, as Deut 14:50 and Exod 4:22 imply.

The expression *bene ha Elohim* is used in three places of the book of Job, at 1:6; 2:1; and 38:7. It is employed elsewhere in the Hebrew Bible at Gen 6:2; Pss 29:1; 82:1; and 89:6; and at Dan 3:25. These imply that the sons of God are most often associated with angels of the heavenly court. Thus, the expression appears to be synonymous with *ṣeba' haš-šamayim*, or "the Hosts of Heaven," at places like Isa 34:4; 37:32; 54:5; Jer 11:17; Amos 5:16; and Ps 11:4.

The sons of God may also be identified with the Hebrew word *mal'akim*, the Hebrew plural of angel. It is used at Job 4:18, and a variety of other places in the Psalms (85:5; 68:17; 78:49; 91:11; 103:20; 104:4; and 148:2, for examples). The NIV, and a few other modern translations, render *bene ha Elohim* simply as "angels." Thomas Aquinas and John Wesley also both prefer this translation, as do most Christian exegetes. Thomas describes the scene as involving "the Lord sitting upon His lofty throne." And, "One should know that the angels here, who are called the sons of God are said to assist the Lord in two ways."[339] Indeed, Thomas distinguishes between the *bene ha Elohim*, or "Good Angels," and those who are "Fallen, or Bad Angels."

Olympiodorus, and many of the early church fathers, identify the *bene ha Elohim* as "fallen angels," as well.[340] The same view is held by Irenaeus, Justin Martyr, Eusebius, Clement of Alexandria, Tertullian, Athenagoras, Lactantius, Ambrose, Augustine, and many other fathers both East and West.[341] Marvin Pope, in his commentary, renders *bene ha Elohim* as "sons of the gods." Pope points to others who render the expression "the gods."[342] Philo says they are "sons of God" because "they were created incorporeal."[343] John Gammie, in his essay "The Angelology and Demonology in the

Septuagint of the Book of Job," renders the phrase as "celestial beings."[344] Philo of Alexandria believes the *bene ha Elohim* are "Cherubim."[345] E. P. Dhorme renders *bene ha elohim* as "*fils d'Elohim*."[346] Leveque, in his *Job et son Dieu*, suggests that the *bene ha Elohim* are "intermediaries between God and man."[347]

Among Jewish scholars, Josephus believes the *bene ha Elohim* are angels. Rashi sees them as "angelic Lords, the sons of lords and judges."[348] Contemporary Jewish scholar Julian Morgenstern, in his essay "The Mythological Background of Psalm 82," suggests that the sons of God are part of the "Assembly of El," or the "Council of El."[349]

The identification of *ha Satan*, the Hebrew text always uses the definite article, with the angels is made clear by the use of the preposition *betoke* that usually means "among." This preposition is often employed to designate a notable member of some class of beings. This can be seen at Gen 23:10 and 45:2, for examples. The first of these says, "Now Ephraim was sitting among the Hittites," where the Hittites is a class and Ephraim, their king, is a notable member of that class. Thus, we are supposed to see *ha Satan* as one of the sons of God, and a notable member of that class.

Ha Satan, the Satan (1:6 and 2:1)

The Hebrew term *ha Satan* comes from the tri-consonant Semitic root STN, that means "Adversary," "Opponent," or "Accuser." The word *Satan* is used as an adjective, a noun, and a verb in the Hebrew Bible. At 1 Sam 29:4 and 1 Kgs 5:4 and 18, the word is used to refer to a military opponent. It is also employed to mean a traitor in battle, as in 1 Sam 29:4. It is also employed to mean an opponent in general, as at 2 Sam 19:23. At Num 22:32, *ha Satan* is used as an antagonist in the way of a human being, in this case Balaam.

Whenever the term *ha Satan* is used in the Hebrew Bible, it is always clear that both good and evil come from God, as 1 Sam 16:14, 1 Kgs 22:22, and Isa 14:7 all imply. The *Genesis Rabbah* says that *ha Satan* came into the world with the creation of woman. The Babylonian Talmud identifies *ha Satan* with the evil imagination, or *yetzer ha ra* of human beings, a nod in the direction of the free will defense motif. The Targum to Numbers (10:10) says that when the shofar is sounded on New Year's Day, Satan is confounded, and that on the Day of Atonement, his power vanishes. In fact, Jewish scholar Mezudat David thinks that *ha Satan* appears on Passover.[350]

Early Christian exegetes, most likely because of the influence of the New Testament, saw the figure of *ha Satan* as a demonic force, at odds with the ways of the Lord. Nevertheless, different church fathers have made very different observations about the figure of Satan in the book of Job. Fifth-century Alexandrian Hesychius, for example, tells us that

> the trial of Job symbolizes the constant struggle of the righteous against the temptation and malice inspired by the passion of the Devil.[351]

Fourth-century Julian of Eclanum, distinguished leader of the Pelagians, tells us, "The power of the Devil can extend only to the limits that were set by God."[352] Ishodad of Merv, ninth-century Syrian scholar, suggests that Job 1:6 means that "even the Devil's thoughts are known to God."[353]

Gregory the Great and Thomas Aquinas both continued the Christian view that Satan and the devil were one and the same figures. Speaking of the distinction between good and bad angels, Thomas tells us:

> One should also consider that those things which are done through good angels are related to the judgment of God in different ways than those which are done by the wicked angels. For the good angels intend that the things they do are related to God . . . but the things done by the wicked angels are not.[354]

In Judaism, both Rashi and Ibn Ezra say, "The Adversary is an angel whose function it is to accuse human beings before the Heavenly Tribunal."[355] This view is contradicted by Saadiah Gaon and other Jewish scholars who believe that *ha Satan* is a human being of particularly bad moral character.[356] Saadiah thinks Satan is simply a human being who resented Job's righteousness and called upon God to put the patriarch to the test, an example of the test theodicy.

Saadiah gives this for his commentary on Job 1:6:

> When it was the day that God's beloved came and presented themselves to The Lord, Job's Adversary was present among them. As for the Adversary, He was an ordinary human being, like those mentioned when scripture says, "The Lord raised an Adversary (Satan) to Solomon, Hadad, the Edomite King [1 Kgs 11:14]."[357]

In more recent times, Henry Cowles, in his 1877 commentary, tells us:

> The Satan's character and work as put here are in full accord with the numerous allusions made to him throughout Scripture. He is the same old serpent, the Devil.[358]

Three other nineteenth-century commentators also make the connection between *ha Satan* and the demonic. In Thomas Scott's 1848 commentary, he says, "Satan is represented as the author of human maladies, by one whose authority is above all the prophets." And, "going to and fro" means "a vigilant execution of the office."[359]

F. W. C. Umbreit, in his 1860 commentary called *The Book of Job with Expository Notes*, also makes the demonic connection when he writes:

> He asks truly Satanic questions, which cunningly seek to awaken God's suspicion, lest Job, from self-interested motives, affected his piety.[360]

Both Cowles and Thomas Scott, then, are advocates of the Influences of Demonic Forces view to explain Job's suffering. *Notes on the Book of Job*, William Kelly's 1879 commentary, points out the absence of the Satan figure after the prologue. He tells us,

"Henceforth, the Adversary vanishes. He has failed no less completely in his renewed malice."[361] Several early twentieth-century commentators also comment on the figure of *ha Satan*. MacFadyen calls Satan "a vagabond of the heavenly court," in his 1917 *The Problem of Pain*.[362] A. S. Peake, in his 1904 commentary, says about Satan:

> He observes the doings of men that he might detect them in sin and then oppose their claims to righteousness before God.[363]

In his 1927 commentary, *The Problem of Pain*, Minos Devine argues strenuously against the demonic view of *ha Satan*. Devine writes:

> It is unfortunate that our version obscures the fact that Satan is not here the name of a person, but that of an office. Though he is represented as a person, his personal standing is only of the slightest consequence, while the role he has played is quite clear. He is an instrument in God's hands to try Job, and when he has done that, he disappears.[364]

Thus Devine is an advocate of the test theodicy. Charles Thomas Walkley, who also completed an early twentieth-century commentary in 1917, goes back to the demonic affiliation of the Satan. Walkley says of Satan, "He never trusts man's goodness. He imputes bad motives. He never sees any good in mankind, he is sneering, beguiling, and always deceiving."[365] Thus, Walkley ascribes to the demonic forces motif to explain Job's suffering, as well.

Among more contemporary commentators, Marvin Pope discusses the role of the Satan among most later twentieth-century exegetes when he says:

> The term is not a title, not yet a proper name . The figure here is not the fully developed character of later Jewish and Christian Satan or the Devil. He is one of the members of the divine court and comes with other attendants to present himself at the celestial court and to report on his fulfillment of his duties. . . . The Satan was a kind of spy, roaming the Earth and reporting to God on the evil he found therein.[366]

J. C. L. Gibson, in his 1985 commentary simply called *Job*, points to some other aspects he sees of the Satan. He observes:

> The Satan has obviously had him under surveillance and knows all about him, for whenever God mentions that He is pleased with Job, the Satan is ready with his answer. . . . The Satan is a nasty piece of work, brazen and impertinent toward God and cynical and sneering toward men.[367]

Solomon Freehof, in his 1958 *Book of Job: A Commentary*, says that "Satan grants that Job is perfect, upright, etc, but these virtues are, he believes, selfish in their origins."[368] In his analysis of the Man from Uz called *Answer to Job*, Jung suggests that God has projected his own unconscious doubts into the Adversary, where God can then more easily accept them.[369]

Skin for Skin (2:4)

There has been a variety of views on the meaning of the expression "skin for skin," uttered by the Satan at 2:4. The Targum of Job, as well as Rashi, renders the line, "member for member," as does Abraham Ibn Ezra (1092–1167).[370] Ephraim the Syrian and Thomas Aquinas render the expression *carneum alienam pro carne sua*.[371] Schultens thinks it should be *cutis supra cute*.[372] Budde (1876), Hontheim (1904), and Olshausen (1852), hold similar views.[373]

Hemd sitzi naher als der Rock, or "The shirt is nearer than the coat."[374] The Septuagint renders the line: "Skin instead of skin," and the Vulgate as *Pellem pro pelle*.[375] J. Parkhurst (1821) translates it as "Skin after skin."[376]

G. R. Noyes supposes that skin for skin means that "any man will give the skin of his life for that of another, whether animal, a person, or his own life."[377] G. M. Good, in his 1812 commentary, points out that the goods and spoils of animals, "in the rude and early ages of man, were his most valuable property."[378] Robert Watson (1892) tells us about skin for skin:

> The proverb put in Satan's mouth carries a plain enough meaning, and yet it is not literally easy to interpret. The sense will be clear if we translate it as, "Hide for skin," yea all that man has he will give for himself.[379]

Watson adds:

> The hide of an animal, lion, or sheep, which a man wears for clothing, will be given up to save his own body. A valuable item of property often will be renounced when it is in danger. The man will flee away naked. In like manner, all possessions will be abandoned to keep oneself unharmed.[380]

Albert Barnes, in his 1847 commentary, cautions against most of the above when he writes:

> This is a proverbial expression, whose origins is unknown, nor is its meaning as a proverb entirely clear.[381]

Barnes continues:

> The general sense of the passage is plain, for it is immediately explained that a man would give everything that he has to save his life; and the idea here is that if Job was so inflicted in his body that he was likely to die, he would give up his religion in order to purchase his life.[382]

H. H. Bernard (1864) renders the line "Limb for limb," while Samuel Davidson (1884) says, "All that a man has he will give up for his life."[383] David Thomas tells us this in his 1878 commentary about skin for skin:

In plain English this means sovereign for sovereign, all the sovereigns that a man has, he will exchange for his life. The idea is that life is dearer to a man than his property, however good that property may be.[384]

F. W. C. Umbreit, in his commentary from 1836, observes, "There is nothing as valuable to a man that he will not exchange it for his life."[385] Duhm (1897), following Calmet (1722), suggests what is being referred to is the skin of an animal in barter.[386] David Clines agrees.

He tells us:

> The most natural view is that the saying comes from the world of bartering, where "one skin for another skin" could well be a phrase for a fair exchange.[387]

Others who hold the bartering view are: Ewald (1836); Franz Delitzsch (1876); Hupfeld (1853); and E. Dhorme (1926).[388] Gregory the Great says about 2:4:

> When we see a blow directed at the face, we put our hands before our eyes to guard against the blow. We present our bodies ready to be wounded, lest they be wounded in a more tender spot.[389]

Saadiah Gaon uses the same simile of holding up one's hands to avoid a blow to the face.[390] Julian of Eclanum also employs a similar image when he writes:

> Humans typically drive away the greatest losses by suffering smaller damages. Often by opposing the hand, we ward off a vital danger to the head.[391]

Olympiodorus (5th c.) says, "One is prepared to sacrifice one member that is less important for another that is more important."[392] Ishodad of Merv (9th-c. Nestorian bishop) and Albertus Magnus (1206–1280) held similar views. Rosenmuller (1824) quotes Exod 21:23 as a parallel and renders it "Life for life."[393] Holscher (1948) cites an Arabic phrase, *ra's bira's*, "one head of cattle for another." Fohrer (1959) mentions a similar expression from Ugarit: *bita kima bita*, or "house for house."[394] It seems to say that if a house falls down at the agency of another, then the agent's house should also fall, a version of retributive justice.

Francis Peloubet (1906) says the general sense of the skin for skin is clear enough, "but the exact force of the proverb is not easy to catch."[395] Peloubet goes on to quote Samuel Cox's 1880 commentary, where Cox mentions the Arabic proverb, "hide for hide,"[396] to save the rest, but give all to save one's life.[397]

Professor Peloubet concludes:

> Satan recognizes no motive, but thinks that Job would make a bargain with God by giving up his property to save his life, which includes health and whatever makes life worth living.[398]

Robert Gordis says, "A man gives up the skin of others to save his own."[399] G. B. Gray (1873) puts it: "Another skin for his own skin."[400] Thomas Aquinas informs us about skin for skin:

> Job was willing to pay with the skin of others, his animals and children, in order to save his own skin.[401]

Edwin Good, in his 1991 commentary, points out that the preposition *be'ad* usually means "beyond" or "up to" a boundary, and not "for." He also says he finds no parallels to "the frequently used idea of exchange." He adds, "The expression is as puzzling in Hebrew as it is in English."[402]

The most compelling explanation of "skin for skin" comes from Tur-Sinai's 1957 commentary. He suggests that a man's heart, his most valuable part, is protected by his skin. He quotes 1 Kgs 20:30 and 22:25 as parallel texts, that speak of "a chamber within a chamber." Tur-Sinai says that the Satan is saying, "Before you did not let me touch him, now let me touch his soul."[403] Something like this was probably the original intention about Skin for skin.

Job's Disease (2:7)

The Hebrew noun used to describe Job's disease at 2:7 is the word *shehin*. This term is used in a variety of ways in the Hebrew Bible, in many places besides the book of Job. It is employed, for example, at Hos 5:13 that tells us:

> When Ephraim saw his sickness [*schechin*] and Judah his wound, then Ephraim went to Assyria, and sent to the great king. But he was not able to cure you or to heal your wound.[404]

At Deut 28:27 and 35, the word *schechin* is also employed. It says:

> The Lord will smite you with boils of Egypt, and with the ulcers and the scurvy and the itch, of which you cannot be healed.[405]

And:

> The Lord will smite you on the knees and on the legs with grievous boils of which you cannot be healed, from the sole of your feet to the crown of your head.[406]

In these two cases, the RSV renders *schechin* as "boils." And in both cases, it speaks of a sickness that cannot be healed. At Exod 9:9–11, the word is also employed to mean "boils," as it does at 2 Kgs 20:7 and at Isa 38:21; but at Lev 18:18–23, the sickness described seems more complicated than a simple boil. This text tells us:

> And when there is in the skin of one's body a boil that has a head, and in the place of the boil there is white color and swelling, or a reddish white spot,

then you should show it to the priest; and the priest shall examine it, and if it appears deeper than the skin and its hairs have turned white, then the priest shall pronounce him unclean. It is the disease of leprosy.[407]

This text and others like it in the RSV translation is connected to the Septuagint's rendering of *schechin* as "*lepra*," which gave rise to the earliest Christian understandings of Job's disease, as well as the initial interpretation of Jewish scholars until about 500 CE. The *Testament of Job*, for example, that was completed sometime between 200 BCE and 200 CE, clearly identifies Job's disease as leprosy.

This same diagnosis was given by Tertullian, Jerome, Saint Augustine, and most of the early church fathers. John of Damascus (777–857), for example, identified Job's disease as leprosy. This tradition also stretches forward to the Reformation, where Theodor Beza and Swiss reformer Ulrich Zwingli also identify Job's disease as leprosy. By the mid-sixteenth century, however, mostly in French texts, Job's disease was known as "*Mal de Job*," a synonym for "syphilis."[408]

This diagnosis of Job's disease being syphilis was revived in the twentieth century in an anonymous article called "Morbus Jobi," written by the librarian of the Army Medical Library, and published by the *Urologic and Cutaneous Review* in 1936.[409] But before the mid-sixteenth century both Jewish and Christian exegetes understood Job's disease to be leprosy. In the Christian tradition, in the thirteenth century, a mass was said called "The Mass of Separation," a celebration for the souls of those who had contracted the disease. In this period, lepers frequently carried clappers or bells and begging bowls, so others knew they were approaching.[410]

By the late eighteenth century, we begin to see more modern understandings of the Man from Uz's illness. In 1802, Bouquillon suggested that Job suffered from erysipelas, an acute inflammation of the skin caused by streptococcus. In France, at the same time, a few other scholars still argued for syphilis.[411]

The mid-nineteenth century saw the emergence of a new diagnosis of Job's malady. Michalis and Lestere suggested that Job suffered from elephantiasis, a hypertrophic fibrosis of the skin and subcutaneous lymph tissue.[412] The chief virtue of this new diagnosis was that the primary culprits in the disease are two species of worms, as in Job 7:5.

The late nineteenth century brought both supporters and critics of the elephantiasis explanation of Job's malady. Supporters of the theory included Davidson, E. C. S. Gibson, and J. F. Genung.[413]

Other nineteenth-century theories about the nature of Job's disease include R. K. Harrison's view that Job had small pox, a theory shared by Frank Balchin and James Hastings, in his celebrated *Dictionary of the Bible*.[414]

J. v. Kinnier Wilson believed Job suffered from scurvy or pellagra.[415] Munch, Bloich, and Preuss favored eczema leprosy; Mastermann, erythema; Guy, dermatitis; and Ball, infected sores.[416] By the mid-twentieth century, three pediatricians, named

Banntyns, Skowron, and Weber, along with a group of British physicians, writing in *Lancet*, both labeled a chronic form of granulomatosis as "Job's Disease."[417] In place of chronic granulomas, S. Levin nominates Yaws, as Job's disease.[418]

In the twentieth century, J. Renie, Buttenwieser, Wallington, Hulse, David Clines, Cochrane, Gramgreg, O'Neill, and S. G. Browne all argue for leprosy.[419] Gemayel, Francis Peloubet, and Marvin Pope think Job's disease was the Biskra Button, while Schapiro sided with those who advocated small pox.[420] The late twentieth century saw a rash of diagnoses of Job's illness that all has psychosomatic origins. William Guy, writing in the *Archives of Dermatology* in 1955, took this approach.[421] James Halliday, in an article for the *Pratitioner*, had a Jungian understanding of Job's malady.[422] Gerber, Kahn, Bakan, Ney, Schimmel, W. S. Taylor, Kapusta, Vogels, Milner, Harvey, and Belzen all gave psychogenic causes to Job's disease.[423] George Howe said Job suffered from "cancerous boils."[424] And William Ho argued for Yaws.[425]

Most recently, Dr. Garibed Eknoyan et al. argue that Job suffered from some sort of "kidney ailment."[426] Kevin Cauley argues for "Black Leprosy,"[427] Ilan Kutz believes Job should be diagnosed and treated in the hematology ward.[428] And Luiz Antonio de Lima Resende et al. argue that Job suffered from an "acute renal failure."[429]

One way to resolve the dilemma in identifying the illness to which Job suffered is to offer an approach like that mentioned by Jeremias Drexelius, seventeenth-century religious scholar and amateur medical historian. Drexelius suggests the sources for Job's maladies were: candor, depression, elephantiasis, arthritis, nephritis, insomnia, among others.[430]

Initially, this lengthy diagnosis provided by Drexelius would seem to suffer from the same problems as both very specific illnesses and very general diagnoses; but in retrospect, Drexelius's diagnosis is not so nonsensical. Perhaps Job's illness cannot be identified because he suffers from a host of ailments, all of which go into the making of Job's malady.

Thus, it is best, we believe, to think of Job's ailment as the "Disease of Diseases." In the same way it is difficult to pinpoint the location of the Land of Uz, it is also just as arduous to settle on the nature of the Man from Uz's illness. It is best to call his ailment: "The Disease of Diseases."[431]

Job's Wife (2:9–10)

The only line that Job's wife utters in the book comes at 2:9. In Hebrew she says, "*Baruch Elohim ve mos*," that usually gets translated as "curse God and die." The word, *barach*, however, at times also means "bless," so it is not entirely clear what Job's spouse intended in her remark.

The words of Job's wife at 2:9 echo the words of Yahweh from 2:3, as well as those from Satan at 2:5, concerning Job's piety. Samuel Cox is right in saying, "Job's wife has been a much maligned woman, both by scholars and the popular imagination, as if she were a kind of scriptural Xantippe."[432] Saint Augustine calls her a *diablo aduitrix*, the "Devil's Assistant."[433]

John Chrysostom thought she was kept alive to be a scourge for her husband, "the last bitter drop of his cup of suffering."[434] Gregory calls Job's wife a "mispersuading woman."[435] Thomas Aquinas suggests that Satan spared Job's wife in ch. 1, precisely so he could use her against Job in ch. 2.[436] Bernard of Clairvaux thinks her comment should be rendered, "Bless God and die." Calvin, in another sermon, calls Job's wife "Satan's tool."[437]

Dhorme points out that the early church fathers emphasized "the role of the wife in the temptation. She acts as an intermediary between Satan and Job, as Eve was between the serpent and Adam."[438]

Indeed, these negative judgments about Job's wife are the primary way she has been depicted in the Christian West. Commenting on this phenomenon, David Clines observes:

> The parallel with Eve, and thus with the archetypal "woman as temptress," has also naturally been drawn.[439]

Thomas Royds, in his 1911 commentary, says that Job's wife is "a second Eve."[440] The name of Job's wife appears in the Talmud and some early rabbinic sources as Dinah (Baba Bathra, 15b). Perhaps this is because Job says his wife "speaks like a foolish woman," and Dinah is the daughter of Jacob in Gen 34:7, where the adjective "folly" is used to describe her.[441]

The Septuagint expands Job's wife's speech for several lines. She says:

> "Behold I wait yet a little while, expecting the hope of my deliverance?" For behold, your memory is abolished from the Earth, your sons and our daughters the pangs and the pain of my womb, which I bore in vain with sorrow; and you yourself seated among the corruption of the worms, spending the night in the open air, and I am a servant and wanderer from place to place and house to house, waiting for the setting of the sun, that I might rest from my labors and my pangs that now beset me; but say something against God and die.[442]

Like most early Christian interpreters of Job's wife, Hesychius stresses the possibility, indeed the certainty in his view, that Job's wife is in league with the devil, which Hesychius continually refers to as "the Betrayer."[443] Thus, Hesychius is an advocate of the demonic forces motif to explain Job's suffering.

In the Jewish tradition, the *Midrash Rabbah on Genesis* (19:12) contrasts Job with Adam. Adam, unlike Job, heeded his wife's bad counsel with disastrous consequences.[444] The *Targum of Job* gives the name of Dinah as Job's wife.[445] The apocryphal *Divrei Iyyov* also speaks of Job having two wives. The first is named Uzit (a transliteration of the Greek Sitidos) and was an Arab woman. Job's second wife was Dinah, the daughter of Jacob, who bore a second set of children after the first ten had died.

In medieval Judaism, Rabbi Jacob ben Meir Tam (1100–1171), the grandson of Rashi, ascribes the best intentions to Job's wife. She speaks as she does because Satan was trying to subvert Job through using her. He says that Job's wife is suggesting that the patriarch commit suicide, simply by cursing God, and this was motivated by seeing her husband suffer so deeply.[446]

Zerahiah Hen, thirteenth-century Jewish Spanish exegete, says that Job's wife, like the Satan, is an allegory for matter, which is the cause of suffering and death.[447] Zerahiah also mentions a parallel between the garden of Eden and Job's wife. Zerahiah writes:

> Just as Eve tempts Adam to eat from the Tree of Knowledge, and thereby causes them to be punished with mortality, so too Job's wife causes him to curse God so that he will die. In both cases, the female represents matter and an attempt to bring death onto the male counterpart, who represents form.[448]

Rabbi Moshe ben Nachman, also known in the West as Nachmanides, says that Job's wife gets her husband to blaspheme because death is better than his current situation. Perhaps her doubts, however, should be seen as a prefiguring of Job's later cursing the day of his birth in ch. 3. Which is worse, to accept one's fate and give up hope as she does, or to wish that one's entire life had never happened, as Job does in the opening of ch. 3?[449]

Finally, Abraham Heschel, in his work *The Prophets*, published in 1955, tells us this about Job and his spouse:

> Job's answer to his wife expresses the essential attitude, "Shall we accept good from the hands of God and not accept evil?"[450]

Most medieval Islamic sources refer to Job's wife as Rahmah, the daughter of Ephraim. Some Muslim exegetes give Job's wife's name as Dinah, Leah, or even Mahkir. Still others call her Dina, presumably a derivation of Dinah. Some say she was the prophet's second wife, who bore him twenty-six new sons. Other Muslim thinkers hold that Job's second wife was given fourteen new sons, double the seven sons in the opening of the book.[451]

Contemporary scholar Anne Catherine Emmerich, in her book *The Life of the Blessed Virgin*, says that Job had four wives in the course of his life (four being from the tribe of Peleg).[452]

George Sale (1697–1736), Canterbury Orientalist and the first great modern English translator of the Qur'an, tells us this about Job's wife:

> His wife (whom some called Rahmah, the daughter of Ephraim, the son of Joseph, and others Mahkir, the daughter of Mannasses) attended him with great patience, supporting him in what she earned with labor; but the Devil appeared to her one day, and after reminding her of her passed prosperity, promised that if she would worship him, he would restore all that they had

lost; whereupon she asks her husband's consent who was so angry at the proposal that he swore that if he recovers, he will give her one hundred lashes.[453]

Unlike Christian medieval depictions of Job's wife extending food to her husband on the end of a stick, lest she have defiling contact with him, in Islamic iconography, *Ayyub*'s spouse is usually shown as a placid, peaceful figure who attends to her husband. One fine example of this is a manuscript owned by the New York City Library (Ms. 456, fol. 109), in which Ayyub is shown accompanied by both the Angel Jibril and his wife.[454] One major difference in this image, however, as well as others like it in the Islamic tradition, is that the Prophet Ayyub is depicted after his sores have been healed.

In the Qur'an, the Angel Jibril instructs Ayyub to strike the ground, and when he does, a healing stream appears that clears up the lesions of the prophet. In the image mentioned above, the healing stream can be seen flowing between the prophet's feet, while his serene wife attends to him.

As in the written sources, Job's wife in Christian iconography is often depicted as a shrew, or an agent of the devil. In a fourteenth-century illumination entitled "Mirror of Human Salvation," for example, Job is seated between his wife and the devil. The Latin subtext reads:

> Job's wife beats him with words, while the Devil beats him with a stick.[455]

By the sixteenth century, artistic renderings of Job's wife are considerably less stern-looking. *Job and His Wife*, by Albrecht Dürer, completed in 1504, is a fine example of this new spirit. The oil painting is a wing of the Jabach Church altarpiece, which was commissioned by Frederick the Wise of Saxony. Job's wife pours water over his body in an act of affection and alleviation. The water appears to bring the patriarch some relief.[456]

Job's wife has been rendered a number of times in drama and fiction. In Archibald MacLeish's *J.B.*, for example, Sarah, the Job's wife character, says this about her husband's situation:

> Sarah: [Speaking of her children.] They are dead and they were innocent. I will not let you sacrifice their deaths, to make injustice justice and God Good.
>
> J.B.: [Covering his face with his hands.] My heart beats. I cannot answer it.
>
> Sarah: If you stay quiet with their innocence ... Theirs or yours ... I will love you.
>
> J.B.: [softly] I have no choice but to be guilty.
>
> Sarah: [her voice rising.] We have the choice to live or die, all of us. Curse God and die![457]

Muriel Spark, in her 1986 novel, *The Only Problem*, has her hero (the Job character) fascinated by a painting by Georges de la Tour, entitled *Job Visited by His Wife*. The painting was completed in the manner of a seventeenth-century painting this way:

> Job's wife tall, sweet-faced, with the intimations of a beautiful body inside the large, tent-like case of her firm clothes, bending, long-necked, solicitous over Job. In her hand is a lighted candle. Job sits on a plain, cube-shaped block. He might be in front of a fire, for the light of the candle cannot alone explain the amount of light that is cast on the two figures. Job is naked, except for his loin cloth. He clasps his hands above his knees. His body seems to shrink, but it is the shrunkenness of pathos rather than want. Besides him is a piece of broken pottery that he has taken to scrape his wounds. His beard is thick. He is not an old man. Both are in their prime, a couple in their thirties. . . . His face looks up at his wife, Imploring some favor, urging some cause. What is his wife trying to tell him? As she bends her sweet face towards him. What does he beg, this stricken man, so serene in his faith, so accomplished in argument? . . . Job and his wife are deeply in love.[458]

Among more contemporary scholars, Norman Habel says, "Job's wife is a realist, whereas Job is nothing if not an idealist."[459] Samuel Terrien says that Job's wife is "a theological method for committing euthanasia."[460] A. B. Davidson tells us, "There is nothing too sharp for an angry woman's tongue."[461] Delitzsch prefers "Blaspheme and die!" for the wife's speech.[462] Robert A. Watson, in his 1882 commentary, says that "the writer probably means here that Job's wife would naturally, as a woman, complicate the sum of his troubles."[463] Søren Kierkegaard, in his book *Repetition*, published in 1843, asks:

> Did Job not have a wife? What do we read about her. Perhaps you think that terror cannot get as much power over a man as the daily thralldom in much smaller adversaries.[464]

Milos Devine, in his 1921 commentary called *The Story of Job*, says this about the Man from Uz's spouse:

> The woman is not introduced for her own sake, and the key to her character is to be found in the way in which her husband understood her attitude is to be explained toward his misfortune.[465]

Devine continues, "We are not to cast a stone at one who shared with him the bitter pangs of bereavement; but that does not alter the fact that her failure imposed an additional strain on his faith."[466]

Albert Schultens suggests "Renounce God and die!" in his 1737 commentary, as does G. R. Noyes in his 1836 translation and commentary.[467] R. F. Hutchinson, in his 1873 commentary, tells us this about the patriarch's wife:

> We are apt to judge harshly Job's wife in thus tempting her husband to sin. But if we remember that she was the mother of ten children buried in the fatal ruins of that house, and that the wife is suddenly reduced from affluence and happiness to poverty and misery, we shall suspend our judgment, and at least think leniently of the poor, half-crazed, old woman.[468]

Driver and Gray tell us:

> Her terse question serves to bring out the uniqueness of Job's character. Many others of normal character would have failed at this point.[469]

Martin Buber agrees that Job's wife's line should read: "Bless God and die!"[470] Marvin Pope notes the parallel of Job's wife to Tobit's wife, Hannah. He also tells us that Saint Jerome had made this same connection, quite explicitly.[471]

Finally, a number of contemporary critics on Job's wife have begun to speak of her role in the context of feminist thought. David Clines, for example, devotes three pages of his massive commentary to what he calls, "Feminist Readings."[472] In this connection, Clines observes:

> The major feminist question, however, for the book is whether its principal concern is in any way a gender-determined one. If it is at all difficult to imagine an alternative version of the Book of Job in which all the protagonists were female and in which at the same time the principal issue arising from the loss of family, social standing, and reputation was a doctrine of retribution and the justice of God, then to that extent the book, however sublime a literary work, may be defective, as yet another expression of an uncritical androcentricity.[473]

Marilyn Yalom, in her 2002 book *A History of the Wife*, also gives a feminist account of Job's spouse. Yalom says about the character, "We hear the bitter voice of the wife and a mother overwhelmed by sorrow and unforgiving of a God deemed responsible for the death of her children."[474]

Finally, the ambiguity of the wife's use of the verb *barak* makes it impossible to determine her intent. It could mean, "Bless Elohim and die victoriously," or "Curse Elohim and get relief through death." Job's response in v. 10, however, suggests that she was speaking in the negative sense.[475]

Job's Lament: Chapter 3

Job Cursing the Day of His Birth (3:1)

Having sat in silence for seven days in the presence of his friends who have come to comfort him, Job finally speaks for the first time in the book in the form of a soliloquy. He begins by cursing the day of his birth and the night of his conception for failing to prevent his sorrow (3:1–10). He then bemoans why he did not die at birth or even stillborn, for then at least he would be at rest, just as those who were great in their life times, or those who had been oppressed (3:11–19). Job also wonders why those who long for death are allowed to linger in life. He concludes by saying that what he most greatly feared in life has now come true—troubles from which there appears to be no rest.

Jeremiah, at 20:14–15, voices a lament comparable to Job's in ch. 3:

> Cursed be the day on which I was born.
>
> The day when my mother bore me,
>
> let it not be blessed!
>
> Cursed be the man
>
> who brought the news to my father,
>
> a son is born to you,
>
> making him very glad.[476]

Rabbi Rava, in the Babylonian Talmud, says about Job 3, "One is not liable for what he says while in pain." He also observes, "If one has friends like Job, it is better off to be dead."[477] Saint Jerome reminds us that with the beginning of ch. 3 "the verses are hexameters in dactyl and spondee."[478] Thomas Aquinas says about Job's lament in ch. 3:

> Note that although to exist and to live are desirable in themselves, yet to exist and to live in misery like this should be avoided, although one may freely sustain being miserable for some purpose. So a wretched life that is not ordered to some good end should not be chosen for any reason.[479]

A few of Calvin's *Sermons on Job* speak of the patriarch cursing the day of his birth. In one of these, he says that Job cursing the day of his birth was actually a blessing.[480] Matthew Henry, in commenting on ch. 3 of Job, observes:

> Long was Job's heart hot within him; and, while he was musing, the fire burned, and the more for being stifled and suppressed. At length, he spoke with his tongue, but not such a good word as David spoke after a long pause. Lord, make me to know my end.[481]

John Hartley, in his commentary, points out that v. 16 of ch. 3 is "one of the great enigmas, for it separates two portions about dealing with Sheol."[482] Dhorme suggests v. 16 should be placed after v. 12.[483] David Noel Freeman, in "The Structure of Job Three," agrees, as does Westermann, who calls the chapter a "self-lament."[484] Not all modern translations of 3:1 say, "After Job opened his mouth and cursed the day of his birth" as the RSV does. The ESV, for example, has it, "I wish the day I was born would be lost forever."[485]

Daniel Simundson, in his 1986 commentary, reminds us that the word for "curse" in 3:1 is "a common word for curse [*qll*], and not the euphemisms which we noted back in the prologue."[486] He adds:

> Job has refrained from cursing God after each level of persecution brought on by the Satan. He still stops short of cursing God in chapter three. He wonders why he was born into a life that has brought so much misery and he wonders why death does not come more quickly to remove him from his painful existence. But he does not curse, blame, renounce, or blaspheme God. Not yet, any way.[487]

W. G. Jordan, in his 1929 commentary, says about Job's lament in ch. 3, "In this passage we have the words wrung from the heart of a man who was fighting a noble battle against fearful odds."[488] John, Bishop of Fredericton, in his 1879 commentary agrees. He says:

> Perhaps no more is meant here than that, in the hyperbolic language of Oriental poetry, he proclaimed his utter wretchedness.[489]

Matitiahu Tsevat, in an essay called "The Meaning of the Book of Job," published in 1966, speaks of the change in style and philosophy at the beginning of ch. 3. Tsevat writes:

> At the beginning of the poetic part we find ourselves in a different world, not only as regards the plot—if we may refer to the regular change of speakers and their ever-increasing animosity—but also as regards to the ideas. The latter, while not unrelated to the ideas of the prologue, assume very different forms, and it is only toward the end of the book, that we recognize them in their earlier formulation.[490]

Finally, David Clines in his recent commentary, also speaks of the lack of theological content in Job's speech from ch. 3. Clines observes:

> It is amazing to find here not one strictly theological sentence, not a single question about the meaning of his suffering, not a hint that it might be deserved, not the slightest nod to the doctrine of retribution. All that will come, in its time, but here we are invited to view the man Job in the violence of his grief. Unless we encounter this man with these feelings, we have no right to listen in on the debates that follow; with this speech we cannot over-intellectualize the book, but must always be reading it as the drama of a human soul.[491]

PART II: THE BOOK OF JOB COMMENTARY

Eliphaz's First Speech: Chapters 4–5

Introduction

Eliphaz was most likely the oldest and wisest of the three friends, so he goes first. Elsewhere in the Hebrew Bible, an Eliphaz is the first son of Esau and Adah. Eliphaz had six sons, of which Omar was the first. A Midrash relates that when Jacob escaped from Esau and fled to his uncle Laban, Esau sent Eliphaz to pursue and kill Jacob, but when they met, Jacob talked him out of it.

Analysis of Chapters 4–5

Many exegetes have pointed out the difficulty of the Hebrew in ch. 4. Kemper Fullerton, in his essay "Double Entendre in the First Speech of Eliphaz," tells us:

> In spite of certain obscurities in its phrasing and connections, probably due to text corruption, the first speech of Eliphaz is one of the most carefully thought-out of the book. Its meaning, however, does not lie on the surface.[492]

W. B. Stevenson, in his 1951 commentary, agrees with the difficulty of the Hebrew of ch. 4. Stevenson observes: "In the first speech of Eliphaz, problems of interpretation are of chief importance."[493] Ibn Ezra suggests that the beginning of Eliphaz's first speech means this: "Should we raise a word against you, you would not weary. Who can go without mentioning the words of the Most High?"[494] Indeed, Eliphaz begins his first speech by praising Job, only to change his mind at v. 7, when he begins to accuse the patriarch of sin.

Ewald believes that Eliphaz "undertakes to correct Job according to his best notions." Ewald continues:

> He is, it is true, already fully convinced of Job's guilt, and speaks to him as a teacher, with superior assurance, like a friend who acknowledges greater experience, as to one who is in error, Still, he speaks, particularly at the beginning and end with great caution and forethought, in order to say what is necessary with as much tenderness and consideration as possible.[495]

Many other exegetes, in both the Jewish and Christian traditions, also see Eliphaz's first speech in very positive light. Rashi says that Eliphaz appears to be a prophet in this first speech. S. R. Driver tells us about Eliphaz's first discourse:

> Job's righteousness should be his confidence, for only sinners are brought to their end by calamity.[496]

Both Dhorme and A. Weiser took Eliphaz's first speech to be intentionally insulting, by assuming him to be the cause of his own suffering.[497] Among the Dead Sea Scrolls, two targum fragments, one from 3:5–9 and the other from 4:16–5:4, were found in Cave IV.[498] David Clines says:

Eliphaz's speech begins with the fundamental assumption that the innocent are never "cut off."[499]

Thomas Aquinas believes that Eliphaz "accuses Job of impatience, when he says, 'Who that was innocent ever perished, or when have the upright been destroyed?'"[500]

This is clearly an application of retributive justice theory. Elaine Phillips, in her essay "Speaking Truthfully: Job's Friends and Job," says that "Eliphaz reaffirms the stability of the moral realm: those who are innocent never perish, and those who are evil reap its fruits."[501] Wesley thinks that Eliphaz speaks with "great modesty" in the beginning of ch. 4.[502] W. G. Jordan, in his 1929 commentary, also takes a positive view of Eliphaz's first discourse. Jordan writes:

> The first speech of Eliphaz, the Temanite, begins with gentle remonstrance reminding Job that one who has seen sorrow and then comes to others and shows sympathy with the sufferer should not be surprised if he is called to bear his share. Surely, his confidence is in his own integrity and knows that just men will not be forsaken by their God.[503]

Jordan assents here to retributive justice theory. Daniel Simundson, in his *Message of Job*, speaks ambivalently about Eliphaz's first speech when he writes, "Eliphaz begins with deference. He wishes not to offend Job, but he cannot keep silent any longer."[504] Paul T. Gibbs, in his 1967 *Job and the Mystery of Wisdom*, observes: "The unmistakable inference is that Job needs to seek God by way of repentance for willful sins."[505] Gibbs, then is an advocate of the Job the penitent motif.

Mezudat David says the key to ch. 4 is v. 7, where Eliphaz says:

> Think hard and try to remember, what innocent people ever perish completely, and where are the upright who were hopelessly destroyed?[506]

Rashi believes the key to Eliphaz's first speech is 4:17, "Can a mortal man be more righteous than God?" Rashi says this question is an interrogatory, and may well be rhetorical.[507]

Countless number of exegetes refer to Eliphaz's vision in 4:13ff. Both Rashi and Ibn Ezra observe:

> When people's thoughts are full of visions in the night, the imaginings that appear to the person in bed comes from seeing things when awake.[508]

Matthew Henry says of Eliphaz's vision, "When we are communing with our hearts, then it is time for the Holy Spirit to commune with us."[509]

Rashi believes that 5:1 refers to angels.[510] Mezudat David says of 5:4, "His sons will distance themselves from man's salvation because of their father's sin, no one will show them any clemency."[511] Mezudat David endorses here a collective form of retributive justice theory.

Rashi observes that at 5:8, Eliphaz is saying:

I would not complain as you are doing, but I would beseech God to release me from my predicament.[512]

Both Rashi and Ibn Ezra say about 5:13, "Any counsel that is planned hastily is quite foolish."[513] One of Calvin's 159 sermons on Job is about 5:17-18. The Targum of Job suggests that the "famine in 5:20 is an allusion to the Egyptian famine of Joseph's time."[514] And W. B. Stevenson, in his 1947 *The Poem of Job*, tells us this about the end of Eliphaz's first speech:

> The last words of Eliphaz's speech are a confident promise that Job's prosperity will be restored and that his life will be prolonged to a perfect close.[515]

Job's First Response to Eliphaz: Chapters 6-7

Introduction to Chapter 6

Job's speech in chs. 6 and 7 picks up a number of key words from Eliphaz's first speech. The word "vexation" (*ka'as*) at 5:2 and 6:2; "hope" (*tiqwah*) at 4:6 and 6:8; "success" (*tusiyyah*) at 5:12 and 6:13; "crush" (*daka*) at 4:19 and 6:9; and "fear" (*yirah*) at 4:6 and 6:14. After the introduction at 6:1, the remainder of the chapter may be divided into four sections (6:2-7; 6:8-13; 6:14-21; and 6:22-30). In the first section, Job continues the assault he began back in ch. 3; in the second, he longs for death; in the final two sections, he addresses the question of the usefulness of Job's friends. In the opening of ch. 6, it is clear that Job speaks to all three friends, not just to Eliphaz. By the end of ch. 6, it is clear that Job speaks directly to God.

Analysis of Chapter 6

6:2-7

David Burrell describes the first section of ch. 6 quite adequately, when he writes:

> In what could be regarded as a poetic master stroke, Job continues to ventilate as though Eliphaz had not spoken, for how else could one hope to meet such insensitive ploys? Yet, while he might be able to dismiss Eliphaz's rhetoric, he frankly despairs of meeting the challenge of affliction at God's hands.[516]

Driver and Gray suggest the "vexation" of v. 2 is "the sense of undeserved treatment that could weigh against his actual suffering."[517] At least one Talmudic sage is shocked at the outburst of Job in v. 2. Rabbi Rav says, "Dust should be put in the mouth of Job because he makes himself the colleague of Heaven by desiring to weigh his pleas in the balance with those of God."[518] Matthew Henry says of 6:2-7:

Job still justifies himself in his complaints. In addition to outward troubles, the inward sense of God's wrath took away all his courage. The inner sense of the wrath of God is harder to bear than the outward sense.[519]

For "heavier than the sand of the sea," at v. 3, Driver and Gray give Prov 27:3 as a parallel. They say of the verse, "Job admits that his words have been rash, but suggests that his suffering is a sufficient excuse for them."[520] Wesley agrees. He says Job's meaning in v. 3 is: "So am I made to possess months of vanity and wearisome nights that are appointed to me?"[521] He points out that "nights" are the saddest time for sick people. Umbreit thinks that Job apologizes in v. 3, "not for having enough words, but for speaking too much and too boldly."[522]

A range of interpretations of v. 4 can be seen, but most interpreters agree with Driver and Gray, who say, "This is the first time Job mentions God as a source for his afflictions."[523] Driver and Gray give some parallels for the "arrows of the Almighty" in v. 4b, including Pss 7:13–14; 38:2–3; 58:5; Deut 32:23–24; and Ezek 5:16.[524]

Mezudat David comments about v. 4, "Job now openly accuses God, the arrow that comes from the Almighty is lodged in me constantly."[525] Rashi observes about v. 4, "It was the custom of the Persians to put poison on the tips of their arrows."[526] Ibn Ezra says about v. 4, "The metaphor changes to that of a hostile army. They are arrayed in war against Job."[527] Gregory informs us that the arrows are "sometimes the utterances of preaching, and sometimes are the arrows of visitation."[528]

About vv. 5–7, Driver and Gray observe:

> Job's complaints are proof of the reality of his pain; does any animal complain when it has its natural and accustomed food? But Job's sufferings are like insipid and repulsive food that no one can bear without complaining.[529]

Umbreit gives Pss 42:3; 80:5; and 102:9 as parallels to Job's sickness being like nauseous food.[530] Reichert, commenting on v. 7, points out that the use of the word *nefesh* probably means the appetites here. He gives Prov 10:3; 13:25; and 27:7 as parallels. Ibn Ezra takes v. 7 literally, "My soul is sick and I shall die."[531]

6:8–13

C. S. Rodd says of these verses:

> The longing for death to end it all is repeated in these verses. He will not commit suicide, but will seek God's final act of annihilation.[532]

Matthew Henry gives a similar interpretation, "Job desires death as the happy ending of his miseries. Job grounds his comfort upon the testimony of his conscience."[533] Peake says that "Job's deepest longing is that God will put him out of his misery."[534] Tyndale says that Job wishes to be killed, "the very thing that Satan was not allowed to do to him."535 Driver and Gray say that despite Job's cry for death, "he does not disregard God's commandments."536

Both Gensius and Umbreit say that the meaning of Job's words in these verses are:

> I would harden myself in sorrow. I would exalt in the pain, if I knew that the pain would hasten my death.537

This is the first time in the book that Job longs for death. Gregory, commenting on v. 12, observes:

> The Holy man, longing for the coming of his Redeemer, under the name of a balance; while he opens his mind in discourse, he instructs us in the earnestness of life.538

Pope Gregory here seems to employ the *Jobus Christi* motif in his comment on Job 6:12. As we shall see throughout in this commentary, the author of the *Moralia in Jobi* frequently used this understanding of the Man from Uz and his book.

6:14–21

Driver and Gray suggest in this third speech of ch. 6 that "Job's friends have abandoned him in his hour of need; they have not shown him the sympathy he was due."539 C. S. Rodd believes that Job in these verses is "now ready to respond to Eliphaz, but his approach is oblique. He speaks of the demands of friendship in a detached way."540 Matthew Henry agrees that these verses are about Job's expectations of his friends. Henry writes:

> In his prosperity, Job formed great expectations from his friends, but then he is disappointed by them; then he compares himself to the failing of brooks in summer. Those who make gold their hope, sooner or later will be ashamed of it. Let us all put our confidence in the Rock of Ages.541

Ibn Ezra renders v. 21 this way: "Now you have become his protagonist, since you see the terror He has brought upon me."542 Peake says the import of vv. 21–22 is:

> Had he pursued on their friendship to ask for a gift that would have cost them anything, he would not have been surprised by their treatment. Such a test of friendship should not be asked to endure.543

Wesley thinks that Job is saying in these verses, "Seeing that you are gracious to others, why may I not hope for the same favor from you? If you don't help me speedily, it will soon be too late."544 Umbreit agrees that Job is addressing God in these verses, but their import is:

If you teach me the right view, I am willing to be set right and "hold my tongue," for I am made to see my error. But if your words are the right ones, why are they so feeble?[545]

6:22–30

Driver and Gray say of vv. 22–23, "He has asked for nothing great from his friends, no money, nor deeds of valor, but mere sympathy."[546] Umbreit observes about vv. 24–25, "If you teach me the right view, I am willing to be set right and 'hold my tongue,' so that I am made to see my error."[547] Rashi says of v. 25, "If you have spoken sincere words, they would be received; but now what does your reasoning prove?"[548] Gregory the Great says of v. 27:

> It is now clear to whom the mind of the stricken man has recourse for hope, seeing that he declares that there was no hope to him in himself, but because he intimates that he was weak.[549]

David Burrell says of vv. 24–26:

> Then he abruptly turns his back on them to address the Lord in a completely different tone. "Teach me, and I will be silent; make me understand how I have gone wrong. . . . Will you consider words of a proof and the speeches of a suffering wind?"[550]

About v. 30, Driver and Gray observe, "Job insists on the soundness of his moral judgments. There is no unrighteousness on nor in his tongue."[551] C. S. Rodd thinks at the end of ch. 6, "Job accuses his friends of heartlessness. He denies in v. 30 that he has lost his sense of what is right."[552] Buttenwieser, reflecting on v. 30 says:

> Since his palate has not lost the power to discern taste, so too his moral sense has not waned.[553]

Introduction to Chapter 7

Chapter 7 continues Job's first response to Eliphaz. The chapter may be divided into two main sections: vv. 1–10, "The Wearisome and Brief Nature of Human Life"; and vv. 11–21, "Job's Bitter Reproach to God." C. S. Rodd gives a good summary of ch. 7. He writes:

> We see that 7:1–6 forms the transition from an address to the friends to a direct appeal to God. Probably these words are also to be taken as part of that appeal. Again, Job moves from a general view to his own particular case. Human beings have a hard time of it. They are like slaves forced to work in the

blazing heat, or a day laborer whose wages have not been paid promptly at the end of the day, and who has no other way of sustaining his life.[554]

Rodd continues his analysis:

> So Job feels himself to be in a wonderfully evocative passage in which he describes his suffering. How long the night seems! His body is covered with sores in which worms breed. He is very aware of the brevity of human life— swifter than a weaver's shuttle flying across the warp, soon to come to an end like a thread that runs out from the shuttle. At last, he speaks to God directly. His appeal is to God's understanding of his condition. Remember, death is not far away, and death is final; and his death will take place directly under the eyes of God.[555]

Analysis of Chapter 7

7:1–10

Ibn Ezra says that the "time of service" in v. 1 means warfare. He cites Num 1:3 and 1 Sam 28:1, as parallels.[556] Mezudat David and Ralbag say the time in question is "an end and appointed time."[557] Rashi thinks it refers to "the limited time a man has to live."[558] Moses Maimonides observes about the first two verses of ch. 7:

> Job complains that his days are numbered and he longs for them to end, as would a hired man.[559]

Saadiah Gaon tells us these verses mean "that man is like an army at a halt, in that the army is encamped in a district and then moves swiftly on."[560] About v. 2, Rashi observes, "As a servant that eagerly longs for shade, or a servant that labors through the long days but seeks the cool shade of the evening."[561] Saadiah says the laborer "keeps his eyes on the shifting of the shade, and grows more and more delightful, as it shifts eagerly waiting release from the drudgery and toil."[562]

About "months of vanity and wearisome nights," Mezudat David explains, "Job now turns from contemplation of the universal misery to lament his own wretched lot."[563] Kissane says he mentions months to contrast them with the day of the hireling. "His term is for months, not for a day, or even a night, unlike the hireling who has no respite."[564] H. H. Rowley points out that the beginning of v. 3 should be rendered, "I am made to inherit . . . "[565]

Driver and Gray tell us this about Job's condition in vv. 4–6:

> This is a graphic condition of the conditions to which his malady has brought him: without hope of recovering relief.[566]

There is much description of Job's sores in these verses. Buttenwieser describes them this way:

Job gives a graphic description of the horrible symptoms of his disease. The hard, Earth-like crusts of his sores alternately gather and run again. . . . In Elephantiasis, the harden boils make the skin look as if it were covered with "dirty" elephant skin.[567]

Gersonides tells us the sores are "broken and obnoxious because of the odious pus that was in them." Mezudat David prefers, "My skin was split." Saadiah, "My skin is ulcered."[568] Rowley says of Job's sores, "Job's ulcers had worms and formed hard crusts which then broke out again."[569] David Clines says, "His body is either covered with open sores that exude pus, or with scabs of sores that are apparently in the course of healing."[570]

The expression "My days are swifter than the weaver's shuttle" is one of the most quoted lines in the book of Job. Browning uses the line in his poem "The Bishop Orders His Tomb."[571] Sophocles has Electra say, "But for me already the most of my life has gone by without hope, and I have no more strength."[572]

Peake explains the image of the weaver's shuttle this way:

> A swift death is preferable to a life in agony; but if life could be lived without constant pain, its brevity is an evil, since none would willingly exchange its warm glow and thrilling interest for the cold and colorless monotony of Sheol.[573]

Kissane points out that elsewhere the passing of life is compared to a courier, to skiffs of reeds, and to an eagle sweeping on its prey.[574] Pope indicates there is a wordplay on the term *tiqwah*, which is rendered as both "hope" and "thread."[575] Thus, Ibn Ezra gives us: "My days have come to an end for lack of thread."[576] The same word is used to describe the scarlet thread that identifies Rahab's house at Josh 2:18–21.

About vv. 7–19, Driver and Gray remark:

> He turns pathetically to God, beseeching Him to remember how brief life is, and for Him to have compassion on him for the short time that remains before he descends forever to the grave.[577]

Driver and Gray give Pss 6:6; 88:6 and 11–13; and Isa 38:18 as parallel texts. Ibn Ezra says that v. 7 is not addressed to Eliphaz, but to God. "They are deeply moving in their pathos and passionate appeal." He cites Ps 78:39 as a parallel.[578] Pope tells us that *ruah*, or "wind," is a symbol for what is transient and unsubstantial, vain and empty. He gives Jer 5:13 and Eccl 1:14 as parallels.[579] About "My eyes will never see good," Pope tells us, "To see or taste good means to experience and enjoy prosperity again."[580] Pope gives 21:13 and 25; 36:11; and Ps 34:11–14 as parallel texts. Rashi says that v. 7 is one of the places where "Job denies the resurrection of the dead."[581] Ishodad of Merv tells us the meaning behind v. 7. He says:

> My eyes will begin to see good again. Here the author refers to the hope that is reserved for people in the new world, that is, the world to come.[582]

Saadiah Gaon informs us that he translates "*ki ruah hayyah*" to mean, "My life is empty," taking *ki ruah* to mean "like the wind." Dhorme thinks that v. 7 means nothing more than, "My life is nothing more than a passing breath."[583] Newsom says, "The sense of tenuousness of life, developed in vv. 5–6, motivates Job's direct appeal to God in v. 7." Clines agrees.[584]

Verse 8 is absent from the Septuagint, and it is also omitted by Dillmann, Budde, and Gray, among others. Others find no reason to incise the verse, and Dhorme points out that the verb "behold," or *Hen!* is a characteristic word of the book, where it appears over a dozen times, and only six times in the rest of the Hebrew Bible.[585] Newton Wray says the meaning of v. 8 is:

> His suffering seems incommensurate with man's importance.[586]

John Edgar McFadyen suggests that v. 7 points to a struggle between two different views of God. He describes these this way:

> We see here the beginning of the struggle between two thoughts of God—One treated him with such inexplicable cruelty and shot his poison arrows at him; and the god who beneath all the torture wishes him well and will miss him and yearn for him when he is gone.[587]

Most exegetes agree with Clines when he says of vv. 9–10, "Job simply expresses the clear conviction of his imminent end, by affirming that even God will not be able to set eyes on him."[588] Clines adds, "His life will end the way clouds break up and disperse."[589] Clines gives 30:15; Isa 44:22; and Hos 13:3 as parallels to the use of the cloud image. The Babylonian Talmud, as well as many other Jewish interpreters, see vv. 9–19 as a denial of resurrection of the dead, as did Rashi and other Jewish interpreters.[590]

Nearly all interpreters agree that vv. 9–10 are an affirmation that in Sheol there is no personal survival of death. Rowley tells us, "Sheol is described here as a land from which there is no return."[591] Dhorme, and many other exegetes, agree. Dhorme writes in regard to 7:9–10: the Babylonians called the netherworld "the land from which there is no return," the abode from which he who enters will never leave.[592] Driver and Gray agree on the pessimistic nature of vv. 9–10, that "no return from Sheol is possible."[593] But John Chrysostom is not so dour in his view. He says, "Job's resignation is much more admirable because he has no clearly defined belief in the resurrection."[594] Gregory the Great is also more optimistic about the understanding of vv. 9–10. Gregory observes:

> As the body's house is a bodily habitation, so it becomes to each separate mind is given over to eternal punishment, he is henceforth no longer recalled from the place he has attached himself in life.[595]

Over and against these views of 7:9–10 is the perspective of Kissane, who believes, "His house and place are to be taken literally, and not to be taken as equivalents to 'family' and 'kinfolk.'"[596] Whether or not this is true, Arthur Peake quotes Mallock's paraphrase of Lucretius's "On Life and Death" as a gloss of vv. 9–10:

> Never shalt thou behold thy dear ones more, never thy wife await thee at the door. Never again thy little climber boy a father's kindness in thine eyes explore.[597]

7:11–21

Rashi says the import of v. 11 amounts to this: "Since you don't desist from me, neither will I restrain my speech in complaining about you."[598] Freehof says v. 11 means:

> Since there is so little time left and my disease is so grave, and my pain is so great that I have nothing left to hope for, I might as well speak out in the bitterness of my heart.[599]

John Fredericton says that the "monster of the deep" in v. 12 is not a whale, but any monster in the sea, or on land.[600] He says that v. 15 should be rendered "emaciated frame," that v. 17 is a parody of Ps 8, and that v. 18 should be translated "take my breath."[601] Daniel Simundson thinks the meaning of the second half of ch. 7 is simply Job saying, "Stop attacking me, I'll soon be dead."[602]

Mezudat David says at v. 20, Job asks, "Even if I have sinned, what have I done to you?" And about v. 21, he says, "Why do you not forgive my transgressions?"[603] Driver says about v. 20, "If I have sinned, why do you assail me for it?"[604] Ewald says about v. 21, "Job may have sinned in his treatment of God."[605] At any rate, this is one of the many times in the book where Job says, *'im*, or "[if] I have sinned."

Bildad's First Speech: Chapter 8

W. F. Albright tells us that "the name Bildad has never been adequately explained, despite the numerous attempts that have been made."[606] Albright is most likely correct, but Franz Delitzsch suggests the identity of *Bir-Daddan*, the name of a king of Arabia in the time of Assur-ban-apal. He explains the name as a compound divine name, much like *Hadad-Rimmon*. Delitzsch also regards *Bir* as the name of a weather god in western Mesopotamia, and offers this as a source for the name.[607]

Delitzsch also mentions *Bedad*, the father of the Idumean king Hadad to support his contention that Bildad is a compound name. But Albright makes this final comment on Delitzsch's surmise: "As plausible as the identification of the name Bildad and *Bir-Dadda* may seem, this writer considers it absolutely impossible."[608]

Elsewhere in the Hebrew Bible, Bildad was a descendant from Shuah, the sixth son of Abraham and Keturah at Gen 25:2. Albright tell us, "Shuah is now generally associated with the place Suhu, on the Euphrates River, south of Cardemish."[609] Thus, it is likely that Shuah was a district of Arabia, to the east of Palestine (see Gen 25:6).

Robert Lowth sums up what we know of Bildad:

> Shuah was one of the sons of Abraham by Keturah, whose posterity were numbered among the people of the East. His position was probably contiguous to that of his brother Midian, and his nephews, Shebah and Dedad (Genesis 25:2–3).[610]

The Septuagint spells the name as "Baldad," as does the Vulgate that spells Shuah as Shuah. The fifteenth-century *Patience of Job* calls the second friend *Baldach*.[611] Most English translations use Bildad.

Introduction to Chapter 8

Chapter 8 is the first of Bildad's speeches. The second friend is far less blunt than the first. Bildad suggests in v. 4 that Job's children may be responsible for his suffering. Chapter 8 is far more theological than what we have seen so far. Chapter 8 is usually divided by scholars into three parts: vv. 1–7, "Bildad Reproves Job"; vv. 8–19, "Hypocrites Will Be Destroyed"; and vv. 20–22, "Bildad Applies God's Just Dealings with Job."

Analysis of Chapter 8

8:1–7

Saadiah Gaon tells us this about the meaning of Bildad's first speech: "This appeal of yours for privileged is itself a sin. Indeed, it is unsound on the face of it, for you must either be right, as you say, or sinful as we say."[612] Both Moses Maimonides and Samuel Ibn Tibbon (1165–1232) identify Bildad's theological orientation in his first speech with that of the Mutazilites, an early medieval school of Islamic philosophy that stressed free will and the providence of God.[613]

In more contemporary Jewish views of Bildad's first speech, Tur-Sinai tells us:

> This chapter presents in the main a consistent, well-ordered response by one of the friends. According to hints contained especially in vv. 3–4, this speech, or part of a speech may have been directed in particular against God's utterances now figuring in chapter XIX.[614]

Tur-Sinai concentrates on Bildad's theological point of view in his opening speech, telling us:

> The friend [Bildad] propounds the unqualified doctrine of retribution, that the just fare well, the wicked ill.[615]

Thus, Tur-Sinai endorses the retributive justice theory here. Solomon Freehof tells us that the most important aspect of Bildad's first speech is that the second friend is responding to Job's discourse from ch. 7. He observes:

> Bildad, who now speaks, ignores Job's bitter complaints of his misery, brushes aside his rebuke of his friends and confines himself to the third part of Job's statement, namely, the misery and injustice of the human lot.[616]

Robert Gordis, on the other hand, thinks the chief import of Bildad's first speech is his employment of a well-known technique in wisdom literature. Gordis tell us about Bildad's opening speech:

> Bildad now dramatizes his faith in God's justice through the use of well-known techniques in Wisdom Literature. In the name of the sages in the past, whom he has invoked, he presents a parable of two plants. One is apparently verdant and fresh, but doomed to shrivel quickly. The other preserves its moisture, even under the hot sun, making its way through stony ground, if need be, and taking root in new soil.[617]

Elsewhere in his commentary, however, Gordis suggests that the primary aspect of Bildad's first speech is theology. He observes, "Here Bildad presents an argument that Wisdom teachers and the ancients are generally regarded as irrefutable, so he appeals to the teaching of the past."[618]

R. P. Scheindlin tells us that the most relevant aspect of Bildad's first speech is his accusing Job's children of sinning at v. 4. Scheindlin writes:

> Bildad centers the discussion on merit, but directly accuses only Job's sons of sinning. He emphasizes the frailty of the wicked man's success and assures Job of restoration, if he will only acknowledge his guilt.[619]

Thus, R. P. Scheindlin appears to be ascribing to a collective, or familial, form of the retributive justice response to the origin of Job's suffering. At v. 4, we find that Job's children may be the cause of the patriarch's suffering. Remember, however, that the narrator, at 1:5, also may have pointed out this possible view, for there Job makes sacrifices for his children "in case they may have sinned in their hearts." Given 1:5, such a view, then, seems out of bounds in the book.

Among the earliest Christian comments on Bildad's first discourse are some remarks by Ephrem the Syrian, John Chrysostom, and Olympiodorus in the early fifth century. Ephrem, commenting on 8:2, tells us:

> So Bildad, the Shuite, reproached Job because he thought that the words that Job has said for the sake of the truth and justice were, in fact, spoken out of arrogance and disdain.[620]

John Chrysostom, writing about vv. 2–3, tells us that Bildad's comments mean, "Do you not perceive the profound justice that reigns in the creation and its profound order? And how everything is regulated and settled?"[621] Olympiodorus, writing about vv. 5–7, says:

> Notice how Bildad demonstrates in this part of his discourse of praise his belief that the happiness of the righteous is found in the goods of the material life.[622]

Julian Eclanum was also among the first Christian exegetes to comment on Bildad's first discourse. He says the key to the speech is to understand that Bildad wants us to "learn from the ancients."[623] If Julian is correct, then this verse is a reference to the view that the ancient Jewish fathers had a wisdom greater than contemporary people. We will call this the "Wisdom of the Fathers" approach.

Thomas Aquinas says that Bildad, "taking Job's words in another direction tries to reduce them to inconsistency."[624] Calvin has mixed feelings about Bildad's first speech, as in this sermon on the beginning of ch. 8:

> The better to profit ourselves by that which is conveyed in this chapter. We must bear in mind what we have declared before, that Job's friend is undertaking an evil case, though he nevertheless has good arguments and good reasons. True, he might misapply them, nevertheless, the doctrine is, in itself, both holy and profitable.[625]

Presumably, the doctrine Calvin has in mind here is retributive justice, that the good should prosper and the wicked receive great ills. Indeed, Bildad's love of retributive justice has attracted a wide range of comments, particularly about v. 4. Didymus the Blind says the meaning of v. 4 is, "If you have not sinned, your sons have."[626] Julian of Eclanum asks about v. 4:

> Do not the sins of your house reflect the guilt of your principles?[627]

Julian, in his question, appears to endorse a collective form of retributive justice theory. Julian continues his analysis by suggesting, "It is useful, however, that you are purified through confession and the offering of prayers."[628] Frederich Spanheim, in his 1670 commentary, as well as Albert Schultens, in his 1736 commentary, both held the view that the speech of Bildad in ch. 8 is a literal transcription of what was said.[629] The same position was held by J. H. Michaelis, in his commentary completed in Halle in 1720.[630]

The comment mentioned above of Julian's on v. 3 about "purification" is one of the earliest endorsements of the moral qualities theodicy. David Clines, in his commentary on vv. 2–7, tells us this about Bildad:

> Bildad, like the other friends, believes firmly that suffering is punishment; but in the way he applies that belief to Job's case differs from the other friends.[631]

H. H. Rowley agrees that retributive justice lies at the heart of Bildad's first discourse. He observes:

> The moral universe, in Bildad's theology, is founded upon the principle of retribution. Any deviation from it would be injustice, and God and justice are mutually compatible terms.[632]

Thus, John Calvin, H. H. Rowley, and Julian of Eclanum all believe that the theological beliefs that lie beneath Eliphaz's first speech in ch. 8 of the book of Job is the theory of retributive justice, or collective retributive justice, while Julian assented to the moral qualities view, as well.

Many nineteenth-century commentators tie Bildad's first speech to the doctrine of retributive justice, as well. Albert Barnes says that Bildad "pursues substantially the line of argumentation that Eliphaz has commenced."[633] Thomas Scott, in his 1848 commentary, agrees. Scott observes:

> Bildad supports the principle of Eliphaz that all sufferings are punishments and necessarily imply previous guilt.[634]

William Bode, in his 1914 commentary, says that "Bildad advances a doctrine, which was not obnoxious to Job, as long as it remains in general terms, but when it became specific, in spite of Job's violent accusations, is it not unjust that Job's children have died an untimely death. It is true, but this was because they were wicked; but Job himself still lives, and if he is really righteous, God's justice will restore his former prosperity."[635]

8:8–19

Comparisons of a lifetime to a shadow are common in Wisdom Literature (see 1 Chr 29:15; Pss 73:12; 92:12). The mention of "shadow" may refer back to 7:6, 7, and 9. The word for shadow is *tsel*. It is used fifteen times in the book. The word *gome* in v. 11 is rendered "papyrus" by the Septuagint. Didymus the Blind says of vv. 11–12, "He seems to mean that big or small, everything in life is subject to Providence, and withers if it does not pay attention to it."[636] Philip the Priest says of vv. 11–12:

> Bildad means that as the papyrus and the reed cannot live without water, so you could not remain in your former happiness without the nourishment and liquid of justice.[637]

The use of plant metaphors to stand for the righteous and reprobate are also common in Wisdom Literature (see Pss 1:3–4; 54:8; 92:12–14; and Jer 17:7–8). Hesychius of Jerusalem says of v. 13, "By preserving the fruit of virtue, Job has caused abundant foliage of this world's goods to bloom."[638] Philip the Priest gives us this meaning for vv. 14–15:

> He who confides in himself and relies on his own strength will not be able to stand, but his arrogance will fall more ruinously.[639]

Olympiodorus observes regarding vv. 14–16, "The impious will suffer the same destiny, when the wrath of God falls upon them."[640] Gregory says that vv. 17–18 are about "hypocrisy."

He tells us:

> For all that the hypocrites do, seeing that in their secret thoughts they look out for the applause of their fellow creatures, like rushes, as it were, they send out roots into the heap of rocks.[641]

Saadiah renders it "sun threads" in v. 14a, a poetic term for "gossamer."[642] The hint of thread may already have been introduced in v. 13b, where *tiqwah* means both "thread" and "hope." Verse 16 provides another metaphor, "the wicked are like *ratab*," "a well watered plant." The same word is employed at 24:8. By analogy, the shoot represents the offspring of a wicked man. (See Ps 128:3.) "What kind of plant this is does not matter, whether a vine or a gourd" (Budde), a tree (Ehrlich), "some obnoxious plant" (Duhm), or "a creeper or crawler" (Fohrer).[643]

Some exegetes turn *gal*, or "rock pile," into a spring or a pile of water in v. 17. Others associate *gal* with *gan*, or "garden," by referring to a passage from Song of Songs 4:12. Thus, Jastrow, Pope, Hartley, and Clines. The verb *bala* in v. 18 usually means "swallow," but here it may mean "destroy." The next verb has a wider range of meanings (lie, deny, and fail). It may mean that the place has a short memory, just as people often do. A parallel passage at Prov 10:7b suggests, "The name of the wicked will rot."[644]

In v. 19, Bildad raises the same query that Eliphaz had at 4:7. The word *masos* means "joy" in sixteen other places in the Hebrew Bible.[645] The Septuagint has it as "catastrophe." Driver says Bildad is being ironic here.[646] Jastrow calls it "sarcasm."[647] Tur-Sinai says "renew," while Dhorme has it as "rotting."[648] Gordis suggests "goes on its way."[649] The NIV and NEB have it as "withers away," by reading *samek* for "sin."[650] At any rate, the subject and verb of v. 19b are incongruent, in that the subject is singular and the verb is plural.

8:20–22

Bildad gives his general theory of retributive justice. God will not reject the innocent, though he may send them chastisements for minor faults. He will not save the wicked from utter ruin. The word *tam* is used again to describe Job. (See 1:8 and 2:3.) David Clines tells us about v. 20:

> This sentence crystalizes the whole retributivist theory and provides a positive statement of the principle of moral order that lay behind the question at v. 3.[651]

Rashi renders v. 20 as, "He will not uphold your enemies who are harming you, until he returns to grant you clemency, and then he will fill your mouth with laughter."[652] The application of Bildad's theory of retributive justice is also at work in v. 21. The MT suggests the active "He will fill," but the next verse favors the passive voice, as do the Peshitta and the Vulgate. The sense of this verse is that Job's enemy, who rejoiced in his downfall, will be confounded when his fortune is restored. The Germans call this *schadenftreuden*. A similar attitude is taken at Prov 24:17. Holscher deletes v. 21 on the ground that it is too friendly to be a comment from Bildad.[653]

The expression "clothed with shame" occurs at Pss 35:26; 109:29; and 132:18. Mezudat David says the verse means:

> He will not reject you and your end will be increased exceedingly, until he fills your mouth with laughter, and your lips will shout with joy in celebration of the great prosperity you have earned.[654]

Most modern exegetes see v. 22 as a positive assertion of the character of Job and his prospects for restoration. Samuel Simundson's comment is typical when he writes on vv. 21–22, "Bildad closes with some words of reassurance for Job, telling him that he will again be able to laugh, while his enemies are appropriately punished."[655]

Three major conclusions may be made about Bildad's first discourse of ch. 8. First, by continually using the particle *'im*, or "if," Bildad raises the possibility that Job is as innocent as he claims to be. Second, Bildad raises the possibility that Job's sufferings come as the result of the sins of his sons, but this seems unlikely given the fact that Job makes sacrifices for these same sons "who may have sinned in their hearts," back at 1:5. And finally, in this chapter, Bildad seems to be an advocate of the doctrine of retributive justice, or collective retributive justice.

Job's First Response to Bildad: Chapters 9 and 10

Introduction

Job's first response to Bildad takes up all of chs. 9 and 10. Thomas Aquinas, Matthew Henry, and Newsom all suggest ch. 9 consists of four separate parts: vv. 1–4; vv. 5–13; vv. 14–24; and vv. 25–35.[656] In regard to ch. 10, Newsom says it is best understood as having three sections: vv. 1–2; vv. 3–17; and vv. 18–22.[657]

Rowley says of these two chapters:

> Job's reply to Bildad seems to concern itself more with things said by Eliphaz than with what Bildad has said. He begins with a sarcastic recognition of the principle enunciated by the friends that man cannot be righteous in the eyes God, because God overwhelms him with His power and refuses to appear with him at the bar of justice.[658]

Many other exegetes concur that the language of chs. 9 and 10 is, at times, quite legalistic. Newsom, for example, says of the opening of ch. 9:

> Job's speech begins with an ironic rhetorical question about the possibility of being "in the right" with God [9:2]. This question leads Job to the image that will dominate not only this speech, but also its whole understanding of his situation: the notion of a lawsuit with God.[659]

Newsom goes on to say more about this view:

> Such a lawsuit is transparently impossible to Job because of the enormous disparity between God's power and his own [9:5–13]. Yet Job cannot leave off his exploration of the idea. Convinced that God's overwhelming power would prevent a just outcome [9:14–21]. Job's conclusion about God becomes increasingly negative
>
> [9:22–24] Lamenting the brevity of his life [9:25–26], Job tries three times to imagine a resolution to his situation [9:27–28; 29–32; and 33–35].[660]

Newsom finishes her introduction to ch. 9:

> The extent to which the image of a lawsuit has taken hold of his imagination is evident from the fact that the impossibility of a resolution is expressed each time in legal language.[661]

Analysis of Chapter 9

9:1–4

McFadyen says of this chapter, "Job points out that there is nothing of God in this speech but pitiless power."[662] Kissane suggests that in these first four verses of ch. 9 Job says:

> Man cannot be just before God, for his adversary is infinitely wise and powerful, having at His command all the forces of nature, such as volcano, earthquake, and the darkness of storm clouds.[663]

Hartley observes that with v. 2, Job "opens with a concession: I know that God does not pervert Justice."[664] Gordis says of v. 2, "Man cannot be just with God, not because man is wicked, but because God overpowers him."[665] Samuel Freehof says that Job's question in v. 2 is this: "How can man prove himself in a discussion with God?"[666] Moses Maimonides thinks that in v. 2, Job is saying, "I know well that God will destroy those who hate Him, and that He will doom the hope of hypocrites."[667]

Duhm says the subject of v. 3 is God. Hartley says Job begins this discussion of a lawsuit with v. 3. Mezudat David says the meaning of v. 3 is this:

If the righteous man would wish to wrangle with God concerning the denial of his just rewards, God would not answer even one question in a thousand.[668]

Rashi says of v. 4, "He is wise in heart 'to contend with Him' and 'mighty in strength' to requite Him."[669] Dhorme says of v. 4:

It would be much too subtle to consider that "wise in the heart and robust in strength" refers to the man who proposes to rebel against God.[670]

Kissane disagrees. He says that v. 4 means little more than, "God has such infinite wisdom and such might to fulfill His wishes that no one can stubbornly resist Him and hope to conquer."[671] Thomas Aquinas thinks that "wise of heart and strong of might" refers to contention of two kinds:

One kind where one contends in debate, and this kind depends on wisdom; and the other kind where one contends by fighting, and this kind depends on strength.[672]

9:5–13

Driver and Gray say these verses are "a description of God's omnipotence as manifested in the mighty works of nature."[673] Gordis believes v. 5 is "a poetic description of an earthquake." He gives 38:6; 1 Sam 2:8; and Ps 105:5 as parallel texts for the earth resting on pillars.[674] Pope gives Ps 18:7; Isa 13:10 and 13; and Joel 2:10 as parallels.[675] John Chrysostom refers to vv. 5–6 in terms of King David, "who touches the mountains as they smoke."[676]

Pope observes that the "darkness" of v. 7 "is the darkness of thunder clouds."[677] Dhorme believes "it does not rise" refers to the "piling up of the clouds."[678] Mezudat David suggests that "He sealed up the stars" in v. 7 means, "He closes off the stars with a partition, and they did not shine."[679] He adds, "This refers to the great flood, when the heavenly bodies did not function."[680] Rowley points out that the word for "sun" (*char'cah*) here is a rare and poetic term, "but it forms an element in some proper names."[681] Ball thinks the name for the sun here comes from the god Horus.[682]

Altogether, the book of Job uses a number of words to signify the sun. At 31:26, it employs the normal word for "light," or *'or*, to represent the sun. At 8:16, the Job poet uses the term *Shemesh* to indicate the sun. At 9:7, we find *ḥeres*, and at 30:28, the poet employs *ḥammah*, one of the usual, classical Hebrew words for "sun."

Gregory believes at vv. 7–8, and their reference to the "heavens," denotes:

That deeply heavenly life of those who preach, of whom the Psalmist speaks, "The Heavens declare the glory of God."[683]

Driver and Gray say vv. 8–9 tell us about "God's power, as shown in the workmanship of control of the billows of the sea."[684] Dhorme believes the verb in v. 9, *hatap* (seize, abduct, or despoil), "stands for a wicked deed committed by one person against another."[685] The constellations of v. 9, *Osh*, *Kesil*, and *Chimah*, have been widely translated in myriad ways. Maimonides thinks they are "signs of the zodiac."[686] Gordis thinks *Chimah* is "*Pleiades*, or possibly *Sirius*."[687] Rowley points out the same three constellations are mentioned at 38:31ff., only in reverse order. The Targum, the Syriac text, the LXX, and the Arabic text, all have them in reverse order as well.[688] Rashi thinks the "chambers of the south" are "rooms where storms are kept." Driver believes it should be rendered "the encirclers of the south," after revocalizing the word for "chambers."[689]

Verses 8–10 are seen as interpolations by Beer, Duhm, Fried, Delitzsch, Budde, and Tur-Sinai.[690] They delete these verses on the grounds that the mention of God's creative works is out of place here.[691]

The Vilna Gaon, Rabbi Elijah ben Solomon Zalman (1720–1797), says the meaning of v. 10 is: "Great deeds are the wonders of nature and supernatural miracles, since the latter are not constant, but occur periodically."[692] Meir Loeb ben Jahiel, also known as Malbim in the West (1809–1879), says of vv. 9–12:

> Job now turns his attention to Bildad's theory that punishment is part of a theory of exchange. He rejects the suggestion that the way to change suffering into an entitlement to benefit him is through prayer. His refusal to accept that although God ignores the justice of his innocence. He will, nevertheless, accept his prayers or can be made to change his mind.[693]

Gregory the Great has entirely different views on the meaning of these verses. Gregory tells us:

> For the human race, to be shut off from interior joy as a result of sin, loses the eye of the mind. Where the mind is now going is the steps of its deserved punishment, it cannot tell.[694]

There is some disagreement about the verb *yahtop* in v. 12. Rashi says it means, "He strikes suddenly."[695] Pope believes it means, "God snatches men away from life and no one can dare question Him."[696] The Targum supposes the meaning is "to remove man from the world."[697] Isaiah di Trani and Mezudat David agree. The LXX renders the verb "He sets free," rather than "He snatches away."[698] Whatever its meaning, *yahtop* is one of the many *hapax Legomena*, but the general sense of "snatching away" can be established from cognates in Akkadian and Arabic.

Rashi says the "helpers of Rahab" in v. 13 are "the proud of Egypt."[699] Kissane says of the helpers of Rahab, "Even powers far superior to man are no match for Him."[700] The use of "Rahab" is a manifest mention of a primitive creation myth. Most modern exegetes of v. 13 agree. Newsom tells us of v. 13:

> Job's final image is drawn from the mythological tradition. Rahab is the name of a Chaos monster, similar to Leviathan. Like the Mesopotamian chaos

monster, Tiamat, Rahab is depicted as having allies. . . . The violent defeat of Rahab is connected with the creation of the world and a just order. That is not, however, the way that Job's following words contextualize the allusion.[701]

9:14–24

Barton says of v. 14, "In striking contrast to the superhuman monsters of v. 13, man is puny; if they were hapless, how much more was he?"[702] Rashi agrees with this interpretation. He says it means, "Surely a weak person like me—how will I answer Him, how will I choose my words to speak with Him?"[703] Mezudat David says of v. 14:

> Although Job states many times that he wants to contend with God, he also changed his mind many times out of his agony and heartache.[704]

Ewald renders v. 15 this way: "I, who if I were right, should not answer, not to my opponent, I should not supplicate."[705] Buttenwieser prefers, "Even if my cause be just, I could not answer. I should have to implore at the mercy of my opponent."[706] Rashi says Job is saying, "I will not reply. I will fear to raise my voice before Him."[707] Barton, on the other hand, observes about these verses:

> Although I am righteous, I should not be answered. I should make many supplications for His Justice.[708]

Rashi gives a parallel of Deut 9:21 for v. 16. He says that Job's wound "oozes blood and pus." Mezudat David observes, "Although Job attributes his suffering to the constellations, he blames God for allowing them to determine his life."[709] Buttenwieser renders v. 16 this way: "If I called and He answered, I would not believe that He had given ear unto my voice."[710]

Ewald calls the *cuwph* of v. 17, a "storm." Buttenwieser, a "tempest."[711] Thomas says of v. 17, "The wearing away of the storm is terrifying."[712] Buttenweiser renders *ruah* as "breath" in v. 18.[713] Thomas prefers, "would not permit my spirit to rest." He adds, "for the spirit rests while the flesh is affected."[714] Rashi has it, "He would not let me bring back my breath."[715] Mezudat David says of v. 18:

> I cannot catch my breath because all day long my soul is bitter until I am satisfied with my bitterness.[716]

Ewald gives this for v. 19: "Is it a matter of strength or might—Behold! Or is it of justice? . . . Who will summon me?"[717] Buttenwieser prefers, "If it is a question of the mighty—behold him, and if it is a question of the right, who dares to summon Him?"[718] Barton says of v. 19, "Job is acknowledging God's omnipotence."[719] Habel believes that *hinne* of v. 19a is either defective for behold, and thus *Hen*, or should be revocalized to get *hinneh*.[720] Robert Gordis agrees.[721]

Habel points out that both verbs of v. 20 should be in the declarative, "so that they are consistent with the legal language."[722] Barton thinks the meaning of v. 20 is:

> If such a meeting could be secured, and he was perfect, he would be so awed by God's greatness that his own mouth would condemn him.[723]

Ewald suggests this for v. 20: "If I am right, my mouth would condemn me. Am I blameless? He makes me crooked."[724] Buttenwieser prefers, "Even though I am righteous, my mouth must condemn me, even if I am innocent, I cannot declare me at fault."[725] The expression "I do not know myself" has occasioned much comment. Habel says it means, "I am distraught."[726] Pope, "I care not for myself." Gordis, "I am besides myself." Ewald, "I will not know myself and despise my own life."[727] Mezudat David, "I do not know my own soul."[728]

Rashi prefers, "I do not know my rest, nor how I will find it."[729] The LXX eliminates the first hemstitch of v. 21.

Hesychius of Jerusalem believes the understanding of v. 22 is:

> Here Job rebuts Bildad's statement that the suffering of the righteous is for the benefit and the suffering of the wicked for their detriment, claiming that all suffering is the same.[730]

Robert Watson says of vv. 23–24, "It is an infinitely sad restatement of what God has been made to appear to him by Bildad's speech that Job begins his reply, 'Yes, yes, it is so.' How can man be just before such a God?"[731] George Noyes believes that "to Bildad, who has charged him with virtually denying the justice of God, Job remarks that he knows full well the greatness and holiness of God, and the weakness and sinfulness of man."[732] Julian of Eclanum says that "in Job's response to Bildad, his words and expressions are of mixed opinions." He adds:

> He approves his general and fairly superficial assertions on God's power and justice, but opposes his conclusion, that is, the notion that his misfortunes derive from sin.[733]

9:25–35

Robert Lowth believes vv. 25–26 refer to the "Elysian Fields."[734] John Chrysostom tells us about the meaning of vv. 25–27 of ch. 9:

> My memories themselves are dead, and I don't even know what I am talking about, as my pain is so great. In the moment itself, in which I speak, as the storm around me is so strong.[735]

Gregory says of vv. 27–28, "Job comes to the realization of his own limits."[736] Saadiah gives 8:12 and Song of Songs 6:11 as parallels for v. 26.[737] Dhorme tells us about v. 27, "Job complains of not seeing happiness, that he has not a moment's respite." Even when he says in vv. 27–28, "If I am ungodly, why have I not died?"[738] Dhorme prefers, "If I am guilty, it is useless to exculpate myself."[739] These verses also contain two more uses of *'im*, or "if" conditionals at vv. 27 and 30.

Francis Peloubet gives Ps 51:7 as a parallel to v. 30.[740] About the personification of clothes in v. 31, Dom Calmet tells us:

> This way of speaking which endows clothes with feelings, such as those of horror and aversion from a sullied body, has something about it that is most striking.[741]

A similar image to Job's complaints at the end of ch. 9 can be seen in Victor Hugo's *La Fin de Satan*, where a leper uses similar language to that of Job.[742] There is some disagreement about how to translate *Mokiah* in v. 33. Dhorme renders it "Judge," who places in his two hands the hands of the two parties and exercises his authority over them. Others render the word "Arbiter," or "Arbitrator," as Newsom and Terrien do.[743]

Ibn Ezra says of v. 35, "I am not a person such as you think as you should hear, for my conscience does not reproach me in that way."[744] Le Hir agrees with this translation. Loisy prefers, "for I am aware of being innocent."[745] John, Bishop of Fredericton, tells us about vv. 34–35:

> Job admits the truth that man can be justified in a fight with God by his own righteousness, but he is altogether perplexed by God's dealings with him.[746]

William Kelly takes another approach to these final verses of ch. 9. He suggests:

> What Bildad urged, Job admits might be true enough; yet, he feels that not only did his first appeal fail, but the real point is no way reached, while the suggestion of hidden sin was as false as it was charitable.[747]

William Bode, in his commentary, sums up ch. 9 in a succinct way:

> Job, in his reply to Bildad's address, which was more direct than Eliphaz's, immediately takes up the first point which had been raised. He, without hesitating, admits it to be so, that God is a god of justice, and that He punishes sins and rewards righteousness.[748]

Solomon Freehof believes:

> The speech of Job that follows Bildad's is an answer to Bildad, but it is also, in a sense, an answer to Eliphaz. It is, in effect, a reaction to the effect which both speeches of the friends have made upon him.[749]

Jantzen gives a different assessment of ch. 9. He says:

The accusation against God in this chapter comes in terms of justice and creative purpose, in terms of the sensibilities of the law court and those of the artisan's workshop.[750]

In whatever way we interpret ch. 9, however, it is difficult not to agree with Robert Gordis when he tells us, "In this chapter, Job reaches the apex of his bitterness."[751] Job is never more acerbic than he is in ch. 9 of his book.

Completion of Job's First Response to Bildad: Chapter 10

Introduction

Job's first response to Bildad is finished in ch. 10. Ewald divides ch. 10 into three parts: 10:2–7; 10:8–17; and 10:18–22. He introduces the first of these parts this way:

> After a vehement beginning of the whole enigma, the question of how the hard treatment of Job harmonizes with the divine omniscience and exultation.[752]

Ewald continues his description of ch. 10:

> Then the melancholy reflection on how the Creator can be so enraged against his own noble work. So determined under all circumstances, whether it is guilty or innocent, to destroy it, an entirely new thought of great force here, which it dwelt upon with great force.[753]

There are also a number of exegetical problems with ch. 10. Duhm, Gray, Ball, Holscher, and Fohrer all reject v. 3, on the grounds that it does not fit the context. The LXX does not translate the first hemstitch of v. 4, and it gives a paraphrase for the rest of the line. A few critics also reject v. 5 (Bickell, Loisy, and Duhm), but say it expresses a new idea. Ehrlich emends v. 7 to get, "Since Thou knowest, I cannot save myself."[754] Beer emends v. 7b and renders it, "There is no iniquity in my hand."[755] Duhm also eliminates v. 4. The Vulgate gives a paraphrase of vv. 13–16. The LXX adds a negative to v. 18 that does not appear in the Masoretic Text.[756]

Analysis of Chapter 10

10:2–7

There is much disagreement about how to translate the opening two verses of ch. 10. The LXX gives us, "Weary in my soul, I will pour my words with groans upon him. I will speak being straightened in the bitterness of my soul."[757] The KJV suggests: "My soul is weary of my life. I will leave my complaint upon myself. I will speak in the bitterness of my soul."[758] The RSV has it, "I loathe my life. I will give free utterance to my complaints. I will speak in the bitterness of my soul."[759] And the NIV gives us, "I loathe my very life. Therefore, I will give free rein to my complaint and speak out the bitterness of my soul."[760]

The second verse has a similar array of interpretations. The LXX says, "And I will say to the Lord, do not teach me to be impious, and wherefore, hast though judged me?"[761] The KJV gives us: "I will say unto God, do not condemn me, show me why you contend with me."[762] The RSV suggests, "I will say to God, do not condemn me, let me know why you contend against me."[763] And the NIV renders the verse, "I will say to God, do not condemn me, but tell me what charges you have made against me."[764]

There is also some variety about what v. 2 means. Dhorme suggests:

> Job gives free rein to his complaints and bitterness. Since God does not come to court, and there is no umpire, this is a whole series of obligations which Job here addresses to his tormentor.[765]

Reichert says of v. 2, "My soul is weary of my life." He gives 7:11 as a parallel in the book.[766] Barton says that the attitude of v. 2 is closer to that of 7:15.[767] Rashi says the meaning of v. 3 is, "Is it not fair that you should oppress me and steal from the righteous."[768]

Reichert thinks in v. 3, "Job seeks to fathom the mysteries that could conceivably cause God's cruel treatment of him."[769] Barton also says about v. 3, "There appears here, in Job's mind, the thought that there should be fairness in God," a view that may indicate retributive justice in that God should give all people what they are due.[770]

Newsom compares the image in v. 3 with Ps 119:73 and Ps 139.[771] Dhorme, Holscher, and Fohrer prefer, "Is it profitable to Thee," while Ewald has, "Is it fitting for Thee."[772] Habel gives Mic 2:2 as a parallel for the verb of v. 3. He says vv. 1–3 is like 7:1–3 and 20. Habel observes, "For El to oppress is to bely his character as Maker." He gives Prov 14:3 as a parallel. Habel also say, "Job brings two charges against El: He spurns His creation and he favors the case of the wicked."[773]

Ball says the sense of v. 4 is: "Are You not liable to errors in judgment? Have You no more insight than my friends?"[774] Barton observes, "If God has limitations, Job should understand why His governance of the world should be so defective."[775] Rowley and Ball think that Job is asking in v. 4, "Are You liable to errors in judgment? Do You have no more understanding than my friends."[776] Rashi also thinks Job is asking about God's fairness in v. 4. Reichert gives 1 Sam 16:7 as a parallel to v. 4. He says Job is saying, "Does God afflict me because He can see no deeper than humans can?"[777]

Rashi believes in v. 5, Job asks God a question, "Are your days like the days of man to pursue and attack me?"[778] Habel says that in vv. 5–6, "Job uses the rhetorical device of disputation by imposing two impossible questions."[779] Dhorme says of v. 6:

> Job returns to the idea from chapter seven: man is so vile and wretched that there seems to be no solid reason why God should pursue him with investigations.[780]

Newsom says of vv. 4–7, "Job parodies the theme of God's complete and effortless knowledge of the individual." She gives Ps 139:2–6 as a parallel.[781] Ibn Ezra believes that v. 7 says, "If I were wicked, I could not escape Your power, for You are Creator."[782] Dhorme agrees about the sense of these verses. He observes, "Job remains helpless in the hands of his Creator."[783]

10:8–17

Jastrow says of these verses, "Job brings a new charge, and one of still bolder character."[784] Habel believes in vv. 8–9, "Job elaborates on his earlier charge against El. You spurn the labor of your hands."[785] The comparison of God to a potter can be seen at Isa 50:9 and Jer 18:4ff. Much debate also has arisen over the images of vv. 10–14. Most critics agree with Barton, who claims that v. 10 "describes the initial processes of procreation," and v. 11 is "the marvelous formation of the child in the womb."[786] But Robert Gordis has the most creative explanations of these verses. He believes they refer to a five-step development:

1. Embryo out of clay.
2. Semen poured out like milk.
3. That solidifies like cheese.
4. Which is then clothed in skin and flesh.
5. And finally, knitted together with bones and sinews.[787]

Dhorme points out that the same verb in v. 15 is also employed at 10:7 and 9:25.[788] Szold construes v. 16 as a question, "Is it a matter of pride that Thou has hunted me?"[789] Both Gordis and Tur-Sinai believe it is not Job who is being compared to a lion, it is God, but Newsom points out the Hebrew is ambiguous about this issue.[790]

Norman Habel says of vv. 15–17:

> Job acknowledges that he is guilty, his fate already is sealed, and thus he can enjoy his lot.[791]

Hesychius of Jerusalem tells us about the lion image of vv. 16–17:

> The human being is called the "lion" with good reason, because he is a royal animal and even more righteous, because by preserving the honor of God's form, he is dreadful to his enemies. That is why in Proverbs, "The righteous are as bold as a lion."[792]

The witness in v. 17 has been variously interpreted. Hartley says that "God keeps sending fresh witnesses to testify his guilt."[793] Rowley believes the witnesses are "Job's sufferings."[794] Ehrlich and Dhorme revocalize to yield, "Thy hostility," which becomes a good parallel to "Thy vexation."[795] Stevenson, Pope, and Steinmann agree.[796] Budde,

Duhm, Gray, Holscher, and Steinmann, all see, "Thou did bring fresh hosts against me," as a series of fresh troops being brought against Job.[797] Barton says the meaning of v. 17 is this:

> Thou renew a host against me. Affliction upon affliction come upon me, like the attacking of an army in waves.[798]

10:18–22

Habel says this about these verses: "Job closes this lengthy speech with a lament reminiscent of his opening cry at 3:1ff., and then gives a brief plea for respite."[799] Hartley says that Job's question in v. 19 is, "Why did you bring me from the womb, only to punish me?"[800] Rashi thinks it is more like, "Would that I had been carried from the womb to the grave."[801] Mezudat David agrees. He adds, "It would be as if I were never born."[802]

Barton observes about v. 20, "Life is very brief, and death simply means gloom in Sheol."[803] Rowley believes that "Job is appealing to God to take His attention off of him, and thus to give him respite."[804] He gives parallels of 3:5 and 7:9ff. Hartley gives 7:19 as a parallel to v. 20.[805] Reichert points out the same verb is translated as "be of good cheer" at 9:27.[806]

Dhorme has v. 20 this way: "Are my days not a trifle, but now cease and depart from me."[807] He gives 7:16 as a parallel.[808] Hartley says the import of vv. 20–22, is, "Job pleads that God grant him some relief in his few remaining days." He gives 7:19 as a parallel text.[809]

Barton points out that the Babylonian text, "Ishtar's Descent," we find:

> Light, they see not. In darkness they dwell.[810]

Barton suggests that the overall idea of v. 22 is that, "in the grave, there is only darkness, without light and brightness."[811] He mentions that Schultens, in his 1735 *Liber Jobi*, compares the Arabic root for light (SDR) in relation to the light.[812] Rashi gives Amos 4:13 as a parallel for v. 22.[813] The LXX paraphrases v. 22. The Syriac Text has, "A land whose eyelid is as the darkness of the shadows of death."[814] Rowley correctly observes that v. 22 is "overloaded with synonyms for darkness." He adds, "Job wishes to emphasize to the utmost the dreary prospects of Sheol."[815]

Driver, on the strength of the Arabic text, renders "chaos" in v. 22 as "without ray of light" amplification.[816] Dhorme says of vv. 21–22, the terse formula "Until I depart and be no more" is reminiscent of Ps 139:14. "The light is as darkness," reminds Pope of Milton's *Paradise Lost*, where he speaks of, "The light in that region where there is no light, but darkness visible."[817] This is an apt parallel. Finally, Newsom points out that vv. 21–22 are traditional ways of describing Sheol, as at Ps 88:7 and 13; and Isa 45:18–19, but that Job "intensifies them." Newsom adds:

He invokes images that suggest chaos prevailing before creation, particularly that the land of death shines like darkness.⁸¹⁸

At any rate, the book of Job has a deep vocabulary when it comes to words related to "dark" and "darkness," particularly in ch. 10 when three different Hebrew terms are employed, including the normal Hebrew word for "darkness," *hasak*. Most of the references to "dark" and "darkness" in the book of Job argue for a view like the contrast motif introduced in the introduction of this work. God is seen associated with "light," and dark and darkness often accompany the wicked, the grave, or language about death or evil.

Altogether, the poet of Job employs six separate Hebrew terms for "darkness." Three of these come from the Semitic root HSK, and three more derive from the PHL root. These words are *'ophel*, *'eyphah*, and *'araphel*, from the latter root, and *ḥošek* and *ḥašak*, from the former root. Counting *ḥasek* mentioned above, also from the ḤŠK root, we now have six words for "darkness" in the Hebrew text of the book of Job.

If we add to this list, two words to indicate "shade" or "shadow," that is, *tsalmavet* and *tsel*, in 10:21 and 22, it brings our total of words for darkness to eight in the final two verses of ch. 10.

Zophar's First Speech: Chapter 11

Introduction

The last of the three friends to speak is Zophar in ch. 11. Most exegetes divide the chapter into two parts: vv. 1–12 and vv. 13–20. The LXX calls the third friend "Zophar, the Minean."⁸¹⁹ The Vulgate spells the name as "Sophar," as does the fifteenth-century French text *La Patience de Job*, a work of seven thousand rhymed verses.⁸²⁰ Strong's *Concordance* suggests the name Zophar comes from a verb, "to depart," or possibly "to hop."⁸²¹ Others say it comes from other verbs, meaning "to chirp," or "to leap."

There is much disagreement over the "Nahman" of the Na'amathites. The *Mikra* has various theories about the location of Nahman. Lowth tells us:

> Nahmathite, or Naamah, was among the cities which fell by lot to the tribes of Judah. In the neighborhood of Idumea. Naamah is enumerated at Josh. 15:21 and 41.⁸²²

Ibn Ezra says that Naamah is a clan. Rabbi Gra says that Zophar and Naamah were brothers, descendants from Nahor, Abraham's brother.⁸²³ During the time of Elisha, there was a Naaman general of Aram, perhaps a descendant. Some say the name Naaman comes from a verb, "to be pleasant."⁸²⁴ Naaman was a commander of the armies of Ben Hadad II, in the time of King Joram. He is mentioned at 2 Kgs 5, where the general is afflicted with leprosy.

Elsewhere in the Hebrew Bible, Naaman is the daughter of Lamech and Zillah and the sister of Tubal-Cain (see Gen 4:22). Abba ben Kahana, fourth-century Iraqi Jew, says that Naaman was Noah's wife and was called pleasant because she was pleasing to God.[825] Most rabbis of the Talmud reject this view and suggest that Naaman was "a foreign woman who sang pleasant songs."[826] Some say Zophar is related to Zipor, the father of Balak (Num 22:2).

Maimonides, for example, gives us, "Tzepho, son of Eliphaz, son of Esau" (Gen 36:15).[827] Maimonides adds, "Tzepho and Zipor may be one and the same as Balak, not a Moabite, because they feared Israel."[828] Naaman is the name of a town in modern Israel. It is identified with the town of Na'nah, a small village six miles south of Lydda.[829] One final view says that Naaman was an Ammonite woman, one of the wives of Solomon. (See 1 Kgs 14:21 and 31; and 2 Chr 12:13, where Naamah is the daughter of Hanun, the son of Nohash, the king of Ammon.)[830]

Whatever the provenance of Naaman, commentators disagree about the place of Job's third friend. Gordis says since he spoke last, he must be the youngest.[831] Hartley strongly disagrees. He writes:

> While many have considered him to be the youngest of Job's companions, little evidence supports this view. All the friends appear to be contemporaries. Nevertheless, Zophar bears the least status, for he only delivers two speeches.[832]

Franz Delitzsch says that Zophar is "the most impetuous of the friends."[833] Maimonides and Rashi agree that the role of Zophar's first speech is that "Job must be brought to the realization that suffering is a wage of sin," a version of retributive justice theory.[834] Victor Reichert says, "Zophar uses language of outspoken cruelty."[835] Gersonides sums up Zophar's first discourse this way:

> Zophar speaks as though it seems that God has concealed full knowledge by Job not endowing him with real powers of conception; yet if he does not understand his real ability, and does not know what is possible for him in making good, then he must surely be a great sinner.[836]

So Gersonides believes that Zophar is an advocate of retribution theory, as well. Roland Murphy says of ch. 11, "The debate is gradually heating up. . . . Job obviously finds Job garrulous."[837] Hartley says Zophar's first speech is "for the most poignant, offering Job little comfort, except for the elaborate pictures of the repentant sinner's peaceful security," a version of the Job penitent motif.[838]

Gutierrez tells us regarding Zophar's words in ch. 11, "In Zophar's mouth these words are a threat, but for Job, they become his hope."[839] Arthur Quiller-Couch calls Zophar "a mean-spirited grey beard."[840] Robert Hillis Goldsmith says of Zophar's speech in ch. 11:

> This miserable comforter disposes of the mystery of human suffering quite easily. For him there is no mystery, suffering is a product of sin.[841]

This, of course, is another reference to retributive justice theory as to the cause of Job's suffering. Goldsmith, as well as many other modern interpreters, believes this is the overarching theological view of the first speech of Zophar in ch. 11.

Maimonides identifies Zophar's philosophical orientation as consistent with the Ash'arites.[842] Manasseh ben Israel (1604–1657) agrees.[843] John Calvin, in a sermon on ch. 11, says that Zophar's words are "an accurate representation of biblical teaching on the majesty and power of God."[844] James Tissot (1836–1902) painted an image of Zophar called *Zophar Condemns Job*, based on 11:3. Job lies on a blanket, his head buried in his clothes. Besides his body, to his left, is an empty bowl. The left arm of Zophar enters from the right. The arms are raised in a gesture of gesticulation.[845]

In Luigi Dallpiccola's 1950 opera, *Giobbe*, Zophar sings the part of a tenor.[846] In Archibald MacLeish's verse play *J.B.*, Zophar plays the part of a conservative, born-again preacher who insists that what separates human beings from the other animals is guilt. Zophar says in *J.B.*:

> Happy is the man whom God correcteth
>
> He tastes his guilt. His hope begins.[847]

Analysis of Chapter 11

11:1–12

After the introduction of the first verse, there is much difference of opinion about how to render the second. Saadiah says, "Shall the man of lips be right?"[848] The Vulgate has it, "Shall one who abounds in words be right?" Marvin Pope prefers: "Shall the glib one be acquitted?"[849] Gersonides, however, thinks v. 2 refers to "Job's falsehoods."[850] Hartley points out that the form of this verse could be declarative, but the context suggests it is a caustic rhetorical question. He asks, "Will his chatter silence other men?"[851]

About vv. 4–6, Newsom remarks:

> Zophar ostensibly quotes Job's words. They are not literally Job's words, however, but a representation of what Zophar has heard Job say, filtering through his own of what is at stake.[852]

Thomas Aquinas says of these verses, "Zophar shows that in divine wisdom, there is something secret which is incomprehensible to man."[853] This, of course, is an assent to the divine plan explanation of Job's suffering. The Hebrew text renders v. 4b, "I am pure in your eyes."[854] About v. 5, Dhorme tells us:

> Job has addressed himself directly to God. He has complained in 9:15–16 that God does not answer him. Now Zophar prays that such an answer might come from above.[855]

Both Jastrow and E. C. S. Gibson agree. Gibson writes, "If only God could take Job at his word and appear and answer him." Jastrow says, "But oh, if God might speak, and open His lips against thee."[856] Kissane takes a different approach to vv. 5–6. He says:

> Zophar is willing to conclude that Job is perfect and upright, in the sense that he is not conscious of any sin. But God's knowledge is infinitely superior to man's, and if God spoke, He would reveal many faults which Job has committed. These are the secrets of God's wisdom.[857]

This appears to be a reference to the omniscience of God in Kissane's comment. Hartley agrees that in v. 5 Zophar asks God to answer Job, but Hartley adds this about these two verses:

> Zophar is so upset with Job he wishes that God might speak to him. Whereas, Job when God speaks, He will make known to Job these secrets of wisdom. This refers to what God knows and humans do not.[858]

Buttenwieser says, "The secrets of wisdom are the things hidden from wisdom." He adds, "The translators fail to realize that *hokmah* is an objective genitive."[859] Some translators render *kiplayim*, which means "double," while others translate it as "manifold." Thus, Dhorme says, "This verse emphasizes the difficulty of understanding ambiguous (two-sided) mysteries, a position consistent with Zophar's view."[860] Pope translates the term as "two-sided." He adds, "This implies a hidden and a manifest side, both known to God."[861] Gordis sees the Hebrew in question as a defective reading of *kipla'im*, or "wonders."[862] Holscher deletes v. 6 because of metrical consistency.[863]

Newsom introduces vv. 7–12 this way:

> Zophar reiterates his argument in these verses, using a traditional figure of speech. The metaphorical image underlying Job's beliefs is a spatial one, the smallness of the human being in a vast world, which itself is only a gesture toward the infinite vastness of divine wisdom.[864]

In Newsom's view, this is yet another nod in the direction of divine plan theory, this time held by Zophar. Dhorme has v. 7 precede v. 4, and cuts vv. 6c, 7–9, and 12. He gives Ps 139:22 as a parallel for v. 7. He says of v. 8, "It is incomprehensible for human thought. It lives beyond all known dimensions."[865] E. C. S. Gibson renders v. 8 this way:

> Heights of Heaven. What canst thou do? Deeper than Sheol. What canst thou know?[866]

All of these views are consistent with divine plan theory because they assert that humans are not capable of ascertaining all that God knows, particularly about Wisdom. Thus, God knows, and humans do not. Pope gives Isa 7:11 as a parallel for v. 8.[867] Franz Delitzsch points out about v. 8, "This refers to the feminine form of expression related to divine wisdom, and amplifies what it says of its transcendent reality."[868] Pope's comment may refer to the female personification of Wisdom that can be found in Proverbs, at places like 3:13–18; 4:5–9; and 9:1–6. About vv. 10–12, Ewald observes, "Zophar seeks here at the same time to turn what Job has said in 9:11 and to mean the exact opposite of its proper meaning."[869] Gersonides thinks that v. 11 "refers to two kinds of ignorance." He adds:

> One ignorance is acquisition, namely a positive one, about where one has erred philosophically; and the other ignorance is due to a lack of knowledge, which is negative, and that is when one does not endeavor to understand existing things.[870]

This is consistent with earlier medieval Jewish philosophers that claim that Job suffers from a lack of intellectual virtues, in Aristotle's terms, such as humility and wisdom, for examples.

E. C. S. Gibson says of v. 12, "This verse is the despair of commentators."[871] Dhorme and others say this verse has the ring of a proverb.[872] Hartley also calls it a proverb "full of alliteration and assonance."[873] Gersonides says that v. 12 means, "Man is like cattle (mentally), when he is first born."[874] Rashi points out that the word for "hollow" also means "empty."[875] Most modern exegetes agree with Newsom, when she writes of v. 12:

> Zophar, in exasperation, applies a proverb about the unlikeliness of an empty-headed person getting understanding.[876]

11:13–20

Newsom introduces these verses this way:

> Having rebuked Job as a donkey brain for not seeing what is evident to himself, Zophar appeals to Job to take necessary steps to restore hope and security for him.[877]

Gibson has a similar understanding of these verses. He writes:

> If Job will only repent and put away his sins, then he need not fear to lift up his face as an innocent man. Even the recollection of his sorrows will pass out of his mind. Once more his life shall be bright, and he will once again be able to sleep securely.[878]

Here, Gibson says, Job displays a version of the Job penitent motif. Franz Delitzsch takes a different view of these verses. He observes:

> While Eliphaz and Bildad, with cautious gentleness, describe suffering more as chastisement than as punishment, Zophar proceeds more boldly, and

demands of Job that he humble himself, as one who incurred punishment from God.[879]

Hartley says what Zophar is doing in these verses is this: "In order to motivate Job to repent, Zophar next paints an ideal sketch of the blessings that attend God's acceptance of a contrite person."[880] The Peshitta in v. 15 replaces "your face" with "your hand."[881] Mezudat David says of the import of v. 15, "Henceforth, you will be strong and not fear any terror, for it shall not come near you."[882] Rashi says of v. 16, "All memory of your misery will be gone."[883] Kissane tells us, "Job will be protected from all danger, and restored to a place of influence, for it is only the wicked who do without hope."[884]

The order of the two hemstitches of v. 17 are reversed in the LXX. Dhorme says of v. 17, "It is conceived on the same pattern as Isa 63:10b."[885] Gersonides says v. 17 implies, "You shall be bright and clear in your new life."[886] Thomas Aquinas sums up vv. 18–20 this way:

> Zophar promised to Job that if he were willing to depart from his iniquity, then "The eyes of the pious will fail, since the good things they wished for they cannot attain."[887]

Hartley says of vv. 18–19, "In his new life, Job will have inner peace. He will have a strong sense of security because he will have genuine hope."[888] The Targum understands the verb of v. 18 to be "digging, in the sense of digging a grave."[889] Reichert says the meaning of the verb is "to search." He gives Deut 1:22 as a parallel text.[890] Dhorme, following Ehrlich, discerns an Arabic root for the verb in v. 18, a root that means "to protect."[891] This word is *hafadh*. Gordis says the verb means "to build a resting place, after the custom of some animals."[892] Driver and Gray prefer "searching out a resting place." Habel says that "searching for a secure abode seems appropriate."[893]

Dhorme says v. 19 "conveys the sense of perfect security." He gives Lev 26:6 as a parallel for the verb.[894] Pope says that v. 19a occurs verbatim at Isa 17:2 and Zeph 3:13. The verb *rbs* is used properly for quadrupeds, but figuratively here for humans, as in Ps 23:2. Pope says that v. 19b literally says, "Many would make sweet your face." The idiom is applied to God at Exod 32:11; Jer 26:19; and Mal 1:9, and to humans at Prov 19:6 and Ps 14:13.[895]

Most exegetes agree with Hartley when he observes about v. 20:

> At the end of this call of repentance, Zophar presents a terse but vivid description of the fate of the wicked.[896]

Gersonides says of the end of Zophar's first discourse, at vv. 20–22, is about "grief and vexation."[897] Gibson says the meaning of the final verse of ch. 11 is, "Be still, and let us remember the fate in store for the wicked."[898] Most interpreters agree that the closing of ch. 11 is much like the closing of ch. 10, where Job reminds us of the pain and suffering of Sheol that is to come for all of us, for the wicked and the righteous alike.

PART II: THE BOOK OF JOB COMMENTARY

Chapter 12: Job's First Response to Zophar (12:1–25)

Introduction

In describing Job's first response to Zophar in ch. 12, Samuel Terrien says this:

> This discourse concludes the first cycle of discussion. Its traditional division into three chapters fits quite accurately its organic plan: (a.) an empirical critique of Providence [12:1–25]; (b.) an indictment of the friends ministrations leading to a new attack upon God [13:1–27]; (c.) a prayerful meditation on the tragedy of life [13:28—14:22].[899]

Other interpreters question the chapter divisions in this lengthy discourse, pointing out that a natural break comes at 13:20. Job first answers his friends (12:1—13:19), and then addresses God directly (13:20—14:22). Nevertheless, the first of these three chapters is usually divided into three main parts (12:1–6; 12:7–12; and 12:13–25).

Rowley describes these three sections this way:

> Stung by Zophar's cruel words, Job now lashes out at his friends. So far, he has been engrossed with the thought of his own misery, and the treatment that God has meted out to him. Now he charges them with trying to curry favor with God whose power and wisdom he recognizes no less than they.[900]

Perdue gives us the following description of chs. 12–14:

> If he cannot prevail upon God to deliver him from death, his only recourse is to revolt. Yet while he hopes to indict and remove the Creator from the throne, what gives Job pause in his thought is his own moral weakness and insignificance.[901]

Analysis of Chapter 12

12:1–6

Hesychius of Jerusalem says that in vv. 1–2, Job is asking, "Is the honor of rational beings really intact with you. Do you know the decisions that God forms with regard to sinners and righteous people?"[902] Newsom says the traditional interpretation is that "Job sarcastically magnifies the opinions of the three friends, as representing the general opinion of mankind."[903]

The word *attem*, "you," is in the second person plural in v. 2, but it is in the second person singular at v. 7. Some, like Duhm for example, have suggested that vv. 4–6 are a redactor's insertion.[904] Duhm also points to the use of "Yahweh" in v. 9. He says that some manuscripts have *Eloah*, which he believes was the original.[905] At any rate, the line is identical to Isa 41:2c.

Dahood says the *'am*, or people in v. 2. comes from the root *'mm* that means "be strong."[906] The article is not expressed with "people," but in Hebrew, nouns in ancient poetry are frequently definite without an article. Thus, there is no need to add it here, as Duhm and Weiser, among others, do.[907] Still less likely is to add gross changes such as "You are knowing ones" (Steinmann and Horst) or "thinking ones" (Klostermann, Peake, Ball, Holscher, and Stevenson).[908] Or "the cunning ones" (Beer) or "the people of the heart" (Kissane, Dhorme, and Tur-Sinai).[909] Fohrer retains a root that means, "You are everybody," that is, "The ones that count."[910]

Rowley thinks that v. 3 is referring to what Zophar has to say at 11:12.[911] Philip the Priest says the meaning of the verse is, "Do you consider yourselves the only ones who are wise. Do you think that after you, there will be no more wise people?"[912] J. K. Burr reminds us that the *levav* or *lev*, "heart," is the seat of the intellect, and the bowels the seat of emotions.[913] Hartley observes about v. 3, "Job responds to the superior attitude of the friends by defending his own wisdom and dignity."[914]

Siegfried and Duhm omit vv. 4–6. They say, "The idea expressed here interrupts the thread from v. 3 to v. 7."[915] The LXX omits v. 4a and b. The special misery of being mocked by one's friends has a parallel at Ps 55:12–15. J. K. Burr has it, "A mockery to his friends am I."[916] Joseph Caryl says of vv. 4–5, "The words of this text are dark."[917] Barton says of v. 5, "In Job's time, and now, the world is ready to kick a man when he is down."[918]

The fifth verse is a difficult one to interpret. The final word, *lappid*, can mean "lamp" or "torch." Ehrlich renders it, "a torch of contempt."[919] The word translated as "thought" in v. 5 is a *hapax*. The verb from which it comes is employed at Jonah 1:6. Another noun from the same verb is used at Ps 146:4. Rashi renders v. 5, "a brand of contempt." He seems to think it means the hell fires of *Gehenna*.[920] The LXX, with the exception of "those who anger the Lord," has nothing to do with the original Hebrew. The NIV divides the first word into the preposition ("for" or "to") and the word *pid* that means "misfortune."

Rowley says of v. 6:

> Job bitterly comments that while the fortunate are kicking the unfortunate who are down, they regard them as wicked, and those who are wicked live at ease.[921]

Fohrer deletes v. 6. Stevenson thinks v. 6 is an interpolation, as do Bickell, Siegfried, Beer, Duhm, Ball, and Steinmann.[922] Julian of Eclanum believes v. 6 is "a charge against God's justice."[923] Ralbag, another name for Gersonides, observes about v. 6:

> This idolator brings the idol in his hand, manufactures it for himself, and then prostrates himself before it, considering that his existence depends on Him.[924]

Ewald says, "In these verses, we are in the density of severe suffering and pain."⁹²⁵ Franz Delitzsch believes, "This strophe is the counterpart to 8:8–10."⁹²⁶ Hartley says of these verses:

> To counter the teachings of the friends, Job claims that marauding bands, those who inflict sudden terror on unsuspecting settlements, are safe and secure in their tents, even though their actions have provoked God. They anger God without suffering any ill consequences.⁹²⁷

Hartley adds this to his analysis of vv. 7–12:

> The strong, assertion conjunction "But!" [*'ulam*] indicates that Job is taking up a new subject. Here he exalts God as Creator of all and affirms that wisdom may be found by listening to the creatures God has created.⁹²⁸

John Chrysostom thinks that in vv. 7–9, the "passion of Christ is foreshadowed."⁹²⁹ This is an obvious reference to the *Jobus Christi* motif.

In v. 8, "the plants of the Earth" is rendered by the KJV, "speaks to the Earth," and implies here that the earth is the netherworld. Some editors use a word meaning "reptile" or "wild beast" in this verse, where it seems to mean the "fish of the sea." Tur-Sinai renders v. 8 as "speaks to the vermin [*torecha*]" and adduces Arabic evidence for that translation.⁹³⁰

About vv. 9–10, Samuel Terrien asks:

> What is the crucial knowledge that every creature understands? In keeping with his rhetorical strategy, Job states it in the form of a well-known saying, "The hand of the Lord has done this."⁹³¹

The use of the word *Yahweh* in v. 9 is surprising. Some manuscripts have *Eloah*, which is most likely the original, or it may be a copyist error. Dhorme believes it is reminiscent of Isa 41:20b, where *Eloah* also appears to be replaced by *Yahweh*.⁹³²

Rowley believes the meaning of v. 10 is, "The issues of life and death are in the hands of God for every creature."⁹³³ Dahood renders the verse, "And the spirit of all flesh is the gift of God."⁹³⁴ Mezudat David says v. 10 refers to: "The Lord in Whose hands is the soul of all living things."⁹³⁵ Barton has it: "Of whose hands is the soul of all living things?" Hartley observes: "Not only does God have control over all creatures, he also has control over every person's life."⁹³⁶ Perhaps this is another reference to the "Book of Deeds" tradition.

Franz Delitzsch says the meaning of v. 11 is this: "The ancients are not to be accepted without being proved."⁹³⁷ Rowley says of the verse, "Job asserts his right to exercise his own critical judgment and to question the judgment of the ancients to which appeal has been made."⁹³⁸ The NEB make vv. 11–12 a parenthesis, with some justification. Hartley says vv. 11–12 resumes the thought of vv. 7–8. He adds:

Job is asking a rhetorical question, implying that God has endowed human beings with the necessary instruments to acquire and test knowledge.[939]

Some scholars delete v. 12, because it is not of the opinion of Job. Thus, Barton renders v. 12 as a question.[940] Rowley says it is better to transfer the *lo* at the end of v. 11 to the beginning of v. 12, and to then read the *lo* as a "not." This would make Job clearly denying the arguments of the friends.[941] Strahan, Holscher, Weiser, and Tur-Sinai, all agree that v. 12 should be an interrogative.[942] John Chrysostom thinks the meaning of v. 12 is this: "Time is needed to understand things."[943]

12:13–25

Samuel Terrien introduces these verses this way:

> Job's rhetorical strategy begins to change in these verses. Whereas before he used platitudes that characterized the friends' speech, now he uses a more traditional hymnic style, but gives the content a decidedly negative cast.[944]

Franz Delitzsch says the meaning of these verses is much simpler: "God is Almighty, and everything in opposition to him is powerless."[945] Newsom takes more of a middle ground on the meaning of vv. 13–25. She writes:

> The sole author of all events (vv. 13–21); not only the fate of the individual, but also the rise and fall of nations depend upon His mighty fiat. (vv. 23–25.)[946]

Barton says of v. 13, "Wisdom in all its varieties belongs to God."[947] Rowley observes about v. 13, "Job here sharply contradicts the idea that wisdom is with the aged. It is with God alone. With him is wisdom (where God is understood)."[948]

Hartley observes that "all aspects of wisdom are connected by four terms: *Hokmah, Gebura, 'eṣa,* and *tebuna,* which all reside in God." He gives Isa 11:2 as a parallel.[949] Philip the Priest believes that vv. 14–15 are "an allusion to Christ's power." This, of course, is an allusion to the *Jobus Christi* motif.[950] Mezudat David, "If a man is shut up in prison, he cannot be released without God's will."[951] The images of v. 15 have attracted many opinions. The LXX has it, "If He should withhold water, He will dry the Earth, and if He should let it loose, He overlooks and destroys it."[952] The KJV takes a similar view, "Behold He withholdeth the waters and they dry up; also, He sendeth them out, and they overturn the Earth."[953] The same word for "withhold" (*'atsar*) appears at 4:2 and 29:9. The word for "overturn" (*haphakh*) is the same term as "overturning mountains" of 9:5. Mezudat David explains v. 15 this way:

> Sometimes He increases the water and sends it to inundate the surface of the Earth, overturning the Earth, and causing much destruction.[954]

Gregory believes the meaning of vv. 16–17 is about "strength and wisdom from God."[955] Rashi says the "one who misleads is *ha Satan*." Thus, Gregory assents here to the influences of demonic forces theory. Pope renders the word for "wisdom" in v. 16 as "victory." He says, "This is efficient wisdom, the kind that leads to successes in one's enterprises."[956] Duhm renders v. 17 this way: "He makes foolish the counselors of the earth."[957] Rashi simply says, "He makes fools." Barton says of v. 17:

> The thought of this verse is that God outwits the wisdom of the crafty counselors and makes the wisdom of the most astute judges to appear foolish.[958]

Hartley agrees about v. 17. He observes, "God is able to outwit human wisdom found in counselors and judges."[959] J. K. Burr believes the "bonds" of v. 18 are "the bonds with which kings bound their subjects."[960] Ephrem the Syrian thinks that vv. 18–19 are "references to Job and Melchizedek."[961] Franz Delitzsch agrees. He observes, "Perhaps Melchizedek of Salem or Jethro of Midian is meant here."[962] Rashi gives Ps 105:22 as a parallel for v. 18.[963]

The noun of v. 19, *kohanim*, Barton renders as "priests." The KJV translates it as "princes." The Vulgate has "priests," the RSV, "priests." Hartley says the meaning of v. 19 is, "Priests are subject to God's authority. They are not exempt from facing woes."[964]

Julian Eclanum thinks that vv. 20–21 "show the absolute power of God over mortals."[965] Barton gives Ps 107:40 as a parallel to these verses.[966] Stevenson says these verses read like a psalm, and may be borrowed from the Psalms. Konig agrees.[967] Hartley says of v. 21:

> Next God pours contempt on mortals, evidence by the people hurling abuse on them. God loosens the girdles of the strong, rendering them infirm.[968]

J. K. Burr says of v. 22, "Though the shadows of death be spread over the deeds of men, God shall bring them to light."[969] Budde deletes v. 22, arguing it is out of context. Dhorme, Steinmann, Fohrer, and Pope, all excise v. 22 as well.[970] Kissane says that v. 22 should follow 11:9.[971] Olympiodorus thinks v. 22 "is a prophecy of Christ's advent," and thus a version of the *Jobus Christi* motif, and Franz Delitzsch says the meaning of the verse is this: "There is nothing so finely spun that God cannot make it visible."[972] Barton takes a similar view of v. 22. He says, "There is no secret so deeply hidden that God cannot penetrate it—no darkness so deep that God cannot see through it."[973] Perhaps this is another reference to the omniscience of God.

About vv. 23–25, Perdue observes:

> Job denies that God has any plan for the nations or any goal toward which He guides History. By contrast, the very gift of wisdom by which rulers successfully direct nations to experience life and well-being is withheld. And without the light of understanding, leaders wander lost in the cosmos.[974]

Franz Delitzsch thinks these verses take up the tone of Eliphaz's speech from ch. 13.[975] Julian the Apostate believes these verses "denote the making and destroying of nations."⁹⁷⁶ The LXX omits one word from v. 24. Ibn Ezra and Moses Maimonides render v. 24 this way:

> He misleads them with false council, and they fail to recognize what is the true way.⁹⁷⁷

The Vulgate renders v. 24 this way:

> He transforms the heart of the leaders of the people on Earth, and misleads those who in vain advance upon the inviolable.⁹⁷⁸

Barton calls the noun in v. 24, "The chiefs of the land."⁹⁷⁹ The KJV calls them, "The chiefs of the people," as does the RSV.⁹⁸⁰ The LXX has it, "The princes of the Earth."⁹⁸¹ Stevenson gives Isa 19:14 and Ps 97:27 as parallels for v. 24.⁹⁸² Mezudat David believes the meaning of the final verse of ch. 12 is this:

> They grope with their hands in the dark places where they have gone and they do not go into a lighted place.⁹⁸³

The LXX has for v. 25, "Let them grope in darkness, and let there be no light, and let them wander like a drunken man."⁹⁸⁴ The KJV employs the verb "staggers," as does the Vulgate.⁹⁸⁵ Gensenius says of v. 25, "The blindness is most intense when the sense of feeling takes the place of sight."⁹⁸⁶

Chapter 13: Job's First Response to Zophar Continued (13:1–28)

Introduction

In ch. 13, Job continues his first response to Zophar. Matthew Henry and others suggest the chapter consists of three main sections. Henry calls them, "Job Reproved His Friends" (vv. 1–12); "He Professes His Confidence in God" (vv. 13–22); and "Job Entreats to Know His Sins" (vv. 23–28.)⁹⁸⁷

Early Christian exegetes describe the content of ch. 13 in similar terms. Didymus, the Blind says of the chapter, "Job's words are sources for moral instruction."⁹⁸⁸ This is an example of the moral qualities view. Gregory agrees. He says, "His teachings here contains references to the near and distant future."⁹⁸⁹ John Chrysostom says of ch. 13, "Silence is better than senseless words."⁹⁹⁰ Olympiodorus takes a more negative view of the chapter. He observes, "God hears false speech here."⁹⁹¹ Hesychius of Jerusalem takes a more positive note on ch. 13. He suggests, "With deep humility, Job seeks to argue his case with God."⁹⁹²

More modern interpreters, in introducing ch. 13, take a view that more describes the relationship of the chapter to what comes before and after it. David Clines, for example, says this about ch. 13:

This chapter both forms an inclusio with 12:2–3, and introduces a new direction to which the speech will move. In referring back to "all" that has just been said, and especially repeating the clause, "I am not inferior to you," (12:3b), Job indicates that the subject of chapter 12 is now at a close; he now has completed his demonstration that his knowledge of God's ways is superior to that of the friends.[993]

Analysis of Chapter 13

13:1–12

Habel says in the opening two verses of ch. 13, "Job's claim to knowledge and wisdom are based on what he has seen and heard personally, not on the wisdom of tradition."[994] Van Heck reminds us that "seeing and hearing can often be linked in order to understand something."[995] David Clines gives us parallel passages that combine hearing and seeing that include: Isa 52:14; Ezek 40:5; and Eccl 1:8. He also points out that seeing and hearing are in reversed order at 29:11.[996] Seeing and hearing are also combined at 42:5.

Mezudat David believes that in v. 2, Job is asking, "Why do you still tell me of God's wonders?" He adds, "Job regards the air of superiority which his friends have assumed is entirely out of place."[997] Clines says the meaning of v. 3 is this:

> What really matters to Job is not the truth in general about the divine character, but the particular confrontation with God, in which he, Job, is involved. Job's uncovering of the divine cruelty has not been an end in itself, as if it were an exposé or an investigative, theological journalist. It was undertaken primarily to demonstrate that his plight cannot be ameliorated by recourse to hackneyed formulae of retribution, that the wisdom of the ages has nothing to offer a righteous man who has been made a laughing stock by God.[998]

Rowley says the verb in v. 3 means "argue," "convince," or "reprove." He also points out that the same verb is employed as a reflexive at Isa 1:18. Rowley adds, "Job is trying here to appeal to God's reason."[999] Moses Maimonides finds that unlikely. He says with v. 3 Job observes, "With such explanations you pretend to heal my wounds so easily."[1000] Habel says of v. 3, "Job is declaring his intentions to proceed with litigation, in spite of the scorn of the friends."[1001]

> Job, a generally good man, is overwhelmed by the evil urge and knows himself to be guilty before God.[1002]

Habel observes about these same verses, "Job closes his speech on wisdom and knowledge with a brief invective similar to his opening at 12:2–3."[1003] Clines points out that the imagery of these verses is not clear, but provides Ps 119:69 as a parallel.[1004] Rowley suggests that "plasterer of lies" has a similar idiom in Akkadian.[1005]

The LXX, under the influence of the next line, took it to refer to "false surgical plasters." Kissane follows the LXX.[1006] Rowley gives Zech 11:17 as a parallel of "healers of worthlessness."[1007] Ewald and Dillmann render "patchers," instead of "healers," by using an Arabic root.[1008] Rashi says the vv. 4–5:

> You are physicians of no value, no substance. Your attention to console me by telling me to repent are of no substance because I have no sins with which I should repent.[1009]

The noun in v. 6, *ribot*, is a term for "pleading," in ancient Israel. The RSV is preferred to the LXX which gives, "The reasoning or reprove of my mouth." Many scholars adopt this view.[1010] Blommerde thinks *ribot* should be in the singular.[1011] Habel gives Deut 17:8 as another parallel.[1012] Hartley tells us about vv. 7–11:

> With a series of questions typical of a disputation, Job sets out to show his friends that they are violating justice by showing favoritism.[1013]

Immanuel Kant quotes vv. 7–11, in showing that "human reason cannot understand divine action."[1014] Rashi says the meaning of these verses is, "Since you come to contend in the place of God, it is not good that you should speak so unjustly."[1015] Habel believes the "lift of the face" in v. 8, as in 32:11, means, "to benefit from a bribe," as in Deut 20:17.[1016] Nahum Glatzer says of v. 8:

> In order to justify God, will you speak unjustly and attach great iniquity toward me?[1017]

Rowley says of v. 9:

> Job continues his sarcasm. God is too great to be deceived by the fawning sycophancy and he will penetrate their shallow souls and then see their insincerity.[1018]

Rashi takes a different view of v. 9. He suggests that Job is asking his friends, "Will it be good when He searches you out and found to be liars?"[1019] Clines says that in asking the question, he means, "What is the friends' motivation for volunteering to defend God?"[1020]

The verb at v. 10 is the same one at v. 3. At v. 10, it indicates "reprove," or "convict." Gordis says the verb should be construed as an interrogatory, with the *he* being supplied from the previous verse, as in 12:12.[1021] Gordis says the meaning of the verse is: "Will you show partiality to one side?"[1022] Tur-Sinai renders the noun *seter* as "mask," or "veil." Habel thinks it means "hiding place,"[1023] while Arthur Peake observes about v. 10:

> It is noteworthy as showing the conflict of feelings in Job, that while he attacks with the utmost boldness, the unrighteousness of God's conduct, he should

have deep-rooted confidence in his righteousness as to believe in him incapable of tolerating a lying defense even of himself.[1024]

Rashi gives Judg 20:38 as a parallel to v. 11. He believes the question of this verse is, "Will not His exultation and His awesomeness terrify you?"[1025] Rowley points out that the verb in v. 11 is derived from a root that is related to "remembering."[1026] The phrase probably means something like "memorable sayings," or "epigrams." Dhorme connects the word *gab* to *gabab*, from which he cites an Arabic term that means "answer."[1027] The verb is also adopted by Beer, Holscher, Steinmann, and Weiser.[1028] Rowley thinks it should be rendered, "Your answers are answers of clay."[1029] I. Eitan takes the same meaning.[1030]

Habel thinks *gabbim* means "backs."[1031] Gordis observes that the word comes from the Aramaic root GWB, as well as the Syriac *gawab*.[1032] Beer concurs, citing the Syriac, GWB.[1033] Guillaume follows an Arabic root with the same meaning of "defenses."[1034] Rashi says of v. 12, "Job is saying to his friends, 'You expect to be compared to Abraham who said at Gen 18:27, "I am only dust and ashes."'"[1035]

13:12–22

Hartley says about these verses:

> This pericope, which stands at the center of the speech, may be construed as part of the second major division of this chapter, but it is to be placed in the first division.[1036]

Hartley goes on to give two reasons to support this view. First, he speaks to his friends in imperatives in vv. 16–17, as in 12:1–12. And second, he speaks to God in the third person in v. 15, while in the next pericope in the second person singular.[1037] Peake says of v. 13, "Job speaks in the plain language of the desperate."[1038] Rowley observes about v. 13, "Job is determined to speak out fearlessly and to brave the consequences."[1039]

The Hebrew of vv. 15–16 has a murky construction, "be silent for me," that is, "stand away from me in silence." The LXX does not have "from me," and consequently many editors delete it. The LXX has it, "that I might desist from anger," apparently reading *hemah* for *mah*. Ball agrees and thus renders it, "and let wrath pass over me."[1040]

Rowley says of v. 14, "This verse begins with 'Why,' which spoils both the sense and the meter."[1041] He adds, "Most editors delete the verse as a dittograph."[1042] Dahood rejects this view and translates it, "till eternity."[1043] A few scholars put v. 14 as the continuation of v. 13 to yield, "what upon what," instead of just "what."[1044] This is also the view of Duhm, Klostermann, Holscher, and Gray.[1045]

Some see in v. 14 confirmation of survival of death. The NIV, for example, renders the line, "So a man dies and he will live again. All the days and service of my life, I will wait for renewal to come."[1046] Similarly, the LXX and the Vulgate put the verse in the declarative, while the RSV has it in the form of a question, "If a man dies, shall he live again?"[1047] Rowley believes "I will put my life in my hands" in v. 14 means, "I will risk my life." He gives Judg 12:3 and 1 Sam 19:5 as parallels.[1048] Ball prefers, "I take my flesh in my teeth" for v. 14a, as does the RSV. Ball believes the image is of a wild beast that takes its prey in its teeth.[1049] Others say it is a wild beast that is disturbed while eating its prey. Rashi renders the line, "My flesh up into my teeth to afflict myself and force myself into silence."[1050] Maimonides thinks the image is asking a question, "Why should I bite my lips to prevent myself from talking or crying out?"[1051]

Verse 15 is one of the most difficult in the entire book. Rowley says the verse has been variously interpreted as, "Though He slay me, yet I will trust in Him." He points out that the kethib has *lo*, meaning "not," and the kere has *lo* meaning "to Him."[1052] The RSV has it, "Behold He will slay me, and I have no hope," as does Duhm, Gray, Holscher, and Weiser.[1053]

The NIV renders v. 15 this way: "You will call and I will answer you. You will come for the creatures you have made."[1054] Horst and Fohrer prefer, "Thou He slays me, yet I will wait for Him."[1055] Ehrlich emends the end of the line and adds, "I will not tremble," as do Dhorme and Pope.[1056] Rashi renders the line, "Behold, He will kill me, and I will hope for Him." He adds this comment:

> Though He slay me . . . I shall not separate myself from Him and shall always trust in Him. Therefore, there is no rebellion and transgressions in my words.[1057]

Archibald MacLeish says of v. 15, "Job will not be brow-beaten."[1058] Nahum Glatzer says it means, "Before I die, I will not put away my integrity from me." He adds, "This verse affirms, I think correctly, that it is not necessary for a man to sin."[1059] Whatever the proper interpretation of v. 15, Rowley concludes about the verse:

> The general sense is clear despite the uncertainty of the details. Job is willing to speak at the risk of his own life.[1060]

Shakespeare quotes v. 15 in sonnet #139. Alexandre Dumas employs it in *The Count of Monte Cristo*, and contemporary American poet Jaime Beirler has a poem entitled "Though He Slay Me, Yet I Will Hope in Him."[1061] Verse 15 also has been the subject matter of a variety of other pieces of art, in both Jewish and Christian traditions.

Joseph Kara says of v. 16, "In all his agony, Job does not abandon his faith that God will be his salvation."[1062] Barton agrees when he writes, "Job's faith remains unswerving."[1063] Rowley says the thought of v. 16 seems to be: "that Job voluntarily, face to face with God, argues his righteousness."[1064] Rashi has a different view of v. 16. He writes:

> He is also just as I am whole-hearted with Him, so He is also my salvation, but you will not find salvation in His eyes.[1065]

Newsom reminds us that in v. 17, the expression, *arakti mishpat* is a technical legal expression and gives a forensic nuance to the following claim, "I shall be found innocent."[1066] Mezudat David, on the other hand, thinks v. 17 is a declarative, "Harken to my words to understand my statements, and let them penetrate in your ears."[1067] David Clines is probably correct when he says of v. 17:

> This verse is omitted by Dillmann, Bickell, and Fohrer, as a prosaic gloss, duplicating in part 21:2, and erroneously continuing the address to the friends. But it can better be seen as introducing a strophe parallel to vv. 13–16, expanding Job's request to the friends from "be silent" to "listen," and invoking their attention as witness to his arguments with God which will begin in v. 20.[1068]

Barton says the meaning of v. 18 is, "I know that I shall be justified."[1069] Rowley points out that the verb used in v. 18 is often used in "marshaling an army."[1070] Here Job is marshaling his arguments, and he is confident he shall win his case. Rowley gives 23:4 and 1 Kgs 3:11 as parallel texts.[1071] Rashi thinks the meaning of v. 18 is, "I have arranged my arguments in my heart."[1072] Mezudat David says of v. 18, "I will be accounted innocent with my arguments."[1073] Maimonides says of the verse:

> I know that God is a Righteous Judge, and if I have not done any foolish things, He will not say that I have sinned.[1074]

Rashi thinks the meaning of v. 19 is, "If I will not contend, I will be silent and perish."[1075] Rowley says, "contend with me" means:

> Plead against me! Job feels that his case is so strong that no one would dream of challenging it. But if one should appear, he would give up his case at once and resign himself to death. He is confident that the God he has known will not dispute his case; but if he should, Job is ready to die, but with an unshakable certainty of the righteousness of his case.[1076]

Rabbenu Meyouchas says of v. 19 that Job is asking, "Who is my opponent with whom I will contend? I do not find my litigant. Soon I will be silent and die for my troubles."[1077] Hartley believes in v. 19 that Job is certain of the outcome of his case.[1078] Mezudat David puts v. 19 in the interrogatory:

> Who is it that dares to confront me in judgment to silence me without just arguments. For now if I remain silent because of invalid arguments presented by my friends, I will perish from the pain of refraining from a reply.[1079]

About v. 20, Peake writes:

> Again and again, Job has challenged God to appear and defend His actions. He has implored him to meet two conditions, to suspend the persecution from which he is suffering, and not to overwhelm him with the dread of His presence.[1080]

Most exegetes point out that Job ceases addressing his friends and turns to God, in the beginning of v. 20. Barton points out that the two things Job requests in v. 20 are the same two he asked for back at 9:34.[1081] Rowley says of v. 20:

> Grant, that is, spare me. This is in formal disagreement with what follows, since one request is positive and one is negative. But the meaning is not in doubt, for the substance of Job's requests. [See 9:34.] God gave to Job peace in his sufferings before he gave him relief from them.[1082]

In v. 21, Horst and Fohrer follow the kere and the Vulgate and get, "Yet, I will wait for Him."[1083] Blommerde follows Dahood that *lo* "not" should be *le*, or "be strong." The verse is thus rendered, "If the Victor slay me, I will still hope."[1084] Gordis says the verb *yhl* denotes the nuance "be silent," as it does at 32:11 and 16.[1085] Rashi has v. 21, "The strength of Your hand of the plague with You has smitten me," as at Exod 9:3.[1086] Rashi believes Job is referring to his sickness here. Mezudat David takes a similar view. He suggests Job is saying in v. 21:

> Distance the plague of Your hand, lest it trouble me, and do not terrify me, lest my arguments be confused. These are the two things Job beseeches God not to do to him.[1087]

Barton observes about v. 22, "Job thinks he can answer any plea that God could make against him."[1088] Hartley says of v. 22, "If God grants these two conditions, the setting for his legal processes will be in place."[1089] Rowley takes another approach in regard to v. 22. He tells us:

> The boldness of Job is without limits. He is equally willing to appear as plaintiff or as defendant. He can defend his case against God, but he also has a strong case against the background of his past experiences of God.[1090]

13:23–28

In v. 23, Hartley says, "Job turns to question God, wanting the particulars of his sins."[1091] Glatzer observes about the verse, "God shows His revelation by hiding His face."[1092] Rowley says hiding the face is a sign of anger (Ps 27:9 and Isa 54:8) or unfriendliness (Ps 30:7).[1093] Peake suggests there should be a pause between vv. 23 and 24.[1094] Rashi thinks that Job's question in v. 23 is this: "Why do You hold Your face from seeing the ways of my righteousness?"[1095] Mezudat David says of the verse in question:

> Job depicts God as commanding that He be castigated and hides His face, lest he see Job's afflictions and have pity on him.[1096]

Glatzer believes, "This is God's chance to show His revelation by hiding His face."[1097] Barton thinks that v. 24 "refers to God's general treatment of Job's afflictions."[1098]

Hartley thinks that in v. 24, Job asks, "Why have You hidden Your face, and seen me as an enemy?" Hartley gives Ps 13:2 and 44:25 as parallel texts.[1099] He gives a version of the Hidden, or Silemt God here.

About v. 25, Hartley observes, "Job probes God's motives for treating him, a frail object, so savagely."[1100] Glatzer thinks v. 25 is about "God's majestic and unintelligible ways."[1101] Barton says the images of v. 25 "are emblems of Job's insignificance as compared to God."[1102] The Targum renders v. 25 this way: "Will you frighten a rattling leaf?"[1103] So too, Rashi, Ibn Ezra, Isaiah di Trani, and Rabbenu Meyouchas.[1104] Mezudat David has it, "Will you break a rattling leaf."[1105] The Talmud suggests the "stubble" of v. 25, is "the straw that remains in the ground when the rest is cut off."[1106]

Tur-Sinai thinks the "writes against" of v. 26, refers to "the assignment of property to an heir."[1107] Hitzig reasons that "writes bitter things" means "prescribes bitter medicine."[1108] Ball has it, "writes upon me bitter things," as does the RSV.[1109] Hitzig thinks this is a reference to the masks of Job's disease.[1110] Dahood says v. 26 means, "writes acts of violence against my account."[1111] The word for "bitter things" is employed at 20:14, where it means "poison," and at 20:25, where it implies "liver" or "gall bladder."[1112]

About the "iniquities of my youth" in v. 26b, Rowley writes:

> Job does not claim that he is sinless. His only claim is that he did not commit any heinous sins as could justify his exceptional suffering. Here he sarcastically suggests that his misfortunes must be a belated requital of the long-forgotten sins of his youth. He means, "Inherit the consequences of them." By the use of this word, Job is saying that youth and manhood are two different persons.[1113]

The Targum seems to believe about v. 26 that Job is saying, "You don't write down the good things that I have done."[1114] Rashi, Ibn Ezra, Saadiah Gaon, Moshe Kimhi, Ralbag, and Rabbenou Meyouchas, all give v. 26 the same understanding.[1115] Barton believes the import of v. 26 is simply, "You prescribe bitter things means You only send me suffering."[1116] Barton says the "stocks" is only here and at 33:11, and thus another *hapax* of the book.[1117] A similar word is used in a Syriac version of Acts 16:24. It was a wooden instrument in which the feet of a prisoner were made secure.

The word employed at v. 27, *cad*, pronounced *sad*, is also used at 38:11. A different term, *'geza*, is employed at 14:8. Some translations, like the RSV, renders this word as "stock," but generally it means a "tree stump." Habel thinks v. 27 refers to the branding of a prisoner's feet.[1118]

Rashi observes about v. 27:

> This refers to the bones of the foot. The stocks press the flesh of the feet, causing much pain. This is analogous to the pain Job is suffering.[1119]

Merx excises v. 27, and makes it follow v. 14:2a.[1120] Duhm and Siegfried think v. 27 should follow v. 14:2b. Budde and Holscher delete v. 27 altogether.[1121] For "like a rotting thing" the LXX has "like a wineskin," so also Beer and Fohrer.[1122] Rowley says the word for "dry chaff" in v. 27 is used to imply "dry rot." He gives Hos 5:12 as a parallel use.[1123] Rowley also believes that Ps 102:26 and Sirach 14:17 are parallels to v. 28.[1124] Cheyney repoints v. 28 to get, "such a one is like a blossom that fades, like a vine that caterpillars have eaten."[1125] Stephen Mitchell, Barton, Habel, and many others, move the final verse of ch. 13 to follow 14:2.[1126] Mezudat David thinks the meaning of v. 28 is this:

> The body You pursue will surely rot away into a decayed object, like a moth-eaten garment. It is beneath Your dignity to pursue such a lowly creature.[1127]

Habel points out that the subject of v. 28 shifts from first person to third.[1128] This is why so many interpreters shift the final verse of ch. 13 to the beginning of ch. 14. Hartley gives us the traditional and modern interpretation of v. 28 when he writes:

> Job compares himself to a rotting piece of wood that is wasting away, or to a garment being eaten by a moth.[1129]

Job's First Response to Zophar Completed (Chapter 14)

Introduction

With ch. 14, Job completes his first response to Zophar, as well as the first round of speeches in the book. Matthew Henry suggests ch. 14 should be divided into three major sections: Job Speaks of Man's Life (vv. 1–6); Of Man's Death (vv. 7–15); and By Sin Man Is Subject to Corruption (vv. 16–22).[1130] Both Newsom and Terrien also divide ch. 14 this same way. Van Hecke tells us about ch. 14:

> Job's strong determination to speak to God Himself comes to a climax in this chapter, Job addresses his friends more directly than ever before, trying to make clear in what respects he differs from his friends.[1131]

Newsom maintains that "the vocabulary and tone of legal challenge are abandoned. In ch. 14, as Job turns instead to contemplate the ephemerality of human existence."[1132] She also points out that many exegetes move the final verse of ch. 13 to follow 14:2.

Analysis of Chapter 14

14:1–6

Many early Christian exegetes, such as Hesychius, Gregory, and John Chrysostom, find original sin in the first six verses of ch. 14. In fact, however, these verses appear to be more about the ephemeral nature of life. Earlier, Job already has lamented on the shortness of life at 7:6ff. and 9:25ff. The Torah, too, at Gen 47:9 speaks of even the longest life being brief. Dhorme tells us that "nothing is so ephemeral as the flower, nothing so fugitive as the shadow."[1133]

Newsom suggests these verses divide into three groups, with the main point expressed in the middle pair. She adds:

> An initial comment on the transient quality of human life [vv. 1–2], leads to the central objection that God bringing Job into judgment is cruelly absurd [vv. 3–4]. The power that God has over the human lifespan becomes an argument for a respite.[1134]

Stevenson renders v. 1, "Earthlings, born of a woman, short-lived and complete with wrath."[1135] Clines remarks about v. 1, "The life of human beings is so fleeting that it seems undignified for God to consecrate so much effort to investigating and judging it."[1136] Malbim suggests in the opening verse of ch. 14 that,

> because he is born of a woman, and because of the matter of which he is composed, his days are short. He is of a humble end because his days are short.[1137]

Mezudat David believes in connection with v. 1, "Job has many fears during his life, it is like he is sated with fears."[1138] Obadiah Sforno says, "He is full of fear due to having to work for a living."[1139] Terrien thinks that Job speaks for all of humankind here, and he adds, "but the present train of thought bears more on the brevity of life than on man's misery."[1140] Hesychius of Jerusalem finds original sin in the opening verse of ch. 14. He adds, "Man is born of a woman and has a short life because he has been ordered to return to the Earth."[1141] The LXX, Peshitta, and Vulgate all read, "and . . . him" rather than "and . . . me."[1142]

Rashi says of v. 2, "He is like a blossom that is cut off immediately, after it emerges, it does not last long."[1143] Dhorme says of the two images in v. 2, "Nothing is so ephemeral as the flower, nothing so fugitive as the shadow."[1144] Clines calls them "two conventional images of the brevity of life."[1145] Malbim says of v. 2, "Man is not in one condition for long because he constantly deteriorates."[1146]

Newsom suggests the meaning of vv. 3–4 comes close to "You cannot make a silk purse out of a sow's ear," or that "Everyone cannot spin gold out of straw."[1147] Gregory takes another view of these verses. He observes about vv. 3–4:

> Job has survived both the power of the Almighty God and his frailty. Before he brought himself and God together, he considered who would come into judgment and who would judge. He saw on one side man, and on the other, his Creator.[1148]

John Chrysostom believes about vv. 4–5, "You see Job taking refuge again in his nature because it is impossible, he says, to be pure." It is clear that John finds original sin here.[1149] Clement of Rome quotes 14:4–5 to establish that "there is none that is free of sin, not even if his life lasts but a day."[1150] Rashi thinks these verses refer to "a putrid drop of semen which is unclean. Not one of them is clean that he should not sin."[1151] Thus, Rashi is against the original sin response to Job's suffering.

Verse 4 is deleted by Bickell, Driver and Gray, Pope, Hurst, and the NEB.[1152] It is also missing in one of the Hebrew manuscripts. Terrien gives Pss 51:5 and 14:3 as parallels. Peake thinks v. 4, is "the sigh of a pious reader, written on the margin, and mistakenly written into the text."[1153]

About vv. 5–6, Clines writes:

> The three cola of v. 5 are best taken as the three-fold reason for the demand of v. 6. Job has twice urged God to "desists" from him, to leave him alone at 7:16 and 10:20, so that he might have some relief in the days he has left. This apparently is a traditional form of lament. [See Ps 39:14.][1154]

Some scholars reduce v. 5 by deleting 5c, as Ball, Fohrer, and others do. Others transfer v. 5c to follow 13:27. Dhorme keeps it where it is, but Holscher and Steinmann delete the entire verse.[1155] Stevenson suggests the *'im* of v. 5 should read, *ki'im*, arguing that the loss of the *ki* may parallel. Presumably 5c has lost its complement.[1156] Didymus the Blind says about v. 6:

> Since God is with Job through hardships He lays upon him, Job says, "Look away!" in the sense of "bring Your anger to an end." God approaches in different ways by allowing participation through anger. The friends have come to the conclusion that Job suffers for his sins. He therefore harshly responds that, "The human being has a short life and is like a withered flower or a shadow."[1157]

The KJV renders v. 6 "that he may rest." Ball adds "from Him." As in 7:16.[1158] Ephrem the Syrian thinks these verses are a prophecy of baptism, while Ibn Ezra observes about v. 6:

> During those few limited days where he can rest from pain until he desires to his old age, and by the weakness of his strength, the day of his death is like a hireling who desires the completion of his day's work.[1159]

Rashi has it, "Until like the hireling, he completes his day."[1160] Others use "day laborer." The KJV has "hireling." The NRSV uses the plural "laborers." The NIV gives "hired man." The RSV has it "hireling." The word in question in the Hebrew is *sakiyr*. It is only used six times in the Hebrew Bible, two in Isaiah (16:14 and 21:14), once in Malachi (3:5), and three times in Job, at 7:1, 7:2, and 14:6.

14:7–15

Stevenson thinks vv. 7–12 is "a meditation which is most appropriate when moved to become the closing words of Job's speech." He adds, "After their removal, vv. 13–21 carry on Job's preceding address to God."[1161] Newsom observes about these verses:

The consequences of the "bounds that humans cannot pass" are worked out in a series of striking comparisons and contrasts with natural phenomenon.[1162]

Terrien thinks these verses about the tree may refer to the "thinking of Egyptian ideas about the afterlife."[1163] Clines reminds us, "The tree, if we speak anthropomorphically, can be said to have hope, a rare commodity in Job's life."[1164] J. G. Weitzstein and Dhorme speak of the practice in Damascus of cutting down old fig trees, walnuts, and pomegranate, along with the vines that have ceased to bear fruit.[1165] The stump, if watered, puts out new shoots the following year that subsequently bear good fruit. Most interpreters agree with Mezudat David, however, when he writes about the tree in 14:7–12, "Even if it is cut off, it will grow again anew."[1166]

There is considerable disagreement about what to do with vv. 13–14. Stevenson says v. 14a is "the note of a critical reader."[1167] Steuernagel believes v. 14a should follow v. 12a.[1168] Dhorme puts it after v. 19.[1169] Fohrer sees it as part of v. 13.[1170] The LXX renders the interrogatory of v. 14 as a declaratory, as does the Vulgate. Some rabbis of the Talmud use Job's remark at 14:14 as evidence he did not believe in the resurrection of the dead. As did Rashi, and some rabbis of the Babylonian Talmud before him.[1171] Newsom writes about v. 14:

> That Job is talking here about resurrection and death is made clear by the rhetorical question of verse 14. He imagines the time in Sheol as a pressed service [*saba*, as in a labor gang or an army, with a set time and an occasion for release]. The same image is employed at Isa. 40:2, to render the exile in Babylon.[1172]

Ibn Ezra calls v. 15 "a supplication." He continues:

> Call to me and I will answer You, so that my case is proven. Call me to take my soul and I will have no strength to resist. It is as though You long to see the work of Your hands, the soul.[1173]

Gregory believes v. 15 is an indication and a foreshadowing of the resurrection.[1174] Thus, Gregory assents to the resurrected Job motif here. Didymus the Blind says of v. 15, "Not only is the body resurrected, but the soul's thoughts are fixed on God."[1175] Rowley observes about v. 15, "Again, we see how two views about God are struggling in his thoughts."[1176] Newsom points out that the words of vv. 14–15 are "the reverse of his words at 13:15," where he said, "I have no hope," whereas now he says, "All the days of my service I shall hope."[1177] Fohrer notes that "counting steps" is never an image of "providential care, but rather of scrutiny of conduct."[1178]

14:16–22

Rashi says of v. 16:

But now you are harming me. You count my steps and you do not wait for my sin to requite me.[1179]

Rowley follows the view of Budde that v. 16 continues the thought of the previous verse.[1180] Fohrer thinks v. 16 should be an interrogatory.[1181] The LXX renders v. 16, "Thou dost not pass over my sins," as does Ewald, Dillmann, Duhm, Gray, and Ball.[1182] Pope thinks the first half of v. 16 refers to an unfriendly numbering, and so he inserts a negative in the verse.[1183] Terrien points out that v. 16 is traditionally interpreted in two, radically different ways. He writes:

> The KJV considers the initial "But now" establishes a brutal contrast between lyrical fancy and present realities. Thus, 16a is rendered, "For Thou now numberest my steps"—a pejorative expression suggesting the watchfulness of a spy.[1184]

The NIV renders v. 16 this way:

> Surely, you will count my steps
> But not keep track of my sins.[1185]

The NRSV, like Pope, adds two negatives to the line:

> For then You would not number my steps,
> You would not keep watch over my sins.[1186]

The Peshitta has it, "Then Thou would not number my sins." Dhorme says that v. 16a refers to the present, while 16b to the future.[1187] There is also much disagreement over v. 17. Rashi thinks it should be rendered, "Sealed up in a cloth bundle, like silver or pearl, lest it be lost."[1188] Mezudat David thinks the meaning of v. 17 is:

> You have added to my iniquities the commission of sins which I did not commit.
> You cause me to inherit the sins of my youth, but after I count the good deeds I
> have performed, I am confident that You will desire me.[1189]

The KJV suggests the idea of sealing a transgression in a bag to the keeping of a memory. Terrien observes, "The allusion is not for the purpose of preservation, but on the contrary, for its concealment and eventual disappearance."[1190] Pope believes in v. 17, "Job's sins were thought of as represented by tally stones placed in a bag."[1191] He points out that O. Eissfeldt has employed the same idea in interpreting 1 Sam 25:29.[1192] Rowley believes, "God treasures up Job's sins and keeps them securely, so that they are not forgotten and so that full punishment will be enacted."[1193]

Newsom points out about vv. 18–22 that "the concluding images of death are governed by the image of separation."[1194] Terrien observes that vv. 18–19 are missing in the Coptic Sahidic Job.[1195] They are marked with an asterisk in the Peshitta. The

LXX begins the verse, "But on the contrary," which may indicate some disturbance in v. 18. The general idea of vv. 18–19, however, is quite clear: "Mountains, rocks, and soil disintegrate under various kinds of erosion, so man's hopes are destroyed little by little, drop by drop." Clines thinks vv. 18–19 take us back to the thought of v. 7, "where we saw that the life of nature is subject to renewal," or the thought of v. 13, where Job, for a few moments, is tantalized.[1196] Philip the Priest says of vv. 18 and 19, "Pride swells up like a mountain, only to fail."[1197] Rowley observes about these verses, "Even the greatest mountains can be shaken and destroyed, how then can man escape destruction?"[1198]

The LXX and Peshitta have "will fall" as the verb for v. 19. Others revocalize and get, "will surely fall" (Holscher, Steinmann, Weiser, Horst, and Fohrer).[1199] Other editors attempt to rearrange the triptych of v. 19. Budde believes v. 12a should follow v. 19a.[1200] Dhorme thinks that v. 14 should precede v. 19a.[1201] Stevenson says, "The grammar, though unusual, is not unprecedented."[1202]

Peake says of v. 20, "In his struggles for life, God worst him, and his defeat is final."[1203] Davidson calls v. 20 "a graphic and pathetic description of death."[1204] Clines takes a different view of v. 20. He writes:

> Death is depicted now as God's victory over human hope for life. Death, that is to say, is not a mere natural process that could perhaps in principle be stalled or cheated. It is a direct divine act that causes a person's death.[1205]

Samuel Terrien tells us about vv. 20–22, "A dead man is unaware of the fate of his progeny. He may retain some sort of psychological consciousness, but his preoccupation is confined to his own fate."[1206] Gray says of these verses, "Dismissed to Sheol, the dead no longer have knowledge of what would, if they were alive on Earth, most intimately concern them."[1207]

The Targum renders v. 22 in two different ways:

> Indeed, his flesh pains him because of the worms
>
> And his soul mourns for him in the Tribunal.[1208]

And the second version:

> Indeed, his flesh pains him until the cover of the coffin is closed,
>
> And his soul mourns for him in the cemetery during the seven days
>
> of mourning.[1209]

Thus, the Targum of Job offers one translation that suggests extinction at death, and another view that indicates survival of the soul, or *nefesh*, after death, in the grave. The former view, as we have indicated earlier, is the predominant one in the book.

Newsom does not believe the final verse of ch. 14 "describes a post-mortem pain," but moves back to the process of dying.[1210] Ibn Ezra says of v. 22, "His flesh that is upon him disintegrates and his soul mourns for the body being devoured by worms."[1211] David Clines points out that ch. 14, like the previous two chapters, ends on the note of death and the underworld.[1212] But Stevenson disagrees. He writes:

> The supposed description of existence in Sheol does not harmonize with OT conceptions as found elsewhere, and the line, on any interpretation, is not a good sequel to v. 21. It may be a reader's note on Job's present condition, "clearly his flesh is in pain and his inner being grieves."[1213]

Buttenwieser, following Konig, makes the final verse of ch. 14 a declarative that man's "kinsmen" and "household" mourn over him when he is dead.[1214] Driver suggests "throat" for "soul," and in v. 22 he renders the verb, "be dry." Thus, he gets, "His throat is parched."[1215] Rowley does not find this interpretation convincing.[1216] Nor do we.

Chapter 15: Eliphaz's Second Speech: 15:1–35

Introduction

Most ancient, medieval, and modern interpreters divide ch. 15 into three parts: vv. 1–5; vv. 6–16; and vv. 17–35. Matthew Henry, Carol Newsom, David Clines, and many other exegetes divide ch. 15 this way. Henry calls the first part, "Job Reproves His Friends."

He calls the second part, "Job Represents His Case as Deplorable," and the third, "I Will Wait for My Renewal to Come."[1217] This seems a sensible way to divide ch. 15.

Analysis of Chapter 15

15:1–5

Thomas Aquinas observes that in these verses, Job is saying, "I have a heart too, just as you do, nor am I inferior to you."[1218] Dhorme says, "Job has boasted his wisdom before at 12:3 and 13:2. Eliphaz turns it into derision."[1219] Wesley believes v. 2 is in the form of a question, "Should a wise man utter vain knowledge, and fill his belly with the east wind?"[1220]

Saadiah Gaon gives us this for v. 2: "Does the wise man offer a love of wind?" He points out that wind is often a metaphor of what is "idle, insubstantial, false, barren, or destructive."[1221] The verb of v. 3, "to be useful" or "profitable," is peculiar to the book of Job. It is also used at 5:17; 22:2; and 35:3. Mezudat David says that Job asks in v. 3, "What difference does it make who is wiser, you or me?"[1222] The Targum and Ibn Ezra render the line, "from which nothing can be learned."[1223] Rashi thinks it asks, "What difference should one debate a matter if one derives no benefit from it?"[1224]

About v. 4, Isaiah di Trani says that Eliphaz tells Job, "You should speak less before the presence of God."[1225] Thomas Aquinas says Eliphaz is saying in v. 4, "You have tried to exclude yourself from the fear of God."[1226] Saadiah says Eliphaz is saying, "I put my discourse before Him." He gives Ps 142:3 as a parallel. Dhorme tells us the meaning of v. 4 is: "The utterances of Job tend to dissuade the pious from recourse to God with his friends."[1227]

Wesley believes that Eliphaz says in v. 5, "You speak wickedness and craftily, you cover your impious principles with a fair pretense to piety."[1228] Thomas Aquinas suggests that in v. 5, Eliphaz observes, "Your words need no other respondent. They destroy themselves."[1229] Dhorme says, "Since your fault inspires your mouth, you adopt the language of the cunning."[1230] Rashi says of v. 5, "Your mouth teaches others your iniquitous beliefs."[1231] Mezudat David agrees. He says Eliphaz says:

> Your evil inclination teaches your mouth to speak such words, but you should have chosen the words of the crafty.[1232]

This reference by Mezudat David, also known as David Altschuler (1689–1769) should be seen, then, as an example of the free will defense, with respect to the cause of Job's suffering. It comes about simply as a by-product of Job's *yetzer ha ra*, or "evil imagination." Altschuler completed a full commentary of the book of Job, which was first published in 1753.

15:6–16

The Peshitta adds, "before me," at the end of v. 6. Dhorme points out that the subject of v. 6 is feminine but it uses a masculine verb.[1233] He thinks in vv. 7–8, "Eliphaz is criticizing the pretensions of Job." He says how difficult it is to acquire wisdom. Zophar made the same point back at 11:7–9. Dhorme suggests in vv. 7–8, we have an undisguised allusion to the discourse of wisdom in Prov 8.[1234] He adds:

> In particular, Prov 8:22–31, which stresses the luxurious display of poetry in the preexistence of wisdom before all things.[1235]

Matthew Henry says of vv. 7–9, "Because he will not grant him the monopoly of wisdom, they will have it as he thought of himself."[1236] John Chrysostom observes about vv. 7–10:

> Eliphaz is just about to say, did you by any chance exist before the entire world, so that you learned about the most ancient times. Or did you learn nothing from the mouth of God?[1237]

Chrysostom used the wisdom of the fathers motif here. Rashi says the meaning of v. 8 is, "You should not boast to God about your extensive knowledge."[1238] Mezudat David thinks v. 8 is in the declarative, "And bring down much wisdom from above to descend upon you."[1239] Dhorme says "the double meaning of 'secret' and 'secret counsel' is apparent in the various translations."[1240] The Targum has "secrets." The RSV, "counsel." The KJV, "secret." The same verb sometimes has the same meaning of "listen," as in 37:2, or as "hear," as in 26:14.

The poet of the book of Job again shows his extensive vocabulary with the variety of words he employs to designate "secret" and "secrets," particularly in chs. 14 and 15. At 15:11, we find the word *'attht* usually is associated with a necromancer or charmer. At 14:3, the poet uses the term *cathar*, pronounced *sawthar*, to indicate "secret." At 15:8 and 29:4, we find the word *cowd*, pronounced *sowd*, to mean "secret." Additionally, the Job poet also employs *ta'amulah*, a female, plural form, as well as the verb, *taman*, that usually indicates "to hide," but also at times designates "secret."

Dhorme says the meaning of vv. 9 and 10 is, "It is always in going back to previous generations that one finds more and more wisdom."[1241] The verb "to have white hair" gives us the noun "white hair," as in 1 Sam 12:2 and Job 41:24. Rashi says the "more" in v. 10 means "more days than your father."[1242] Dhorme thinks that Eliphaz says in vv. 9 and 10, "Job does not have a monopoly on wisdom."[1243] Eliphaz repeats in v. 9, Job's question from 12:3c and 12:9,

Gregory says of vv. 11–13:

> It is as if Eliphaz has said to Job in plain words, "If you would amend your profession of faith, you might have long ago have possessed consolation in your many scourges."[1244]

Saadiah renders *tahumot* in v. 11 as "warning" or "admonition," and *la'at* as "hidden," on the basis of 1 Kgs 19:13 and 1 Sam 18:23.[1245] Rashi says the "fatness" in v. 11 refers to his "plenty."[1246] Thomas Aquinas says that in v. 11, Eliphaz says, "It is easy for God to lead you back to a state of prosperity."[1247] Dhorme says the pronoun is used in v. 12 in the sense of "why," as in 7:21.[1248] The verb implies being "unhinged by passion" or "to be carried away by passion," that is, "beyond the bounds of good sense."[1249] Dhorme gives Prov 6:25 as a parallel text.[1250]

Saadiah says in v. 13, Eliphaz observes:

> Do you not fear God and the punishment that He has warned you of, when you responded in anger to your Lord with the things you have been saying.[1251]

Thus, Saadiah seems to be assenting to a version of retributive justice here. Saadiah gives Ps 139:7 as a parallel to v. 13. Ehrlich has the first hemstitch as, "that you may give back your soul to God," on the strength of Eccl 12:7.[1252] The word *ruah*, "breath," or "spirit" in v. 13 is sometimes used to imply "anger," as in Judg 8:3 and Prov 16:32. Thomas Aquinas says of Eliphaz in v. 14, "Eliphaz impugns this statement because of frailty of the human condition, through which man avoids sin with difficulty."[1253]

Olympiodorus of Thebes, fifth-century exegete, says of vv. 14–16, "Who is the person, Eliphaz says, who can be blameless or can proclaim, 'I am righteous!'?"[1254] Isaiah di Trani says v. 15 means, "According to the Sages, this verse refers to the righteous, who, despite their holiness, cannot be trusted to avoid sin."[1255] This is another use of the wisdom of the sages motif in the book. Ishodad of Merv says of v. 16, "The author uses these words to show that human beings enjoy uttering blasphemies."[1256] Dhorme thinks v. 16 is the conclusion of Eliphaz's argument.[1257]

15:17–35

Gregory says that vv. 17–19 are "further proof of Eliphaz's pride."[1258] Saadiah says these verses mean that "the tradition must be continuous each generation, receiving it from another as reliable as themselves."[1259] Rashi says that v. 18 means, "Wise men confess their transgressions. They do not hide their iniquities from their fathers."[1260] Dhorme agrees. He says of v. 18, "Like Bildad at 8:8, Eliphaz invokes tradition. Wise men do not possess their wisdom intrinsically. They hold it from their fathers, and transmit it to their sons, 'a version of Collective Retributive Justice.'"[1261]

Wesley observes about v. 19, "God watches over these holy men, so that no enemy could invade them, could have done over you, if you had been such a one."[1262] Rashi says v. 19 implies, "No stranger passes in their midst."[1263] John Chrysostom believes vv. 20–24 means this:

> "No stranger marched against them" means that the wise are those who enjoy peace and transmit it to their descendants.[1264]

Ephrem the Syrian thinks the meaning of these verses is, "The wicked are defeated by distress."[1265] John Wesley finds that the import of v. 20 is, "He knows how short the time of life is, and therefore lives in a state of continuous fear in losing it." About the next verse, v. 21, Wesley observes: "Even when he feels no evil, he is tormented with perpetual fears."[1266]

Dhorme says of v. 22, "The aim here is not to give a warning to the wicked man, but to describe his state of mind."[1267] Wesley observes that the import of v. 22 is, "When one falls into trouble, he despairs of deliverance, by reason of his guilty conscience."[1268] Saadiah renders the Hebrew *galmud* by employing the Arabic *mayshum* that literally means "luckless."[1269] Le Hir has v. 23, "He sees the evil day looming ahead."[1270] Ernest Renan agrees. He writes of v. 23, "He knows that dark days are prepared for him."[1271]

Both the Vulgate and the Peshitta have, "like a king quick to attack," for v. 24. Both Duhm and Ball excise v. 24, on the grounds that it is a gloss of v. 26. Rashi says v. 24 means, "The anguish is stronger than he and it will prevail over him."[1272] Mezudat David renders v. 24 as, "He will seize him forcibly."[1273] Saadiah says the import of v. 24 is this: "Just as the sphere surrounds the globe of the Earth, so does trouble encompass the unjust."[1274]

Philip the Priest observes about vv. 25–27, "By mentioning the fatness of the neck, Eliphaz has indicated an over-abundant and almost excessively flowing arrogance."[1275] Wesley says of v. 25:

He sinned against God with a high hand. The Almighty—which aggravates the madness of this poor worm who fights against omnipotence.[1276]

Mezudat David says of v. 25, "He stretched out his hand to blaspheme God."[1277] Rashi says v. 26 is "an expression of height," as in Ezek 16:24.[1278] Many interpreters understand this verse as the idea of innate evil, perhaps a nod in the direction of original sin theory. Saadiah renders v. 27 as, "and made fat upon his flanks." He gives Lev 3:15 as a parallel.[1279] Dhorme observes about v. 27:

> Here the author invokes a picture of the godless man as a bloated egoist who in his greed puts on fat.[1280]

Wesley says the meaning of v. 27 is that, "Because he was fat, rich, potent, and successful, as this expression signifies, the fat means his only care is to pamper himself."[1281] Rashi says it refers to "the collops of fat on his loins."[1282] Mezudat David says, "He has indulged himself until his flesh became so fat that it covers his whole face."[1283]

About vv. 27–28, Olympiodorus observes:

> He describes the absolute solitude of the impious, and says that because of their misery, they inhabit desolation instead of prosperous cities and houses. In fact, Eliphaz says, "their wealth will not last."[1284]

Rashi implies of v. 28, "This is the custom of haughty people to build ruins for a name."[1285] Ibn Ezra observes that this verse means, "They secluded themselves so that they may plot evil."[1286] Dhorme observes the import of v. 28 is this:

> The tyrant has ravaged and reduced to barrenness the regions around him in order that he may settle in the rooms of others.[1287]

About v. 29, Dhorme says:

> We return here to the theme of punishment of the wicked which was first described as the torments of remorse.[1288]

Thus, Dhorme finds retributive justice theory in v. 29. Mezudat David says of v. 29, "He will not become wealthy because of his arrogance, nor will he retain his riches."[1289] Thomas Aquinas thinks the verse has just the opposite implication—"This means that he will acquire wealth again."[1290] About the next verse, v. 30, Thomas observes:

> By the proud of his words, so that he could not in any way hope for recovery, not even if it came from God.[1291]

Gregory the Great introduces vv. 31–33 this way:

> As often as we do alms after sin, we, as it were, pay a high price for all of our bad actions.[1292]

Saadiah renders v. 31 as, "His words trust not in fairness." He gives Prov 26:4 and 8:11 as parallels.[1293] He adds, "The errant person does not place his trust in truth an equity but in falsehood and fraud."[1294] Saadiah renders *timmale* in v. 32 as "casts down." Matthew Henry says the meaning of v. 33 is, "They shall die in the beginning of their days and never come to maturity."[1295] Saadiah renders *yahmos* as "shall scatter." He gives Lam 2:6 as a parallel.[1296]

Philip the Priest says of the final two verses of ch. 15:

> With these words, Eliphaz identifies holy Job as a robber and a pretender who hides his violent actions. He has also spoken so in his first speech, when Eliphaz compared him with a lion, a lioness, and a cub of lions and tigers. But we must believe in God, who by praising Job did not call him a deceiver, but declared him to be innocent and simple.[1297]

Rashi observes about v. 35:

> They conceive trouble and bear iniquity. This means they commit evil and are recompensed. The recompense of the birth is in accordance with conception.[1298]

Saadiah says the importance of v. 35 is, "Do not pretend to have experiences that you have not."[1299] Thomas Aquinas says of v. 35, "He has contrived in his heart how to inflict pain on another, and the conception of his pain indeed produced harm unjustly afflicted."[1300] Mezudat David says of the final verse of ch. 15: "It is the heart that prepares deceit, so it will receive its just recompense."[1301] Ibn Ezra implies, "The belly represents hidden thoughts," in v. 35.[1302] This brings us to an essay on the "East wind" (15:2) in the Hebrew Bible and the book of Job.

The East Wind in Old Testament and Book of Job

The ancient Hebrew expression "East Wind" is found throughout the Old Testament, as well as the book of Job. It occurs, for examples, at Hos 13:15; Gen 41:22–24; Ezek 19:10–12; Isa 32:1–2; and Ps 55:6–8. The Hebrew of this expression is *kedem ruwach*. It refers to the hot wind that comes from the east. Specifically from the deserts of Arabia, Mesopotamia, and Babylon.

Jeremiah, at 13:24, refers to the East Wind as the "Wind of the wilderness." Altogether "East" and "East Wind" appear twelve times in the book of Job, including 15:2 and 27:21. Job 1:3 tells us that Job "was the greatest of all the people of the East." Job 1:19 speaks of a "great wind" that came across the wilderness, most likely the East Wind. Besides 15:2, the East Wind is also mentioned at 27:21.

Although the desert land east of Palestine was called the *Kedem*, the Far East in the Old Testament is known as the *Misrach*. At Job 37:17, Elihu mentions the "South

Wind." The South Wind in the Old Testament is usually cool, because it comes from the Mediterranean Sea.

Chapter 16: Job's Second Response to Eliphaz

Introduction

Calvin divides the sixteenth chapter into three parts: vv. 1–5; vv. 6–16; and vv. 17–22.[1303] About the first of these parts, Calvin says:

> Eliphaz has represented Job's discourse as without profit, and nothing to the purpose. Job here shows him the same character.[1304]

J. C. L. Gibson says of Job's remarks in ch. 16, "Job is overwhelmed by the new turn of events in the friends' arguments."[1305] No longer is there even a pretense to guiding him back to the right.[1306] C. F. Keil and Franz Delitzsch also take a negative view of Job's second discourse to Eliphaz. They say, "This speech is meant to be comforting. It is primarily an accusation. It wounds instead of soothing."[1307]

Chapter 16 employs the word *edh*, or "witness," twice, at vv. 8 and 19. Some exegetes connect this term to the *Goel* of 19:26 and the "angel mediator," in the Elihu speeches at 33:23. Job also speaks of his symptoms in ch. 16, particularly at vv. 13–17. Job also makes a number of comments in ch. 16 about how God is his enemy. (See vv. 7 and 11, for examples.)

Analysis of Chapter 16

16:1–5

Kissane says of vv. 2–6:

> Nothing but empty words, where he has reason to expect sympathy.[1308]

Ball believes that in v. 2, Job is saying, "I have heard many things like this before."[1309] Thomas Aquinas observes about the beginning of this speech, "Eliphaz has spoken harshly against Job in his answer, so Job accuses him of unfitting consolation in the beginning of this speech."[1310] Wesley thinks "Job reproves Eliphaz here for needless repetition. You tell me nothing I did not already know."[1311] Matthew Henry says in v. 3, Job asks, "When will you put an end to these impertinent discourses?" The "windy words" of v. 3 are literally "words of air."[1312]

The word for "heap" in v. 4 is *chabar*. It is a primitive root that means "to join." Ball says the verse should be rendered, "If your soul were in the place of my soul."[1313] Rashi thinks the words mean, "I know how to chide as you do."[1314] Mezudat David believes v. 4 is about "the fear of retribution." Another indication of retributive justice theory.[1315]

Matthew Henry says in vv. 4–5, "Job accuses his friends of violating the rules of friendship."[1316] Good says v. 5 should be rendered, "With my own mouth, I shall overpower you," followed by, "I will strengthen you with my mouth and the moving of my lips should assuage your grief."[1317] Driver translates v. 5 this way:

> But I would strengthen you with my mouth, and the solace of my lips should assuage your grief.[1318]

Stevenson thinks the verses of chs. 15 and 16 are out of order. He says Eliphaz's second speech should go from 15:2 to v. 12, and then on to v. 17, followed by v. 27, then 31, then 30, and finishing with 16:3.[1319] He begins Job's fifth speech at 16:2, then jumps to 16:7, followed by 16:15, 22, and 17:1.[1320]

16:6–16

Calvin says of this second section of ch. 16:

> Here is a doleful representation of Job's grievances. What reason do we have to bless God, as we make such complaints?[1321]

About vv. 6–7, Matthew Henry observes, "Though I speak, my grief is not assuaged; but now He has made me weary. Thou has made desolate all my company."[1322] Driver also believes these verses are in the interrogatory:

> Though I speak, my grief is not assuaged. And though I forbear, what am I eased? But now He hath made me weary; Thou has made desolate all my company.[1323]

Rashi agrees. He says v. 6 should be rendered, "Should I speak my pain would not cease, and should I stop, what would that leave me?"[1324] Driver says v. 7 should say "exhausts me," for "made weary" is not strong enough.[1325] Ball believes v. 6 "seems superfluous."[1326] Keil and Delitzsch render v. 6 as, "Thou hast destroyed all my testimony," another verse that indicates a law case.[1327]

Kissane introduces vv. 7–11 this way:

> How different their treatment of him. Eliphaz is his accuser and his enemy. The others mock and buffet him in misery. And God has delivered them up to their insults, and refuse to answer his prayers for his redress.[1328]

Umbreit thinks the "band of witnesses" in v. 8 is himself.[1329] The expression "shriveled me up," or "fill me with wrinkles," in v. 8 is the Hebrew *qamat*. This verb only appears here and at 16:8 and 22:16. Ball gives Ps 27:12 as a parallel for v. 8.[1330] Rashi agrees that Job "is a witness to his own iniquity."[1331] Umbreit says v. 9 means, "Job would not ascribe hatred to God." He gives Ps 50:22 as a parallel.[1332]

Matthew Henry thinks v. 10 shows that "Job was a type of Christ," thus he ascribes to the *Jobus Christi* motif here.[1333] Both Schultens and Wetzstein render v. 10,

"Altogether they eat themselves, full upon me."[1334] Mezudat David explains v. 10 this way:

> They opened their mouths at me, and with words of disdain, they struck me on the cheek. It is as though they use these disdainful words to strike me on the cheek, embarrassing me with such a blow.[1335]

Again, Matthew Henry says of v. 11, "As Christ was given up to the wicked, so too Job is delivered into the hands of the wicked."[1336] Again, this is a version of the *Jobus Christi* motif. J. C. L. Gibson tells us in v. 11, "God surrenders him to the wicked and ungodly."[1337] Rashi says in v. 11, "that God delivers Job to be a fool."[1338] Keil and Delitzsch observe about v. 12:

> He was prosperous and contended, but all at once God began to be enraged against him.[1339]

Mezudat David believes in v. 12, "God makes Job a target for His arrows."[1340] Driver has it, "set me up for the mark."[1341] He gives 7:20 and Lam 3:12 as parallels.[1342] Mezudat David says in v. 12, "the pains of my suffering," refers again to the shooting of arrows, with God as the archer.[1343] Umbreit says the archer is "whoever is Job's enemy and directs his arrows at him."[1344]

In v. 15, Matthew Henry again sees Job, "as a type of Christ, as many of the ancients make him."[1345] This is another instance of the *Jobus Christi* motif. The Geneva Bible says v. 15 means "Job's glory was brought low."[1346] Ball thinks in v. 15, the cloth mentioned, "sackcloth in the KJV and RSV, is probably an Aramaism."[1347] The word is *saq*. It comes from the Aramaic root ʿSQ.

Thomas Aquinas describes the import of v. 16, this way:

> Having described his enemies, he shows now his humiliation, first regarding his external dress, "I stitched a cloth over my skin."[1348]

Driver also renders v. 15 as "sackcloth upon my sin."[1349] Ralbag says in v. 16, "Job's face became smeared with mud and filth."[1350] Ball says of v. 16, "My belly is burned from weeping."[1351] Keil and Delitzsch say of the verse, "His hands are clean from wrong-doing, free from violence and oppression."[1352]

16:17–22

Calvin introduces this third section of ch. 16 this way:

> Job's condition was very deplorable, but he had the testimony of his conscience and thus he allowed no gross sins for himself.[1353]

Kissane introduces these same verses this way:

His call for redress against the unjust attacks of the friends has already reached the Heavens to plead with God on his behalf, that his innocence be vindicated, and he be restored to happiness before it is too late.[1354]

Kissane and others think v. 17 should follow v. 14. About v. 17, he observes, "All of this has come to me for reasons known to God alone."[1355] This is an indication of the divine plan perspective. Driver renders v. 17 this way:

> Although there is no violence in mine hands
>
> And my prayer is pure.[1356]

Mezudat David says that in v. 17, Job is saying, "All this came to me for nothing, not for any violence I have committed."[1357] Rashi says that v. 17b means, "I did not curse my friend, nor did I think any evil against him."[1358] Mezudat David observes about v. 18:

> Job prays that the Earth should not cover the blood oozing from his wounds but leave them exposed, so that passersby should see them and pray for his recovery.[1359]

Kissane thinks the blood mentioned in v. 18 is "blood that lies undiscovered and unavenged."[1360] Thomas Aquinas observes that in v. 18, "Job describes his innocence."[1361]

Thomas adds:

> He proceeds further to the vain consolation and thus he begins with the words, "My wordy friends."[1362]

Adam Clarke thinks v. 18 is an allusion to the murder of Abel.[1363] At Gen 4:10, Abel's blood cries from the grave. Umbreit gives 16:9 as a parallel to v. 18.[1364] Ball says of v. 18:

> If left uncovered the blood of a murdered man was believed to call down the vengeance of Heaven on the murderer.[1365]

Mezudat David observes about v. 19, "Even now I have found a witness on my behalf, for the uprightness of my heart, and He is the Lord Who knows all."[1366] Rashi says the witness of v. 19 is "My Creator, Who knows my ways."[1367] The Geneva Bible renders v. 19, "Behold my witness is in Heaven, and my record is on high."[1368] This may be another reference to the Book of Deeds motif in ancient Judaism. Adam Clarke says, "I appeal to God in my innocence."[1369] Driver renders v. 19 this way:

> Even now, behold, my witness is in Heaven And He that voucheth for me is on high.[1370]

Thomas Aquinas says this about v. 19:

> The dissipation of my members not only causes me sensible pain, but it also bears witness against me.[1371]

John Wycliffe, in his commentary on the book of Job, believes that the "witness" of v. 19 is "God Himself."[1372] A number of other commentators agree that the "Witness" in v. 19 is God. Among these are Matthew Henry and Albert Barnes in his commentary on the book of Job, published in 1834.[1373] Whatever the identity of the "witness" in v. 19, most interpreters suggest that it is connected to the *Goel*, or "Redeemer" in 19:25–27.

The first two words of v. 20 are problematical. *Melisay re'ay*, or "my scorners are my friends." The word *melis* is related to the verb "to scorn." *Lis*, in Wisdom Literature, means "mediator," as in 33:23, or "interpreter." Adam Clarke translates v. 20 this way:

> My friends scorn me, they deride and insult me, but my eye is toward God.
>
> I look to Him to vindicate my cause.[1374]

Driver has v. 20:

> My friends scorn me
>
> But my eyes pour out tears unto God.[1375]

Umbreit thinks the "scorners" in v. 20 means, "my mockers, my friends."[1376] In his understanding of v. 21, Umbreit writes, "Job says that God must support me against God."[1377] Driver also thinks v. 21 is about "the right of Job himself against God."[1378] Rashi says of v. 21, "If only there was someone I could reason with."[1379]

Thomas Aquinas says about the meaning of v. 22:

> Behold the short years pass away because man only lives for a short time.[1380]

Good says v. 22 implies, "But the years numbered to me are few."[1381] Ball says of the verse, "Job still expects a few years of life, but only a few."[1382] J. C. L. Gibson observes that the import of the final verse of ch. 16 is, "Job, as he looks around, sees the open derision of his friends."[1383] Keil and Delitzsch give us the final word on ch. 16. They write:

> Job establishes that the heavenly witness will not allow him to die a death that he and others would see as the death of a sinner.[1384]

Blood in Old Testament and Book of Job

Dam or *dammo*, the ancient Hebraic words for "blood," appear throughout the Old Testament in many different context. One of those is in Job 16:18, which we will discuss below. In other Old Testament contexts, blood is equivalent to life itself, such as Gen 49:11–12 and Isa 63:6. Blood is also employed in the context of Old Testament sacrifice. Leviticus 16:14–16, for example, tells us that the priest sprinkles blood on the Mercy Seat on the Day of Atonement. Psalm 58:19 implies there is a difference between the blood of the righteous and the "blood of the wicked."

Genesis 17:24 speaks of God making a "blood covenant" with humans. Several passages in the Old Testament suggest the ancient Jews had a prohibition against the eating of blood, such as Deut 12:15–16 and 21–25. Numbers 35:19, in addition to Job 18:25–26, speaks of an Avenger of Blood, or *Goel*. This appears to be family member who is obligated to avenge the blood of a relative. Several Old Testament passages, however, appear to argue against the idea of collective retributive justice. Among these passages are: Deut 24:16; 2 Kgs 14:6; 2 Chr 25:4; Jer 31:21–30; and Ezek 18:20.

There are a number of verses in the book of Job where blood appears. One comes at Job 16:8, where Job asks that his blood "not be covered" in Sheol. This most likely indicates that he wishes his actions to be vindicated and in the God Speeches, at ch. 39:30, God talks about the eagle "sucking up the blood of its young," for "where the slain are, there is He." We turn now to ch. 17.

Chapter 17: Job's Second Response to Eliphaz Continued

Introduction

Matthew Henry divides ch. 17 into two parts: vv. 1–9 and vv. 10–16. He calls the first section, "Job Appeals from Man to God." Henry labels the second section, "His Hope Is Not in Life, But in Death."[1385] Newsom and Samuel Terrien also give similar descriptions in dividing ch. 17 into two major parts, vv. 1–9 and vv. 10–16.[1386]

Chapter 17 completes Job's lament to his first friend, Eliphaz's second discourse. Much of this chapter, like the several chapters preceding it, are taken up with the patriarch's preoccupation with death, for there are numerous references in the chapter to death, Sheol, and the Pit.

Chapter 17 also shows the depth of the poet's Hebrew vocabulary. In the chapter he employs: *yashar* (v. 8); the preposition *betoke*, at v. 10; the "desires of the *leb*," or "heart" (v. 11); and the "darkness" of v. 13, one of the six words for "darkness" in the book, as we have seen earlier.

Analysis of Chapter 17

17:1–9

There is a great deal of disagreement about how to translate the first verse of ch. 17. The LXX has it, "I am perishing, borne away by the wind. I beg for the grave and do not attain it."[1387] Duhm has the beginning of v. 1, "His spirit has destroyed my days, the grave is left to me."[1388] Driver has it, "My spirit is consumed, my days are extinct, and the grave is ready for me."[1389] Ibn Ezra begins the verse, "My days are shattered."[1390] Coverdale translates it, "I am harde at deathes dore."[1391] The word for "grave" in the

129

verse (*qinrah*) is in the plural, thus, the Targum renders 1a as, "They are preparing tombs for me." The KJV also uses the plural, while the NIV has it as a singular. The plural may be used to suggest the place where graves are to be found, the cemetery. Altogether, there are eleven references to the "grave" in the book of Job. Five of those use the noun *Sheol*; five employ the word, *qeber*; and a single instance is in the book of the word, *be'y*, that also sometimes means "tomb."

Verse 2 in the LXX has only one hemstitch. The language of v. 2 looks very much like 30:25 and 31:36. The beginning of v. 2 is in the form of an oath, thus the "surely" in the RSV. It might be rendered, "I swear that . . . ," as at 31:36. Dhorme suggests, "In bitterness, my eyes pass the night."[1392] Holscher thinks it is closer to, "My eyes are weary of their contentiousness." Fohrer agrees.[1393] Rashi thinks v. 2, is "an expression of provocation."[1394] Wesley believes it should be an interrogatory: "Do not my friends mock me, instead of comforting?"[1395]

Verse 3 is marked with an asterisk by Jerome. The Hebrew has, "Lay down my pledge." Ehrlich says, "My pledge, my earnest."[1396] Rashi says of v. 3, "Job turns to address the Omnipresent and says, 'Now turn Your attention to me.'"[1397] Dhorme says about the third verse:

> The pledge which he offers to God consists in his suffering, as it were an anticipation of his death.[1398]

Rowley agrees. He says:

> Job turns here to address God, beseeching Him to act as a Guarantor for Job to himself.[1399]

The same phrase, "give now a pledge," is used at Gen 42:34. Isaiah di Trani thinks that v. 3 implies, "If you accept him in surety and You will not harm me, then I will not fear."[1400] Peake compares v. 3 to Heb. 6:13ff., where God can find no one greater than himself to swear by, and thus he swears by himself.[1401]

Verse 4 is omitted by Bickell, Duhm, and Ball, following the LXX, which omits vv. 3b to 5a. The "their" in this verse must be God. Dhorme has v. 4b, "Therefore, their hand is not raised."[1402] Driver says the meaning of v. 4 is:

> God has blinded his friends from perceiving the truth about him.[1403]

Mezudat David renders v. 4 this way:

> You have hidden their hearts from understanding. Therefore, your glory will not
>
> be exulted through them.[1404]

Wesley believes v. 4 is closer to, "Thou hast blinded the faith of my friends. Therefore, I desire a more wise and able Judge."[1405] Dhorme says of v. 4:

Job has just declared that no one can stand as guarantor for him. Naturally, he is thinking of his friends. The latter have egregiously failed to understand the situation of Job.[1406]

The Peshitta renders the first hemstitch of v. 5, "And friend rises against friend."[1407] Le Hir has it, "He who delivers up his friend as his prey." Renan: "The man who betrays his friends."[1408]

Rashi says of v. 5b, "Each of them speaks to his friends, and this will come to them. Their children's eyes will fail."[1409] Mezudat David says of v. 5b, "He who tells thoughts of flattery, his children's eyes will fail."[1410] This, of course, is an endorsement of the collective retributive justice motif.

Dhorme believes in v. 6, Job returns to his lament of 16:19. He says Job "has ceased to regard God as the cause of his ills."[1411] Keil and Delitzsch render v. 6 this way:

> And He hath made me a proverb to the world. And I became as one who in whose face they spit.[1412]

In v. 6, God is referred to in the third person. The LXX has it, "Thou hast made me."[1413] Rowley tells us that spitting in the face "is a grievous insult." He cites Deut 25:9; Isa 50:6; and Matt 20:67 as confirmation. The word *topet*, or "spit," in v. 6 is another hapax in Job. About v. 6b, Driver observes:

> This refers to neighboring tribes who suddenly hear of Job's misfortunes and then at once treat him as an example of an egregious sinner.[1414]

Dhorme has the verb of v. 6 as third person, singular, passive form.[1415] In most versions the word *binate*, or "members," is seen as a plural. It is likely the word comes from the Babylonian *banu*, that means "a limb."[1416]

There is some disagreement about how to translate v. 6b. The RSV has it, "And I am one before whom people spit." But a literal rendering of the Hebrew says, "I have become like Tophet of old." Tophet was a place in the Valley of Hinnom where human sacrifices were made to the Canaanite god Moloch. (See Jer 19:11–14; 7:31–32; Isa 30:33; 2 Kgs 23:10.)

There is some disagreement about the rendering of v. 7. Mezudat David has it:

> My eyes become dim because of my great anger, as one suffering pain is angry with himself.[1417]

The same verb for eyesight failing is employed at Gen 27:1 and Deut 34:7. Beer says v. 7b should be translated, "My members fail as a shadow."[1418] Budde has "my imaginations" for my members.[1419] Ralbag renders v. 7b, "The features of my face are like a shadow."[1420]

Wesley says of the "shadow" in v. 7b:

> I have grown so poor and thin that I am not to be called a man, but the shadow of a man.[1421]

Driver suggests, "My eyes dim as a reason of my vexation." He says the translation "sorrow" suggests "a false idea" for the verse.[1422] Freehof renders v. 7b as, "All my limbs have shriveled up."[1423] Rashi says these limbs are the "ones with which he was born."[1424] Keil and Delitzsch render v. 7 this way:

> Then my eyes became dim with grief. And all my members were as if a shadow.[1425]

Many exegetes think vv. 8–19 are out of place. Thus, Duhm, Gray, Ball, Holscher, Stevenson, and Fohrer.[1426] Peake, Kissane, and Pope believe only v. 8 is out of place.[1427] Verse 11 does follow quite nicely from v. 7. Duhm puts vv. 8–10 after 18:3, Bildad's speech.[1428]

Dhorme retains the place of vv. 8–10, as does Davidson.[1429] Freehof thinks these verses are meant to be sarcastic.[1430] Keil and Delitzsch render v. 8 this way:

> The upright were astonished at it. And the innocent are stirred up over the godless.[1431]

Dhorme expresses his admiration for v. 9. He says of the verse, "The human spirit rises here to the height of moral grandeur."[1432] The Peshitta adds "and he will remain steadfast" to the end of v. 9. Franz Delitzsch says of v. 9, "These words of Job are like a rocket that shoots above the tragic darkness, lighting it up suddenly."[1433] Mezudat David believes the meaning of v. 9 is that "righteous men will be handsomely rewarded with spiritual pleasures in the Hereafter."[1434]

17:10–16

Verse 10 recalls 6:29. The verb in v. 10 is also used at Prov 1:23. Wesley says that Job is saying in v. 10, "Come and renew the debate, as I see you are resolved to do so."[1435] Rashi thinks that Job says in the verse, "I will not find any wise men among you because you mock my lamentations."[1436] Freehof agrees. He says Job observes, "It is in vain that you return and give the same arguments."[1437] Keil and Delitzsch render v. 11 that way, as well.[1438]

Verse 11 literally says, "The inheritance of my thoughts has been broken."[1439] Budde renders v. 11, "My days have been spent dying."[1440] Duhm has it:

> My days have been spent without hope, the desires of my heart have been destroyed.[1441]

Rowley says the meaning of v. 11 is, "Job feels that death is near, being once more convulsed with pain."[1442] Jewish interpreters divide v. 11 in many different ways because of differences in styles of cantillation. Dhorme observes this about v. 11:

> The idea of "cords" or "fibers" of the heart breaking would be a rather attractive thought.[1443]

Verse 12 is absent from the LXX. Rowley says of v. 12:

> This verse represents the false comfort of Job's friends who pretend that night is day, and hold out false hopes that light is at hand.[1444]

Wesley believes that v. 12 is about Job's sleep, or lack thereof. He writes:

> My thoughts so incessantly pursue me and disturb me that I can no longer sleep in the night.[1445]

Freehof gives Isa 5:20 as a parallel for v. 12.[1446] Le Hir renders the line, "My nights have turned into days."[1447] Dhorme says of v. 12, "Job complains of being unable to sleep, in consequence of his nightmares."[1448] Loisy gives this poetic translation, "In vain, they say that night dawns when, for me, it is darkness."[1449] In v. 13, Rowley observes, "Job returns to his morbid desire for death."[1450] Wesley believes the "waiting" in v. 13 refers to "deliverance."[1451]

Dhorme puts v. 13 in the interrogatory:

> Can I hope again,
> Sheol is my house.[1452]

The Targum has v. 13, "If I await the tomb as my house," while the Peshitta has it, "If I wait for Sheol." Duhm thinks vv. 13–14 are a "series of truisms."[1453] Keil and Delitzsch give this rendering of v. 13:

> If I hope, it is for Sheol as my house, in darkness I have made my bed.[1454]

The noun "pit" in v. 14 is in the feminine. Wesley says, "This verse refers to the corruption of the grave."[1455] Keil and Delitzsch render v. 14 this way:

> I cry to corruption. Thou art my father. To the worm, thou art my mother and sister.[1456]

The RSV has the verse:

> If I say to the Pit, You are my father, and to the worm, you are my mother or my sister.[1457]

Dhorme observes about v. 15, "Job explains that his days have not seen happiness."[1458] Mezudat David puts v. 15 in the form of two questions, "Why is my hope deferred? How can I see the good I am hoping for?"[1459] Rowley observes about v. 15:

> Poor is the prospect that Job sees before him, quite other than the hope of a rosey restoration that the friends predicted, if only he were able to confess his sins.[1460]

Guillaume gives an Arabic sense to "my hope," and renders it instead, "My steadfast piety."[1461] Keil and Delitzsch give a similar translation to v. 15: "Where now, therefore, is my hope, and my hope that sees it?"[1462] Wesley believes the hope in v. 15 is, "The happiness you would have me expect."[1463]

The verb in v. 16 is in the feminine plural. Rabbi Meyouchas renders v. 16 this way:

> Will my hopes and desires descend into the boundaries of the grave? Or will they descend after me into the grave?[1464]

Keil and Delitzsch have v. 16:

> To the bars of Sheol, it descends.
> When at the same time there is real rest in the dust.[1465]

Wesley says these bars in v. 16 are "the innermost part of the Pit. My hopes are dying and they will be buried in the grave."[1466] Rowley, however, says "the meaning of bars is doubtful, and if it is correct, they stand for the gates of Sheol."[1467] The LXX has "with me in Sheol."[1468] Ibn Ezra renders v. 16b as "the threshold of the netherworld."[1469] Le Hir and Renan have it, "the gates of Sheol."[1470] Driver translates v. 16 this way:

> Will they go down with me into Sheol,
> Or shall we descend together into the dust?[1471]

Gersonides believes v. 16b refers to "the depths of the underworld."[1472] Rashi observes about v. 16, "These are the limbs of my body that ultimately will descend to the grave."[1473] Dhorme says the meaning of the final verse in ch. 17 is this: "Hope and happiness are not to follow a dying man."[1474] However we interpret the images of ch. 17 it is clear that Job in this chapter continues the preoccupation with death we have seen in the last few chapters.

Chapter 18: Bildad's Second Speech

Introduction

Matthew Henry divides ch. 18 into three sections: vv. 1–4; vv. 5–10; and vv. 11–21.[1475] Hartley, Rowley, and Newsom divide the chapter into only two parts, vv. 1–4 and vv. 5–21.[1476] We will follow Henry's analysis below. He calls the first section, vv. 1–4, "Bildad Reproves Job." He labels the second section of ch. 18, "Ruin Attend the Wicked," and the third, vv. 11–21, "The Ruin of the Wicked."[1477]

About this second speech of Bildad, Rowley observes:

> Bildad now returns to the attack with less subtlety than Eliphaz, though in no less doctrinaire a way. Whereas Eliphaz had described that fears bred evil in the wicked, Bildad describes the miserable experiences he encounters.[1478]

Solomon Freehof thinks Bildad's opening remarks in ch. 18 do not add anything new to the argument.[1479] Others believe that Bildad's remarks in ch. 18 contain some new views of the origin of Job's suffering, as well as some old perspectives. Chapter 18:21, for example, seems to imply retributive justice, a very old view, while 18:18 might suggests the contrast view in relationship to the patriarch's ills.

Hartley describes Bildad's second speech in ch. 18 this way:

> Bildad takes up the task of instructing Job for the second time. His speech is developed quite simply into two sections: a complaint against Job [vv. 2–4], and a discourse on the terrible fate of the wicked [vv. 5–21].[1480]

One aspect that makes this chapter so difficult to interpret are a number of grammatical and vocabulary puzzles in the chapter, particularly in vv. 2–3, v. 11b, and vv. 25–27. Finally, the Vulgate spells Bildad's name as "Baldad." The *Testament of Job* renders the name of the second friend as "Baldas."

In ch. 18 of Job, in vv. 8–10, the poet refers to a "net," "trap," "snare," "rope." These are: *sebakah*, or "snare" (v. 8); *resheth*, "net," in v. 8; *chabol*, or "snare," in v. 10; *malkadoth*, "trap," in v. 10. At 19:6, the text also uses *matsowd*, another word for "net." Verses 13–15, describe some of the symptoms of Job's illness. Verse 18 implies the contrast view as an explanation of Job's suffering, as does v. 6. Verse 17 suggests that Job's name will "perish" after his death; so he will lack a social form of immortality; and v. 19 again employs the preposition *betoke*, or "among," the same word used when the Satan is first introduced in the Prologue of Job.

Analysis of Chapter 18

18:1–4

In the *Testament of Job*, Baldas asks the patriarch, "If you place your hope in God, how then does He act unjustly toward you?" (37:5–8).[1481] Baldas goes on to accuse Job of not being a follower of God, and also that Job is insane, while he echoes the words of vv. 2–4.[1482] Hesychius of Jerusalem says of vv. 2–4, "Bildad practices ignorance and callousness toward Job's points and opinions."[1483] Julian of Eclanum agrees. He says that "Bildad is full of malice and bad faith."[1484] John Chrysostom also accuses Bildad of "enmity and bad faith."[1485] Gersonides believes that Bildad in vv. 1–4 is suggesting, "You are like a man who, because of much vexation, devours and destroys his own soul."[1486] Thomas Aquinas observes that Bildad "accuses Job of inefficient speech and an empty multiplication of words."[1487]

Ewald believes that Bildad uses the plural in v. 2 because, "He treats Job as being in the company of the wicked."[1488] The LXX has a singular verb in the first hemstitch, "How long will you cease talking?"[1489] Dhorme prefers, "How long will you restrain your words." He bases this on the Akkadian word *kinsu*, which means "bridle."[1490]

The verb "consider" in v. 2b again is in the plural. Many translators change it to the singular. With the change of a single consonant, Dhorme suggests "listen," rather than "consider."[1491] Guillaume connects the verb in v. 2b to an Arabic root, *wahihan*, and renders the verb, "express yourself plainly."¹⁴⁹² Peake thinks in the opening verses of ch. 18, Bildad is asking, "Do you imagine that the order of things will be deranged for your sake?"¹⁴⁹³ Dhorme thinks that Bildad "raises the level of Job's anxiety to its highest point."¹⁴⁹⁴ Ewald observes that "Bildad is deeply offended and finds in Job a touch of madness."¹⁴⁹⁵ G. V. Garland surmises:

> The opening words of Bildad suggest the idea that he has interrupted Job, as he was describing his hopeless condition.¹⁴⁹⁶

Umbreit tells us that Bildad in the opening of ch. 18, "advances violently and arrogantly against Job, full of displeasure on account of empty speeches of his associates, and ascribes to him a deep and cutting wisdom."¹⁴⁹⁷

David Thomas observes that "Bildad has made similar observations in his first discourse in chapter eight."¹⁴⁹⁸ Davidson believes that several things in Job's last discourse have offended Bildad. Davidson goes on to enumerate these things:

1. Job has used very harsh words toward his friends, and has called them annoying comforters.
2. He spoke impiously of God, saying that he tore himself in anger.
3. He appeals to the earth and nature to rise up on his side.¹⁴⁹⁹

Robert Gordis, in *The Book of God and Man*, tells us this about the opening of Bildad's second discourse, "Job's misery invokes not one friendly word from Bildad. He feels keenly that he and his friends have been insulted."¹⁵⁰⁰ T. F. Royds argues that "Bildad protests against Job's discourse is one of the most passionate effusions of the phlegmatic speaker."¹⁵⁰¹ Scott says, "Bildad is manifestly aroused and expresses himself with great dignity and power."¹⁵⁰²

C. S. Rodd says, "Bildad condemns Job's complaints and tells him to be silent."¹⁵⁰³ George Noyes, in his 1843 commentary, says that Bildad "comes forward full of resentment against Job on account of the low estimation to which he held their discourses."¹⁵⁰⁴ Dhorme points out that the opening of ch. 18 is repeated by Job himself at 19:1–2.¹⁵⁰⁵ Both Duhm and Beer wish to eliminate vv. 2–3, in that it uses plural forms.¹⁵⁰⁶ Terrien observes that the plurals "may easily be explained as a dittograph."¹⁵⁰⁷

Driver and Gray have "beasts" in v. 3. They say, "unintelligent animals." They give Ps 73:22 as a parallel.¹⁵⁰⁸ Hartley thinks in v. 3, "Bildad particularly calls him out for speaking down to the friends."¹⁵⁰⁹ Newsom says that Bildad's objection that Job treats them like "cattle," is acute. She adds:

> Even though Job has not used such a term, he has ridiculed the herd mentality embedded in the clichéd and platitudinous language of the friends.¹⁵¹⁰

Kissane connects v. 4 to the previous verse, suggesting it should be "brute beasts who exhibit their wrath."¹⁵¹¹ E. C. S. Gibson believes v. 4 is "about the law of retribution fixed by God."[1512] Thus, a nod in the direction of retributive justice theory. Gibson adds:

> Job may rage and tear himself as he wills, but this law will remain powerful to rule over evil-doers.[1513]

Driver gives 2 Kgs 9:31 as a parallel for v. 4.[1514] Freehof says of v. 4, "Your wild words simply add to your miseries."[1515] Rashi believes the "rock being removed" is his Creator.[1516] Duhm says Bildad's emotions "run away with him."[1517] Fohrer deletes the first line of v. 4, suggesting it is a gloss.[1518] Hartley observes of v. 4, "Bildad renounces Job further with a biting rhetorical question."[1519]

18:5–10

Many of the verbs in these verses are in the passive voice. Bildad also employs the passive voice at 8:11–13, where he describes a plant that withers without water. The images of light and darkness to symbolize the righteous and the wicked are common in Wisdom Literature. (See 3:20; 10:21–22; 15:22; 17:13, for examples.) The expression, "The lamp of the wicked goes out," is also a traditional proverb for the Wisdom writers. It is employed at Prov 13:9; 20:20; and 24:10, for examples. Gregory the Great says, "The light of the wicked is put out because they quickly come to a great end."[1520] Rashi thinks v. 5 refers to the moral character of the wicked.[1521] Gersonides translates v. 5 this way:

> The light of their thoughts and their counsel is darkened, and therefore they walk in darkness in all that they do.[1522]

David Thomas tells us about the extinguished lamp, "Instead of having the lamp and fire of prosperity burning in his home, the dark, cold night will soon set in."[1523] Marvin Pope believes vv. 5–6 "reaffirm the dogma of retribution."[1524] C. S. Rodd thinks vv. 5–6 have to do with the importance placed on fire in the ancient world. He writes:

> In any age, when starting a fire was more difficult than striking a safety match, it was normal to keep a light permanently burning. The lamp became a symbol for well-being.[1525]

Olympiodorus says of vv. 7–10, "Bildad uses here the metaphor of birds or animals caught in a net."[1526] Thomas Aquinas observes, "The same way one is willing to put his foot in a net and prepare to be captured, so are those who throw themselves into sinning."[1527] Rashi says of these verses, "The rope is a trap with which he will be caught."[1528]

He continues:

> The trap is hidden in the path just as they hide the noose that eventually traps birds.[1529]

Hartley observes about vv. 8–10, "Bildad illustrates the fact that the wicked person is sure to stumble on the path he is taking by enumerating the many traps that are set for him."[1530]

Rowley says there develops in these verses "a thought of perils into which the wicked walks with firm and wide steps."[1531] Driver and Gray say what we have in vv. 8–10 is:

> The piling up of terms related to snares and traps, that indicates the strength of Bildad's conviction.[1532]

Jerome marks v. 9 with an asterisk. The expression "catch by the heel" reminds us of the birth of Jacob at Gen 25:26. Rowley gives Ps 18:5 as a parallel for v. 10. The same word for "rope" is used at Prov 5:22. The RSV has it as "toils," rather than rope. Dhorme says, "This is a rope that is destined to catch him. It denotes the act of stealing a gin."[1533]

18:11–21

The images of ch. 18 shift from hidden menace to agents of death and the underworld, represented as a group of hungry predators. Verse 11 describes the chase; v. 12, the cornering of the prey; vv. 13–14 describe the devouring of the prey by agents of death, in images reminiscent of the "hounds of Hell." Here they are called "the King of Terrors," and the "First-born son."

The LXX fuses v. 11b with v. 12a, to get a single sentence. The Vulgate gives a vague translation of v. 11, "*et involent pedes ejus.*"[1534] Driver says the meaning of v. 12 is, "Terrors shall make him afraid on every side, and shall chase him at his heels."[1535] Hesychius of Jerusalem suggests the words of v. 12 "are appropriate to the impious, but not to Job."[1536] Driver and Gray say the verb of v. 12b should be "famished."[1537] Habel personifies death in v. 13 as "the Hungry One." He renders the verse:

> The Hungry One shall be his strength. Calamity is ready as his escort. He consumes his skin with both hands. The First-Born Death consumes with both hands.[1538]

Gersonides says the meaning of v. 13 is, "His limbs shall be consumed by the most deadly of diseases."[1539] Rowley says of v. 13, "This is death in its most terrible form."[1540] Dhorme believes it refers to a plague demon.[1541] Marshall, "the worms of corruption."[1542] While Tur-Sinai translates v. 13 this way:

> He shall eat the strips of his hide; the starving First-Born shall eat his own flesh strips.[1543]

Newsom thinks v. 13 is a reference to the Ugaritic god Mot—the god of death.[1544] Rowley points out that the first word of v. 13 may be rendered "his iniquity" or "his trouble."[1545] Dhorme cites Le Hir and takes the first option, "His iniquity yawns before him."[1546] Many others have followed the second option, like Zockler, for example, who says, "His calamity shows itself hunger."[1547]

Rashi says the meaning of v. 14 is, "He will be torn away from his wife."[1548] He adds, "Although it literally says from his tent, it means his wife."[1549] Gersonides says of v. 14, "The insecurity of his tent shall make him flee into places where terror reigns."[1550] Driver and Gray say, "The wicked man is torn away from his home at death."[1551] Hartley believes, "The wicked man is torn from his secure tent, which has been the center of his security."[1552] Mezudat David, as well as other Jewish exegetes, believe that "Job will be torn from his wife."[1553] Rowley points out that the verb used in v. 14 is often employed in the pulling out of tent pegs.[1554] Thus, Ball renders the line, "His cords are broken away from his tent."[1555]

Chapter 18 shifts to images of annihilation in vv. 15–19. Driver and Gray say of v. 15, "After his death, the wicked man's house lies uninhabited and cursed."[1556] Gersonides says the house was not his "because it was obtained in robbery."[1557] Ibn Ezra observes about v. 15, "Strange animals and noxious weeds will roam and grow where formally he dwelt."[1558] Ehrlich thinks the use of "sulphur" in v. 15b is for "disinfectant purposes."[1559] Dhorme agrees, adducing testimony to show that the ancients knew of its disinfectant properties.[1560] Homer, in the *Odyssey*, has Ulysses demand sulphur so he can cleanse the room that has been sullied by corpses (sect. XXII).[1561] At v. 15, we may have a similar meaning.

The verbs of v. 16 are in the perfect tense. Reichert suggests v. 16 shows, "The entire family of the wicked that will perish." He gives Amos 2:9 as a parallel.[1562] Driver and Gray take a similar approach. They render v. 16 this way:

> The wicked man leaves no prosperity; his whole family perishes with him; consequently, he not only dies, he is also forgotten.[1563]

This is another version of retributive justice theory. Rowley says in v. 16, "Bildad returns to the comparison of the wicked with vegetative life."[1564] Ephrem the Syrian suggests the words of vv. 15–16, are about "the punishment of the impious that will resemble the punishment of the Sodomites."[1565] Ephrem uses the retributive justice theme here. Jerome marks v. 17 with an asterisk. The word for "street" in v. 17 may also mean "countryside." Julian of Eclanum, in reference to vv. 17–19, describes what will happen "to the impious in general, but also obliquely refers to Job, because he suffers these things under the scourge of God."[1566] Hartley observes that the meaning of v. 17 is, "The memory of the wicked person vanishes from the Earth."[1567]

Driver and Gray say:

> He is forgotten in the cultivated country, in which his own homestead and fields lay, and beyond where his animals were permitted to graze.[1568]

Driver and Gray think v. 18 "repeats the idea of 16:14 and 19."[1569] Rowley points out the verbs in v. 18 again are in the passive voice and are in the plural.[1570] Ball makes them singular and in the active voice.[1571] Thus, he gets, "He shall thrust Him," and understands the subject as God. In fact, Beer adds the word "God" to v. 18b for metrical reasons, or so he says.[1572]

Mezudat David says of v. 19:

> Among his people no son or grandson shall remain in the place where he lived.
> Some of them will die and some will go into captivity in another nation.[1573]

Ewald says v. 19 indicates that "the impious man has no place in the future."[1574] The same words of v. 19 are also found together at Gen 21:23. Reichert believes v. 19 to be an "alliterative proverb."[1575] Thus, Moffat has, "neither son nor scion."[1576] Ball suggests, "neither chit nor child."[1577] Tur-Sinai prefers, "neither breed nor broad."[1578] Rowley points out that the dread of having no descendants was "a much dreaded fate."[1579] He gives Deut 7:14 as a proof text.

The LXX is without v. 21. Julian of Eclanum says the meaning of vv. 20–21 is, "The memory of the wicked shall be lost."[1580] Gregory the Great thought v. 20 is a reference to the Anti-Christ, and v. 21, "to the quality of human hypocrisy."[1581] Thomas Aquinas says of these verses, "With respect to the ultimate end of the impious, it is either through disobedience or through disbelief that he does not know God."[1582]

Rashi thinks the "latter people" of these concluding verses are "those who do not witness the downfall of the wicked."[1583] David Thomas tells us this about the conclusion to ch. 18:

> This is the conclusion of the whole matter, and was aimed undoubtedly at Job. He means to say that all the wicked men must meet with a terrible end; you are wicked, and your end must be terrible.[1584]

Again, David Thomas assents here to the retributive justice motif. Schultens thinks the "easterners and westerners" of these verses are "two civilized parts of mankind, Occident and Orient."[1585] Francis Andersen says vv. 20–21 show "how preoccupied Bildad is with externals."[1586] The second hemstitch of v. 21 may be compared to 8:13a. Robert Gordis sums up the import of Bildad's second speech with these words: "Bildad proceeds to describe the punishment of the sinner, his person, his family, his very name, all will be destroyed."[1587] Perhaps this is a version of the collective retributive justice motif.

Much of contemporary scholarship on the end of ch. 18 agrees with C. S. Rodd's conclusion when he writes, "All we find in this chapter is a stern theology passionately defended."[1588] Driver and Gray say the meaning of v. 20 is, "The whole world is horrified at the wicked man's fate."[1589] About v. 21, they write:

> This verse clinches the argument implicit in the previous description of the wicked; such a fate, and none other, awaits the wicked.[1590]

C. S. Gibson believes the "day" in v. 20 is "the day of disaster, or the day of death."[1591] Budde thinks that Sheol is the subject matter of vv. 20–21.[1592] Rowley observes about v. 21:

> This verse summarily assures Job that the facts are as Bildad has stated them, and that wickedness and the fate of the wicked he has described are directly linked as cause and effect.[1593]

Newsom believes vv. 20–21 are related to other portions of the text. She observes:

> This description concludes by evoking the horrified reaction of the whole world to the spectacle of annihilation of the wicked (v. 20). Picking up the reference to habitation (*miskam*) (v. 15) and tent (*ohel*) (vv. 6, 14, and 15), Bildad uses these terms as metaphors for the existence of those "who do not know God."[1594]

Hartley takes a similar view of the closing of ch. 18. He says:

> Bildad closes with a summary statement marked off by the particle '*ak*, "Surely." Not to know God is to have no fellowship with God.[1595]

Chapter 19: Job Answers Bildad's Second Speech (Chapter 19:1–29)

Introduction

Samuel Terrien, Carol Newsom, and Matthew Henry all divide ch. 19 into three parts: vv. 1–7; vv. 8–22; and vv. 23–29. The latter of these three parts contains Job's proclamation of his *Goel*, or "blood avenger," a controversial and grammatically difficult passage, particularly vv. 25 and 26. Matthew Henry calls the first of these three parts of ch. 19, "Job Complains of Unkind Usage." The second section, Henry refers to as, "God Was the Author of His Affliction." "Job's Belief in the Resurrection" is the name that Henry gives to the closing section of ch. 19.[1596]

John Wycliffe, on the other hand, suggests that ch. 19 consists of two parts, vv. 1–22, "Job's Anger at His Friends," and vv. 23–29, "Job's Discovery of His Redeemer."[1597] In our analysis, we will follow Terrien, Newsom, and Henry. Chapter 19 also contains another mention of the Book of Deeds in v. 23. In vv. 21 and 22, we get more of a description of the symptoms of Job's disease; and v. 17 has the only other mention, besides at 2:9 and 31:10, to Job's spouse, or *ishah*, in the book.

Chapter 19 also contains a variety of nouns to signify God. *Eloah* is used three times; *El* is also employed three times; and if the *Goel*, or Redeemer, is God, then we have a seventh mention of the Divine, as well.

Analysis of Chapter 19

19:1–7

Rashi believes v. 2 is an expression of grief. The reference to "ten times" in v. 3, Rashi says, means this:

> This means Job's five addresses and the five addresses of his companions, two each by Eliphaz and Bildad, and one by Zophar.[1598]

John Wesley interprets the number ten as "many times." He adds, "a certain number for an uncertain."[1599] The LXX, as well as many other interpreters, read the singular *hirhiq* as "He makes distant," or "He alienates."[1600] Thus, they render the verb as a plural and as an intransitive, for there is no object. The Masoretic Text implies in v. 3 that God is the ultimate cause of Job's social isolation.

Bildad has begun both his speeches with "How long?" Job retorts by turning it against Bildad, as well as the other friends. Solomon Freehof renders v. 4, as, "And be it indeed that I have erred, mine error remains with myself."[1601] Rashi sees v. 4 to mean, "And even if I have indeed erred, let my error stay with me." Rashi adds:

> Even if I did possibly commit a sin, that sin is known only to me. Why then do you rebuke me? You cannot know my secrets.[1602]

Mezudat David, in his commentary, takes the same view of v. 4.[1603] The LXX extends v. 4 to make the verse a conditional sentence. These added words from the LXX are accepted by Beer, who says the verse is infinitely connected to vv. 5–9.[1604] Stevenson thinks v. 4 "is not likely to be correct" because of the extended Greek text.[1605] Rashi and Ibn Ezra, as well as the Targum, say of v. 5, "If you have added to my troubles, then you have shown and reprove me to my face."[1606] Ibn Ezra says it means, "My error is hidden deep within me, if indeed I have erred, then how can you know it to rebuke me?"[1607] Freehof follows Rashi on v. 5 to say the verse means, "You add your abuse to my grief."[1608] Mezudat David says that v. 5b means:

> You wish to prove that I have sinned, as evidence by the fact of his suffering.[1609]
> About v. 6, he adds, "Your contention is untrue, but you who are debating with me should know that God is preventing my cause."[1610] Mezudat David adds about v. 6: Even the net that he has spread around me to trap me is unjust, and is not for any sin that I have committed.[1611]

Bildad uses the same verb at v. 6 at 8:3. Freehof thinks the import of v. 6 is, "You blame me for sins which you say I have committed, but I say that God has done me an injustice, and He gives me no opportunity to prove that I am innocent."[1612] Rashi says the meaning of v. 7 is, "I cry out, but I am not answered."[1613] Wesley takes a similar view of the verse. He observes, "Behold, I cry out of wrong, but I am not heard. I cry aloud, but there is no judgment."[1614] The LXX and Vulgate begin v. 7 with "Behold," or

Hen! in Hebrew, while the Peshitta makes it a conditional and thus, uses *'im* or "If," to begin the line. Dhorme renders v. 7 this way:

> If I cry out, "Violence," I receive no reply. In vain do I cry for help, there is no judgment.[1615]

19:8–22

The LXX translates the beginning of v. 8 as, "He has blocked my way so that I cannot get through."[1616] Dhorme gives a similar rendering for v. 8a.[1617] Rowley has it, "walled up my way." He gives Lam 3:7–9 and Hos 2:6 as parallels. He also observes that the verse is like 3:23; 13:27; and 14:5, where "Job has complained about restrictions which hemmed him in."[1618] Rowley adds, "At 1:10, the Satan had spoken of protective barriers raised by God around Job."[1619]

About v. 9, Rowley tells us:

> God has stripped Job of the honorable reputation that he once enjoyed, and has removed from his head the crown which serves as a metaphor for the esteem in which he was once held. Honor is a garment to be worn or stripped off.[1620]

Dhorme renders v. 9:

> Of my glory he has stripped me, and the crown he has removed from my head.[1621]

Wesley says the "glory" to which Job refers is "his estate, children, authority, and all his comforts."[1622] Mezudat David has v. 9 as, "He has stripped me of my honor and removed the crown from my head." He adds, "and I am humiliated." He says:

> Some interpret this to mean that Job has lost his money, others that he was branded by his friends as a sinner.[1623]

The *Ohev Mishpat* takes a similar view. Rashi believes v. 10 is an "expression of uprooting." Stevenson says that v. 10 is "barely coherent." He observes, "He demolished me all around" cannot be well understood of Job's personal fate, although it might describe the attacks on his home and land.[1624] The verb in v. 10 has been interpreted to mean "to perish" from the Arabic *halak*, but that "would not adequately describe Job's present condition."[1625]

Stevenson suggests, therefore, that v. 10 be moved to stand after v. 12.[1626] The Peshitta gives an alternative understanding of v. 10. "He has uprooted me from all of my surroundings, and removed my hopes like a tree."[1627]

Freehof renders v. 12 this way:

> His troops come together, and cast their way against me. And encamp around about my tent.[1628]

Freehof says of this verse, "Here he repeats the description of God's attack that he used in the answer to Eliphaz at 16:13–14, namely the picture of himself as a besieged city and God as his Attacker."[1629] Mezudat David renders v. 12 this way:

> Together His troops advance, they build their road against me, and they camp around my tent.[1630]

He explains this rendering this way:

> All the troops of His pains advance and go on a paved road, none of them turning off. Instead, they camped around my tent and did not leave immediately.[1631]

Mezudat David says the proper interpretation of v. 13 is, "He has distanced my brothers from me." He further observes about v. 13:

> The troops of pain distance themselves my relatives from me because they considered me a sinner, to be evidence by these pains.[1632]

Rowley translates v. 13 as:

> He has put my brethren far from me, and my acquaintances are wholly estranged from me.[1633]

Rowley points out that "many editors follow this approach."[1634] The LXX has apparently read one word, 'akzaru, as two words, ak zaru, and has understood it as a denominative from akzar, or "cruel." But the verb as it stands is not used elsewhere. Most interpreters point out that the first two words of v. 15 should be joined to v. 14, or so say Beer, Bickell, Duhm, and Peake.[1635] Rowley points out that the KJV has v. 14, "My kinfolk have failed, and my familiar friends have forgotten me." He observes, "This first line is thus short and v. 15 is over-loaded."[1636]

Rowley adds:

> Most modern editors redivide to yield four normal lines in two verses, as the RSV does. For the first line then Duhm proposes to read, "My kinfolk has ceased to know me," which Peake and Strahan approve, but Gray and Dhorme reject. As divided the verses are excellently balanced.[1637]

John Wesley gives a very different translation of v. 15. He has it, "They that dwell in mine house, and my maids, count me for a stranger. I am an alien in their sight."[1638] He adds about these maids, "who, by reason of their sex, commonly have more compassionate hearts than men."[1639]

Rowley interprets v. 16 to mean, "Instead of Job's slaves obeying the slightest sign of his hand, they ignore his wishes when he humbles himself to implore them to attend to him."[1640]

About v. 16, Dhorme observes:

The servant must be ready to obey the slightest sign [Ps 123:2]. But here the roles are reversed. The servant does not condescend to answer. Job is obliged to humiliate himself, to beseech in vain.[1641]

Rowley renders v. 17 this way:

I am repulsive to my wife, loathsome to the sons of my own mother.[1642]

Rowley takes this to mean, "My breathe is strange." Rowley adds of v. 17:

The verb is probably to be connected to a different root, meaning, "to be loathsome." For "my breathe" Beer needlessly proposes to read, with a slight change, "my smell."[1643]

Habel points out that *ruhi*, literally "my wind" or "my spirit" has been rendered "my breathe" (Dhorme); "my odor" (Driver and Gray); "my desire, passion" (Gordis); and "my sighing" (Tur-Sinai).[1644]

Habel continues:

Presumably the Driver and Gray rendering was based on the suggestion of G. Beer that we vocalize the MT as *rehi*, or "my smell." It is preferable, however, to retain the "spirit/breathe" connotation. It is more than Job's smell that is repulsive to his wife.[1645]

Wesley renders v. 18 this way:

Yea, young children despised me; I arose and they spake against me.[1646]

About "arose," Wesley remarks, "From my seat, to shew my respect to them, though they were my inferiors."[1647] Dhorme says the meaning of v. 18 is, "When Job rises to leave the company, the youngsters begin to jeer at his company."[1648] Rashi remarks about v. 18, "I was despised in the eyes of children, surely in the eyes of princes."[1649] Wesley translates v. 19 this way:

All my inward friends abhorred me; and they whom I have loved have turned against me.[1650]

About the word "skin," Wesley observes, "Immediately, the fat and flesh next to the skin being consumed."[1651] Rashi says Job's bones are cleaved "because I am emaciated from the thickness of my flesh."[1652] He adds, "All his skin was afflicted with boils and worms except his gums."[1653] Mezudat David and Isaiah di Trani agree with this view by saying, "I escaped complete affliction only by the gums, which were left unaffected."[1654] Moses Maimonides explains the end of v. 20 by saying:

I escaped total extinction by the skin of my teeth with which I chew. He had no more teeth with which to chew, only the skin at the base of his teeth.[1655]

Freehof thinks "by the skin of his teeth" may well be a proverbial phrase, as were the words of Satan in the prologue, "skin for skin."[1656] Gersonides agrees with this approach.[1657] Szold says, "I have been wasting away, and if I am still alive, it is due only to a little food I could masticate with my gums."[1658]

Verse 20 has a number of difficulties in the Hebrew text. The first hemstitch is much too long, for the bones to cleave to the skin (Lam 4:8), or to the flesh (Ps 102:6), but not to both at once.[1659] Le Hir proposes to see these affects as the "result of fever."[1660] Mezudat David thinks that Job asks in v. 21 for his friends "to have pity on him." He says:

> You, my friends, and do not continue to disgrace me, because the hand of God has touched me, and that pain suffices.[1661]

Sforno believes the import off v. 21 is, "Supplicate for me, my friends, who are closer to me than brothers."[1662] Freehof observes about vv. 21 and 22:

> He pleads with his friends to stop giving him the traditional arguments as proof that he is a sinner, to stop merely acting as a vehicle of tradition, but to act as sympathetic friends and to have pity for his misery. God is persecuting him for whatever mysterious reasons He has, but why should not his own friends have pity on him?[1663]

Mezudat David says the meaning of v. 22 is Job asking, "Why do you persecute me like God? Why do you hurt me by disgracing me?"[1664] Strahan says of v. 22, "The whole tragedy of the book is packed into these extraordinary words. Job's complaint of his friends is they are too God-like."[1665] Wesley takes another approach to v. 22. He says Job asks, "Why do you persecute me as God, and are not satisfied with my flesh?"[1666] He says of "not satisfied," "They are like wolves or lions that are not content with devouring the flesh of their prey, but also breaks their bones."[1667]

19:23–29

This pericope is one of the most famous, and the most difficult, in the book, for it contains the celebrated *Goel*, or Redeemer, passage at vv. 25–27. Before we get there, however, at vv. 23 and 24, Job asks three times for a written work, some written evidence of his genuine righteousness. The first two of these is are in v. 23, that Freehof renders as, "Oh that my words were now written, oh that they were inscribed in a book."[1668] Freehof goes on to explain his translation:

> With neither friends nor God on his side, who can do justice to him? Perhaps no one can do justice for him in the present. If that is so, perhaps there is hope that justice will come in the future. So he wishes that his cause was written in a book or engraved with metal upon a rock.[1669]

Job may be referring to the Hebrew tradition of a "Book of Deeds," in which the activities of all people are written in a book by God. (See Rev 20:12.) Dhorme thinks by v. 23, "May this be recorded for future generations to come."[1670] He says in regard to v. 24, "The material on which the engraving is done is not lead but brass and rock, for the inscription must last forever."[1671] Habel says, "The noun *sepher*, that normally means 'book,' probably has the meaning here of inscription, stela, or monument."[1672] He gives Isa 30:8 as a parallel, where *sepher* is parallel with *luah*, or "tablet."[1673] Habel adds, "This rendering is supported by the context."[1674] About v. 24, Habel describes some of the difficulties:

> The precise recording process described here is in dispute. Driver and Gray argue that "lead" refers to a lead tablet on which the inscription is made, a process known to ancient classical authors. The suggestion made by Rashi that lead was poured into letters incised in the stone to form an inlaid inscription has been attested by the inscription of Darius at Behistun.[1675]

Rowley observes about v. 23, "Job is thinking of the protestation of his innocence, which he longs to be preserved after his death."[1676] Tur-Sinai says v. 24 refers to "a plaque of iron and lead."[1677] C. R. Conder takes the meaning in v. 24 to be "red lead," and that the reference refers to letters being painted red after they have been incised.[1678] Stevenson thinks v. 23 refers to the Assyrian *siparru* (bronze or copper), "because of it being combined with engrave, and because the inscription would be a more permanent record than writing in a book."[1679] Both Dhorme and Holscher accept this argument.[1680]

Stevenson says the probable meaning of the clause in v. 24a, "with a pen of iron on lead," is a more clear rendering than the Masoretic Text. Theodosius has it, "with an iron pen and lead."[1681] The Peshitta, "with an iron pen and stylus of lead," and the Vulgate, "with an iron pen and a sheet of lead."[1682] Mezudat David describes v. 23 this way:

> Who will give me a man, and where is the one who will do it, so that my words will be written, etc.[1683]

About v. 24, Mezudat David observes:

> That they will melt lead and pour it into the grooves to preserve the script for posterity. Thus, future generations could judge who was right, for Job's friends did him great harm by continually accusing him of neglecting his study of God.[1684]

In the midst of Job's second response to Bildad, at vv. 25–27, Job voices a hope that has become the object of a good deal of disagreement in Judaism and Christianity. The relevant passage is rendered this way in the RSV:

> For I know that my Redeemer lives, and at last he will stand upon the earth;
> And after my skin has been destroyed, then without my flesh I will see God,

> Whom I shall see on my side, and my eyes shall behold, and not another. My heart faints within me.[1685]

Christian commentators from very early on have come to see this pericope as an Old Testament precursor of Christ, as well as a confirmation of survival after death, specifically resurrection of the body. It has been used in the traditional, Christian burial service, for example, because of its supposed simple surety about resurrection. But to gain some sense of what this text may have meant for those who wrote it, we must return to two other places where Job calls for assistance. In the first round of speeches, Job calls for a *mokiah*, or "arbiter," who might serve as a judge between him and his adversary (9:32–33). In the second round, at 16:19, Job's longing becomes a conviction that somewhere there is an *'edh*, or "witness," who is ready to testify on his behalf:

> Even now, in fact, my witness is in heaven, and he that vouches for me is on high.[1686]

Finally, now at 19:25–26, the longing and conviction becomes a desire for a "blood avenger," or *Goel*, who in early Judaism was duty-bound to see that justice was done for a member of his family or clan. Second Samuel 14:11, gives us a good indication of how the term *Goel* was employed by writers in Israel in the sixth century BCE. This text tells us:

> Then she said, "Pray, let the king invoke the Lord your God, that the avenger of blood [the *Goel*], slay no more, and my son not be destroyed."[1687]

In this passage a woman wishes to spare her son from the swift and sure vengeance of the *Goel*. But it is significant that here the RSV translates the word as "blood avenger." It is also clear, we believe, that the *Goel* is to be a human being. The temptation to make the *Goel* a supernatural character, or even a god, as a hidden reference to Jesus, is perhaps, quite great. But nowhere else in the Hebrew Bible is the word *Goel* used to describe anyone other than a person who seeks revenge for some wrong done to a member of his family or clan.

David Clines, in his recent commentary, has suggested that Job's *mokiah*, *edh*, and *Goel*, may, in fact, be Job himself. He says that Job, above all else, is his best "own witness." So, at least for Clines, the arbiter, the witness, and the redeemer is nothing more than the patriarch himself, the Man from Uz, speaking of his own salvation.[1688]

As it stands, the Hebrew of v. 25b is quite corrupted. There appears to be a preposition missing. As it stands it reads this way:

> That he the last shall stand upon the Earth.[1689]

This has led many translators to add "at" between "he" and "the." Whether or not this is a wise insertion, or whether it is the only possible insertion, are matters of some debate. Verse 26 suffers from even more profound textual difficulties. As Samuel Terrien puts the matter:

> Verse 26 is in a state of textual corruption which defies the resources of exegesis. The Hebrew view of the Masoretic text is syntactically incoherent.[1690]

A literal reading of v. 26a gives us something like this:

> And after my skin they have peeled off [or mutilated] this [feminine pronoun] (she/her).[1691]

We think that Terrien is essentially correct about v. 26. Any reconstruction of this pericope, at least on the basis of the Hebrew, is ultimately a matter of a series of guesses. Any translation of vv. 25–27 will tell us far more about the exegete than it does the Hebrew text. The Babylonian Talmud (sect. 16a) contains a number of views that show that in these verses "Job denied the resurrection of the dead."[1692] The LXX renders vv. 25–26 this way:

> I know that my Redeemer lives,
> And that in the end he will stand upon the Earth,
> And after my skin has been destroyed
> Yet in my skin I shall see God.[1693]

The KJV translates vv. 25–26 in a slightly different way. It gives us:

> For I know that my Redeemer liveth, and that he shall stand at the latter day upon the Earth. And though after my skin worms destroy this body, yet in my flesh I shall see God. Whom I shall see for myself, and mine eyes shall behold, and not another, though my reins be consumed within me.[1694]

Clement of Rome, in the first century CE, sees Job 19:25–27 as a proof text for resurrection of the body.[1695] Jerome, as well, tells us this passage "proves the hope and reality of resurrection."[1696] Jerome assents here to the *Jobus Christi* and the resurrected Job motifs. Indeed, about v. 26, Jerome suggests:

> When all flesh shall see the salvation of God, and Jesus as God, then I also shall see Him, and no stranger, the Redeemer and Savior, and my God.[1697]

The Vulgate renders the *Goel* passage as "*Redemptor meus*."[1698] Most Christian exegetes to the eighteenth century also gave this understanding of 19:25–27. In Judaism, on the other hand, this view is not adopted. Saadiah Gaon, for example, says the *Goel* "refers to a human being, rather than to a God."[1699] Gersonides takes the position of the Talmud that "Job did not believe in the resurrection, but since he lived before the time of the Torah, there is no reason to expect he would have known it."[1700] Rashi observes about v. 25:

This *vav* refers to the above. You persecute me, but I know that my Redeemer lives to requite me, and he will endure and rise. After all earthly dwellers have perished, He will endure and last.[1701]

In the Christian tradition, the pericope continued to be read as a prophecy of the resurrection. Thomas Aquinas, for example, says that "Job knows his Redeemer that lives through the certitude of his faith." He adds, "Now this glory is the hope for a future resurrection."[1702] Like Jerome, Thomas also assents here to the *Jobus Christi* as well as the resurrected Job motifs. Before Thomas, both John Chrysostom and Ephrem the Syrian saw the *Goel* passage in similar ways. Ephrem observes, "Here the blessed Job predicts the future manifestations of Emmanuel in the flesh at the end of time."[1703] John Chrysostom tells us this about vv. 25–27:

> Notice the state of the soul of those in distress; they want not only those who are seeing these events now, but also those who will come later, to be witnesses of their own misfortune. Did Job know the doctrine of the resurrection? I believe so.[1704]

Clearly, Chrysostom, Ephrem, and Thomas Aquinas were all advocates of the resurrected Job motif, as well as the *Jobus Christi* image. This also was true in general of ancient and medieval Christian views of the Man from Uz and his book. Job 19:25–27 has been extensively employed in European music from the seventeenth and eighteenth centuries. Heinrich Schutz's *Geistliche chormusik* made the passage the centerpiece of his cantatas.[1705] Handel's *Messiah* and its contralto aria, "I Know That My Redeemer Liveth," is on Handel's grave at Westminster Abbey.[1706] Georg Phillip Schutz uses vv. 25–26 as a confirmation of the resurrection.[1707] And F. G. Klopstock's *Der Messias*, first published in 1748, also sees that the *Goel* passage has a similar function.

The passage has also inspired a number of other pieces of Christian art. One of the finest of these is Vittore Carpaccio's *Meditation on the Passion*. It is a tempera on wood painting, completed around 1495. It was designed to explore the relationship of Job's suffering to that of Jesus Christ.[1708] Another work of Carpaccio, entitled *Job and the Dead Christ*, explores the same theme. It is also a tempera on wood painting, completed sometime between 1505 and 1510.[1709] Another fine piece of art inspired by Job 19:25–27 is Koren der Harootian's *Job Standing Erect*, a 1950 sculpture.[1710]

In more modern, Christian scholarship from the eighteenth century to the present, we may find the same Redeemer as Christ view, in John Wesley, for example.[1711] But one also begins to see a change in the interpretation of the *Goel* passage in the nineteenth century. Wesley says of v. 25:

> The word *Goel* here used properly agrees to Jesus Christ, for this word is primarily used of the next kinsman whose office it was to redeem by a price paid, that sold or mortgaged estate of his deceased kinsman; to revenge his death, and to maintain his name and honor, by raising up seed to him. All which more fully agrees to Christ, Who is our nearest kinsman and brother.[1712]

Some nineteenth-century Christian interpreters continue the view that the *Goel* passage is a "*Jobus Christi*" understanding of the text in question. G. H. A. Ewald, for example, observes, "This is the undoubted utterance of the truth of the higher hope which looks joyfully beyond physical death into the immortality of the soul."[1713] Samuel Davidson agrees. He writes:

> This passage expresses a hope of immortality. In it the Spirit of Job pierces beyond Sheol into the future, confidently looking for a vision of God to vindicate his righteousness.[1714]

A number of other nineteenth-century exegetes take other views about the passage in question. Joseph Jacobs, in his 1896 commentary, traces the history of the passage and says it has a "savage origin." He adds, "The Church and Synagogue recognized the principle of survival of the fittest, long before modern biology."[1715] Arthur Peake thinks the purpose of the passage is to show that Job will be vindicated and found innocent. Peake observes:

> This reaches its climax in the famous passage, 19:25ff., in which Job expresses his conviction that his vindicator lives, and that his innocence will be at last established. And though he does not look forward to a vindication in this lifetime, yet he believes that he will be permitted to know that his character is cleared.[1716]

Charles Walkley also likens the Redeemer passage of 19:25–27 to the "triumphant entry of Jesus Christ into the city of Jerusalem."[1717] John, Bishop of Fredericton agrees.[1718] These, of course, are other applications of the *Jobus Christi* motif we have introduced back in the introduction.

Albert Barnes, in his 1847 commentary, takes a more neutral view of the passage. He observes, "There are few passages in the Bible which have excited more attention than this . . . or in respect to which the opinions of expositors have been more divided."[1719] William Kelly, in his 1875 commentary, also takes a neutral approach to the Redeemer passage. He writes:

> Then does the truth of God's intervention at the end flash so brightly. Before his soul . . . He knows his Kinsman-Redeemer lives, and, the Last One shall stand on the dust; and no matter what the ravages of this mortal, from his flesh he shall see Eloah—see Him for himself.[1720]

George R. Noyes, and many other nineteenth-century Christian interpreters, think the Redeemer passage is about vindication. Noyes remarks, "What Job longs for in this passage is a vindication of his character by God."[1721] But F. R. Budde disagrees. He says, "This passage contains no reference to God's appearance after Job is dead."[1722] K. Kautzsch, on the other hand, in his 1876 commentary, suggests, "This line means Job's vindication is to take place before his death."[1723]

Francis Andersen, in his commentary, concentrates on the difficulties of the passage. He says:

> This passage is notoriously difficult. Much depends on the authenticity and meaning of its central affirmation, "My Redeemer lives." Unfortunately, it is followed by several lines which are so unintelligible that the range of translations offered are bewildering.[1724]

Ernest Renan takes a much more neutral approach to interpreting 19:25–27. He writes:

> Whatever form he gives his belief, whatever symbol he employs to invest his affirmations of the future, the just man has the right to say with the old patriarch from Idumea, "Yes, I know that my redeemer liveth and that he will appear in the latter days upon the Earth."[1725]

Twentieth-century interpreters of 19:25–27, for the most part, have argued against the resurrection understanding of the passage in question. H. H. Rowley says of the passage, "This is one of the most cryptic passages in the book, and both text and interpretation are far from clear."[1726] Robert Gordis has this to say about the *Goel* passage:

> In a moment of mystic ecstasy, he sees his vindication through a redeemer, who will act to revenge his suffering. The term he uses, *goel*, means a kinsman, a blood avenger, who in earlier Hebrew law, was duty bound to see that justice was done by his aggrieved brother.[1727]

Elsewhere, in the same book, Gordis adds:

> By and large, the idea that Job is referring here to the afterlife is finding less and less favor among commentators.[1728]

Edwin Good, in his 1990 commentary, also takes a negative view of the Redeemer passage. He says:

> The central word is not "redeemer," and it especially is not "Redeemer." Some may not distinguish the former from the latter.[1729]

Mezudat David says about v. 27, "All these sores are plainly visible at all, but what I alone see is that my kidneys are consumed within me."[1730] Nahmanides says of v. 27:

> From the fact that my flesh is consumed and I am still alive, I perceive the power of God over His creatures, that He brings man to the point of being crushed.[1731]

Stevenson says about v. 27:

> Too much has been read into the Hebrew of this clause by those who make no change in the wording. The bare word "kidneys" does not specify the kind of

emotion or feeling that has its seat in the kidneys (whether longing, or joy, or sorrow).[1732]

Renan renders v. 28, "And the right will be found on my side."[1733] Le Hir has it, "You who flatter yourselves that you have found me guilty."[1734] Crampon and Segond prefer, "And the justice of my cause will be recognized."[1735] Habel points out that the opening *ma*, or "How" of v. 28 could be an interrogatory or an exclamation, but the meaning of the verse is much the same.[1736]

Habel also points out that v. 29 has been problematical and has been variously rendered, "for wrath brings the punishment of the sword" (RSV); "The sword that sweeps away all iniquity" (NEB); "For yours are crimes deserving the sword" (Gordis); "For wrath will destroy the ungodly" (Duhm).[1737] Some scholars read *hemma*, or "these things," for *hema*, "wrath" or "anger." The "these things" probably refer back to the actions of the friends.[1738]

Other nineteenth-century Christian interpreters point to the many textual difficulties of the passage in question. John Edgar McFadyen, for example, in his *The Problem of Pain*, remarks:

> The obscurity of the original is seen in the intrusion of the very important and conceivably misleading words.[1739]

Stevenson observes about v. 29c, "There is no logical connections between this clause and the rest of the verse. Possibly it depends on a principal clause now lost."[1740] Ewald, Ball, and Wright read *Shaddai* for *saddin*.[1741] Fohrer translates it as, "That you may know there is a Judge."[1742] Ewald, Wright, and Ball prefer, "That you shall know Shaddai."[1743] Dhorme defends the translation of the RSV that gives us:

> Be afraid of the sword,
>
> For wrath brings the punishments of the sword
>
> That you may know there is a judgment.[1744]

The preposition "from" employed in v. 26 is ambiguous. It may also mean "in" or "without," though the latter meaning is not attested elsewhere in the Hebrew Bible where a verb of perception is used. Job still regards death as imminent given the present state of his body being rapidly destroyed by disease. John Wycliffe suggests that the *Goel* passage indicates that "God is his Kinsman," rather than a "stranger."[1745]

Chapter 20: Zophar's Second Speech (Chapter 20:1–29)

Introduction

In his first speech (ch. 11), Zophar reiterated the doctrine of retributive justice, and suggested that Job actually deserves more punishment than he has received (11:6b). Zophar also speaks at length about the inability of human beings to understand the mysteries of God, a sort of bow to the divine plan point of view. In ch. 11, Zophar concluded with an exhortation for Job to repent, so that his life might again have an upswing. This second speech of Zophar, ch. 20, adds little that is new theologically. Retribution and the fate of the wicked remain important themes in this chapter.

Chapter 20 is most often divided into three sections: vv. 1–9; vv. 10–22; and vv. 23–29. Matthew Henry refers to the first section as, "The Short Joy of the Wicked." The second section as, "Ruin of the Wicked," and the final section by the name, "Portion of the Wicked."[1746] Most modern exegetes also divide ch. 20 the same way. H. H. Rowley introduces Zophar's second speech of ch. 20 this way:

> Hot to take up the argument, Zophar bursts out in passionate and intemperate speech to dwell on the brevity of the prosperity of the wicked and the retribution he [Job] brings on himself.[1747]

Strahan says of the speech, "Every syllable of his remorseless invective, whether true or false in the abstract, is tragically irrelevant and cruelly unjust in its application."[1748] Strahan adds, "He is sure that God is as hot and impatient as himself, for when the zealot makes his own opinions and sentiments the standard of divinity."[1749] Rowley adds about Zophar, "There is a magnified Zophar on the throne of the universe."[1750]

Chapter 20 also contains a number of theological responses to the cause of Job's suffering. Verse 5 suggests retributive justice theory; v. 19 indicates the free will defense; and vv. 28 and 29 look much like the divine plan view.

The word for "food" at the end of v. 23 is the Hebrew *basar*, or "flesh." The same noun is employed in v. 14. At the close of ch. 20, the Divine is called *El* three times in vv. 28 and 29. At v. 8 of ch. 20, we see another of the many visions and dreams that are alluded to in the book. Also see: 4:12–21; 7:13–14; 20:8; and 33:14–18.

Analysis of Chapter 20

20:1–9

Peake thinks that the idea of a colloquy between Zophar and his thoughts is an artificial one.[1751] Duhm proposes that v. 2 should read, "My thoughts disturb me," and Strahan and Gray follow. Kissane prefers, "My thoughts appall me," while Dhorme renders it, "My thoughts bring me back."[1752] Rashi has it, "My thoughts cause me to answer." He adds:

> My thoughts will answer me with a reply in my mouth, and because I keep my peace and remain silent, as I put my silence within me, my thoughts will then give their reply.[1753]

The poet of Job employs three separate words for "thought" and "thoughts." The first of these is *mowrash*, which is used at 17:11. The second is *machashabah*, that can be found at 21:27. The third classical Hebrew term for "thoughts" is *ca'if*, pronounced *saw'if*. The Job poet uses it at 4:13 and 20:2, for examples.

At any rate, Mezudat David begins v. 3 with the words, "The chastisement of my disgrace." He says it means, "A desire arising from my understanding, compels me to answer."[1754] The LXX translates v. 4a as part of v. 2b, thus vv. 2b to 3 were omitted in the Greek text. Duhm renders v. 3, "And you answer me by wind without understanding."[1755] Ehrlich has it, "An impulse of my understanding prompts me to reply."[1756] The RSV's "I have censure which insults me" is preferable to the KJV: "putteth me to shame."

The Masoretic Text begins v. 4 with, "Do you know this from of old?" The RSV adds a *lo*, or "not," to get, "Do you not know from of old?" The Peshitta and the Vulgate are both without the "not." Kissane takes v. 4 to be the "utterance of the inner voice which speaks to Zophar."[1757] Zophar follows the lead of Bildad (8:8) and Eliphaz (15:18–19) in appealing to the wisdom of the fathers motif. Habel points out that in v. 5, "Zophar cites a standard doctrine on the brevity of happiness for the wicked."[1758] Rashi says of that happiness, "In a short time, it will end."[1759] Rowley gives Ps 37:18ff. as a parallel text to v. 5.[1760] Dhorme thinks the meaning of v. 5 is, "The relation of the wicked is near, in the sense that it is a phenomenon that does not cover a long distance."[1761] Strahan says of v. 6, "It is not Zophar's sermon against pride that makes him a false prophet, but his application of it to Job."[1762] Rowley gives Amos 9:2 and Isa 14:13ff. as parallels for v. 6.[1763] Habel observes about Zophar's comment in v. 6:

> The hubris of the wicked compels them to reach for the Heavens, where God dwells in his glory, or for the clouds which he mounts in theophanic splendor.[1764]

Habel adds about v. 6, "Zophar's comment is an insulting innuendo that Job's greatness derives from his lust for power."[1765] Mezudat David says v. 6 is "an allegory representing great prosperity."[1766] Driver says in v. 6, "Zophar claims to speak out of his understanding, not to utter empty words."[1767]

Freehof thinks the meaning of v. 7 is, "After the wicked has disappeared, he will immediately be forgotten."[1768] Driver points out that v. 7 is in the present tense, "does perish," as opposed to the RSV that has it, "will perish."[1769] Rashi says what is perishing in v. 7 is "dung."[1770] Ibn Ezra agrees. He tells us:

> He will perish forever, like his dung which quickly disappears, and those who saw his prosperity will say, "Where is he? No trace will remain of him."[1771]

Mezudat David says the import of v. 7 is this:

> He will become very successful and then suddenly he will become as repulsive as dung.[1772]

The Peshitta has "like a whirlwind," rather than "like his dung."[1773] Alter has, "like his turd." Ewald has it, "according to his greatness." Dhorme, "like a ghost."[1774] The "Where is he?" of v. 7 reminds us of 14:10. Habel says of this section, "Ironic barbs adorn Zophar's portrait."[1775] Saadiah renders v. 7, "Still, at their furling would he be lost utterly." He believes the rolling up is like the scroll at Isa 34:4.[1776] The noun at the end of v. 7 is *gaylel*, a word that usually means "dung," as Ezek 4:12 shows. It comes from *gelel*, "to spoil," or "to soil."

Saadiah Gaon has this for v. 8:

> Like a dream, shall he fly, and they shall find him not, restless as a vision of the night.[1777]

Dhorme believes vv. 8–9 develop the idea contained in v. 7. He gives Isa 29:7 as a parallel text.[1778] Mezudat David observes about v. 8:

> He is like a dream which flies away when the person awakens. So will he fly away from the world, and no one will find him.[1779]

Stevenson points out that the LXX's rendering of vv. 8–9 are a paraphrase.[1780] Rowley gives Ps 73:20 and Isa 29:7 as parallels for v. 8, and Ps 103:16 for v. 9.[1781] Verse 9 is marked with an asterisk by Jerome.[1782] Duhm says that v. 9 is a paraphrase of v. 7b and a quotation of v. 10.[1783] The verb *sazap* also occurs at 28:7. The KJV and RSV render it as "scorched," but in v. 9 it is used as a synonym of *sadap*, or "blighted," also found at Gen 41:6.

20:10–22

Freehof points out that the two clauses of v. 10 would read better if they were in reverse order. He says:

> His own hands will have to restore his (stolen) wealth, and after his death his children will also need to appease the poor whom he has robbed during his lifetime.[1784]

Tur-Sinai believes that it involves more than simply "appease." The children will have to work out their father's embezzlements by laboring like slaves for the poor, whom he had robbed.[1785] Budde agrees. He suggests adding one letter to get, "his children," which would improve the parallel with "his sons."[1786]

Rowley translates v. 11a as "His bones are filled with youthful vigor," meaning, "He will die prematurely full of the sins of his youth."[1787] Rashi has it, "His bones are full of his youth." He adds, "This means the strength of his youth."[1788] Rashi renders v. 11b as, "And he will lie on the dust with him."[1789] Rashi says of the line, "because he will die suddenly with his strength."[1790]

Freehof translates v. 12 this way:

> Though wickedness be sweet in his mouth,
>
> Though he hides it under his tongue.[1791]

Freehof says the meaning of v. 12b is, "It tastes so sweet to him that he does not want to swallow it."[1792] Rowley believes, "It is hidden in his mouth as long as possible, so as to extract the maximum pleasure from its taste."[1793] Rashi says the sweetness "refers to the custom of the wicked man":

> If evil is sweet in his mouth and he does not see now the moment when it was to take effect.[1794]

Dhorme says this about vv. 12–15:

> The images contained in this description of the wicked man relishing the sweets of his sin well conveys the idea of this gloomy pleasure. Evil is like a sweet that the guilty man lingerly sucks, and which he keeps under his tongue and on his palate until he has savored its delights to the full.[1795]

Rashi believes the import of v. 14 is that, "His food will turn into the venom of the cobra, within him."[1796] Mezudat David observes about v. 14:

> His punishment will be that his food will turn over in his innards in an unusual way—by vomiting. It will be like snake venom in his stomach, and he will perforce vomit it up because it is indigestible. The intention is that in all his undertakings, he will stumble in unusual ways.[1797]

Rashi says of v. 15, "Although he swallowed up the wealth, it will not remain in his possession. He will vomit it up and God will cast it out of his belly."[1798] Rowley says of v. 15, "The figure of God administering the emetic is coarse and powerful, as befits Zophar."[1799] Habel says the meaning of v. 15 is, "The meal eaten with relish leads to food poisoning."[1800] He says in the verse, *El* is introduced "as the decisive punitive power."[1801] He gives Deut 32:35 as a parallel text. Stevenson believes v. 16 should follow v. 13, "to which it gives a better sequence" than v. 14. He says, "After its removal, vv. 15, 17, and 18 run in harmonious sequence."[1802] Freehof renders v. 16 this way: "He shall suck the poison of asps; the viper's tongue shall slay him."[1803] For v. 17, he translates:

> He shall not look upon the rivers,
>
> The flowing stream of honey and curd.[1804]

Freehof thinks the "honey and curd" refer back to the sweetness in v. 12.[1805] Rashi says v. 17 "refers to the rivers of Paradise."[1806] He observes:

> The wicked will not be privileged to behold them. But as the verse stands it means that he will not long enjoy the rivers of the Earth, and it also means the "streams of honey," the rivers of sweet prosperity.[1807]

THE BOOK OF JOB

Rowley thinks the meaning of v. 17 is, "The time of enjoyment to which the wicked look forward, he will not live to see."[1808] Klostermann suggests v. 17a should be "rivers of oil."[1809] This yields a good parallel to "the streams of honey and curd."[1810] Peake, Gray, and Dhorme all follow this approach.[1811]

Strahan calls v. 18 "lumbering."[1812] Mezudat David says of v. 18, "He will not return what is quite unusual because it has three hemstitch, rather than the customary two."[1813] The Vulgate interprets all of v. 18 as retribution. Evil actions performed by the evildoers.[1814] Rowley says the import of v. 19 is that "the wicked have callously left the poor to their fate, after he has oppressively treated them."[1815] Habel says of v. 19:

> The wicked will not participate in celebrating the Earth's blessings. Instead, they will be forced to relinquish the riches gained by unjust appropriation and false trading.[1816]

Habel also tells us that the verb of v. 18a, *swb*, or "disgorge," carries the "dual connotations" of "bring back / return [wealth]," and "bring up / disgorge [food]."[1817] Gersonides thinks that "after he crushed the poor, then he dies."[1818] Szold says the sense of v. 20 is that, "He robs a man of his house and yet compels the victim to keep it in a state of disrepair."[1819] Driver says the import of v. 20 is, "He will not live in it, but enjoy it."[1820] Habel says of vv. 21–22, "The eating metaphor here is expressed as gluttony."[1821] Rashi says in v. 21, "He left nothing of his food to share with the poor, therefore, his goods shall not prosper." Rashi also believes the verse refers to the people of Sodom "who were stingy with travelers."[1822]

Habel points out that Zophar uses the term *amal*, or "trouble," to describe the disaster which strikes those who are sated with sin.[1823] This is another sharp jab delivered by the third friend, Zophar. For Zophar, the *amal* that Job experiences only happens when "one is fully evil." Instead of being a paragon of virtue, Job is "riddled with corruption," or so Zophar has it.[1824]

20:23–29

Norman Habel introduces vv. 23–25 this way:

> The ills which result naturally from the inherent destructiveness of evil deeds are complemented by expressions of divine anger. God's fury penetrates the bellies of the wicked, which are sated from the gluttonous obsession with evil [v. 23a and b]; the manna they will experience will be a downpour of divine anger, not a shower of miraculous blessings [v. 23c]. When they cease to flee one of God's attacks they will be confronted by another [vv. 24–25].[1825]

Habel says the "weapons" of v. 24 are "probably arrows," though Robert Gordis believes they are swords.[1826] The *qeset*, or "bow" of v. 24b is an obvious reference to arrows. Zophar may be referring to Job's earlier description of Shaddai as an "Archer," who fires arrows of poison at Job in the style of the Canaanite god Reshef. In v. 25 the arrows fly forward and penetrate through the victim's back, pierce the gall bladder, and then create panic. The *merora*, or "gall," of v. 25 recalls the poison of the asps that the wicked experience in their bellies.[1827]

Freehof points out correctly that the metaphor shifts in vv. 24–25 from food to battle. "The wicked shall be transfixed by a spear or a bow."[1828] He also says that the Targum suggests the "fire not blown by man" in v. 26, "refers to the fire of Gehenna."[1829] Many other Jewish exegetes take the same view. Rowley renders v. 26 this way: "All darkness is laid up for his hidden things."[1830] The LXX eliminates the word "hidden." Driver says the fire in v. 26 is "one not kindled by man, but by God."[1831] Dhorme understands the "what is left?" in v. 26 to mean "whoever survives."[1832]

Rowley believes the meaning of v. 27 is this:

> Heaven and Earth will combine against him.[1833]

Other interpreters think the verse is a reference that Job's witness is in heaven, and his appeal to the earth is not to cover up his blood.[1834] Gray finds this view doubtful.[1835] Budde transposes v. 27 to follow v. 28, as does Dhorme as well.[1836] Saadiah interprets v. 28 to mean, "The goods of his house are swept away," on the strength of a reading of Gen 29:10.[1837] Rashi thinks the "recompense" of v. 29 is "the inheritance of the person about whom God speaks by decreeing this upon him."[1838]

Chapter 21: Job's Second Reply to Zophar (Chapter 21:1–34)

Introduction

Chapter 21 is Job's second response to his third friend, Zophar. It also brings the second round of speeches to a close. This chapter is one of the most theological in the book. Job responds to many of the theological explanations for Job's suffering that have been made by Eliphaz, Bildad, and Zophar in previous chapters. He even suggests a few theological views that the friends have not made, and then still counters them.

Chapter 21 also has a number of *hapax Legomena*, words that only appear once in Hebrew scripture, making them at times difficult to interpret. We will point to a number of these in our analysis. Carol Newsom, Samuel Terrien, and Matthew Henry all divide ch. 21 into four sections.[1839] For Newsom, these parts are: vv. 1–6; vv. 7–16; vv. 17–26; and vv. 27–34.

Matthew Henry, who divides the chapter the same way, gives the following names to the four parts: vv. 1–6, "Job Entreats Attention"; vv. 7–16, "The Prosperity of the Wicked"; vv. 17–26, "The Dealings of God's Providence"; and vv. 27–34, "The Judgment of the Wicked Is in the World to Come."[1840]

Newsom gives this introduction to the chapter:

Throughout the second cycle of speeches, the friends have focused on one theme only: the fate of the wicked (chapters 16–17 and 19). Now, however, in his final speech in this cycle, Job addresses the cumulative arguments of the friends concerning the fate of the wicked.[1841]

Robert Gordis agrees that this is the correct understanding of the chapter. He tells us:

> In contrast to Zophar's mythical picture of the misery of the sinner and his offspring, Job pictures the actual ease and contentment of the malefactor, the well-being of his family, and finally his quick and easy death.[1842]

Gordis continues his analysis of ch. 21:

> In this, Job's closing speech in the second cycle, he follows the practice he employed at the end of the first cycle (chapter 12), by quoting and then demolishing the arguments of the friends. Job cites four of the arguments that have been advanced and refutes them in turn.[1843]

Gordis goes on to enumerate these four arguments:

1. The sinner's descendants are punished. Since it was he who sinned, why is he himself not punished?

2. God is too exalted to be taught or judged by man. Job counters this contention, not directly but obliquely. He contrasts the happy lot of the wicked with the misery of the righteous. This inevitably raises questions about the divine wisdom.

3. "Where is the house of the prosperous sinner? It is sure to be utterly destroyed." Far from it; any passer-by can point out the mansion standing in all its glory.

4. God spares the wicked only to the day of doom. "Why the delay?" Job asks. Why not immediate punishment for his evil doing?[1844]

Gordis finishes his analysis of ch. 21:

> Job adds one finishing touch to his portrait of the prosperous sinner. There is a final indignity: even in death there is no moment of truth. The evil doer is given an elaborate funeral and is borne to his grave in pomp and honor.[1845]

John Wycliffe sums up the content of ch. 21 of Job by telling us:

> After a prefatory request for attention [vv. 2–6], he proceeds to undermine the opposition by exposing the fallacy in their analyses of the fortunes of the wicked [vv. 7–34].[1846]

PART II: THE BOOK OF JOB COMMENTARY

Analysis of Chapter 21

21:1–6

In these opening verses, Job asks for a hearing, sarcastically granting the friends permission to mock him when he is through (vv. 2–3). The "consolation" of v. 2b is an echo of 15:11. In v. 3, the verbs change from the plural to the singular, suggesting he is not only speaking to one of the friends, but all the versions, except the Targum, have the plural. About v. 4, Rowley says:

> Job's complaint is against God and not against men. If it were against men, he might expect sympathy from other men; but none dare offer him sympathy, when his complaint is against God.[1847]

The "impatient" (*qasar*) at the end of v. 4 literally says, "My spirit is short." This reminds us of a similar expression at 4:5. Mezudat David says the meaning of v. 4 is, "Why should you make an issue of my complaint. Am I complaining to a man like me that he should listen to me?"[1848] Rashi thinks the meaning of v. 4 is:

> Am I speaking to a man, that I should think he is not attending to my complaints to reply to me ? I am speaking to God.[1849]

Rashi says the import of v. 5 is, "Be astonished at my words because you will not know what to answer."[1850] Rowley has it, "be appalled." He says, "What has astounded Job will also astound his friends."[1851] The expression "put your hand on your mouth" in v. 5b, Rowley says, "is a gesture of awed silence." He gives 29:9, 40:4, and Mic 7:16 as parallels.[1852] Dahood believes that v. 5 is a "gesture of amazement, rather than silence."[1853]

Mezudat David and Rashi say the significance of v. 6 is this:

> I become frightened for I see the wicked men of the flood. When I remember these things, I become frightened and quaking seizes my flesh because these deeds are displeasing to me.[1854]

Saadiah Gaon renders v. 6 this way:

> Still when I call one thing to mind, I am dumbfounded and tremors seize my body.[1855]

Rashi says of v. 6:

> Job's old faith in God is shattered when he faces the facts of experience, and he shudders at the fact that there is no more a moral basis of the universe.[1856]

21:7–16

In this section, Job begins by describing the prosperity of the wicked, first in general terms (vv. 7–16), then in contradiction to the friends' specific representations of the cause of Job's sufferings (vv. 17–26). Finally, he relies on self-defense in vv. 27–34, or so says Wycliffe's commentary on the chapter.[1857] Zophar has said at 20:11 that the wicked die prematurely. In v. 7, Job says they live to old age. Mezudat David says, "This is the question: Why do the wicked live on?"[1858] Newsom says, "Job announces the topic of his complaint," in v. 7. "Contrary to what should be, the wicked actually live long and prosperous lives."[1859] Verse 8 has a peculiar Hebrew construction. It literally says, "Before them, with them." Kissane transfers the "with them" to v. 8b, and with the change of a vowel he gets, "their kinfolk" (and their offspring).[1860] Ball makes a similar transfer and then adds a consonant to get, "their offspring abide."[1861] So too Dhorme.[1862]

The "rod" of v. 9 recalls Eliphaz's statement at 5:24. Rowley says of the verse, "Eliphaz has promised Job safety in his tent if he accepts his misfortunes as divine chastisement and repented. Job here sets the security of the wicked against this."[1863] Mezudat David believes the meaning of the "rod" in v. 9 is, "They have never experience any divine retribution."[1864] Samuel Terrien says the import of v. 10 is this:

> Not only do they and their household prosper, but their own livestock appear to be unfailingly fertile.[1865]

Saadiah renders v. 10 this way:

> His cattle carry without aborting, and when his kine deliver, it is without stillbirth.[1866]

Stevenson has v. 10 as, "The bull of each one of them . . ."[1867] Rowley says, "The fertility in herds and flocks was regarded as a mark of divine blessing." He gives Deut 28:14 and Ps 144:13ff. as parallel texts.[1868] The word *aviyl*, or "little ones," in v. 11, usually means "babe." It comes from the Semitic root *uwl*. Newsom calls them, "the mischievous, teasing, and attractive urchins."[1869] Rashi renders the word "infants."[1870] Ibn Ezra says the meaning of v. 12 is this:

> They would raise their voice in song with the tambourine and harp. The flute is only an expression of sensual laughter.[1871]

Rowley says this about vv. 11–12:

> The picture of the children frolicking like lambs and singing and playing suggests most vividly peace and happiness. The instruments mentioned are a percussion instrument, a stringed instrument, and a wind instrument.[1872]

Rowley says the import of v. 13 is, "Not only do the wicked know unbroken prosperity, but they come to a peaceful end in their ripe old age."[1873] Saadiah has v. 13:

They spend their days in good living,

And in a moment return to the Earth without illness.[1874]

The LXX has "in tranquility." Beer says the sense of the verse is, "In a moment they are frightened and descend to Sheol."[1875] All the verbs in v. 14 are singular in the LXX. Rowley says that v. 14 "are not the men who drift away from God, but those who deliberately reject Him."[1876] Eliphaz repeats the wording of v. 14 at 22:17. Mezudat David thinks v. 14 refers to "the generation of the flood who refused God's assistance."[1877]

Verse 15 is omitted by the LXX, most likely because it seemed blasphemous. Davidson cites Coverdale's translation of v. 15, "What maner of felowe is the Almightie that we shulde serve him?"[1878] The verb of v. 15 usually implies "meet," or "encounter," but here it appears to mean, "meet with a request," or so says Rowley.[1879]

Fohrer deletes v. 16 as a gloss.[1880] Habel renders the verse, "Our happiness is not his doing."[1881] John Wesley gives this meaning to v. 16:

But the wicked men have no reason to reject God, because of their prosperity, but only kept by God's power and favor. Therefore, I am far from approving their opinion, of following their course.[1882]

Saadaih Gaon renders v. 16 this way:

See, the upright have not their good in their hands.
And His sentence upon the evil has been far delayed.[1883]

The LXX translates v. 16b as, "The counsel of the wicked is far from him." Stevenson thinks v. 16 is a "reader's remark," as does Ball.[1884] It certainly is not the view of the friends, coming as they do directly after the comments of the miscreants. Merx, Beer, Duhm, and Tur-Sinai all eliminate the "not," or *lo* in v. 16.[1885]

21:17–21

In this section of ch. 21, Job challenges the statistics about sin and suffering provided by the friends (v. 29). Although Job too exaggerates, he is much nearer to the truth than are his opponents. In v. 19a, Job anticipates a possible evasion (see 5:4 and 20:10), and then rebuts it in vv. 19b–21. The verbs in vv. 19b–21 have the force of a command. "Let his own eyes see his destruction." Job argues that the traditional theory of retribution constitutes a disguised criticism of the actual ways of God.

Verse 17c appears to be a detached half line which gives an appropriate parallel to v. 19a, so it helps to solve the problems of v. 19. The removal of v. 17c leaves v. 18 to be a smooth continuation of the question of v. 17a and b. The noun in v. 17c is usually rendered as "birthpains," but here and elsewhere, Job 17:1 and Mic 2:10, for example, the stem has the broader connotation of "injury," or "ruin." The nouns of v. 18, *teben*, or "stubble," and *mots*, or "chaff," are both unusual terms in ancient Hebrew. Habel describes vv. 17–18 this way:

> The wicked who relished committing the wrongs which enabled their rise to power will eventually face total frustration. They will not enjoy the results of their labor to the full.[1886]

Habel says that "rivers of oil" and "streams of milk/honey" seem to symbolize "the quality of prosperity which seems to derive from divine blessing." Canaan, as the land of blessing, flowed with milk and honey, as Exod 3:8 and 17 suggest.[1887] When *El* dreams of Baal's restoration to life and to fertility, he exclaims:

> The Heavens rain oil.
>
> And the ravines run with honey.[1888]

The verb for v. 18a, from the *ʾswb* root, carries a dual connotation. It could mean to "bring back" or "return" wealth, or "bring back" or "disgorge" food. Samuel Terrien says the sense of v. 17 is to ask, "How many times does He [God] destroy the wicked in his anger?" He takes the noun of v. 17c to be the "pangs of labor."[1889] Stevenson and others say v. 17c should be moved to follow v. 19a.[1890] Terrien says the import of vv. 19–21 is that:

> God stores up their iniquity for their sons.[1891]

If this is the proper interpretation of v. 19a, then it refers to a collective form of retributive justice. Earlier, Bildad used this view at 8:4. Newsom agrees. She says:

> Job cites a possible objection, that even if a wicked person is not punished, it is because God has stored up the punishment for the wicked person's children.[1892]

The idea that God might punish subsequent generations for the sin of the father is a common theme in ancient Israel. One may find it at: Exod 20:5; Deut 5:9; 2 Sam 12:13–14; and Lam 5:7, for examples; but both Jeremiah, at 31:29–31, and Ezek 18:1–4, argue against that same view, as does Job 1:1 and 5, for that matter.

The word for "destruction" in v. 20 is a *hapax*. It is sometimes rendered as "craft," or as "misfortune." Ehrlich translates it as "cup." Pope and Dahood render it "weapons," as does Wright.[1893] A. F. I. Beeston argues for the meaning "condemnation."[1894] Rowley says of v. 20:

> Job is here continuing to express his view that the wicked ought to experience retribution themselves (but commonly do not), rather than entail it for their children.[1895]

Stevenson renders *abdeneh* of v. 20 as "destruction," but the word only appears here, so it is difficult to say if he is correct.[1896] A different word to signify "destruction," *kiyd*, is also employed in the book. Rashi renders v. 20 as, "Let his eyes experience his ruin."[1897] He makes this observation about v. 21:

> What does he desire or care about his house after his death, to worry in his life time about the retribution destined to befall them, since the number of his months has been cut off and they will end before the evil that the Omnipresent has promised them.[1898]

Rashi thinks the meaning of v. 21 is, "This is what I said to you in v. 5, 'Turn to me and be silent.'"[1899] John Wesley thinks v. 21 is a declarative, "Have pity on me, oh you my friends, for the hand of God has touched me."[1900] Newsom says the import of v. 21 can be explained as, "In death, all knowledge and all concerns for one's descendants are cut off."[1901]

21:22–26

John Wesley thinks that v. 22 should be an interrogatory:

> Why do you persecute me as God has done, and are not simply satisfied with my flesh?[1902]

Newsom believes that these verses are a "comparison between one person's fate and that of another." She says, the poet "introduces his argument with a citation of a common cliché: no one can teach God understanding since God is the judge of all, as well as being the Highest."[1903] Samuel Terrien says the significance of vv. 23–26 is that, "Death comes indiscriminately to all men alike."[1904] Stevenson agrees about these verses. He observes:

> The verses treat the inequalities of human life, without special reference to the Miscreants.[1905]

Stevenson then adds the following:

> There is no literary connection between these lines and their immediate connection. They have something of the character of closing reflexions, yet cannot be confidently transferred to stand after vv. 27–34, which are themselves an appropriate ending to Job's speech. It is likely that additional lines, which joined them more closely in their context, have been lost.[1906]

Whether or not Stevenson is correct about these verses is not clear. What is clear, however, is that v. 24 contains the Hebrew term *atiyn*, which is another *hapax*, and thus gives interpreters trouble. The parallel at v. 24b seems to suggest a part of the body. The LXX and Vulgate render it "bowels." The Peshitta, "sides." The Targum has it as "breasts,"[1907] to agree with the Masoretic Text's "milk." The next line, v. 27, refers to thoughts and arguments and not to purpose, whether good or bad. So the word *atiyn* remains something of a mystery.

21:27–34

In this section, Job recognizes his image in the veiled descriptions of the friends. For the most part, however, Job displays his views of the relationship between sin and subsequent retribution. This is made clear in his question in v. 30, "Why is the wicked man spared in the day of calamity?"

Rowley observes about these verses the following:

> Job's meaning is that he know that when his friends talk of the fate of the wicked they really meant himself, and that they concluded from his sufferings that he must pay for the price of his sins.[1908]

Rowley thinks the "Prince" in v. 28 is to be understood in a bad sense here, meaning "the oppressor."[1909] Job clearly anticipates in these verses that his friends will bring forward their declarations that the wicked leave no memory among men. It is for this reason that he appeals in the following verses to independent testimony. The testimony in v. 29 is of world travelers.[1910] Kissane, on the other hand, says that v. 29 refers to "the man on the street," but this seems unlikely.[1911]

The KJV and RSV appear in v. 30 to have Job say the opposite of what he is actually contending.[1912] Rowley renders the verb "reserved to the day." Some render it "is withheld." Dillmann, Gray, and Fohrer prefer "He is saved," while Ball thinks that v. 30b should be translated "He escapes."[1913] Dhorme has it, "He is merry,"[1914] but the parallel to v. 30a prefers the RSV's rendering:

> The wicked man is scared in the day of his calamity,
>
> That he is rescued in the day of wrath.[1915]

Verse 32 contains two more words that are rarely used in the Hebrew Bible. The first of these is *qeber*, usually translated "grave." It is also used at 3:22 and 5:26. The other is *gadiysh* that is rendered "tomb" by most interpreters. Most exegetes agree with Wycliffe, however, when he writes:

> It is far from clear how the clods or pebbles of the valley could be "sweet" to the dead man.[1916]

Often in the Old Testament, as well as the book of Job, the word *Sheol* is employed as a synonym for the "grave." In Job, this is true at 7:19; 14:13; 17:13; 21:13; and 24:19. In addition to *qeber* and *Sheol*, a third word is used in Job to stand for the grave. It is *be'iy*, and can be seen at 30:24. Altogether, then, there are eleven references to the grave in Job, five *Sheol*, five *qeber*, and one *be'iy*.

Ball emends the line somewhat weakly to get "He is quiet among the clods," or "He is at rest among the clods."[1917] The use of "clods" most likely comes from the Vulgate's *glebae*, which is also used at 21:33. Some render the noun as "pebbles," or even as "stones" or "gravel." The word *ragab* may be derived from the Arabic *raqam*, usually employed for small stones. The Peshitta gives the connotation of "caves," thus it has, "Caves of the valley swallow him."[1918] Some say the reference is to "rock tombs." Stevenson thinks the lines refers to "rock-tombs."[1919] Rowley says of v. 22, "The dead man is poetically depicting as consciously sharing in his own funeral, enjoying the splendid mound that covers him."[1920]

Again v. 34 contains two other Hebrew words of significance. The first is the word *hebel* that means a variety of things, including the KJV's "vanity," throughout Ecclesiastes. Here it seems more to mean "nothing," or as the RSV has it, "empty nothings." The other term is *ma'al*, that is connected to the usual word for "false" or "falsehood." Thus, the RSV gives us for v. 34b, "There is nothing left but your falsehoods."[1921] John Wesley, for v. 34, gives us:

> How then confort ye me in vain,
>
> In your answers there remaineth falsehood.[1922]

Rowley agrees with this analysis. Reflecting on v. 34, he tells us:

> In view of all this and the lack of moral principles to explain the inequalities among men, Job dismisses the arguments of the friends as hollow and as meaningless.[1923]

Habel and most other exegetes take a similar approach to the meaning of v. 34. He says:

> Job's companions have proven to be disloyal, by deferring to God rather than by being genuine friends.[1924]

John Wycliffe believes that at Job 21:34 the proper meaning of the verse is this:

> By punctuating the balloon of airtight retribution, Job leaves his accusers clinging to falsehood.[1925]

Something like that is most likely the proper interpretation of the final verses of ch. 21 of the book of Job. At any rate, at the close of ch. 21, we come to the end of the second round of speeches in the book. The third cycle goes from 22:1 until 31:40, to which we now turn.

Chapter 22: Eliphaz's Third Speech (22:1–30)

Introduction

Chapter 22 begins the third round of speeches. It is also the final words from Job's first friend, Eliphaz. Matthew Henry, Samuel Terrien, and Carol Newsom all divide ch. 22 into four principal parts.[1926] Henry has these four parts as: vv. 1–4; vv. 5–14; vv. 15–20; and vv. 21–30. Henry names these four parts thusly: "Man's Goodness Profits Not"; "Job Accused of Oppression"; "The World Before the Flood"; and "Eliphaz Exhorts Job's Repentance."[1927]

Habel calls ch. 22 "Eliphaz's Indictment of Job."[1928] Most exegetes give the chapter similar names.[1929] Samuel Terrien describes the four sections of ch. 22 this way:

> Eliphaz plunges into his third discourse with intemperate abruptness (vv. 2–5) and he gives substance to this new accusations with plain lies (vv. 6–10.) Yet, he not only hopes that Job will not follow "the ancient road" (vv. 11–20) but even invites him not to make his peace with God and to be saved (vv. 21–30).[1930]

John Wycliffe, on the other hand, divides ch. 22 into only three parts: vv. 1–7; 8–23; and 24–30. He describes these three parts in terms of questions. He calls the first part, "As God lives, who has taken away my right?" The second, "What is the hope of the Godless man when God cuts him off?" The third part of ch. 22 is labeled, "If you lay gold in the dust?"[1931]

Chapter 22 of the book of Job is another section of the text where the poet's vocabulary is on display. In the space of thirty verses, he employs *Eloah* four times; *Shaddai*, three times; *El*, once; and *Elohim*, one time. He uses the *tam* of Job 1:1, in vv. 3 and 19. The poet also puts forth a version of the contrast theodicy in v. 11; retributive justice in v. 16; and the moral qualities view or the test theodicy in vv. 29–30.

Analysis of Chapter 22

22:2–5

Terrien maintains that "Eliphaz fails to reply to the main arguments presented by Job in chapter 21, but he should not be accused of ignoring them deliberately."[1932] He thinks that Eliphaz asks in v. 2, "Can a man be profitable to God?"[1933] Newsom points out that Eliphaz does not begin with the customary "introductory complaint about windy words, lack of wisdom, or insulting speech."[1934] Habel points out that "the meaning of the root *skn* is disputed in v. 2."[1935]

Gordis, on the basis of the Aramaic of the Babylonian Talmud, gets the following question, "Can a man endanger God?"[1936] The Masoretic Text's *alemo*, "to him," should be read *'olam*, or the "Eternal One." This allows the prepositional *lamed* of v. 2a to be used as double duty. The patriarchal "*El Olam*," as at Gen 21:33, would be appropriate to the world of Eliphaz and his friends.

Newsom says about vv. 4–5, "Eliphaz's words assert the impartiality of God."[1937] She gives 35:6–8 as a parallel.[1938] Job's claims to innocence at 9:21 and 16:7 seem to be impossible to Eliphaz. Rashi says the import of v. 4 is, "Will He reason with you because he fears you?"[1939]

Mezudat David has it, "Does he castigate you because he fears you?"[1940] Rashi thinks the sense of v. 5 is to ask, "Is it not so that He knows that your evil is great?" He says that Eliphaz answers Job on behalf of the Almighty (*Shaddai*). He adds:

He is justified in causing you to suffer, because your evil is great. That is, against a great man like you, every infraction of the law is accounted as a grave sin because many will learn from your example. Therefore, your iniquities are endless, because all their sins are the results of your actions and are attributed to you.[1941]

Rashi assents here, of course, to retributive justice theory. Many other exegetes also take this same view about v. 5. Jerome marks v. 5 with an obelisk. He renders the line, "Is it not because your wickedness is great?"[1942] Dhorme renders the line the same way. The "no end" or "no limit" to v. 5b has a parallel use at Eccl 4:8 and 16. The RSV renders v. 5 this way:

> Is not your wickedness great?
>
> There is no end to your iniquities.[1943]

The KJV renders v. 5 differently. It gives us:

> Is not thy wickedness great,
>
> And thine iniquities infinite?[1944]

Saadiah Gaon's translation of v. 5 is much like the KJV and RSV:

> Is not thine evil great,
>
> And are not thy offenses endless?[1945]

22:6–14

Saadiah says the meaning of v. 6b is, "and the clothing of the naked has been stripped, that is, people became naked as a result."[1946] Mezudat David gives a similar reading. He says of v. 6b, "and you strip the naked of their clothes." He adds:

> You take the shirts off peoples' backs, causing them to go naked. They are naked because of this end: stripped of their clothes, they are left naked.[1947]

Mezudat David says the meaning of the following verse, v. 7, is, "You gave the faint no water to drink."[1948] Saadiah has it, "Thou hast not given water to the fainting."[1949] Newsom gives this description of the import of vv. 7–9:

> Callous disregard for elemental human solidarity is reflected in the accusation that Job refused water to the thirsty or bread to the hungry (v. 7). Response to or rejection of these basic needs was the touchstone of human decency and faith-fullness to the creator of all. . . . Similarly, protection of the widow and orphan (v. 9) was one of the most fundamental obligations of those possessing power and position within ancient society.[1950]

Stevenson points out that v. 8 is in the third person, thus it supports the parallel of v. 2. He also says the verbs of v. 9 are all incongruous, second, singular masculine in v. 9a, and third, singular masculine active in v. 9b.[1951] Mezudat David says of v. 9:

> You sent widows away, but when you heard of an injustice committed by a widow, You took all her belongings and banished her from the land, crushing the strength of her sons—now orphans—whom has no one to turn to.[1952]

He says the meaning of v. 10 is that, "In payment for their sins, traps are set around you, and the fear of falling suddenly into a trap terrifies you."[1953] Dhorme says the basis for the "darkness" of v. 11, or *hasak*, or "the light has become darkened."[1954] The word *hosek*, or "darkness," is a major symbol of doom in the view of Eliphaz, and throughout Wisdom Literature, as we have seen earlier.

Habel believes the imperative "see" in v. 12 may be vocalized by the particle *ro' e*, that is "the one who sees." This provides an appropriate parallel to God in v. 12a.[1955] Dahood thinks *gobah* is to be read as *gaboeh*, or the "Lofty One."[1956] But this would seem to destroy the parallelism of the "head of the stars" and the "heights of Heaven." Newsom points out that "shielding dark clouds are associated with theophanies, in referring to v. 14." She gives Exod 20:21 and 1 Kgs 8:12 as parallel texts.[1957] Rashi thinks that v. 14 refers to "thick clouds that are a concealment, that are before him, so he cannot see."[1958] He thinks that the "old way" of v. 15 is, "The way of the ancients, in the time of yore."[1959] Stevenson maintains that much of this speech is "an address to Everyman, or to his representative who has just spoken for the skeptics."[1960] Rashi appears to be alluding to the wisdom of the fathers motif.

22:15–20

Stevenson believes v. 15 is part of the address to Everyman. He also points out that both verbs of the following verse, v. 16, should be in the same tense. He thinks, as is, the verse may be ironic.[1961] Rashi assents here, of course, to the idea that the "ancients" have wisdom. Rashi says v. 16 refers to "those who were cut off before their time," and the "river" or "washed away" of v. 16b refers to the Flood, or to "the brimstone of Sodom being poured into the foundation."[1962]

Mezudat David renders v. 17 this way:

> Who says to God, "He has turned away from us,"
> So what will the Almighty do to them?[1963]

Stevenson thinks there is a scribal error in v. 17, as does Budde, Beer, and Tur-Sinai.[1964] Verses 17–19 are very close to the wording of Job's at 21:14–16. Both Eliphaz and Job agree that the wicked contemptuously dismiss God. Job represents them as denying that God can do anything for his friends.

Stevenson wishes to delete v. 17, so that it follows much more smoothly and closely to v. 16. Mezudat David gives the following for v. 18:

> Although God filled their houses with good, they denied divine Providence. Indeed the counsel of those wicked people is beyond me. Why did they deny Divine Providence when God filled their houses with good?[1965]

Mezudat David, and many others, believe that v. 19 recalls Noah and the flood. He observes about the verse:

> Noah and his sons, who were righteous, saw their downfall and rejoiced, because they had followed God wholeheartedly and were not drawn after an erroneous belief of their wicked contemporaries.[1966]

Rowley gives Pss 56:6ff. and 69:32 as parallels to the idea of rejoicing over the exultation of the righteous in v. 19.[1967] One of Jean Calvin's 159 sermons on the book of Job is on 22:12–17. Calvin alludes in the sermon to Isa 66:1, "Heaven is My throne, and the Earth is My footstool."[1968] In the sermon, Calvin puts emphasis on God's transcendence and his imminence:

> God then is not enclosed in Heauen . . . there is in Heauen as it were such a marke of maiestic and glory, that when we lift vp our eyes thither, we must needs be moved therewith.[1969]

The word for "adversaries," *qimanu*, in Hebrew is another *hapax* in v. 20. Merx has it "their possessions," as do Wright, Dhorme, Weiser, and Fohrer.[1970] Kissane prefers "their greatness." "Their adversaries" seems to be more appropriate, since both the wicked and their possessions were destroyed (v. 16).[1971] Stevenson says, "'Our opponents' may be preferred because it gives a welcome definition of those referred to and supplies an antecedent to the suffix 'their,' in v. 20b." Some modern critics derive *qimanu* from the noun *qim*, that means "adversary" or "opponent."

22:21–30

The Hebrew *tebo'ateka* of v. 21b should be interpreted as a verb that means "will come to you." Blommerde reads the following *toba* as an allusion to God as the "Good One."[1972] Thus, he renders the line, "Then your gain will be the Good One." This is a sense supported by v. 25.[1973] Stevenson thinks v. 21 should be moved to the end of Eliphaz's speech. He thinks just before v. 29 is the best place to put it.[1974] Rashi thinks the import of v. 21 is, "And you will be complete, lacking nothing."[1975] Mezudat David translates v. 22 this way:

> Now take into your heart the Torah that was given from His mouth, as would one who believes in Divine Providence.[1976]

Rowley thinks that in v. 22, Eliphaz clearly thinks of himself as the mouthpiece of God.[1977] Dahood renders v. 22b "write his words," rather than the RSV's "lay up his words."[1978] Mezudat David says of v. 23, "You shall be built up, from your present decrepit condition."[1979] The LXX reads *tapeinoses* for the verb in v. 23a, or "you will humble yourself."[1980] The RSV takes the same view.[1981]

Stevenson points out that in v. 24, "the text and meaning of this line are quite uncertain. It may have belonged to another context."[1982] Rashi says v. 24 means, "Then you will make fortifications on the Earth."[1983] His reasoning also suggests that v. 25 means, "The Almighty shall be the Judge over your enemies."[1984] Stevenson says of v. 25b, "No certain translation is possible and no plausible correction has been offered."[1985] The word *to'apa* in v. 25 is a very rare one in the Hebrew Bible. Parallel texts at Num 23:22 and Ps 95:4 suggest it may mean "horn" or "peak."

The wording of v. 26 looks very much like 10:2 and 16:20. Mezudat David says the meaning of the verse is this: "When you return to God you will delight in His support, for He will bring delight to your soul."[1986] He adds about v. 27, "And you will pay your vows, and will be confident in your sacrifices. The payments of your vows will be accepted."[1987] Rowley says the meaning of v. 27 is, "Job's present complaint is that God hides His face from him and thus will not hear him."[1988] He says of v. 28:

> All his undertakings will prosper, instead of the darkness in which he now walks . . .
>
> His paths will be light.[1989]

Mezudat David says that v. 28 means:

> When you decide to do something, the Omnipresent will accomplish that thing for you.[1990]

Rabenu Meyouchas agrees. He says of v. 28, "Whatever you ask God by decree, He will give to you, as a favorite child asks his father for nuts and is given them, or asks for pomegranates and is given them."[1991] He says v. 28 "is the origin of the popular maxim, 'A righteous man decrees, and the Holy One, blessed be He, fulfills.'"[1992]

Rashi believes the meaning of v. 29 is this: "If you see your generation humble, then pledge that it will be uplifted, and it will be uplifted."[1993] Rowley thinks the verse should say, "God abases the proud."[1994] The Masoretic Text literally says: "When they humble, you shall say, 'Pride!'"[1995] Dhorme has it, "He abases pride."[1996] Holscher, "He abases the one who speaks proudly."[1997] The word *gewa* in v. 29 is "pride," but the English "courage" may be a better rendering. The subject of v. 29b appears to be God, but it does not say so explicitly in the Hebrew.

Stevenson thinks that v. 30a is far too short. There is no satisfactory restoration among the modern exegetes. He also comments that the persons, the verbs, and the pronoun suffixes, as they stand, do not agree.[1998] Mezudat David says v. 30 should be translated:

> He will deliver the innocent from woe, and you will be delivered by the purity of your hands, and with your merit.[1999]

Ibn Ezra has "an innocent island," rather than "innocent delivers the man who is not innocent."[2000] The RSV emends the *Io* "not" to *ish*, or "man," as do many modern translations.

At any rate, Eliphaz's final words of ch. 22 urge Job to return to God in hope of peace and blessing, and remind us that in spite of all, he was a friend in the family of faith. The consolation is vitiated, however, by the Pharisaic spirit and its incessant repetition of false accusations against Job. In their own distorted way, these promises were prophetic. Note especially 22:30:

> He delivers the innocent man. You will be delivered through the cleanliness of your hands.[2001]

Chapter 23: Job's Third Answer to Eliphaz (23:1—24:25)

Introduction

In the first portion of ch. 23, Job leaves aside what Eliphaz has said and he gives new expression to his idea of undeserved punishment. Again, he yearns for an opportunity to argue his case with God. Though, at the same time, he appears terrified of *Shaddai*, or the Almighty.

Later in the chapter, he turns to the injustices of the world, where the strong often oppress the weak, while God does nothing. Nowhere in the chapter does Job address the friends directly. Chapter 23 begins Job's third response to Eliphaz. The chapter is one of the shortest in the book, containing only seventeen verses. Samuel Terrien, Carol Newsom, and Matthew Henry all suggest ch. 23 has three main sections.[2002] Henry gives the first section, vv. 1–7, the name, "Job Complains That God Has Withdrawn." He calls vv. 8–12, "He Asserts His Integrity," and vv. 13–17, "The Divine Terrors."[2003]

Rowley gives the following description to ch. 23:

> In the first part of his reply, Job leaves aside what Eliphaz has said and gives now expression to his consciousness of undeserved suffering, and yearns afresh for the opportunity to argue his case with God, though at the same time he is afraid of God. He then turns again to the injustices of the world, where the strong oppress the weak, while God does nothing. Nowhere in this speech does Job directly address the friends. Some verses, 24:18–25, do not seem appropriate to the lips of Job, and some editors think they are out of place here.[2004]

In his commentary on the book of Job, John Wycliffe divides ch. 23 into only two parts. Verses 2–9 is called, "Even today, my complaint is rebellious." Wycliffe calls the second part of ch. 23, vv. 10–17, "But He knows the way I take."[2005] In ch. 23, Job makes a number of references to his "Law Case," particularly vv. 1–7. In this chapter, there is also another assertion by Job of his innocence, at vv. 12–14. His urgent pleas in ch. 23 look very much like those Job had uttered back at 9:34ff. and 13:1–2. As then, he declares that he is either ready to set out his own defense or to reply to God's accusations.

In ch. 23, we also see some of the poet's legal vocabulary that exists throughout the book. He uses words like *shapat*, or "judge"; *naqah*, or "acquit"; and *riyb*, or "case" or "complaint," in the opening seven verses of ch. 23. The Hebrew language of the court will be returned to in ch. 31, and elsewhere in the book. Indeed, later we will say more about "Job as a Law Case," in appendix A.

Analysis of Chapter 23:1—24:25

23:1–7

Rowley introduces this section this way:

> Protesting anew against his sore affliction, Job desires that he might meet God, and is sure that if he did so, he would convince him of his innocence.[2006]

Strahan says this of these verses, "The undimmed light of his normal consciousness illuminates for him the very way that leads unto God."[2007] Saadiah says of v. 2, "When he says, 'My plaint is counter,' he means that his complaint each day is at variance with what it was the day before."[2008] Mezudat David says of v. 2, "Even today, after I have given vent to my anger and have complained to God to the utmost of my ability."[2009] Rashi thinks the meaning of v. 2b is, "The bitterness of my speech remains in its place, for there is no consolation in your words."[2010] Mezudat David explains about v. 3, "Would that I knew God's place so that I could find him, and I will find Him."[2011] Stevenson believes that the LXX on v. 3 is a paraphrase. Rowley says of v. 3:

> It is the chief distinction between Job and his friends that he desires to meet God and they do not.[2012]

Strahan makes the same point about ch. 23, and about v. 3 in particular.[2013] Rowley believes the "seat" in v. 3 is "His judgment seat, or tribunal." He points out the word means "a fixed or prepared place."[2014] Some render the word for seat as "dwelling." Rashi calls it "a prepared place."[2015] He says the following about v. 5:

> Even if He stops me from speaking before Him, perhaps He would speak with me and I would know the words with which He would answer me.[2016]

Rowley observes about v. 5, "Job is ready not alone to face God with his charges, but to hear any counter-charges God might bring against him. . . . If only God would give him a chance to understand why he was suffering, he would be satisfied."[2017] About the following verse, v. 6, Rowley tells us, "He is confident that God will give him a fair hearing, and would not simply overwhelm him with His power."[2018] Rabbenu Meyouchas renders v. 6b, "Will He contend me with much power?"[2019] Mezudat David gives a similar translation. Stevenson points out that the Vulgate's "*magnitudinus suae mole*" is a paraphrase of the noun that both the LXX and Peshitta use.[2020]

Stevenson also suggests that v. 7a is a better sequel to vv. 4–6 and a better parallel to v. 7b.[2021] Habel says of v. 7b:

> Since God is Job's adversary at law with His heavy hand on Job [v. 2], it seems better to read *mishpati*, "my judgment case," with the Vulgate, rather than the MT's *missopeti*, "from my Judge."[2022]

Rashi thinks the import of v. 7 is, "The propriety of my deeds will be proven revealed and it will appear to Him."[2023] Rowley says that v. 7 is an expression of:

> An unshakable confidence in the strength of his case and the certainty of his acquittal possesses Job.[2024]

Driver, with a slight change, translates for v. 7b, "There would he affirm his case and argue with me."[2025] Rather than, "my Judge," in v. 7b, some editors read "my suit," and take the meaning to be: "I should receive my right." Strahan says, "Job does not want to be delivered from his Judge, but wants his innocence vindicated."[2026]

23:8–12

Saadiah Gaon says of v. 8:

> That is, God knows that I am in the right. Job interprets God's silence as avoidance of the confrontation which he seeks, since in a direct encounter God Himself would admit the justice of God's cause. God's silence is a display of arbitrariness of His power, as Job interprets it.[2027]

Rowley observes about vv. 8–12:

> Though Job cannot find God wherever he seeks him, he is assured that God knows his ways and that in the end he will be vindicated and come forth as gold from the refiner.[2028]

Habel suggests the points on the compass is the subject matter of vv. 8 and 9. He observes, "The four points of the compass are determined on the basis of the Israelite facing East." Thus, east is also "before," and west is "behind."[2029] Rashi takes the same view.[2030] Rowley also agrees. He says:

> Forward is to the East, and backward to the West; on the left is to the North, and on the right is to the South.[2031]

Duhm says in these verses, "Job asks if any man could seek God in this particular fashion."[2032] Rashi says the meaning of v. 10 is this: "Because he knows the way with me, He has tested me, but I will emerge like gold."[2033] Thus, Rashi thinks the text endorses a version of the test theodicy here. Stevenson thinks v. 10 should follow v. 7, and that these two verses together "describe an imaginary trial."[2034] If this is so, we have another reference to Job's "Law Case."

Saadiah believes the meaning of v. 10 is:

> He describes how they load down the wheat with grain, yet let them grow hungry.[2035]

There has been some disagreement about the translating of v. 10. The MT has, "the way with me." The Syriac, "my way and standing." Dhorme and Beer, "the way of my standing." J. Reider translates it, "the way of my life."[2036] Even so, the meaning is very clear. In contrast to Job's inability to find God, he is sure that God will find Job.

Rowley gives Ps 17:5 as a parallel to v. 11. He observes, "The divine testimony to the unswerving integrity of Job (vv. 2–3) is matched by his unwavering loyalty to the law of God."[2037] Stevenson thinks vv. 11–12 should follow vv. 7 and 10. He even says they might rightly follow v. 2, or suitably follow v. 8.[2038] He seems to think the order of these verses is not entirely clear.[2039] We agree with this judgment. Mezudat David says v. 12 refers "to the previous verse, 'I kept His way.'"[2040] Rashi says of v. 12:

> More than my daily food, I was eager to keep the words of His mouth.[2041]

Rashi gives Prov 30:8 as a parallel text for v. 12.[2042] Sforno thinks the prohibitions in v. 12 are moral and dietary. He observes:

> The commandments concerning forbidden foods, blood and the limbs of a live animal, I have kept. I would not remove these commandments from my daily bread. I kept the words of His mouth in my heart, so as not to forget them.[2043]

Many editors follow the LXX on v. 12 and read *beheqi*, "in my bosom" for *mehuqqi*, as the MT has it.[2044] Pope gives Ps 119:11 as a parallel to v. 12.[2045] Stevenson observes about v. 12, "The words here are badly arranged."[2046] Others read *mehuqqi* as *mekukki*, or "more than my law," but as is, it is obscure and unclear.

23:13–17

Rowley thinks the import of v. 13 is that, "God freely chooses His course, and His power is irresistible."[2047] Saadiah has an entirely different sense of v. 13. He renders it:

> They are of those who, as the light declines, seem not to be sure of its ways, and sit not in its pathways, out of shame.[2048]

Stevenson says the meaning of v. 13 is this: "God is not what He might be expected to be. He will not fulfill Job's hopes."[2049] He thinks that v. 14, "applies the statement of v. 13 to Job's case and to the world in general."[2050] Rashi says of v. 14:

> I know that He will not draw back His hand until He completes the sentence of His decrees, the retribution that He has decreed against me.[2051]

Rashi says of v. 15, "Therefore, since He does not requite man according to His ways, I am startled by Him; and when I ponder His ways, I am frightened by Him."[2052] Rowley takes a similar view of v. 15. He says, "When Job thinks of the inexplicable ways of God with men, his terror returns."[2053] Saadiah believes vv. 15–16 are about a thief and what he does with his gains.[2054] Rashi says of v. 16, "Yea, God has made my heart faint."[2055] He adds:

> In addition to the pains and suffering, He has brought faintness to my heart, in order to frighten me in an exceeding way.[2056]

Rashi renders the final verse of ch. 23, this way:

> Because I was not cut off from before the darkness, and because He did not cover the thick darkness from before me.[2057]

Habel points to the difficulties of v. 17 when he writes:

> This verse has caused scholars difficulty. The negative *lo* in the first line negates the intention of the second line.[2058]

The RSV omits the negative. The NAB reads *lu* or "would that." Dhorme points to the Aramaic root SMT, or "silent," and renders, "I have not been silent because of the darkness."[2059] A solution might be to recognize an emphatic *lu*, "indeed, really," rather than *lo*, or "not."

Chapter 24: Job Continues His Third Response to Eliphaz

Introduction

In ch. 24, Job completes his final response to Eliphaz. Traditionally, ch. 24 is divided into three main sections. Samuel Terrien, Carol Newsom, and Matthew Henry all divide the chapter that way.[2060] Henry suggests the three sections are: vv. 1–12; vv. 13–17; and vv. 18–25. He labels the first part, "Wickedness Is Often Unpunished." "The Wicked Shun the Light," is Henry's name for the second section of ch. 24. He calls vv. 18–25, "Judgment for the Wicked."[2061]

Rowley introduces ch. 24 this way in a chiastic form:

> It seems it may be wise to ask whether the chapter is a unified speech. Contrary to the opinion of most scholars, we would argue that a basic unity and coherence is throughout, but is making concessions to the previous speaker.[2062]

Rowley goes on to divide the chapter this way:

a. The Question in Dispute (v. 1).

b. Concessions concerning Exploitation in Society (vv. 2–12).

b1. Concessions concerning Flagrant Evildoers (vv. 13–17).

c. Acknowledged Destiny of the Wicked (vv. 18–20).

b2. Recapitulation concerning the Exploitation of Evil (v. 21).

d. Resolution of the Question (vv. 22–24).

e. Closing Challenge (v. 25).[2063]

Like Henry, Terrien, and Newsom, then, Rowley says the chapter consists of three parts: vv. 1–12; vv. 13–17; and vv. 18–25. We will examine the chapter by looking carefully at each of these three parts. There has been considerable discussion among modern scholars, however, about whether Job is indeed the speaker of this speech.

Analysis of Chapter 24

24:1–12

Rowley also says this about the beginning of ch. 24:

> In typical disputational style the speech begins with the question to be resolved (v. 1.) That question is not a why of lament against God (as in 3:11, 12, 20; and 7:20); but the problem posed for debate. As such, the question reflects a claim of the protagonist which requires refutation. In the design of the speech, however, the resolution of the issue only appears in the closing lines (vv. 22–24.) In the intervening verses, two apparently contradictory positions in the debate are elaborated.[2064]

The question about v. 1 is expressed clearly in the RSV translation:

> Why are not times of judgment kept by *Shaddai*,
>
> And why do those who know Him never see His days?[2065]

The LXX does not have the negative in v. 1a. Andersen says of v. 2:

> Evidently the grammatical subject of this sentence has been lost. The differing words supplied by the versions must for the most part be stopgaps.[2066]

The removal of "landmarks" in v. 2 refers to where "the lands of another begins and ends," as S. R. Driver tells us.[2067] Habel tells us about vv. 2–4, "The speaker concedes that society is filled with numerous cases of exploitation typical of the ancient world."[2068] He says about the landmarks, or *gebulah*, in Hebrew in v. 2, "These were necessary to preserve one's inheritance."[2069] Habel gives Deut 19:14 and 27:17 as parallels.[2070] But these parallels are in the singular, *gebul*, and not the plural, as in v. 2. The Semitic root, GBL, often means to "set a boundary."

The stealing of the goods of widows and orphans was considered a grave sin in ancient Israel (see v. 3). The widow and the orphan were symbols of vulnerability. Taking a widow's garment in pledge was an offense detailed in ancient Hebrew law codes (see Deut 24:17).

Andersen thinks vv. 5–6 expressly speak of "the robbery of the poor by the rich man's fields and vineyards."[2071] Habel observes correctly that in vv. 5–8, "the focus shifts from the crimes of the oppressor to the plight of the victims."[2072] Habel continues:

> The lead metaphor designates the destitute as "wild asses, forced to live as scavengers in the wilderness" (v. 5); their daily toil is to forage for food; their only source of supply is the barren wilderness. Like wild asses they are forced to find "fodder" in the fields, and to glean grapes from the vineyards. The "wicked" in v. 6b are presumably the rich owners of the fields and vine-yards, whom the poor are driven to steal from, or to serve as enforced laborers. The misery of the hungry poor is intensified by their lack of clothing and shelter. They are forced to brave the elements at night and huddle together among the rocks (vv. 7–8).[2073]

The image of the wretched clinging to a rock, or *sur*, may be an allusion to God being a "Rock for His people" at Deut 32:15; Isa 17:19; and Pss 31:3 and 62:8. Verse 9 resumes the thought of v. 3. Indeed, many scholars place it after v. 3. Rashi says the meaning of vv. 8–9 is:

> From the stream that flows from the mountains, these naked people became wet and damp because they have no cover. They have no refuge under which to cover themselves. They hide in the crevices of rocks, and even from there the stream flows down and sprays on them wet and moist.[2074]

Rashi thinks in v. 10, "They go without clothing." He adds about the verse:

> And from the hungry they took sheaves of gleaming which are left for the poor. And those who were carrying the sheaves are made hungry, because they were robbed of them, so they remain hungry.[2075]

Rashi also observes that vv. 11 and 12 are about "the owners of oil trees, and the owners of vineyards."[2076] Rowley points out the great range of approaches to rendering v. 11. The verb for "they make oil," in v. 11 is only found here, and thus another *hapax* in Job. It may be a derivative of the word *yishar*. Others say the verb derives from the word for "noonday," as do the Vulgate, the Peshitta, and Kissane, for example.[2077] Scholars also disagree about the final noun of v. 12 (*tipla*, in Hebrew). Some say it should be "folly," while others render it as "unseemliness."

24:13–17

John Wycliffe tells us this about 24:13–17:

> Economic tyrants, such as those just described, often operate with legal technicalities. In addition to them, wanton and violent men overrun the Earth. These are murderers, adulterers, and thieves, all lovers of darkness.[2078]

Wycliffe gives Exod 20:13–15 as parallel verses to 24:13–17.[2079] Norman Habel introduces this section this way:

> The preceding section (vv. 2–12) focused on sins of exploitation which could perhaps be perpetuated publically within the bounds of the law, but which violated acceptable norms of compassion and common justice. The evildoers of this section (vv. 13–17) are those who flagrantly break the laws of society. They are active rebels against the accepted social order who are identified with the seemy side of society.[2080]

Habel also thinks the crimes being enumerated in these verses are "burglary, murder, and adultery."[2081] Rashi says the people described in v. 13 "are the generation of the Flood."[2082] Mezudat David explains v. 14 this way:

> Because of the light, the murderers rise early; he slays the poor and the needy who are on their way to work, and, in the middle of the night, he acts just like a thief.[2083]

Rashi says in v. 15, "The transgressor puts on a mask, so he could commit the transgressions." Again, he identifies the miscreants of v. 15 with the "people of the age of the Flood."[2084] Rowley says that in v. 15, "the prostitute is represented as beginning her operations at dusk. Here the adulterer has the equal covers of darkness and disguise."[2085]

The Masoretic Text has, "He digs," for the verb in v. 16. The RSV, NIV, and other modern translations have, "They dig," though this is certainly not the way thieves would find their way into a house. The verb for v. 16b usually means "seal," but the RSV has "shut." The KJV has "had marked."[2086] The Job poet employs both *shawar*, at 22:15, and *chamets*, at 24:16, to indicate "marked."

The "deep darkness" of v. 17 reminds us of 3:5. The first two words of v. 17 are most likely part of v. 16, ending it "to them."[2087] Rashi renders v. 17 this way:

> For together morning is to them as the shadow of death, for he recognizes the terrors of the shadow of death.[2088]

Habel says of v. 17, "Since they do not know the light (v. 16c), they view the morning as being alien to them."[2089] The dawn is their darkness and represents death rather than life. The dawn would expose their deeds for what they are. Proverbs frequently

24:18–25

S. R. Driver believes vv. 18–21 "express the opposite of what Job has been saying, the view taken by the friends." He writes, "The sinner, they say in v. 18, is rapidly borne away on a stream. The passers-by as they see his desolated homestead, utter a curse over it. He no more visits his well-planted vineyards."[2090] Verse 20a has a present tense verb. It should be "forgets," or "shall forget." The arrangement of v. 20 is a bit confusing. "Is not remembered" is parallel to "is forgotten." The RSV gives us the following for the verse:

> The squares of the town forget them;
>
> Their name is no longer remembered;
>
> So wickedness is broken like a tree.[2091]

Most modern translations follow the RSV on v. 20. Rowley observes about v. 21, "The reference is once more to the wicked man who exploits and oppresses the weak and the unfortunate. But here he meets with swift retribution."[2092] Stevenson thinks v. 21 is to be taken as an irony.[2093] Rashi says v. 21 refers to "the barren woman who is fed, but does not bear offspring."[2094] He says v. 22 refers to "the Holy One, blessed be He, Who draws those mighty men with his strength to retribution and to sustenance by the reprieve that He granted them."[2095] Thus, Rashi assents to the retributive justice theory here.

Rowley says that v. 22 "presents the picture of God recovering the wicked to health when they are at death's door."[2096] The KJV and RSV present the picture in v. 22 of God using his power over the mighty to destroy their confidence.[2097] Rowley says, "It is a question of whether God rises to power or the wicked rises to health."[2098]

A chief question about the rendering of v. 23 is whether it should read "and his eyes" (RSV) or "but his eyes" (KJV.) In the former view, God grants the wicked support and a sense of security, while watching over them with care. In the latter view, God allows them to feel secure, while he watches closely. The latter view, is probably preferred. Dhorme and Pope take this stance on v. 23.[2099]

The Hebrew of v. 24 has a number of difficulties. For one thing it moves from "they" to "he." In fact, throughout the verses it is difficult to determine whether it is singular or plural. The sense of the verse, however, is quite clear. The wicked, in the midst of their exaltation are cut off like a flower, or like heads of grain during the harvest season. Kissane has for v. 24, "They are exalted for a little while and then vanish."[2100] Rashi has it, "They are taken away in a second and he is no more."[2101] He says the second verb in v. 24 is "crushed," and he concludes the line, "like all, they are gathered in, and like the tip of a piece of grain, they are cut off."[2102] Habel says the meaning of v. 24 is this: "The wicked may rise high in their powerful positions, but ultimately they have no stability."[2103] Saadiah says in v. 24, "He is only continuing the same argument he had from the start."[2104] Stevenson agrees that v. 24 should be translated, "They are exalted for a while and then vanish." He also says that v. 24b is "corrupted beyond emendation, except by violent conjecture."[2105] If one omits the preposition in v. 24c, and makes the verb singular, it may then be translated, "and the best of grain shall wither."

Stevenson says of v. 25, "It may be the concluding line of Job's eighth speech, although nothing beyond v. 12 can be assigned certainly to it."[2106] The question of v. 25, "Who will prove me false?," is a challenge. "Let someone of you prove me false!" Rashi says, "If this is not so, then make my words nought."[2107] Habel takes a similar view to the closing verse of ch. 24:

> In typical disputational style, the speaker closes with a challenge for the gainsayer to refute the preceding argument.[2108]

S. R. Driver, commenting on v. 25, tells us this:

> This verse describes how the sinner, though of course he must die like all other men, enjoys a long life, and has at the end a quick and painless death.[2109]

Chapter 24:25 reminds us very much of 21:13. Rashi says of the closing verse of ch. 24, "If it is not as I say, then let anyone of you prove me a liar."[2110] Mezudat David makes the same conclusion about the verse:

> If you claim that what I said is not true, where is the man who can prove it is a lie, saying that such people do not enjoy great prosperity.[2111]

Job, being sure of his facts, issues a challenge to his listeners in the final verse of ch. 24:

> If it is not so, who will prove me a liar, and show there is nothing in what I say?[2112]

Chapters 22–27: The Organization of the Third Round of Speeches

Before moving on to ch. 25, we might do well to make some comments on the organization of the third cycle of speeches in the book of Job. As it is, Bildad's third discourse consists of only six verses, and Zophar's third speech does not appear at all in the book. This is exacerbated by the fact that Job's third response to Bildad begins in ch. 26 and continues all the way until the end of ch. 31—much longer than any of his other responses to the friends.

Leo Perdue, commenting on these facts and the condition of the third cycle, tells us this:

Perhaps the knottiest literary problem to unravel in the Book of Job is the obvious disarray of the third cycle. Following the consistent pattern of the first two cycles of the debate, one anticipates that the third cycle would have three speeches of Job, alternating with three from the friends. However, in the present arrangement, Zophar has no third speech at all, while Bildad gives a truncated speech in 25:1–6.

Further, the lengthy Job speeches appear to include material quite uncharacteristic of his earlier arguments, but more appropriate for the position consistently argued by the friends (especially 27:13–23 and probably 26:5–14.)[2113]

There have been countless attempts to restore the third cycle of speeches in the book of Job. The simplest rearrangement to achieve a proper order for the third cycle is the following:

- Chapter 21 Job
- Chapter 22 Eliphaz's Third Speech
- Chapter 23 Job
- Chapter 24 Zophar's Third Speech (and 27:13–33)
- Chapter 25:1–6
- Chapter 26:5–14 Bildad's Third Speech
- Chapter 26:1–4
- Chapter 27:1–12 Job[2114]

Chapter 28 also gives us a number of further questions. For one thing, vv. 12–28 is a hymn to Wisdom, or *Hokmah*, that seems to have nothing to do with what comes before it (28:1–11), nor what comes after it (ch. 29). This suggests to many scholars that the Hymn to Wisdom may have been an addition. More will be said about this when we get to ch. 28.

Chapter 25: Bildad's Third Speech

Introduction

Following the outline we have suggested above, we will examine 25:1–6 and 26:5–14 together, because we believe they constitute Bildad's final discourse. Thus, our analysis will be in two parts, 25:1–6 and 26:5–14. Since the first part is only six verses, we may provide a suitable English translation:

Then Bildad the Shuite answered: [v. 1]

Dominion and fear are with God; [v. 2]
He makes peace in His High Heaven.

Is there any number to His armies? [v. 3]

Upon whom does His light not arise?

How then can man be righteous before God? [v. 4]

How can he who is born of a woman be clean?

Behold, even the moon is not bright. [v. 5]

And the stars are not clean in His sight;

How much less man, who is a maggot, [v. 6]

And the son of man, who is a worm.[2115]

Analysis of Chapter 25

25:1–6

Freehof tells us this about these verses:

> The speech contains only six verses and obviously is incomplete. The thought expressed in this fragment is virtually identical with that voiced by Eliphaz in Chapter 4:17–19, namely that even the angels and the heavenly bodies are imperfect in God's sight. How then can man expect to be perfect?[2116]

Rowley thinks the import of v. 2 is that, "God is supreme Lord of the universe, and His power inspires terror."[2117] Rashi says the dominion and fear of v. 2 is "directed toward what Job has said at 23:4." Saadiah renders v. 2 this way:

> Power and terror are with Him.
> And He makes His peace in the heights.[2118]

Rowley also believes "the beginning of this speech is probably now lost, since we have none of the reproach or impatience which usually marks the opening words of the speeches."[2119]

He adds, "Some antecedent to the pronoun may have stood in the lost opening passage."[2120] The LXX has "his ambush" (*'orbo*) rather than "his light" (*'orehu*), with the change of one letter. Duhm, Dhorme, and Fohrer follow this approach.[2121] Mezudat David translates v. 3 as, "Have His troops a number?" He adds this commentary on the verse:

> Do God's troops, the heavenly angels, have a number? This demonstrates the greatness of His ruling power. Accordingly, they are awestruck by His exultation.[2122]

The sense of v. 5a suggests that we follow Robert Gordis's approach and read *mittahat*, or "beneath," with v. 5a, rather than v. 5b. He also makes this argument in terms of the meter of the two lines.[2123] Saadiah renders v. 5 this way:

Lo, even the moon does not shine.

And the stars are not pure in His presence.[2124]

Saadiah says, "The word *ya'ahil* is the same as *yahel*, or 'shine,' as in 31:26 with an infixed *alif*."[2125] Saadiah translates v. 6 this way:

How then, man, who is a worm,

Or the son of Adam, who is a grub?[2126]

Rashi has, "He removes the moon and it will not shine, and the stars are not pure in His eyes."[2127] Rowley gives 15:15 as a parallel to v. 5, and 4:19 and 15:16 to v. 6.[2128] David Kimhi renders the word *ad* as "even," thus he gets, "Behold the moon, even it has no brightness."[2129]

Tur-Sinai has it, "He commands the moon not to shine."[2130] This makes the thought of 25:5 similar to 9:7, where "He commands the sun and it does not rise."[2131] About v. 6, Rowley observes:

> The littleness of man, and his humble origin, are evidence to Bildad of his moral worthlessness. It is hard to see how Bildad could suppose that any of this was an answer to Job.[2132]

Mezudat David tells us this about v. 6:

> How much less a man, who is destined to become devoured by worms, and who is humble and lowly before the Almighty? Surely, man's disobedience to the Creator is considered a grave transgression.[2133]

Stevenson thinks v. 6 has some difficulty. He observes:

> If this line is a sequel to the emended form of v. 5, it makes an elliptical statement about God's treatment of men. But God's display of might in human affairs, very briefly stated, is not a suitable link between vv. 1–5 and 26:5–14, assuming those latter lines to be a part of Bildad's speech.[2134]

Stevenson adds that v. 5 "may be an unskilled addition of someone who misunderstood the meaning of v. 4 in the MT."[2135] S. R. Driver points out that the Hebrew of v. 6 uses two words for "worm."[2136] The first denotes the worm of decay and corruption (see 7:5 and 17:14).

The second expresses the idea of extreme abasement, as in Ps 22:6.[2137] The repetition of the English word "worm" thus weakens the understanding of the verse. Thus, some exegetes render the second word for "worm" as "grub."

Altogether, worm/worms are mentioned seven times in the book of Job. Four of those times, it uses the word *rimmah*; three more times, as well as *tole'ah*, the second word in 25:6. The other verses that use "worms" are at: 7:5; 17:14; 21:26; 24:20; and, of course, 25:6, twice.

THE BOOK OF JOB

26:5–14

INTRODUCTION

Given the outline above, these verses complete Bildad's third and final discourse. Habel labels vv. 5–9, "The Awesome Mystery of God." He calls vv. 10–14, "The Establishment of Cosmic Order." Stevenson also believes Bildad's third speech continues with these verses. He says he makes these judgments on "metrical and grammatical reasons."[2138] Rowley gives 15:15 as a parallel to v. 5. He says, "Here physical brightness is linked with ethical purity." He adds:

> The heavenly bodies are again linked in thought with the angels associated with them, and the clearness of their light accepted as the proof of their moral protection.[2139]

Freehof believes in vv. 5–6, "Job speaks of the world of the shades, or *Rephaim*. They imply that even the hidden world of the dead is open to the eyes of God."[2140] Mezudat David takes a similar view. He observes, "If you wish to recite the greatness of God, I know more than you, and I too can recite 'Behold Gehinnom, the place of the dead.'"[2141] This would imply that Mezudat David takes a divine plan view of vv. 5 and 6. The word *Rephaim* is sometimes translated as "the dead" or "the shades," in various Old Testament passages, such as Ps 88:10; Prov 2:18; 9:18; 21:16; and Isa 14:9 and 26:14 and 19; in addition to Job 26:5.

The noun *Abaddon* used at v. 6b is also employed at 28:26, as well as Ps 88:11 and Prov 15:11 and 27:20. Abaddon is the name of a place. It appears to be an intensive form of the Semitic stem *abad*, that means "perish" or "destroy." This stem is used 184 times in the Hebrew Bible. In the New Testament, the same place is known as *Apollon*, which is an active participle of *apollymi*, that also means "to destroy." (See Revelation 8 and 9.)

The expression *belima*, or "without anything," is linked with the word *tohu*, or "chaos," giving us a subtle variation of the expression *tohu wabohu*, from Gen 1:2 and Jer 4:23. Mezudat David thinks the meaning of v. 7 is, "He spreads the world over empty space, with nothing to support it." He also says, "The world is referred to as the 'north' because the main civilizations of the world are in the north."[2142] The word "North" in v. 7 is *Taphon*, which is also the name of a city east of the Jordan in Gad's territory. (See Josh 13:27; Num 32:35; Ps 48:2; and Isa 14:13.)

Rashi says, "The cloud does not split" in v. 8 means, "It never splits so that its water may fall together to the Earth."[2143] The "closes in" of the next verse, v. 9, is "He closes in with walls the face of His throne, or He makes darkness His secret place."[2144] Ibn Ezra says the throne represents the heavens, as in Isa 66:1.[2145] Some scholars follow Ibn Ezra and vocalize *kese*, or "full moon," for *kisse*, or "throne."[2146]

In v. 10, the Masoretic Text's *hoq haq*, "with a limit, he encircled," is correct, instead of *ḥag ḥoq*, or "He traced a circle." Rashi believes it means, "He encircled a boundary."²¹⁴⁷ Rowley has it, "He has described a circle," or "He has drawn a limit to the circle."²¹⁴⁸ He says the "pillars of the Heavens," in v. 11 are "the great mountains which support the sky, like the Atlas Mountains in classical mythology."²¹⁴⁹

Mezudat David says of v. 11:

> The Earth is known as the pillars of the Heavens because it is in the center, and it is as though the Earth supports the Heavens.²¹⁵⁰

The verb "tremble" in v. 11 is found only here, but its meaning is not in doubt. The verb "stilled" in v. 12 may also mean "stir up," as in Isa 51:15 and Jer 31:35. Rowley says of the verse, "What the author has in mind is the controlling of the primeval waters of creation."²¹⁵¹ Dhorme defends "divides," rather than "stilled."²¹⁵² Rahab in v. 12 appeared earlier at 9:13. Driver says of Rahab, "This is doubtless the mythical dragon which personifies the raging sea."²¹⁵³ The "By His wind" of v. 13 could also be "By His spirit," or "By His breath," but the reference here is probably to the wind that blows away the clouds and brings clear skies. They "were made fair" is literally "becomes fairness," in v. 13. The verb of v. 13b, like at Isa 51:9, should probably be translated "pierced." The "fleeing serpent" of v. 13b, Rowley says, "is the defeat of the flying serpent, or Leviathan." He gives 3:8 and Isa 27:1 as parallel texts.²¹⁵⁴

S. R. Driver translates v. 14 this way:

> Lo, these are but the outskirts of His ways;
>
> And how small of a whisper do we hear of Him?
>
> But the thunder of His power, who can understand?²¹⁵⁵

Freehof says the verse means:

> All these marvels are but the slightest whisper of God's power. His real strength is as much greater as the thunder is greater than a whisper.²¹⁵⁶

Rowley is impressed with the poetic quality of 26:14. He tells us:

> Skillfully the author evokes the sense of the infinite range of God's power, of which he has mentioned but in an insignificant whisper.²¹⁵⁷

Rashi sums up this third response to Bildad's this way:

> Job castigates Bildad for reciting facts already known to all and neglecting to tell the wonders of God. He proceeds to recite some of God's wonders, but does not refute Bildad's arguments, that, in respect to God's exaltation and man's lowliness, any disobedience is regarded as a grave sin, because, if that were so, the wicked too should be punished severely for their sins.²¹⁵⁸

Bildad seems to avoid the challenge of Job at 24:35. Instead, in his third speech Bildad appears to have repeated ideas he has introduced or has held earlier in the dialogue. In fact, Bildad repeats ideas expressed earlier by Eliphaz at 4:17ff. and 15:14ff.

Bildad also appears to accept ideas confirmed by Job at 9:2 and 14:4. Bildad's brief third effort represents his rapidly expiring breath. The lack of Zophar's third speech may be the silence of the vanquished.

Chapter 26:2–4 and 27: Job's Answer to Bildad

Introduction

Following the outline suggested above in regards to the order of the third cycle of speeches, as well as W. B. Stevenson and other scholars, Job's response to Bildad's third discourse consists of the following:

- Chapter 26:2–4.
- Chapter 27:2–6, 11–12, and 22.

In our analysis, we will consider Job's third response to Bildad in these terms. These verses are Job's ninth speech in the book. Presumably, the heading was written after the displacement of 26:5–14 by one who knew or suspected that these words were those of Bildad.

Analysis of Chapter 26

26:2–4

These verses begin Job's third response to Bildad. In v. 2, Jastrow tells us, "The 'one without power,' and the 'one without strength,' are not intended to describe Job, but God, though, of course, in a sarcastic way."[2159] Freehof says of the first four verses of ch. 26:

> In this chapter, Job begins vv. 1–4 with, as he always does, dismissing the value of the speech of the friends. Then he follows with a description of God's grandeur in nature, much as he did in chapter nine.[2160]

Mezudat David observes about v. 2, "Have you not helped with your words one who himself is powerless to comprehend Divine Providence?"[2161] About the following verse, he observes, "What counsel have you given to the one who has no wisdom of his own?"[2162] Rowley, as well as other modern exegetes, think that v. 2 introduces an "oath." He "swears by the God who has harmed him."[2163] This is one of the many oaths referred to in the book. (See, for examples, 5:19; 22:27; ch. 31; and 33:26.)

The reference to "my breath" in v. 3 "derives from Gen 2:7, where the breath of God animates human beings." Jastrow believes that v. 4 is an insertion. He says of the verse, "A pious commentator in order to give a different turn to Job's bold insistence, inserts v. 4."²¹⁶⁴ Habel tells us that the meaning of vv. 4–5 is clear: "If even the celestial realms are not free of guilt, how can a mortal be found innocent before God?"²¹⁶⁵

27:2–6, 11–12, and 22

Chapter 27:1–6 is the second time that oaths, vows, or promises are mentioned in the book. At 22:27, Eliphaz instructs Job to pay his vows, using the plural form of the noun *sebu'a*. At 27:1–6, Job makes his own vow or promise (*nedar*) to God. There are a number of varieties of oaths, vows, and promises in the Old Testament. Many of these invoke God, such as Judg 8:19 and 1 Sam 19:6. Others are prohibitions against the invoking of foreign gods, such as at Jer 5:7 and 12:16.

We also see in the Old Testament a ritual by which oaths, vows, and promises were to be kept in ancient Israel. Both Gen 24:9 and 47:29 speak of the parties of a promise holding each other's genitals in their hands, as a sign that each will keep the promise. At any rate, dozens of oaths, vows, and promises may be seen throughout the Old Testament.

Analysis of Chapter 27

27:2–6, 11–12, and 22

The use of the word *masal* is the normal word for "proverb," in ancient Hebrew. Indeed, Rashi renders it "parable" in v. 1. The opening of v. 2, "As *El* lives," is a standard formula introducing an oath. It calls for a curse on the speaker, if it does not come true (see 1 Sam 14:39 and 45). Earlier Job was ready to summons God to court, or for God to summon him (13:22.) He had issued challenges (13:19), made accusations (9:22 and 28), and protested his innocence (9:20–21). His goal was to pursue litigation, so that his innocence might be established.

Now Job takes the final step. He speaks of an oath to the court as if it were in session. In his oath, he refers to the hearing, whether one is listening or not. The Hebrew text of v. 3 is quite ambiguous. It could mean, "My soul is yet whole in me," or "My soul is bitter in me." Mezudat David renders v. 4, "My lips will speak no injustice." He seems to suggest "If my lips speak injustice, may I be punished for it."²¹⁶⁶

Rashi observes about v. 5:

> It would be disgraceful for me to speak hypocritically and to admit they are right and that I have dealt wickedly, since I do not believe it in my heart. Until I die, I will not give up my innocence.²¹⁶⁷

Rowley says about v. 5, "To admit that the friends charges were true would be a violation of his duty to God, and that so long as he lived, he will not repudiate his integrity."²¹⁶⁸ Habel points out that the *halila li* of v. 5a, or "far be it from me," is a "formula for introducing a serious declaration that carries with it self-imprecation."[2169] He says by vv. 5–6, Job is saying, "May I be damned if I declare you in the right."[2170]

Saadiah believes v. 6 is an argument against dualism: Light and darkness are not gods "because they limit one another."[2171] Stevenson says of v. 6b, "The unexpressed object of the verb is clearly Job himself."[2172] Rowley says of the meaning of v. 6 is this:

> Job affirms that, as he looks back over his life, his conscience does not reproach him. In what has survived in this speech Job advances nothing new, but merely scorns Bildad's defense of God and reaffirms his own innocence. It is this that makes it probable that part of this speech has been lost.[2173]

Mezudat David says the meaning of v. 6 is clear: "The righteousness that I practiced was always steady, never incidental. I clung tenaciously to it without slackening, and my heart never deviated from it."[2174] Rashi says the import of v. 11 is, "I will instruct you what the standard is that is in God's hands, and what is with *Shaddai*, I will not conceal."[2175] S. R. Driver says that v. 11 is about, "The methods of God's Providence, in particular, His treatment of the wicked."[2176] Freehof says of v. 12:

> The true evidence of a man's innocence is his desire to remain in communion with God. How, therefore, can you falsely and vainly call me wicked, when you yourself have seen how I constantly sought to converse with the Almighty?[2177]

Rashi says the meaning of v. 22 is, "The one who casts evil upon him will show no compassion."[2178] Driver says the "clapping of hands" in v. 22, "is a token of malicious delight."[2179] He gives Lam 2:15 as a parallel text. "By the force of Thy hand, Thou torturest me / Thou liftest me up with the wind," is how Jastrow ends v. 22.[2180] This is a far cry from the RSV's:

> It hurls at him without pity;
> He flees from its power in headlong flight.[2181]

Or from the KJV's:

> For God shall cast upon him, and not spare.
> He will fain flee out of his hand.[2182]

Chapter 28: Mining and the Hymn to Wisdom

Introduction

Nearly all modern critics divide ch. 28 into two parts. The first of these parts, vv. 1–11, describes the activities of miners in the ancient Near East. The second part, vv. 12–28, is a hymn to the concept of *Hokmah*, or wisdom. Freehof is surely correct when he describes ch. 28 this way:

This chapter is a song in praise of Wisdom. It begins with a vivid description of mining operations and the engineering skill involved. Then it moves to the thought that in spite of man's great skill and in spite of all his explorations in the depth of the earth, he has found no true wisdom.[2183]

John Wycliffe tells us about ch. 28:

> Some commentators regard this chapter as a hymnic interlude inserted by the poet to separate the dialogue from Job's final summing up in chapters 29 to 31.[2184]

Here it is treated as a continuation of Job's instruction "concerning the hand of God." As such, it further demonstrates that Job's piety is both genuine and fervent. Like Newsom and Matthew Henry, Wycliffe divides ch. 28 into four sections: vv. 1–11; vv. 12–19; vv. 20–27; and v. 28. We will follow that division in our analysis.

Analysis of Chapter 28

28:1–11: *Miners and Mining*

Newsom describes this passage this way:

> The first part of the poem, concerning the God-like power of human beings to search out and mine precious minerals, is divided into a series of small strophes. In vv. 1–2, the topic is announced. Verses 3–4 recount the search for minerals in a distant and inaccessible land. Verses 5–6 describe the land and its subterranean riches. The extra-ordinary human achievement locating the source of such riches is underscored by contrasting the animals' ignorance concerning its location (vv. 7–8.) The climax comes in the account of the mining operation itself and the successful bringing to light the hidden treasures.[2185]

The text of Job 28 begins in v. 1 with the noun *moṣa'*, usually rendered as "mine." The noun derives from the verb *yasa* that means "to go into," or "to come out of." The word *moṣa'* is nominative in v. 1a. Rowley says the initial *ki* is an "asseverative particle."[2186] Pope translates *moṣa'* as "smelter," from an Arabic root meaning "to be clean."[2187] Blommerde thinks the preposition *min* in the expression *me'apar* does double duty to mean "from dust" and from *'eben*, or "stone."[2188]

Robert Gordis takes the subject of v. 2a as "stone," and reads, "Ore is poured out of copper."[2189] The RSV, on the other hand, has it:

> Iron is taken out of the Earth,
> And copper is smelted from the ore.[2190]

Rashi also believes that v. 1 means, "Gold has a place where they refine and smelt it, and where copper is smelted from stone."[2191] Dhorme also takes the verb of v. 2 to be rendered "is smelted," but adds the adjective "hard." Thus he has, "A hard stone becomes copper."[2192] The first verb of v. 3 "puts" is in the singular, but most modern translations put it in the plural. Thus, the RSV has, "Men put . . ." Rowley agrees that "the verb is ambiguous," but it makes more sense to say "mortals" are the subject.[2193] The noun in v. 3, *qes* in Hebrew, is variously interpreted as "end," "extremity." It is parallel to the noun *taklit*, or "limit" in the following line. Newsom points out that many of the expressions in vv. 3-4 are used "to describe the darkness of Sheol," as at 10:21-22, for example.[2194] Rowley says that v. 4c "refers to miners suspended by ropes into the shaft of a mine."[2195]

In order to make v. 5b more parallel, Gordis reads *lehem*, or bread, as "heat," citing a variant form at 20:23.[2196] Holscher says the Vulgate's *bemo* for *kemo*, and thus renders the line "like fire,"[2197] rather than the "by fire" of the RSV. Freehof thinks v. 4 "describes the shaft dug in far-off, lonely lands, where the metal is discovered."[2198] He agrees that the verse describes "miners swinging, as they hang."[2199] Tur-Sinai thinks the swinging does not refer to the miners, but to the mines, "which are far from human habitation."[2200]

Freehof says, "The path no bird knows," "describes the shafts which neither bird of prey, with its keen eyes, have never seen, nor the lion of the desert has ever passed. Yet man, who refers 'to a path unknown to brigands.'"[2201] He explains v. 7b this way:

> When the end comes to the place from which sapphires are mined, it becomes totally desolate, so that even the desert birds do not frequent it.[2202]

The "proud beasts" of v. 8 is literally "the sons of Pride" in the Hebrew text. The same expression occurs again at 41:34. The word for "lion" in v. 8 is the same used at 4:10. Dhorme has "leopard."[2203] Others, like S. Monwinckel, for example, thinks the reference is to a mythical beast of the serpent variety, related to Leviathan.[2204] Mythical creatures, however, seem out of place here, so we think that meaning is not likely the proper one.

Rashi thinks this entire section, vv. 4-9, refer to "the people of Sodom and Gemorrah and their destruction."[2205] Mezudat David observes about these verses:

> This is a general description of various things in the world, each having its beginning and its end, which Job will ultimately contrast with wisdom, which has neither a beginning nor an end. In v. 9, he depicts the final destruction of the flinty rocks. God stretches forth His hand and overturns them from the root by means of the wind, which is locked up in the bowels of the Earth.[2206]

Rashi says this about v. 11:

> When it comes time for the rivers to end, God binds them up in the depths, that is, He stops them up. When the Earth will come to an end, He will bring out His hidden spring into the light, and its waters shall increase and cover the face of the Earth.[2207]

Rashi adds about the verse, "As it is true that all physical things come to an end, physical success is of no value."[2208] Rowley says the meaning of v. 11 is, "Man has explored the sources of rivers by penetrating underground to their springs."[2209] Newsom agrees about v. 11. She says,

> It contrasts God's "forcing open" streams and channels with God's drying up the rivers.[2210]

Jastrow, on the other hand, thinks that vv. 10–11 are about "the gathering place of all living things, that is, death."[2211]

28:12–27: The Hymn to Wisdom

Samuel Terrien describes the opening of the psalm to wisdom in ch. 28 of the book of Job this way:

> There can be little doubt that this magnificent poem on the inaccessibility of wisdom does not belong to the discourses of Job. It is not written in his style; it is not connected with the Joban context (either 27:2–6 or 29:1ff.). If Job had uttered it, the rebuke of Yahweh to him (chaps. 38–41), would be either considerably weakened or even completely uncalled for.[2212]

Verse 14 uses the terms *tehom* (the "deep") and *yam* (the sea). Terrien asks of this usage:

> Is this merely a poetic adornment, or does the poet refer to these words to the cultic practices of ancient Egyptian and Semitic polytheism?[2213]

Rowley believes "the deep" is the "primeval abyss, the subterranean reservoir from which the sea is fed and the floods emerge."[2214] He gives Gen 7:11 and 49:25 as parallel texts. About v. 15, Rowley observes, "Not only can wisdom not be found, wherever it may be sought, but if it could be found no wealth could equal it."[2215] The word for "gold" in v. 15 is found only here. It comes from a root that means "to enclose." Gray renders it "sterling gold."[2216] Indeed, this passage has a profusion of words for "gold," five separate words between v. 15 and v. 19.

The verb in v. 16 is only found here and in v. 19. It is a by-form of a word in Lam 4:2, and it appears to mean "to weigh against." The expression, "the gold of Ophir" has been variously discussed. The word for "gold" used in v. 17 is the same word at v. 1. The KJV gives the noun "crystal" after the conjunction at the beginning of v. 17a. The word only appears here. Glass was a very rare commodity in the ancient Near East, and the word for "glass" or "crystal" is another hapax in Job.

The MT has "a vessel of fine gold" at v. 17b, but other versions usually make it a plural. Thus, the RSV has "jewels of fine gold." The RSV has "coral" and "glass" for the nouns of v. 18a. The word for "coral" is also found at Ezek 27:16. Delitzsch and Holscher both think the first noun should be "pearls."[2217] The second noun, *gabis* in Hebrew, is found only here. A related term, from the GBS root, is *'elgabis*, means "hailstones" at Ezek 13:11 and 13.

The RSV gives "topaz" for the first noun in v. 19. This follows Theodosius and the Vulgate.[2218] The Targum renders it, "green pearl." It is most likely a borrowed foreign word. It perhaps suggests that the color of the stone is yellow. The "Ethiopia" of v. 19 is probably correct. Pliny tells us there was an island in the Red Sea region called "Topazos."[2219]

Verse 20 repeats the question at v. 12, except here we have "whence comes," rather than "where shall be found?" Some exegetes change v. 12 so it more resembles v. 20. Peake says if uniformity is a goal, v. 20 should be conformed with v. 12, not the other way around.[2220] The "all living" of v. 21 implies all animals and people, as at 30:23, where it just means all people. Abaddon is personified in v. 22, along with Death. Rowley gives 26:6 as a parallel text.[2221]

Terrien says of v. 22:

> Religious techniques, as well as scientific achievements, are futile of themselves in the domain which matters most for human existence.[2222]

Rowley gives Ps 44:1–2 as a parallel to v. 22b.[2223] Saadiah says that v. 23 should be rendered "God comprehends its way," because it is analogous to the first acts of creation, which he alone comprehends.[2224] Ibn Ezra, Rashi, and Mezudat David translate the two nouns at the beginning of v. 22 as "Destruction and Death."[2225] Mezudat David explains:

> The destruction and death are those who have died long ago, who said that they heard the praise of wisdom from others, and that no one can achieve it because of its preciousness. Only God knows its location, as well as how to reach it.[2226]

Samuel Terrien introduces vv. 23–28 this way:

> When all human efforts have failed, and only then, is man ready to come to himself and acknowledge that the God who created the cosmos and remains still "the faithful Creator" (vv. 24–26), understands the way to wisdom ... and knows its place (v. 23.) For wisdom is the supreme possession of God. The poet does not say that God created it (cf. Prov. 8:22–31 and Ecclus. 1–9), but he insists in his climactic verse that God, at the moment of His creative activity, took cognizance of its reality.[2227]

Mezudat David observes about v. 27, "He prepares wisdom for the creation by arranging it in its best possible order and then searched it out to know its secrets." He adds, "This is an anthropomorphism expressing the idea that God understands its way because God had used it in days of yore."[2228] In Mezudat David's view, these may be another instance of the wisdom of the fathers motif.

28:28

The closing verse of ch. 28, that is, v. 28, is omitted by some editors because only here, and at 12:9, does the MT use the divine name *Yahweh*, "Lord," or "*Adonai*"; and because v. 28 appears to be disconnected to what follows it in ch. 29, as well as what preceded it at vv. 12–27. Terrien believes that v. 28 is a "choral interlude," that "subtly prepares Job for the higher level of the theophany to follow" (38:1—42:6).[2229] Rashi observes about "fear of the Lord" and "wisdom" in v. 28, "One requires the other, and wisdom is unseemly without the fear of the Lord."[2230]

Mezudat David explains v. 28 this way:

> Because human intelligence cannot fathom the depths of wisdom, it is as though God said to man that fear of the Lord is the introduction to wisdom, and shunning evil is the introduction to understanding; i.e., through the fear of God one can achieve the knowledge of hidden matters, naturally unattainable, for then God will have bestowed wisdom upon him. All of this refers back to the beginning of the chapter, "For silver has a mine and gold has a place where it is refined." That is, that wisdom is superior to everything in the world, and it cannot be attained except through the fear of God. Thus, if even the same incident befalls a righteous man and a wicked one, it is worth being righteous in order to attain the mysteries of wisdom.[2231]

One interesting feature of 28:28 is that the Hebrew refers to God as *Adonai*, and not as *Yahweh*, the ancient Hebrew name that could not be pronounced. Mezudat David seems to assent to the divine plan theory with respect to 28:28, principally because of the word *Adonai* and the "mysteries of Wisdom" which that name implies.

However we interpret Job 28:28, it is clear that the verse tells us, and Job understands, that man must reverently acknowledge that he and his world are subject to their Creator. A man begins to be wise when he ceases to strive for wisdom independently of God. He advances through the attainment of wisdom through the laws of God and the observations of nature. The fear of the Lord is the beginning of wisdom.

One final aspect of the Hymn to Wisdom in ch. 28 is the extensive vocabulary of the poem, particularly when it comes to words for "gold." In a space of nineteen verses, the author(s) use four different words for gold. These are: *zahab* (vv. 1, 6, and 16); *sagur* (v. 15); *paz* (v. 17); and *kethem* (also v. 17).

Chapters 29–31: Job's Final Discourse

Introduction

These three chapters are the final laments from Job. In this sense, they match the patriarch's first lament in ch. 3. Chapter 29 looks back to the past, to happier times before Job's sufferings began. Chapter 30 deals with the present and to the woeful state into which he has fallen. In ch. 31, Job's asks for an urgent request that God hear his lament, so he might present his case.

These three chapters, 29–31, are Job's final response to the friends, as well as the closing of the dialogue portion of the book. Both Samuel Terrien and Matthew Henry believe ch. 29 should be divided into three sections.[2232] The first of these is vv. 1–6, which Henry calls "Job's Former Comforts." The second section is vv. 7–17, which Henry labels, "The Honor Paid to Job." Henry refers to part three of ch. 29 as "The Crown of Job's Prosperity."[2233]

Chapter 29, as we shall see, also contains one of the most controversial verses in the book. It comes at v. 18a, where the word *chol* appears. Some have rendered the word as "ostrich." Others as the "phoenix." And still others as "sand," or even "palm tree." More will be said at the end of our analysis of ch. 29.

Analysis of Chapter 29

29:1–6

Chapter 29, as with ch. 27, again opens with the observation that Job again takes up his discourse. This may imply that he has been interrupted. If this was the case, then the poem of wisdom separates Job's reply to Bildad in ch. 27, from this, his final speech. In these opening verses, Job laments the life that he has lost. As Newsom says of these verses, "Job first recounts his sense of God's protective presence (vv. 2–4.) His language is personal, relational, and richly emotive."[2234]

Rashi thinks v. 2 says, "Would that I were in my early months, like the early days when I was in my greatness."[2235] He says that v. 3 is "an expression of light and joy."[2236] Mezudat David observes about v. 3, "When the light of His bestowal of plenty shone on my head."[2237] Rowley agrees that the lamp and the light are symbols of blessing. He gives 2 Sam 22:29 as a parallel to v. 3, as well as Ps 36:9.[2238]

Rowley believes the expression "my autumn days" in v. 4 means, "the ripeness of my days." He adds:

> The autumn is the season of maturity, when the fruits are gathered. It is the time of life in which a man reaps what he has sown, a time which ought to be a mellow, fruitful, happy season for the righteous man.[2239]

In v. 5, Rowley believes "Job refers to the loss of his children." He says the line is purposely shortened to add to the poignancy.[2240] Both Theodosius and the Vulgate render v. 4, "autumn days, denoting the time of youth," or so says Andersen.[2241] Mezudat David says of v. 5:

> When the Almighty was still with me, or benefit me, and my young were still around me, to serve me.[2242]

Nineteenth-century Russian rabbi Malbim maintains that v. 5 is about "Job's success with his children. God has blessed him with sons, who stood around him."[2243] Mezudat David thinks that v. 6 refers to "the places where he walked were washed with cream that was so plentiful that it spread on the ground, and no one else would bother to gather it up."[2244] Newsom says the *hema* of v. 6, "denotes a yogurt-like food often associated with gestures of hospitality."[2245]

She gives Gen 18:8 and Judg 5:25 as parallel texts.

29:7–17

Most critics point out that in vv. 7–10 the venue shifts from the family and home to the city and its gate, the place for political speech and debate. (See Deut 21:19 and Ruth 4:1–2.) These verses clearly show the honor that Job is given by his peers, first by young men and then by the sages of the city. The latter arise in his presence and wait for him to be seated. As Newsom describes these verses, "Job is the dynamic center that reorganizes social space."[2246] Both Rashi and Mezudat David believe v. 7 refers to "a high ceiling, prepared for a chair for the elders of the city to sit, and when I was in the city they prepared my seat."[2247] Rashi says v. 8 means, "The youth hid and the old men rose in my presence."[2248] Rowley agrees. He observes about v. 8:

> Job's arrival was marked by the deference paid to him by the young and the old. The young modestly withdrew, while the old men remained standing respectfully until Job sat.[2249]

The nouns in vv. 9–10 are variously translated. Rowley has "princes and nobles."[2250] The NIV has "chief men and nobles." The RSV, "princes and nobles." The KJV, "princes and nobles."[2251] Clearly, the first nouns means the "chief magistrates of the city," and the "nobles" are most likely the next in order of authority.

Rowley says of the meaning of v. 11:

> Job's prosperity and prestige did not earn him the envy and hatred of others, because it bred no arrogance in him.[2252]

Rashi says of v. 11:

> All of this came to me because of the uprightness of my ways, for the ear that heard of the propriety of my act would praise me, and the eye that saw the goodness of my ways would bear witness for me.[2253]

Mezudat David says of v. 12:

> My custom was that at all times I would deliver the poor man who would cry out to me because of oppressors, and also the orphan, and the one who had no one to help him because of his bad luck.[2254]

Jastrow thinks that v. 11 means that "God looked upon me as fortunate."[2255] The KJV has "robe and diadem" for the final two nouns of v. 14.[2256] The NIV has "robe and turban," as does the RSV. Newsom remarks about vv. 12–17, "Here the focus shifts from the inner circle of Job's peers to persons occupying a more marginal place on the social map: the poor, the orphan, and the wretched."[2257]

Mezudat David says the meaning of v. 16 is, "If I did not know the truth of a claim, I shall investigate it."[2258] Ralbag says of the following verse, v. 17, "This represents the unjust taking of the property of the poor by force."[2259] Newsom says, "His metaphor in v. 17 is implicitly that of a shepherd, someone like David, who would risk his own life to rescue a sheep carried off by a predator."[2260] She gives 1 Sam 17:34–35 as a parallel text.

29:18–25

Freehof points out that v. 18 is a difficult text. He renders the line, "I shall die with my nest and multiply my days as the Phoenix."[2261] He says of v. 18a, "He means because of my righteousness, I was confident of having a happy life to the very end."[2262] Mezudat David translates it as, "multiply my days as numerous as the grains of sand."[2263] Tur-Sinai has a similar translation.[2264] Habel says of v. 18:

> The key issue in this crux, is whether the word *ḥol* is to be rendered "sand" or "Phoenix."[2265]

Marvin Pope favors "sand," and challenges the evidence for those who say "phoenix."[2266] John Wesley observes about v. 18, "Multiply. See how apt even good men are, to set death at a distance to them."[2267] The LXX has "like a palm tree," as do Ball and Kissane.[2268] This involves reading *kannahol* for *chol*, with the *nahal* being a rare term for "palm tree." The Septuagint translates *stelekos phonikos*, "like the Phoenix," while the Masoretic Text reads, *kachol*, where *ka* is the preposition "like," and *cohl*, is "sand," or even "palm tree." Also see Judg 21:21 and 22 and Jer 23:19, as parallel texts. Rabbinic opinion, for the most part, sided with the "phoenix" theory. William Albright says he found this bird in Ras Shamra mythology.[2269] The phoenix is a symbol both of longevity and immortality, but it is improbable that this is what Job has in mind at v. 18. "Sand" is the most likely translation, as Edward Greenstein has suggested in his recent translation published by Yale University Press in 2019.[2270]

Rowley says of vv. 19–20:

> Fine poetic figures for the basis of Job's confidence mark this and the following verse.[2271]

Rowley gives Ps 1:3; Jer 17:8; and Ezek 31:7 as parallels for vv. 19–20.[2272] Hoffmann wishes to read *kidon* for *kabod* to mean a word parallel to a "bow."[2273] The bow, of course, is a symbol of strength. (See Gen 49:24; Ps 46:9; Jer 49:35.) Wesley agrees.

He says, "My strength is signified by my bow because in ancient times, the bow and arrow were the principal instruments of war."[2274]

Habel says of vv. 21–24:

> Job resumes the theme of vv. 7–10, where he was a respected leader and judge of his community. Job's words were authoritative and final. His counsel was heeded by all. His wisdom was awaited as people await the rain, especially the spring rain of March and April, which was vital for crops.[2275]

Freehof agrees with this analysis. He writes:

> From v. 21 to the end of the chapter, Job elaborates the thoughts expressed in vv. 8–11, that everyone listened to him at the gate when he spoke.[2276]

Rashi explains v. 24 this way:

> Even when I mock them, they took my laughter seriously out of respect for me.[2277]

Ibn Ezra says of v. 24, "A ruler should be very serious with his dignity, but with me, when I laughed, I was undignified, though they still respected me."[2278] Rowley renders v. 24 as:

> I smiled on them when they had no confidence,
> And the light on my countenance they did not cast down.[2279]

Wesley has "laughed" for the first verb in v. 24. He says of the verse, "I carried myself so familiarly with them, that they could scarce believe their eyes and ears."[2280] Rashi says the meaning of v. 24 is, "They were afraid to get near me and to become familiar with me."[2281] Mezudat David observes, "They did not become familiar with me to lower my stature."[2282] He adds, "They did not look at the features of my countenance."[2283]

Rashi explains the final verse of ch. 29, v. 25, this way:

> I would choose their way. All their ways and their counsel, I would choose for them, for they would ask me, "Which way shall we go and what shall we do?"[2284]

Habel says that v. 25 "is an important summative statement delineating Job's status in the society."[2285] Ewald thinks the final verse "provided a transition of what is to follow in the form of a barbed reminder to the friends that they had so miserably failed to comfort Job."[2286] John Wesley observes about v. 25, "They sought me out for advice in all difficult cases, and I directed them about the methods they should take."[2287] Tur-Sinai translates the phrase in v. 25 as "as one comforts the mourners."[2288] Szold says v. 25 means: "A King sits among the troops after the battle and comforts the mourners among them for those who were slain."[2289] Pope and Dhorme prefer,

"Where I led them, they were willing to go."[2290] Kissane believes that v. 25 is a "summary of Job's relations with the elders (v. 25a), with the people in general (v. 25b), and with those in trouble (v. 25c.) The final clause referring back to vv. 11–13."[2291] This views seems the most likely.

Chapter 30: Job Continues His Final Response

Introduction

Chapter 30 continues Job's final speech in the book. Freehof tells us this about ch. 30:

> This is the second half of the speech which began in chapter 29. Chapter 29 talked of his erstwhile prosperity and now he speaks of his present misery. He describes first, in vv. 1–15, the worthless people who now mock him. Verse 16 to the end refers again to his physical and mental suffering.[2292]

Although Freehof divides ch. 30 into only two parts, other scholars like Matthew Henry and Samuel Terrien prefer to see the chapter as having four parts. Terrien calls the entire chapter by the name, "The Suffering in the Present Time,"[2293] and divides it into the following four parts: vv. 1–8, which he calls, "Irreverence of Worthless Men"; the second section, vv. 9–15, Terrien gives the name, "Hostility of Society"; vv. 16–23 of ch. 30, Terrien calls, "Cruelty of God"; and he labels the final section of ch. 30 "Misery and Dereliction."[2294]

In ch. 30, Job turns to his present state. C. S. Rodd, in his 1990 commentary on the book, tells us this about the chapter:

> As he turns to his present suffering we detect a new bitterness. He is mocked by the young outcasts of society, and this brings him to describe those who scoff at him in words that show little sympathy for his plight. He declares that he would not have put their fathers on a level with his own watch dogs.[2295]

Chapter 30 of Job, like many previous passages, also contains several verses that describe the symptoms of Job's disease, particularly vv. 16–23 and 30. The chapter also contains many of the Hebrew words of the poet's characteristic vocabulary. He employs, for examples, the word *nefesh* in v. 16; *afar va efer*, or "dust and ashes," in v. 19; and the verb *'emas*,' "abhor" or "despise," that is also used in Job 42:5–6.

Analysis of Chapter 30

30:1–8

H. H. Rowley describes these opening verses of ch. 30 this way:

From his former state Job now turns to the present, and in this chapter he sets the misery he now experiences against the honor of the past. He begins by describing the off-scourings of the people who now treat him with disdain.[2296]

Both Duhm and Peake believe that these verses are misplaced and belong to the description of the outcasts at 24:5ff.[2297] Peake retains v. 1, which Duhm thinks is a transition verse; so too Strahan.[2298] Budde removes only vv. 3–7.[2299] The contempt that Job shows to outcasts here seems to be beyond his normal views in the rest of the book. The verb "make sport of" in v. 1 is also employed at 29:24, but the preposition in 30:1 is different. Here it is vulgar mockery, at 29:24, a gracious smile.

Rowley says that v. 2, "would seem to refer to the fathers, who were degenerate weaklings, unfit for honest work."[2300] Freehof observes about v. 2, "These are such useless people that even their crops are destroyed under their hands."[2301] Rashi says the meaning of v. 2 is:

> In those days they were useless, and they were useless, for trouble came because of them.[2302]

Mezudat David remarks about v. 2, "I despised them, not only because they were low people with no redeeming qualities, but also because, as I said their strength was of no value. It was scant, and not enough to save the sheep from predators."[2303] Rashi says of v. 3:

> Because of their poverty and because of their hunger, they were ashamed to mingle in people's company and so dwelt in solitude.[2304]

Verse 3 contains some of the best alliteration in the book: *'emesh sho'ah umesho'ah*, or "the darkness of the desolate dunes." Rowley says the word for "hunger" in v. 3 is rendered "famine" here.[2305] Hitzig has the line, "They are rolled up with hunger," but that seems not to be an improvement over the RSV's "Through want and hard hunger."[2306] At v. 3a, Terrien says the meaning of vv. 3–4 is this: "Their physical weakness was the result of their hunger, which in turn was due to the fact that they were expelled from society (vv. 5–7)."[2307] The word *gew* in v. 5 in an Aramaism, but there is a Phoenician word *gew* that means "community." In fact, the *min*-gew is the first in a whole series of obscure places in this chapter that have other Semitic origins.

Rowley says of v. 6, "It is bitter to Job to realize that people who live in such squalor and degradation feel able to taunt him, now that he is an outcast and relegated to his dung-heap."[2308]

Gray thinks "bray" in v. 7 is "the cry of lust," but Dhorme says it is "the hoarse cry of hunger."[2309] The Hebrew verb *yinhaqu* is generally used for donkeys. The precise plant mentioned in v. 7b cannot be identified. Dhorme thinks it is "nettles."[2310] Mezudat David agrees. The word for the plant in v. 7, *pirhah*, is another hapax. He thinks it is a particularly coarse variety of "couch grass."[2311]

How to translate v. 8a is not so easy. It literally says, "sons of a senseless person," or "sons of a nameless person," in the MT. Rashi has it, "sons of ignoble people." The Targum agrees. The RSV translates v. 8 this way:

> A senseless, a disreputable brood,
>
> They have been whipped out of the land.[2312]

Rashi prefers, "were broken in my days from the land," for v. 8b. Ibn Ezra says of v. 8b:

> They were crushed and humbled more than the Earth, or more than the people of the Earth.[2313]

Rowley has it, "They were thrust out of the land," for v. 8b.[2314] Saadiah says the meaning of v. 8 is this:

> Everyone has some senseless babble which he takes for words of wisdom in trying to unriddle my downfall.[2315]

30:9–15

Samuel Terrien introduces this second section of ch. 30 this way:

> Whatever the significance of the preceding verses, there is little doubt that in the present passage, Job is developing the familiar theme of his own social isolation He explains it as the result of his physical exhaustion which even the lowest samples of humanity interpret as an act of God.[2316]

Terrien suggests that vv. 12–14 "confirm the fact that Job has lost his nobility and salvation." He gives Ps 51:12 as a parallel text.[2317] Rowley takes another approach. He says of these verses:

> Whereas he was once treated with deference by great and small, and those whom he helped blessed by his name, now he is scorned and condemned, and treated as one abandoned by God. On all sides he is besieged, until he feels like a city being breached by its foes. His honor is cast to the wind and his prosperity has vanished like a cloud.[2318]

Jastrow translates vv. 14–15 this way:

> They block my path (v. 14).
>
> They scale my bulwark.
>
> As through a wide breach they come;
>
> As a storm they roll themselves upon me (v. 15).
>
> My honor is chased as the wind.

And my welfare passes away as a cloud.[2319]

Jastrow rightly points out that v. 15 has three lines, rather than the customary two in this chapter. Rashi translates v. 15 this way:

> Terrors turned upon me,
>
> They pursue my nobility as a spirit.[2320]

Rashi says the "nobility" in v. 15b "is the noble spirit that rested upon him from the beginning," and that the "terrors," of v. 15a are "demons."[2321] Mezudat David, on the other hand, remarks about v. 15:

> A group of terrors turned upon me, it pursued my soul as a wind, etc. It pursued me like the chaff of the mountains, and the salvation which usually would have come to me passed swiftly away, as a cloud moving from place to place.[2322]

Ibn Ezra says of v. 15:

> This refers to Job's early days when he enjoyed prosperity. When terrors turned upon me, my luck would pursue them as a wind, and a cloud, my salvation would quickly pass to me. And now . . .[2323]

In v. 15, the translation *netivati*, or "my path," is employed in several versions. The Syriac Version, however, reads it *nedivati*, or "my nobility." John Alter in 15b suggests that Job says, "My rescue like a cloud passes on." Many other interpreters, however, give exotic meaning to the Hebrew *yeshu'ati*.

C. S. Rodd is probably correct when he relates about vv. 15–19:

> The only excuse for showing such contempt for such wretched outcasts is that Job has sunk so low that even the most despised rejects of society now are able to taunt him.[2324]

30:16–23

Samuel Terrien introduces this section of ch. 30 this way:

> The physical pains that Job endures are indeed due to the direct will of the Deity. So for the last time, Job addresses his divine tormentor and utters his accusation against Him. Not only does God refuse to answer his proud prayer (notice the possible implications of the verb "I stand up" in v. 20b, but he also intensifies his strokes (vv. 21–22), until death comes (v. 23).[2325]

Jastrow thinks that vv. 16–24 are part of Job's third response to Bildad, and v. 25 should be transferred to Job's "supplementary speech."[2326] Freehof says that the meaning of v. 18 is "either that his body is so swollen that his clothes are too tight, or in the restlessness of his sleepless nights, his clothes become uncomfortable."[2327] Rodd believes the picture in v. 18 is of a man choking in his own phlegm, though the meaning of the simile is not clear. "God" has been added in v. 19 to indicate who the subject of the verb is. Without naming him, Job blames God for his misfortunes.[2328]

30:24–31

Freehof believes that v. 25 is in "the form of an oath." "May this and this calamity come upon me."[2329] If Freehof is correct, this is the fourth time in the book where we see oaths, vows, or promises. (See 5:19; 22:27; 27:1–6.) Rashi says of v. 25:

> You know and recognize whether I was compassionate and did not weep for the poor, who had difficult times, and whether my soul did not grieve for the needy, this that befell me because of all these.[2330]

Rowley points out that the word for "grieve" is another hapax of the book. An adjectival version of it is at Isa 19:10.[2331] With various changes, Driver renders vv. 24–25 this way:

> Surely no begger would put out his hand,
>
> If he had found no relief in his plight.
>
> Without my having wept for one hardly treated by life
>
> And my soul being grieved for the needy.[2332]

Driver's approach is quite ingenious, but not convincing. Stevenson says that v. 25 is "quite alien to the context." He thinks it might belong to 31:19f.[2333] He also says the repetition in v. 26 "seems to add to the effectiveness of the line and so there is no indication of textual error."[2334] The "my heart" of v. 27 is literally "my bowels," for the ancient Jews, the seat of the emotions. Rashi says v. 27b should be rendered, "The days of affliction come to meet me, and I am silent."[2335] He says the meaning of v. 28 is, "The sun did not gaze upon me, yet my skin is blackened."[2336] This is another reference to the symptoms of Job's ailment.

Freehof says of v. 29:

> Jackals and ostriches live in the wilderness. Job here means, "I live in the desert. I have no friends left. My only companions are the denizens of the desert, the jackals and the ostriches."[2337]

Rowley points out that the cry of the jackal was a plaintive call. The claim here is probably that Job's cries are like theirs.[2338] The Targum renders the nouns of v. 29, "dragons and ostriches."[2339] Many modern exegetes think these animals are "two species of owls that make their plaintif cries at night."[2340] Mezudat David sees v. 30 speaking about the darkening of Job's skin, his "external covering," and that v. 31 is about "weeping and mourning."²³⁴¹ Rowley believes the music of v. 31 is "the glad music of his former life."²³⁴² Jastrow has it:

> An associate to jackals have I become,
>
> And a companion to ostriches.²³⁴³

Jastrow adds, "Jackals and ostriches are frequently used in biblical poetry as symbols of desolation and mourning."²³⁴⁴ Mezudat David agrees. He says of v. 31:

> Instead of listening to the harp and the flute, as I was accustomed to doing, I now engage in mourning and weeping.²³⁴⁵

Rodd makes four points about these final verses of ch. 30. First, Job cannot abandon his belief that goodness should be rewarded. Second, "he returns to the charity that he used to give beggars." Third, the "ferment in his bowels" continues the description of his illness. And finally, "the joyful music of his earlier life has turned into weeping and a dirge."²³⁴⁶ From our perspective, this is a good summary of the final verses of ch. 30.

Chapter 31: The Completion of Job's Final Speech

Introduction

Chapter 31 is the final chapter of Job's monologue of chs. 29–31. Driver and Gray, as well as Matthew Henry, divide the chapter in the following parts: vv. 1–8, "Job Develops His Uprightness"; vv. 9–15, "His Integrity"; vv. 16–23, "Job Respectful"; vv. 24–31, "Violence"; and vv. 32–40, "Job's Final Lament." Samuel Terrien calls the whole of ch. 31, "The Final Oath of Innocence."²³⁴⁷ He tells us:

> The happiness of the past (ch. 29) has been swallowed up in the sorrow and shame of the present (ch. 30). There is no future to contemplate except death, and therefore, nothingness (ch. 30:23, 31). Nevertheless, Job still asserts his righteousness. So he ends his soliloquy with the most solemn and elaborate protest of innocence that he has ever tried to express. For this purpose, he examines a series of more than sixteen concrete hypotheses of sinful acts, each one beginning with the conjunction "If," or *'im*.²³⁴⁸

C. S. Rodd and the editors of the NEB, and REB among others, transpose vv. 2–4 to follow v. 5 in ch. 31.²³⁴⁹ One element of the character of Job's final speech are the number of "oaths" that the chapter contains. Another element of ch. 31 is the meaning of the final verse of the chapter. Finally, as Terrien remarks, ch. 31 has the overall character of an "oath." More will be said later about this phenomenon.

THE BOOK OF JOB

Analysis of Chapter 31

31:1–8

Terrien points out that the "lack of a transition from chapter 30 is somewhat confusing."[2350] In fact, the first four verses of ch. 31 are not in the LXX. Franz Delitzsch says that "Job begins with the duty of chastity in v. 1." He adds about vv. 2–3:

> The question of v. 2 is proposed in order that it may be answered in v. 3, again in the form of a question: In consideration of the just punishment which the injurer of female innocence meets, Job disavows every unchaste look.[2351]

Freehof points out, "Except for a few words after God's speeches from the whirlwind, Job says nothing more." Thus the chapter closes with, "The words of Job are ended."[2352] Buttenwieser believes that ch. 28, the chapter on Wisdom, belongs after ch. 31.[2353] Saadiah renders v. 1 this way:

> I had made a compact with mine eye not to look upon a blooming girl.[2354]

The word for "compact" is *berith*, the same word employed at Gen 15, where Abraham makes a "covenant" with God. The word *bahkalah*, or "blooming girl," for Saadiah, is a "fair maiden."[2355] Jastrow has it, "I made a covenant with my eyes/never to have a thought of a virgin."[2356] He appears to be right about that for the noun is *bethulah*, or "virgin," and not *almah*, or "young woman." Jastrow thinks that vv. 2–4, "are the beginning of Zophar's third speech."[2357] About v. 2, Rowley observes, "Here Job describes his expectations in times of prosperity." And about v. 3, "This is the principle on which Job thought he could count."[2358] This is a clear reference to divine plan theory. Mezudat David says of v. 4, "Job says this according to his companions who believe in divine providence, if, as they claim, God guides the happenings of the world, He surely sees my ways."[2359] Rowley writes about v. 4, "It is possible that Job is here still thinking back to the old days and the confidence that he had then."[2360]

Mezudat David says that Job remarks about God in v. 5:

> He will see whether I went with men of falsehood to learn their ways and to be like them, and whether my feet went in the way of deceit.[2361]

Mezudat David renders v. 6 this way:

> May He weigh me with a just scale, and may God know my innocence.[2362]

Rowley reminds us that "God had borne witness to Job's integrity in 2:3, where the same word is used in v. 6." About v. 7, Rowley observes:

> It is here made clear that Job's covenant with his eyes was wider than the example in v. 1. They have never led him to stray from the path of rectitude or to cover what was another's.[2363]

Mezudat David says that v. 7 means:

> If my foot had turned away from the road and my heart had gone after my eyes,
>
> and any wrong-doing has clung to my hands.[2364]

Sforno says that v. 7 asks, "If I have strayed in my philosophical speculation or whether my heart strayed after my eyes by unchaste imagination."[2365] Rashi says of v. 8, "May I sow and another eat, and my produce be uprooted." He adds, "As in the previous verse, this is to be understood as a curse."[2366] Rowley agrees about v. 8. He says of the verse:

> Job here invokes a curse upon himself, if he has sinned in thought or deed in the ways indicated.[2367]

There are five different words in Job to designate "curse." *Barak*, which also at times means "bless," is employed at 1:5, 11; 2:5 and 9; *alah* is used at 31:30; *naqab*, at 31:8; *arar* is employed at 3:8; and finally, *qalal*, that comes from the QLL Aramaic root, is used at 3:1 and 24:18. *Naqab* is the verb at 31:8.

Rowley gives Deut 28:30 and Isa 65:22 as parallels to v. 8. Franz Delitzsch also agrees that Job "calls down upon himself a curse." He also gives Deut 28:30 as a parallel. He says, "What he sows, let strangers reap and eat; and even when that which is sown does not fall into the hands of strangers, let them be uprooted."[2368]

31:9–15

Rowley tells us that "the sin of adultery is here repudiated," meaning v. 9.[2369] Samuel Terrien observes about vv. 9–12:

> If he has committed adultery (v. 9), let his own wife belong to another man (v. 10).
>
> And let him perish in the fire (vv. 11–12).[2370]

Franz Delitzsch says that v. 12 is about "a fire consuming him who allows the sparks of sinful desire to rise up within him."[2371] He says that v. 13 "denotes a maid who is not necessarily his slave, as in chapter 19:15."[2372] Rowley points out about v. 13, "The rights of slaves were few, though the lot of the slave in Israel was better than elsewhere." He gives Exod 21:1–11, as a parallel text.[2373]

Franz Delitzsch says of v. 15:

> One and the same God has fashioned us in the womb, without our cooperation, in equally animal way, which smites down all pride, in like absolute conditionedness.[2374]

Rowley agrees about v. 15. He says of the verse, "Job had spoken of the care that God had lavished upon him in the process of birth."[2375] He continues:

> Now he acknowledges the same care had been lavished upon the meanest slave. He and the slaves are creatures of the same God, so that the person of the slave was no less sacred than his own.[2376]

Mezudat David asks about v. 15:

> Is he lower than I? Did not the one who made me in my mother's womb also not make him in his mother's womb? I was in my mother's womb and he was in his mother's womb. Did not one Creator form both of us?[2377]

Samuel Terrien makes a similar interpretation of v. 15:

> Did not He who made me in the womb not also have made him?[2378]

Terrien adds this note: "This awareness of the equality of birth among men is high as the ethical level of the New Testament."[2379] Rowley agrees. He adds about v. 15, "The lofty ethical character of this passage is very remarkable in the setting of the ancient world."[2380]

Compared to other cultures around them, the ancient Jews treated their slaves much better. Here Job recognizes that the slaves are human, created by God as he was, and that Job listened to their complaints. Job acknowledges to God that he is responsible for the treatment of his slaves.

31:16–23

C. S. Rodd tells us about this section of ch. 31:

> The poor, widows, and the fatherless were those members of society without protection and with no one to secure their rights.[2381]

Samuel Terrien comments on this section this way:

> Job now turns to sins against charity, and he indirectly sets forth the most comprehensive program of social responsibility.[2382]

He observes about vv. 16–17:

> If I have withheld anything that the poor desired . . . or have eaten my morsel alone.[2383]

Rowley, commenting on v. 16, says:

> How far from the truth Eliphaz was in 22:7ff. Job now makes plain. In mercy he has failed no more than in justice. To the poor, the widow, and the fatherless, all so easily exploited, he had ministered in their need, and never had they looked in vain to him for aid.[2384]

Freehof maintains that "the eye of the widow to fail" in v. 16 means, "to languish, or cease to look forward to hope." He gives Ps 69:4 as a parallel text.[2385] Rashi asks about v. 17, "How commendable is this trait, which the author puts into Job's mouth, that he never sat down is more relevant here."[2386]

About v. 18, Rashi observes:

> This virtue raised me as a father who raised me and taught me. So did the uprightness of my heart teach me from my youth.[2387]

Rowley believes v. 18 is to be read as a parenthesis, "since it breaks the prorasis which leads up to v. 22." He adds, "Here Job claims that he went far beyond mere charity to the needy, and gave them fatherly care."[2388] Mezudat David says of v. 18:

> Although human nature resists this trait somewhat, constant practice from my youth implanted it into my very nature.[2389]

Freehof points out that v. 18 uses two different genders. He says "they refer back to v. 16."[2390] At v. 20, Mezudat David thinks Job asks:

> Did not that man's loins bless me because I dressed him? Indeed, they blessed me. This is a figure of speech for the poor man's gratitude. Indeed, I made him a garment from the fleece of my lambs.[2391]

Rowley thinks at v. 20, the "loins" is used for the whole body, here the part that is especially protected from the cold, where the bones are credited with speech.[2392] Driver renders v. 20, "without his loins having blessed me."[2393] Duhm, Budde, Strahan, and Gray render v. 21 "against the perfect," rather than "against the fatherless."[2394] The upright man, however, is not necessarily weak, whereas the orphan is, and therefore the more relevant here. Rowley observes about v. 22:

> Here follows the imprecation pronounced by Job against himself, if he has done any of these things. It is related especially to v. 21, "If he has raised his hand in threat against the weak, may his arm fall helpless and broken."[2395]

Rowley gives Ps 137:5 as a parallel for v. 22. The word "socket" in v. 22 is only used here in this sense. Gray thinks it means the "hollow tube of the reed."[2396] Kissane takes it to mean "the elbow joint." Dhorme translates it "humerus." Pope says it is the "upper arm." Rashi says it's the "shoulder blade."[2397] At any rate, this is another hapax in the book. Dhorme says of v. 22:

> What restrained Job from exploiting his power over others was in dread of the power of God, who was ever-present in his thoughts.[2398]

The first line of v. 23 is literally: "For a terror unto me was a calamity from God." The LXX and Peshitta have, "For the terror of God restrained me."[2399] Driver has, "The terror of God came upon me."[2400] The meaning is clear: Job feared that God would bring him calamity. The KJV renders the second line of v. 23, "By reason of His majesty, I was powerless." So too the RSV. Bickell moves v. 23 to follow v. 18, while Duhm believes it should be immediately after v. 18.[2401]

Rashi makes vv. 23–24 a little clearer by commenting:

> The calamity which God sends to the wicked was always a terror to me, and therefore, I would do none of these evil things.[2402]

31:24–31

Rowley gives Ps 49:6ff. as a parallel to v. 24. He says of the verse, "Here Job repudiates that charge which Eliphaz has made against him at 22:24ff."[2403] Rashi, Ibn Izra, and Freehof all maintain that in vv. 26–27, "Job is taking an oath that he never worshipped Idols."[2404] Freehof adds:

> When he saw the Sun in its splendor, his heart was never enticed to worship the Sun and the moon.[2405]

Ibn Ezra maintains that the "kissing of the hand" in v. 27b is "one of the gestures of idolatrous worship," but Szold takes the line figuratively and says, "If when the Sun has shone upon me when I was prosperous."[2406] Both Szold and Malbin think the shining of the sun is a symbol of prosperity.[2407] Ewald finds an indication of the spread of Zoroastrianism in the beginning of the seventh century BCE.[2408] Delitzsch believes it is a "reference to ancient heathenism of Western Asia."[2409] He points out that "it is questionable whether v. 28 is to be regarded as a conclusion" with Umbreit and others, or as a parenthesis with Ewald and Hahn.[2410]

About v. 28, Delitzsch says the meaning is:

> His worship of God would have been hypocrisy, if he had disowned in secret the God whom he acknowledged openly and outwardly.[2411]

About v. 29, Delitzsch explains:

> He did not rejoice at the destruction of his enemy who was full of hatred towards him.[2412]

Exodus 23:4ff., on the other hand, enjoins us to "help our enemies."[2413] Mezudat David asks about v. 29:

> Did I rejoice because of the misfortune of my friend, and did not become aroused to rise up against him to recompense him when evil befell him, thinking that, just as he has commenced to fall, he would continue to do so.[2414]

Franz Delitzsch thinks this strophe closes with v. 30. Rowley says of v. 30, "Not only has Job rejoiced over his enemies troubles, he has never in his heart wished them harm."[2415] He says the reference to "my mouth" in v. 30 is "literally 'my palate,' implying that the cursing of one's enemies was a dainty morsel which Job never suffered himself to taste."²⁴¹⁶ The LXX, at v. 31, renders: "that his maids would have willingly eaten him, their kind master."²⁴¹⁷ Rowley observes about v. 31, "Job's spirit of hospitality has been shared by his servants, who eagerly desired that others might be."²⁴¹⁸

31:32–40

Freehof says of vv. 35–37:

> These verses return to a thought which Job has expressed frequently before. He wishes that God would make clear wherewith he has sinned, so that he may have had an opportunity to answer and defend himself. But since these three sentences interrupt the sequence of the various oaths in this chapter, Tur-Sinai believes they were misplaced from some earlier chapter.²⁴¹⁹

Mezudat David says in v. 35, Job asks, "Would that I were given a man who would listen to me to fill my desire."²⁴²⁰ Ibn Ezra translates, "Lo, here is my mark," for v. 36.²⁴²¹ Mezudat David says that in v. 37, Job's says, "I will tell him the number of my steps to that man," presumably the man in v. 35.²⁴²²

Rowley says of v. 37:

> Job is prepared to defend his integrity to God, and to submit his life to the fullest examination. Not as a criminal would he appear before God, but as an innocent man with head held high like a prince.²⁴²³

Rashi says the import of v. 38 is:

> If my soul complains about me concerning the gleanings, the forgotten sheaves, and the end of the field, as well as tithes, claiming that I did not extract tithes properly.²⁴²⁴

Duhm supposes that the meaning of v. 38 is that "the land should testify that Job has not observed the year of his release, or the law against sowing two kinds of grain."²⁴²⁵ Rowley agrees with this interpretation of v. 38. He gives Lev 19:19 as a parallel text.²⁴²⁶ Duhm excises v. 39, though it seems to follow naturally from v. 38. Indeed, Terrien points out about vv. 38–40:

> Most modern commentators think that these verses are accidentally displaced and should be transferred between vv. 34 and 35.²⁴²⁷

Rowley, however, says of v. 40, "The imprecation fits the hypothetical crime. If Job had wrongfully acquired the fruits of the land, let it cease to bear fruit. Instead of useful grains, wheat and barley, let it yield thorns and rank-smelling weeds."²⁴²⁸ He also points out that "the words of Job have ended" in v. 40 "is generally held to be an editorial note."²⁴²⁹ But since the end of ch. 31 is followed by the Elihu speeches—that may have been an addition to the text—Rowley and others may not be right about that.

Terrien says of the close of ch. 31:

Job knows that if he had obtained his fields in a criminal fashion, he, like Cain would have been "cursed from the ground."[2430]

Freehof renders v. 40 this way:

> Let thistles grow instead of wheat
> And noisome weeds instead of barley.[2431]

Rowley gives Ps 77:20 and Jer 51:64 as parallel texts to v. 40.[2432] Franz Delitzsch says of vv. 38–40, "These verses must be regarded as a final rounding off (not as the beginning of a fresh chain of thought)."[2433] Mezudat David gives this meaning to v. 40:

> Instead of wheat, my punishment should be that thistle would emerge, and instead of barley, noisome weeds should grow.[2434]

More on Oaths in the Old Testament and the Book of Job

The Hebrew Bible uses three separate words to designate an "oath" or "promise to God."

These are *saba*, *sebu'a*, and *alah*. The oath was a manner of guaranteeing a promise in Israelite society and the ancient Near East. The idea of an oath was connected to the idea of the covenant or *Berith* in classical Hebrew. The person taking an oath would raise his right hand and swear (Deut 32:40), or even raise both hands (Dan 12:7). Oaths were solemn commitments and were not to be given lightly.

In the Old Testament an oath might also bind one's descendants (see Gen 50:25–26; Josh 9). These texts, as well as others at Gen 24:9 and 47:29–31, speak of the symbolism before the swearing of an oath. Oaths became more complicated in intertestamental Judaism. The Mishnah contains an entire tractate on the subject called *Sebu'oth*.

One reason for believing that ch. 31 of Job is an extended oath is the multiple uses of the word *'im*, or "if," in that chapter. If-then constructions were often a sign of oaths in ancient Hebrew. Chapter 31 begins with a mention of a "covenant," another sign that an oath is to follow. This is followed by the employment of eighteen if-then expressions, at vv. 5, 7, 7, 9, 13, 16, 19, 20, 20, 21, 24, 25, 26, 27, 31, 33, 38, and 39.

Chapters 32–37: The Elihu Speeches

Introduction

A considerable amount of debate has arisen about whether these chapters were an original part of the book of Job. Both traditional and more modern scholars have weighed in on this issue. It is our opinion that the Elihu speeches were, in fact, not original to the book. We have made this claim for a number of reasons, some about the structure and content of the book, some theological, and some grammatical and etymological.

Among the reasons for saying that the Elihu speeches were an addition to the book are the following: First, when the friends of Job are introduced in 2:11–13, Elihu is not among them. Second, God addresses Eliphaz "and his two friends," at 42:7, but Elihu is nowhere mentioned. Third, at 31:35, the end of Job's final speech of the dialogue, Job asks for the Almighty to show up and tell him why he is suffering. If we take out Elihu's speeches, that is precisely what happens next when God speaks from the whirlwind, beginning in 38:1ff.

Fourth, the first six verses of the Elihu speeches, that is 32:1–6, are written in prose. This is the only prose of the book besides the prologue and epilogue. Could it be that a redactor chose to introduce the fourth friend in prose, just as the other three friends were introduced in ch. 2, and God, Satan, and Job in ch. 1 in prose?

Fifth, the final words of ch. 31 are, "The words of Job are ended." This appears to be an indication that the patriarch will speak no more, and the book may have come to an end. In fact, Job speaks two more times, at 40:3–5 and 42:1–6. Sixth, Elihu refers directly to the other three friends and to Job, but none of the other characters refer to Elihu. Seventh, Elihu quotes Job word for word at 33:8–11 and 13:24; 34:5–9 and 27:3; 35:3 and 7:20. The other three friends do not quote Job directly. Eighth, Elihu calls Job by name in several places in the book (32:12; 33:1; 34:5; 36:16; and 37:13–14). The other three friends never do this.

Ninth, and finally, Job responds to all of the speeches of Eliphaz, Bildad, and Zophar, but he does not respond to anything said by the fourth friend, the young Elihu. Perhaps this is because his theological point of view is vastly different than the retributive justice views of Eliphaz, Bildad, and Zophar.

Indeed, in terms of theological reasons for believing that the Elihu speeches are an inclusion to the book, the principal one is that the fourth friend provides theological responses to the suffering of Job that the other friends have not introduced earlier. It is true that at times Elihu seems to argue for retributive justice, as Eliphaz, Bildad, and Zophar have done.

The fourth friend, however, also suggests theories of suffering not uttered by the first three friends. Three approaches in particular that Elihu suggests are what we earlier have called the "moral qualities view," the "test perspective," and the "divine plan theory." The first of these approaches, we will remember, says that God uses evil and suffering in order to develop certain, significant moral qualities, such as patience and fortitude. At 33:19, Elihu tells us:

> Man is also chastened with pain upon his bed
> And with continual pain in his bones.[2435]

At 36:15, Elihu again observes:

> He delivers the afflicted by their affliction
> And opens their ear to adversity.[2436]

The test perspective can be seen in the Elihu speeches at 33:16; 34:3; and 34:36. This view, as we have shown earlier in this work, suggests that God uses evil and suffering to test the characters of good men. In this regard, Elihu at 34:3 tells us to:

> Hear my words, you wise men, and give ear to me, you who know
>
> for the ear tests words, as the palate tastes food.[2437]

A few verses later, at 34:36, Elihu exclaims:

> Would that Job were tried to the end because he answers like wicked men.[2438]

It appears in Elihu's view that the agent for testing or trying is God himself, and presumably, after being tested the patriarch from the Land of Uz will come out in flying colors and attest to his character of being *tam va yashar*, or blameless and upright. In fact, one way to understand the entire prologue of Job is in terms of the test perspective, where in the end, the patriarch comes out very well in the test.

The divine plan point of view essentially argues that God knows more about the meaning of Job's suffering than human beings do. Thus, it might be said that God has a divine plan, whereby everything works out for the good. Something might be seen as evil or suffering in the short run, but in the long run everything will be seen to work out for the good.

This divine plan perspective can be seen at: 33:12; 34:31–32; 36:22 and 26–30; and 37:23–24 in the Elihu discourses. In the first of these Elihu says:

> Behold, in this you are not right. I will answer you
>
> God is greater than man.[2439]

At 36:22, Elihu reminds us:

> Behold God is exalted in power;
>
> Who is a teacher like him?[2440]

Another example of a belief in divine plan may be seen at 36:26, where Elihu remarks:

> Behold, God is great and we know Him not;
>
> The number of His years is unsearchable.[2441]

And at 36:29–30, where Elihu asks:

> Can anyone understand the spreading of the clouds,
>
> the thunderings of his pavilion.
>
> Behold, He scatters His lightning about Him.
>
> and covers the roots of the sea.[2442]

These, of course, are rhetorical questions, questions about the power and wisdom of God much different from queries made by Eliphaz, Bildad, and Zophar. In that regard, the first three friends look backward, to discuss the reason for Job's suffering through retributive justice theory, while Elihu looks forward, to explain Job's suffering with divine plan theory.

Before the appearance of Elihu, most of the arguments made by the other three friends were directly related to retributive justice. This approach can also been seen in the Elihu discourses at: 33:26; 34:12; 34:22; 34:24–26; 34:36–37; 35:5–6; 36:6; 36:10; 36:13; 36:21; and 37:24; but one might say that with these three new arguments of the test view, moral qualities perspective, and divine plan theory, Elihu shifts the theological debate from looking backward (retributive justice) to looking forward (divine plan). In philosophical terms, we might say that the book moves from a deontological approach to ethics (retributive justice) to a teleological view of ethics (divine plan).

A final theological argument about the Elihu speeches is related to what follows them, God's responses from the whirlwind. One curious fact about ch. 37 is that much of Elihu's words to be found there look surprisingly like the language God uses in his discourses beginning in 38:1ff. In this sense, the end of the Elihu speeches may be a foreshadowing of the divine discourses to follow. In this sense, ch. 37 may be seen as an introduction to what was to follow. More will be said about this is our explication of ch. 37.

At the level of grammar, vocabulary, and etymology, we also see a number of reasons for believing the Elihu speeches, as well as the Hymn to Wisdom in ch. 28, are very different from the rest of the book. For one thing, there are far more hapax logomena in the Elihu chapters than the remainder of the book. Altogether, there are 119 hapaxes in the book of Job, but there is a greater concentration of these words that appear only once in the Hebrew Bible in the Elihu speeches, and ch. 28. Hapaxes can be seen, for examples at: 28:17; 32:6; 33:9; 33:24; 33:25; 34:36; 35:15; 36:27; and 37:9, as well as many other verses in 28 and 32–37.

In the last of these, Elihu employs the word *cupawh*, or "whirlwind," a hapax. But this is not the word that appears at 38:1, where God speaks from a *Ce'arah*, or "whirlwind," "storm," or "tempest." The root word for this noun in 38:1 is *ce'ar*, that sometimes means to "take hold of." The vocabulary of Elihu looks far more like postexilic Judaism than does the rest of the book. Finally, there are many more Aramaisms in the Elihu speeches than can be detected in the rest of the book of Job. Kautzsch suggests that chs. 32–37 contain eighty-four Aramaic words spread over thirty-two verse of those chapters, far more than any six chapters of the dialogue.[2443] Other scholars suggest similar numbers of Aramaisms. These are far more than are to be found in the dialogue chapters.

More specifically, more than any of the other characters in the book, Elihu employs a broader range of terms for the divine in his speeches. In most of the chapters of Elihu speeches, he regularly shifts back and forth from *El*, *Eloah*, and *Elohim*, as well as *Shaddai*, or the "Almighty," which the fourth friend employs five times at 32:8; 33:4 and 12; 35:13; and 37:23.[2444] If we add ch. 28's hymn to Wisdom, we can add *Yahweh* to this list, for that name for God appears at 28:28. We also should add 37:23, where the word "Power" is employed to refer to God.

Altogether, in the six short chapters devoted to the Elihu speeches, the fourth friend makes thirty different references to the Divine. He employs *El*, *Eloah*, *Elohim*, *Shaddai*, or "Almighty," *Kabbir*, or "Mighty," and *Asah* and *Pa'al*, or "Maker." If we add the *Yahweh* used at 28:28, and "Power" employed at 37:23, we have nine different names for the Divine used in ch. 28 and 32–37—a range far greater than any other six chapters of the book.

At times, Elihu uses a much broader set of literary techniques, like the use of if-then constructions and the expression, *Hen!* or "Behold!" as in ch. 33. Elihu also has a much wider vocabulary of words related to ethics and morality. For example, he regularly uses the words *mishpat*, *binah*, and the root SDQ, that is the base for words related to "right" and "moral."[2445] Words for wisdom, uprightness, righteousness, understanding, and right, just and justice, judgment, and power occur far more often in chs. 32–37 than elsewhere in the book. Many of these words appear at: 28:28; 32:7, 9, 13; 33:23 and 26; 34:16–17; 35:2 and 7; 36:17; and 37:23. Another grammatical reason for believing that the Elihu speeches are later than the dialogue is to look at how terms related to "word" and "words" are employed in the book. All told, three separate terms are used to signify "word" and "words." These are *'emer*, *devar/devarim*, and *milleh/milin*. These words are used thirty-nine times in the book of Job. The Aramaic *milin* is employed thirty-four times of the thirty-eight instances in the entire Hebrew Bible.

This Aramaic term replaces the Early Hebrew *devar/devarim*. This may reflect a moment in the history of the text when Aramaic was in the process of replacing Classical Hebrew as the vernacular language of the Judean population. Of the thirty-four examples of *milin*, with the Aramaic plural ending of "n" rather than the Hebrew's "m," twenty of those are in the Elihu speeches.

Elsewhere, we have suggested that the final date for the book of Job is in the late sixth century BCE, or early fifth century. This is consistent with what we have said here about words related to words in the book of Job. The term *'emer* is only employed three times in the Torah, one in Genesis (49:21) and twice in Numbers (22:7 and 24:16). But it is not used again until the *Kethuvim*, particularly in Psalms and the book of Job.

In fact, in the Elihu speeches there is a greater variability of the use of these words—three *debar/debarim*, seven *millin*, and five *'emer*. This is another example of the wide vocabulary to be found in the speeches of Job's fourth friend. The word *'emer*, that generally means "speech" or "utterance," is employed forty-nine times in the Hebrew Bible, but a dozen of those are in Job, including 32:12, 14; 33:3; and 34:37.

Putting all of this together, then, we conclude that the speeches from the fourth friend, the brash, young Elihu, in chs. 32–37, appear to be a later inclusion in the book of Job. As we have seen, this may also be true of the second half of ch. 28, the "Hymn on Wisdom" as well. Opinions about the fourth friend, Elihu, have varied over time in both Judaism and Christianity. The Babylonian Talmud pronounced that he was "one of the seven prophets of the Gentiles."[2446] Rabbi Akiba says that Elihu was Balaam, and Rabbi Eleazer says that he represented Isaac because his name was "barachel."[2447] Rabbi Judah argues that Job's words were in praise of God, much more than those of Elihu. In the *Testament of Job*, a Greek apocryphal work, the figure of Elihu appears as a Satanic beast.[2448]

Many medieval Jewish accounts of Elihu are more positive in judging the fourth friend. Ibn Ezra, for example, in his commentary from 1140, says, "The true solution to the problem is to be found in Elihu's words."[2449] Moses Maimonides, in his *Guide to the Perplexed*, also gave a much more positive account of the figure of Elihu, as did Saadiah Gaon.[2450]

The earliest church fathers were not great admirers of the figure of Elihu. Jerome in his commentary agrees with the opinion of the Talmudists that he is to be identified with Balaam, and therefore, he is a false prophet.[2451] Gregory the Great thinks that Elihu had a "proper understanding of the problem of Job," but Elihu's words, Gregory believes, are "proud and arrogant."[2452] Theodore of Mopsuestia says that Elihu's words are "more offensive than those of the other friends."[2453]

It was not until the beginning of the nineteenth century, first with the commentary of Stuhlmann in 1804, that it was argued that the Elihu speeches are an addition to the original poem.[2454] Since that time, interpreters are in two basic camps, those who think Stuhlmann was right and those who think he was wrong.

In the former camp, we find Gesenius, Rosenmueller, Umbreit, Stickel, Hahn, Cornill, and Budde.[2455] Against the genuineness of the Elihu speeches as part of the original work, we have: Stuhlmann, Eichhorn, Ewald, Hirzel, Renan, Dillmann, Merx, Hitzig, Davidson, Wright, Hoffmann, Driver, Bickell, Siegfried, Duhm, A. S. Peake, Friedrich Delitzsch, and Kuenen.[2456]

From the above discussion, it should be clear that our view is in the camp of those with Stuhlmann, with the dozen arguments we have given above that Elihu is an addition to the original book of Job. Another feature of the Elihu speeches is how often the fourth friend uses names or adjectives related to the Divine. If we add ch. 28 to 32–37, we see six different names for God, including: five *Elohim*; thirteen *El*; five *Eloah*; five *Shaddai*, or "Almighty"; one *Yahweh*; and three *Kabbir*, or "Mighty." Like ch. 28, the Elihu speeches also have a vocabulary quite different from the rest of the book, particularly in regard to ethics and the good.

Among the words regularly employed by Elihu are: *nefesh* and *neshumah*, both related to "soul." *Ruah*, or "spirit." *Hokmah*, or "wisdom," and words related to the SDQ Semitic root that usually designate "right" "correct," or "moral." Like ch. 28, the Elihu speeches have a much broader vocabulary than Job and the other three friends, particularly in regard to words associated with ethics and morality.

Analysis of Chapter 32

Introduction

The figure of Elihu was descended from Nahor, according to 32:2 and 34:1. He is said to have descended from Buz, who may be from the line of Abraham. At Gen 22:20–21, a Buz is mentioned as a nephew of Abraham. Of the four friends, only with Elihu do we have his clan, his tribe, and his home country, with the other three we only get their country.

Both Samuel Terrien and Matthew Henry divide ch. 32 into three portions. Part one, for both men, is the prose introduction at vv. 1–5. The second section consists of vv. 6–14. And the third part, vv. 15–22. Henry calls part one, "Elihu Displeased at the Dispute between Job and His Friends." He labels the second section of ch. 32, "He Reproves Them." Henry calls the closing section of ch. 32, "He Speaks Without Partiality."[2457]

Of all the figures in the book of Job, Elihu has been the most controversial. Andersen calls him "prolix and pompous."[2458] Good, "insufferably pompous."[2459] Rowley says he is "self-important," while Whedbee observes that Elihu is "a buffoon, a comic figure whom the author ridicules."[2460] Fohrer believes that the fourth friend is guilty of "righteous indignation."[2461] Hartley says much the same about Elihu.[2462] De Wilde believes that Elihu's anger is in response "of what Job has gotten away with."[2463] Good calls Elihu a "pompous, insensitive bore."[2464] Duhm calls him "impertinent and smug."[2465] Habel observes that Elihu "boasts too much about his own integrity."[2466] Dhorme observes that "Elihu talks to hear himself talk."[2467] And Hartley believes Elihu's "wordiness may be a sign of insecurity."[2468] Rowley thinks that Elihu's impartiality "only makes him look more ridiculous,"[2469] while Peake thinks it is "sincerely meant."[2470]

In the Jewish tradition, both the LXX and the Peshitta eliminate a number of verses in the Elihu discourses. Among these are: 33:14; 34:36; 36:21; and 36:29. The *Testament of Job* thinks that the fourth friend is "imbued with the Spirit of Satan."[2471] The Talmud, as well, takes a negative view of Elihu. It says he is "Balaam in disguise," and that "it must be difficult to breathe at such heights."[2472]

In the medieval Jewish period, Saadiah in the tenth century says this about Elihu:

> Job heard this discourse, but held his peace, offering no rebuttal to Elihu. His silence at this point may indicate one of two things, either acquiescence or reservation. And it is for this reason that God addresses him to exhort him to acknowledge Elihu's arguments and to leave behind his fancies and suppositions, which, in effect, constitute his failing—although God does not say directly, lest the people think little of Job's forbearance.[2473]

Saadiah raises the question of why God, nor Job did not respond to Elihu. One possible answer to that question is that the fourth friend has a theological point of view that is perfectly consistent with that of the God Speeches that are to follow. We must also remember that at 42:7–8, where God castigates Eliphaz, Bildad, and Zophar, the fourth friend, Elihu, is nowhere to be found. Perhaps this is true because Elihu's overall theological view is the morally proper one.

Rashi thinks that Elihu "points out the relative insignificance of man in the cosmos, and this is one of the most important judgments of the fourth friend."[2474] In commenting on 33:24, Rashi observes, "Elihu tells Job, 'He reproves you because he loves you,'" a reference to the moral qualities perspective.[2475] But Moses Maimonides takes a more positive view of Elihu. He says, "Among the friends, his is the most perfect in knowledge."[2476]

The *Zohar* in a number of passages frequently discusses Divine judgment, mercy, and the meaning of suffering in terms of the Elihu character.[2477] Gersonides thinks, "The Elihu passages are primarily a precursor to the God speeches."[2478] He adds, "The fourth friend promises God's help and then God gives it in the form of a mild rebuke."[2479]

In more modern Jewish scholarship, Samuel Freehof says this about Elihu:

> There is a sharp difference in style between the Dialogue and the Elihu Speeches. The Hebrew of the Elihu speeches is much more Aramaic in form. There are many more Aramaic words, which indicates a different era for the respective authors.[2480]

Robert Gordis thinks that Elihu "occupies a middle ground between Job and his friends."[2481] He describes Elihu this way:

> A young, brash bystander, probably one of several witnesses to the debate. He has been following the arguments with growing impatience. He is angry, not only with Job for impugning God's justice, but also with the friends for defending His cause so inadequately.[2482]

Leon Roth, in his essay "The Jews and Judaism," in *Judaism: A Portrait*, observes this about the fourth friend of Job:

> Elihu declares that God is just, and yet suffering may rightly come to the innocent as a discipline and warning.[2483]

Thus Roth ascribes to the moral qualities response with respect to the cause of Job's suffering, or perhaps to the test view. Professor Roth goes on to tell us:

> The Elihu chapters nevertheless, are an organic part of the book . . . in that he argues for Divine Providence.[2484]

Robert Eisen agrees about the importance of Elihu. He writes:

> The notion added by Elihu and not mentioned by one of the others is that which he expresses parabolically when he speaks of the intercession of an angel.[2485]

The "Angel Mediator" about which Eisen speaks can be found at Job 33:23. This text tells us:

> If there be for him an angel mediator, one of a thousand to declare to man what is right for him; and he is gracious to him saying, "Deliver him from going down into the pit."[2486]

Louis Finkelstein, in an article called "Insight into Our Deep Need," written for *Life* magazine, points out that "the character of the book of Job with whom Archibald MacLeish apparently identifies himself is Elihu." Elihu does not appear in the play, but his point of view is always in evidence.[2487]

Among the earliest Christian understandings of Elihu, Jerome says of him, "The fourth friend has neither the understanding nor the wisdom of Job and the other friends."[2488] Gregory the Great says of the figure of Elihu, "He is an emblem of confident arrogance."[2489] The Venerable Bede, following the Talmud, says, "Elihu is to be confounded with Balaam."[2490] Thomas Aquinas, in his commentary, also takes a positive view of the fourth friend. He writes:

> Elihu's debate against Job is added here, and he, of course, uses sharper arguments against Job than the prior speakers, and approaches closer to the truth.[2491]

Thomas makes this judgment primarily because the fourth friend of Job assents to the divine plan theory, unlike Eliphaz, Bildad, and Zophar. John Calvin, in one of his 159 sermons on the book of Job, tells us this about the fourth friend, Elihu—something that implies what we have called the moral qualities view:

> The purpose of these speeches is to show that we should rather seek to learn than to teach others, except where necessity restrains us.[2492]

Among other early modern views of the book of Job, Strigel, in his 1571 commentary, calls Elihu "an ambitious orator."[2493] Herder calls him "arrogant and bold."[2494] Robert Lowth, in his *Lectures on the Sacred Poetry of the Hebrews*, says the following about Elihu:

> Elihu interposes as an arbiter of the controversy; he reproves the severe spirit of his friends, as well as the presumption of Job, who trusted far too much in his own righteousness.[2495]

J. H. Michaelis, in his 1720 commentary, says of Elihu, "The young man, with high conceit of himself, and censures his speech as little or nothing to the purpose."[2496] In the early nineteenth century, G. H. Ewald observes about Elihu:

> The consideration of the real meaning of these speeches conducts to the following view or their origin. A poet, some century or two later than our author, observed in the book many questionable, dangerous, and offensive thoughts

that had been uttered by Job with great force and without any hesitation. This poet sets out to repair those errors.²⁴⁹⁷

Ewald, then, was among the first to declare that the speeches of Elihu were an addition by a later writer than the original.²⁴⁹⁸ Barnes, in his 1844 commentary, tells us that the name Elihu means, "God is He."²⁴⁹⁹ He adds about the fourth friend:

> Elihu was full of words and felt constrained to speak. It was not because he forced himself to do it, not because he did it as a mere matter of duty, but he was so impressed with the subject that it would be a relief for him to give utterance of his views.²⁵⁰⁰

Barnes speaks specifically about ch. 33 when he says:

> In the following chapter [ch. 33] the main design is to convince Job that he has erred in the views which he has expressed to God, and to state the true design of his afflictions.²⁵⁰¹

James Anthony Froude, in his book *Short Studies on Great Subjects*, observes about the authenticity of the Elihu discourses:

> The speeches of Elihu, which lie between Job's last words and God's appearance is now decisive. It is pronounced by Hebrew scholars not to be a genuine part of the book.²⁵⁰²

Rosenmuller (1824), Umbreit (1832), and Stickel (1842) also all argue that the Elihu speeches were not an original part of the text.²⁵⁰³ At the end of the nineteenth century, as we shall see, Noyes says this of Elihu, "In so far as Elihu's relation to the three friends is concerned, it is not easy to find any great differences between his conception and theirs."²⁵⁰⁴

V. Garland, in his 1898 commentary, entitled *The Problems of Job*, points out that

> Elihu directs the attention of his hearers to the approaching tempest, as a manifestation of God's Almighty power.²⁵⁰⁵

M. Le Hir, in his 1873 commentary, was among the first French scholars to argue that the Elihu speeches were written at a later date than the rest of the book.²⁵⁰⁶ George R. Noyes, in his 1838 commentary, introduces the Elihu discourses this way:

> With chapter 32 commences a new division of the poem, the design of which seems to be to prepare the way for the appearance of the Deity.²⁵⁰⁷

David Thomas begins his introduction to the Elihu speeches in his 1878 commentary by observing that "the name Elihu means, 'Whose God is He.'"²⁵⁰⁸ T. K. Cheyne, in his 1887 commentary, says that the Elihu speeches "come from a considerably later period than the original work."²⁵⁰⁹ William Kelly, in speaking of Elihu in his 1879 commentary, writes:

> The second discourse of Elihu has for its scope to prove that the divine equity in government is in no way to be doubted, and that Job, who did not venture to impeach it, is himself deserving of good censure, as giving countenance in word and deed, to the evil and the scornful.[2510]

John Fredericton's 1879 commentary introduces the Elihu speeches in this manner:

> For the first time in the controversy, the great purposes of affliction is distinctly brought out. It is to hide pride from man, to humble and purify him.[2511]

The first half of the twentieth century also saw the emergence of many observations about Elihu. W. G. Jordan, in his 1929 commentary, writes of the fourth friend:

> It is very obvious that the long discourse of Elihu may be an interpolate or an afterthought—a fresh attempt by the author or some later writer to correct the errors into which Job and his friends are suppose to have fallen.[2512]

Francis Peloubet's 1906 commentary observes about Elihu:

> It is said that Elihu adds nothing to what the friends have said. But he does bring out in clear, shining vision, what the friends only hinted at, the hints also being obscured by the passionate trend of their argument.[2513]

William Jennings, in his 1912 commentary, says that "Elihu's part is to show that the three friends have failed in their arguments."[2514] Minos Devine, on the other hand, in his 1921 commentary, declares about the fourth friend, "Elihu has done more to meet Job's necessity than all the proverbial wisdom in the minds of the other friends."[2515] Edward Kissane says of Elihu, "He is compelled to speak in defense of God's honor."[2516] G. Rawlinson, in his 1913 commentary, published by Funk and Wagnalls, calls Elihu speeches, "The weak and rambling speech of a boy."[2517] He goes on to suggest the moral qualities view as Elihu's response to suffering, when he writes:

> At such times, Elihu holds, God gives men spiritual wisdom and instructs them, makes them understand His dealings with them, and His purposes with respect to them.[2518]

Rawlinson adds about Elihu:

> Suffering is not vindictive punishment of sin, nor is it the work of a malignant or even indifferent being. It has been sent by God for the wholesome discipline of his children.[2519]

This is another application of the moral qualities view, though he does criticize the retributive justice and demonic forces views in this passage. Among critics in the second half of the twentieth century, Francis Andersen says, "In terms of the overall design of the book, Elihu comes in abruptly, and when he has finished speaking, is never heard from again."[2520] Andersen adds about the Elihu speeches:

> The theological content of the Elihu material has been given a low rating by some scholars. Others have esteemed it highly as a needed complement to the rest of the book.[2521]

John Hartley observes about Elihu:

> Believing that his insight into God's ways is inspired, Elihu exhorts Job and his friends to listen to him while he offers his own view. He promises speeches that are wise and just.[2522]

Seton Pollock, in his book *Stubborn Soil*, says of Elihu, "At first sight there seems to be a marked similarity between the speeches of the Lord and those of Elihu."[2523] Pascal Parente, in an article for the *Catholic Biblical Quarterly*, published in 1944, says this of the fourth friend:

> Elihu, the fourth of these friends, is not included in God's condemnation of them because he seems to have offered the key to the solution of the problem.[2524]

C. A. Row, in his book *Future Retribution*, says of Elihu:

> A fifth interlocutor is introduced who undertakes to throw light on the subject under discussions . . . but ultimately leaves the difficulty unsolved.[2525]

Emil Kraeling, in his *The Book of the Ways of God*, published in 1938, also suggests that the figure of Elihu shows Job that suffering has a "pedagogical purpose."[2526] So Kraeling assents to the moral qualities theory, as well. Marvin Pope, however, in his Anchor Bible commentary, tells us that "Elihu is flatulent with words."[2527]

Three American philosophers in the mid-twentieth century also made comments on the figure of Elihu. These are Paul Weiss, Gilbert Murray, and Josiah Royce. The latter observes, "The speeches of Elihu contain the most hints on the nature and purpose of suffering."[2528] Paul Weiss disagrees. He says, "Elihu is a brash youngster who repeats in principle what his elders have said."[2529] Gilbert Murray, twentieth-century scholar of the classics, observes about the fourth friend, Elihu:

> Elihu the Buzite is thoroughly shocked by this attitude of Job. His belly becomes like wine that has no vent; it is ready to burst with indignation, much like new bottles.[2530]

Finally, Plate XII of William Blake's illustrations of the book of Job depicts Elihu. The younger man stands in the left of the image. He gestures to Job, his wife, and his three friends. His left foot is forward. To the right of the figure can be seen Job's wife, then the patriarch, and finally, the three friends, Eliphaz, Bildad, and Zophar.[2531]

Analysis of Chapter 32

32:1–5

The name Elihu means "My God is He," or "He is My God." The name Elihu is the grandfather of Elkanah at 1 Sam 1:1; the name of one of Manasseh's soldiers, at 1 Chr 12:20; the name of a Levite at 1 Chr 26:20; and a brother of King David, 1 Chr 27:18. The name Barachel means, "Bless, oh God," or "Bless God." Genesis 22:21 tells us that Buz was a brother of Uz, and thus the fourth friend is more closely related to Job than the other three friends.

Rowley says of v. 1 that the friends "give up the debate as useless because of Job's incorrigible self-righteousness."[2532] Solomon Freehof renders v. 2b as "against Job because he justified himself rather than God."[2533] The RSV has it, "because he was righteous in his own eyes."[2534] Rashi gives a similar translation. Ibn Ezra says the meaning of v. 3 is that "they accused Job of being wicked."[2535] Freehof says of verse 3:

> The friends should not have been able to justify God against Job's accusation, but they had failed. Elihu, therefore, feels the need of speaking in behalf of God.[2536]

Rowley says that v. 3 originally ended with "and declared God in the wrong." This would mean, then, that in abandoning the debate, they were conceding the verdict to Job and thereby condemning God.[2537] This approach is followed by Duhm, Strahan, Ball, Dhorme, Kissane, Fohrer, and Pope, among others.[2538]

Terrien observes about vv. 4–5:

> Elihu's anger exploded the more violently because he had to contain himself during the discussion on account of his inordinate youth. v. 4a is either corrupt or rather awkward, for it literally reads, "Elihu waited for Job with words," as the KJV has it.[2539]

Terrien points out that the text does not say that Job and the three friends were older than Elihu, rather it emphasizes the youthfulness of the fourth friend.[2540] Mezudat David says of v. 5, "When he saw that they had no answer, he became angry at them too and no longer waited."[2541] Rowley says of v. 5:

> Elihu denies that wisdom is reserved for the aged, though he had given his elders a chance to vanquish Job's argument before he ventured to speak.[2542]

However we interpret the first five verses of ch. 32, they are written, like the Prologue and Epilogue, in prose. This may be because all the other characters to this point in the book have been introduced in prose—God, Satan, Job, Bildad, Eliphaz, and Zophar. Or there may be some other reason (s) for these verses to appear in prose.

32:6–14

Samuel Terrien introduces vv. 6–10 this way:

> The new speaker reveals a remarkable mixture of timidity and boldness. On the one hand he acknowledges that he has kept silent because he felt the restraint of his youth. . . . On the other hand, he was not lacking in opinion or knowledge, a "definite conviction."[2543]

Rowley points out that the verb "was timid" only appears here in v. 6, thus another hapax in the Elihu speeches.[2544] Freehof says v. 7 means, "Those who have had many days should have the privilege to speak."[2545] He says about v. 8:

> Elihu means that while he waited for the wise old men to speak, he realized that the old have no monopoly on wisdom. Wisdom is due to "the spirit in man." God can also give understanding to the young. Therefore, he is emboldened to speak.[2546]

The verb "listen" in v. 10 is in the singular, addressed to Job. Other versions have it as a plural, so it is likely that Elihu was addressing the friends, as well as Job. Mezudat David understands v. 10 to mean, "Since wisdom depends on man's spirit, I said to Job, 'Listen to me. I too will express my opinion. Although I am younger, because perhaps my spirit is more receptive to wisdom.'"[2547] He says about v. 11:

> I have duly observed the rules of etiquette by patiently waiting for you to finish your speech and by listening attentively to your reasons until you searched out the matters.[2548]

Rowley observes about v. 11, "Pompously Elihu repeats in other words what he has just said. He suggests 'All their laborious efforts to comfort Job have been less successful than his inspired genius will prove.'"[2549] Rashi says the import of v. 12, "Yes, I attended to you and saw there is no one to convince Job."[2550] He adds:

> There is no one who can clarify these matters to him. I have heard no one reply with words appropriate for him True, I have heard many speeches, but they all consist of empty words.[2551]

Rashi says about v. 13, "We have found wisdom by remaining silent in order not to provoke him anymore."[2552] Freehof says that Rashi means that "wiser men have remained silent."[2553] Rowley says of v. 13, "The friends have found in Job a wisdom which only God can refute."[2554] Rowley says of v. 14, the verb "marshalled" shows that Elihu has "heavier artillery than the other friends have used."[2555]

32:15–22

Mezudat David says the import of v. 15 is this:

The foolishness of their answers caused them dismay, because Job refuted their arguments and they could find no answer for him.[2556]

Rashi says that v. 15 shows "that words have turned away from him."[2557] Freehof points out that v. 15 is one of those places where the text changes from second to the third person.[2558] In the LXX, vv. 15–16 are absent. Dhorme believes these verses are "Elihu's reflection to an imaginary audience, he depicts the friends of Job, standing agape and dumbfounded. They became dismayed and ceased to reply."[2559] Budde and many others omit vv. 15–16.[2560]

Dhorme points out that a number of exegetes rearrange the order of vv. 15–17. The LXX retains only the final of vv. 14b to 16. About v. 18, he observes:

> Elihu has just declared that he proposes to make a reply. He is not in the situation of Job's friends with whom words fail, "for I am full of words."[2561]

In v. 19, we get a comparison, "My belly is like a wine which is not opened," that is, which is sealed and unable to find any outlet, no means of escape. Mezudat David believes that v. 19 means:

> I cannot restrain myself because I am full of words, and the space in my belly is cramped because of all the statements in it. This is a figurative expression.[2562]

Rowley says that "only at v. 19 does the word for 'wineskins' have this meaning." The same word, elsewhere in the Hebrew Bible, is associated with necromancy.[2563] Verse 19 is the third time the word *yayin*, or "wine," has appeared in the book. Also see 1:13 and 1:18. Samuel Terrien suggests in these verses:

> In the third part of this preamble Elihu continues his reflections in the style of a soliloquy, perhaps in order to indicate his contempt for the impotent professionals (vv. 15–16) and reveal his opinion (v. 17). He is so full of words that he cannot contain them, and the spirit within him [literally, "his belly"] constrains him (v. 18.)[2564]

Rowley says of v. 21, "Elihu gives himself another certificate, this time for impartiality. He is doubtless deadly sincere, for he takes himself so seriously."[2565] Rashi disagrees. He says Elihu's words in v. 21 mean, "I will not change my words to replace them with milder expressions in defense of Job's honor."[2566] Dhorme believes the expression "to lift up one's face," means to feel shame in v. 21.[2567] The LXX takes the same view. Freehof thinks v. 21 is addressed to the friends.[2568]

Rowley thinks the meaning of the final verse of ch. 32 is this:

> Not only is Elihu a stranger to anything that savors of impartiality. He also would be afraid of immediate divine vengeance if he gave way to it.[2569]

Dhorme points out about v. 22:

Note the juxtaposition of two personal verbs, the second dependent on the first. (6:28; 10:16; 19:3) "For I did not know how to give titles of distinction." Elihu will remain faithful to his habits. He has a weighty reason for doing so. This reason is his Creator would not suffer him to do otherwise.[2570]

Driver points out that the construction of v. 22 is in the imperfect, more like the Peshitta than the Masoretic Text. Saadiah renders v. 22 this way:

> Just as I was never wont to use such a manner of address.
>
> Nay, I had done so just a little,
>
> My maker would have summoned me ere now.[2571]

Dhorme gives only two lines for v. 22, and a completely different sense. He says:

> For I do not know how to flatter,
>
> else would my Maker soon put an end to me.[2572]

Elihu uses one of his many words for God in v. 22. This time it is *'asah*. Other words for "Maker" employed by the Job poet include *pa'al*, *abhadh*, *Nathan*, and *yatsagh*, a word that also implies "to set up." These terms may be found at: 4:17; 10:8; 35:10; 36:3; 40:19; 40:24, in addition to 32:22.

Dhorme's translation is the same as the RSV, while the KJV gives us:

> For I know not to give flattering titles.
>
> In so doing, my Maker would soon take me away.[2573]

Chapter 33: Elihu's Second Discourse

Introduction

This chapter continues the discourses of Elihu, the fourth friend. In ch. 33, we see much of the specialized, Hebrew vocabulary of the fourth friend, as we shall see below. Both Samuel Terrien and Matthew Henry suggest ch. 33 has five basic parts. Henry gives the following names to these sections:

- vv. 1–7: Elihu Offers to Reason with Job.
- vv. 8–13: Elihu Blames Job for Reflecting upon God.
- vv. 14–18: God Calls Men to Repentance.
- vv. 19–28: God Sends Affliction for Good.
- vv. 29–33: Elihu Entreats Job's Attention.[2574]

Analysis of Chapter 33

33:1–7

Unlike the other three friends, Elihu calls Job by name in v. 1, as he does at 34:5, 7; 35:1ff. and 16. Rowley says of this opening verse, "With interminable prolixity he repeats himself at 32:10."[2575] About v. 2, Rowley adds:

> The self-importance of Elihu is boundless, and he is the master of banality.[2576]

Peake says of the opening of ch. 33, "It would show a strange lack of literary tact to edit the great genius to whom we owe the poem with such bathos as this."[2577] Rowley remarks about Peake's comment, "But whoever wrote the Elihu speeches probably deliberately put such banal words into his mouth, since his purpose was rather to expose this type of character than to exalt it."[2578]

In the Masoretic Text, v. 3 has no verb. For "The uprightness of my heart," Duhm proposes, "My heart overflows."[2579] Beer has it, "My heart is astir."[2580] Dhorme, "My heart will repeat."[2581] And Holscher, "My heart affirms."[2582] The second line of v. 3 reads, "and the knowledge of my lips they speak purely." Clearly, there is a want of balance in the two lines of v. 3, so many exegetes transfer the first word of v. 3a to v. 3b to get "my lips speak purely." Kissane, with a slight change in vowels, yields the most acceptable translation: "My heart will reveal words of knowledge."[2583] It seems that Elihu is once again bragging about his own ability.

Both Peake and Dhorme transfer v. 4 to follow v. 6, while Kissane has it follow 32:13;[2584] Gray defends v. 4 as is in the RSV, and in its present position.[2585] Both Budde and Duhm eliminate v. 4.[2586] Rowley observes about v. 4:

> Elihu is not saying here that he is like all men in having the breath of God in all men, but that he in particular is inspired by God, so that his words alone are not sincere, but of special value.[2587]

Of the expression "set your words in order," in v. 5b, "words" does not appear in the Masoretic Text. The verb usually means "arrange," or to "put in order." It is often employed in marshaling arguments, as in 32:14, or arranging troops for battle, as at 6:4 and 1 Sam 17:8. Dhorme understands the verb here in the sense of arranging troops for battle.[2588]

About v. 6, Rowley tells us:

> Elihu, like Job, is human. He and Job stand on the same footing, so that Elihu will have no advantage over Job in this respect. At the same time, he is persuaded that Job will stand but a poor chance against his superior armory.[2589]

In v. 6, Elihu says that he speaks in "God's stead." Peake says about v. 7, "One can imagine how the poet's scorn would have crushed this presumptuous meddler," meaning that the speeches of Elihu are not of the same quality as those lines from the original poet.[2590] The noun "pressure" in v. 7b is another hapax, but the verb appears in Prov 16:26. The LXX has "My hand," with the omission of one letter. But it seems a pity to omit a rare word that makes good sense as "pressure," as the RSV has it, as opposed to the KJV that renders v. 7b, "My hand be heavy." The word in question is *paynim*. Samuel Terrien thinks Elihu, in v. 7, "is merely expressing his fear of the Deity."[2591]

33:8–13

Terrien points out in these verses, "the new interlocutor is compelled to quote from the hero's earlier statements." He suggests that vv. 8–11 are a repeat of 9:21, as well as 10:7; 16:17; 23:10–12; 27:5–6; and 31:1ff.[2592] Elihu also seems to attribute to Job words that he did not actually utter. For example, the "innocent" of v. 9 and "occasions" in v. 10 are words not found in Job's discourses. Additionally, Elihu at times seems to misrepresent the words of Job in places, as in v. 12a, for example. Job never says, "Behold, in this you are right," but he does say, "God is greater than man."[2593]

The LXX at v. 12c says, "He that is above men is eternal."[2594] Duhm uses this to construct, "He did removeth himself from men."[2595] Traditionally, this line has had two separate meanings. Either God is too great to be called upon by men, or that God is above the petty feelings of Job. The latter is Elihu's more probable meaning.

Rowley says that in v. 13, Elihu means, "Why do you make it a ground of complaint against Him that He does not answer?"[2596] He suggests that v. 13b should be translated, "saying, 'he will answer none of my words,'" but the word "saying," does not appear in the Hebrew text; and it has "His words," rather than "my words." This may refer to "man" in the previous verse.[2597] Hitzig, and many others, substitute "Thy words," as the Vulgate has it. Bickell, Duhm, and many others agree with the RSV rendering of v. 13b: "Saying, 'He will answer none of my words.'"[2598] Dhorme and Kissane both point out that the Peshitta wrongly has it, "my words," arguing instead for "His words."[2599]

33:14–18

John Calvin wrote several sermons on ch. 33 of Job. About vv. 13–17, for example, he says:

> God speaks not of an absolute or lawless power, but as a power that is matched with rightfulness.[2600]

In regard to the same passage, in the same sermon, Calvin observes:

> Wherefore, let us be sure that our damnation shall be the greater, if we not be quiet about our afflictions, but fall to grudging, and although our mouth speak not a word, yet we be full of such heart burning within that we play the mule which chaweth upon his bit.[2601]

Samuel Terrien says the meaning of v. 14 is this:

> Job is wrong in thinking that God is deaf to his appeals, for Job thereby implies that there is no difference between infinity and finitude, creativity and creature-liness, and he forgets that "God is greater than man." ... The voice of the Almighty is clear to everyone who has ears to hear it.[2602]

Rowley thinks vv. 12ff. has inspired v. 15. He points out that the "opens the ear" of v. 16 is an expression that sometimes means to inform.[2603] He gives Ruth 4:4 and 1 Sam 20:2, 12, and 13 as parallels. The RSV has "and terrifies them with warnings," for v. 16b, but the Masoretic Text has, "and seals their bond."[2604] Dahood agrees.[2605] The Peshitta and the Vulgate have, "their correction."[2606] The general sense would appear to be clear from the RSV.

The Masoretic Text has a singular object for v. 17b, thus "deed." The RSV agrees. The KJV translates, "that he may withdraw man from his purpose."[2607] Bickell proposes, "from his iniquity."[2608] So too Duhm, Strahan, and Pope.[2609] The Hebrew has "pride from man he covers," for v. 17b. The KJV and RSV take it to mean "hide His pride from man." Dillmann proposes, "puts an end He [God] hides from man his action," but this does not seem convincing and it seems best to follow Dillmann.[2610]

Rowley says of v. 18:

> In all of God's actions they are beneficient, in that it is designed to save him from a worse fate.[2611]

The use of the "Pit" in v. 18a reminds us of 17:14. The "perishing by the sword" in v. 18b is most likely a corruption. The verb usually means "to pass through" and though the noun often means a weapon, this does not seem to be relevant here, where we expect a parallel to the Pit. Thus, Duhm proposes, "going down to Sheol." Strahan agrees.[2612]

33:19–28

About v. 19, Rowley observes:

> Elihu now passes to a second channel of divine communication in warning, and with continual strife in his bones.[2613]

Terrien says of vv. 19–22:

> In the second place God chastens man by physical pain (v. 19), which produces fasting (v. 20) and thus a leanness (v. 21) and awareness of mortality (v. 22).[2614]

He continues:

> Elihu concedes, however, that neither dreams in the lonely hours of the night nor bodily ailments carries in itself the words of God to man. Suffering is not

the instrument of divine revelation, but only its possible channel. It merely prepares man to listen.[2615]

Rowley points out that the word "life" in v. 20 probably means "appetite," as at 38:39.[2616] This makes it parallel to "soul" which it means at Ps 107:9. The verb for v. 20a, usually rendered "loathes," is another hapax in this form. The word is *zaham*, an adjectival form of the same word is employed at 6:7.

The RSV translates "loathes." The KJV translates "abhoreth." The "dainty food" of v. 20b is literally "food of desire" in the Hebrew text. Rashi has, "And his living spirit causes him to abhor food." He adds, "The soul and the life of the sick person cause him to abhor all tasty food." He renders v. 21 this way: "His flesh is consumed from sight."[2617] Mezudat David gives this for v. 21:

> Then the fat of his flesh will become emaciated and will be withdrawn from sight. It will be consumed so quickly that the consumption of the flesh will virtually be visible.[2618]

Ibn Ezra, on the other hand, takes the opposite view. He explains about v. 21, "His flesh will be consumed until it no longer will be visible."[2619] Rashi says the import of v. 21b is this: "And his bones are dislocated means they are out of their place."[2620] Holscher proposes, "the bones stick out."[2621] Dhorme says, "the bones are thin."[2622] Others suggest, the bones "are laid bare." Rowley says this means there is little flesh left to cover them.[2623] He suggests, "and his life is one close to death," much like the RSV.

Rowley introduces v. 23 this way:

> When reduced by illness until he is at death's door, God seeks again to reclaim him, this time by sending an angel to him. The angel is a messenger of God, or may be human or superhuman, here probably the former.[2624]

Rowley renders the second noun, *luwts*, of v. 23 as "mediator." He says the word elsewhere means "interpreter," as of dreams at Gen 42:23. The "one of a thousand" of v. 23b, Rowley suggests, means, "No sick man need fear that there are not enough angels deputed for this service to serve all needs. The heavenly court is a large one."[2625] Verse 23c literally says, "his uprightness," but most translators render it "what is right for him," as has the RSV.[2626] Rowley and many others agree. Mezudat David renders v. 23 this way:

> If there is an angel over him, one out of a thousand.[2627]

He says about v. 23a, "When he is judged in the Heavenly Tribunal," and about v. 23b, "One of a thousand who testify to his guilt, and intercedes with his uprightness."[2628] Samuel Terrien says of the angel-mediator of v. 23, "In as much as man is not paying heed to this disclosure of his obligations, the angel-mediator truly mediates not only the will of God to man, but also the weakness of man to God."[2629]

Rashi thinks, "He is gracious to him," of v. 24, refers to "the Omnipresent."[2630] Ibn Ezra thinks the angel of v. 24 is "one appointed as his guardian."[2631] Rashi indicates the "I have found a ransom" of v. 24b refers to:

> This one merit suffices to save his soul, even though the angels who testify to his guilt greatly outnumber the one who testify to his merit.[2632]

Both Budde and Steuernagel introduce God as the subject of v. 24a.[2633] But it is more probable that the subject is the angel, who after his implied success in reclaiming or the sick man, a ransom should be provided. Bickell, Budde, and others add "of his soul" after the ransom of v. 24b.[2634] Dillmann thinks the ransom is the implied repentance of the sick man; so too Kissane.[2635] But the ransom appears to be provided by the mediator, as an expression of his graciousness. After reclaiming the sufferer, he buys him an extended life.

There are a variety of words for "ransom" in the Hebrew Bible. Verse 34 uses the most common one, *kopher*. It is also employed at 36:18. Two other words for ransom are *pidyom* and *padah*. The former is used at Exod 21:30, the latter, at Hos 13:14.

Rowley says in v. 25, "The sick man is restored to life, and his flesh once more clothes his bones."[2636] The "become fresh," as the RSV has v. 25a, is another hapax. Siegfried changes one letter to yield, "to become plump."[2637] Dhorme proposes *yirtab*, or "become fresh," as does the RSV. H. H. Nichols suggests *yerak*, or "becomes tender," but the word remains a mystery.[2638]

Most exegetes suggest that after the angel's successful mediation, the restored man's prayers are now accepted, and he is admitted to the presence of God. Some commentators think the "come into his presence" in v. 26b is a reference to coming to the holy of holies in the temple.[2639] This would only be true, of course, if the setting is to be that of Israel, rather than Edom or elsewhere. It makes more sense to say it refers to worship in general, without specifying a particular place.

The "He recounts to men his salvation" in v. 26c literally says, "He restores his righteousness" in the Hebrew text.[2640] This seems to be out of place here, however, since he already has been accepted as righteous earlier. Mezudat David says of v. 26, "He entreats God, and placates Him in prayer."[2641]

About v. 27, Rashi exclaims:

> He makes a row of men because when he is saved from his illness and confesses before them to his Creator, but I have no profit in these matters.[2642]

Rowley says the verb in v. 27a (*shuwr*) is "sings," but the KJV and RSV render it "looketh."[2643] Dhorme finds the verb "repeat," which is also employed in vv. 3 and 14. But this is a doubtful root and it is best to follow the RSV, where the meaning is the restored man sings for joy, as he tells of his recovery.[2644]

J. Reider reads *yaser* for *yasor* to get the meaning, "He confesses."[2645] Guillaume, using an Arabic root, translates, "He says joyfully."[2646] Rowley thinks that v. 27b is too short and the verb usually means "to be equal."[2647] Budde reads *sillem* instead of *sawah*, as does Fohrer.[2648] He also adds God as the subject, while Duhm adds "according to my iniquity" at the end of v. 27b, and Bickell has it, "according to my sin."[2649]

Verse 28 is the fourth time in this chapter that "going down into the Pit" is mentioned ("from the Pit," in v. 18; "unto the Pit/Grave," in v. 22; "going down to the pit" in v. 24). This phrase is used nowhere else, and the verb means "passing through." Dhorme finds it equivalent to the verb in v. 28b, where the same verbal idiom is employed.[2650] The "shall see" or "may see" of v. 28b is another idiom used elsewhere for "to gloat over." (See Ps 22:17.) Here it means "looking for relief and joy on the light, rather than going down into Sheol, or the Pit." Mezudat David translates v. 28a as "he redeems his soul." He says of the verse:

> With this confession, he redeemed his soul from perishing in the pit of the grave, and his living spirit will see the light of life, that is, the saving from death is due to the confession, and none of his good deeds are deducted because of this rescue.[2651]

33:29–38

The expression "twice, three times" means repeatedly in v. 29. Rashi observes about the verse:

> He chastises him for his iniquities with his illness in order not to destroy him, but if he provokes Him further, he should be concerned with Gehinnom.[2652]

Rashi adds about v. 29:

> If a person commits a transgression once, God forgives him; a second time, God forgives him; a third time, God forgives him; the fourth time, however, God does not forgive him.[2653]

The Hebrew text has, "that he may be enlightened with," for v. 30b. Duhm has, "to enlighten him with," so too Pope, while Budde, on the basis of the Peshitta, read, "to bring back his soul from the Pit."[2654] This makes the idiom the same as in v. 28. Mezudat David says the import of v. 30 is "to bring back the soul from the grave and enable him to become enlightened in light of the eternal life in the World to Come."[2655] Rabbenu Maeyouchas explains v. 30 this way: "The entire verse is referring to this life, in this world."[2656]

In v. 31, Elihu again mentions Job by name. Mezudat David believes the verse means:

> I have answered your questions as to why God does not answer people, namely, that it is not so, for the dreams and the pain are God's words. Now hearken yet and listen to me, remaining silent until I answer your other questions.[2657]

Rowley says about v. 31, "Filled with a sense of his own importance, Elihu frequently demands attention."[2658] Mezudat David observes about v. 32:

> If you have words to refute what I have said, speak up and tell me what is on your mind, because my sole intention is to justify you. Thus, it is to your benefit to speak your mind, and I will try to set you straight on the path of truth and righteousness. If you remain silent, however, and keep the words in your belly, you will remain with your false ideas, and you will not be justified.[2659]

H. H. Rowley says of v. 32:

> After telling Job to be silent and listen, Elihu tells him to speak if he has anything to say. But Elihu cannot imagine anyone having an answer to make to him.[2660]

Szold says the meaning of v. 32 is nothing more than, "I seek to set you aright."[2661] The LXX, perhaps because of Elihu's arrogance or verbosity, deletes vv. 31b to 33.[2662] Rashi believes the "wisdom" of v. 33 is "the Wisdom of Divine Providence." Perhaps the divine plan view.[2663] He adds, "Elihu emphasizes that he wishes to justify Job, not to condemn him as his friends have done."[2664] Samuel Terrien believes the final verse of ch. 33 is about "unilateral transcendence and contemplation."[2665]

Chapter 34: The Continuation of Elihu's Speech

Introduction

Chapter 34 continues Elihu's discourse. Matthew Henry divides the chapter into four sections. Samuel Terrien, however sees the chapter having five sections. He labels these sections in the following way:

- The Need to Test Words (vv. 1–4).
- The Irreligion of Job (vv. 5–9).
- The Defense of Divine Justice (vv. 10–20).
- Divine Omnipotence Is Absolute (vv. 21–28).
- The Meaning of Divine Silence (vv. 29–37).[2666]

Elihu continues to employ his special vocabulary, with many Aramaic words in this chapter. He also employs several names for God in the chapter, including: *El*, *Eloah*, *Shaddai*, and even *Elohim* in v. 37. We also find characteristic terms like *binah* (vv. 10 and 33); *mishpat* (v. 12 and 23), *ruah*, at v. 14; *kabbir* (vv. 17 and 24); and words associated with the SDQ Semitic root, usually connected to "right," or "moral."

Chapter 34 contains another hapax in the book of Job. This one comes at v. 36. It appears to be related to a verb connected to "try" or "test." Thus, the verse may be assenting to the test theodicy here. Several other of our theological responses to the cause of Job's suffering also are employed in ch. 34. Verse 3 is akin to the test theodicy, as well. Verses 12–13 are related to retributive justice theory; and v. 27b, that speaks of Job "having no regard for His ways," appears to be a version of divine plan theory.

Analysis of Chapter 34

34:1–4

Rowley describes this first section of ch. 34 this way:

> Elihu now turns to defend the character of God against the charges Job has made, continuing to ignore the particular situation of Job, he deals in generalities, and while Job has argued from the particular to the general, from his own case to the character of God, then confirmed by other injustices around him. Elihu deals with the general concept of his theology, and concludes from it the sin of Job.[2667]

He adds about v. 2, "The wise men" of v. 2a "could hardly be the three friends, after what Elihu has said of them in 32:11ff. It may be the presumed audience of bystanders, from among whom Elihu himself has emerged."[2668] Driver agrees. He says, "not Job's three friends, but impartial bystanders, whom Elihu pictures as being present."[2669] Freehof observes about v. 2:

> Whom is Elihu addressing? It sounds as if he is speaking to a group which would be an indication also that this is a later insertion, as if the writer forgot that he put Elihu into the small company of the four debaters. Of course, he may be addressing the three friends and Job scornfully as "wise men."[2670]

Freehof renders v. 3 this way:

> For the ear trieth words,
> As the palate tasteth food.[2671]

Freehof here endorses the test view. He adds about this verse:

> In introducing a number of harsh words which Job made and which he, Elihu, intends to refute, he uses one of Job's own introductory phrases 12:11), "the palate tasteth its food." Then follows a series of quotations from Job's speeches in which Job claims to be righteous and to be unfairly attacked. In vv. 7–9, Elihu reminds Job that such scornful speeches are typical speeches of wicked people, and that by taking this road, "Job walketh with wicked men" (v. 8).[2672]

Rowley thinks that "discriminate" is a better translation than "choose" in v. 4. He says, "What Elihu means is to choose after careful examination."[2673] Mezudat David says it should be, "Let us choose judgment." He adds:

Let you and me decide judgment to clarify the truth, and let us know between ourselves what arguments are valid and which are invalid.[2674]

Rowley suggests the following for v. 4:

Let us choose what is right

And let us determine among ourselves what is good.[2675]

The word for "good" here is the normal word for "judgment." The meaning is probably something like, "Let us arrive at a sound conclusion."[2676] Driver gives 9:21 and 27:2 as parallels for v. 4.[2677] Terrien says of vv. 3–4, "Elihu here seems to contradict himself, as he appeals no longer to a 'testing' the truth of the interpretive beliefs concerning life is like 'tasting' a wine or a piece of cheese (cf. 12:11). It is, therefore, within the reach of man as man."[2678]

34:5–9

Many exegetes point out that in these verses Elihu directly quotes from Job's previous speeches, as we already have shown he did back at 33:8–11. Rowley gives 27:2 as a parallel to v. 5. He observes about the verse:

Elihu here in part cites what Job has said and in part summarizes Job's position.

His method here, as in the previous speech, was to take Job's views to pieces.[2679]

Driver translates v. 6 this way:

Notwithstanding my right

I am counted a liar.[2680]

He says, "This means, 'I maintain my innocence,' while some say 'falsely admit my guilt.'"[2681] Verse 6 says, "I am counted a liar" in most translations, though the Hebrew text simply says, "I lie." The KJV renders it, "Should I lie" (against my right), that is, "Should I confess guilt when I am innocent?"[2682] Dhorme repoints to yield, "I am deceived."[2683] Others say, "I am made a liar," which is the sense of the RSV. Kissane reads *'aksar* with the further change of *'al mishpat*, to get "in spite of my right."[2684] None of these changes, however, appear to be necessary. Mezudat David thinks that Elihu believes that Job has said, "I accuse my Judge of being a liar, because he did not judge me fairly."[2685] Presumably he means God here.

At v. 7, Elihu speaks of "scoffing for iniquity." Job earlier spoke of God scoffing at the calamity of the innocent at 9:23. Zophar suggests that Job scoffs at sound doctrine at 11:3, and Eliphaz speaks of the innocent scoffing in delight as the misfortunes of the wicked at 22:17. Here, however, Job is regarded as a public menace, scoffing at religion and thereby subverting morality. Sympathy appears to have no place in the heart of Elihu.

Many modern translation have v. 8a as, "Who goes in company with evildoers." The Hebrew, however, literally says, "Who takes the path of evil-doers?" Rowley gives 22:15 as a parallel to v. 8.[2686] Rowley says the meaning of v. 9 is that Elihu maintains that Job believes that "virtue is useless."[2687] But in fact Job did not say this at all. On the contrary, he has clung to virtue for its own sake, and not for what it has brought him.[2688] Mezudat David says v. 9 means, "A man derives no benefit if he perfects his ways," implying that Job had done just that.[2689] Driver says of v. 9, "Job has never expressed this doctrine in so many words, but it would be a natural inference from such passages as 9:22; 10:3; and 21:7ff."[2690]

34:10–20

"Men of understanding" in v. 10 is literally "men of heart" in the Hebrew. Mezudat David points out this means "men of an understanding heart." He says of v. 10b, "Far be it for God to commit wickedness, that is, to withhold the reward from one who deserves it."[2691] About v. 11, Rowley makes the following observation:

> Elihu like all the friends and like every wise theologian, is persuaded that God is not unjust. Where they err in tracing all human experience to the working of this one principle, and refusing to consider anything that might imperil it. A theology that must wear blinkers is an inadequate one. From the story of Cain and Abel on, the Bible recognizes that dessert and fortune are not precisely matched.[2692]

Rowley says about v. 12, "Elihu cannot bear to repeat what he said in v. 10."[2693] Mezudat David maintains v. 12 should be translated:

> Surely, God does not condemn
> And the Almighty does not pervert justice.[2694]

This, of course, is an assent to the retributive justice theory. He adds about the verse:

> Surely God does not condemn the righteous to repay one who did no evil with the punishment that was due the wicked. He does not pervert justice by withholding one's rightful reward.[2695]

Rashi prefers this translation for v. 13:

> Who gave him a charge over the Earth,
> And who disposes of the entire world?[2696]

Driver points out, of course, that this is a rhetorical question. He says the answer should be, "No one but Himself."[2697] Rowley says the meaning of v. 13 is clear: "Because God is supreme and not answerable to anyone, therefore, He can do no wrong.

He can have no possible motive for doing so."²⁶⁹⁸ Job already has said that God does not answer to anyone at 9:12, but he asks, "Why should all the injustices of life be placed at his door" at 9:24.

The Hebrew of v. 14 gives us: "If he should set his heart upon him (that is, man) or should gather to himself his spirit and his breath."²⁶⁹⁹ The LXX and Peshitta are closer to, "If he should take back unto himself" (to God).²⁷⁰⁰ The thought of v. 14 seems to be, "Since all men are alike and equally dependent on God, there is no reason why he should favor one over another."

Verse 15 has parallels at 12:10 and 28:21. In the former, we saw, "all living." In the latter, "every living creature." Here, in v. 15, we get, "all flesh," to indicate that when the breath is withdrawn, only the lifeless flesh remains. Terrien gives Ps 104:29–30 as another parallel to v. 15.²⁷⁰¹

The question of v. 16a, "If you have understanding . . . ," the "you have" does not appear in the Hebrew. At any rate, in this verse, Elihu changes to the singular, and appears to ask for Job's attention. Freehof says this about v. 17:

> Even if you hate or dislike the judgment passed, will you then condemn the righteous Judge?²⁷⁰²

Szold takes this verse to mean, "Even on Earth, one who hates right governs men, will you for that reason condemn God?"²⁷⁰³ Ibn Ezra takes a view on v. 17 quite like that of Freehof.²⁷⁰⁴ Many exegetes think that Elihu begs the question in v. 17. The suggestion that government guarantees justice is far from the truth in many places. The verb "govern" in v. 17a is literally "bind up" in the Hebrew. Here it has the sense of keeping a kingdom under control.

Both the KJV and RSV have, "Is it fit to say?" That none would denounce the king to his face is evidence of power and not of righteousness. To rebuke Job for daring to accuse God, who is mightier than any king, could be understood as an appeal to prudence in v. 18. Rowley says about v. 19:

> The reason why God can treat all impartiality is that all are the creatures of His hand.²⁷⁰⁵

Ibn Ezra thinks that v. 19 is connected to v. 18 in that, "if it is not right to despise and scorn earthly rulers, certainly it is wrong to scorn the Divine Ruler who 'respects not the person of princes, nor regards the rich more than the poor.'"²⁷⁰⁶ Freehof says about v. 19:

> God is powerful enough to have destroyed everybody for their sins, and yet he does not do so. This demonstrates His mercy. Besides, it would be improper to use scornful terms of a human king. How much more wrong is it of the Eternal and the Just God?²⁷⁰⁷

Rowley explains v. 20 this way:

The proof of God's impartiality is in the swift destruction he sends on the mighty.[2708]

Driver translates v. 20 this way:

> In a moment they die, even at midnight;
>
> The people are shaken and pass away;
>
> And the mighty are taken away without hand.[2709]

Driver believes that v. 20c means "through no human agency, by the unseen power of God." He gives Dan 2:24 as a parallel to v. 20, as well as Lam 4:6.[2710] Rashi observes about v. 20:

> They die in a moment when a sudden death, such as a pestilence, comes upon them as punishment for sin Then both die in one moment, the prince just like the poor man.[2711]

34:21-28

Mezudat David describes v. 21 this way:

> For the Omnipresent observes all of man's ways, and when he sins against Him, He immediately sends him to eradicate him from the world; rich or poor, few or many, without a prior natural cause to which to attribute the death.[2712]

Freehof gives Jer 16:7 as a parallel text for v. 21.[2713] Rowley gives 24:23 and 31:4 as parallels. He observes about v. 21:

> Elihu means that because God is omniscient, when disaster falls, it is the evidence that he has seen wickedness. Job believes that God is omniscient, and therefore, he must know that Job is innocent.[2714]

Rowley adds about v. 21, "The Prologue shows that Job is right on this issue. Where he goes wrong is in concluding that God is indifferent in moral issues."[2715] Rowley provides Ps 139:11ff. and Jer 23:24 as parallel texts to v. 22. He says of the verse:

> God's all-seeing eye can penetrate the deepest darkness, and no act of man is concealed from Him.[2716]

Samuel Terrien says the meaning of v. 22 is that "Job had complained that God refused to go to trial with him."[2717] Rowley observes about v. 23:

> Job has lamented that he could not go to law with God (9:32), though he has also recognized that God would be not only be an adversary but Judge (10:2.) Elihu says that God does not need to go through the process of the court to

establish guilt. Because He knows all, His just sentence can be pronounced and executed at any time without summoning a man to the tribunal.[2718]

Freehof agrees in regard to v. 23. He writes:

> God does not need to hold a court hearing with man as you, Job, have frequently demanded. He knows all the truth and sends just punishment when needed. This is stated in the next six verses. God's judgment, based upon His complete knowledge, applies to individuals and to nations.[2719]

The "without inquiry" or "without investigation" in v. 24, literally says "no investigation" in the Hebrew. Similar phrases are employed at 5:9 and 9:10. The KJV has, "in ways past finding out."[2720] The point here appears to be that God is so arbitrary that he brushes any examination or investigation aside. Rowley says of v. 24, "His power matches His will, and He can execute justice as well as pronounce it."[2721]

Rowley proposes that v. 25 be moved to follow directly v. 22.[2722] Dhorme, Kissane, and Fohrer also believe it would fit better there.[2723] F. Zimmermann, using evidence from Syriac and Arabic, gives the following for v. 25b, "Therefore, he repudiates their works."[2724] If the verse is transferred, however, this is quite unnecessary, and the ordinary sense is appropriate. There is a clear lack of balance in the two lines of v. 26. The Hebrew text has "under wicked men," while the KJV and RSV prefer, "as wicked men." In Ugaritic, the preposition can mean "among" as well as "under," so we must render it, "among wicked men," as Wright does.[2725] The beginning of v. 27, "Because" consists of three Hebrew words. Dhorme transfers the first of these to v. 26.[2726] Bickell omits the other two words.[2727] Beer omits the third word and transposes the other two,[2728] but most other exegetes leave the translation alone.[2729] Both Rashi and Mezudat David explain v. 27 this way:

> The people were destroyed because they turned away from following God,
> and they did not understand even one of His ways.[2730]

S. R. Driver believes the meaning of v. 27 is, "God's omniscience enables him to act without any special investigation."[2731] Mezudat David says the import of v. 28 is:

> God destroys the wicked in order to bring upon each one of them the punishment due them because of the cry of the poor whom he has oppressed.[2732]

The verb "caused" in v. 28a is an infinite, and it could be rendered as a singular or a plural. Davidson prefers the singular and took the meaning to be, "By destroying the wicked God brought the cry of the oppressed to Himself."[2733] Peake, however, objects to this, and he prefers the plural.[2734] Terrien says the meaning of v. 28 is, "It is not true to say that God does not hear the cry of the oppressed.[2735]

34:29–37

Terrien says the import of v. 29 is clear: If God is silent, no human being has the right to condemn Him."[2736] Rowley points out that v. 29ff. is very cryptic, but the import seems to be, "If God remains quiet and does not intervene to punish the wicked, no one has any right to condemn Him."[2737] Hitzig transposes two letters in the second verb to get, "who can make trouble?" for v. 29a.[2738] Dhorme renders the first verb in v. 29a as "casts down."[2739] Ehrlich emends the second verb to get "who can be saved?" He also transposes two consonants, so that he renders the verse:

> If He declares a man just,
>
> Who can condemn?[2740]

Kissane emends vv. 29c and 30 to translate:

> With a nation or with a man, he is compassionate
>
> delivering a miscreant from the snares of affliction.[2741]

This approach is not convincing. Dhorme moves "godless" to the next verse to make a much better parallel to v. 29c, "that no one of those who ensnare the people should reign."[2742]

But this still makes it long for a short verse. It is more probable that a word or words have been lost in vv. 29c and 30. Rashi says of v. 30, "Over the poor, who reigned because of the snares of the people who were guilty of iniquity, and concerning such a God you should not have said, 'scoundrel!' and 'wicked!'"[2743]

The expression "has one said to God" is emphatic, as is "to you" in v. 31. Rowley observes about the verse:

> If confusion is made to God, why should he have to get Job's permission before accepting it? Is Job setting himself before God.[2744]

Rashi says of v. 31:

> To be said to him, it is fitting and proper for all those who suffer pain to say, "I bear, accept, and tolerate Your judgments, and I will not destroy myself." Further, the one who is judged must say, "Besides what I see, that is, what I know to perceive in Your words. You instruct me, and if I have committed Injustice, I will not continue."[2745]

Rowley gives us, "Teach me what I do not see," at v. 32.[2746] The Hebrew literally says, "apart from that which I see."[2747] Dhorme prefers, "until I see."[2748] But this seems incorrect. The verse is clearly a confession and a promise of obedience to God, so there is no necessity to emend v. 32.

Mezudat David says of v. 33:

> Should the speculation concerning God's judgment end with you? Should you alone decide, because you despise everyone else's opinion? Will you choose the truth of the matter and not I. I too have understanding equal to yours. Now what do you know of philosophic theories, to ascertain whether they are correct?[2749]

And of v. 34, Mezudat David adds:

> I know that men of understanding will say to me that they agree with all that I say, and every wise man will listen to my words and not deviate from them.[2750]

Rowley observes about v. 34:

> Possibly we should suppose that Elihu paused to give Job a chance to reply, but it is probable that it occurred to Elihu that anyone should think about replying to the cogent arguments he thought he was using.[2751]

Samuel Terrien says in vv. 35–36, "Job speaks without knowledge, and deserves to be tried to the end, since he adds rebellion to his sin and multiplied his words against God." Terrien adds about these verses:

> Once more Elihu discerns that the specifically theological character of Job's guilt. His position is close to that held by the three friends in the poetic discussion because he cannot accept the validity of Job's attacks upon the righteousness of God. But unlike the three friends, he has so far been careful to argue on the basis of the sufferer's blasphemous criticism of the divine will, not on the presumption of the sufferer's moral guilt. He has not attempted to justify the hero's misery by charging him with ethical turpitude.[2752]

The natural meaning of the Hebrew words for "would that" in v. 36a is "my father," as the Vulgate translates. But this makes no sense. The KJV has it, "My desire is that . . . " taking from the root meaning "to desire," or *arbeh*.[2753] Others take the meaning from Arabic meaning, "to entreat," and thus, "I pray." The meaning, then, is not a wish that Job's trial might continue, but rather, the reason why Job must expose his errors. Most exegetes think the RSV's sense is preferable:

> Would that Job were tried until the end
>
> because he answers as wicked men do.[2754]

Duhm and others delete the words, "He claps his hands among us." "The hands" is not in the Hebrew text.[2755] Ehrlich emends "among us" to get "our face," and thus, "He slaps our face."[2756] Dhorme repoints the word for "he claps," and understands the line according to Aramaic and thus translates, "In our midst, he casts doubts upon."[2757] Duhm reads the first line of v. 37, "He adds to his sin"; so too Marvin Pope.[2758] If we retain the Hebrew text and add "his hands," the line becomes a castigation of Job for the contempt he has shown God.[2759]

PART II: THE BOOK OF JOB COMMENTARY

Chapters 35–36: Elihu's Discourse Continues

Introduction

Chapters 35 and 36 continue Elihu's discourses. Elihu again shows his range of referring to the Divine, making eleven more references to God in these chapters, including his employment of *El, Elohim, Eloah, Shaddai, Kabbir,* and two references to "Maker," at 35:10 and 36:3. The word used at 35:10, the Hebrew *a'sah*, is also employed at 4:17 and 32:22; but a different term is used at 36:3, the Hebrew *pa'al*, a noun form of the verb "to make."

In chs. 35 and 36, Elihu also reveals his range of answers that he proposes about the cause of Job's suffering. At 36:5–7, he endorses retributive justice. At 36:10 and 15, he suggests a response closer to what we have labeled the moral qualities view; and at 36:26, Elihu presents a version of the divine plan perspective, as we have indicated earlier.

Elihu also continues his characteristic Hebrew vocabulary in chs. 35 and 36. He employs, for example, the word *Hen!* or "Behold!" at 35:5 and 36:5, 22, 26, and 30. He uses *mishpat* at 35:7 and 36:17; *kabbir* at 36:5; and words related to the SDQ root at 35:2 and 36:6. Chapter 36:2 is one of the many Aramaic sentences in the Elihu speeches; and the word for "mist" in 36:27 is another hapax legomena in the Elihu discourses. The term is *'ed*, and may be related to words from a root meaning "vapor" or "mist." The word "drops," or *nazal*, is another unusual word, at 38:28.

Nearly all interpreters divide ch. 35 into two main sections, vv. 1–8 and vv. 9–16. Some exegetes, like Samuel Terrien, further divide the chapter into the following four parts:

- Rights of Man before God (vv. 1–4).
- Freedom of God from Man (vv. 5–8).
- Gift of God to Man (vv. 9–12).
- Vanity of Job's Arguments (vv. 13–16).[2760]

In our analysis of ch. 35, we shall follow Terrien's division of the chapter. One final element of ch. 36 is that at vv. 27–33, the language of Elihu looks very much like the language of God and his speeches from the whirlwind in ch. 38 to follow, another indication that Elihu is a Prelude to the Theophany.

Analysis of Chapter 35

35:1–4

Terrien observes about these verses:

With remarkable penetration, Elihu understands that Job became a blasphemer when he deemed religion and morality were unprofitable to him.[2761]

H. H. Rowley introduces ch. 35 this way:

> Elihu now proceeds to deal with Job's declaration that virtue is of no avail, and argues that neither virtue nor sin can affect God, but that both affect man.[2762]

Kissane changes one letter in "my right" to yield, "I am righteous."[2763] Rather than "before God" in v. 2a, both the KJV and RSV have, "more than God." The "have I" of v. 3a, Dhorme understands "to God."[2764] Indeed, the Hebrew text has "to Thee." The Hebrew of v. 3b is not "How am I better off." Rather, it is "How am I profited by my sin?" We must remember, however, that Job never suggests his sin was the cause of his suffering. Ehrlich suggests, "What do I do if I have sinned?" So too Dhorme, Kissane, and Larcher, among others.[2765]

Rowley comments about v. 4:

> Elihu is prepared to instruct Job and his friends, for whom Elihu already has expressed contempt.[2766]

Dhorme believes the onlookers are the reference to the plural "you" in v. 4a.[2767] Peake says of v. 4, "Elihu proceeds to appropriate the thoughts of his friends is no proof that he cannot be professing to instruct them; such conduct would be quite characteristic of him."[2768]

Mezudat David explains v. 4 this way:

> Just as I differ with you so too I differ with your companions, because they judge that your suffering came because of your many sins, and I do not believe that.[2769]

Mezudat David, then, appears to be consenting to retributive justice theory as an interpretation of Job's suffering that Elihu proves at 35:4. The fourth friend reverts to this theory in a number of other places, as well. Among these are: 34:12; 35:8; and 36:14.

35:5–8

Terrien gives 22:12 and 11:7ff. as parallels to v. 5.[2770] Rowley observes about v. 5, "Job too has acknowledged that God controlled the heavens at 9:8ff."[2771] The thought here is that God is so far above us, He is beyond the reach of our actions.[2772] Thus, Terrien assents here to the divine plan answer to Job's suffering. Rashi says about the "gazing at the Heavens" of v. 5:

> Since He is high and you are low, and He has no benefit from your wickedness and His righteousness, why do you boast to him about your righteousness.[2773]

In v. 6, Elihu quotes Job's line at 7:20, and v. 7 looks very much like Eliphaz's comment at 22:3. Mezudat David thinks Elihu is asking in v. 7, "If you are righteous, what do you give to God, or what does He take from you of His own accord?"[2774] Rashi says the meaning of v. 8 is:

> Your wickedness or your righteousness can and will bring benefit. Observe there are many wicked men who . . .[2775]

Rowley says that in v. 8, "Elihu does not mean that a man's righteousness or wickedness only profits or injures himself, but another man like himself."[2776] Terrien makes this observation about vv. 5–8:

> With a somber bit authentic awareness of divine transcendence, Elihu suggests that God, who is above the heavens and the clouds, is not affected by human sin. Much more important still, God does not need man's righteousness.[2777]

Freehof agrees that Elihu follows "the argument of the speech of Eliphaz at ch. 22, Namely, that man does not do a favor to God by being righteous, nor harm to God by being evil. Elihu continues this same argument here in v. 8."[2778]

35:9–12

Solomon Freehof says of v. 9:

> Verse nine to the end takes up another argument of Job. Job, particularly in chapter 24, had complained of the social injustice on earth. He speaks of all the homeless and the miserable and ends up by saying that God does not seem to consider it wrong (24:12) Yet, God imputeth it not for unseemliness. Elihu answers that God who knows all things must certainly have the case of the unfortunate in His mind and intend to rectify it.[2779]

Rowley says of v. 10, "They merely cry out against their oppressors. They are not driven by their sorrows to seek God."[2780] Peake observes about v. 10b, "If only the author could have kept to this height."[2781] Kissane prefers, "Who gives succor in the night," for v. 10b.[2782] Rashi translates v. 10 this way:

> Where is God, my Maker,
>
> Who deals destruction at night.[2783]

Dhorme thinks the songs in the night are "the crashes of thunder."[2784] Ehrlich alters the text to yield "lights,"[2785] while Wright renders it "constellations."[2786] But it would seem a pity to rob Elihu of such a poetic line. Rashi says the meaning of v. 11 is, "He teaches us more wisdom than He does the beasts. He esteemed us and made of greater than the beasts and the birds."[2787]

Rowley gives 12:7 as a parallel to v. 11. Freehof agrees with this understanding of v. 11. He writes:

> The great blessing of God to man is that He gives him a higher intelligence than that of the animals. This is also the theme of Psalm 8. This idea is consistent with the rest of the thought of Elihu, namely, that God is our great Guide and Teacher. He teaches us through our dreams and through our sorrows.[2788]

Most exegetes point out that v. 12 seems to follow the thread at v. 9, thus, Kissane, and many others have v. 12 follow v. 9.[2789] This is another place where Elihu goes back to something he already has said, or that Job has said earlier. Rashi observes about v. 12:

> They cry out and see that there the poor cry out because of the pride of those who oppress them, and He does not answer.[2790]

Freehof says that most Jewish commentators take v. 12 to be another example of the "foolish things that people say who forget about God's Providence when they see the oppression in the world."[2791] Rashi explains v. 12 this way:

> Do not say foolishly there they cry because of the haughtiness of the oppressors, and their God gives no answer.[2792]

35:13–16

Rowley says of v. 13, "The cry here is not really addressed to God, but to the void. Therefore, God does not hear it."[2793] The Hebrew has "Only vanity God does not hear." The word translated "vanity" (*shav*) can also be rendered "false." Thus, Ibn Ezra translates, "It is false to say that God will not hear."[2794] Tur-Sinai also follows this translation.[2795]

Rowley says of v. 14:

> If God does not listen to those who do not turn to him, how much less will He listen to Job who complains against Him. Job's cry is only not to God, but it is directed against Him.[2796]

S. R. Driver renders v. 14 this way:

> How much less when thou sayest
>
> Thou beholdest him not.
>
> The cause is before him, and thou waitest for him.[2797]

Driver believes by v. 15, Elihu means that "God is indifferent to suffering, such that righteousness profits a man no more than sin."[2798] Verse 15 is clearly one of the most obscure of the book. Davidson says of the verse, "It competes worthily with the original in darkness."[2799]

Freehof points out that v. 16 "is almost the exact ending of chapter 34."[2800] He adds:

> But since chapter 34 spoke chiefly of the majesty of God, the closing sentence in chapter 35 is "Job multiplied his words against God." Since God speaks of the intelligence which God has given us, the chapter ends, "He multiplies words without knowledge."[2801]

Chapter 36: Elihu Continues His Discourse

Introduction

Chapter 36 appears to continue the speech begun in ch. 35. Both Matthew Henry and Samuel Terrien suggest that ch. 36 has four sections. Terrien gives these four parts the following names:

- Elihu Desires Job's Attention (vv. 1–4).
- The Methods of How God Deals with Men (vv. 5–14).
- Elihu Counsels Job (vv. 15–23).
- The Wonders in the Works of Creation (vv. 24–33).[2802]

In our analysis, we will follow the divisions of Professor Terrien, which is only slightly different than that of Matthew Henry.

Analysis of Chapter 36

36:1–4

Again in v. 2 of ch. 36 Elihu announces that he has something to say on God's behalf. The "bear with me" in v. 2b, elsewhere in the Hebrew Bible this same verb means "to surround," for example at Judg 20:43. Here the meaning seems to be "wait," which is a common use in Syriac. Several other words in v. 2 are also Aramaisms.

What Elihu seems to suggest by v. 3 is that he will display his range of knowledge, another indication of the fourth friend's haughtiness. Szold suggests that v. 3 means, "I will get my knowledge from God whom we see at a distance."[2803] Again, in v. 4 as Rowley says, "Elihu is a stranger to modesty, and frequently finds it necessary to certify his own genius."[2804] The use of the word "perfect" in v. 4b is the same word *tam/tamim*, blameless that describes Job in the Prologue. Freehof says the "upright in mind is with thee" refers to God. So too Ibn Ezra.[2805] Freehof remarks about v. 4:

> God the Benificient and the Benevolent is present and He will testify as to the truth of what I say.[2806]

Tur-Sinai follows this explanation of v. 4, and calls attention to a parallel at 1 Sam 2:3, "For the Lord is a God of knowledge."[2807] Szold holds a similar view about v. 4.[2808] Verse 4 also contains the only instance of the word *sheqer*, or "false," in the verse.

36:5–14

In v. 5 there is a repetition of the word "mighty" (*kabbir*) and there is no object to the verb "despise," much like at 42:6. The word "any" that completes v. 5a does not appear in the Hebrew text. Duhm reduces the verse to get simply, "See, God despises the stubborn of heart."[2809] So too Beer and Strahan,[2810] while G. B. Gray reduces it to yield: "God does not reject the perfect."[2811] Steinmann holds a similar view.[2812] Fohrer translates v. 5, "Lo, God rejects the mighty."[2813]

Dhorme and Marvin Pope read, "Lo, God is mighty in strength and despises not the pure of heart," for v. 5.[2814] Kissane transfers the "mighty in strength" to v. 6, leaving v. 5 simply as, "Look, God rejects not the pure of heart."[2815]

Rowley believes in v. 6, Elihu says that Job has asked, "Why are the wicked aloud to live?"[2816] Elihu replies by saying they do not. "God destroys the wicked and rights the wrongs suffered by those who are reduced to poverty by their oppression."[2817] Mezudat David observes about v. 6:

> As a rule, He does not supervise the wicked, but when He gives the humble poor their sustenance, He separates the wicked from them and does not sustain him with them.[2818]

Solomon Freehof says of v. 7, "With kings on the throne, God will exalt the righteous, and give them the dignity of kings."[2819] For "his eyes" Bickell suggests "his right."[2820] So too Budde, Beer, Peake, and Dhorme.[2821] But there seems no good reason here to change the Hebrew text. To say that God does not rob the righteous of their rights is inferior to saying he has them forever in his watchful gaze.

H. H. Rowley says the following about v. 8:

> When the righteous suffer before God has delivered them from their wicked oppressors, it is because he is seeking through discipline to refine them.[2822]

The reference to "discipline" suggests the moral qualities view. Dhorme thinks that v. 8 continues to deal with the kings in v. 7, "who may be reduced to captivity for their discipline."[2823] But it seems unlikely that Elihu would believe that all kings were righteous, and here the discipline appears to be for those who are fundamentally good men, though not without some moral flaws.

Rowley observes about v. 9:

> The purpose of their affliction is to bring home to them their sins, and to awaken them to a recognition that their exaltation has bred pride in them.[2824]

Rashi says about v. 9, "He tells them their deed with these sufferings. He lets them know that they sinned before Him." He adds:

> All the words of Elihu were complete consolations and not chidings, that is, do not worry about the sufferings if you are righteous, because they are for your own good, and He says that with sufferings, they will soon repent of iniquity.[2825]

Freehof says in regard to v. 12:

> According to Elihu, the tragedy of life is not sufferings in themselves. All of our sufferings may teach us much and misfortune may lead us on the path of nobility. The real tragedy is to suffer and not to learn anything from it. . . . The heaviest blow a man may sustain is to "die without knowledge."[2826]

Mezudat David has a similar view to the meaning of v. 12. He writes, "They will pass away from the world by the sword, and die because they lack the knowledge of understanding and to repent of their iniquity."[2827] Rowley also takes a similar view of the verse. He says, "If they will not learn from their discipline, final doom will overtake them."[2828] What most interpreters point out about these verses is that Elihu employs what we have called the moral qualities view, whereby suffering acts as a kind of discipline for developing certain moral traits like trust and fortitude.

Many modern translators render v. 13 this way:

> The godless in heart cherish anger;
> They do not cry for help when he binds them.[2829]

This is the translation of Pope, the RSV, as well as the NRSV. We believe that this is the best rendering of Job 36:13. The Hebrew text says "put anger." This has been understood by some to mean "lay up God's anger," but more commonly it means to "nourish anger" in their hearts, instead of realizing that their chastisement is for their own good. Dhorme makes this meaning explicit by rendering, "keeps their anger." Rowley gives Amos 1:11 and Jer 3:5 as parallels for v. 13.[2830]

Solomon Freehof observes about v. 14:

> Those who suffer and do not turn to God risk a corruption of the spirit because all that they then retain in their minds and hearts is bitterness, resentment, and despair; but those who turn to God find that God "delivereth the afflicted and openeth their ear by tribulation."[2831]

S. R. Driver believes that v. 14 refers to one who "complains that he can't find God." He gives 13:24; 23:8ff.; and 30:20 as parallel texts for v. 14.[2832] Duhm suggests that the meaning of v. 14 is this: "These persons who are attached to shrines for infamous purposes, commonly expire quite early."[2833] This is a version of the "good die young" adage. There is much confusion about how to translate the end of v. 14b. Dhorme renders it, "in adolescence." The RSV and Rowley prefer "in shame."[2834]

36:15–23

Rowley is sure that v. 15 means:

> Those who profit by their discipline are delivered. Elihu restates his view that the meaning of discipline to lead on to his application of the principle to the case of Job.[2835]

Again, in this section we see references to the moral qualities point of view. As we have suggested earlier, this is one feature of the book that sets Elihu apart from the other friends who put much more emphasis on the retributive justice theory. Nevertheless, Freehof says the meaning of v. 18 is this:

> Prosperity may tempt us to pride and evil. Guard yourself in your time of sufficiency for it may lead you to evil. This is also possibly a hint from Elihu that Job's sufferings came in the dangerous days when he was at the height of his prosperity.[2836]

Many modern translations of v. 18 give us this:

> Beware lest wrath entice you into scoffing;
> And let not the greatness of the ransom turn you aside.[2837]

The Hebrew text gives us, "for wrath, lest it entices you." Clearly the word "entice" here means "entice to evil." The KJV here takes the wrath to be God's, the RSV understands it to be Job's. Another problem with v. 18 is that the two lines appear to have nothing to do with each other. The word "scoffing" is translated as "sufficiency" at 20:22. This is yet another Aramaism that is found in the Elihu speeches.

Verses 19–20 are two of the most difficult in the Hebrew text. Thus, Dhorme rejects them as a gloss.[2838] The word rendered "your cry" is not found elsewhere with this meaning, or it may be connected to a word for "rich" (*soa*). Similarly, the word for "from distress" (*besar*) could also be pointed as *beser*, or "gold." There have been too many renderings that are too varied to make good sense of these lines. Gray rightly says of v. 20, "This is perhaps the most unintelligible of all these verses."[2839]

The construction for v. 21b is quite unusual, and the Hebrew could more naturally mean, "on account of this." Budde renders v. 21b, "unrighteousness you have chosen."[2840] The Peshitta, however, understands the verb in its Aramaic meaning of "test," and thus it gives us, "you have been tested." This is followed by Wright, Dhorme, and many others.[2841] This seems more apropos. As Rowley observes, "The affliction of which he complains is rather being traced to his iniquity, as described in the previous verse."[2842] If "tested" is the proper view, then Elihu refers here to the test perspective, or the moral qualities view, as he did at 33:16 and 36:15. Both Freehof and Szold believe that v. 22 means, "God raises up the humble by His power."[2843] Rowley says of the verse, "Elihu now turns to the purpose of the suffering which Job's iniquity has entailed, and in accordance with what he has said above, he declares that God is teaching him about it."[2844] Again, if this is the proper meaning of v. 22, then it is another instance of the moral qualities theodicy. Almost all translators say the meaning of the next verse, v. 23, is that "God is supreme, and there is none over Him and is subject to the judgment of no one." Similarly, v. 24 is generally seen as a humble recognition of the works of God. But nowhere else has Job claim the right to punish God, so it seems highly unlikely here.

If God being Supreme is the proper view of v. 23, then Elihu is assenting again to the position that God knows all and is All-Powerful, and he has a plan, or 'esa, which he knows, but to which humans are not privy.

36:24–33

Freehof points out the similarity of these verses to ch. 37, a praise of God's grandeur in nature. Rashi says the import of v. 24 is like that at Num 24:17.[2845] Mezudat David explains the verse this way:

> Keep in mind to remember that His works, because by yourself, you will magnify his works, which men saw. These deeds that are known and which reveal to all the greatness of His Providence, in addition to those works that are unknown to us.[2846]

Mezudat David's understanding of v. 24 is consistent with what we have called the divine plan theory of Job's suffering. Man is far too puny to understand the workings of God.[2847] Rashi thinks the reference to "from afar" in v. 25 refers to "from the creation of the world until now."[2848] Rowley thinks the meaning of v. 25 is that, "Man cannot see the works of God close at hand, and therefore cannot understand it completely."[2849] If this is the proper view, then Elihu again argues for the divine plan theory.

Rashi takes v. 26 to show, "The number of His years are unfathomable."[2850] Duhm concludes from this verse that the author of it lived some two centuries later than the author of the Divine speeches.[2851] Gersonides says v. 29 refers to the "crashing of the pavilion of clouds and the crashing of thunder."[2852] Driver gives Ps 18:11 as a parallel to v. 29.[2853] Tur-Sinai suggests we read *taswit*, or "bed," for *te'su'ot*.[2854] The word for "pavilion" in v. 29b means "canopy" at Ps 18:11, where the clouds are described as "the pavilion of God."[2855] The verb "scatters" in v. 30a comes from the same root as the "spreading" of v. 29a. The Hebrew has "light," rather than "lightning" in v. 30a. The same word appears to mean "lightning" in v. 32, but most scholars render it "mist," that is *edo* for *oro*. Pope changes "about him" (*alaw*) to *'alily*, and finds here a divine name, *'Alily*, from which the Ugaritic evidence suggests.[2856]

Rosenmuller points out the lack of agreement on any two translators in regard to v. 32.[2857] Newer interpretations have arisen on the verse, but there is still considerable disagreement over the verse. Freehof maintains about v. 32:

> The traditional interpreters object to the idea that lightning springs from God's hands to mean "clouds." Both Gersonides and Szold, however, take it to mean "hands," but translate the sentence, "With His two hands, He spreads the lightning."[2858]

Peake gives more than thirty explanations of v. 33. The early versions are in disagreement as to the meaning of many words in the verse. Freehof thinks the *telleth* of v. 33 means that "even the animals are aware of God's works."[2859] Driver changes some of the vowels in v. 33 to yield the following:

> As one that is jealous with anger against unrighteousness.[2860]

Two final aspects of ch. 36 pertain to the vocabulary in the chapter. In the RSV, the translators use the word "Behold" to begin several verses in the chapter, at vv. 5, 22, 26, and 30. In three of these, they are a translation of the word *Hen*. The fourth instance, which occurs at v. 24, uses an entirely different, unconnected word, *shiyr*. At v. 25, we see the use of the verb "beholds," a word that comes from the same root as *shiyr*.

Second, in ch. 36 the author uses the word *tam*, "blameless" or "perfect," that was employed to describe Job in the Prologue. Third, the chapter uses a number of words often seen in wisdom literature, such as "righteous," in v. 7, and "judgment," in v. 27. Finally, ch. 36, like the other chapters of Elihu's speeches employs multiple names for God. The name that predominates in ch. 36 and the first half of 37 is *El*, though we also find *Eloah* and *Shaddai* at 37:15 and 37:23, respectively.

Chapter 37: The Close of Elihu's Discourses

Introduction

In ch. 37, we see the close of Elihu's discourses, as well as the dialogue portion of the text that began in ch. 3 and continued until the end of what Elihu has to say in ch. 37. In ch. 37, Elihu also continues his more teleological explanations of Job's suffering, and a movement away, in Elihu, from more deontological responses, like retributive justice. In ch. 37, Elihu continues his use of the divine plan view, as well as the moral qualities approach.

Both Matthew Henry and Carol Newsom divide ch. 37 into three basic sections. The initial of these Henry calls "Elihu Observes the Power of God" (vv. 1–13). The second section, vv. 14–20, Henry labels "Job Required to Explain the Works of

Nature." "God Is Great and Is to Be Feared" is Henry's name for the final section of ch. 37.[2861]

Chapter 37 contains two more hapax logomena, at vv. 7 and 9. The first of these is the verb "seals up," and the other is the noun for "whirlwind," where the Hebrew word is *cupuwh*, and not the *ce'arah* employed at 38:1 when God speaks from a tempest or whirlwind.

Chapter 37 also continues Elihu's tendency to employ a number of Hebrew terms to designate the Divine. He makes six references to God in the chapter: four references to *El*; one to *Eloah*; and one to *Shaddai*, in v. 23. In ch. 37, Elihu also continues to use his characteristic Hebrew vocabulary. In the chapter, he uses words like *tam*, or "blameless"; *mishpat*, or "justice"; and *ruah*, or "spirit" "wind," or "breath."

Finally, much of the language of ch. 37, particularly vv. 1–7 and 14–24 look very much like the Hebrew to be found in the God speeches, beginning in ch. 38. Elihu employs nouns connected to "thunder," "light," and "lightning," and "wind," that later will be found profusely in the God's speeches.

Analysis of Chapter 37

37:1–13

Newsom introduces vv. 1–5 this way:

> Elihu develops the themes of lightning in these verses. A new section is marked off first by his reference to his own emotional reaction to the dramatic sense he has just described (v. 1) and by his call to others to listen (v. 2.) Here, even more explicitly, thunder is described as the voice of God in a manner reminiscent of Psalm 29. The function of this passage is sensuous, inviting the reader to "listen, listen" (v. 2). In v. 5b, Elihu returns to the theme he announced in 36:26, the inability of humans to comprehend God and God's works.[2862]

Most modern translations of v. 1 have "My heart," though the LXX has "Thy heart."[2863] So too Bickell and Duhm, but Budde notes that Job is not actually addressed until v. 14.[2864] In v. 1b, the verb is plural and thus should be "leaps." It is found only here and at Lev 11:21 and Hab 3:6, where it is transitive. The word for "thunder" (*ra'am*) in v. 2 is rendered as "troubling" at 3:17. In Arabic, a similar root means the rumbling of the sea. The image of thunder as the voice of God was also seen earlier at 28:28.

Verse 3 looks like a parallel to 28:24. The "it" in v. 3a refers to the lightning. The verb is another Aramaism. It means "to release," or "to let go." The "his voice" in v. 4a, the LXX has "a voice." The verb "roars" in v. 4 is often employed of lions, as with Judg 14:5 and Amos 3:4 and 8, for examples.

Duhm reads *yar'enu*, or "shows us" for *yar'em*, or "thunder."[2865] He also gives "wondrous things" instead of "wondrously," in v. 5.[2866] So too Strahan, Holscher, and

Fohrer.[2867] Budde suggests we take "thunder" out of v. 5, and wishes violently to emend to get, "He does wondrous things past finding out, great things which we cannot comprehend."[2868] Dhorme is also dissatisfied with the thunder of v. 5. He translates it, "God by His voice works [*ya'emol*] wonders."[2869] All these changes, however, seem unnecessary. All that is needed is to understand that v. 5 provides a transition from the thunder storm to the winter frost.

The verb "fall" here is in its Aramaic form. The KJV has "be" for this verb. The RSV has "fall." The Hebrew text has "sower of rain and shower of rains" for v. 6b.[2870] The Peshitta omits the second reference to rains. The RSV renders v. 6b, "and the shower and the rain." The final words of v. 6, "be strong" literally says, "of his strength."

Verse 7 describes the suspension of agricultural pursuits while the winter rains and snow prevail. Hitzig and many others read the preposition *be'ad*, instead of *be'yad*, "the hand of."[2871] Thus with this translation we get the idiom at Gen 7:16, "he seals up every man." Rashi explains v. 7b this way:

> By the side of every man it seals, that is, the rain seals a person in his house, not permitting him to go out to do his work in the fields.[2872]

Mezudat David says of v. 7b:

> God seals the knowledge of the rain within the hand of every man, lest he learn of it in advance; thus, every man knows to hasten to do his work, lest the rain prevents him from doing so.[2873]

Newsom points out that v. 7 is obscure, but it is clearly parallel to v. 8. She observes:

> Just as animals go into their dens to avoid winter storms, so also people stay in doors.[2874]

Thus, Newsom prefers translating, "He shuts in every person, so that all people may know his work."[2875] In v. 9, Newsom tells us:

> The image of humans and animals shut up tight in their dwellings is complemented by the cold storm wind emerging from its chamber.[2876]

Newsom gives 38:22–24 and Ps 135:7 as parallels to v. 9.[2877] Elihu employs two separate poetic images of the wind. One is a wind stored away and called forward at God's command (v. 9). The other is wind as the "breathe of God" (v. 10). Elihu again speaks of rain and lightning in v. 11. Rashi thinks in v. 11 Elihu refers to "*Aph Beri*" the name of an angel who is the ruler of the clouds and scatters the Omnipresent's storm clouds.[2878]

Newsom says of vv. 12–13:

> He brings this section of the poem to a close with an observation about the moral purposes of such natural phenomena.[2879]

Newsom points out, quite rightly, that the language of command and guidance in v. 12 is quite like the language of God in ch. 38 and following, particularly at 38:10–12. Rowley says the import of v. 12 is:

> Here Elihu emphasizes the thought that all these natural forces obey the will of God, and fulfill His purposes.[2880]

Both Duhm and Dhorme say the meaning of v. 12 is, "The cloud goes round in circles, wheeling according to His plans."[2881] The word *mithappek* can also be found at Gen 3:24, where it describes the turning around of a flaming sword. The word "guidance" in v. 12 should be "plans" or "purposes." At Prov 12:5, the RSV renders it "counsels." The "for correction" in v. 13a is literally "for the rod," in the Hebrew text. Freehof remarks about v. 13:

> Elihu is fond of the thought that everything that God does may have a pedagogic purpose, so he says of the rain, "Whether it is for human correction or whether merely to water the Earth."[2882]

Freehof thinks that v. 13 is a blending of retributive justice and divine plan theories. Newsom says that vv. 12–13, "These terms describe a range of divine purposes: punishment, acceptance, and love."[2883] Rashi says of v. 12:

> He causes the clouds and the wind to encompass the mountains, so that they should be watered from all sides.[2884]

Rashi observes about v. 13;

> Whether for the punishment of men, He lets them fall on mountains and hills, which are not places for sowing.[2885]

37:14–20

Newsom thinks the purpose of these verses and the general theme is the "human inability to comprehend the ways of God."[2886] She adds:

> Elihu mimics the style of the divine speeches, with a series of rhetorical questions designed to contrast God's power and wisdom with Job's ignorance and lack of control.[2887]

At v. 14 we see another time when Elihu calls Job by name, something not done by the other three friends. Mezudat David remarks about v. 14, "With your ears harken to my address, and with your heart, ponder the wonders of God, which are ascribed to God, and not to constellations."[2888] This is clearly an argument against astrological Determinism. Moses Kimhi believes v. 16 refers to "the weight of the clouds."[2889] Ibn Ezra thinks it is "the balancing of the clouds,"[2890] Rowley agrees it should be "balancing," much like 36:29.[2891]

Gray suggests the "idea of the clouds laden with moisture being poised in the sky."[2892] Duhm reconstructs v. 16b and then translates, "making a deluge to pour down at the thunder,"[2893] but this is not to be preferred.[2894]

Freehof says the meaning of v. 17 is this:

> Thou whose garments are warm. The thought seems to be: Thou, o man, who must accommodate thyself to all the changes of the wind. Does Thou think thou can help God to spread out the skies.[2895]

The verb "spread out" in v. 18 is literally to "beat out" or "to flatten." The noun "firmament" is derived from the same verb. The adjective "hard" in v. 18b is used for a "solid mass," as at v. 10. Rowley gives this description of v. 19:

> With biting sarcasm Elihu asks Job to instruct how he should approach God Since he himself would never dare to approach him. The reference to drawing of a case is doubtless an allusion to Job's expressed desire to meet God in a court of law The term here for drawing up a case is the same verb employed for setting in order preparations for battle, as at 13:18.[2896]

Rowley thinks the "darkness" of v. 19b, "is the darkness that God conceals from us."[2897] Gersonides believes about v. 19, "Teach us what to say because we mortal and limited men are unable to grasp the nature of God. We are in mental darkness."[2898] Rowley says of v. 20:

> Elihu shrinks from the very idea of such an encounter with God, which would simply be to court destruction.[2899]

Newsom thinks in v. 20, "Elihu mocks Job's eagerness to talk with God by rejecting with horror the notion that God should be informed that Elihu wishes to speak with God, for that would be tantamount to a death wish."[2900] Dhorme translates v. 20 this way:

> When a man has spoken, is he informed?[2901]

Fohrer gives a similar rendering of v. 20.[2902] Rashi thinks in v. 20 Elihu is asking, "Need it be told to Him when I speak. Is He like human beings that He might be told what we are saying?"[2903] Mezudat David says the meaning of v. 20 is this:

> I cannot set up words before Him because my words are compared to darkness, and if I speak who would dare to tell Him, will he be able to do so? He will be destroyed and die.[2904]

The Targum translates v. 20, "If a man dare speak to God, will he be punished, i.e., swallowed up?"[2905] Driver renders the verb "annihilated." He adds, "as a man would expect to be if he presumed to contend with the Almighty."[2906]

37:21–24

Newsom suggests that these final verses of ch. 37 have two purposes, "To sum up Elihu's main points and to prepare the way for the theophany."2907 The difficulty of looking directly at the sun, or *owr*, "light," is implicitly compared to the impossibility of "contending with God."2908 Rowley says the return to natural phenomenon in v. 21 is curious.2909 Kissane believes that vv 21–24 should come directly after v. 8.2910 Pope moves v. 21 to follow v. 18.2911 Rashi thinks the meaning of v. 21 is, "Elihu returns to chide Job's three friends for not coming up with an appropriate answer to the meaning of Job's suffering."2912

Newsom adds about the close of ch. 37:

> Elihu cannot conclude without an explicitly moral comment. As he has been at pains to argue throughout this speech, God's power is coordinated with justice and righteousness.2913

Rashi thinks the final verse of ch. 37, that is v. 24, "Those who boast of their wisdom are self-regarded by God."2914 Szold interprets the verse this way: "Though all men revere Him, even the wisest cannot behold Him."2915 Rowley provides a similar meaning to v. 24, when he writes:

> Men reverence God because He is so great and good. He is high above men and even the wisest of them are utterly beneath his notice.2916

Rowley appears here to endorse the divine plan theory. Many modern translators render v. 24b as "wise in their own conceit," but there is no justification for this nuance, though it is found in the Vulgate Version.2917 The Hebrew simply says, "the wise of heart," a phrase also found at 9:4, where it has no pejorative connotation. It is best to translate v. 24b as the RSV does:

> He does not regard any who are wise in their own conceit.2918

Chapter 38–39: The First Speech of God

Introduction

From the beginning of ch. 38 until the end of ch. 41, we get God's two speeches out of the whirlwind. The first goes from 38:1 to 39:40. God's second speech begins at 40:6 and ends at 41:34. At the close of each of these discourses, Job responds to God, first at 40:1–5, and then at 42:1–6. The first of God's speeches is a series of interrogatories (38:2–38.) The remainder of ch. 38 and all of ch. 39 speak about the animal kingdom, God's creation and the inaccessibility of God to humans.

God's second speech, 40:1—41:34, contains descriptions of two great beasts, Behemoth and Leviathan. The former occurs at 40:16–24, and the latter at 41:1–34. This is followed by Job's second response to God at 42:1–6, where the poetry of the book of Job comes to an end.

The two God Speeches have a number of similarities. First, each begins with a pronouncement that the God Yahweh will speaks from a whirlwind (38:1 and 40:6). Second, both speeches then move to a challenge to Job (38:2–3 and 40:7–14). These challenges incorporate the pronouncement for Job to "gird up his loins and to answer Yahweh's questions" (38:3 and 40:7). Fourth, both of the speeches begin by using a moral category in relationship to Yahweh. In the first speech, the author employs the term *'esa*, or Plan (38:2); the second speech uses the word *mishpat* at 40:7, a word usually rendered as "judgment" or "justice." Finally, both of the speeches of Yahweh consist of two main parts, according to their content.

In the first speech, God speaks first about cosmology and phenomena of the weather. In the second section of the first speech of the Lord, God speaks of ten members of the animal kingdom. The second speech consists of a single pair of beasts, Behemoth and Leviathan. After the completion of Yahweh's first discourse, God specifically asks for a response from Job, at 40:1–2. Job then declines to speak (40:3–5). Following the second discourse of Yahweh, Job replies without a specific divine invitation at 42:1–6.

Analysis of Chapters 38–39

Chapter 38 is usually divided into two parts, vv. 1–3 and vv. 4–38. A third portion of the first speech of Yahweh begins at 38:39 and ends at 39:30. We will examine these three sections of the first speech of the Lord, one at a time, and in order, beginning with 38:1–3. Robert Watson, in his 1892 commentary on the book of Job, explains what he sees as the meaning for God's first speech in ch. 38. He tells us:

> The aim of the author throughout the speech from the storm is to provide a way of reconciliation between man in affliction and perplexity and the Providence of God that bewilders and threatens to crush him.[2919]

Both Peake and Strahan suggest that in the divine speeches, "the author of Job proves himself to be one of the supreme poets of nature, a writer gifted with descriptive powers almost without parallel."[2920]

38:1–3

Verse 1 uses the divine name Yahweh as in the Prologue and the Epilogue, and in 40:1, 3, 6; and 42:1. In the dialogue, it also has been used at 12:9 and 28:28, as we have shown earlier. The storm described in v. 1 is the word *ca'ar*. The same term is employed at 40:6. Two other Hebrew words for "storm" also are employed in the book. The first of these is *cuwphah*, a hapax, used at 27:20 and 37:9. The other is *se'arah* and was employed early in the book at 9:17.

Throughout the Hebrew Bible, appearances of God, specifically Yahweh, are accompanied by storms. Ezekiel 1:4; Nah 1:3; and Zech 9:14 are three good examples of this phenomenon. It becomes clear in v. 2 that the first speech from God is not a response to Elihu who was the previous speaker. Rather, it is a response to a mortal, Job. The word "counsel" in v. 2a is the Hebrew term *'esa*, that also means "Plan." So Yahweh announces in the beginning of his first discourse that there is a "divine plan" about which he wishes to speak. In fact, the divine plan view is the overall response to evil and suffering to be found in the God speeches.

Dhorme renders the "words without knowledge" in v. 2 as "Providence."[2921] Proverbs 19:21 and Isa 19:17 are parallel passages to v. 2, as is 35:16. The "girding of the loins" in v. 3a is to prepare oneself for a hard task or test that was to follow. Both Jer 1:17 and Isa 5:27 are parallels to v. 3. Some exegetes say it may be a reference to belt-wrestling, but that seems not to be necessary to the context. Verse 3 will be repeated at 40:7. The verse is absent from the Peshitta and the Vulgate. The Old Testament has a variety of Hebrew verbs for "girding," and one for "girding up." Four different verbs are translated as "gird." These are *'azar, 'aphad, chagar, and chabash*.

The final two are employed the most often in the Old Testament. The word *shanas* is the verb for "girding up." It is only used one time in the OT. There are three verbs in Koine Greek for the verb "to gird," as well. These are *zonnumi, diazannumi, and perizannumi*. The Old Testament also has three separate nouns for "loins." "Loins" or their girding are discussed or mentioned in several places in the book of Job, including 12:18; 38:3; 40:7; and 40:16, where the loins of Behemoth are described.

38:4–38

Dhorme says of v. 4, "Yahweh reduces the problem to a question of origins." He adds:

> In order to understand the things that happen in the world and to apprehend the Divine counsel, it would have been necessary to be present at the origins of things. Before everything else, God founds the Earth and the Heavens. Where was Job at the creation? Are you the first man to have been born, and were you brought forth before the hills?[2922]

Stevenson thinks that v. 4 conflicts with the questions posed at v. 5ff. He proposes to read v. 4 as an infinitive, and without a suffix, and thus he proposes, "When the Earth was founded."[2923] Dhorme says in v. 5, "The Earth is likened to a building."[2924] Rowley observes that in v. 5 "its measurements" were "as though the builder's plans had been drawn up before hand."[2925]

The "bases" in v. 6 refer to the fact that the ancient Hebrews believed the earth rested on great pillars. At 26:7, the earth is shown as suspended from above and resting on nothing. At Ps 24:2, the earth appears to rest on the sea. The verb "sunk" is also employed of the mountains being sunk into the ground at Prov 8:25. Some say the pillars on which the earth rests are the mountains.

When the foundations of the Second Temple were being laid, there was music and song (Ezra 3:10–11). In v. 7, the laying of the foundation of the world is represented as being accompanied by music and song. But since human beings have not yet been created, it was the stars, the planets, and the angels who did the singing. At Gen 1:16, the stars are created after the earth.

The "Or who shut," in v. 8a reads "and He shut" in the Hebrew text. The Vulgate reads "who shut," as does Merx, Wright, Dhorme, Fohrer, and many others.[2926] The verb used in v. 8 is the same as at 1:10 and 3:23. Gray proposes reading "Where were you when the sea was born?" to make a clearer parallel to the second line.[2927] The "burst forth" of v. 8b compares a turbulent sea to a child breaking out of the womb. The figure of birth is carried over to v. 9. As the child is wrapped in swaddling clothes, so too the sea was wrapped in clouds. The noun as the end of v. 9b, "swaddling band," is another hapax in the noun form, though a verbal form is employed at Ezek 16:4.[2928]

The verb, "prescribed" in v. 10 usually means "broke," as the LXX and Vulgate have it. Dhorme transposes the two verbs in v. 10, and thinks that after the divine imposition of "bounds," the "doors" of v. 8 are no longer needed.[2929] Fohrer reads *esgor*, or "I shut it within its . . . "[2930] So too Dillmann and Duhm.[2931] Amos 1:5 and Jer 51:30 are both parallels to v. 10.

The second line of v. 11 says in the Hebrew text, "Here He will put on the pride of the waves." This only makes sense if a limit is supplied as the object of the verb, as the LXX has it, according to Budde, and others.[2932]

In v. 12, we come to a description of the succession of night and day, which must become carefully regulated if the world is to follow the *'esa*, or Plan, of Yahweh. In v. 13, night is depicted as a blanket covering the earth that the dawn takes hold of by the finger tips of its rays and shakes it out. The works and actions of the wicked are carried out under the cover of darkness, and are shaken out of the blanket. It is a common image in wisdom literature to see the cloak as a coverlet at night, and this is why the blanket should be returned when night falls.

The "skirts" of v. 13a is translated as "ends" by the KJV and RSV. The same noun is used at 37:3, where it is sometimes rendered as "corners." Jewish interpreters have tended to see v. 14 as a reference to death and resurrection. The first hemstitch they say represents the earthy clothes. It is quite difficult, however, to extract this meaning from the Hebrew text. The most common understanding of v. 14 is that it shows the awakening of nature in the first rays of light in the dawn, like the behavior of clay under a seal. This is the understanding that Dhorme and Rowley give to the verse.[2933]

The "light" mentioned in v. 15 is clearly the light of the wicked which is in "darkness." With the coming of the day, darkness is banished. G. R. Driver thinks the reference to the wicked in v. 15 means the "Dog-stars, Canis Major and Canis Minor" whose light is cut off.²⁹³⁴

He also thinks the "uplifted arm" of v. 15b is the "Navigator's Line," "a line of stars that extends like a bent arm across the sky from the horizon to the zenith, passing through Sirius, Procyon, Castor, and Pollux."²⁹³⁵ The arm is broken, however, as one star after another fades before the oncoming light of the day.

In v. 16, Job is challenged to display his knowledge, not of the origins of things, but of the range and extent of things that cannot be seen by the human eye. The word for "springs" in v. 16, *nebek*, is another hapax. The springs of the sea here are the subterranean depths from which the seas were believed to be replenished.

The "gates of death" in v. 17 is a reference to the entrance of Sheol. Parallel texts may be found at Ps 9:13–14, 107:18, and Isa 38:10. Guillaume renders gates as "boundaries."²⁹³⁶

The "deep darkness" in v. 17b is clearly again a reference to the darkness of Sheol, as is the parallel at 3:5. The Targum has the "gatekeepers," rather than the gates. The noun "expanse" in v. 18a is only found here and at 36:16. In v. 18, it is in the plural form, intensifying the idea of a "vast expanse."

In v. 19, light and darkness are personified as two separate beings, each with its own abode from which it come forth daily and then returns. The Targum has "the Land of the Garden of Eden" in v. 18a, rather than the "expanse of the earth."²⁹³⁷ Ibn Ezra thinks v. 19 asks:

> Do you understand all that has been done until the breadth of the Earth? If you know it tell Me. If you do not know it, then how can you fathom My behavior?²⁹³⁸

This view is another reference to divine plan theory. Mezudat David remarks about v. 19, "Do you understand which is the way to which the light dwells and as for darkness?"²⁹³⁹ In v. 20, the pronouns are singular, but the reference must still be to the light and darkness of v. 19. The verb "discern" in v. 20b is sometimes controversial. Hoffmann, by the addition of two letters, reads it as "bring it into."²⁹⁴⁰ Dhorme, on the other hand, compare it to 28:23, and reads it as is.²⁹⁴¹

Dhorme believes that v. 21 is a complement to v. 4 above, "Where were you ... "²⁹⁴² At any rate, Yahweh is shown here as a master of sarcasm. Ibn Ezra explains v. 21 this way:

> Did you know then, before you were born, how many would be the number of your days?²⁹⁴³

This is another example of the many references to the idea of a "Book of Deeds," that contains all the actions of each human being possessed by God. Mezudat David agrees. He observes about v. 21:

THE BOOK OF JOB

Did you know then that you would be born, and do you know now how many days have been allotted to you, how may days that you will live?[2944]

About v. 22, Mezudat David says:

Have you come in your speculation to the treasures of the snow, and do you see in your mind the treasures of hail, in order to comprehend their essence?[2945]

H. Rowley says of v. 22ff:

Snow and hail are thought of as being kept in store by God, ready to be brought out as required, in times of crisis, and especially in battle.[2946]

Rowley gives Josh 10:11; Exod 9:22ff.; and Isa 28:17 as parallel texts of hail as a weapon of God in battle. For the use of hail in theophanies, he gives Ps 18:12ff. and Isa 30:30 as parallel texts.[2947] The noun in v. 22b, "storehouses," Guillaume again finds a different word. He translates "large rocks [of the hail]."[2948] Dhorme believes it signifies that, "The snow and the hail are stored up for God's disposal and used in the great crises of history."[2949]

The "light" in v. 24 brings us back to v. 19; but this parallel between light and the "east wind" seems to make little sense. Hoffmann proposes to read *'ed*, or "mist," instead of *owr*, or light. This approach has been widely followed.[2950] Wind and weather are a much clearer parallel than wind and light. Others propose instead of light, we translate as *ruah*, or wind. So Ewald, Merx, and others.[2951] Siegfried sees *kepor* as "hoar frost," Beer as *kitor*, or smoke. Driver renders it "parching heat," as does Guillaume.[2952] Tur-Sinai says the word translated as "light" in v. 24 means "the west wind." Thus, he translates, "Which way the west wind and the east winds blow."[2953]

The Peshitta omits v. 25a. The Targum says the verse refers to "clouds which pour out rain to the accompaniment of thunder."[2954] The second hemstitch of v. 25 is identical to 28:26b. The word for "channel" in v. 25a is used elsewhere as a "conduit," as at Isa 7:3, or as "trench" at 1 Kgs 18:32. Dhorme says the import of v. 25 is, "The desert is uninhibited and uninhabitable, and yet it rains there."[2955]

Rowley observes about v. 26:

God's Providence extends to more than man. His rains fall on lands where no life can be found.[2956]

Peake says about v. 26, "It is not merely Job's ignorance of things he could not know, it is his narrow outlook . . . for which Yahweh rebukes him."[2957] Two different words for "man" are employed in v. 26. Dhorme believes v. 27 is a "continuation of the description" begun in v. 26.[2958] He says the meaning of v. 27 "to make grass grow in a desert place."[2959] The expression "waste and desolate land" looks very much like 30:3. Rowley says the second hemstitch should be translated, "to cause to sprout a sources of vegetation."[2960]

Both Bickell and Duhm omit v. 28; but the verse seems to be closely linked to v. 29.[2961] Gray calls v. 28, "a beautiful verse."[2962] The word for "drops" v. 28b is another hapax of the book, but there is little doubt about the meaning of the word. Mezudat David thinks that v. 28 asks, "Has the rain a father who commands it to fall?" He calls v. 28b "waves of dew," rather than "drops of dew."[2963] He asks of the following verse, v. 29, "From whose womb is it commanded to freeze?"[2964] The word "ice" in v. 29 also has been employed at 6:16 and 37: Here it appears to mean "frost," as it does at Gen 31:40 and Jer 36:30.

The verb, "becomes hard" in v. 30 is connected to a word that means "hide." Hitzig and others take the verb to signify "coagulate," and thus we get the RSV's:

> The waters become hard like a stone,
>
> And the face of the deep is frozen.[2965]

The word for "chains" in v. 31a is only found elsewhere in the Hebrew Bible at 1 Sam 15:32. Rowley thinks that two letters have been damaged and renders the verb in v. 31a as "bind." Verses 31–32 speak of four constellations, the Pleiades, Orion, Mazzaroth, and the Bear. In Job 9:9, three of these starry systems are mentioned, but not Mazzaroth. It is not entirely clear which constellation is meant by Mazzaroth, for the word is another hapax of the book. Rowley and others identify Mazzaroth with *mazzalot*, a word used at 2 Kgs 23:5 that means "constellation." Driver thinks the word is *mazarot*, or "girdling stars," referring to the circle of the zodiac.[2966]

At v. 33, the Hebrew text asks the question, "Do you know the ordinances of the Heavens." Rowley says this refers to, "the laws which govern the movements of the heavenly bodies."[2967] The word "rule" or "dominion" in v. 33b is another hapax in the book. Dhorme takes it to mean, "what is written."[2968] The word in question is *mishtar*. Job is asked in v. 33b if he can direct the influence of the heavenly bodies in any way, an obviously rhetorical question. The second line of v. 34 is identical with 22:11b. The LXX has "answer you," rather than "cover you" in v. 34b, but the Hebrew seems to be more expressive than that.

Two uncertain words make the meaning of v. 36 quite difficult to interpret. These are words rendered as "clouds" and "mist." The KJV gives "heart" and "clouds." The RSV, "inward parts" and "mind." The first word is also used at Ps 51:6–8, where the RSV has "inward being," but that word may not have the same meaning here. The Targum provides two separate translations, the first being "heart"; but the context appears to be the actions of nature, so that translation makes little sense. Freehof renders "wisdom in the inward parts, as does the KJV." Freehof says:

> The same phrase is used in Psalm 51:8, "Truth in the inward parts . . . wisdom in mine inmost heart." However, this verse speak of wisdom in the minds of the living, interrupts the sequence in this passage which continues in the next two verses, and finishes the theme of the rain and the storm. In this verse 36, speaking of wisdom were read as following verse 38. It would then serve as an

introduction to the discussion beginning in v. 39 and continuing through the next chapter which speaks of the marvelous instincts of the animals, and the wonderful things they do because of the wisdom that God has put in them.[2969]

Erhlich connects the verb "number" to an Arabic root that means to "chase away."[2970] Driver believes the thought of v. 37 is "the clouds scuddling across the sky."[2971] Rowley says the import of v. 38 is quite simple:

> When the rains descend the particles of dust are joined together to form a single mass again.[2972]

In the expression "runs into a mass," the noun and the verb are cognates, the latter also at 37:10. The verb means "flow," or "cast," as with metals. But this does not seem to be appropriate here, where the reference is to the fusing of the dust into mud, just like molten metal.

38:39—39:30

These verses constitute the second part of God's first discourse. Here the poet gives in review in brilliant verses a number of animals and birds, and God asks if Job knows the secrets of their lives. The most famous and brilliant of them all is the description of the battle horse in 39:18–20.

We will divide this section into the following parts:

- vv. 39–41 of ch. 38: lions and ravens.
- 39:1–12: wild ass, wild ox, and others.
- vv. 13–18: ostrich, wild beast, and horse.
- vv. 19–25: more on battle horse.
- vv. 26–30: wisdom and the eagle.[2973]

Robert Watson, in his 1892 commentary says about the ordering of these beasts presented in chs. 38 and 39, "The reasoning is from the lesser to the greater."[2974] He might be right about that, but later we will suggest another understanding related to domestication. The animals go from the most domesticated to the "hawk" or "vulture," "Behemoth" and "Leviathan," of which humans have no control.

38:39–41

This section begins with the "King of beasts," the lion. Does Job provide the lion with its prey, while it waits in its den. And yet, God cares deeply for the lion and he has given it its strength and cunning in the stalking of its prey. He also causes the prey to come into his vicinity.

Rowley gives Ps 104:21 as a parallel text.[2975] The Malbin says of v. 39:

The scripture delineates the individual providence on the earth over all species of animals and surely over the most esteemed of all. He begins with the providence concerning the food necessary for their sustenance starting with the strongest and weakest creatures . For the old lions that go out to prey on other beasts, God hunts the prey; for the young lions who wait for their food to be brought to them, God constantly satisfies their appetites.[2976]

Verse 40 continues the questions about the lion: "when they crouch in their dens, or lie in wait in their covert." The word "covert" is the same word rendered "lairs" or "dens" at 37:8. Rashi says of v. 40, "They stand crouching to lie in wait, so it is the habit to crouch and bend themselves so that they will not be recognized."[2977]

Rowley observes about v. 41:

> The position of the raven between the lion and other wild animals has seemed suspect to some. Wright reads 'ereb, or "evening" for 'oreb, or "raven." Thus, "Who provides the lion's prey in the evening?"[2978]

Both Duhm and Beer take the same approach to v. 41.[2979] This, then, requires us to go back to v. 39 to discover the reference to "its" The word for "prey" in v. 41 is not the same word used at v. 39. The KJV renders the noun "his food," others think the noun is related to hunting and translates the noun "what is taken in hunting." Rowley says that either translation may be justified.[2980]

The raven of v. 41 is indeed black. Rashi says about v. 41:

> When the raven's eggs are hatched, they are white and the father suspects that his wife has been unfaithful . Therefore, he hates his young and does not feed them. God prepares food for them by creating gnats from the dung, etc.[2981]

39:1–12

In this section, the focus shifts from nature and the weather to members of the animal kingdom. Verse 1 describes the mountain goat. Rashi says of the species:

> It hates its young, and when preparing to give birth, it goes to the top of high rocks, so that its young should fall to the earth and die.[2982]

Rowley believes the animal in v. 1a may be an "ibex," that is found in the high mountains. The KJV translates "wild goats" for the same noun. Rowley gives Ps 104:18 as a parallel to the verse. He says that v. 2a, "concerns the period of pregnancy," and v. 2b, "the season of foaling."[2983] Duhm wishes to change the verb of v. 2b to yield "appoint," but this seems to be unnecessary.[2984] Mezudat David agrees that v. 2a refers to "the months of their pregnancies, to know when they will be filled, in order to help deliver their young."[2985] The verb "crouch" used in v. 3a is employed when a woman is in childbirth, as at 1 Sam 4:19. Rowley says of this line:

It is commonly thought that this line refers to the ease with which the ibex bears its young, But rabbinical commentators understood it of the difficulty of their bearing, doubtless owing to the common meaning of the word rendered "their young."[2986]

The verb "bring forth" in v. 3a usually means "cleave," as it does at 16:13 and Ps 141:6. This meaning, however, does not seem to fit here. Mezudat David observes about v. 3, "They kneel after receiving a snake bite, and they require no help in their delivery. They merely kneel and bring forth their young."[2987] Rashi thinks the verb in v. 4b should be "go forth." He continues, "from themselves in the birth at the moment that I [God] prepare for them."[2988]

Ibn Ezra says of v. 4, "They grow in strength." He adds:

> When they are a little grown, they are raised on the grain, on seeds and grasses, and they do not require the raising by their father or mother.[2989]

Rowley observes about the wild ass of v. 5:

> The wild ass roaming the steppes, is conceived here as being a domestic ass, that patient drudge released from bondage. The fine description perhaps reflects the sympathy of the author with the untamable creature.[2990]

The "wild ass" also appears at 6:5, 11:12, and 24:5. The "swift ass" at the end of v. 5 is from an Aramaic word found only here in the Hebrew Bible. The "steppes" mentioned in v. 6a is depicted here as a desert. Both of these terms and the "salt land" are also mentioned together at Jer 17:6. "Salty soil" for the ancient Jews is land that is infertile, as Ps 107:34 suggests. Ralbag says the salt land is land where, "No man is able to domesticate him and raise him in civilization."[2991] So too says the *Ohev Mishpat*.[2992]

Mezudat David says of v. 7, "He mocks the tumult of the city because he is not there, and he does not harken to the shouts of the driver who wishes to drive him to work."[2993] The word for "driver," *nagas*, in v. 7b is sometimes used for the overseer in forced labor. Here it is used as a driver of animals. Malbim explains v. 7 this way:

> He rejects the tumult of the city, preferring the wilderness where he will not hear the shouts of the driver.[2994]

The Targum, Rashi, and Mezudat David, all explain v. 8 in this manner:

> He spies out the mountain for his pasture.[2995]

Rowley points out about v. 8:

> In the desert pasturage is scarce, and the wild ass must roam far and wide in search of it.[2996]

Davidson tells us that "the Arab poets compare a deep abyss or a ravine" to the "belly" of the wild ass, which is often empty for want of food.²⁹⁹⁷ In other words, it pays the price for its freedom. At Jer 14:6 we see a parallel to v. 8. Ralbag renders v. 8a this way: "The springs of the mountain is his pasture."²⁹⁹⁸ Rowley points out about v. 9:

> The domestic ass and ox are often mentioned together in the Old Testament, so here the wild ox follows the wild ass. Like the wild ass, it is untamable and its great strength cannot be harnessed to the service of man.²⁹⁹⁹

Some believe the "wild ox," like the KJV, is a "unicorn." This animal is mentioned nine times in the Hebrew Bible. The animal in question certainly has two horns (Deut 33:17) and it was thought to be some kind of an ox (Ps 29:6; Isa 34:7). It was very powerful and the frequent reference to its horns suggest that it was very dangerous. Rashi translates, "Did you tie a wild ox because of the furrow of your ox?"³⁰⁰⁰

Malbim says of v. 10, "The verse speaks of the smoothing out the furrows of the field, after the field already has been plowed."³⁰⁰¹ He adds, "Even to perform such an easy task, the wild ox will not submit to you."³⁰⁰² Ibn Ezra thinks that v. 11 asks, "Will you leave your work [plowing and sowing], which you usually give to the oxen, to this wild ox?"³⁰⁰³ Rowley observes about v. 11:

> The wild ox has great strength which might be useful to man if he could harness it. But his inability to do this is matched by the unreliability of the wild ox, which cannot be trusted to do what was wanted.³⁰⁰⁴

Mezudat David says the meaning of v. 12 is this:

> Will you believe him that he shall return your seed. He will surely flee with your seed to the deserts.³⁰⁰⁵

Malbim says, "You surely cannot believe him because he will devour it. Who sustains these creatures, if not I? How then can you say that I do not guide the earthly creatures?"³⁰⁰⁶ Terrien believes the wild animal in vv. 9–12 may be an "Asiatic buffalo." He says the word for "wild ox" may come from the Akkadian *remu*.³⁰⁰⁷ The KJV renders the noun *re'em* as "unicorn."

The noun is employed six times in the KJV, all are rendered as "unicorn."

39:13–18

These verses do not appear in the LXX. Stevenson says of them, "They are probably a separate composition by the author of the poem of Job."³⁰⁰⁸ Rowley mentions that the "series of rhetorical questions is broken by this section."³⁰⁰⁹ At v. 17, God is spoken of in the third person. The *renaim* in v. 13, Mezudat David tells us, "is the name of a huge bird," called in the language of the Mishnah. Rashi thinks it a "peacock."³⁰¹⁰ The RSV renders the animal as "ostrich." The word *renaim* appears nowhere else. Freehof also thinks it is an ostrich. He writes:

> One of the most difficult verses in the book, especially the second half of the verse.[3011]

Buttenwieser says it is untranslatable. The translations of v. 13 are quite varied in their explanations.[3012] Ibn Ezra says the bird is called *renaim* "because of its pleasant voice."[3013] Mezudat David says the name comes "from its happiness with its beautiful plumage."[3014] He explains v. 14 this way:

> For she leaves her eggs on the ground and she goes and warms them, but she warms them on the dust of the Earth, that is, they are left to warm themselves on the dust of the roads.[3015]

Rashi says of v. 15:

> God did not endow the ostrich with motherly love for her potential offspring. Therefore, she leaves her eggs in the sand, and not concern herself that a person may inadvertently trample the eggs, or an egg-eating beast intentionally step on it to squeeze out its contents.[3016]

Rashi observes in regard to the "hardened" of v. 16, "She deals harshly with her young ones, distancing them from her heart, as though they were not hers."[3017] Mezudat David says of v. 16:

> Even after the eggs are hatched, the ostrich does not care for her young. The most she ever does is to place an unfertilized egg over the fertilized eggs, so that she hides them in the ground. The egg rots and becomes wormy, and with these worms she feeds her young.[3018]

The verb "deals cruelly," is employed at Isa 63:17, where it is used for the "hardening" of the heart. Lamentations 4:3 is a parallel for v. 16. The "no fear" of v. 16 means "to have no concern." Dahood prefers to render v. 16b, "without a flock."[3019] Mezudat David observes about the following verse, that is v. 17:

> For God caused her to forget wisdom. The reason for this neglect is that God caused her to forget wisdom and did not give her a share of understanding to watch her eggs as other birds do.[3020]

Rowley says v. 17 is about an Arab proverb, "more stupid than an ostrich."[3021] The verb "rouses" herself to flee in v. 18 is only used here in the Hebrew Bible. The KJV has, "lifted herself on high." Some have said the "on high" implies flying. Dhorme says the verb means, "to rear herself up."[3022] But in Arabic, the verb means "to whip," particularly a horse. Gray translates it, "spurs herself."[3023] Terrien says of vv. 13–18:

The ostrich is ugly and foolish (vv. 14–16 and 17.) This is probably a marginal comment which has crept into the main text, but it is able to outrun a horse.[3024]

39:19–25

Verse 19 begins a description of the wonderful assets of the horse, and especially the war horse. Mezudat David thinks v. 19 asks a question, "Are you the one that gave the horse its strength to be braver than other animals?"[3025] About v. 20, he observes: "Like a locust, he skips and leaps and he shakes himself all over."[3026] The word "leap" in v. 20a usually means "quiver" or "shake." But this does not seem appropriate here. The reference, most likely, is to the galloping of a horse. The word "snorting" in v. 20b is a variant of a word found at Jer 8:16. It comes from a root meaning "to blow," as at Jer 6:29. From this root also comes the word for "nostril."

The verb "paws," or *chaphar*, in Hebrew, in v. 21a usually means "to dig." This is the only time in the Hebrew Bible where it implies a pawing of the earth. A cognate word in Arabic means a "hoof." The Hebrew text has "they paw," but the LXX, Peshitta, and Vulgate all translate it as a singular. The reference to "valley" in v. 21b is connected to the fact that armies in the ancient near-east were often formed in valleys. (See Gen 14:8 and Judg 7:1.) Dahood proposes to render the line, "He paws vigorously."[3027] The term employed for "valley" in v. 21b is *emeq*, a little used word.

The "rattle" at v. 23 is only used here. It is probably a by-form of a verb which means "raise a ringing cry." In Arabic, it is the word employed to speak of the vibration of the bow string after an arrow has been released. But here the quiver is doing the rattling. Rashi says of v. 23:

> The quiver is full of arrows, and they knock against each other, and by this a sound is heard.[3028]

Ibn Ezra says it might also be the sound of an arrow "that comes out of the quiver."[3029] Rashi says the meaning of v. 24 is, "He makes holes with his feet."[3030] Rowley renders v. 24a this way:

> With fierceness and rage, he swallows the ground.[3031]

Rowley gives parallels to v. 24 of Ps 77:18 and Isa 14:16. The verbs from which the nouns of v. 24 are rendered "shake" and "tremble."[3032] Both nouns, therefore, imply excitement rather than anger. Thus Gray renders it, "quivering and excited, he dashes into the fray."[3033] Mezudat David says of v. 25:

> Not only is the horse not concerned with when he hears the sound of the *shofar*, but in fact he is happy even when he hears the sound of many *shofaroth*.[3034]

He continues:

He smells battle from afar. He is able to sense the voice of the enemy in battle, even from afar, so that the soldiers are able to detect from the horse's behavior that an army is rapidly upon them.[3035]

39:26–30

The Hebrew of v. 26 literally says, "The hawk grows a wing." Mezudat David says it refers to, "the hawk's southward migration in the winter time." "It is because of your understanding that the hawk flies, that is spreads its wings to the south."[3036] Rowley thinks it should be in the interrogatory:

> Does Job inspire the migration of the hawk, or to direct the eagle to build its nest on the lofty crag—so unlike the ostrich (v. 14.) They are joined together here because both are birds of prey.[3037]

Rashi renders v. 27 as:

> Or is it by your order that the eagle flies high.[3038]

The RSV gives us:

> Is it at your command that the eagle mounts up
> And makes its nest on high.[3039]

Stevenson says it is likely that, "Verse 27 has been worked into the text from Jer 49:16.[3040] But the mention of a second bird would be contrary to all the other descriptions of animals, including 38:39–40."[3041] The word rendered "eagle" (*nesher*) in v. 27 is also sometimes translated as "vulture." The LXX, for example, has "vulture," the Vulgate, "eagle."[3042]

Rowley gives Jer 49:16 as a parallel for v. 28. Rashi observes about v. 28, "He dwells on the rock and lodges." He adds:

> Aaron was confident when he placed the censer with the incense on the foundation stone of the Holy of Holies.[3043]

Samuel Terrien tells us about the closing verses of ch. 39:

> By God's intelligence, and by God's command—not Job's—the hawk soars in the sky and the eagle swoops down upon its prey.[3044]

Terrien concludes:

> Now the poet has completed his gallery of vignettes on animal life—all designed to give the hero his sense of insignificance—and return to the essential question as Yahweh directly challenges Job.[3045]

Mezudat David says of these closing verses of ch. 39:

God illustrates to Job His Providence over His creatures in all aspects of their lives. In supplying them with food, in their conception, their birth, their habitat, their egg-laying habits, their migratory habits, and the heights to which they fly. God surely bestows His Providence upon man, the choice of the Creation, the creature crowned with the crown of intelligence and created in His image.[3046]

The verb "suck up" in v. 30 is another hapax in the God's speeches. With the addition or subtraction of a single letter, the verb may be connected to an equivalent of the verb employed at 1 Kgs 21:19, where it means, "to lick up."[3047] This is the RSV's understanding of the verb. The verb in question is *'ala'*. Before moving to the discussion of ch. 40, we will first return to the issue of the order of the animals in chs. 38 and 39.

In short, the litany of creatures in those chapters appears to have proceeded from the most often domesticated to the inability to domesticate, that is, Behemoth and Leviathan, with the added proviso that even if humans cannot control the actions of the soaring hawk, or the vulture, and Behemoth and Leviathan, Yahweh can.

Analysis of Chapter 40

Introduction

In these verses we see Job's response to Yahweh's first speech from the whirlwind. Yahweh calls on Job in v. 1 to answer the speech he has just given. Job, in abasement, confesses that he has been reduced to silence. Thus, in v. 4, Job lays his hand over his mouth, a sure sign that only silence will follow. Later, in 42:1–6, Job will conclude the second stage of his abasement, where the patriarch responds to the second speech of the Lord.

40:1–5

Rowley introduces these first five verses of ch. 40 this way:

> Summarily, Yahweh calls on Job to answer the speech he has just listened to, and Job, in abasement confesses that he is reduced to silence. If the second divine speech is secondary, Job's speech is continued in 42:2–6.[3048]

The opening verse of ch. 40 is absent in the LXX. Many modern exegetes omit it as well, on the grounds that it separates the last verses of the first divine speech, from the remainder of the speech. Alternatively, Yahweh may have paused after his first discourse to see if Job had been listening or had any reply.

In the first three verses of ch. 40, the author employs three separate names for God. In vv. 1 and 3, he uses Yahweh. At v. 2, both *Shaddai* and *Eloah* are used. Later in the chapter, at vv. 9 and 19, the text uses a fourth name, *El*. Rowley renders "a faultfinder," in v. 2a. The KJV has it, "He that contendeth." The noun used here is only used here in the entire Hebrew Bible. It comes from a common Semitic root that means "correct" or "reprove." Ehrlich reads it as a finite verb, *yasur*, or "depart."³⁰⁴⁹ Dhorme similarly reads *yasur*, but with a meaning of "turn aside."³⁰⁵⁰ The verb "contend" (RSV) or "contendeth" (KJV), some read the participle "contender." "Will he who argues with Shaddai yield?"

The KJV renders v. 4a as, "Behold, I am vile; what shall I answer thee. I will lay my hand upon my mouth."³⁰⁵¹ The object *ashuwq*, is translated "vile" by the KJV. The RSV is closer to the truth of the verse when it renders it:

> Behold, I am of small account; what shall I answer thee?
>
> I lay my hand on my mouth.³⁰⁵²

The NIV paraphrases v. 4 to say, "I am unworthy—how can I reply to you? I put my hand over my mouth."³⁰⁵³ The NRSV gives a more accurate rendering of the verse. It translates:

> See, I am of small account; what shall I answer you?
>
> I lay my hand on my mouth.³⁰⁵⁴

The "of small account" usually means "be swift," or "be light." The Hebrew term is *qalal*, or "small." It is the opposite of *kabed*, or "heavy," as is clear at 2 Sam 6:22, where both of these terms are employed.³⁰⁵⁵ Genesis 16:4ff., 1 Sam 2:30, and Nah 1:14 are parallel texts for the verse. The reference to the "hand on my mouth" is indicative of being silent. The same expression is employed at 21:5 and 29:9. Newsom says of the phrase, "This is a gesture of deference and respect."³⁰⁵⁶

The "I will not answer" of v. 5b is translated by Hitzig, with the change of a single letter, as "I will not repeat it."³⁰⁵⁷ Many modern translators have followed this lead to yield a closer parallel to the second line, "twice, but I will proceed no further." But this change seems to be unnecessary. Job is challenged by Yahweh to answer, and he declines, having already said all that he would say.

Rashi explains v. 5 this way:

> I have spoken a little and I will add no more.³⁰⁵⁸

Mezudat David explains v. 5 thusly:

> One question that I have asked, that is, why did You deliver guidance of the world to the constellations. I will not repeat because now I see that, in fact, You did not do that. But the other two questions that I asked, that is, why the wicked prosper and why do the righteous suffer, have not yet been answered. However, I will not continue to ask them because I fear to criticize You.³⁰⁵⁹

This is, of course, an endorsement of retributive justice theory.

Malbim agrees about the two questions. He says, "Job, satisfied with the answer to the first question, requests that God answer the second question, after which he will no longer continue to ask."³⁰⁶⁰ Freehof observes about v. 5: "Job now realizes how little he is compared to God, and how small his knowledge is. So he decides he will not complain further."³⁰⁶¹ So Freehof also sees v. 5 as an example of the retribution theory. The two traditional understandings of the action of covering his mouth are an indication he will be silent, or it is a sign of deference and respect. Either, or both, seem appropriate.³⁰⁶²

40:6–14 and 15–24

Introduction

The remaining verses of ch. 40 consists of two sections. The first of these, vv. 6–14, is a brief, thematic introduction. In the other section and the final portion of the chapter, vv. 15–24, Job is instructed to "look at Behemoth." This is followed in ch. 41 with a description of the great sea monster, Leviathan.

40:6–14

Rowley introduces these verses this way:

> After Job has confessed and submitted, a second divine speech comes, as Peake says, perilously near nagging. It is probable that the parts of this speech dealing with Behemoth and Leviathan. We should then be left with only a few verses [vv. 7–17], for the second speech. In that case, it may be best to join these verses to the first speech and Job's words of submission in 40:4ff.³⁰⁶³

Rowley points out that most modern exegetes see the passages on Behemoth and Leviathan to be a later addition to the book. Thus, the wisdom chapter 28, the Elihu speeches of chs. 32–37, and the descriptions of Behemoth and Leviathan all may be additions to the original book of Job, though the notion that Behemoth and Leviathan are not original seems less likely.

Rowley says of these verses, "Job is invited to assume the throne of the universe." He adds:

> If Job's condemnation of the injustice which marks God's rule is justified, then he ought to be able to show God how it should be governed. He is therefore invited better.³⁰⁶⁴

Freehof says of vv. 7–14:

> God asks Job, then, whether he believes that he can manage the affairs of men.³⁰⁶⁵

The "put me in the wrong" of v. 8a is literally "break my judgment." About this verse, Rowley remarks:

Had Job only defended his own integrity, he would have been wholly justified, as the Prologue makes clear. But beyond this, he has impugned the righteousness of God, and had declared that God was in the wrong, and had challenged God's moral right to be in charge of the world.[3066]

About v. 9, most modern exegetes suggest that even if Job had the wisdom necessary to rule the world, and the integrity as well, did he also have the power? Mezudat David says of the verse, "Do you have an arm like God? Man is created in God's image if he does not deviate from God's ways to an extent, he is endowed with great power. He may even rule over the heavenly host, as Joshua was able to stop the sun and the moon, during the Battle of Gibeon."[3067]

The "arm of God" in v. 9 is a common expression in the Old Testament. It can be found at Deut 4:34; Isa 40:10; Ps 44:3; Ps 77:15; Ps 89:10, 13; Ps 98:1; as well as at Job 40:9.

About v. 10, Mezudat David observes:

> Try to test the matter; bedeck yourself with pride and excellence, and clothe yourself with glory and beauty in order to perform wondrous deeds.[3068]

H. H. Rowley agrees. He says of v. 10, "Job is invited to adorn himself with the attributes of power."[3069] He gives Ps 104:1 as a parallel to v. 10b, where similar terms are employed. The expression, "spendour and glory" recurs at Ps 21:5; 96:6; and 111:3. Mezudat David translates v. 11a as, "scatter your raging anger." He adds, "at the wicked to punish them with the breath of your lips."[3070] He renders v. 11b as, "see any haughty man." He adds: "Look at him and humble him, as befits a perfectly righteous man."[3071] Malbim explains v. 11 this way:

> If you see a haughty man who oppresses his fellows, humble him physically by weakening him.[3072]

Rowley says of v. 11, "Here Job is invited to exercise his power. He has supposed that the moral government of the world requires the swift punishment of the wicked, and he is initiated to effect it."[3073] The first line of v. 12 is identical to v. 11b, with the exception of the verb, "bring him low." This appears to be a synonym for "abasement." Duhm proposes the change in a letter for the word "proud," giving it as "lofty."[3074] Both Dhorme and Kissane follow this same approach.[3075] But Fohrer and others find no good reason to make this change. Indeed, some exegetes strike v. 12a altogether. Rashi translates v. 12b as "and crushed the wicked in their place."[3076] He continues:

> If you have the power, crush the wicked in his place. Further on, Scriptures cite two examples of proud creatures, the Behemoth on the dry land and the Leviathan in the sea.[3077]

The "in the dust," or *aphar* in Hebrew, in v. 13 probably means the grave. We have seen the cutting off of the wicked as something pointed out by the friends earlier in the book, but Job has denied earlier that this does not happen in experience. Here he is invited to effect the cutting off of the wicked.

Mezudat David observes about v. 13:

> Hide them all in the dust, and bind their faces in the hidden places. That is, decree upon them humility and submission, and see whether your decree is executed.[3078]

Ralbag says of v. 13:

> Imprison them. This verse is to be understood literally, that they be slain and buried.[3079]

Rowley believes the "hidden places" in v. 13a is "probably the dark recesses of Sheol."[3080]

He observes about v. 14:

> If Job is able to assume the authority and to exercise this government of the world, then God would acknowledge his power, for God is one whose power is equal to His purposes.[3081]

Rowley gives Ps 98:1 and Isa 59:16 and 63:5 as parallel texts to v. 14. He says further about v. 14, "Let Job show that his power is equal to the purposes he would impose upon God."[3082] Mezudat David says of "I too will confess to you" of v. 14a:

> When you will be on such a level that the merit of your right hand will save you; When you will have such power in your arm, I too will admit that you are completely righteous. But now, agree that it is not so; what is it about you to bless and praise as a righteous man?[3083]

40:15–24

Introduction

This section introduces the great land animal Behemoth. The name is the plural form of the word *behemah*, which is commonly used to refer to four-legged animals such as cattle. The employment of *Behemah* here may be a use of the *pluralis excellentiae*, or the "plurality of excellence," similar to the royal "We."

The word Behemoth is used elsewhere in the Hebrew Bible at Gen 6:7 and 9:10; Pss 36:6; 73:22; 135:8; 147:9; Isa 30:6; and Job 39:15. In most of these, the word is singular and translated as "beast." At Ps 73:22, for example, the text tells us:

> I was stupid and ignorant,
> I was like a beast toward thee.[3084]

Analysis of Behemoth Narrative

The expression in v. 1, "which I had made you," is absent from the LXX. Duhm, Dhorme, and Fohrer omit it in their translations.[3085] Besides the Septuagint, the oldest Jewish reference to Behemoth comes in the *Apocalypse of Enoch*, a second-century BCE text. It gives the following description of the origins of Behemoth:

> And in that day two monsters will be parted, one monster as a female, Leviathan, in order to dwell in the abyss of the ocean over the fountain of water; and the other a male called Behemoth, which holds its chest in an invisible desert whose name is Dundayin, east of the Garden of Eden.[3086]

Fourth Esdras (6:47–52), written in the late first century CE, also mentions both Behemoth and Leviathan. It reveals:

> Then you keep into existence two living creatures. The name of one was called Behemoth, and the name of the other Leviathan. And you separated one from other, for the seventh part when the water had been gathered together could not hold both of them. And you gave Behemoth one of the parts which had been dried up on the third day, to live in it, where there are a thousand mountains.[3087]

A Jewish haggadic tradition suggests that at the end of time, Behemoth, along with Leviathan and Ziz, a great bird, will become food for the righteous in a great Banquet. The Babylonian Talmud (74b) also speaks of this banquet story at the end of time.[3088] There is a Jewish hymn recited on the festival of Shavout, celebrating the giving of the Torah to Moses, known as the *Akdamut*. The text tells us:

> They sport with Leviathan and the ox [Behemoth], when they were interlocked with one another, and engaged in combat. With his horns, the Behemoth will gore with strength the fish.[3089]

This is most likely a reference to belief in a cosmic struggle of God with Behemoth and Leviathan at the end of time. Three things can be concluded about these earliest Jewish reference to Behemoth. First, he is a primeval beast, the king of land animals. Second, he is not conquerable by human beings. Third, Behemoth and Leviathan may have been involved in a cosmic battle of some sort, whereby Yahweh defeats them both.

The medieval Jewish tradition contains comments from several scholars on Behemoth, including Rashi, Ibn Ezra, Gersonides, Mezudat David, and Rabbenu Meyouchas. Rashi alludes to the rabbinic maxim in *Baba Bathra* 74b, that Behemoth is destined to be the fare of the righteous in the future life.[3090] He points out:

> Although the word appears in the plural, the context indicates that Behemoth is the name of a great beast, making it a singular noun.[3091]

Ibn Ezra interprets the "with you," of v. 15b, to indicate that Behemoth was created on the same day as man.[3092] Mezudat David thinks the "grass," of v. 15c refers to the fact that Behemoth was herbivorous throughout his long life.[3093] Rashi interprets v. 16a to mean:

> His testicles are crushed and hidden, and have not been completely torn off.[3094]

Rashi apparently alludes to the fact that Yahweh castrated the male of the species and made the female barren, lest they multiply and overrun the world.[3095] Rashi interprets v. 19 to mean, "Behemoth is the first of God's ways, that is, He was created at the beginning to be the chief of all the animals."[3096]

In regard to the mountains yielding food for Behemoth in v. 20, a parallel text can be found at Ps 50:10 that informs us:

> For every beast [behemah] of the forest is mine,
> The cattle of a thousand hills.[3097]

Mezudat David says the following in regard to v. 21:

> Can he lie under the shade of trees? He is too huge for any shade to shelter him.
>
> It is only through My Providence that he lives unprotected by shade.[3098]

Ibn Ezra says that v. 24 is "connected with the previous verse, which says he is not afraid of the river."[3099] Gersonides gives the following explanation of v. 24:

> When he gets to the bottom of the river, he fearlessly thrust his nose into the snares hidden there.[3100]

Gersonides prefers this translation for v. 24b;

> Shall it be possible in anyone's eyes that he can pierce the Behemoth's nose with a snare or a hook?[3101]

The Hebrew of v. 24 merely says this:

> With his eyes he takes it to him,
> And with his snare he thrusts his nose.[3102]

Saadiah Gaon, in the tenth century saw Behemoth as a natural creature, not associated with the demonic.[3103] Moses Maimonides mentions the banquet at the end of time, but he says it is symbolic of "the enjoyment of the intellectual life."[3104]

More modern Jewish scholars who have made observations about Behemoth include Solomon Freehof, Robert Gordis, and many others. Freehof begins his description of vv. 15–24 by saying, "From verse 15 to 24, is the development of Behemoth, now usually taken to mean the hippopotamus."[3105] Robert Gordis also sees Behemoth as a natural creature and not a mythological one. He too says Behemoth as a hippopotamus.[3106] Contemporary Jewish scholar, Ariela Pelaia, however, thinks that both Behemoth and Leviathan are mythological creatures from ancient Jewish Literature, in her essay, "What is Behemoth?"[3107]

Among the earliest Christian sources on Behemoth are comments by John Chrysostom, Julian of Eclanum, Philip the Priest, Ephrem the Syrian, Gregory, Ishodad of Merv, Albertus Magnus, and Thomas Aquinas. Some early, Christian Gnostics thought that Behemoth and Leviathan are "two of the seven circles through which the soul must travel to be purged of its sins, and thus, worthy of salvation."[3108]

Both Julian of Eclanum and John Chrysostom think, "Behemoth was created to inspire the fear of God."[3109] Chrysostom adds, "God has not created such enormous beasts to show what is useful for us, but what is done according to His will."[3110] Ephrem the Syrian, fourth-century Christian scholar, says that "Behemoth is a Dragon, that is, a land animal, just as Leviathan is an aquatic beast."[3111] Gregory the Great says of Behemoth, "The mercy of the Lord has set limits on the powers of Behemoth." He says the two great beasts in the end of the book of Job, Behemoth and Leviathan, are "disguises used by Satan in his dealings with humans."[3112] This is one of the many places where Gregory employs the influences of demonic forces theory. Phillip the Priest, another fourth-century thinker, agrees. He observes that "Behemoth is an allegory of the Devil, enslaving carnal people. It is the absolute influence of the Devil."[3113]

Ishodad of Merv, another Syrian Christian in the ninth century, says, "Behemoth is a dragon without equal. He is a representation of the Devil who must be opposed and defeated by the righteous."[3114] Thus, another application of the demonic forces motif. Thomas Aquinas thinks Behemoth is the elephant, while his mentor, Albertus Magnus, says the tail of Leviathan is a euphemism for the "genital member."[3115]

Urbain Brandier, a French Catholic priest of the seventeenth century, was convinced that Behemoth "is a demonic creature."[3116] John Milton writes about the birth of Behemoth in "Paradise Lost." He identifies Behemoth and Leviathan as "the river horse and the scaly crocodile."[3117] Collin de Plancy, in his *Dictionnaire Infernal*, published in 1861, suggests that "Behemoth rules over the domain of gluttony, and is said to be the butler and high cupbearer of Hell."[3118]

Among early nineteenth-century exegetes, Thomas Scott in his 1848 commentary, writes this about Behemoth:

> The beast described in these verses is called Behemoth. This name signifies the beast by way of eminence, or the greatest among beasts. The elephant and the river horse lay claim to it.[3119]

Arthur Peake agrees. He says of Behemoth:

> The word has been used as a Hebraized form of the Egyptian "water ox." The word is an intensive plural of the common Hebrew word for "beast." It simply means, "a huge beast."[3120]

G. R. Noyes, in his 1838 commentary, agrees that Behemoth is the "river-horse."[3121] Ewald remarks about Behemoth, "Behemoth appears to be the Hebrew form of the Egyptian hippopotamus, an apparently very dangerous and really almost harmless, herbivorous animal."[3122] R. F. Hutchinson, in his 1873 commentary, suggests that Behemoth is an elephant.[3123] Driver and Gray call Behemoth "a colossal beast."[3124] John Fredericton, in his 1879 commentary, says that Behemoth "is generally supposed to be the hippopotamus."[3125] George Garland's 1898 commentary says that Behemoth is the "African river-horse."[3126] G. H. Fielding in his 1898 commentary, renders v. 15 as, "Behold now the river-horse."[3127]

Francis Peloubet agrees that Behemoth is a hippo in his 1906 commentary.[3128] William Jennings, in his 1912, *The Dramatic Poem of Job*, says that "Behemoth fits better an antediluvian monster," a cosmic mythological beast.[3129] A. B. Davidson, in describing Behemoth, writes:

> The tail of the hippopotamus is short, naked, and muscular, resembling that of a hog. The great strength of the animal may be inferred from the muscular stiffness of the tail, which bends like a branch or young stem of a cedar.[3130]

William Bode, in his 1914 commentary, also argues for the Hippo.[3131] J. S. Exell, in his 1913 *Pulpit Commentary*, remarks that

> authorities are divided equally between the elephant and the hippopotamus; but the best recent Hebraists and naturalists incline toward the latter.[3132]

Among contemporary scholars of the book of Job, John Gibson in his 1985 commentary says the Behemoth is "the beast *par excellence*."[3133] Hartley observes about the beast:

> Behemoth, like Job, is God's creation, and both are servants of God. Endowed with a hearty appetite, this huge beast cuts a swath through a grassy plain. It can devour an entire field of grain, impoverishing a village.[3134]

George Soper Cansdale in his 1970 work, *Animals of Bible Lands*, simply calls Behemoth a "huge beast."[3135] Jean Bodin, in a 1992 article, thinks Behemoth is "the Egyptian Pharaoh who persecuted the Israelites."[3136] Pierre de Lancre, in his book *On the Inconstancy of Witches*, says that Behemoth is "a monstrous animal, who can disguise himself as a dog, an elephant, a fox, or a wolf."[3137] I. Steinmann, in his 1955 commentary, *Le Livre de Job*, as does Morris Jastrow, believe that Behemoth is a mythological creature and that his tail is a euphemism for the penis.[3138] Marvin Pope also believed that both Behemoth and Leviathan were mythological creatures.

Indeed, H. H. Rowley points out that Gunkel, Cheyne, Pope, and many others also take the view that Behemoth is a mythological creature.[3139] G. R. Driver identifies Behemoth with the crocodile.[3140] In medieval iconography, Behemoth is usually depicted as an ox. The *Liber Floridus*, a twelfth-century manuscript, shows a horned devil riding

THE BOOK OF JOB

the back of an ox-like creature, the Behemoth.[3141] One of William Blake's illustrations of the book of Job depicts both Behemoth and Leviathan in a single image.

In Blake's image, Behemoth looks like a hippopotamus and leviathan is a twisting sea monster. Above them, in the image, can be seen Job, his wife, and three friends. And above these figures can be seen God, flanked by two angels on either side.[3142]

Chapter 41: Leviathan

Introduction

All thirty-four verses of ch. 41 of the book of Job are about the figure of Leviathan. The word Leviathan comes from the Semitic root LVT, related to the verb, "to twist," or "to coil." In modern Hebrew the word Leviathan means "Serpent." In many eastern European languages, the word Behemoth means "hippopotamus," and Leviathan means "sea monster." The figure of Leviathan appears elsewhere in the Hebrew Bible at: Isa 27:1; Ps 74:14; and 104:25–26, and also elsewhere in Job at 3:8.

Carol Newsom introduces ch. 41, the narrative on Leviathan, this way:

> Whereas Behemoth's extraordinary power finds its artistic representation in images of repose and security, Leviathan is rendered in images of violence, fire, and turmoil. The segue between the two poems is hunting imagery, which closes the poem on Behemoth (40:24), and opens the one on Leviathan (41:1.) As a motif, hunting is much more extensively developed in the Leviathan section, since it provides a way to talk about Leviathan's dangerous violence.[3143]

Indeed, one interesting feature of the descriptions of both Behemoth and Leviathan is that at both 40:24, and at 41:1, the text asks two rhetorical questions about whether humans can "pierce his nose with a hook" and "draw out Leviathan with a hook?" The implied answers, of course, is, "No, but God can." This, of course, are other examples of how God can control all of his created beings, while man cannot.

Newsom continues her description of Leviathan:

> Unlike "Behemoth," the name "Leviathan" brings with it a well-developed set of symbolic associations. Both in Ugaritic mythology and in the Bible, "Leviathan" [or "Lotan"] is the name of a sea monster with which Yahweh, Baal, and Anat do Battle. In the Baal Epic, the god Mot refers to a victory of Baal "when you killed Lotan, the Fleeting Serpent, the seven-headed monster." Elsewhere, the goddess Anat says, "Didn't I demolish El's Darling Sea? Didn't I finish off the divine river, Rabbim? Didn't I snare the Dragon? I enveloped him, I demolished the Twisting Serpent, the seven-headed monster."[3144]

In the Bible, the psalmist praises Yahweh, saying, "It was you who split open the Sea by your power; / you broke the heads of the monster in the waters. / It was you who crushed the heads of Leviathan; / and gave him as food to the creatures of the desert."³¹⁴⁵ For Pope, this is further evidence that Behemoth and Leviathan are to be seen as mythological creatures.

Matthew Henry and Newsom, among others, divide ch. 41 into the following six parts:

- vv. 1–8
- vv. 9–12.
- vv. 13–17.
- vv. 18–21.
- vv. 22–24.
- vv. 33–34.³¹⁴⁶

In our analysis of ch. 41, we will follow this outline of Henry's in regard to the great sea monster, Leviathan.

Analysis of Chapter 41

41:1–8

Rowley begins his analysis of the beginning of ch. 41 with these words:

> That Leviathan was a mythological creature is beyond question, and some editors so understand the name here. Gunkel identifies Leviathan with Tiamat. Pope cites passages from the Ras Shamra Texts showing beyond doubt the mythological character of Leviathan, which was generally recognized before these texts were known.³¹⁴⁷

Rowley continues his analysis when he writes, "But this does not prove that a mythological creature is being described here."³¹⁴⁸ By this comment, Rowley points to a controversy among modern scholars about whether Behemoth and Leviathan are to be considered as real, natural creatures, or as mythological beasts, like in the many ancient near-east accounts of the clashes of God with these mythological beasts.

The "fish hook" of v. 1a is a word found only here and at Isa 19:8 and Hab 1:15. The passage in Isaiah speaks of "fishermen who cast a hook." The verse is Habakkuk uses the word in a similar context. The "press down" in v. 1b literally says "causes to sink." The verb is from a root found at Amos 8:8 and 9:5, where it means "to sink." The same root is employed at Lev 8:13, where it implies "to bind," and Dhorme finds this meaning here, as well.³¹⁴⁹

The use of the noun "tongue" in v. 1b has generally been rejected by modern scholars. Peake renders the line:

> Can you put a rope around his tongue and lower jaw when you have caught him?³¹⁵⁰

This context might require more "bind" than "cause to sink" here. The "rope" in v. 2a is literally the word for "reed," as in Isa 9:14. Thus, it is most likely a rope made of reeds. This image is of the binding of prisoners, which is well attested in Assyrian. Dhorme cites an inscription of Ashurbanipal that speaks of a prisoner's jaw being bound with a reed rope.[3151]

Verse 3 seems to speak of Leviathan as if he were a human prisoner. Would he plead for mercy, as a human prisoner might. Many modern commentators speak fancifully of "crocodile tears." The following verse, v. 4, speaks of the possibility of domesticating Leviathan. Will he make a "covenant," or *berith*, so that he is called into the service of someone? At Exod 21:5ff. we see a parallel to v. 4.

Verse 5 asks if Leviathan can be made into a child's toy, like a captive bird. On the evidence of Arabic cognates, D. W. Thomas translates, "Will you tie him with a string like a young sparrow?"[3152] Robert Gordis also follows a similar reading. The "traders" or "merchants" of v. 6 is probably workers in groups or partnerships, and divide the work into several jobs. Such work might also demand a certain amount of haggling among the partners, as in v. 6b suggests.[3153]

The two nouns used in v. 7, often rendered as "harpoons" and "fishing spears" are both two more hapaxes. The first word is related to the noun "thorns." (See Num 33:55.) The second noun comes from a Semitic root meaning "to whir." One of the words for "locust" in the Hebrew Bible, such as at Deut 28:42, comes from the same root. A word for "cymbals" also is derived from this root. Both of these nouns clearly describe dangerous weapons. The first one with "barbs." The second, capable of being thrown and whizzed through the air. At v. 8, we see some advice: If you get close to Leviathan, think carefully first of what the consequences might be. No one lives to repeat such folly. S. R. Driver thinks that v. 8 is "an indirect way of saying that no one has any claim against God, or a ground of complaint against Him, such as Job has raised."[3154] But then Driver adds:

> But a reference to God hardly seems in place here, and it is possible with slight changes to read "him" rather than "me" at the end of v. 10.[3155]

41:9–12

Many interpreters suggests that ch. 41 really begins with v. 9, in that the description of Leviathan seems to be resumed in v. 9. Duhm transfers these verses to make the culmination of the Behemoth description.[3156] The "the hope of a man" in the RSV's rendering of v. 9a, actually says, "his hope" in the Hebrew text. Rowley thinks this hope "refers to that of any assailant."[3157] Budde reads, "thy hope." So too Kissane Larcher, Fohrer, and many others.[3158] Dhorme transposes v. 9 with v. 10.[3159] This is probably best to follow.

In regard to "he is laid low even at the sight of him," of v. 9b has an interrogative particle at the beginning of this line. But it is omitted by Gray, Dhorme, and many others.³¹⁶⁰ Budde translates the line, "thou art laid low."³¹⁶¹ Kissane changes the vowels to secure "even a mighty man is flung down at his sight."³¹⁶² Gunkel suggests, "his appearance cast down even a god." So too Cheyne.³¹⁶³ Pope translates, "were the gods not cast down at the sight of him."³¹⁶⁴ Pope adduces Ugaritic or Mesopotamian material in explaining v. 9.³¹⁶⁵ But there seems to be no necessity for this. The sense is clear: any man who would lay a hand on Leviathan, he will have a bitter reason to regret it.

The "no one is so fierce" in v. 10a, the "fierce" is literally "cruel" in the Hebrew text. Gray renders it, "Is he not too fierce for one to stir him up?"³¹⁶⁶ Dhorme translates v. 10a as, "Is he not cruel, as soon as he is awakened?"³¹⁶⁷ Kissane has it, "Is he not fierce if one rouses him up?"³¹⁶⁸ So too Steinmann and Pope.³¹⁶⁹ All of these scholars agree that the first half of v. 10 is a warning not to rouse Leviathan. The "before me" of v. 10b, most exegetes suggest, "If it is wrong to rouse Leviathan, how much more wrong would it be to arouse Yahweh?" Many early manuscripts, as well as the Targum have "before him," keeping the emphasis on Leviathan and not the Divine.

Most modern translations of v. 11a, render it, "Who has given to me that I should repay him?" The Hebrew text, however, says, "Who has confronted me?" The LXX has it, "Who will confront me and remain silent," presumably meaning "and remain safe."³¹⁷⁰ This would have to involve reading *wayyislam* for *waa'sallem*, which is also followed by Merx, and many other editors.³¹⁷¹

The "whatever is under the whole of heaven is mine," does not refer to Leviathan, but rather is a claim made about God, since he is the Owner of all that there is. If we make a slight change of the Hebrew *li hu* "is mine" to get *lo hu*, or, *lo ehad*, that is, "there is no one," or *mi hu*, or "who indeed," are all possible readings. Many exegetes follow one or the other of these approaches. The meaning of v. 11b, then, would be, "There is no one under the whole heaven who could face Leviathan and survive? Who indeed."

Verse 12 now turns to the more minute details of Leviathan. Rashi translates v. 12a as, "From his nostrils, smoke go forward."³¹⁷² Mezudat David says of the line:

> The vapor that emerges from his nostrils is due to the great heat of his body. It is so thick and copious that it resembles smoke, and it also resembles the steam that rises from a bubbling pot.³¹⁷³

Rashi believes v. 12b refers to an "earthenware vessel," or pot.³¹⁷⁴ Most modern translations, however, give an entirely different sense to the verse. The RSV, for example, renders v. 12 this way:

> I will not keep silent concerning his limbs,
>
> or his mighty strength or his goodly frame.³¹⁷⁵

The Hebrew of v. 12 is closer to the RSV. It literally says, "and the word of might, and the grace of his arrangement."³¹⁷⁶ If the Leviathan is a crocodile, one would scarcely associate grace with the creature. With slight changes, Dhorme reads, *waʾaʾbabber*, or "and I will tell" for *udebar*, or, "and the word of his incomparable might."³¹⁷⁷ Pope suggests the following for v. 12:

> Did I not silence his boasting
>
> By the powerful word *hayyin* prepared?³¹⁷⁸

In this translation, Pope thinks that *hayyin* is an epithet of a particular Ugaritic deity, here believed to stand for a "Master Enchanter" who casts spells before a battle;³¹⁷⁹ but it seems unnecessary in an encounter between Yahweh and Leviathan to make this kind of change in v. 12.

41:13–17

In regard to "his outer garment" in v. 13a, the Hebrew text literally says, "the face of his garment." This is believed by many editors to refer to the scales of the crocodile's skin. Dhorme thinks it refers to the front on the garment, as opposed to the back.³¹⁸⁰ The "double coat of mail" or "his goodly frame," as some versions have it, literally says, "and the word of might and the grace of his arrangement." The Hebrew has, "his double bridle." This is taken to mean his upper and lower teeth. The LXX reads *siryon*, or "armor," instead of *resen*, or "bridle," as do most other modern editors.³¹⁸¹ Jeremiah 46:4 and 51:3 are parallels to v. 13.

Verse 14, most editors maintain, refers to Leviathan's formidable teeth, which inspire much terror in humans. The upper jaw of the crocodile, Rowley informs us, has thirty-six teeth, while the lower jaw has thirty.³¹⁸² Rather than "of his face" in v. 14a, the Peshitta has "of his mouth."³¹⁸³ Some exegetes needlessly follow this view.

The opening of v. 15, in the Hebrew text says, "his pride," but most modern interpreters emend it to get "his back." In fact, the LXX, Aquila, and the Vulgate, all have "his back" or cover the animal's back.³¹⁸⁴ The "shut up closely, as with a seal," most editors interpret to mean that the scales are tightly packed together that no air or moisture can seep between them. The word *sar*, or "closely," the LXX reads as *sor*, or "stone." The thought then would be that there is a hardness to the rock-like seal with which the scales are compared.

Presumably, vv. 16–17 continues the thought of the tightness of the scales in the previous verse. Not even air can get between them. Newsom agrees. She says, "The rows of shields are Leviathan's teeth, set so close together that there is no space between them."³¹⁸⁵

41:18–21

The KJV uses the obsolete "neesings" for the first noun in v. 18a. The word is *atiyshaw*. Most modern exegetes translate it as "sneezings." The noun appears to indicate the vapor or spray of moisture that emits from Leviathan's nostrils. Pope, who interprets Leviathan as a purely mythological creature, finds in v. 18 the breathing out of a "flame of fire."[3186] The "like the eyelids of the dawn" of v. 18b is, perhaps, a reference to the reddish hue of the eyes of the crocodile. Newsom says it refers to "dawn's light that has a reddish hue."[3187] She refers to the German expression, *morgenrot*, that literally means, "the red of morning."[3188]

Rowley observes about vv. 18–19:

> When the crocodile issues from the water, it expels its pent-up breathe together with water in a hot steam from its mouth, and this looks like a steam of fire in the sunshine.[3189]

Peake thinks that the author may have embroidered his picture with his own reminiscences of stories of fire-breathing dragons.[3190] Pope also sees this description in just such terms.[3191] The word for "nostrils" in v. 20 is another hapax of the book. The Hebrew term is *nekeer*. The same root occurs at 39:20, where it is usually translated as "snorting." It comes from the NKR root, that is the source for words like *nachray*, or "snore," the verb *nachar*, and *nacharah*, a verb that means "to snort."

The RSV's "boiling pot and burning rushes" in v. 20b does not have the word "burning" in the Hebrew text. The word for "rushes" is the same term employed at 41:2, where it probably means "rope." The Peshitta and the Vulgate have "a seething and boiling pot" for v. 20b, reading *'ogem* for *agmon*. This also was proposed by Bickell and is generally followed by most modern editors.[3192] Verse 21 is clearly connected to the description in v. 19. Strahan believes the hyperbolic language lends more credence to the mythological interpretation of the beast, as does Marvin Pope.[3193]

41:22–24

The "neck" of v. 22 is not a prominent feature for strength in the crocodile, but elsewhere in the Hebrew Bible, the neck is seen as a seat of strength. (See Job 15:26 and Ps 75:5, for examples.) Newsom believes in these verses, "[we] move from the face to the neck." She adds:

> The poet traces Leviathan's neck, the folds of flesh below the neck and the chest.[3194]

Newsom adds about vv. 22–24:

> Those features if Leviathan raised itself up, which is precisely what is described in the following verse [41:25].[3195]

Rowley thinks the "terror" or "sorrow" of v. 22b should be read "dismay." The word, however, is found only here, so it is difficult to make sense of it here, for it is another hapax in the book. The word in question is *de'abah*. It comes from a root that means "to languish." Here it represents the "dismay" which Leviathan inspires, a dismay which is said to dance before him. Frank Cross, with the change of a pair of letters, reads "strength," instead of "terror." He justifies this by using a Ugaritic passage.[3196] The RSV's "folds" or KJV's "flakes" of v. 23a is literally, "fallings." The Hebrew is *mappal*. Rashi says v. 23 should be rendered:

> He makes the deep seethe like a pot
>
> He makes the sea like a seething mixture.[3197]

The word "hard" in v. 24, that modifies "stone" is the same term employed at v. 23, where it is rendered as "hard as a stone" in the RSV. The triple repetition of this word, Rowley says, "is perhaps deliberate to emphasize the effect."[3198] But many other editors believe the style of the verse would be quite inelegant, and thus Duhm, and many others reject v. 23b and all of v. 24.[3199] The noun rendered "nether millstone" at the end of v. 24, Rowley observes, was "heavier and harder than the upper millstone for obvious reasons."[3200] The Hebrew for this noun is *tachli rekeb*, the first word is related to the underworld, and the second to a millstone.

Kissane transfers v. 25 to follow 40:18, but this transfer appears to be quite arbitrary.[3201] Verse 25 is quite difficult and has occasioned much discussion. Some editors prefer "at his majesty," to "when he raises himself up," which Dhorme and others prefer.[3202] The expression "the mighty" in v. 25a might also be translated as "the gods," as the Peshitta and the Targum have it.[3203] The Vulgate, on the other hands, translates the noun as "angels." Pope follows this approach and cites both Mesopotamian and Ugaritic sources to bolster that mythological view.[3204]

41:26–31

Newsom introduces these verses this way:

> The raising-up of Leviathan should present an adversary the opportunity to strike it. Yet even the gods are terrified of Leviathan because it is unvulnerable to any weapon.[3205]

Newsom goes on to suggest that vv. 26–29 is a "catalogue of weapons—sword, spear, dart, javelin, iron, bronze, arrow, slingstone, club, lance."[3206] Rowley observes about these verses:

> Every kind of weapon is useless to bring against Leviathan. His natural defenses render him impervious to them all.[3207]

The word for "clubs" or "darts" [*towthach*] employed in v. 29a is yet another hapax of the book. Most translators get that meaning from an Arabic cognate. The word for "javelin" or "spear" in v. 29b is not the same word used at v. 26b, but it is used at 39:23. The Hebrew term is *kedown*. The KJV and RSV give "underpants" for the first noun of v. 30, but some translate it "under him." The "like the sharp potshards" of v. 30a literally says "the sharp points of potshards," in the Hebrew text.

Newsom adds:

> The physical description of Leviathan, interrupted by the catalogue of weapons, resumes in 41:30.³²⁰⁸

The KJV gives "his underpants" for the noun in v. 30a. The KJV has "under him." The "like sharp potshards" in the verse is literally, "the sharp points of potshards" in the Hebrew text. Many commentators cite a passage in Aelian's *De Natura animalium* [X, 24] in which the same comparison of the scales of the crocodile, on its back, with potshards is made.³²⁰⁹

Rowley says with v. 31, "We now have the evidence of Leviathan's motion in the water, which he chums up to a great foam."³²¹⁰ Habel believes that *tit*, or "mire," as well as *mesula*, or "the depths" and *tehom*, or "the deep," are all "evocative of the chaotic, as is the image of churning water."³²¹¹ The word for "pot" in v. 31a is an ordinary household utensil. The same word is employed at Jer 1:13. The verb "boil" in v. 31a is the same verb used at 30:27. The comparison made at v. 31b is interpreted in a large number of ways. According to some, it is the foam on the top surface of a boiling pot. Others say it is the smell of the ingredients all simmering together.

41:32–34

Newsom begins her analysis of these verses at the close of ch. 41 this way:

> As God declared Behemoth status as "first in rank" among the works of God, so Leviathan's place is proclaimed. Leviathan is no threat to God, but upon Earth it is supreme.³²¹²

The word for "without equal" is spelled the same way as the phrase "none can dominate him" (*en moslo*). Here both meanings are probably intended. The previous poem is ample testimony to that claim, and to the claim that Leviathan is made "without fear." Newsom remarks about these verses:

> As in chapter 39, the conclusion of the poem is marked by an inclusion, as 41:34 echoes 40:11b. There Job was challenged to "look on every proud beast that brings it low." Here it is said that Leviathan "looks on all that are haughty." Far from being brought low, Leviathan is the King.³²¹³

Perdue agrees. He says of v. 33, "Peerless and without fear, Leviathan is the king of beasts and is feared by all."[3214] In regard to the verb of v. 34a, "He beholds," many scholars with slight changes translate "everything . . . fears him," which provides a better contrast to the previous line. Leviathan knows no fear, while at the same time he inspires it in humans.

Rashi also translates, "He is king over all the sons of pride."[3215] He means here the "proud beasts." Job 28:8 is a parallel to v. 34, where the same Hebrew expression appears. Mezudat David renders the verse this way:

> Although he is in the water, below the Earth, he sees all the high and mighty creatures upon the Earth, and although he knows of all the wondrous creatures, he is dismayed by none of them, because he is king over all proud beasts and is prouder than all of them. God is saying to Job, "I have shown you the wonder of My creations. From this you can deduce the extent of My greatness."[3216]

Leviathan in Art

The oldest artistic depiction of Leviathan can be seen on a cylinder seal from the Tell Asmar excavations from the twenty-fourth century BCE. It shows two men fighting with a seven-headed monster, most likely Lotan or Leviathan.[3217] The seal was discovered among the clay sealings and tablets of an ancient Mesopotamian Palace, excavated in the early 1930s by an archeological team from the University of Chicago.

A number of medieval Christian painters did renderings of Behemoth and Leviathan, often together, or depicted along with the figure of Ziz, a representation of another ancient, Jewish myth of a large bird that can block out the sun. One good example of this motif are the sixth-century mosaic pavements in the city of Cyrenaica, and the fifth-century House of Kyrios Leontis at Beth Shean. These pieces of art show Behemoth as an ox, and Leviathan as a crocodile.[3218]

Another early Christian rendering of Behemoth and Leviathan is a wood beam painting in Saint Catherine's Monastery in the Sinai. It shows the battle between Behemoth and Leviathan. Again the former looks like a great ox, while the latter appears to be a crocodile.[3219] In later Christian art, Leviathan was often depicted as the Mouth of Hell.[3220] One good example is Simon Marion's "Hellmouth," from the Getty's *Les Visions du Chevalier Tondal*. The painting is dated around 1474. Marion was born in Amiens around 1452.[3221]

Other Leviathans as Hellmouth can also be seen in the Westchester Psalter, from around 1225. It shows the damned being swallowed into a toothy Hellmouth that also has a Hell's Gate locked behind it.[3222] The Wenhaston Doom is another example of Leviathan as Hellmouth. It is situated on a side wall of Saint Peter's Church in Suffolk, England. It was most likely produced at the end of the fifteenth century, and then whitewashed over by the Puritans. It was rediscovered during the Victorian era, after heavy rains dissolved the lime-based wash.[3223]

Other depictions of Leviathan as Hellmouth can also be seen in the following places:

1. At the west doorway of the Abbey of Conques-en-Rouergue (11th c.).
2. The west front portal of the Lincoln Cathedral, mid-twelfth-century church.
3. An early thirteenth-century manuscript of the Paris National Library (MS. Fr. 403, fol. 40r).
4. The Fitzwaren Psalter, a mid-fourteenth-century manuscript at the Paris National Library (MS. Lat. 765, fol. 15).
5. A 1440 illuminated manuscript owned by the Pierpont Morgan Library in New York City (MS. 945, fol. 158v).[3224]

The only Islamic depiction of Leviathan can be seen in a mid-sixteenth-century Turkish miniature from the *Qisas al-Anbiya*, or "Stories of the Prophets," by Ishaq al-Nashapuri. It associates Leviathan with the sea monster that swallowed Jonah. The image is owned by the Chester Beatty Library, in Dublin (Ms. 231, fol. 156).[3225]

Abraham Bosse (1602–1676), a French Huguenot painter, illustrated Thomas Hobbes's 1651 *Leviathan*, in which Leviathan is shown as a giant human. He holds a sword in his right hand and a scepter in the left. The image is accompanied by passages from the Vulgate version of the book of Job, particularly the passages from ch. 41, the Leviathan chapter.[3226]

One of William Blake's 1824 illustrations of the book of Job pictures both beasts in a single work. Behemoth is shown as a hippopotamus and Leviathan as a large Sea Serpent.[3227] Gustave Doré also depicts Leviathan as a Sea Serpent who is being engulfed by water, while above, in the clouds, Christ appears, looking radiant. Doré called the image *Destruction of Leviathan*, which is dated at 1865.[3228]

The twentieth century saw the production of a number of paintings with Leviathan as the subject matter. These include the following:

1. *Leviathan*, by Julian Levi (1900–1982). Abstract oil on canvas. This 1960 painting is owned by the Smithsonian American Art Museum.
2. Seymour Lipton's 1963 *Leviathan*. It is a metal sculpted piece, part of the City of Philadelphia's Public Art Displays.
3. Salvador Dali completed a *Leviathan* in 1969.[3229]

In addition, there are also two twenty-first-century artists who have depicted Leviathan. The first of these is called *The Head of Leviathan*. It is a Surrealistic acrylic painting, a black-and-white image that looks like a ghost wearing a KKK hood. The painting is owned by the Kazuya Akimoto Art Museum in Tokyo.[3230] The other twenty-first-century image is entitled *Rage of Leviathan*, by a man named Zanakan. It shows a large, scaly sea creatures with an open mouth that reveals sharp teeth with which he destroys a ship with its tail.[3231]

Leviathan in Literature and Culture

The earliest references to Leviathan in literature and culture comes from the Talmud. At the *Avoda Zara*, section 3b, for example, we get the following description:

> Rav Yehuda says there are twelve hours in the day. In the first three hours, God sits alone and studies the Torah; in the second three hours, He sits and judges the world; in the third three hours God feeds the entire world; and in the fourth three hours, God plays with Leviathan, for, as it is written, "The Leviathan which You have created to play with."[3232]

The *Moed Katan* (section 25b) also mentions Leviathan. It tells us:

> Rav Ashi said to Bar Kipok, "What will be said at your funeral?" He answered, "If a flame can fell a cedar, what hope does a small tree have? If a Leviathan can be hooked and hauled to land, what hope has a fish in a puddle?"[3233]

The *Pirke de Rabbi Eliezer*, a midrashic text says that the whale that swallowed Jonah narrowly avoided being eaten by Leviathan, which generally eats a whale a day.[3234] In another archeological dig at Bet Zavit, the relic bones and perhaps a foot print of ancient Sea animals have been discovered. Some think these served as the origins of the developing creation myth about Behemoth and Leviathan.[3235]

In a hymn by Kalir, the Leviathan is a serpent that surrounds the earth and has its tail in its mouth, much like the Greek *Ouroborus* and the Nordic *Midgard* Serpent.[3236] There is also a parallel to Leviathan in Greek mythology, where Zeus faces off with a many-headed dragon named Typhon.[3237]

In more modern literature and culture, John Milton mentions Leviathan in *Paradise Lost*. He uses the term to describe the power and strength of Satan.[3238] Thomas Hobbes called his 1651 work about the state of nature and the social contract *Leviathan*.[3239] Herman Melville identifies Leviathan with the great white whale in *Moby Dick*.[3240] *Leviathan* was the name of a ship at the Battle of Trafalgar that was captained by a Commander Trotter.[3241] Lord Byron refers to a boat in an 1818 poem as "an oak Leviathan."[3242] Edmond Burke, in referring to the Duke of Bedford, called him "a Leviathan among the creatures of the crown."[3243] A Leviathan is depicted in the *Shor-ha Bar*, a piece of nineteenth-century Polish folk art. It was made by R. Lilientalowa in Cracow in 1908.[3244]

George Oppen's 1962 poem "Leviathan" shows the beast as an all-consuming force of history, which Oppen believes is a threat to human survival.[3245] Leviathan is a major character in the 1975 science fiction novel *The Illuminatus Trilogy*, by Robert

Shea and Anton Wilson.[3246] And Karl Shuker, a cryptozoologist, in his book *In Search of Prehistoric Survivors*, suggests that Leviathan is a myth inspired by sightings of a Mosasaur Sea Monster.[3247]

Views of Leviathan: 19th and 20th Centuries

Scholar	Natural or Mythological	Animal or Myth
19th Century		
William Blake (1825)	N	Hippo or Sea Serpent
Noyes (1838)	N	Crocodile
Albert Barnes (1844)	?	Fierce Animal of Deep
Franz Delitzsch (1872)	N	Hippo or Crocodile
Hutchinson	N	Whale
Thomson (1878)	N	Crocodile
John of Fredericton (1879)	N	Crocodile
William Kelly (1879)	N	Water Ox/Hippo
T. K. Cheyne (1887)	M	Creation Monsters
Ewald (1882)	N	Hippo or Crocodile
William Cowles (1887)	N	Whale
Toy (1892)	M	Creation Monsters
Gunkel (1895)	M	Creation Monsters
Watson (1895)	N	Hippo or Crocodile
Early 20th Century		
H. Wilkinson (1901)	N	River Ox or Hippo
Penn-Lewis (1903)	N	Whale
S. R. Driver (1906)	N	Crocodile
A. S. Peake (1906)	N	Crocodile
Francis Pelubet	N	Crocodile
Royds (1911)	N	Crocodile
Jennings (1912)	N	Crocodile
William Bode (1914)	N	Massive Rhino or Hippo
S. Ridout.	N	Crocodile
Morris Jastrow (1920)	M	Great Sea Monster
Driver and Gray (1923)	N	Hippo or Crocodile
Stevenson (1951)	M	Creation Monsters

Scholar	Natural or Mythological	Animal or Myth
Later 20th Century		
Freehof (1958)	N	Crocodile
Pope (1965)	M	Creation Monsters
Tur-Sinai (1967)	M	Creation Monsters
Archer (1982)	M	Creation Monsters
Habel (1985)	M	Creation Monsters
Hartley (1988)	Mix of M and N	Mix of two views
C. S. Rodd (1990)	N	Crocodile
James Williams (1992)	M	Creation Monsters
D. A. Deal (1999)	N	T. Rex

Chapter 42: Job's Second Response to Yahweh

Introduction

The final chapter of the book of Job, ch. 42, is divided into two portions. The first of these is vv. 1–6 that contains Job's final words to his God. The second section, vv. 7–17, like the prologue, sits as a prose epilogue. Newsom introduces ch. 42 this way:

> Immediately following God's speech concerning Behemoth and Leviathan, Job replies. As the decisive word that Job speaks in God's presence, this reply provides the dramatic climax anticipation since the Satan's prediction that, once deprived of his family, possessions, and health, Job would curse God to his face [1:11 and 2:5].[3248]

Chapter 42:1–6 is a counter-balance to Job's lament in ch. 3. These lines also continue, or complete, Job's reconciliation or apology began at Job 40:3–5. Wycliffe believes this confession marks "Job's final bruising of Satan, and the final redemption of Yahweh's vindication before Job."[3249]

Analysis of Chapter 42

42:1–6

Rowley and many other editors connect these verses directly to 40:4ff., Job's response to God's first speech. This "continues," as Rowley says, "Job's response to Yahweh in submission and surrender."[3250] The "purpose" or "thought" of v. 2b is connected to Gen 17:11, where the same verb is used. The word "purpose" refers to the divine plan, whereby the entire universe eventually unfolds according to the Purpose of the Almighty. If Job had not understood this purpose before, he certainly does now. Perhaps Job comes to the realization that God's omnipotence and omniscience go hand and hand with his moral character, his "omnibenevolence." The Hebrew word for "purpose" or "thought" in v. 2b is *me'zimmah*.

The book of Job employed a separate word for "thought," at 12:5. The term is *ashtoth*, and it is only used this single time in ch. 12. The first line of v. 3 is a variation of 38:2, which most editors regard as a marginal note here. S. R. Driver, however, thinks it might be original, it being cited for the purpose of admitting the justice of its implied rebuke.[3251] Franz Delitzsch, Zockler, and Kissane make similar judgments about v. 3.[3252]

Verse 4 repeats, with slight variations 33:31, 38:3, and 40:7. Again, most editors delete v. 4 as a marginal gloss. It cannot, in any case, be regarded as what Job is now saying to God, but at best it is a reminiscence of what God had earlier said to him. Rashi says that v. 4 means, "I did not understand so much as You informed me, for many wonders are hidden and are concealed from me, which I do not know."[3253] If this is the proper view, then Job, in the end ascribes to the divine plan point of view.

Ibn Ezra observes about v. 5 of the final chapter:

> From this verse it appears that Job had not prophesied prior to this message from God. He had merely heard that there were prophets in the world, such as Abraham, Isaac, and Jacob.[3254]

Rowley says about vv. 5 and 6:

> These verses terminate the main part of the book, devoted to discussion, and they give the conclusions of the matter. Job is no longer tortured with doubts and blasphemous complaints, but lifted to a new plane of peace. His intellectual problem is left unsolved, but he has transcended it. He does not simply resign himself passively to the impossibility of a solution, but yields himself in active reverence to find peace in the living presence of a God he believed he had lost. His restless spirit found rest when he rested in God.[3255]

The "my eyes see thee" is not a reference to physical sight. The verb "to see" (*chazah*), like in English, also means "to know" or "to understand." One way to help to understand v. 5 is to remember that these people live in a desert, which is now in the midst of a whirlwind. Anyone who has ever been in the desert during a wind storm knows that one cannot see anything. In this sense, Job may be saying, "Now I see that I cannot see." Meaning, I now understand that God has an overall plan that I am incapable of understanding. Arthur Peake says that v. 5 "is the most precious thing the book has to offer us. Theodicy is transcended in religion."[3256] If Peake is correct about that, it is because 42:5–6 ascribes to the divine plan theory about the cause of Job's suffering.

There has been a bit of controversy surrounding the meaning of v. 6. Rowley says of the verse, "Job's repentance is not of any sin which has brought his suffering on him, such as the friends had called for. It was of the things he had said in his ignorance during the course of the debate."[3257] Rashi renders v. 6a, "I despise my life."[3258] S. R. Driver has it, "I abhor myself."[3259] John, Bishop of Fredrichton, in his 1879 commentary, translates v. 6a as "I retract."[3260] Saadiah Gaon renders it, "Therefore, I do spurn what I formerly have said."[3261] The verb *emas* means "despise," "reject," or "regard with little value." The object, "myself," as the RSV has it, does not appear in the Hebrew text. Thus, the object has to be supplied by the translators. Some editors give "what I have said" as the object. Pope points out that the verb here, as well as at 7:16, is intransitive, so no object is needed. At any rate, the two most prominent alternatives are either that Job "abhors himself," or he is "rejecting what he has said." The KJV renders the line:

> Wherefore, I abhor myself,
>
> And repent in dust and ashes.[3262]

The verb *emas* is employed without a direct object three other times in the Old Testament. All of these come in the book of Job. These can be found at: 7:16; 34:33; and at 36; 5, in addition to 42:6. The second verb in v. 6 is *niham*. Since it is first person singular and followed by a preposition, the Hebrew is *nihamti al*. The verb *niham* means either "to repent" or "to be comforted." The preposition *al* could mean "in," or it could also express "about." Thus, Job may be repenting in dust and ashes, or he may be comforted about dust and ashes. In the first interpretation, Job would be submitting to Yahweh. In the second interpretation, he may simply be saying that he is comforted by his finitude—that his suffering may soon come to an end—and he is happy about that.

The fragment of Job found in Cave 11 of the Dead Sea Scrolls, renders 42:6, "Therefore, I am poured out and boiled up" (or dissolved).[3263] J. B. Curtis translates 42:6 this way: "Therefore, I feel loathing and contempt towards you, oh God; and I am sorry for being a frail man."[3264] In an essay entitled "Job: Repentant or Rebellious?," B. Lynne Newell renders 42:6 thusly:

> Therefore, I will have nothing more to do with the sins of which you charge me that I committed by speaking without understanding, and I repent in dust and ashes.[3265]

Similarly, Edward Greenstein in his recent translation of the book of Job renders 42:5–6 this way:

> As the hearing of the ear I have heard you.
>
> And now my eyes have seen you
>
> That is why I am fed up.
>
> I take pity on dust and ashes.[3266]

Like Curtis, Greenstein suggests that Job is not repenting in vv. 5–6. Instead, he expresses that he is "fed up," and is content with his finitude. Rarely in Judaism or Christianity can one find such a translation of what is clearly the punch line of the book.

There also have been some negative responses to Job's comment in 42:5–6. George Bernard Shaw mocks Job's response.[3267] Eli Wiesel holds that Job should have pressed God more by not capitulating.[3268] But both of these critics assume that everything that takes place in God's universe ought to be explained to humans; but, perhaps, there may be some things that people are not meant to understand, for we are not God.

Other Translations of 42:6: 19th and 20th Centuries

Scholar	Translation
Delitzsch (1872)	"Therefore, I am sorry and repent in dust and ashes."
John Fredericton (1879)	"Wherefore, I retract and repent on dust and ashes."
Ewald (1882)	"Therefore, I retract what I have said and repent in dust and ashes."
R. A. Watson (1892)	"Wherefore, I repudiate my words, and repent in dust and ashes."
S. R. Driver (1906)	"Wherefore, I abhor myself and repent in dust and ashes."
Moffatt (1918)	"Therefore, I despise myself and repent in dust and ashes."
Jastrow (1920)	"Therefore, I recall and repent in utter worthlessness."
Driver and Gray (1923)	"Wherefore, I repudiate what I had said and repent in dust and ashes."
Dhorme (1926)	"I sink down and repent in dust and ashes."
Rowley (1946)	"Therefore, I despise myself and repent in dust and ashes."
Terrien (1954)	"Wherefore, I despise myself and repent in dust and ashes."
Freehof (1958)	"Wherefore, I abhor my words and repent, seeing I am dust and ashes."
Pope (1965)	"So I recant and repent in dust and ashes."
Habel (1985)	"Therefore, I retract and repent of dust and ashes."
Simundson (1986)	"Therefore, I despise myself and repent in dust and ashes."

In some more recent scholarship, a number of interpreters have suggested that Job is not repenting at 42:5-6. Among these are Carl Jung, D. A. Robertson, K. Fullerton, and in a 1979 essay by J. B. Curtis mentioned earlier. Robertson thinks Job's response is "hypocritical."[3269] Jung believes that what Job does is "prostrate himself because Yahweh cannot be judged morally."[3270] J. B. Curtis, in his 1979 essay entitled "On Job's Response to Yahweh," also argues that Job does not repent, but he does totally and unequivocally reject Yahweh. Curtis tells us that Job "is totally disenchanted with his God."[3271]

Curtis suggests the following rendering of 42:6:

> Therefore, I feel loathing, contempt, and revulsion toward you, O God And I am sorry for being a frail man.[3272]

Thus, in Curtis's view, Job totally, and finally, rejects this unjust, unfeeling, and irrelevant deity. This radical suggestion of Curtis would seem to indicate that we should reevaluate what has traditionally been the sense that has been made at Job 42:5-6. Curtis believes that Job does not acquiesce at the end of the book.

Further evidence that Job is merely saying that he is comfortable with his finitude at 42:6 is the only two other uses of *'afar va 'efer*, or dust and ashes, in the Hebrew Bible. At both Gen 18:27, where Abraham is contended with his finitude, and Job 30:19—where the expression clearly means comfort about creatureliness—the conclusion about 42:6b may be similar to what Curtis and Greenstein suggest.

42:7-17

With v. 7 the book reverts back to prose, much like at the beginning of the book. Also, the references to God in this epilogue all use the word Yahweh, and not the El, Elohim, Eloah, and Shaddai we saw in the dialogue. Verse 7 tells us that God speaks to "Eliphaz, and his two friends," presumably meaning Bildad and Zophar. Elihu is nowhere to be found. Nor is the Satan figure we were introduced to in the Prologue. Yahweh tells the three, "You have not spoken the truth like My servant Job." You have not said of Me, "what is right." Rowley observes about these verses, "Since the Epilogue was demanded by the Prologue, so the focal point should be the subject of the trial, and on that the friends have spoken wrongly and Job rightly."[3273]

The sacrifices that Yahweh requires of the friends in vv. 8-9 recall the burnt offerings made by Job for his sons, "in case they might have sinned" at 1:5. The sacrifices here are very large ones. Numbers 23:1ff. is perhaps the best parallel of these verses. The mentioning that Job will pray for the friends after they make the sacrifices perhaps speaks of the value of intercessory prayer, which is often recognized in the Hebrew Bible. (See Gen 18:23ff. and 20:7, for examples.)

In vv. 10-17, Job's fortunes are doubled, and his friends and family bring presents to him. The number of children, seven sons and three daughters, equal the number he possessed in the Prologue. Whether this is the first set of children brought back to life by Yahweh, or it is a new set of children is not clear from the Hebrew text. The expression "restored to fortune" in v. 10 is translated as "turned the captivity" in the KJV and RSV.

The "piece of money" in v. 11 is the Hebrew word *kesita*, an anachronistic value of currency. The word is so old, we no longer know its value. The word is only used elsewhere at Gen 33:19 and Josh 24:32. This may be evidence that Job lived in the patriarchal age. Rowley points out that coined currency was not made in ancient Israel until the sixth century BCE.[3274]

The "ring of gold," or *nezem*, in v. 11 was worn by ladies in their noses (see Gen 24:27 and Isa 3:21), and by both men and women in their ears. (See Prov 11:22 and Gen 35:4.) Abraham's servant carried a ring as a gift, when he traveled to seek a wife for Isaac (see Gen 24:22). The numbers in v. 12 are precisely double those in the opening of the book at 1:3. The form for the word "seven" (*sheteph*) is unusual. Hence, the Targum reads it as "double seven," and thus gives Job fourteen sons in the end of the book. Ehrlich, Dhorme, and Steinmann, among others, interpret the seven just that way.[3275] But Arthur Peake thinks it is a "fine trait that the number of children is the same."[3276]

One interesting feature about vv. 12–13 is there is nothing of the "many servants" we were told Job had back at 1:3. At 42:12 and 13, we find double the number of animals, sheep, camel, oxen, and asses, but nothing about the *'ebadim*, or "servants" in the opening chapter of the book.

The names of the three daughters in v. 14 are Jemimah, Keziah, and Keren-happuch. The first means "dove." The second, "cinnamon," and the third, "eye shadow." Jezebel at 2 Kgs 9:30 wears similar makeup. It is a dark mineral powder used on the eyes. The other significant thing about these three daughters is that they are given property rights in v. 15. Numbers 27:1ff. sketches out the laws of inheritance for children. Daughters are only entitled to a share of the inheritance if there were no male heirs. This is another item, besides their beauty, that sets them apart from other women.

What we can say is the final word on Job's daughters is that they look good, smell good, and come with substantial dowries. These are not attributes to suggest that the daughters have rights like their brothers—and thus a feminist interpretation—rather they are three attributes that in the ancient world would be very attractive to potential suitors.

The 140 years prescribed for Job in v. 16 is twice the "three score and ten" mentioned at Ps 90:10. (Also see Gen 50:22ff. as a parallel.) The "four generations" in v. 16b is a sign of great blessing in the Hebrew Bible, though only three generations are mentioned in the Job text. The mention of Job "dying old and full of days" again is said only of the holiest of the patriarchs. The LXX adds an addendum to the end of

v. 17 that Job will share in the resurrection of the dead at the end of time. It makes this claim on the authority of the "Syriac book," presumably meaning the Peshitta.

Mezudat David observes about v. 17:

> Since he died among great wealth and prosperity, seeing his children and their offspring before him, and achieving all of his desires, he did not yearn to live any longer, but was sated with the days he had.[3277]

Hapax Legomena in Book of Job

Altogether most scholars identify 1,703 *hapax legomena*, words that appear once and only once in the Bible. In the book of Job, we can find 119 of these words. They appear throughout the book, but there is a larger concentration of them in the Elihu Speeches, chs. 32–37. In the speeches of the fourth friend of Job, we see the following Hebrew words:

- 32:6, "anxious."
- 32:19, "bag or skin bottle."
- 32:24, "ransom."
- 33:7, "hand."
- 33:9, "clean."
- 33:20, "loathsome."
- 33:24, "ransom."
- 33:25, "strong" or "free."
- 34:8, "company."
- 34:9, "dead."
- 34:25, "to be strong."
- 34:36, "would that."
- 35:5, "be bright."
- 35:15, "arrogance."
- 36:2, "to wait."
- 36:18, "enough," or "mockery."
- 36:19, "exertion."
- 36:27, "to draw out."
- 36:27, "drops."
- 35:9, "cry."
- 37:2, "to wait."
- 37:18, "wondrous works."

- 37:18, "mirror."
- 37:21, "dusky."

Other hapax legomena in the book may be organized this way:

Round I:

- 2:8, "to scrape oneself."
- 3:4, "daylight."
- 3:5, "light."
- 3:5, "rain cloud."
- 3:5, "darkening."
- 3:13, "rest" or "exhausted."
- 4:10, "to be broken out."
- 4:13, "error" or "craziness."
- 5:2, "destruction."
- 5:17, "to dry up."
- 5:25, "destruction."
- 6:6, "ox tongue."
- 6:6, "white of egg."
- 6:9, "to strip off."
- 6:10, "to jump."
- 6:10, "labor pains."
- 6:12, "bronze."
- 6:14, "discouraged."
- 6:17, "to dry up."
- 6:17, "be burning."
- 6:21, "terrors."
- 7:4, "restlessness."
- 7:5, "crust," or "clod."
- 7:15, "suffocation."
- 7:20, "target."
- 8:16, "moist," or "juicy."
- 8:19, "what is rotten."

- 9:6, "to shudder."
- 9:9, "constellation."
- 9:12, "to snatch away."
- 9:18, "to be bitter."
- 9:26, "swooping."
- 9:26, "cane."
- 10:2, "regulation" or "order."
- 10:10, "cheese."
- 10:22, "order."
- 12:5, "opinion."

Round II:

- 15:12, "to wink."
- 15:24, "small."
- 15:24, "onslaught" or "battle," or "attack."
- 15:27, a collop of fat.
- 15:32, "to be leafy" or verdant.
- 16:11, "to cast."
- 16:13, "kidneys."
- 16:15, "to insert."
- 16:15, "skin," or "crust."
- 16:19, "witness."
- 15:29, "property."
- 16:8, "wrinkles."
- 16:15, "skin."
- 16:19, "witness."
- 17:1, "extinct" or "extinguish."
- 17:6, may be "to spit."
- 18:2, "snare" or "trap."
- 18:2, "chase."
- 8:3, "stupid" or "foolish."
- 18:5, "spark."

- 18:10, "trap" or "snare."
- 19:3, "impudent."
- 19:14, "unintentional sin."
- 19:20, "bald."
- 20:6, "excellence."
- 20:22, "excess," or "plenty."
- 20:26, another word for "trap."
- 21:20, "destruction."
- 21:24, *Atinim* "utters."
- 21:24, "bone-marrow."
- 21:32, "tomb."

Round III

- 22:20, "adversaries."
- 24:11a, "walls" or "terraces."
- 24:11b, "to press oil."
- 24:20, "wet."
- 25:5, "bright."
- 26:9, "to spread out."
- 26:11, "to sway" or "to tremble."
- 26:11, "understanding."
- 26:13, "fair" or "beautiful."
- 28:15, "gold."
- 28:17, "glass."
- 28:17, "exchange."
- 28:18, "crystal."
- 29:18, "sand" or "Phoenix." Or "palm tree."
- 28:19, "pure gold."
- 29:30, "sulk."
- 30:4, "sea purslane."
- 30:6, "gullies" or "slopes."
- 30:8, "to cast out."

- 30:12, "brood of youth."
- 30:13, "to tear open."
- 30:15, "arrogance."
- 30:24, "pray" or "cry."
- 30:25, "to be sad."
- 30:25, "to bow down."
- 31:28, "a Judge's decision or action."
- 31:33, "bosom."
- 33:9, "clean."
- 33:20, "loathsome."
- 33:24, "deliver."
- 33:25, "fresh" or "green."
- 34:36, "O that."

Chapters 38–42

- 38:9, "swaddling clothes."
- 38:10, "spring."
- 38:16, "sources."
- 38:22, "Constellations."
- 38:26, "drop."
- 38:28, "a store of goods."
- 38:31, "band."
- 38:31, "bracelet" or "fetter."
- 38:32, "stars."
- 38:33, "domain."
- 38:36, "cock" or "rooster."
- 39:5, "wild ass."
- 39:18, "to paw the ground."
- 39:19, "horse's neck" or "mane."
- 39:20, "snorting."
- 39:23, "to rattle."
- 39:26, "to soar" or "fly."

- 39:30, "to drink."
- 40:12, "to tread down."
- 40:16, "muscle" or "sinew."
- 40:17, "to hang."
- 40:17, "rod."
- 40:18, "hammering stave."
- 40:31, "harpoon," or "sharp weapon."
- 40:31, "fish lance."
- 41:4, "graceful."
- 41:10, "torn out."
- 41:11, "spark."
- 41:11, "sneezings" or "nostrils."
- 41:14, "strength."
- 41:14, "to dance," or "to leap."
- 41:18, "sneezings."
- 41:18, "small arrow."
- 41:18, "error."
- 41:19, "leap."
- 41:19, "decay."
- 41:20, "nostrils."
- 41:21, "missiles," or "spike."
- 41:21, "club."
- 41:25, "similarity."
- 42:3, "to become dark" or "black."
- 42:13, "twice seven."

Aramaisms in the Book of Job

One feature that sets the book of Job apart from many other biblical works is the number of Arabic, Aramaic, Syriac, and Akkadian words phrases, and sentences in the book. Among scholars, these have come to be called "Aramaisms." Altogether, we have identified eighty-three Aramaisms. Among these Aramaisms are the following:

- 2:8, "to scratch" (Ugaritic).
- 2:22, "wrong" (Akkadian).
- 3:4, "day" (Arabic).
- 3:5, "gloom" (Aramaic).
- 3:7, "barren" or "sterile" (Arabic).
- 3:22, "shaking" or "shivers" (Aramaic).
- 4:15, "ruins" (Akkadian).
- 5:5, "baskets" (Aramaic).
- 5:22 and 30:3, "famine" (Aramaic).
- 6:2, "ruin" (Akkadian).
- 6:6, "unsavory" or "tasteless" (Aramaic).
- 7:5, "clods of earth" (Ethiopic).
- 9:4, "to prosper" (Aramaic).
- 8:17, "cleave in two" (Aramaic).
- 9:16, "wonders" (Akkadian).
- 9:26, "light cane ships" (Ugaritic).
- 10:10, "curd" or "cheese" (Arabic).
- 12:6, "perfect," or "accusations" (Aramaic).
- 12:12, "pronouncements" (Akkadian or Arabic).
- 13:7, "explication" (Aramaic).
- 13:17, "declare" (Arabic).
- 13:26, "hold account" (Aramaic).
- 15:29, "rich" (Aramaic).

- 15:34, "fruitless" (Arabic).
- 16:4, "shake my head" or "harangue" (Babylonian).
- 16:15, "skin" (Arabic).
- 16:19, "witness" (Aramaic).
- 17:1, "to extinguish" (Syriac/Ugaritic).
- 17:2, "mockeries" (Aramaic).
- 17:6, "to spit" (Aramaic).
- 17:10, "for" (Akkadian).
- 17:15; 19:6; 19:23; and 24:25, "now that" (Ugaritic).
- 17:19, "clean" (Aramaic).
- 18:3, "to be foolish," "demean" (Arabic).
- 18:20, "attaches" or "cements" (Aramaic).
- 19:3, "impudent" (Aramaic).
- 19:29, "demons" (Aramaic).
- 21:5, "desolation" (Aramaic).
- 21:10, "to impregnate" (Aramaic).
- 21:20, "condemnation" (Aramaic).
- 21:27, "contemplate" or "thoughts" (Syriac).
- 21:33 and 38:38, "clod" (Aramaic).
- 2:24 and 25, "gold and silver ore."
- 22:30, "not" (Arabic).
- 23:2, "hand" (Syriac).
- 23:11, "not turned aside" (Aramaic).
- 24:22, "his life" (Aramaic/Arabic).
- 24:24, "grass" (Arabic).
- 25:2, "dominion" (Akkadian).
- 25:13, "net" (Babylonian).
- 26:7, "nothing" (Ugaritic).
- 26:10, "circle" (Aramaic).
- 28:8, "crystal" (Akkadian).
- 28:17, "glass" (Ugaritic).
- 28:20, "channels" (Arabic).

- 29:4, "autumn days" (Akkadian).
- 30:3, "fruitless" (Arabic).
- 30:6, "gully" (Aramaic).
- 31:3, "misfortune," or "disaster" (Ugaritic).
- 31:33, "bosom" (Arabic).
- 31:33, "man" or "men" (Aramaic).
- 32:6, "to be shy" (Arabic).
- 32:10, "pretexts" (Syriac).
- 33:9, "clean" (Syriac).
- 33:11, "stocks" (Syriac).
- 33:24, "to free" (Aramaic).
- 33:25, "fresh" or "juicy" (Ugaritic).
- 34:4, "correct" or "right" (Aramaic).
- 34:25, "the doing" (Ugaritic).
- 35:15, "arrogance" (Arabic).
- 35:16, "to be great" (Ugaritic).
- 36:2, the entire line is Aramaic.
- 36:16, "distress" (Ugaritic).
- 36:18, "scorn" (Aramaic).
- 36:18, "look," or "beware" (Aramaic).
- 36:19, "forces" (Aramaic).
- 36:19, "cry for help" (Arabic).
- 36:22, "Master" or "God" (Aramaic).
- 36:29, "can any understand" (Aramaic).
- 36:33, "storm" (Aramaic).
- 37:11, "to burden" (Aramaic).
- 37:11, "fullness" (Ugaritic).
- 37:16, "wonder" (Ugaritic).
- 37:18, "mirror" (Akkadian).
- 37:19, "North winds" (Ugaritic).
- 38:24, "West Wind" (Akkadian).
- 38:28, "pools" (Arabic).

- 38:31, "cluster" (Ugaritic).
- 39:21 "strength" (Akkadian).
- 40:17, "drops" (Arabic).
- 40:25, "press down" (Aramaic).
- 41:7, "spears" (Akkadian).
- 41:7, "pride" (Aramaic).
- 41:12, "cauldron" (Aramaic).
- 41:14, "vigor" (Aramaic).

Of these 98 Aramaic, Arabic, Syriac, Ugaritic, and Akkadian words we have discovered in the book of Job, there are many more in ch. 28 and the Elihu Speeches than any other parts of the book. In fact, nearly half of the total. Indeed, in this sample of forty-six of the total ninety-eight, twenty-three are from those two sources. This may be another reason for suggesting that the Hymn to Wisdom and the Elihu Speeches were later additions to the book.

Endnotes

1. Vicchio, 1:95–116.
2. Vicchio, 1:158–76.
3. Vicchio, 1:130–31.
4. Vicchio, 1:119–22.
5. Vicchio, 1:158–76.
6. Vicchio, 1:158–76.
7. Vicchio, 1:158–76.
8. Vicchio, 1:158–76.
9. Vicchio, 1:158–76.
10. Vicchio, 1:158–76.
11. Vicchio, 1:158–76.
12. Vicchio, 1:158–76.
13. Vicchio, 1:158–76.
14. Vicchio, 1:158–76.
15. Vicchio, 1:158–76.
16. Vicchio, 1:139–57.
17. Vicchio, 1:139–57.
18. Vicchio, 1:139–57.
19. Vicchio, 1:139–57.
20. Vicchio, 1:139–57.
21. All in Simonetti and Conti, *Ancient Christian Commentary*.
22. All in Simonetti and Conti, *Ancient Christian Commentary*.
23. The Holy Qur'an 4:163.
24. The Holy Qur'an 6:84.
25. The Holy Qur'an 21:83–84.
26. The Holy Qur'an 38:41–44.
27. The Holy Qur'an 38:41–44.
28. Vicchio, *Sweet Uses of Adversity*, 56.
29. Vicchio, *Sweet Uses of Adversity*, 56.
30. Vicchio, 1:3.
31. Vicchio, 1:3.
32. Aristotle, *Generations of the Animals*.
33. Gaon, *Book of Theodicy*.
34. Gaon, *Book of Theodicy*, 97.

35 Vicchio, 2:87–115.
36 Vicchio, 2:87–115.
37 Vicchio, 2:87–115.
38 Vicchio, *Voice from the Whirlwind*, 129–30.
39 Vicchio, 2:87.
40 Vicchio, 2:90.
41 Vicchio, 2:95.
42 Vicchio, 2:91.
43 Vicchio, 2:91.
44 Vicchio, 2:91.
45 Vicchio, 2:91.
46 Vicchio, 2:92.
47 Vicchio, 2:92.
48 Vicchio, 2:92.
49 Vicchio, 2:92.
50 Vicchio, 2:93.
51 Vicchio, 2:100.
52 Vicchio, 2:100.
53 Vicchio, 2:101.
54 Rashi, quoted in Vicchio, 2:100.
55 Rashi, quoted in Vicchio, 2:100.
56 Rashi, quoted in Vicchio, 2:100.
57 Rashi, quoted in Vicchio, 2:100.
58 Rashi, quoted in Vicchio, 2:101.
59 Rashi, quoted in Vicchio, 2:101.
60 Rashi, quoted in Vicchio, 2:101.
61 Rashi, quoted in Vicchio, 2:101.
62 Rashi, quoted in Vicchio, 2:102.
63 Rashi, quoted in Vicchio, 2:102.
64 Rashi, quoted in Vicchio, 2:102.
65 Rashi, quoted in Vicchio, 2:102.
66 Rashi, quoted in Vicchio, 2:103.
67 Rashi, quoted in Vicchio, 2:103.
68 Rashi, quoted in Vicchio, 2:103.
69 Rashi, quoted in Vicchio, 1:101.
70 Rashi, quoted in Vicchio, 2:101.
71 Rashi, quoted in Vicchio, 2:101.
72 Rashi, quoted in Vicchio, 2:102.
73 Moses Maimonides, quoted in Vicchio, 2:107.
74 Vicchio, 2:114–15.
75 Vicchio, 2:114–15.

76. Vicchio, 2:114–15.
77. Vicchio, 2:112.
78. Vicchio, 2:112.
79. Vicchio, 2:112.
80. Vicchio, 2:112.
81. Vicchio, 2:112.
82. Vicchio, 2:112.
83. Vicchio, 2:113.
84. Vicchio, 2:113.
85. Vicchio, 2:113.
86. Vicchio, 2:113.
87. Aquinas, *Summa Theologica*, pt. 1, q. 2.
88. Laato, *Theodicy in the World of the Bible*, xxxviii.
89. Laato, *Theodicy in the World of the Bible*, xxxviii.
90. Laato, *Theodicy in the World of the Bible*, xxxviii.
91. Laato, *Theodicy in the World of the Bible*, xxxviii.
92. Gersonides, quoted in Vicchio, 2:114–15.
93. Gersonides, quoted in Vicchio, 2:114–15.
94. Gersonides, quoted in Vicchio, 2:116.
95. Gersonides, quoted in Vicchio, 2:116.
96. Gersonides, quoted in Vicchio, 2:116.
97. Gersonides, quoted in Vicchio, 2:115.
98. Gersonides, quoted in Vicchio, 2:116.
99. Gersonides, quoted in Vicchio, 2:116.
100. Gersonides, quoted in Vicchio, 2:116.
101. Gersonides, quoted in Vicchio, 2:117.
102. Gersonides, quoted in Vicchio, 2:117.
103. Gersonides, quoted in Vicchio, 2:118–19.
104. Gersonides, quoted in Vicchio, 2:119.
105. Gersonides, quoted in Vicchio, 2:119.
106. Gersonides, quoted in Vicchio, 2:118.
107. Gersonides, *On the Book of Job*.
108. All in Simonetti and Conti, *Ancient Christian Commentary*.
109. Vicchio, 2:7–8.
110. Vicchio, 2:12–13.
111. Vicchio, 2:12–13.
112. Vicchio, 2:13.
113. Vicchio, 2:13–14.
114. Vicchio, 2:15.
115. Vicchio, 2:20.
116. Job 14:4 KJV.

117 Job 14:4 KJV.
118 Augustine, *City of God*, book I, 23–24.
119 Augustine, *City of God*, book I, 23–24.
120 Augustine, *City of God*, book I, 23–24.
121 Ambrose, *Job and David*, quoted in Vicchio, 2:19.
122 Ambrose, *Job and David*, quoted in Vicchio, 2:19.
123 Gregory, quoted in Vicchio, 2:30.
124 Gregory, quoted in Vicchio, 2:30.
125 Gregory, quoted in Vicchio, 2:30.
126 Gregory, quoted in Vicchio, 2:31.
127 Gregory, quoted in Vicchio, 2:31.
128 Gregory, quoted in Vicchio, 2:33.
129 Gregory, quoted in Vicchio, 2:33.
130 Gregory, quoted in Vicchio, 2:34.
131 Gregory, quoted in Vicchio, 2:35.
132 Gregory, quoted in Vicchio, 2:35.
133 All in Simonetti and Conti, *Ancient Christian Commentary*.
134 Bessermann, *Legend of Job*, 72–73.
135 Bessermann, *Legend of Job*, 56.
136 Bessermann, *Legend of Job*, 76–79.
137 Bessermann, *Legend of Job*, 76–79.
138 Aquinas, quoted in Vicchio, 2:136–37.
139 Aquinas, quoted in Vicchio, 2:136–37.
140 Aquinas, quoted in Vicchio, 2:137.
141 Aquinas, quoted in Vicchio, 2:138.
142 Aquinas, quoted in Vicchio, 2:140.
143 Aquinas, quoted in Vicchio, 2:139.
144 Aquinas, quoted in Vicchio, 2:140.
145 Aquinas, quoted in Vicchio, 2:140.
146 Aquinas, quoted in Vicchio, 2:142–43.
147 Aquinas, quoted in Vicchio, 2:143.
148 Aquinas, quoted in Vicchio, 2:145–47.
149 Aquinas, quoted in Vicchio, 2:145.
150 Aquinas, quoted in Vicchio, 2:146.
151 Aquinas, quoted in Vicchio, 2:146–47.
152 Aquinas, quoted in Vicchio, 2:147.
153 Aquinas, quoted in Vicchio, 2:147.
154 Luther on Lyra, quoted in Vicchio, 2:148.
155 Luther on Lyra, quoted in Vicchio, 2:148.
156 Luther on Lyra, quoted in Vicchio, 2:148.
157 Luther on Lyra, quoted in Vicchio, 2:148.

158 Luther on Lyra, quoted in Vicchio, 2:148.
159 Luther on Lyra, quoted in Vicchio, 2:148.
160 Ibn Ishaaq, quoted in Vicchio, *Biblical Figures*, 115.
161 Al-Thabani, quoted in Vicchio, "Image of Ayyub," 4.
162 Al-Thabani, quoted in Vicchio, "Image of Ayyub," 5.
163 Al-Thabani, quoted in Vicchio, "Image of Ayyub," 5.
164 Al-Tabari, quoted in Vicchio, 2:75.
165 Al-Tabari, quoted in Vicchio, 2:75.
166 Al-Zamakhshari, quoted in Vicchio, 2:75.
167 Abn Asakir, quoted in Vicchio, 2:75.
168 Abn Asakir, quoted in Vicchio, 2:76.
169 Abn Asakir, quoted in Vicchio, 2:75.
170 Al-Hanbeli, quoted in Vicchio, 2:75–76.
171 Ibn Kathir, quoted in Vicchio, 2:75.
172 Al-Baydawi, quoted in Vicchio, 2:76.
173 Al-Baydawi, quoted in Vicchio, 2:76.
174 Al-Baydawi, quoted in Vicchio, 2:76.
175 Duran was a Spanish rabbi, as was Joseph Albo; Abravanel was Portuguese. He completed his Job commentary in 1517; Farissol was a French rabbi. His commentary was published in 1518; De' Sommi was also from France; Yagel was an Italian rabbi. Many of the quotes on Duran come from Eisen, *Book of Job*, 175–202.
176 Duran, *Ohev Mishpat*.
177 Duran, *Ohev Mishpat*.
178 Duran, *Ohev Mishpat*, 49.
179 Duran, *Ohev Mishpat*, 49.
180 Duran, *Ohev Mishpat*, 31.
181 Duran, *Ohev Mishpat*, 31.
182 Duran, *Ohev Mishpat*, 32.
183 Duran, *Ohev Mishpat*, 32.
184 Job 28:10 (Masoretic Text).
185 Duran, *Ohev Mishpat*, 111.
186 Albo, *Sefer Ha-'Ikkarim*, 2:36.
187 Albo, *Sefer Ha-'Ikkarim*, 2:235.
188 Albo, *Sefer Ha-'Ikkarim*, 2:236.
189 Albo, *Sefer Ha-'Ikkarim*, 1:17 and 4:291.
190 Albo, *Sefer Ha-'Ikkarim*, 2:200.
191 Abravanel, *Six Lectures*.
192 Abravanel, *Six Lectures*, 100.
193 Farissol, *Sefer Iyyov*.
194 Farissol, *Sefer Iyyov*, 143.
195 Farissol, *Sefer Iyyov*, 293.

ENDNOTES

196 Farissol, *Sefer Iyyov*, 256.
197 Farissol, *Sefer Iyyov*, 256.
198 Farissol, *Sefer Iyyov*, 338.
199 Farissol, *Sefer Iyyov*, 200.
200 Farissol, *Sefer Iyyov*, 177.
201 Farissol, *Sefer Iyyov*, 177.
202 Sommi, *Performing Arts*, 39.
203 Sommi, *Performing Arts*, 39.
204 Yagel, *Valley of Vision*, 259.
205 Yagel, *Valley of Vision*, 259.
206 Yagel, *Valley of Vision*, 260.
207 Vicchio, 3:34.
208 Vicchio, 3:34.
209 Vicchio, 3:34.
210 Spinoza, quoted in Vicchio, 3:35.
211 Spinoza, quoted in Vicchio, 3:35.
212 Spinoza, quoted in Vicchio, 3:35.
213 Spinoza, quoted in Vicchio, 3:36.
214 Spinoza, quoted in Vicchio, 3:36.
215 Spinoza, quoted in Vicchio, 3:36.
216 Vicchio, 2:214–15. All these sources can be found in Besserman, *Legend of Job*.
217 Vicchio, 2:214–15.
218 Vicchio, 2:242–43.
219 Calvin, quoted in Vicchio, 2:243.
220 Luther, quoted in Vicchio, 2:177.
221 Luther, quoted in Vicchio, 2:177.
222 Luther, quoted in Vicchio, 2:178.
223 Luther, quoted in Vicchio, 2:178.
224 Luther, quoted in Vicchio, 2:178.
225 Luther, quoted in Vicchio, 2:178.
226 Luther, quoted in Vicchio, 2:178.
227 Luther, quoted in Vicchio, 2:178.
228 Luther, quoted in Vicchio, 2:178.
229 Luther, quoted in Vicchio, 2:178.
230 Vicchio, 2:179.
231 Vicchio, 2:179.
232 Vicchio, 2:179.
233 Vicchio, 2:179.
234 Calvin, quoted in Vicchio, 2:184.
235 Calvin, quoted in Vicchio, 2:184.
236 Calvin, quoted in Vicchio, 2:186–87.

237 Calvin, quoted in Vicchio, 2:187.
238 Calvin, quoted in Vicchio, 2:187.
239 Calvin, quoted in Vicchio, 2:188.
240 Beza, quoted in Vicchio, 2:188.
241 Beza, quoted in Vicchio, 2:189.
242 Kallen, *Book of Job as a Greek Tragedy*.
243 Vicchio, 3:189.
244 Vicchio, 2:214–16.
245 Vicchio, 2:217.
246 Goldsmith, quoted in Vicchio, 3:217.
247 Vicchio, *Sweet Uses of Adversity*, 56.
248 Vicchio, *Sweet Uses of Adversity*, 56.
249 Vicchio, *Biblical Figures in the Islamic Faith*, 116–17.
250 Sale, quoted in Vicchio, *Biblical Figures*, 117.
251 Vicchio, 2:76.
252 Vicchio, "Image of Ayyub," 2–3.
253 Weitzstein, quoted in Vicchio, "Image of Ayyub," 3.
254 Weitzstein, quoted in Vicchio, "Image of Ayyub," 3.
255 Vicchio, 2:81.
256 Vicchio, 2:81.
257 Mendelssohn, *Philosophical Writings*, 277.
258 Mendelssohn, *Philosophical Writings*, 277.
259 Aaron Hale-Wolfssohn. The rabbi's Job commentary is out of print, but his play, where he also speaks of Iyyov, in the introduction, the rabbi speaks of the Man from Uz.
260 Ottenhosser, *Das Buch Hiob*.
261 Ottenhosser, *Das Buch Hiob*.
262 Mendelssohn, *Hiob Cantata* (1831). Thorofon Records published an e-print of the score in 1998.
263 Vicchio, 3:168–69.
264 Vicchio, 2:82–86.
265 Vicchio, 2:89–90.
266 Vicchio, 2:89–90.
267 Vicchio, 3:95–96.
268 Vicchio, 3:100–15.
269 Vicchio, 3:128–29.
270 Vicchio, 3:144–48.
271 Vicchio, 3:158–62.
272 Vicchio, 3:158–62.
273 Vicchio, 3:158–62.
274 Susman, *Book of Job*, in Glatzer, *Dimensions of Job*, 86–92.
275 Zapffe, *Om det tragiske*.

276 Vicchio, 2:217–18.
277 Dhorme, *Le Livre de Job* (Paris, 1926).
278 Vicchio, 3:163–65.
279 Rudolph Otto, in Glatzer, *Dimensions of Job*, 225–27.
280 Gilbert Murray, in Glatzer, *Dimensions of Job*, 194–96.
281 G. K. Chesterton, in Glatzer, *Dimensions of Job*, 228–36.
282 Vicchio, 3:177–78.
283 Vicchio, 3:181.
284 Vicchio, 2:224–26.
285 Vicchio, 2:219.
286 Vicchio, 2:219.
287 Kafka, *The Trial*.
288 Vicchio, 2:228–29.
289 Vicchio, 2:219.
290 Vicchio, 2:222–26.
291 Vicchio, 2:222–26.
292 *Critical Perspectives on the Book of Job*. Vicchio, 2:227.
293 *Critical Perspectives on the Book of Job*. Vicchio, 2:227.
294 Glatzer, *Dimensions of Job*.
295 Vicchio, 3:177–88.
296 Clines, *Book of Job*.
297 Lewis, *Viktor Frankl and the Book of Job*.
298 Dhorme, *Le Livre de Job*.
299 W. F. Albright, "Islam and the Religions of the Ancient Orient," *Bulletin of the American Schools of Oriental Research* 9.3.
300 W. M. Flinders Petrie, *The Tell el Amarna Letters* (London: Forgotten Books, 2016), 112.
301 "Job," in Orr, *International Standard Bible Encyclopedia*, 240; Hitchcock, *Bible Names Dictionary*.
302 Terrien, *Job*, 908.
303 Ewald, *Commentary on the Book of Job*, 84.
304 Gordis, *Book of God and Man*, 66–67.
305 Fohrer, quoted in Rowley, *Job*, 29.
306 Gregory, quoted in Vicchio, 2:33–34.
307 Lam 4:21 RSV.
308 Vicchio, "Image of Ayyub," 2–3.
309 Zuck, *Sitting with Job*, 245–47.
310 Rowley, *Job*, 28.
311 Moritz, *Das Buch Hiob*, 18.
312 Gregory, quoted in Vicchio, 2:30.
313 Josephus, *Antiquities*, 31.
314 Vicchio, "Image of Ayyub," 1–4.

315 Dhorme, "Le Pays de Job."
316 Tur-Sinai, *Sefer Iyyob*, note on 1:1.
317 Pope, *Job*, 3–4.
318 Dhorme, *Le Livre de Job*, xxv.
319 Jerome, *Collected Works*, 2233.
320 Saadiah, *Book of Theodicy*, 174.
321 Luther, "Preface to the Old Testament," 235.
322 Luther, "Preface to the Old Testament," 235. Pope, *Job*, 1.
323 Pope, *Job*, 1.
324 Dhorme, *Le Livre de Job*, xxv.
325 Gersonides, *On the Book of Job*, 13.
326 Terrien, *Job*, 909; Gibson, *Book of Job*, 42.
327 Rashi, in Rosenberg, *Job*, 11.
328 Wesley, *Explanatory Notes*, 444–45.
329 Geneva Bible, 339.
330 Clines, *Book of Job*, 2.
331 Zuckerman, *Job the Silent*, 13; Rodd, *Book of Job*, 1; Habel, *Book of Job*, 11.
332 Scheindlin, *Book of Job*, 55.
333 Freehof, *Book of Job*, 55.
334 Clarke, *Commentary on Job*, 3.
335 Rowley, *Job*, 28; Bergant, *Israel's Wisdom Literature*, 15; Wilcox, *Bitterness of Job*, 55.
336 Gregory, *Moral Reflections*, 11.
337 Aquinas, *Commentary on the Book of Job*, 138–39.
338 Driver and Gray, *Book of Job*, 119.
339 Aquinas, *Commentary on the Book of Job*, 139.
340 Olympiodorus, quoted in Simonetti and Conti, *Ancient Christian Commentary*, 15.
341 All listed in Vicchio, 2:33–35.
342 Pope, *Job*, 1 and 10.
343 Philo, 17.
344 Gammie, "Angelology."
345 Philo, 17.
346 Dhorme, *Le Livre de Job*, 22.
347 Leveque, *Job et Son Dieu*.
348 Rashi, in Rosenberg, *Job*, 7.
349 Morgenstern, "Mythological Background," 4.
350 *Targum on Iyyov* (Tel Aviv, 1972).
351 Hesychius, quoted in Simonetti and Conti, *Ancient Christian Commentary*, 5.
352 Julian of Eclanum quoted in Simonetti and Conti, *Ancient Christian Commentary*, 5.
353 Ishodad, quoted in Simonetti and Conti, *Ancient Christian Commentary*, 230.
354 Aquinas, quoted in Vicchio, 2:140.
355 Rashi, in Rosenberg, *Job*, 12.

356 Saadiah, quoted in Vicchio, 2:91.
357 Saadiah, quoted in Vicchio, 2:91.
358 Cowles, *Book of Job*, 244.
359 Scott, *Book of Job*, 9.
360 Umbreit, *Book of Job*, 9.
361 Kelly, *Book of Job*, 12.
362 McFadyen, *Problem of Pain*, 16.
363 Peake, *Job*, 22.
364 Devine, *Problem of Pain*, 12.
365 Walkley, *Commentary on the Book of Job*, 8.
366 Pope, *Job*, 10–11.
367 Gibson, *Book of Job*, 21.
368 Freehof, *Book of Job*, 41.
369 Jung, *Answer to Job*, 1–32.
370 Targum of Job.
371 Ephrem, quoted in Simonetti and Conti, *Ancient Christian Commentary*, 9.
372 Schultens, *Liber Jobi*, 1:23.
373 All on Rowley, *Job*, 37.
374 All on Rowley, *Job*, 37.
375 All on Rowley, *Job*, 37.
376 All on Rowley, *Job*, 37.
377 Noyes, *Book of Job*, 14.
378 Good, *Commentary on the Book of Job*, 17.
379 Watson, *Book of Job*, 19–20.
380 Watson, *Book of Job*, 19–20.
381 Barnes, *Book of Job*, 27.
382 Barnes, *Book of Job*, 27.
383 Bernard, *Le Livre de Job*, 15; Davidson, *Book of Job*, xx.
384 Freehof, *Book of Job*, 50.
385 Umbreit, *Book of Job*, 10.
386 Duhm, *Das Buch Hiob*, 11; Calmet, *Commentary on the Book of Job*, 9.
387 Clines, *Job 1–20*, 43.
388 Dhorme, *Le Livre de Job*, 14.
389 Gregory, quoted in Simonetti and Conti, *Ancient Christian Commentary*, 11.
390 Saadiah, *Book of Theodicy*, 173–74.
391 Julian, quote in Simonetti and Conti, *Ancient Christian Commentary*, 11.
392 Olympiodorus, quoted in Simonetti and Conti, *Ancient Christian Commentary*, 11.
393 Ishodad, quoted in Simonetti and Conti, *Ancient Christian Commentary*, 12.
394 Holscher, *Das Buch Hiob*, 15.
395 Peloubet, *Book of Job*, 19.
396 Peloubet, *Book of Job*, 19.

397 Cox, *Commentary on the Book of Job*, 23.

398 Peloubet, *Book of Job*, 10.

399 Gordis, *Book of Job*, 4.

400 Gray, quoted in Rowley, *Job*, 34.

401 Aquinas, quoted in Vicchio, 2:138–39.

402 Good, *In Turns of Tempest*, 52.

403 1 Kgs 20:30 and 22:25.

404 Hos 5:13.

405 Deut 28:27.

406 Deut 28:35.

407 Lev 18:18–23.

408 Vicchio, 2:239.

409 Vicchio, 2:239.

410 Vicchio, 2:241.

411 Vicchio, 2:241.

412 Vicchio, 2:241.

413 Vicchio, 2:241–42.

414 Vicchio, 2:241–42.

415 Kinnier Wilson, as quoted in Pope, *Job*, 21–22.

416 Vicchio, 2:242.

417 Vicchio, 2:243.

418 Vicchio, 2:243.

419 Vicchio, 2:244.

420 Vicchio, 2:244–45.

421 Vicchio, 2:245.

422 Vicchio, 2:245.

423 Vicchio, 2:246.

424 Vicchio, 2:245.

425 Vicchio, 2:248.

426 Vicchio, 2:248.

427 Cauley, "Job's Affliction," 1104.

428 Kutz, "Job and His Doctors," 1616.

429 Resende, "Solving the Conundrum of Job," 1616.

430 Drexelius, quoted in Vicchio, 2:250–51.

431 Drexelius, quoted in Vicchio, 2:250–51.

432 Cox, *Commentary on the Book of Job*, 41.

433 Augustine, quoted in Simonetti and Conti, *Ancient Christian Commentary*, 14.

434 Chrysostom, quoted in Simonetti and Conti, *Ancient Christian Commentary*, 14.

435 Gregory, quoted in Vicchio, 2:32.

436 Thomas, quoted in Vicchio, 2:xx.

437 Bernard of Clairvaux, *Steps of Humility*, 41.

438 Dhorme, *Le Livre de Job*, 17.
439 Clines, *Job 1-20*, xlix, and 51-52.
440 Royds, *Job and the Problem of Suffering*, 29.
441 Gen 34:7 RSV.
442 LXX, p. 27.
443 Hesychius, quoted in Simonetti and Conti, *Ancient Christian Commentary*, 13.
444 *Midrash Rabbah* on *Genesis*, 19:12.
445 Targum of Job, p. 21; *Divrei Iyyov*, p. 23.
446 Meir Tam, quoted in Eisen, *Book of Job*, 120.
447 Zerahiah Hen, quoted in Eisen, *Book of Job*, 120.
448 Zerahiah Hen, quoted in Eisen, *Book of Job*, 120.
449 Nachmanides, quoted in Eisen, *Book of Job*, 114.
450 Heschel, *Prophets*, 158.
451 See Vicchio, 2:74-80.
452 Emmerich, *Life of the Blessed Virgin*, 100.
453 Sale, quoted in Vicchio, 2:76.
454 See Vicchio, 2:78.
455 "Mirror of Human Salvation," at l'Agence photograhique de vi Reunion de mussees Nationaux (14th c.).
456 Albecht Dürer, "Job and His Wife" (1604; Frankfurt State Museum).
457 MacLeish, quoted in Vicchio, 2:224.
458 Spark, quoted in Vicchio, 2:221.
459 Habel, *Book of Job*, 96.
460 Terrien, *Job*, 25-26.
461 Davidson, *Book of Job*, 46.
462 Delitzsch, *Biblical Commentary on the Book of Job*, xx.
463 Watson, *Book of Job*, 55.
464 Kierkegaard, quoted in Flatzer, 260.
465 Devine, *Problem of Pain*, 31.
466 Devine, *Problem of Pain*, 31.
467 Schultens, *Liber Jobi*, 1:49; Noyes, *Book of Job*, 50.
468 Hutchinson, *Commentary on the Book of Job*, 23.
469 Driver and Gray, *Book of Job*, 24-25.
470 Martin Buber, quoted in Glatzer, *Dimensions of Job*, 58.
471 Pope, *Job*, 19-21.
472 Clines, *Job 1-20*, 50-51.
473 Clines, *Job 1-20*, 50-51.
474 Yalom, *History of the Wife*, 117.
475 Crenshaw, *Reading Job*, 45.
476 Jer 20:14-15 RSV.
477 Babylonian Talmud, 16a.

478 Jerome, "Prologue to the Translation of Job," *Vulgate*.
479 Aquinas, https//:ahspriority.org/Thomas/Aquinas/englis//ssjob/html./#031.
480 Calvin, *Sermons from Job*, 45.
481 Henry, *Commentary on the Holy Bible*, 220.
482 Hartley, *Book of Job*, 88–89.
483 Dhorme, quoted in Rowley, *Job*, 41.
484 Freedman, "Structure of Job Three," 504–5.
485 Westermann, *Structure of the Book of Job*, 8–9.
486 Simundson, *Message of Job*, 46–47.
487 Simundson, *Message of Job*, 46–47.
488 Jordan, *Commentary on the Book of Job*, 27.
489 Fredericton, *Book of Job*, 29–30.
490 Tsevat, "Meaning of the Book of Job," 79–80.
491 Pope, *Job*, 27–28.
492 Fullerton, "Double Entendre," 324–25.
493 Stevenson, *Critical Notes*, 46.
494 Ibn Ezra, *Job*, 122.
495 Ewald, *Commentary on the Book of Job*, 104–5.
496 Driver, quoted in Rowley, *Job*, 50–51.
497 Clines, *Job 1–20*, 36. Dhorme, *Le Livre de Job*, xx.
498 Vicchio, 1:181.
499 Clines, *Job 1–20*, 36.
500 Thomas, *Book of Job*, xx.
501 Phillips, "Speaking Truthfully," 43.
502 Phillips, "Speaking Truthfully," 43.
503 Wesley, 1292.
504 Wesley, 1292.
505 Gibbs, *Job and the Mysteries of Wisdom*, 93.
506 Mezudat David, in Rosenberg, *Job*, 66.
507 Rashi, in Rosenberg, *Job*, 66.
508 Rashi, in Rosenberg, *Job*, 66.
509 Henry, *Commentary on the Holy Bible*, 111.
510 Rashi, in Rosenberg, *Job*, 67.
511 Mezudat David, in Rosenberg, *Job*, 67.
512 Rashi, in Rosenberg, *Job*, 67.
513 Rashi and Ibn Ezra, in Rosenberg, *Job*, 67.
514 Sokoloff, *Targum to Job*, 49. Calvin, quoted in Vicchio, 2:185.
515 Stevenson, *Poem of Job*, 38.
516 Burrell, *Deconstructing Theodicy*, 28.
517 Driver and Gray, quoted in Rowley, *Job*, 67.
518 Rabbi Rav, BB. 16a.

519 Henry, *Commentary on the Holy Bible*, 121.
520 Driver and Gray, quoted in Rowley, *Job*, 68.
521 Wesley, 1303.
522 Umbreit, *Book of Job*, 61.
523 Driver and Gray, quoted in Rowley, *Job*, 68.
524 Driver and Gray, quoted in Rowley, *Job*, 68.
525 Mezudat David, in Rosenberg, *Job*, 72.
526 Rashi, in Rosenberg, *Job*, 72.
527 Ibn Ezra, *Job*, 72–73.
528 Gregory, quoted in Simonetti and Conti, *Ancient Christian Commentary*, 34.
529 Driver and Gray, quoted in Rowley, *Job*, 69.
530 Umbreit, *Book of Job*, 62.
531 Reichert, *Job*, 59.
532 Rodd, *Book of Job*, 19.
533 Henry, *Commentary on the Holy Bible*, 123.
534 Peake, quoted in Rowley, *Job*, 70.
535 Tyndale, *Old Testament Commentaries*, 41.
536 Driver and Gray, quoted in Rowley, *Job*, 72.
537 Gensius, *Hebrew Grammar*, 100; Umbreit, *Book of Job*, 63.
538 Gregory, quoted in Simonetti and Conti, *Ancient Christian Commentary*, 36–37.
539 Driver and Gray, quoted in Rowley, *Job*, 72.
540 Rodd, *Book of Job*, 19.
541 Henry, *Commentary on the Holy Bible*, 125.
542 Ibn Ezra, *Job*, 74.
543 Peake, *Job*, 42–43.
544 Wesley, 1309.
545 Umbreit, *Book of Job*, 64.
546 Driver and Gray, quoted in Rowley, *Job*, 73.
547 Umbreit, *Book of Job*, 65.
548 Rashi, in Rosenberg, *Job*, 73.
549 Gregory, quoted in Simonetti and Conti, *Ancient Christian Commentary*, 38–39.
550 Burrell, *Deconstructing Theodicy*, 29.
551 Driver and Gray, *Book of Job*, 74.
552 Rodd, *Book of Job*, 19–20.
553 Buttenwieser, quoted in Rowley, *Job*, 75.
554 Rodd, *Book of Job*, 20.
555 Rodd, *Book of Job*, 20.
556 Ibn Ezra, *Job*, 75.
557 Mezudat David, in Rosenberg, *Job*, 75.
558 Rashi, in Rosenberg, *Job*, 75.
559 Moses Maimonides, quoted in Vicchio, 2:111.

560 Saadiah, *Book of Theodicy*, 206.
561 Rashi, in Rosenberg, *Job*, 76.
562 Saadiah, *Book of Theodicy*, 206.
563 Mezudat David, in Rosenberg, *Job*, 76.
564 Kissane, quoted in Rowley, *Job*, 81.
565 Rowley, *Job*, 77.
566 Driver and Gray, quoted in Rowley, *Job*, 78.
567 Buttenwieser, quoted in Rowley, *Job*, 78.
568 Saadiah, *Book of Theodicy*, xx.
569 Rowley, *Job*, 77.
570 Clines, *Job 1–20*, 74.
571 Browning, "Bishop Orders His Tomb," 57–60.
572 Sophocles, *Electra*, 192.
573 Peake, quoted in Rowley, *Job*, 79.
574 Kissane, quoted in Rowley, *Job*, 79.
575 Pope, *Job*, 60.
576 Ibn Ezra, *Job*, 77.
577 Driver and Gray, quoted in Rowley, *Job*, 79.
578 Ibn Ezra, *Job*, 77.
579 Pope, *Job*, 60.
580 Pope, *Job*, 60.
581 Rashi, in Rosenberg, *Job*, 77.
582 Ishodad, quoted in Simonetti and Conti, *Ancient Christian Commentary*, 41–42.
583 Saadiah, *Book of Theodicy*, 208.
584 Newsom, *Book of Job*, 133–34.
585 Clines, *Job 1–20*, 167–68.
586 Wray, *Book of Job*, 49.
587 McFadyen, *Problem of Pain*, 51.
588 Clines, *Job 1–20*, 167.
589 Clines, *Job 1–20*, 167.
590 Baba Batra, 16a.
591 Rowley, *Job*, 79.
592 Baba Batra, 16a.
593 Driver and Gray, quoted in Rowley, *Job*, 79.
594 John Chrysostom, quoted in Simonetti and Conti, *Ancient Christian Commentary*, 43.
595 Gregory, quoted in Simonetti and Conti, *Ancient Christian Commentary*, 43.
596 Kissane, *Book of Job*, 81.
597 Peake, quoted in Rowley, *Job*, 88.
598 Rashi, in Rosenberg, *Job*, 80.
599 Freehof, *Book of Job*, 41.
600 Fredericton, *Book of Job*, 45.

ENDNOTES

601 Fredericton, *Book of Job*, 45.
602 Simundson, *Message of Job*, 57–58.
603 Mezudat David, in Rosenberg, *Job*, 80.
604 Driver and Gray, quoted in Peake, *Job*, 88.
605 Ewald, *Commentary on the Book of Job*, 120–21.
606 Albright, "Name of Bildad," 31–32.
607 Delitzsch, *Biblical Commentary on the Book of Job*, 1:63.
608 Delitzsch, *Biblical Commentary on the Book of Job*, 1:63.
609 Albright, "Name of Bildad," 330–34.
610 Lowth, *Lectures on Sacred Poetry*, 206.
611 *La Patience de Job*, 11–12.
612 Saadiah, *Book of Theodicy*, 207.
613 Maimonides, Ibn Tibbon, xx.
614 Tur-Sinai, *Book of Job*, 55.
615 Tur-Sinai, *Book of Job*, 55.
616 Freehof, *Book of Job*, 84–85.
617 Tur-Sinai, *Book of Job*, 56.
618 Gordis, *Book of Job*, 100.
619 Gordis, *Book of Job*, 145.
620 Scheindlin, *Book of Job*, 57.
621 John Chrysostom, quoted in Simonetti and Conti, *Ancient Christian Commentary*, 44.
622 John Chrysostom, quoted in Simonetti and Conti, *Ancient Christian Commentary*, 44.
623 Julian, quoted in Simonetti and Conti, *Ancient Christian Commentary*, 45.
624 Aquinas, quoted in Vicchio, 2:114.
625 Calvin, quoted in Vicchio, 2:185.
626 Didymus the Blind, in Simonetti and Conti, *Ancient Christian Commentary*, 44–45.
627 Julian, quoted in Simonetti and Conti, *Ancient Christian Commentary*, 44–45.
628 Julian, quoted in Simonetti and Conti, *Ancient Christian Commentary*, 44–45.
629 Spanheim, *Das Buch Hiob*; Shultens, *Das Buch Hiob*.
630 Michaelis, *Das Buch Hiob*, 48.
631 Clines, *Job 1-20*, 197–98.
632 Rowley, *Job*, 83.
633 Barnes, *Book of Job*, 47.
634 Scott, *Book of Job*, 51.
635 Bode, *Book of Job*, 53.
636 Didymus the Blind, in Simonetti and Conti, *Ancient Christian Commentary*, 47.
637 Philip the Priest, in Simonetti and Conti, *Ancient Christian Commentary*, 47.
638 Hesychius, quoted in Simonetti and Conti, *Ancient Christian Commentary*, 47.
639 Olympiodorus, in Simonetti and Conti, *Ancient Christian Commentary*, 47.
640 Philip, the Priest, in Simonetti and Conti, *Ancient Christian Commentary*, 47.
641 Gregory in Simonetti and Conti, *Ancient Christian Commentary*, 47–48.

642 Saadiah, *Book of Theodicy*, 211.
643 All quoted in Rowley, *Job*, 83–84.
644 Prov 10:7b RSV.
645 See, for examples, Isa 24:8; 32:13 and 14.
646 LXX (author's translation); Driver, *Book of Job*, 101.
647 Jastrow, *Book of Job*, 63.
648 Tur-Sinai, *Book of Job*, 53.
649 Gordis, *Book of Job*, 59.
650 NIV, "wither away." NEB, "sin."
651 Clines, *Job 1–20*, 200.
652 Rashi, in Rosenberg, *Job*, 93.
653 Holscher, *Das Buch Hiob*, 60.
654 Mezudat David, in Rosenberg, *Job*, 87.
655 Simundson, *Message of Job*, 58.
656 Henry, *Commentary on the Holy Bible*, 151.
657 Newsom, "Job and His Friends," 154–55.
658 Rowley, *Job*, 89–90.
659 Newsom, "Job and His Friends," 156.
660 Newsom, "Job and His Friends," 156.
661 Newsom, "Job and His Friends," 156.
662 McFadyen, *Problem of Pain*, 68.
663 Kissane, *Book of Job*, 60.
664 Hartley, *Book of Job*, 165.
665 Gordis, *Book of Job*, 67.
666 Freehof, *Book of Job*, 60.
667 Maimonides, *Guide to the Perplexed*, 153.
668 Duhm, *Das Buch Hiob*, 67; Hartley, *Book of Job*, 167; Mezudat David, in Rosenberg, *Job*, 88.
669 Rashi, in Rosenberg, *Job*, 82.
670 Dhorme, *Le Livre de Job*, 77.
671 Kissane, *Book of Job*, 61.
672 Aquinas, 188.
673 Driver and Gray, quoted in Rowley, *Job*, 91.
674 Gordis, *Book of Job*, 70.
675 Pope, *Job*, 70.
676 Chrysostom, quoted in Simonetti and Conti, *Ancient Christian Commentary*, 50.
677 Pope, *Job*, 70.
678 Dhorme, quoted in Rowley, *Job*, 92.
679 Mezudat David, in Rosenberg, *Job*, 90.
680 Mezudat David, in Rosenberg, *Job*, 90.
681 Rowley, *Job*, 92.
682 Ball, quoted in Rowley, *Job*, 92.

683 Gregory, quoted in Simonetti and Conti, *Ancient Christian Commentary*, 50.
684 Driver and Gray, quoted in Rowley, *Job*, 92.
685 Dhorme, quoted in Rowley, *Job*, 92.
686 Maimonides, *Guide to the Perplexed*, 59.
687 Gordis, *Book of Job*, 68.
688 Targum, Peshitta, and Septuagint, on 9:9.
689 Rashi, in Rosenberg, *Job*, 95; Driver and Gray, quoted in Rowley, *Job*, 92–93.
690 All quoted in Rowley, *Job*, 93.
691 Rowley, *Job*, 93.
692 Rabbi Gra [Zalman], *Rav Pe'alim*, 36.
693 Rabbi Jahiel, *Buch Iyyov*, 41.
694 Gregory, quoted in Simonetti and Conti, *Ancient Christian Commentary*, 51.
695 Rashi, in Rosenberg, *Job*, 93.
696 Pope, *Job*, 71.
697 Targum of Job, 14.
698 Mezudat David, in Rosenberg, *Job*, 91; Trani, *Sefer Iyyov*, 27.
699 Rashi, in Rosenberg, *Job*, 83. Trani, *Sefer Iyyov*, 30.
700 Kissane, quoted in Rowley, *Job*, 96.
701 Newsom, *Book of Job*, 159.
702 Barton, *Commentary on the Book of Job*, 61.
703 Rashi, in Rosenberg, *Job*, 96.
704 Mezudat David, in Rosenberg, *Job*, 91.
705 Ewald, *Commentary on the Book of Job*, 137.
706 Buttenwieser, quoted in Rowley, *Job*, 94.
707 Rashi, in Rosenberg, *Job*, 96.
708 Barton, *Commentary on the Book of Job*, 61.
709 Rashi, in Rosenberg, *Job*, 93; Mezudat David, in Rosenberg, *Job*, 92.
710 Buttenwieser, quoted in Rowley, *Job*, 94.
711 Ewald, *Commentary on the Book of Job*, 125.
712 Thomas, quoted in Vicchio, 2:115.
713 Buttenwieser, quoted in Rowley, *Job*, 94.
714 Thomas, quoted in Vicchio, 2:115. Buttenwieser, quoted in Rowley, *Job*, 94.
715 Rashi, in Rosenberg, *Job*, 93.
716 Mezudat David, in Rosenberg, *Job*, 91.
717 Ewald, *Commentary on the Book of Job*, 138.
718 Buttenwieser, quoted in Rowley, *Job*, 94.
719 Barton, *Commentary on the Book of Job*, 64.
720 Habel, *Book of Job*, 182.
721 Gordis, *Book of Job*, 70.
722 Habel, *Book of Job*, 183.
723 Barton, *Commentary on the Book of Job*, 65.

724 Ewald, *Commentary on the Book of Job*, 126.
725 Buttenwieser, *Book of Job*, 95.
726 Habel, *Book of Job*, 183.
727 Gordis, *Book of Job*, 71.
728 Mezudat David, in Rosenberg, *Job*, 93.
729 LXX, p. 111.
730 Hesychius, quoted in Simonetti and Conti, *Ancient Christian Commentary*, 53–54.
731 Watson, *Book of Job*, 77.
732 Noyes, *Book of Job*, 70.
733 Julian of Eclanum, quoted in Simonetti and Conti, *Ancient Christian Commentary*, 54.
734 Lowth, *Lectures on Sacred Poetry*, 112.
735 John Chrsostom, quoted in Simonetti and Conti, *Ancient Christian Commentary*, 55.
736 Gregory, quoted in Simonetti and Conti, *Ancient Christian Commentary*, 55.
737 Saadiah, *Book of Theodicy*, 109.
738 Dhorme, quoted in Rowley, *Job*, 98.
739 Dhorme, quoted in Rowley, *Job*, 98.
740 Peloubet, *Book of Job*, 72.
741 Calmet, *Commentary on the Book of Job*.
742 Hugo, *La Fin de Satan*, 43.
743 Dhorme, *Le Livre de Job*, 144–45.
744 Ibn Ezra, *Job*, 99.
745 Le Hir, *Le Livre de Job*, 77.
746 Fredericton, *Book of Job*, 51.
747 Kelly, *Book of Job*, 73.
748 Bode, *Book of Job*, 79.
749 Freehof, *Book of Job*, 174.
750 Jantzen, *Job*, 87.
751 Gordis, *Book of Job*, 72.
752 Ewald, *Commentary on the Book of Job*, 142–43.
753 Ewald, *Commentary on the Book of Job*, 143.
754 Bickell, Loisy, and Duhm, quoted in Rowley, *Job*, 100–101.
755 Bickell, Loisy, and Duhm, quoted in Rowley, *Job*, 100–101.
756 Bickell, Loisy, and Duhm, quoted in Rowley, *Job*, 100–101.
757 LXX, 10:1–2.
758 KJV, 10:1–2.
759 RSV, 10:1–2.
760 NIV, 10:1–2.
761 LXX, 10:2.
762 KJV, 10:2.
763 RSV, 10:2.
764 NIV, 10:2.

765 Dhorme, *Le Livre de Job*, 146–47. Reichert, *Job*, 60.
766 Barton, *Commentary on the Book of Job*, 68.
767 Rashi, in Rosenberg, *Job*, 98.
768 Reichert, *Job*, 60.
769 Barton, *Commentary on the Book of Job*, 63.
770 Barton, *Commentary on the Book of Job*, 63.
771 Newsom, *Book of Job*, 158.
772 Dhorme, Holscher, and Fohrer, all quoted in Rowley, *Job*, 100–101.
773 Habel, *Book of Job*, 198–99.
774 Ball, quoted in Rowley, *Job*, 101.
775 Barton, quoted in Rowley, *Job*, 101.
776 Barton, quoted in Rowley, *Job*, 101.
777 Reichert, *Job*, 61.
778 Rashi, in Rosenberg, *Job*, 98.
779 Habel, *Book of Job*, 198.
780 Dhorme, *Le Livre de Job*, 148.
781 Newsom, *Book of Job*, 159.
782 Newsom, *Book of Job*, 159.
783 Dhorme, *Le Livre de Job*, 148–49.
784 Jastrow, *Book of Job*, 49.
785 Habel, *Book of Job*, 198.
786 Barton, *Commentary on the Book of Job*, 64.
787 Gordis, *Book of Job*, 75.
788 Dhorme, *Le Livre de Job*, 154.
789 Szold, *Sefer Iyyov*, 48.
790 Newsom, *Book of Job*, 160.
791 Habel, *Book of Job*, 200.
792 Hesychius, quoted in Simonetti and Conti, *Ancient Christian Commentary*, 59.
793 Hartley, *Book of Job*, 64.
794 Rowley, *Job*, 104.
795 Ehrlich and Dhorme, quoted in Rowley, *Job*, 104.
796 Pope, *Job*, 81.
797 Budde, Duhm, Gray, Holscher, and Steinmann, all quoted in Rowley, *Job*, 104.
798 Barton, *Commentary on the Book of Job*, 66.
799 Habel, *Book of Job*, 200–201.
800 Hartley, *Book of Job*, 65.
801 Rashi, in Rosenberg, *Job*, 99.
802 Mezudat David, in Rosenberg, *Job*, 99.
803 Barton, *Commentary on the Book of Job*, 67.
804 Rowley, *Job*, 104.
805 Hartley, *Book of Job*, 65.

806   Reichert, *Job*, 65.
807   Dhorme, *Le Livre de Job*, 154.
808   Dhorme, *Le Livre de Job*, 154.
809   Hartley, *Book of Job*, 66.
810   Barton, *Commentary on the Book of Job*, 67.
811   Barton, *Commentary on the Book of Job*, 67.
812   Schultens, *Liber Jobi*, 2:66.
813   Rashi, in Rosenberg, *Job*, 100.
814   Peshitta and Septuagint, 10:22.
815   Rowley, *Job*, 105.
816   Driver, quoted in Rowley, *Job*, 105.
817   Dhorme, *Le Livre de Job*, 155.
818   Newsom, *Book of Job*, 162.
819   Septuagint, Vulgate, 11:1–2.
820   *La Patience de Job*, quoted in Besserman, *Legend of Job*, 65.
821   Strong, *Exhaustive Concordance*, 1510.
822   Lowth, *Lectures on Sacred Poetry*, 91.
823   Rabbi Gra and Ibn Ezra, 101.
824   2 Kgs 5.
825   Abba ben Kahana, *Derushim*, 93.
826   Baba Batra, 16a and 16b.
827   Maimonides, *Guide to the Perplexed*, 47.
828   Maimonides, *Guide to the Perplexed*, 47.
829   Naaman, six miles south of Lydda, in contemporary Israel.
830   1 Kgs 14:21 and 31 RSV.
831   Gordis, *Book of Job*, 83.
832   Hartley, *Book of Job*, 67.
833   Franz Delitzsch, in Rowley, *Job*, 105.
834   Moses Maimonides, 100.
835   Reichert, *Job*, 66.
836   Gersonides, *On the Book of Job*, 74–75.
837   Gersonides, *On the Book of Job*, 74–75.
838   Hartley, *Book of Job*, 70.
839   Gutiérrez, *On Job*, 47.
840   Quiller-Couch, quoted in Mason, *Gospel according to Job*, 41.
841   Goldsmith, "Healing Scourge," 7–8.
842   Maimonides, *Guide to the Perplexed*, 49.
843   Manesseh ben Israel, 94.
844   Calvin, *Sermons from Job*, 52.
845   James Tissot, "Zophar Condemns Job" (1885).
846   Dallpiccola, Luigi, "Giobbe" (1950).

847 MacLeish, *J.B.*, 27.
848 Saadiah, *Book of Theodicy*, 218.
849 Pope, *Job*, 84.
850 Gersonides, *On the Book of Job*, 74–75.
851 Gersonides, *On the Book of Job*, 74–75.
852 Newsom, *Book of Job*, 164.
853 Aquinas, 127.
854 Masoretic Text, 11:4b.
855 Dhorme, *Le Livre de Job*, 158–59.
856 Gibson, *Job*, 63.
857 Kissane, *Book of Job*, 64.
858 Hartley, *Book of Job*, 207.
859 Buttenwieser, quoted in Rowley, *Job*, 106–7.
860 Dhorme, *Le Livre de Job*, 159.
861 Pope, *Job*, 84–85.
862 Gordis, *Book of Job*, 84.
863 Holscher, quoted in Rowley, *Job*, 107.
864 Newsom, *Book of Job*, 165.
865 Dhorme, *Le Livre de Job*, 159.
866 Gibson, *Job*, 64.
867 Pope, *Job*, 86.
868 Delitzsch, *Biblical Commentary on the Book of Job*, 1:107.
869 Ewald, *Commentary on the Book of Job*, 147.
870 Gersonides, *On the Book of Job*, 75.
871 Gibson, *Job*, 65.
872 Dhorme, *Le Livre de Job*, 160.
873 Hartley, *Book of Job*, 208–9.
874 Gersonides, *On the Book of Job*, 76.
875 Rashi, in Rosenberg, *Job*, 101.
876 Newsom, *Book of Job*, 166.
877 Newsom, *Book of Job*, 166.
878 Gibson, *Job*, 66.
879 Gibson, *Job*, 66.
880 Hartley, *Book of Job*, 69.
881 Peshitta, 11:15.
882 Mezudat David, in Rosenberg, *Job*, 105.
883 Rashi, in Rosenberg, *Job*, 103.
884 Kissane, *Book of Job*, 65.
885 Dhorme, *Le Livre de Job*, 165.
886 Gersonides, *On the Book of Job*, 78.
887 Aquinas, 131.

888 Hartley, *Book of Job*, 70.
889 Targum of Job, p. 22.
890 Reichert, *Job*, 68.
891 Dhorme, *Le Livre de Job*, 166–67.
892 Gordis, *Book of Job*, 86.
893 Driver and Gray, quoted in Rowley, *Job*, 110.
894 Dhorme, *Le Livre de Job*, 166–67.
895 Pope, *Job*, 87.
896 Hartley, *Book of Job*, 70.
897 Gersonides, *On the Book of Job*, 79.
898 Targum of Job, p. 24.
899 Terrien, *Job*, 117.
900 Rowley, *Job*, 111.
901 Perdue, *Voice from the Whirlwind*, 62.
902 Hesychius, quoted in Simonetti and Conti, *Ancient Christian Commentary*, 67.
903 Newsom, *Book of Job*, 170.
904 Duhm, quoted in Rowley, *Job*, 112.
905 Duhm, quoted in Rowley, *Job*, 112.
906 Dahood, quoted in Rowley, *Job*, 112.
907 Duhm, quoted in Rowley, *Job*, 112.
908 All quoted in Rowley, *Job*, 112.
909 Kissane, Dhorme, and Tur-Sinai, all quoted in Rowley, *Job*, 112.
910 Fohrer, quoted in Rowley, *Job*, 112.
911 Rowley, *Job*, 112.
912 Phillip the Priest, quoted in Simonetti and Conti, *Ancient Christian Commentary*, 70.
913 Burr, quoted in Rowley, *Job*, 112.
914 Hartley, *Book of Job*, 221–22.
915 Siegfried and Duhm, quoted in Rowley, *Job*, 113.
916 Burr, quoted in Rowley, *Job*, 113.
917 Caryl, *Directory of the Afflicted*, 29.
918 Barton, *Commentary on the Book of Job*, 75.
919 Ehrlich, quoted in Rowley, *Job*, 113.
920 Rashi, in Rosenberg, *Job*, 104.
921 Rowley, *Job*, 113–14.
922 Fohrer and Stevenson, quoted in Rowley, *Job*, 114.
923 Julian, quoted in Simonetti and Conti, *Ancient Christian Commentary*, 68.
924 Gersonides, *On the Book of Job*, 88–89.
925 Ewald, *Commentary on the Book of Job*, 151.
926 Delitzsch, *Biblical Commentary on the Book of Job*, 1:109.
927 Hartley, *Book of Job*, 72.
928 Hartley, *Book of Job*, 72.

929. Chrysostom, quoted in Simonetti and Conti, *Ancient Christian Commentary*, 68.
930. Tur-Sinai, quoted in Rowley, *Job*, 115.
931. Terrien, *Job: Poet of Existence*, 44.
932. Dhorme, *Le Livre de Job*, 123–24.
933. Rowley, *Job*, 114.
934. Dahood, quoted in Rowley, *Job*, 114.
935. Mezudt David, 106.
936. Barton, quoted in Rowley, *Job*, 114.
937. Delitzsch, *Biblical Commentary on the Book of Job*, 110.
938. Rowley, *Job*, 114.
939. NEB, 12:11–12.
940. Barton, quoted in Rowley, *Job*, 115.
941. Rowley, *Job*, 115.
942. All quoted in Rowley, *Job*, 115.
943. Chrysostom, quoted in Simonetti and Conti, *Ancient Christian Commentary*, 70.
944. Terrien, *Job: Poet of Existence*, 46.
945. Delitzsch, *Biblical Commentary on the Book of Job*, 111.
946. Newsom, *Book of Job*, 161.
947. Barton, quoted in Rowley, *Job*, 115–16.
948. Rowley, *Job*, 116.
949. Hartley, *Book of Job*, 213–14.
950. Phillip, quoted in Simonetti and Conti, *Ancient Christian Commentary*, 70.
951. Mezudat David, in Rosenberg, *Job*, 108.
952. LXX, 12:15.
953. KJV, 12:15.
954. Mezudat David, in Rosenberg, *Job*, 108.
955. Gregory, quoted in Simonetti and Conti, *Ancient Christian Commentary*, 70–71.
956. Pope, *Job*, 93.
957. Duhm, quoted in Rowley, *Job*, 116.
958. Rashi, in Rosenberg, *Job*, 105.
959. Hartley, *Book of Job*, 76.
960. Burr, quoted in Rowley, *Job*, 117.
961. Ephrem, quoted in Simonetti and Conti, *Ancient Christian Commentary*, 71.
962. Delitzsch, *Biblical Commentary on the Book of Job*, 113.
963. Rashi, in Rosenberg, *Job*, 106.
964. Barton and Hartley, quoted in Rowley, *Job*, 117.
965. Julian, quoted in Simonetti and Conti, *Ancient Christian Commentary*, 71.
966. Barton, quoted in Rowley, *Job*, 117.
967. Stevenson and Konig, quoted in Rowley, *Job*, 117.
968. Hartley, *Book of Job*, 76.
969. Burr, quoted in Rowley, *Job*, 117.

970 Budde, quoted in Rowley, *Job*, 117.

971 All quoted in Rowley, *Job*, 117.

972 Kissane, quoted in Rowley, *Job*, 117.

973 Olympiodorus, quoted in Simonetti and Conti, *Ancient Christian Commentary*, 72.

974 Barton, *Commentary on the Book of Job*, 114.

975 Perdue, *Voice from the Whirlwind*, 64.

976 Delitzsch, *Biblical Commentary on the Book of Job*, 114.

977 Julian, in Simonetti and Conti, *Ancient Christian Commentary*, 72–73.

978 Ibn Ezra, *Job*, 96; Maimonides, *Guide to the Perplexed*, 99.

979 Vulgate, 12:24.

980 Barton, quoted in Rowley, *Job*, 119.

981 LXX, 12:25.

982 Stevenson, *Critical Notes*, 11.

983 Mezudat David, in Rosenberg, *Job*, 110.

984 LXX, 12:26.

985 KJV, 12:25.

986 Gensius, *Hebrew Grammar*, 139.

987 Henry, *Commentary on the Holy Bible*, 209.

988 Didymus, in Simonetti and Conti, *Ancient Christian Commentary*, 74.

989 Gregory, in Simonetti and Conti, *Ancient Christian Commentary*, 76–77.

990 Chrysostom, in Simonetti and Conti, *Ancient Christian Commentary*, 74.

991 Olympiodorus, in Simonetti and Conti, *Ancient Christian Commentary*, 74.

992 Hesychius in Simonetti and Conti, *Ancient Christian Commentary*, 73.

993 Clines, *Job 1–20*, 288.

994 Habel, *Book of Job*, 88.

995 Van Heck, "From Conversation about God," 119–20.

996 Clines, *Job 1–20*, 289.

997 Mezudat David, in Rosenberg, *Job*, 110.

998 Clines, *Job 1–20*, 289.

999 Rowley, *Job*, 120.

1000 Maimonides, *Guide to the Perplexed*, 191.

1001 Habel, *Book of Job*, 89.

1002 Habel, *Book of Job*, 89.

1003 Habel, *Book of Job*, 89.

1004 Clines, *Job 1–20*, 290.

1005 Rowley, *Job*, 120.

1006 LXX, 13:3.

1007 Rowley, *Job*, 120.

1008 Ewald, *Commentary on the Book of Job*, 166–67. Dillmann, quoted in Rowley, *Job*, 120.

1009 Rashi, in Rosenberg, *Job*, 111.

1010 Rowley, *Job*, 120.

1011 Blommerde, *Northwest Semitic Grammar*, 39.
1012 Habel, *Book of Job*, 219. Hartley, *Book of Job*, 80.
1013 Hartley, *Book of Job*, 80.
1014 Kant, as quoted in Kivistö and Pihlström, "Kantian Anti-Theodicy," 347–49.
1015 Rashi, in Rosenberg, *Job*, 112.
1016 Habel, *Book of Job*, 219.
1017 Glatzer, *Dimensions of Job*, 19.
1018 Rowley, *Job*, 121.
1019 Rashi, in Rosenberg, *Job*, 112.
1020 Clines, *Job 1–20*, 291.
1021 Gordis, *Book of Job*, 104.
1022 Gordis, *Book of Job*, 104.
1023 Tur-Sinai, quoted in Rowley, *Job*, 121.
1024 Peake, quoted in Rowley, *Job*, 121.
1025 Rashi, in Rosenberg, *Job*, 112.
1026 Rowley, *Job*, 121.
1027 Dhorme, *Le Livre de Job*, 185.
1028 All quoted in Rowley, *Job*, 121.
1029 Rowley, *Job*, 121.
1030 Eitan, "Job Thirteen," 2–3.
1031 Habel, *Book of Job*, 230–31.
1032 Gordis, *Book of Job*, 105.
1033 Beer, *Das Buch Hiob*, 1:121.
1034 Guillaume, quoted in Rowley, *Job*, 121.
1035 Rashi, in Rosenberg, *Job*, 113.
1036 Hartley, *Book of Job*, 83.
1037 Hartley, *Book of Job*, 83.
1038 Peake, quoted in Rowley, *Job*, 123.
1039 Rowley, *Job*, 123.
1040 LXX, 13:15.
1041 Rowley, *Job*, 123.
1042 Rowley, *Job*, 123.
1043 Dahood, quoted in Rowley, *Job*, 123.
1044 Rowley, *Job*, 123.
1045 Duhm and Klostermann, quoted in Rowley, *Job*, 123.
1046 NIV, 13:14.
1047 Septuagint and Vulgate, 13:14.
1048 RSV, 13:15.
1049 Ehrlich, quoted in Rowley, *Job*, 123.
1050 Ball, quoted in Rowley, *Job*, 123.
1051 Rashi, in Rosenberg, *Job*, 115.

1052 Maimonides, *Guide to the Perplexed*, 100.
1053 Rowley, *Job*, 123.
1054 RSV, 13:15.
1055 NIV, 13:15.
1056 All quoted in Rowley, *Job*.
1057 Quoted in Rowley, *Job*.
1058 Rashi, in Rosenberg, *Job*, 115.
1059 MacLeish, *J.B.*, 44.
1060 Glatzer, *Dimensions of Job*, 19.
1061 Shakespeare, sonnet 139.
1062 Kara, *Sefer Iyyov*, 100.
1063 Barton, quoted in Rowley, *Job*, 123.
1064 Berleir, 113 and Dumas, *Count of Monte Cristo*, 19.
1065 Rashi, in Rosenberg, *Job*, 116.
1066 Newsom, *Book of Job*, 175.
1067 Mezudat David, in Rosenberg, *Job*, 115.
1068 Clines, *Job 1–20*, 292.
1069 Barton, quoted in Rowley, *Job*, 124.
1070 Rowley, *Job*, 124.
1071 Rowley, *Job*, 124.
1072 Rashi, in Rosenberg, *Job*, 117.
1073 Mezudat David, in Rosenberg, *Job*, 116.
1074 Maimonides, *Guide to the Perplexed*, 195.
1075 Rashi, in Rosenberg, *Job*, 118.
1076 Rowley, *Job*, 124.
1077 Meyouchas, *Sefer Iyyov*, 16.
1078 Hartley, *Book of Job*, 89.
1079 Mezudat David, in Rosenberg, *Job*, 113.
1080 Peake, quoted in Rowley, *Job*, 124.
1081 Barton, quoted in Rowley, *Job*, 124.
1082 Rowley, *Job*, 124.
1083 All quoted in Rowley, *Job*, 124.
1084 Dhorme, *Le Livre de Job*, 191–92.
1085 Gordis, *Book of Job*, 110.
1086 Rashi, in Rosenberg, *Job*, 116.
1087 Mezudat David, in Rosenberg, *Job*, 113.
1088 Barton, quoted in Rowley, *Job*, 124–25.
1089 Hartley, *Book of Job*, 88.
1090 Rowley, *Job*, 124.
1091 Hartley, *Book of Job*, 88.
1092 Glatzer, *Dimensions of Job*, 88.

1093 Rowley, *Job*, 124.
1094 Peake, quoted in Rowley, *Job*, 124.
1095 Rashi, in Rosenberg, *Job*, 114.
1096 Mezudat David, in Rosenberg, *Job*, 114.
1097 Glatzer, *Dimensions of Job*, 19.
1098 Barton, quoted in Rowley, *Job*, 124–25.
1099 Hartley, *Book of Job*, 90.
1100 Hartley, *Book of Job*, 90.
1101 Glatzer, *Dimensions of Job*, 19.
1102 Barton, quoted in Rowley, *Job*, 125.
1103 Targum of Job, p. 27.
1104 Rosenberg, *Job*, 213.
1105 Mezudat David, in Rosenberg, *Job*, 114.
1106 Baba Mezia, 103a.
1107 Tur-Sinai, quoted in Rowley, *Job*, 125.
1108 Hitzig, quoted in Rowley, *Job*, 126.
1109 Ball, quoted in Rowley, *Job*, 125.
1110 Hitzig, *Das Buch Hiob*.
1111 Dahood, quoted in Rowley, *Job*, 121.
1112 Dahood, quoted in Rowley, *Job*, 121.
1113 Rowley, *Job*, 125.
1114 Targum of Job, 13:26.
1115 See Gersonides, *On the Book of Job*, 90.
1116 Barton, quoted in Rowley, *Job*, 125.
1117 Barton, quoted in Rowley, *Job*, 125.
1118 Habel, *Book of Job*, 231.
1119 Rashi, in Rosenberg, *Job*, 118.
1120 Merx, quoted in Rowley, *Job*, 125.
1121 Budde and Helscher, quoted in Rowley, *Job*, 125.
1122 LXX, 13:27.
1123 Rowley, *Job*, 125–26.
1124 Rowley, *Job*, 125–26.
1125 Cheyney, quoted in Rowley, *Job*, 125.
1126 All mentioned in Rowley, *Job*.
1127 Mezudat David, in Rosenberg, *Job*, 116.
1128 Habel, *Book of Job*, 225–26.
1129 Hartley, *Book of Job*, 92.
1130 Henry, *Commentary on the Holy Bible*, 299.
1131 Newsom, *Book of Job*, 165. And Terrien, *Job*, 930.
1132 Newsom, *Book of Job*, 165.
1133 All in Simonetti and Conti, *Ancient Christian Commentary*, 78–83.

1134 Newsom, *Book of Job*, 165. And Dhorme, *Le Livre de Job*, 194.
1135 Stevenson, quoted in Rowley, *Job*, 127.
1136 Clines, *Job 1-20*, 294.
1137 Leibush [Malbim], 111.
1138 Mezudat David, in Rosenberg, *Job*, 117.
1139 Sforno, *Sefer Iyyov*, 119.
1140 Terrien, *Job*, 932.
1141 Hesychius, quoted in Simonetti and Conti, *Ancient Christian Commentary*, 79.
1142 LXX, 14:1-3.
1143 Rashi, in Rosenberg, *Job*, 121.
1144 Dhorme, *Le Livre de Job*, 194.
1145 Clines, *Job 1-20*, 295.
1146 Leibush, 112.
1147 Newsom, *Book of Job*, 166.
1148 Gregory, quoted in Simonetti and Conti, *Ancient Christian Commentary*, 79.
1149 Chrysostom, quoted in Simonetti and Conti, *Ancient Christian Commentary*, 79.
1150 Clement, quoted in Simonetti and Conti, *Ancient Christian Commentary*, 79.
1151 Rashi, in Rosenberg, *Job*, 121.
1152 All quoted in Rowley, *Job*, 130-31.
1153 Peake, quoted in Rowley, *Job*, 131.
1154 Clines, *Job 1-20*, 296.
1155 Dhorme, *Le Livre de Job*, 196.
1156 Stevenson, quoted in Rowley, *Job*, 131.
1157 Didymus, quoted in Simonetti and Conti, *Ancient Christian Commentary*, 82.
1158 KJV, 14:6; Ball, *Book of Job*, 70.
1159 Ephrem, quoted in Simonetti and Conti, *Ancient Christian Commentary*, 81. And RSV, 14:6.
1160 Rashi, in Rosenberg, *Job*, 122.
1161 Stevenson, quoted in Rowley, *Job*, 132.
1162 Newsom, *Book of Job*, 167.
1163 Terrien, *Job*, 934.
1164 Clines, *Job 1-20*, 297.
1165 Weitzstein and Dhorme, quoted in Rowley, *Job*, 128-29.
1166 Mezudat David, in Rosenberg, *Job*, 119.
1167 Stevenson, quoted in Rowley, *Job*, 129.
1168 Steuernagel, *Das Buch Hiob*, 66.
1169 Dhorme, *Le Livre de Job*, 204.
1170 Fohrer, quoted in Rowley, *Job*, 129.
1171 LXX, 14:19. And Baba Batra, 16a.
1172 Newsom, *Book of Job*, 168.
1173 Ibn Ezra, *Job*, 122.
1174 Gregory, in Simonetti and Conti, *Ancient Christian Commentary*, 82.

1175 Didymus, quoted in Simonetti and Conti, *Ancient Christian Commentary*, 82.
1176 Rowley, *Job*, 130–31.
1177 Newsom, *Book of Job*, 168.
1178 Fohrer, *Studien zum Das Buch Hiob*, 74.
1179 Rashi, in Rosenberg, *Job*, 123.
1180 Rowley, *Job*, 131.
1181 Fohrer, *Studien zum Das Buch Hiob*, 74.
1182 All quoted in Rowley, *Job*, 131.
1183 Pope, *Job*, 108–9.
1184 Terrien, *Job*, 935. And KJV, 14:16.
1185 NIV, 14:16. And Pope, *Job*, 109.
1186 NRSV, 14:16; Pope, *Job*, 109.
1187 Dhorme, *Le Livre de Job*, 207.
1188 Rashi, in Rosenberg, *Job*, in Rosenberg, *Job*, 247.
1189 Mezudat David, in Rosenberg, *Job*, 120.
1190 Terrien, *Job*, 936.
1191 Pope, *Job*, 32.
1192 Pope, *Job*, 32.
1193 Rowley, *Job*, 131.
1194 Newsom, *Book of Job*, 170.
1195 Terrien, *Job*, 937.
1196 Clines, *Job 1–20*, 300.
1197 Phillip, quoted in Simonetti and Conti, *Ancient Christian Commentary*, 83.
1198 Rowley, *Job*, 131.
1199 Septuagint and Peshitta, 14:19; Holscher, Steinmann, Weiser, Horst, and Fohrer, all quoted in Rowley, *Job*, 131.
1200 Budde, *Das Buch Hiob*, 70.
1201 Dhorme, *Le Livre de Job*, 204.
1202 Stevenson, quoted in Rowley, *Job*, 131.
1203 Peake, *Job*, 82.
1204 Davidson, *Book of Job*, 81.
1205 Clines, *Job 1–20*, 300.
1206 Terrien, *Job*, 937.
1207 Gray, quoted in Rowley, *Job*, 132.
1208 Targum of Job, 12:22.
1209 Targum of Job, 12:22.
1210 Newsom, *Book of Job*, 171.
1211 Ibn Ezra, *Job*, 133.
1212 Clines, *Job 1–20*, 300.
1213 Stevenson, quoted in Rowley, *Job*, 132.
1214 All quote in Rowley, *Job*, 132.

1215 Driver, *Book of Job*, 87.
1216 Rowley, *Job*, 132.
1217 Henry, *Commentary on the Holy Bible*, 329.
1218 Aquinas, *Commentary on the Book of Job*, 82.
1219 Dhorme, *Le Livre de Job*, 208.
1220 Wesley, 299.
1221 Saadiah, *Book of Theodicy*, 81.
1222 Mezudat David, in Rosenberg, *Job*, 124.
1223 Targum of Job, 15:3. Ibn Ezra, *Job*, 151.
1224 Rashi, in Rosenberg, *Job*, 200.
1225 Trani, *Sefer Iyyov*, 80.
1226 Aquinas, *Commentary on the Book of Job*, 83.
1227 Saadiah, *Book of Theodicy*, 81.
1228 Wesley, 300.
1229 Aquinas, *Commentary on the Book of Job*, 83.
1230 Dhorme, *Le Livre de Job*, 208–9.
1231 Rashi, in Rosenberg, *Job*, 200.
1232 Mezudat David, in Rosenberg, *Job*, 200.
1233 Peshitta, 15:6.
1234 Dhorme, *Le Livre de Job*, 209.
1235 Dhorme, *Le Livre de Job*, 209.
1236 Henry, *Commentary on the Holy Bible*, 321.
1237 Chrysostom, quoted in Simonetti and Conti, *Ancient Christian Commentary*, 88.
1238 Rashi, in Rosenberg, *Job*, 201.
1239 Mezudat David, in Rosenberg, *Job*, 201.
1240 Dhorme, *Le Livre de Job*, 209.
1241 Targum of Job, 15:9. And Dhorme, *Le Livre de Job*, 209.
1242 Rashi, in Rosenberg, *Job*, 201.
1243 Dhorme, *Le Livre de Job*, 211.
1244 Gregory, quoted in Simonetti and Conti, *Ancient Christian Commentary*, 85.
1245 Saadiah, *Book of Theodicy*, 82.
1246 Rashi, in Rosenberg, *Job*, 201.
1247 Aquinas, *Commentary on the Book of Job*, 83.
1248 Dhorme, *Le Livre de Job*, 212–13.
1249 Dhorme, *Le Livre de Job*, 212–13.
1250 Dhorme, *Le Livre de Job*, 212–13.
1251 Saadiah, *Book of Theodicy*, 83.
1252 Ehrlich, quoted in Rowley, *Job*, 136.
1253 Aquinas, *Commentary on the Book of Job*, 83.
1254 Olympiodorus, quoted in Simonetti and Conti, *Ancient Christian Commentary*, 86.
1255 Trani, *Sefer Iyyov*, 82.

1256 Ishodad of Merv, in Simonetti and Conti, *Ancient Christian Commentary*, 86.
1257 Dhorme, *Le Livre de Job*, 214.
1258 Gregory, quoted in Simonetti and Conti, *Ancient Christian Commentary*, 87–88.
1259 Saadiah, *Book of Theodicy*, 83.
1260 Rashi, in Rosenberg, *Job*, 202.
1261 Dhorme, *Le Livre de Job*, 214–15.
1262 Wesley, 302.
1263 Rashi, in Rosenberg, *Job*, 203.
1264 Chrystom, quoted in Simonetti and Conti, *Ancient Christian Commentary*, 88.
1265 Ephrem, quoted in Simonetti and Conti, *Ancient Christian Commentary*, 88.
1266 Wesley, 302.
1267 Dhorme, *Le Livre de Job*, 216–17.
1268 Wesley, 302.
1269 Saadiah, *Book of Theodicy*, 84.
1270 Le Hir, *Le Livre de Job*, 63.
1271 Renan, *Le Livre de Job*, 70.
1272 Rashi, in Rosenberg, *Job*, 203.
1273 Mezudat David, in Rosenberg, *Job*, 202.
1274 Saadiah, *Book of Theodicy*, 85.
1275 Philip the Priest, quoted in Simonetti and Conti, *Ancient Christian Commentary*, 88.
1276 Wesley, 303.
1277 Mezudat David, in Rosenberg, *Job*, 202.
1278 Rashi, in Rosenberg, *Job*, 203.
1279 Saadiah, *Book of Theodicy*, 86.
1280 Dhorme, *Le Livre de Job*, 221.
1281 Wesley, 304.
1282 Rashi, in Rosenberg, *Job*, 204.
1283 Mezudat David, in Rosenberg, *Job*, 202.
1284 Olmpiodorus, quoted in Simonetti and Conti, *Ancient Christian Commentary*, 88.
1285 Rashi, in Rosenberg, *Job*, 203.
1286 Ibn Ezra, *Job*, 169.
1287 Dhorme, *Le Livre de Job*, 221.
1288 Dhorme, *Le Livre de Job*, 222.
1289 Dhorme, *Le Livre de Job*, 222.
1290 Mezudat David, in Rosenberg, *Job*, 203.
1291 Aquinas, *Commentary on the Book of Job*, 86.
1292 Gregory, quoted in Simonetti and Conti, *Ancient Christian Commentary*, 92–93.
1293 Saadiah, *Book of Theodicy*, 86.
1294 Saadiah, *Book of Theodicy*, 86.
1295 Henry, *Commentary on the Holy Bible*, 335.
1296 Saadiah, *Book of Theodicy*, 86.

1297 Philip, quoted in Simonetti and Conti, *Ancient Christian Commentary*, 89.
1298 Rashi, in Rosenberg, *Job*, 204.
1299 Saadiah, *Book of Theodicy*, 86.
1300 Aquinas, *Commentary on the Book of Job*, 87.
1301 Mezudat David, in Rosenberg, *Job*, 203.
1302 Ibn Ezra, *Job*, 203.
1303 Calvin, *Sermons from Job*, 115.
1304 Calvin, *Sermons from Job*, 115.
1305 Gibson, *Job*, 56.
1306 Gibson, *Job*, 56.
1307 Keil and Delitzsch, *Commentary on the Old Testament*, 55.
1308 Kissane, *Book of Job*, 51.
1309 Ball, quoted in Rowley, *Job*, 145.
1310 Aquinas, *Commentary on the Book of Job*, 89.
1311 Wesley, 302.
1312 Henry, *Commentary on the Holy Bible*, 332.
1313 Ball, quoted in Rowley, *Job*, 145.
1314 Rashi, in Rosenberg, *Job*, 204.
1315 Mezudat David, in Rosenberg, *Job*, 203.
1316 Henry, *Commentary on the Holy Bible*, 332.
1317 Good, *In Turns of Tempest*, 55.
1318 Driver, quoted in Rowley, *Job*, 145.
1319 Stevenson, quoted in Rowley, *Job*, 145.
1320 Stevenson, quoted in Rowley, *Job*, 145.
1321 Calvin, *Sermons from Job*, 116.
1322 Henry, *Commentary on the Holy Bible*, 33.
1323 Driver, quoted in Rowley, *Job*, 151.
1324 Rashi, in Rosenberg, *Job*, 204.
1325 Driver, quoted in Rowley, *Job*, 151.
1326 Ball, quoted in Rowley, *Job*, 146.
1327 Keil and Delitzsch, *Commentary on the Old Testament*, 56.
1328 Kissane, *Book of Job*, 52.
1329 Umbreit, quoted in Rowley, *Job*, 146.
1330 *Qamat* is among the many hapaxes in the book.
1331 Rashi, in Rosenberg, *Job*, 205.
1332 Umbreit, quoted in Rowley, *Job*, 160–61.
1333 Henry, *Commentary on the Holy Bible*, 334.
1334 Both quoted in Rowley, *Job*, 161.
1335 Mezudat David, in Rosenberg, *Job*, 205.
1336 Henry, *Commentary on the Holy Bible*, 334.
1337 Gibson, *Job*, 58.

1338 Rashi, in Rosenberg, *Job*, 205.
1339 Keil and Delitzsch, *Commentary on the Old Testament*, 58.
1340 Mezudat David, in Rosenberg, *Job*, 205.
1341 Driver, quoted in Rowley, *Job*, 148.
1342 Driver, quoted in Rowley, *Job*, 148.
1343 Mezudat David, in Rosenberg, *Job*, 205.
1344 Umbreit, quoted in Rowley, *Job*, 148.
1345 Henry, *Commentary on the Holy Bible*, 334.
1346 Geneva Bible, 16:15.
1347 Ball, quoted in Rowley, *Job*, 149.
1348 Aquinas, *Commentary on the Book of Job*, 90.
1349 Driver, quoted in Rowley, *Job*, 149.
1350 Gersonides, *On the Book of Job*, 105–6.
1351 Ball, quoted in Rowley, *Job*, 149.
1352 Keil and Delitzsch, *Commentary on the Old Testament*, 60.
1353 Calvin, *Sermons from Job*, 116.
1354 Kissane, *Book of Job*, 53.
1355 Kissane, *Book of Job*, 53.
1356 Driver, quoted in Rowley, *Job*, 149.
1357 Mezudat David, in Rosenberg, *Job*, 206.
1358 Rashi, in Rosenberg, *Job*, 205.
1359 Mezudat David, in Rosenberg, *Job*, 206.
1360 Kissane, *Book of Job*, 53.
1361 Aquinas, *Commentary on the Book of Job*, 91.
1362 Aquinas, *Commentary on the Book of Job*, 91.
1363 Clarke, *Commentary on Job*, 79.
1364 Umbreit, quoted in Rowley, *Job*, 149–50.
1365 Ball, quoted in Rowley, *Job*, 150.
1366 Rosenberg, *Job*, 102.
1367 Rashi, in Rosenberg, *Job*, 205.
1368 Geneva Bible, 16:19.
1369 Clarke, *Commentary on Job*, 80.
1370 Driver, quoted in Rowley, *Job*, 150.
1371 Aquinas, *Commentary on the Book of Job*, 92.
1372 Wycliffe Bible, p. 201.
1373 Henry, *Commentary on the Holy Bible*, 335.
1374 Clarke, *Commentary on Job*, 81.
1375 Driver, quoted in Rowley, *Job*, 150–51.
1376 Umbreit, quoted in Rowley, *Job*, 151.
1377 Umbreit, quoted in Rowley, *Job*, 151.
1378 Driver, quoted in Rowley, *Job*, 151.

ENDNOTES

1379 Rashi, in Rosenberg, *Job*, 206.
1380 Aquinas, *Commentary on the Book of Job*, 92.
1381 Good, *In Turns of Tempest*, 57.
1382 Ball, quoted in Rowley, *Job*, 151.
1383 Gibson, *Job*, 59.
1384 Keil and Delitzsch, *Commentary on the Old Testament*, 61.
1385 Henry, *Commentary on the Holy Bible*, 337.
1386 Newsom, *Book of Job*, and Terrien, *Job*.
1387 LXX, 17:1.
1388 Duhm, quoted in Rowley, *Job*, 152.
1389 Driver, quoted in Rowley, *Job*, 152.
1390 Ibn Ezra, *Job*, 205.
1391 Coverdale, *Writings and Translations*, 398.
1392 LXX, 17:2; RSV, 17:2; Dhorme, *Le Livre de Job*, 243.
1393 Holscher, quoted in Rowley, *Job*, 152–53.
1394 Rashi, in Rosenberg, *Job*, 207.
1395 Wesley, 305.
1396 Ehrlich, quoted in Rowley, *Job*, 153.
1397 Rashi, in Rosenberg, *Job*, 207.
1398 Dhorme, *Le Livre de Job*, 244.
1399 Rowley, *Job*, 152–53.
1400 Trani, *Sefer Iyyov*, 86.
1401 Peake, quoted in Rowley, *Job*, 153.
1402 All quoted in Rowley, *Job*, 153.
1403 Driver, quoted in Rowley, *Job*, 153.
1404 Mezudat David, in Rosenberg, *Job*, 207.
1405 Wesley, 305.
1406 Dhorme, *Le Livre de Job*, 245.
1407 Peshitta, 17:5.
1408 Le Hir, *Le Livre de Job*, 81, and Renan, *Le Livre de Job*, 101.
1409 Rashi, in Rosenberg, *Job*, 207.
1410 Mezudat David, in Rosenberg, *Job*, 206.
1411 Dhorme, *Le Livre de Job*, 246–47.
1412 Keil and Delitzsch, *Commentary on the Old Testament*, 62.
1413 LXX, 17:6.
1414 Driver, quoted in Rowley, *Job*, 154.
1415 Dhorme, *Le Livre de Job*, 247.
1416 Rowley, *Job*, 154.
1417 RSV, 17:6b; Mezudat David, in Rosenberg, *Job*, 207.
1418 Beer, quoted in Rowley, *Job*, 154–55.
1419 Budde, quoted in Rowley, *Job*, 155.

1420 Gersonides, *On the Book of Job*, 113–14.
1421 Wesley, 306.
1422 Driver, quoted in Rowley, *Job*, 155.
1423 Freehof, *Book of Job*, 63.
1424 Rashi, in Rosenberg, *Job*, 208.
1425 Keil and Delitzsch, *Commentary on the Old Testament*, 66.
1426 All quoted in Rowley, *Job*, 155.
1427 All quoted in Rowley, *Job*, 155.
1428 Duhm, quoted in Rowley, *Job*, 155.
1429 Dhorme, *Le Livre de Job*, 248–50.
1430 Freehof, *Book of Job*, 63.
1431 Keil and Delitzsch, *Commentary on the Old Testament*, 67.
1432 Dhorme, *Le Livre de Job*, 249.
1433 Peshitta, 17:9; Delitzsch, *Biblical Commentary on the Book of Job*, 1:77.
1434 Mezudat David, in Rosenberg, *Job*, 207.
1435 Wesley, 306.
1436 Rashi, in Rosenberg, *Job*, 207.
1437 Freehof, *Book of Job*, 64.
1438 Keil and Delitzsch, *Commentary on the Old Testament*, 67.
1439 Author's translation.
1440 Budde, quoted in Rowley, *Job*, 156.
1441 Duhm, quoted in Rowley, *Job*, 156.
1442 Rowley, *Job*, 156.
1443 Dhorme, *Le Livre de Job*, 251.
1444 Rowley, *Job*, 156.
1445 Wesley, 307.
1446 Freehof, *Book of Job*, 65.
1447 Le Hir, *Le Livre de Job*, 83.
1448 Dhorme, *Le Livre de Job*, 152–253.
1449 Loisy, quoted in Rowley, *Job*, 156.
1450 Rowley, *Job*, 156.
1451 Wesley, 307.
1452 Dhorme, *Le Livre de Job*, 255.
1453 Targum of Job, 17:14; Peshitta, 17:14; Duhm, quoted in Rowley, *Job*, 156.
1454 Keil and Delitzsch, *Commentary on the Old Testament*, 68.
1455 Wesley, 307.
1456 Keil and Delitzsch, *Commentary on the Old Testament*, 68.
1457 RSV, 17:14.
1458 Dhorme, *Le Livre de Job*, 254–55.
1459 Mezudat David, in Rosenberg, *Job*, 206.
1460 Rowley, *Job*, 157.

1461   Guillaume, "Arabic Background," 17.
1462   Keil and Delitzsch, *Commentary on the Old Testament*, 68.
1463   Wesley, 307.
1464   Meyouchas, *Sefer Iyyov*, 34.
1465   Keil and Delitzsch, *Commentary on the Old Testament*, 69.
1466   Wesley, 307.
1467   Rowley, *Job*, 157.
1468   LXX, 17:16.
1469   Ibn Ezra, *Job*, 205.
1470   Le Hir, *Le Livre de Job*, 84; Renan, *Le Livre de Job*, 75.
1471   Driver, quoted in Rowley, *Job*, 157.
1472   Gersonides, *On the Book of Job*, 113–14.
1473   Rashi, in Rosenberg, *Job*, 208.
1474   Dhorme, *Le Livre de Job*, 255–56.
1475   Henry, *Commentary on the Holy Bible*, 350.
1476   Rowley, *Job*, 158–64.
1477   Henry, *Commentary on the Holy Bible*, 350.
1478   Rowley, *Job*, 157–58.
1479   Freehof, *Book of Job*, 71.
1480   Hartley, *Book of Job*, 322–23.
1481   *Testament of Job*, 37:5–8, in Vicchio, 1:122–23.
1482   *Testament of Job*, 37:5–8, in Vicchio, 1:122–23.
1483   Hesychius, quoted in Simonetti and Conti, *Ancient Christian Commentary*, 97.
1484   Julian, quoted in Simonetti and Conti, *Ancient Christian Commentary*, 97.
1485   Chrysostom, quoted in Simonetti and Conti, *Ancient Christian Commentary*, 97.
1486   Gersonides, *On the Book of Job*, 119–20.
1487   Aquinas, *Commentary on the Book of Job*, 92.
1488   Ewald, *Commentary on the Book of Job*, 196–97.
1489   LXX, 18:1–2.
1490   Dhorme, *Le Livre de Job*, 257.
1491   Dhorme, *Le Livre de Job*, 257.
1492   Guillaume, "Arabic Background," 18.
1493   Peake, quoted in Rowley, *Job*, 157.
1494   Dhorme, *Le Livre de Job*, 257.
1495   Ewald, *Commentary on the Book of Job*, 197.
1496   Garland, *Book of Job*, 70.
1497   Umbreit, quoted in Rowley, *Job*, 158.
1498   Thomas, *Book of Job*, 217.
1499   Davidson, *Book of Job*, 77.
1500   Gordis, *Book of God and Man*, 73.
1501   Royds, *Job and the Problem of Suffering*, 66.

1502 Scott, *Book of Job*, 61.
1503 Rodd, *Book of Job*, 37–38.
1504 Noyes, *Book of Job*, 70.
1505 Dhorme, *Le Livre de Job*, 257.
1506 Duhm and Beer, quoted in Rowley, *Job*, 157.
1507 Terrien, *Job*, 950.
1508 Driver and Gray, quoted in Rowley, *Job*, 157.
1509 Hartley, *Book of Job*, 324.
1510 Newsom, *Book of Job*, 175.
1511 Kissane, *Book of Job*, 62.
1512 Gibson, *Job*, 62.
1513 Gibson, *Job*, 62.
1514 Driver, quoted in Rowley, *Job*, 159.
1515 Freehof, *Book of Job*, 140–41.
1516 Rashi, in Rosenberg, *Job*, 210.
1517 Duhm, quoted in Rowley, *Job*, 159.
1518 Fohrer, quoted in Rowley, *Job*, 159.
1519 Hartley, *Book of Job*, 324.
1520 Gregory, quoted in Simonetti and Conti, *Ancient Christian Commentary*, 100.
1521 Rashi, in Rosenberg, *Job*, 210.
1522 Gersoniddes, 119–20.
1523 Thomas, *Book of Job*, 218.
1524 Pope, *Job*, 133–34.
1525 Rodd, *Book of Job*, 38.
1526 Olmpiodorus, quoted in Simonetti and Conti, *Ancient Christian Commentary*, 99.
1527 Aquinas, *Commentary on the Book of Job*, 99.
1528 Rashi, in Rosenberg, *Job*, 210.
1529 Rashi, in Rosenberg, *Job*, 210.
1530 Hartley, *Book of Job*, 324.
1531 Rowley, *Job*, 160–61.
1532 Driver and Gray, quoted in Rowley, *Job*, 161.
1533 Vulgate, 18:9; Dhorme, *Le Livre de Job*, 262.
1534 Vulgate, 18:11.
1535 Driver and Gray, quoted in Rowley, *Job*, 161.
1536 Hesychius, quoted in Simonetti and Conti, *Ancient Christian Commentary*, 103.
1537 Driver and Gray, quoted in Rowley, *Job*, 161.
1538 Habel, *Book of Job*, 69.
1539 Gersonides, *On the Book of Job*, 119.
1540 Rowley, *Job*, 162–63.
1541 Dhorme, *Le Livre de Job*, 264.
1542 Marshall, quoted in Rowley, *Job*, 263.

1543 Tur-Sinai, *Book of Job*, 150.

1544 Newsom, *Book of Job*, 177.

1545 Rowley, *Job*, 162.

1546 Dhorme, *Le Livre de Job*, 264.

1547 Zockler, quoted in Rowley, *Job*, 162.

1548 Rashi, in Rosenberg, *Job*, 210.

1549 Rashi, in Rosenberg, *Job*, 210.

1550 Gersonides, *On the Book of Job*, 119.

1551 Driver and Gray, quoted in Rowley, *Job*, 162.

1552 Hartley, *Book of Job*, 325.

1553 Mezudat David, in Rosenberg, *Job*, 209.

1554 Rowley, *Job*, 162–63.

1555 Ball, quoted in Rowley, *Job*, 163.

1556 Driver and Gray, quoted in Rowley, *Job*, 163.

1557 Gersonides, *On the Book of Job*, 119.

1558 Ibn Ezra, *Job*, 209.

1559 Ehrlich, quoted in Rowley, *Job*, 163.

1560 Dhorme, *Le Livre de Job*, 266.

1561 Homer, *Odyssey*, sect. XXII.

1562 Reichert, *Job*, 79.

1563 Driver and Gray, quoted in Rowley, *Job*, 163.

1564 Rowley, *Job*, 163.

1565 Ephrem the Syrian, quoted in Simonetti and Conti, *Ancient Christian Commentary*, 99–100.

1566 Vulgate, 18:17. Julian, quoted in Simonetti and Conti, *Ancient Christian Commentary*, 100.

1567 Hartley, *Book of Job*, 326.

1568 Driver and Gray, quoted in Rowley, *Job*, 163.

1569 Driver and Gray, quoted in Rowley, *Job*, 163.

1570 Rowley, *Job*, 163.

1571 Ball, quoted in Rowley, *Job*, 163.

1572 Beer, quoted in Rowley, *Job*, 163.

1573 Mezudat David, in Rosenberg, *Job*, 213.

1574 Ewald, *Commentary on the Book of Job*, 219.

1575 Reichert, *Job*, 81.

1576 Moffat, quoted in Rowley, *Job*, 164.

1577 Ball, quoted in Rowley, *Job*, 164.

1578 Tur-Sinai, *Book of Job*, 152.

1579 Rowley, *Job*, 164–65.

1580 LXX, 18:21; Julian, quoted in Simonetti and Conti, *Ancient Christian Commentary*, 97.

1581 Gregory, quoted in Simonetti and Conti, *Ancient Christian Commentary*, 98.

1582 Aquinas, *Commentary on the Book of Job*, 100.

1583 Rashi, in Rosenberg, *Job*, 214.

1584 Thomas, *Book of Job*, 220.

1585 Schultens, *Liber Jobi*, 2:68.

1586 Andersen, *Book of Job*, 158.

1587 Gordis, *Book of God and Man*, 80.

1588 Rodd, *Book of Job*, 37–38.

1589 Driver and Gray, quoted in Rowley, *Job*, 165.

1590 Driver and Gray, quoted in Rowley, *Job*, 165.

1591 Gibson, *Job*, 62.

1592 Budde, quoted in Rowley, *Job*, 165.

1593 Rowley, *Job*, 165.

1594 Newsom, *Book of Job*, 178.

1595 Hartley, *Book of Job*, 327.

1596 Henry, *Commentary on the Holy Bible*, 362.

1597 Wycliffe Bible, 19:23–29.

1598 Rashi, in Rosenberg, *Job*, 213.

1599 Wesley, 318.

1600 LXX, 19:2.

1601 Freehof, *Book of Job*, 79.

1602 Rashi, in Rosenberg, *Job*, 213.

1603 Mezudat David, in Rosenberg, *Job*, 212.

1604 Mezudat David, in Rosenberg, *Job*, 212.

1605 Stevenson, quoted in Rowley, *Job*, 165.

1606 Rashi, in Rosenberg, *Job*, 213.

1607 Ibn Ezra, *Job*, 208.

1608 Freehof, *Book of Job*, 79.

1609 Mezudat David, in Rosenberg, *Job*, 212.

1610 Mezudat David, in Rosenberg, *Job*, 212.

1611 Mezudat David, in Rosenberg, *Job*, 212.

1612 Freehof, *Book of Job*, 79.

1613 Rashi, in Rosenberg, *Job*, 214.

1614 Wesley, 319.

1615 Dhorme, *Le Livre de Job*, 272–73.

1616 LXX, 19:8.

1617 Dhorme, *Le Livre de Job*, 272–73.

1618 Rowley, *Job*, 168.

1619 Rowley, *Job*, 168.

1620 Rowley, *Job*, 168.

1621 Dhorme, *Le Livre de Job*, 273.

1622 Wesley, 320.

1623 Mezudat David, in Rosenberg, *Job*, 213.

1624 Stevenson, quoted in Rowley, *Job*, 167–68.

1625 Stevenson, quoted in Rowley, *Job*, 167–68.
1626 Stevenson, quoted in Rowley, *Job*, 167–68.
1627 Peshitta, 19:10.
1628 Freehof, *Book of Job*, 80.
1629 Freehof, *Book of Job*, 80.
1630 Mezudat David, in Rosenberg, *Job*, 213.
1631 Mezudat David, in Rosenberg, *Job*, 213.
1632 Mezudat David, in Rosenberg, *Job*, 213.
1633 Rowley, *Job*, 168.
1634 Rowley, *Job*, 168.
1635 All quoted in Rowley, *Job*, 168.
1636 Rowley, *Job*, 168.
1637 Rowley, *Job*, 169.
1638 Wesley, 323.
1639 Wesley, 323.
1640 Rowley, *Job*, 169.
1641 Dhorme, *Le Livre de Job*, 277.
1642 Rowley, *Job*, 169.
1643 Rowley, *Job*, 169.
1644 Dhorme, *Le Livre de Job*, 278–79; Gordis, *Book of God and Man*, 83; Habel, *Book of Job*, 100.
1645 Habel, *Book of Job*, 100.
1646 Wesley, 324.
1647 Wesley, 324.
1648 Dhorme, *Le Livre de Job*, 278.
1649 Rashi, in Rosenberg, *Job*, 215.
1650 Wesley, 324.
1651 Wesley, 324.
1652 Rashi, in Rosenberg, *Job*, 215.
1653 Rashi, in Rosenberg, *Job*, 215.
1654 Mezudat David, in Rosenberg, *Job*, 214; Trani, *Sefer Iyyov*, 138.
1655 Maimonides, *Guide to the Perplexed*, 229.
1656 Freehof, *Book of Job*, 46.
1657 Gersonides, *On the Book of Job*, 123–25.
1658 Szold, *Sefer Iyyov*, 90.
1659 Szold, *Sefer Iyyov*, 90.
1660 Mezudat David, in Rosenberg, *Job*, 217, and Le Hir, *Le Livre de Job*, 66.
1661 Mezudat David, in Rosenberg, *Job*, 217.
1662 Sforno, *Sefer Iyyov*, 100.
1663 Freehof, *Book of Job*, 81.
1664 Mezudat David, in Rosenberg, *Job*, 217.
1665 Strahan, quoted in Rowley, *Job*, 171.

1666 Wesley, 325.
1667 Wesley, 325.
1668 Freehof, *Book of Job*, 81.
1669 Freehof, *Book of Job*, 81.
1670 Dhorme, *Le Livre de Job*, 281–82.
1671 Dhorme, *Le Livre de Job*, 281–82.
1672 Habel, *Book of Job*, 101.
1673 Habel, *Book of Job*, 101.
1674 Habel, *Book of Job*, 101.
1675 Habel, *Book of Job*, 102.
1676 Rowley, *Job*, 171–72.
1677 Tur-Sinai, *Book of Job*, 155.
1678 Conder, quoted in Rowley, *Job*, 172.
1679 Stevenson, quoted in Rowley, *Job*, 172.
1680 Dhorme, *Le Livre de Job*, 281.
1681 Stevenson, quoted in Rowley, *Job*, 172.
1682 Theodosius, 181.
1683 Mezudat David, in Rosenberg, *Job*, 217.
1684 Mezudat David, in Rosenberg, *Job*, 217.
1685 RSV, 19:25–27.
1686 Job 16:19 (author's translation).
1687 2 Sam 14:11 (author's translation).
1688 Clines, *Job 1–20*, 366.
1689 Job 19:25 (author's translation).
1690 Terrien, quoted in Vicchio, 1:84.
1691 Job 19:26a (author's translation).
1692 Baba Batra, 16a; Terrien, quoted in Vicchio, 1:84.
1693 LXX, 19:25–26.
1694 KJV, 19:25–26.
1695 Clement, quoted in Vicchio, 1:144.
1696 Vulgate, 19:25.
1697 Vulgate, 19:26.
1698 Vulgate, 19:26.
1699 Saadiah, *Book of Theodicy*, 116.
1700 Gersonides, *On the Book of Job*, 123–24.
1701 Rashi, in Rosenberg, *Job*, 222.
1702 Thomas, *Book of Job*, 240.
1703 Ephrem, quoted in Simonetti and Conti, *Ancient Christian Commentary*, 105.
1704 Chrysostom, quoted in Simonetti and Conti, *Ancient Christian Commentary*, 105.
1705 Schutz, *Geistliche chormusik*.
1706 Handel, "I Know That My Redeemer Liveth."

1707 G. P. Schutz, *Das Buch Hiob*.
1708 Carpaccio, *Meditation on a Passio*.
1709 Carpaccio, *Job and the Dead Christ*.
1710 Harootian, *Job Standing Erect*.
1711 Wesley, 329.
1712 Wesley, 329.
1713 Ewald, *Commentary on the Book of Job*, 208–11.
1714 Davidson, quoted in Rowley, *Job*, 172–73.
1715 Jacobs, *Commentary on the Book of Job*, 93.
1716 Peake, quoted in Rowley, *Job*, 173.
1717 Walkley, *Commentary on the Book of Job*, 80.
1718 Fredericton, *Book of Job*, 119.
1719 Barnes, *Book of Job*, 89.
1720 Kelly, *Book of Job*, 84.
1721 Noyes, *Book of Job*, 87.
1722 Budde, quoted in Rowley, *Job*, 173.
1723 Kautzsch, *Das Buch Hiob*, 88.
1724 Andersen, *Book of Job*, 86.
1725 Renan, *Le Livre de Job*, 87.
1726 Rowley, *Job*, 172–73.
1727 Gordis, *Book of God and Man*, 82.
1728 Gordis, *Book of God and Man*, 131.
1729 Good, *In Turns of Tempest*, 54.
1730 Mezudat David, in Rosenberg, *Job*, 220.
1731 Nachmanides, *Sefer Iyyov*, 100.
1732 Stevenson, quoted in Rowley, *Job*, 173.
1733 Renan, *Le Livre de Job*, 88.
1734 Le Hir, *Le Livre de Job*, 92.
1735 Crampon and Segond, quoted in Rowley, *Job*, 174.
1736 Habel, *Book of Job*, 103.
1737 RSV, 19:29; NEB, 19:29; Gordis, *Book of God and Man*, 83.
1738 Rowley, *Job*, 174.
1739 McFadyen, *Problem of Pain*, 81.
1740 Stevenson, quoted in Rowley, *Job*, 174.
1741 All quoted in Rowley, *Job*, 175.
1742 Fohrer, *Studien zum Das Buch Hiob*, 85.
1743 All quoted in Rowley, *Job*, 175.
1744 Dhorme, *Le Livre de Job*, 287–99.
1745 Wycliffe Bible, 19:29.
1746 Henry, *Commentary on the Holy Bible*, 378.
1747 Rowley, *Job*, 175–76.

1748 Strahan, quoted in Rowley, *Job*, 175.
1749 Strahan, quoted in Rowley, *Job*, 175.
1750 Rowley, *Job*, 175.
1751 Peake, quoted in Rowley, *Job*, 176.
1752 Dhorme, *Le Livre de Job*, 289–90.
1753 Rashi, in Rosenberg, *Job*, 220.
1754 Mezudat David, in Rosenberg, *Job*, 219.
1755 LXX, 20:4.
1756 Ehrlich, quoted in Rowley, *Job*, 176.
1757 Kissane, quoted in Rowley, *Job*, 176.
1758 Habel, *Book of Job*, 302–3.
1759 Rashi, in Rosenberg, *Job*, 220.
1760 Rowley, *Job*, 176.
1761 Dhorme, *Le Livre de Job*, 290.
1762 Strahan, quoted in Rowley, *Job*, 177.
1763 Rowley, *Job*, 177.
1764 Habel, *Book of Job*, 104.
1765 Habel, *Book of Job*, 104.
1766 Mezudat David, in Rosenberg, *Job*, 220.
1767 Driver, quoted in Rowley, *Job*, 177.
1768 Freehof, *Book of Job*, 75.
1769 RSV, 20:7.
1770 Rashi, in Rosenberg, *Job*, 213.
1771 Ibn Ezra, *Job*, 211.
1772 Mezudat David, in Rosenberg, *Job*, 220.
1773 Peshitta, 20:7.
1774 Dhorme, *Le Livre de Job*, 292.
1775 Habel, *Book of Job*, 104.
1776 Saadiah, *Book of Theodicy*, 83.
1777 Saadiah, *Book of Theodicy*, 83.
1778 Dhorme, *Le Livre de Job*, 293.
1779 Mezudat David, in Rosenberg, *Job*, 220.
1780 Stevenson, quoted in Rowley, *Job*, 177–78.
1781 Rowley, *Job*, 178.
1782 Vulgate, 20:9.
1783 Duhm, quoted in Rowley, *Job*, 178.
1784 Freehof, *Book of Job*, 85.
1785 Tur-Sinai, quoted in Rowley, *Job*, 178.
1786 Budde, quoted in Rowley, *Job*, 178.
1787 Rowley, *Job*, 178.
1788 Rashi, in Rosenberg, *Job*, 214.

1789   Rashi, in Rosenberg, *Job*, 214.
1790   Rashi, in Rosenberg, *Job*, 214.
1791   Freehof, *Book of Job*, 85.
1792   Freehof, *Book of Job*, 85.
1793   Rowley, *Job*, 178.
1794   Rashi, in Rosenberg, *Job*, 214.
1795   Dhorme, *Le Livre de Job*, 295–96.
1796   Rashi, in Rosenberg, *Job*, 214.
1797   Mezudat David, in Rosenberg, *Job*, 213.
1798   Rashi, in Rosenberg, *Job*, 214.
1799   Rowley, *Job*, 179.
1800   Habel, *Book of Job*, 106.
1801   Habel, *Book of Job*, 106.
1802   Habel, *Book of Job*, 106.
1803   Freehof, *Book of Job*, 152–53.
1804   Freehof, *Book of Job*, 152–53.
1805   Freehof, *Book of Job*, 152–53.
1806   Rashi, in Rosenberg, *Job*, 214.
1807   Rashi, in Rosenberg, *Job*, 214.
1808   Rowley, *Job*, 179.
1809   Klostermann, *Job*, 179.
1810   Klostermann, *Job*, 179.
1811   Dhorme, *Le Livre de Job*, 297–98.
1812   Strahan, quoted in Rowley, *Job*, 179.
1813   Mezudat David, in Rosenberg, *Job*, 214.
1814   Vulgate, 20:18.
1815   Rowley, *Job*, 179.
1816   Habel, *Book of Job*, 105.
1817   Habel, *Book of Job*, 105.
1818   Gersonides, *On the Book of Job*, 129–30.
1819   Szold, quoted in Rowley, *Job*, 180–81.
1820   Driver, quoted in Rowley, *Job*, 181.
1821   Habel, *Book of Job*, 105.
1822   Rashi, in Rosenberg, *Job*, 215.
1823   Habel, *Book of Job*, 105.
1824   Habel, *Book of Job*, 105.
1825   Habel, *Book of Job*, 106.
1826   Habel, *Book of Job*, 106.
1827   Job 20:25 (author's translation).
1828   Freehof, *Book of Job*, 8.
1829   Freehof, *Book of Job*, 84.

1830 Rowley, *Job*, 182.
1831 LXX, 20:26; Driver, quoted in Rowley, *Job*, 182.
1832 Dhorme, *Le Livre de Job*, 304–5.
1833 Rowley, *Job*, 182–83.
1834 Rowley, *Job*, 182–83.
1835 Gray, quoted in Rowley, *Job*, 182.
1836 Budde, quoted in Rowley, *Job*, 182–83; Dhorme, *Le Livre de Job*, 298.
1837 Saadiah, *Book of Theodicy*, 86.
1838 Rashi, in Rosenberg, *Job*, 215.
1839 Newsom, "Job and His Friends," 491–92.
1840 Henry, *Commentary on the Holy Bible*, 397.
1841 Newsom, "Job and His Friends," 491.
1842 Gordis, *Book of God and Man*, 86.
1843 Gordis, *Book of God and Man*, 86.
1844 Gordis, *Book of God and Man*, 87.
1845 Gordis, *Book of God and Man*, 87.
1846 Wycliffe Bible, 21:7–34.
1847 Rowley, *Job*, 184.
1848 Mezudat David, in Rosenberg, *Job*, 215.
1849 Rashi, in Rosenberg, *Job*, 216.
1850 Rashi, in Rosenberg, *Job*, 216.
1851 Rowley, *Job*, 184.
1852 Rowley, *Job*, 184.
1853 Dahood, quoted in Rowley, *Job*, 184.
1854 Mezudat David, in Rosenberg, *Job*, 215.
1855 Saadiah, *Book of Theodicy*, 88.
1856 Rashi, in Rosenberg, *Job*, 220.
1857 Wycliffe Bible, p. 33.
1858 Mezudat David, in Rosenberg, *Job*, 216.
1859 Newsom, "Job and His Friends," 484.
1860 Author's analysis; Kissane, *Book of Job*, 143.
1861 Ball, quoted in Rowley, *Job*, 185.
1862 Dhorme, *Le Livre de Job*, 328–29.
1863 Rowley, *Job*, 185.
1864 Mezudat David, in Rosenberg, *Job*, 216.
1865 Terrien, *Job*, 963.
1866 Saadiah, *Book of Theodicy*, 88.
1867 Stevenson, quoted in Rowley, *Job*, 185.
1868 Rowley, *Job*, 185.
1869 Newsom, "Job and His Friends," 484.
1870 Rashi, in Rosenberg, *Job*, 216.

1871 Ibn Ezra, *Job*, 210.
1872 Rowley, *Job*, 185.
1873 Rowley, *Job*, 185.
1874 Saadiah, *Book of Theodicy*, 89.
1875 LXX, 21:13.
1876 Rowley, *Job*, 185.
1877 Mezudat David, in Rosenberg, *Job*, 217.
1878 Davidson, quoted in Rowley, *Job*, 185.
1879 Rowley, *Job*, 185.
1880 Fohrer, quoted in Rowley, *Job*, 185.
1881 Habel, *Book of Job*, 107.
1882 Wesley, 330.
1883 Saadiah, *Book of Theodicy*, 90.
1884 LXX, 21:16; Ball, quoted in Rowley, *Job*, 185.
1885 All quoted in Rowley, *Job*, 185–86.
1886 Habel, *Book of Job*, 107.
1887 Habel, *Book of Job*, 107.
1888 Habel, *Book of Job*, 107.
1889 Terrien, *Job*, 965.
1890 Stevenson, quoted in Rowley, *Job*, 187.
1891 Terrien, *Job*, 965.
1892 Newsom, "Job and His Friends," 493.
1893 Pope, *Job*, 159.
1894 Beetson, quoted in Rowley, *Job*, 185.
1895 Rowley, *Job*, 185.
1896 Stevenson, quoted in Rowley, *Job*, 185.
1897 Rashi, in Rosenberg, *Job*, 216.
1898 Rashi, in Rosenberg, *Job*, 216.
1899 Rashi, in Rosenberg, *Job*, 216.
1900 Wesley, 325.
1901 Newsom, "Job and His Friends," 493.
1902 Wesley, 325.
1903 Newsom, "Job and His Friends," 493.
1904 Terrien, *Job*, 965.
1905 Stevenson, quoted in Rowley, *Job*, 189–90.
1906 Stevenson, quoted in Rowley, *Job*, 189–90.
1907 Peshitta, 21:24b, and Stevenson, 190.
1908 Rowley, *Job*, 190.
1909 Rowley, *Job*, 190.
1910 Rowley, *Job*, 190.
1911 Kissane, quoted in Rowley, *Job*, 190.

1912   KJV and RSV, 21:30.
1913   All quoted in Rowley, *Job*, 191.
1914   Dhorme, *Le Livre de Job*, 322.
1915   RSV, 21:30.
1916   Wycliffe Bible, 21:32.
1917   Ball, quoted in Rowley, *Job*, 199.
1918   Peshitta, 21:32.
1919   Stevenson, quoted in Rowley, *Job*, 199.
1920   Rowley, *Job*, 199.
1921   RSV, 21:34b.
1922   Wesley, 326.
1923   Rowley, *Job*, 192.
1924   Habel, *Book of Job*, 108.
1925   Wycliffe Bible, 21:34.
1926   Terrien, *Job*, 1072; Newsom, "Context of Imagination," 162–64.
1927   Henry, *Commentary on the Holy Bible*, 405.
1928   Habel, *Book of Job*, 108.
1929   See Rowley, *Job*, 196.
1930   Terrien, *Job*, 972.
1931   Wycliffe Bible, ch. 22.
1932   Terrien, *Job*, 972.
1933   Terrien, *Job*, 972.
1934   Newsom, "Job and His Friends," 499–500.
1935   Habel, *Book of Job*, 109.
1936   Gordis, *Book of God and Man*, 88; BB 16b.
1937   Newsom, "Job and His Friends," 500.
1938   Newsom, "Job and His Friends," 500.
1939   Rashi, in Rosenberg, *Job*, 220.
1940   Mezudat David, in Rosenberg, *Job*, 219.
1941   Mezudat David, in Rosenberg, *Job*, 219.
1942   Rashi, in Rosenberg, *Job*, 220; Vulgate, 22:5.
1943   Dhorme, *Le Livre de Job*, 327; RSV, 22:5.
1944   KJV, 22:5.
1945   Saadiah, *Book of Theodicy*, 104.
1946   Saadiah, *Book of Theodicy*, 104.
1947   Mezudat David, in Rosenberg, *Job*, 219.
1948   Mezudat David, in Rosenberg, *Job*, 219.
1949   Saadiah, *Book of Theodicy*, 105.
1950   Newsom, "Job and His Friends," 500.
1951   Stevenson, quoted in Rowley, *Job*, 194.
1952   Mezudat David, in Rosenberg, *Job*, 219.

1953 Mezudat David, in Rosenberg, *Job*, 219.
1954 Dhorme, *Le Livre de Job*, 331–32.
1955 Habel, *Book of Job*, 109.
1956 Dahood, quoted in Rowley, *Job*, 194.
1957 Newsom, "Job and His Friends," 501.
1958 Rashi, in Rosenberg, *Job*, 218.
1959 Rashi, in Rosenberg, *Job*, 218.
1960 Stevenson, quoted in Rowley, *Job*, 194–95.
1961 Stevenson, quoted in Rowley, *Job*, 194–95.
1962 Rashi, in Rosenberg, *Job*, 218.
1963 Mezudat David, in Rosenberg, *Job*, 217.
1964 Stevenson, quoted in Rowley, *Job*, 195.
1965 Mezudat David, in Rosenberg, *Job*, 217.
1966 Mezudat David, in Rosenberg, *Job*, 217.
1967 Rowley, *Job*, 196.
1968 Calvin, *Sermons from Job*, 62.
1969 Calvin, *Sermons from Job*, 62.
1970 All quoted in Rowley, *Job*, 195.
1971 Kissane, quoted in Rowley, *Job*, 195.
1972 Blommerde, quoted in Rowley, *Job*, 197.
1973 Blommerde, *Northwest Semitic Grammar*, 17.
1974 Stevenson, quoted in Rowley, *Job*, 197.
1975 Rashi, in Rosenberg, *Job*, 218.
1976 Mezudat David, in Rosenberg, *Job*, 217.
1977 Rowley, *Job*, 197.
1978 Dahood, quoted in Rowley, *Job*, 197; RSV, 22:22.
1979 Mezudat David, in Rosenberg, *Job*, 218.
1980 LXX, 22:23.
1981 RSV, 22:23.
1982 Stevenson, quoted in Rowley, *Job*, 197.
1983 Rashi, in Rosenberg, *Job*, 218.
1984 Rashi, in Rosenberg, *Job*, 218.
1985 Stevenson, quoted in Rowley, *Job*, 197.
1986 Mezudat David, in Rosenberg, *Job*, 217.
1987 Mezudat David, in Rosenberg, *Job*, 217.
1988 Rowley, *Job*, 197.
1989 Rowley, *Job*, 197.
1990 Mezudat David, in Rosenberg, *Job*, 217.
1991 Meyouchas, *Sefer Iyyov*, 92.
1992 Meyouchas, *Sefer Iyyov*, 92.
1993 Rashi, in Rosenberg, *Job*, 218.

1994 Rowley, *Job*, 199.
1995 Job 22:29 (author's analysis).
1996 Dhorme, *Le Livre de Job*, 341.
1997 Holscher, quoted in Rowley, *Job*, 199.
1998 Stevenson, quoted in Rowley, *Job*, 199.
1999 Mezudat David, in Rosenberg, *Job*, 217.
2000 Ibn Ezra, *Job*, 213.
2001 Job 22:30 (author's translation).
2002 Newsom, "Job and His Friends," 507–8.
2003 Henry, *Commentary on the Holy Bible*, 416.
2004 Rowley, *Job*, 200.
2005 Wycliffe Bible, ch. 23.
2006 Rowley, *Job*, 200.
2007 Strahan, quoted in Rowley, *Job*, 200.
2008 Saadiah, *Book of Theodicy*, 90.
2009 Mezudat David, in Rosenberg, *Job*, 218.
2010 Rashi, in Rosenberg, *Job*, 219.
2011 Mezudat David, in Rosenberg, *Job*, 218.
2012 Stevenson, quoted in Rowley, *Job*, 200; LXX, 23:3.
2013 Strahan, quoted in Rowley, *Job*, 200.
2014 Strahan, quoted in Rowley, *Job*, 200.
2015 Rashi, in Rosenberg, *Job*, 219.
2016 Rashi, in Rosenberg, *Job*, 219.
2017 Rowley, *Job*, 200.
2018 Rowley, *Job*, 200.
2019 Meyouchas, *Sefer Iyyov*, 94.
2020 Stevenson, quoted in Rowley, *Job*, 215.
2021 Stevenson, quoted in Rowley, *Job*, 215.
2022 Habel, *Book of Job*, 114.
2023 Rashi, in Rosenberg, *Job*, 219.
2024 Rowley, *Job*, 201.
2025 Driver, quoted in Rowley, *Job*, 201.
2026 Strahan, quoted in Rowley, *Job*, 201.
2027 Saadiah, *Book of Theodicy*, 109.
2028 Rowley, *Job*, 201–2.
2029 Habel, *Book of Job*, 114.
2030 Rashi, in Rosenberg, *Job*, 219.
2031 Rowley, *Job*, 202.
2032 Duhm, quoted in Rowley, *Job*, 202.
2033 Rashi, in Rosenberg, *Job*, 219.
2034 Stevenson, quoted in Rowley, *Job*, 202.

2035 Saadiah, *Book of Theodicy*, 209.
2036 Reider, quoted in Rowley, *Job*, 202.
2037 Rowley, *Job*, 202.
2038 Stevenson, quoted in Rowley, *Job*, 202.
2039 Stevenson, quoted in Rowley, *Job*, 202.
2040 Mezudat David, in Rosenberg, *Job*, 218.
2041 Rashi, in Rosenberg, *Job*, 217.
2042 Rashi, in Rosenberg, *Job*, 217.
2043 Sforno, *Sefer Iyyov*, 63.
2044 LXX, 23:12.
2045 Pope, *Job*, 172.
2046 Stevenson, *Poem of Job*, 49.
2047 Rowley, *Job*, 203.
2048 Saadiah, *Book of Theodicy*, 210.
2049 Stevenson, quoted in Rowley, *Job*, 203.
2050 Stevenson, quoted in Rowley, *Job*, 203.
2051 Rashi, in Rosenberg, *Job*, 219.
2052 Rashi, in Rosenberg, *Job*, 219.
2053 Rowley, *Job*, 203.
2054 Saadiah, *Book of Theodicy*, 210.
2055 Rashi, in Rosenberg, *Job*, 220.
2056 Rashi, in Rosenberg, *Job*, 220.
2057 Rashi, in Rosenberg, *Job*, 220.
2058 Habel, *Book of Job*, 115; Job 23:17 (author's analysis).
2059 Dhorme, *Le Livre de Job*, 352.
2060 Newsom, "Job and His Friends," 510.
2061 Henry, *Commentary on the Holy Bible*, 422.
2062 Rowley, *Job*, 204.
2063 Rowley, *Job*, 204.
2064 Rowley, *Job*, 204.
2065 RSV, 24:1.
2066 LXX, 24:1.
2067 Driver, quoted in Rowley, *Job*, 204.
2068 Habel, *Book of Job*, 115.
2069 Habel, *Book of Job*, 115.
2070 Habel, *Book of Job*, 115.
2071 Andersen, *Book of Job*, 83.
2072 Habel, *Book of Job*, 116.
2073 Habel, *Book of Job*, 116.
2074 Rashi, in Rosenberg, *Job*, 221.
2075 Rashi, in Rosenberg, *Job*, 221.

ENDNOTES

2076 Rashi, in Rosenberg, *Job*, 221.
2077 Vulgate and Peshitta, 24:11.
2078 Wycliffe Bible, 24:13–17.
2079 Wycliffe Bible, 24:13–17.
2080 Habel, *Book of Job*, 117.
2081 Habel, *Book of Job*, 117.
2082 Rashi, in Rosenberg, *Job*, 221.
2083 Mezudat David, in Rosenberg, *Job*, 220.
2084 Rashi, in Rosenberg, *Job*, 221.
2085 Rowley, *Job*, 209.
2086 RSV, 24:16b.
2087 Rashi, in Rosenberg, *Job*, 221.
2088 Rashi, in Rosenberg, *Job*, 221.
2089 Habel, *Book of Job*, 116.
2090 Driver, quoted in Rowley, *Job*, 204.
2091 RSV, 24:20.
2092 Rowley, *Job*, 204.
2093 Stevenson, quoted in Rowley, *Job*, 204.
2094 Rashi, in Rosenberg, *Job*, 221.
2095 Rashi, in Rosenberg, *Job*, 221.
2096 Rowley, *Job*, 212.
2097 KJV and RSV, 24:22.
2098 Rowley, *Job*, 212.
2099 Dhorme, *Le Livre de Job*, 366; Pope, *Job*, 176.
2100 Kissane, quoted in Rowley, *Job*, 213.
2101 Rashi, in Rosenberg, *Job*, 221.
2102 Rashi, in Rosenberg, *Job*, 221.
2103 Habel, *Book of Job*, 117.
2104 Saadiah, *Book of Theodicy*, 211.
2105 Stevenson, quoted in Rowley, *Job*, 213.
2106 Stevenson, quoted in Rowley, *Job*, 213.
2107 Rashi, in Rosenberg, *Job*, 221.
2108 Habel, *Book of Job*, 118.
2109 Driver, quoted in Rowley, *Job*, 213.
2110 Rashi, in Rosenberg, *Job*, 221.
2111 Mezudat David, in Rosenberg, *Job*, 220.
2112 Mezudat David, in Rosenberg, *Job*, 220.
2113 Perdue, *Voice from the Whirlwind*, 71.
2114 Author's arrangement of Third Cycle.
2115 Job 25:1–6 (author's translation).
2116 Freehof, *Book of Job*, 84.

2117 Rowley, *Job*, 213, and Rashi, in Rosenberg, *Job*, 222.
2118 Saadiah, *Book of Theodicy*, 212.
2119 Rowley, *Job*, 213.
2120 Rowley, *Job*, 213.
2121 LXX, ch. 25.
2122 Mezudat David, in Rosenberg, *Job*, 223.
2123 Gordis, *Book of God and Man*, 90.
2124 Saadiah, *Book of Theodicy*, 212.
2125 Saadiah, *Book of Theodicy*, 212.
2126 Saadiah, *Book of Theodicy*, 212.
2127 Rashi, in Rosenberg, *Job*, 224.
2128 Rowley, *Job*, 215.
2129 Kimhi, *Commentary on the Prophets*, 149.
2130 Rowley, *Job*, 215.
2131 Rowley, *Job*, 215.
2132 Rowley, *Job*, 215.
2133 Mazudat David, in Rosenberg, *Job*, 223.
2134 Stevenson, quoted in Rowley, *Job*, 215.
2135 Stevenson, quoted in Rowley, *Job*, 215.
2136 Driver, quoted in Rowley, *Job*, 215.
2137 Author's analysis.
2138 Stevenson, quoted in Rowley, *Job*, 217.
2139 Rowley, *Job*, 215.
2140 Freehof, *Book of Job*, 84.
2141 Mezudat David, in Rosenberg, *Job*, 223.
2142 Mezudat David, in Rosenberg, *Job*, 223.
2143 Rashi, in Rosenberg, *Job*, 224.
2144 Rashi, in Rosenberg, *Job*, 224.
2145 Ibn Ezra, *Job*, 210.
2146 See Rowley, *Job*, 217.
2147 Rashi, in Rosenberg, *Job*, 224.
2148 Rowley, *Job*, 219.
2149 Rowley, *Job*, 219.
2150 Mezudat David, in Rosenberg, *Job*, 223.
2151 Rowley, *Job*, 219.
2152 Dhorme, *Le Livre de Job*, 384–85.
2153 Driver, quoted in Rowley, *Job*, 219.
2154 Rowley, *Job*, 219.
2155 Driver, quoted in Rowley, *Job*, 219.
2156 Freehof, *Book of Job*, 85.
2157 Rowley, *Job*, 220.

2158 Rashi, in Rosenberg, *Job*, 225.
2159 Jastrow, *Book of Job*, 90.
2160 Freehof, *Book of Job*, 85.
2161 Mezudat David, in Rosenberg, *Job*, 224.
2162 Mezudat David, in Rosenberg, *Job*, 224.
2163 Rowley, *Job*, 216–17.
2164 Jastrow, *Book of Job*, 90.
2165 Habel, *Book of Job*, 120.
2166 Rashi, in Rosenberg, *Job*, 225; Mezudat David, in Rosenberg, *Job*, 224.
2167 Rashi, in Rosenberg, *Job*, 225.
2168 Rowley, *Job*, 221.
2169 Habel, *Book of Job*, 120.
2170 Habel, *Book of Job*, 120.
2171 Saadiah, *Book of Theodicy*, 212.
2172 Stevenson, quoted in Rowley, *Job*, 221.
2173 Rowley, *Job*, 221.
2174 Mezudat David, in Rosenberg, *Job*, 224.
2175 Rashi, in Rosenberg, *Job*, 225.
2176 Driver, quoted in Rowley, *Job*, 221.
2177 Freehof, *Book of Job*, 86.
2178 Rashi, in Rosenberg, *Job*, 225.
2179 Driver, quoted in Rowley, *Job*, 221.
2180 Jastrow, *Book of Job*, 91.
2181 RSV, 27:22.
2182 KJV, 27:22.
2183 Freehof, *Book of Job*, 87.
2184 Wycliffe Bible, ch. 28.
2185 Newsom, "Job and His Friends," 528–29.
2186 Rowley, *Job*, 227.
2187 Pope, *Job*, 197.
2188 Blommerde, *Northwest Semitic Grammar*, 125.
2189 Gordis, *Book of God and Man*, 93.
2190 RSV, 28:2.
2191 Rashi, in Rosenberg, *Job*, 226.
2192 Dhorme, *Le Livre de Job*, 399–400.
2193 Rowley, *Job*, 227.
2194 Newsom, "Job and His Friends," 528–29.
2195 Rowley, *Job*, 227.
2196 Gordis, *Book of God and Man*, 93.
2197 Vulgate, 28:5; Holscher, quoted in Rowley, *Job*, 227.
2198 Freehof, *Book of Job*, 88.

2199 Freehof, *Book of Job*, 88.
2200 Tur-Sinai, *Book of Job*, 160.
2201 Freehof, *Book of Job*, 88.
2202 Freehof, *Book of Job*, 88.
2203 Dhorme, *Le Livre de Job*, 404.
2204 Monwinckel, quoted in Rowley, *Job*, 228.
2205 Rashi, in Rosenberg, *Job*, 226.
2206 Mezudat David, in Rosenberg, *Job*, 225.
2207 Rashi, in Rosenberg, *Job*, 226.
2208 Rashi, in Rosenberg, *Job*, 226.
2209 Rowley, *Job*, 228.
2210 Newsom, "Job and His Friends," 530.
2211 Jastrow, *Book of Job*, 92.
2212 Terrien, *Job*, 979.
2213 Terrien, *Job*, 979.
2214 Rowley, *Job*, 230–31.
2215 Rowley, *Job*, 230–31.
2216 Gray, quoted in Rowley, *Job*, 231.
2217 Both quoted in Rowley, *Job*, 231.
2218 Vulgate, 28:17; RSV, 28:17; Targum of Job, 28:17.
2219 Pliny, *Natural History*, 214.
2220 Peake, quoted in Rowley, *Job*, 231.
2221 Rowley, *Job*, 232.
2222 Terrien, *Job*, 980.
2223 Rowley, *Job*, 233.
2224 Saadiah, *Book of Theodicy*, 215.
2225 Mezudat David, in Rosenberg, *Job*, 226.
2226 Mezudat David, in Rosenberg, *Job*, 226.
2227 Terrien, *Job*, 980.
2228 Mezudat David, in Rosenberg, *Job*, 226.
2229 Terrien, *Job*, 980.
2230 Rashi, in Rosenberg, *Job*, 227.
2231 Mezudat David, in Rosenberg, *Job*, 226.
2232 Terrien, *Job*, 984.
2233 Henry, *Commentary on the Holy Bible*, 428.
2234 Newsom, "Job and His Friends," 537–38.
2235 Rashi, in Rosenberg, *Job*, 228.
2236 Rashi, in Rosenberg, *Job*, 228.
2237 Mezudat David, in Rosenberg, *Job*, 227.
2238 Rowley, *Job*, 235.
2239 Rowley, *Job*, 235.

2240 Rowley, *Job*, 235.
2241 Vulgate, 28:5; Theodosius, 24.
2242 Mezudat David, in Rosenberg, *Job*, 226.
2243 Leibush, 100.
2244 Mezudat David, in Rosenberg, *Job*, 226.
2245 Newsom, "Job and His Friends," 537–38.
2246 Newsom, "Job and His Friends," 538.
2247 Rashi, in Rosenberg, *Job*, 228; Mezudat David, in Rosenberg, *Job*, 226.
2248 Rashi, in Rosenberg, *Job*, 222.
2249 Rowley, *Job*, 236.
2250 Rowley, *Job*, 236.
2251 KJV.
2252 Rowley, *Job*, 236.
2253 Rashi, in Rosenberg, *Job*, 228.
2254 Mezudat David, in Rosenberg, *Job*, 226.
2255 Jastrow, *Book of Job*, 77.
2256 KJV.
2257 Newsom, "Job and His Friends," 540.
2258 Mezudat David, in Rosenberg, *Job*, 226.
2259 Gersonides, *On the Book of Job*, 236.
2260 Newsom, "Job and His Friends," 540.
2261 Freehof, *Book of Job*, 187–88.
2262 Freehof, *Book of Job*, 187–88.
2263 Mezudat David, in Rosenberg, *Job*, 227.
2264 Tur-Sinai, quoted in Rowley, *Job*, 240.
2265 Habel, *Book of Job*, 403–5.
2266 Pope, *Job*, 213.
2267 Wesley, 200.
2268 LXX, 29:18.
2269 Albright, "Name of Bildad," 35.
2270 Greenstein, *Job*, 122.
2271 Rowley, *Job*, 240.
2272 Rowley, *Job*, 240.
2273 Hoffman, "Relation between the Prologue and the Speech Cycle."
2274 Wesley, 201.
2275 Habel, *Book of Job*, 405.
2276 Freehof, *Book of Job*, 190–91.
2277 Rashi, in Rosenberg, *Job*, 229.
2278 Ibn Ezra, *Job*, 221.
2279 Rowley, *Job*, 240.
2280 Wesley, 201.

2281 Rashi, in Rosenberg, *Job*, 230.
2282 Mezudat David, in Rosenberg, *Job*, 239.
2283 Mezudat David, in Rosenberg, *Job*, 239.
2284 Rashi, in Rosenberg, *Job*, 241.
2285 Habel, *Book of Job*, 411–12.
2286 Ewald, *Commentary on the Book of Job*, 293.
2287 Wesley, 202.
2288 Tur-Sinai, quoted in Rowley, *Job*, 241.
2289 Szold, quoted in Rowley, *Job*, 241.
2290 Pope, *Job*, 215.
2291 Kissane, quoted in Rowley, *Job*, 241.
2292 Freehof, *Book of Job*, 91.
2293 Terrien, *Job*, 986.
2294 Terrien, *Job*, 986.
2295 Rodd, *Book of Job*, 57.
2296 Rowley, *Job*, 241–42.
2297 Duhm and Peake, quoted in Rowley, *Job*, 242.
2298 Strahan, quoted in Rowley, *Job*, 242.
2299 Budde, quoted in.
2300 Rowley, *Job*, 242.
2301 Freehof, *Book of Job*, 92.
2302 Rashi, in Rosenberg, *Job*, 239.
2303 Mezudat David, in Rosenberg, *Job*, 238.
2304 Rashi, in Rosenberg, *Job*, 239.
2305 Rowley, *Job*, 243–44.
2306 Hitzig, quoted in Rowley, *Job*, 244.
2307 Terrien, *Job*, 987.
2308 Rowley, *Job*, 244.
2309 Gray, quoted in Rowley, *Job*, 244.
2310 Dhorme, *Le Livre de Job*, 434.
2311 Mezudat David, in Rosenberg, *Job*, 238.
2312 Rashi, in Rosenberg, *Job*, 239.
2313 Ibn Ezra, quoted in Rosenberg, *Job*, 228.
2314 Rowley, *Job*, 244.
2315 Saadiah quoted in Rowley, *Job*, 244.
2316 Terrien, *Job*, 987.
2317 Terrien, *Job*, 987.
2318 Rowley, *Job*, 245–46.
2319 Jastrow, *Book of Job*, 101.
2320 Rashi, in Rosenberg, *Job*, 240.
2321 Rashi, in Rosenberg, *Job*, 240.

2322 Mezudat David, in Rosenberg, *Job*, 239.
2323 Ibn Ezra, *Job*, 228.
2324 Rodd, *Book of Job*, 57.
2325 Terrien, *Job*, 988.
2326 Jastrow, *Book of Job*, 98.
2327 Freehof, *Book of Job*, 93.
2328 Rodd, *Book of Job*, 57.
2329 Freehof, *Book of Job*, 94.
2330 Rashi, in Rosenberg, *Job*, 241.
2331 Rowley, *Job*, 250.
2332 Driver, quoted in Rowley, *Job*, 250.
2333 Stevenson, 100.
2334 Stevenson, 100.
2335 Rashi, in Rosenberg, *Job*, quoted in Rosenberg, *Job*, 229.
2336 Rashi, in Rosenberg, *Job*, quoted in Rosenberg, *Job*, 229.
2337 Freehof, *Book of Job*, 95.
2338 Rowley, *Job*, 251.
2339 Targum of Job, 30:29.
2340 Rowley, *Job*, 251–52.
2341 Mezudat David, in Rosenberg, *Job*, 240.
2342 Rowley, *Job*, 251–52.
2343 Jastrow, *Book of Job*, 99.
2344 Jastrow, *Book of Job*, 99.
2345 Mezudat David, in Rosenberg, *Job*, 240.
2346 Rodd, *Book of Job*, 56–57.
2347 Terrien, *Job*, 990.
2348 Terrien, *Job*, 990.
2349 Rodd, *Book of Job*, 58–59.
2350 Terrien, *Job*, 990.
2351 Delitzsch, *Biblical Commentary on the Book of Job*, xx.
2352 Freehof, *Book of Job*, 100.
2353 Buttenwieser, quoted in Rowley, *Job*, 261.
2354 Saadiah, *Book of Theodicy*, 220.
2355 Saadiah, *Book of Theodicy*, 220.
2356 Jastrow, *Book of Job*, 101.
2357 Jastrow, *Book of Job*, 101.
2358 Rowley, *Job*, 264–65.
2359 Mezudat David, in Rosenberg, *Job*, 240.
2360 Rowley, *Job*, 265.
2361 Mezudat David, in Rosenberg, *Job*, 240.
2362 Mezudat David, in Rosenberg, *Job*, 240.

2363 Rowley, *Job*, 253.
2364 Mezudat David, in Rosenberg, *Job*, 240.
2365 Sforno, *Sefer Iyyov*, 206.
2366 Rashi, in Rosenberg, *Job*, 241.
2367 Rowley, *Job*, 254.
2368 Delitzsch, *Biblical Commentary on the Book of Job*, 291.
2369 Rowley, *Job*, 254.
2370 Terrien, *Job*, 991.
2371 Delitzsch, *Biblical Commentary on the Book of Job*, 292.
2372 Delitzsch, *Biblical Commentary on the Book of Job*, 292.
2373 Rowley, *Job*, 255.
2374 Delitzsch, *Biblical Commentary on the Book of Job*, 292.
2375 Rowley, *Job*, 255.
2376 Rowley, *Job*, 255.
2377 Mezudat David, in Rosenberg, *Job*, 241.
2378 Terrien, *Job*, 992.
2379 Terrien, *Job*, 992.
2380 Rowley, *Job*, 255.
2381 Rodd, *Book of Job*, 58–59.
2382 Terrien, *Job*, 994.
2383 Terrien, *Job*, 994.
2384 Rowley, *Job*, 255.
2385 Freehof, *Book of Job*, 103.
2386 Rashi, in Rosenberg, *Job*, 242.
2387 Rashi, in Rosenberg, *Job*, 242.
2388 Rowley, *Job*, 256.
2389 Mezudat David, in Rosenberg, *Job*, 242.
2390 Freehof, *Book of Job*, 105.
2391 Mezudat David, in Rosenberg, *Job*, 242.
2392 Rowley, *Job*, 256–57.
2393 Driver, quoted in Rowley, *Job*, 257.
2394 All quoted in Rowley, *Job*, 257.
2395 All quoted in Rowley, *Job*, 257.
2396 All quoted in Rowley, *Job*, 257.
2397 Dhorme, *Le Livre de Job*, 459; Rashi, in Rosenberg, *Job*, 243.
2398 Dhorme, *Le Livre de Job*, 459.
2399 Peshitta, 31:23.
2400 Driver, quoted in Rowley, *Job*, 257.
2401 Bickell and Duhm, quoted in Rowley, *Job*, 257.
2402 Rashi, in Rosenberg, *Job*, 243.
2403 Rowley, *Job*, 257–58.

2404 Rashi, in Rosenberg, *Job*, 243.
2405 Freehof, *Book of Job*, 105.
2406 Ibn Ezra, *Job*, 230.
2407 Szold and Lubisch, quoted in Rowley, *Job*, 258.
2408 Ewald, *Commentary on the Book of Job*, 288–89.
2409 Delitzsch, *Biblical Commentary on the Book of Job*, 293.
2410 Delitzsch, *Biblical Commentary on the Book of Job*, 293.
2411 Delitzsch, *Biblical Commentary on the Book of Job*, 294.
2412 Delitzsch, *Biblical Commentary on the Book of Job*, 294.
2413 Delitzsch, *Biblical Commentary on the Book of Job*, 294.
2414 Mezudat David, in Rosenberg, *Job*, 242.
2415 Mezudat David, in Rosenberg, *Job*, 242.
2416 Rowley, *Job*, 259.
2417 LXX 31:31.
2418 Rowley, *Job*, 259.
2419 Freehof, *Book of Job*, 107.
2420 Mezudat David, in Rosenberg, *Job*, 243.
2421 Ibn Ezra, *Job*, 225.
2422 Mezudat David, in Rosenberg, *Job*, 243.
2423 Rowley, *Job*, 261.
2424 Rashi, in Rosenberg, *Job*, 245.
2425 Duhm, quoted in Rowley, *Job*, 261.
2426 Rowley, *Job*, 261.
2427 Terrien, *Job*, 996.
2428 Rowley, *Job*, 262.
2429 Rowley, *Job*, 262.
2430 Terrien, *Job*, 996.
2431 Freehof, *Book of Job*, 108.
2432 Rowley, *Job*, 261.
2433 Delitzsch, *Biblical Commentary on the Book of Job*, 294.
2434 Mezudat David, in Rosenberg, *Job*, 244.
2435 Job 33:19 (author's translation).
2436 Job 36:15 (author's translation).
2437 Job 34:3 RSV.
2438 Job 34:36 RSV.
2439 Job 33:12 RSV.
2440 Job 36:22 RSV.
2441 Job 36:26 RSV.
2442 Kautzsch, *Das Buch Hiob*, 209.
2443 Author's analysis.
2444 Author's analysis.

2445 Baba Bathra, 15b.
2446 Baba Bathra, 15b.
2447 Baba Bathra, 15b.
2448 Baba Bathra, 15b.
2449 Ibn Ezra, *Job*, 233.
2450 Maimonides, *Guide to the Perplexed*, 163; Saadiah, *Book of Theodicy*, 221.
2451 Vulgate, ch. 32.
2452 Gregory, quoted in Simonetti and Conti, *Ancient Christian Commentary*, 164.
2453 Theodore, quoted in Simonetti and Conti, *Ancient Christian Commentary*, 163.
2454 Stuhlmann, *Das Buch Hiob*, 31.
2455 All in bibliography.
2456 All in bibliography.
2457 Henry, *Commentary on the Holy Bible*, 448.
2458 Andersen, *Book of Job*, 100.
2459 Good, *In Turns of Tempest*, 319.
2460 Whedbee, "Comedy of Job," 28.
2461 Fohrer, quoted in Rowley, *Job*, 263.
2462 Hartley, *Book of Job*, 169.
2463 De Wilde, quoted in Rowley, *Job*, 263.
2464 Good, *In Turns of Tempest*, 320.
2465 Duhm, quoted in Rowley, *Job*, 263.
2466 Habel, *Book of Job*, 252.
2467 Dhorme, *Le Livre de Job*, 472–73.
2468 Hartley, *Book of Job*, 169.
2469 Rowley, *Job*, 263.
2470 Peake, quoted in Rowley, *Job*, 263.
2471 Testament of Job, 21.
2472 Baba Bathra, 15b.
2473 Saadiah, *Book of Theodicy*, 222.
2474 Rashi, in Rosenberg, *Job*, 246.
2475 Rashi, in Rosenberg, *Job*, 246.
2476 Maimonides, quoted in Vicchio, 2:112–13.
2477 Berg, *Essential Zohar*.
2478 Gersonides, *On the Book of Job*, 190–91.
2479 Gersonides, *On the Book of Job*, 190–91.
2480 Freehof, *Book of Job*, 207.
2481 Freehof, *Book of Job*, 208.
2482 Gordis, *Book of God and Man*, 104–5.
2483 Gordis, *Book of God and Man*, 104–5.
2484 Roth, in Glatzer, *Dimensions of Job*, 73.
2485 Eisen, *Book of Job*, 209–10.

2486 Eisen, *Book of Job*, 210.
2487 Finkelstein, "Insight into Our Deep Need," 29.
2488 Vulgate, ch. 32.
2489 Gregory, quoted in Simonetti and Conti, *Ancient Christian Commentary*, 164.
2490 Bede, quoted in Simonetti and Conti, *Ancient Christian Commentary*, 166.
2491 Aquinas, quoted in Vicchio, 2:141.
2492 Calvin, quoted in Vicchio, 2:187.
2493 Strigel, *Das Buch Hiob*, 227.
2494 Herder, in Glatzer, *Dimensions of Job*, 143.
2495 Lowth, in Glatzer, *Dimensions of Job*, 136.
2496 Michaelis, *Das Buch Hiob*, 226.
2497 Ewald, *Commentary on the Book of Job*, 326–27.
2498 Ewald, *Commentary on the Book of Job*, 326–27.
2499 Barnes, *Book of Job*, 220.
2500 Barnes, *Book of Job*, 220.
2501 Barnes, *Book of Job*, 221.
2502 Froude, "Book of Job," 33.
2503 All in bibliography.
2504 Noyes, *Book of Job*, 224.
2505 Garland, *Book of Job*, 247.
2506 Le Hir, *Le Livre de Job*, 127.
2507 Noyes, *Book of Job*, 225.
2508 Thomas, *Book of Job*, 188.
2509 Cheyne, *Job*, 197.
2510 Kelly, *Book of Job*, 206.
2511 Fredericton, *Book of Job*, 123.
2512 Jordan, *Commentary on the Book of Job*, 194.
2513 Peloubet, *Book of Job*, 230.
2514 Jennings, *Commentary on the Book of Job*, 199.
2515 Devine, *Problem of Pain*, 197.
2516 Kissane, quoted in Rowley, *Job*, 264.
2517 Rawlinson, *Job*, 209.
2518 Rawlinson, *Job*, 209.
2519 Rawlinson, *Job*, 210.
2520 Andersen, *Book of Job*, 188.
2521 Andersen, *Book of Job*, 188.
2522 Hartley, *Book of Job*, 174.
2523 Pollock, in Glatzer, *Dimensions of Job*, 268.
2524 Parente, "Book of Job."
2525 Row, *Future Retribution*, 207.
2526 Kraeling, quoted in Glatzer, *Dimensions of Job*, 205–14.

2527   Pope, *Job*, 228–29.

2528   Royce, quoted in Vicchio, 3:184–87.

2529   Weiss, quoted in Glatzer, *Dimensions of Job*, 181–93.

2530   Murray, quoted in Glatzer, *Dimensions of Job*, 194–97.

2531   Blake, "Image of Elihu," discussed in Vicchio, 3:109.

2532   Rowley, *Job*, 263–64.

2533   Freehof, *Book of Job*, 211.

2534   RSV.

2535   Ibn Ezra, in Rosenberg, *Job*, 219.

2536   Freehof, *Book of Job*, 208.

2537   Rowley, *Job*, 264.

2538   All quoted in Rowley, *Job*, 264.

2539   Terrien, *Job*, 998.

2540   Terrien, *Job*, 998.

2541   Mezudat David, in Rosenberg, *Job*, 220.

2542   Rowley, *Job*, 264.

2543   Terrien, *Job*, 998.

2544   Rowley, *Job*.

2545   Freehof, *Book of Job*, 209.

2546   Freehof, *Book of Job*, 209.

2547   Mezudat David, in Rosenberg, *Job*, 249.

2548   Mezudat David, in Rosenberg, *Job*, 249.

2549   Rowley, *Job*, 265.

2550   Rashi, in Rosenberg, *Job*, 250.

2551   Rashi, in Rosenberg, *Job*, 250.

2552   Rashi, in Rosenberg, *Job*, 250.

2553   Freehof, *Book of Job*, 209.

2554   Rowley, *Job*, 265.

2555   Rowley, *Job*, 265.

2556   Mezudat David, in Rosenberg, *Job*, 249.

2557   Rashi, in Rosenberg, *Job*, 250.

2558   Freehof, *Book of Job*, 209.

2559   LXX, 32:15–16.

2560   Budde, *Das Buch Hiob*.

2561   Dhorme, *Le Livre de Job*, 481–82.

2562   Mezudat David, in Rosenberg, *Job*, 249.

2563   Rowley, *Job*, 267.

2564   Terrien, *Job*, 999.

2565   Rowley, *Job*, 267.

2566   Rashi, in Rosenberg, *Job*, 250.

2567   Dhorme, *Le Livre de Job*, 482.

2568 Freehof, *Book of Job*, 60.
2569 Rowley, *Job*, 267.
2570 Dhorme, *Le Livre de Job*, 485.
2571 Driver, quoted in Rowley, *Job*, 267.
2572 Dhorme, *Le Livre de Job*, 485.
2573 Dhorme, *Le Livre de Job*, 485.
2574 Henry, *Commentary on the Holy Bible*, 435.
2575 Rowley, *Job*, 268.
2576 Rowley, *Job*, 268.
2577 Peake, quoted in Rowley, *Job*, 268.
2578 Peake, quoted in Rowley, *Job*, 268.
2579 Duhm, quoted in Rowley, *Job*, 268.
2580 Beer, quoted in Rowley, *Job*, 268.
2581 Dhorme, *Le Livre de Job*, 486–87.
2582 Holscher, quoted in Rowley, *Job*, 268.
2583 Kissane, quoted in Rowley, *Job*, 268.
2584 Peake, quoted in Rowley, *Job*, 268; Dhorme, *Le Livre de Job*, 487.
2585 RSV, 33:12.
2586 Budde and Duhm, quoted in Rowley, *Job*, 269.
2587 Rowley, *Job*, 269.
2588 Dhorme, *Le Livre de Job*, 486–87.
2589 Rowley, *Job*, 269.
2590 Peake, quoted in Rowley, *Job*, 269.
2591 Terrien, *Job*, 1000.
2592 Terrien, *Job*, 1000.
2593 Author's analysis.
2594 LXX, 33:12c.
2595 Duhm, quoted in Rowley, *Job*, 270–71.
2596 Rowley, *Job*, 271.
2597 Rowley, *Job*, 271.
2598 All quoted in Rowley, *Job*, 271.
2599 All quoted in Rowley, *Job*, 271.
2600 Calvin, quoted in Vicchio, 2:187.
2601 Calvin, quoted in Vicchio, 2:187.
2602 Terrien, *Job*, 1001.
2603 Rowley, *Job*, 271.
2604 Masoretic Text, 33:17b.
2605 Dahood, "Northwest Semitic Philology."
2606 Peshitta and Vulgate, 33:16–17.
2607 Masoretic Text, 33:17.
2608 Bickell, quoted in Rowley, *Job*, 271–72.

2609 All quoted in Rowle, *Joby*, 272.
2610 Dillmann, quoted in Rowley, *Job*, 272.
2611 Rowley, *Job*, 272.
2612 Both quoted in Rowley, *Job*, 272.
2613 Rowley, *Job*, 272.
2614 Terrien, *Job*, 1002.
2615 Terrien, *Job*, 1002.
2616 Rowley, *Job*, 272–73.
2617 Rashi, in Rosenberg, *Job*, 303.
2618 Mezudat David, in Rosenberg, *Job*, 304.
2619 Ibn Ezra, *Job*, 238.
2620 Rashi, in Rosenberg, *Job*, 304.
2621 Holscher, quoted in Rowley, *Job*, 273.
2622 Dhorme, *Le Livre de Job*, 499.
2623 Rowley, *Job*, 273–74.
2624 Rowley, *Job*, 274.
2625 Rowley, *Job*, 274.
2626 RSV, 33:23.
2627 Mezudat David, in Rosenberg, *Job*, 251.
2628 Mezudat David, in Rosenberg, *Job*, 251.
2629 Terrien, *Job*, 1004.
2630 Rashi, in Rosenberg, *Job*, 252.
2631 Rashi, in Rosenberg, *Job*, 252.
2632 Rashi, in Rosenberg, *Job*, 252.
2633 Both quoted in Rowley, *Job*, 274.
2634 Quoted in Rowley, *Job*, 274.
2635 Both quoted in Rowley, *Job*, 274.
2636 Rowley, *Job*, 274.
2637 Siegfried, quoted in Rowley, *Job*, 274.
2638 Nichols, quoted in Rowley, *Job*, 274.
2639 See Num 7:89.
2640 Author's analysis.
2641 Mezudat David, in Rosenberg, *Job*, 252.
2642 Rashi, in Rosenberg, *Job*, 255.
2643 Rowley, *Job*.
2644 Dhorme, *Le Livre de Job*, 503–4.
2645 Reider, quoted in Rowley, *Job*, 274.
2646 Guillaume, quoted in Rowley, *Job*, 274.
2647 Rowley, *Job*, 274.
2648 Rowley, *Job*, 274.
2649 Bickell, quoted in Rowley, *Job*, 274.

2650 Dhorme, *Le Livre de Job*, 504.
2651 Mezudat David, in Rosenberg, *Job*, 251.
2652 Rashi, in Rosenberg, *Job*, 252.
2653 Rashi, in Rosenberg, *Job*, 252.
2654 Pope, *Job*, 299.
2655 Mezudat David, in Rosenberg, *Job*, 251.
2656 Meyouchas, *Sefer Iyyov*, 207.
2657 Mezudat David, in Rosenberg, *Job*, 251.
2658 Rowley, *Job*, 276.
2659 Mezudat David, in Rosenberg, *Job*, 251.
2660 Rowley, *Job*, 276.
2661 Szold, quoted in Rowley, *Job*, 276.
2662 LXX, 33:31–33.
2663 Rashi, in Rosenberg, *Job*, 252.
2664 Rashi, in Rosenberg, *Job*, 252.
2665 Terrien, *Job*, 1008.
2666 Terrien, *Job*, 1006.
2667 Rowley, *Job*, 276–77.
2668 Rowley, *Job*, 276–77.
2669 Driver, quoted in Rowley, *Job*, 277.
2670 Freehof, *Book of Job*, 215.
2671 Freehof, *Book of Job*, 215.
2672 Freehof, *Book of Job*, 211.
2673 Rowley, *Job*, 277.
2674 Mezudat David, in Rosenberg, *Job*, 252.
2675 Rowley, *Job*, 278.
2676 Author's analysis.
2677 Driver, *Canaanite Myth*, 99–100.
2678 Terrien, *Job*, 1007.
2679 Rowley, *Job*, 278.
2680 Driver, quoted in Rowley, *Job*, 278.
2681 Driver, quoted in Rowley, *Job*, 278.
2682 KJV, 34:6.
2683 Dhorme, *Le Livre de Job*, 510–11.
2684 Kissane, quoted in Rowley, *Job*, 277.
2685 Mezudat David, in Rosenberg, *Job*, 253.
2686 Rowley, *Job*, 277.
2687 Rowley, *Job*, 277.
2688 Rowley, *Job*, 277.
2689 Mezudat David, in Rosenberg, *Job*, 252.
2690 Driver, quoted in Rowley, *Job*, 277.

2691 Mezudat David, in Rosenberg, *Job*, 252.
2692 Rowley *Job*, 279.
2693 Rowley, *Job*, 279.
2694 Mezudat David, in Rosenberg, *Job*, 253.
2695 Mezudat David, in Rosenberg, *Job*, 253.
2696 Rashi, in Rosenberg, *Job*, 253.
2697 Driver, quoted in Rowley, *Job*, 279.
2698 Rowley, *Job*, 279.
2699 Masoretic Text, 34:14.
2700 Septuagint and Peshitta, 34:14.
2701 Terrien, *Job*, 1008.
2702 Freehof, *Book of Job*, 217.
2703 Szold, quoted in Rowley, *Job*, 279–80.
2704 Freehof, *Book of Job*, 217–18.
2705 Rowley, *Job*, 281.
2706 Rosenberg, *Job*, 49–50.
2707 Freehof, *Book of Job*, 218.
2708 Rowley, *Job*, 281.
2709 Driver, quoted in Rowley, *Job*, 281.
2710 Driver, quoted in Rowley, *Job*, 281.
2711 Rashi, in Rosenberg, *Job*, 253.
2712 Mezudat David, in Rosenberg, *Job*, 252.
2713 Freehof, *Book of Job*, 218.
2714 Freehof, *Book of Job*, 218.
2715 Rowley, *Job*, 281.
2716 Rowley, *Job*, 281.
2717 Terrien, *Job*, 1009.
2718 Rowley, *Job*, 282.
2719 Freehof, *Book of Job*, 218.
2720 Rowley, *Job*, 282.
2721 Rowley, *Job*, 282.
2722 Rowley, *Job*, 282.
2723 Fohrer, quoted in Rowley, *Job*, 282.
2724 Zimmermann, quoted in Rowley, *Job*, 282.
2725 Peshitta, 34:25.
2726 Dhorme, *Le Livre de Job*, 519.
2727 Bickell, quoted by Rowley, *Job*, 282.
2728 Beer, quoted by Rowley, *Job*, 282.
2729 Mezudat David, in Rosenberg, *Job*, 253.
2730 Mezudat David, in Rosenberg, *Job*, 253.
2731 Driver, quoted in Rowley, *Job*, 282.

2732 Mezudat David, in Rosenberg, *Job*, 253.
2733 Davidson, quoted in Rowley, *Job*, 282.
2734 Peake, quoted in Rowley, *Job*, 282.
2735 Terrien, *Job*, 1010.
2736 Terrien, *Job*, 1010.
2737 Rowley, *Job*, 283.
2738 Hitzig, quoted in Rowley, *Job*, 283.
2739 Dhorme, *Le Livre de Job*, 523–24.
2740 Ehrlich, quoted in Rowley, *Job*, 283.
2741 Kissane, quoted in Rowley, *Job*, 283.
2742 Rowley, *Job*, 283.
2743 Rashi, in Rosenberg, *Job*, 254.
2744 Rowley, *Job*, 285.
2745 Rashi, in Rosenberg, *Job*, 254.
2746 Rowley, *Job*, 283.
2747 Masoretic Text, 34:32.
2748 Dhorme, *Le Livre de Job*, 524.
2749 Mezudat David, in Rosenberg, *Job*, 253.
2750 Mezudat David, in Rosenberg, *Job*, 253.
2751 Rowley, *Job*, 285.
2752 Terrien, *Job*, 1012.
2753 Vulgate, 34:34.
2754 RSV, 34:34.
2755 Duhm, quoted in Rowley, *Job*, 285.
2756 Ehrlich, quoted in Rowley, *Job*, 285.
2757 Dhorme, *Le Livre de Job*, 522.
2758 Pope, *Job*, 260.
2759 Duhm, quoted by Rowley, *Job*, 285.
2760 Terrien, *Job*, 1015.
2761 Terrien, *Job*, 1015.
2762 Rowley, *Job*, 287.
2763 Kissane, quoted in Rowley, *Job*, 287.
2764 Dhorme, *Le Livre de Job*, 472–73.
2765 Ehrlich, quoted in Rowley, *Job*, 287.
2766 Rowley, *Job*, 287–88.
2767 Dhorme, *Le Livre de Job*, 473.
2768 Peake, quoted in Rowley, *Job*, 288.
2769 Mezudat David, in Rosenberg, *Job*, 254.
2770 Terrien, *Job*, 1016.
2771 Rowley, *Job*, 288.
2772 Rowley, *Job*, 288.

2773 Terrien, *Job*, 1017.
2774 Mezudat David, in Rosenberg, *Job*, 254.
2775 Rashi, in Rosenberg, *Job*, 255.
2776 Rowley, *Job*, 288.
2777 Terrien, *Job*, 1016.
2778 Freehof, *Book of Job*, 220–21.
2779 Freehof, *Book of Job*, 220–21.
2780 Rowley, *Job*, 289.
2781 Peake, quoted by Rowley, *Job*, 289.
2782 Kissane, quoted by Rowley, *Job*, 289.
2783 Rosenberg, *Job*, 50.
2784 Dhorme, *Le Livre de Job*, 533.
2785 Ehrlich, quoted in Rowley, *Job*, 289.
2786 Wright, quoted in Rowley, *Job*, 289.
2787 Rashi, in Rosenberg, *Job*, 256.
2788 Rowley, *Job*, 289.
2789 Kissane, quoted in Rowley, *Job*, 289.
2790 Rashi, in Rosenberg, *Job*, 256.
2791 Freehof, *Book of Job*, 221.
2792 Rashi, in Rosenberg, *Job*, 256.
2793 Rowley, *Job*, 289.
2794 Ibn Ezra, *Job*, 250.
2795 Tur-Sinai, quoted in Rowley, *Job*, 289.
2796 Rowley, *Job*, 290.
2797 Driver, quoted in Rowley, *Job*, 290.
2798 Driver, quoted in Rowley, *Job*, 290.
2799 Davidson, quoted in Rowley, *Job*, 290.
2800 Freehof, *Book of Job*, 222.
2801 Freehof, *Book of Job*, 222.
2802 Terrien, *Job*, 1022.
2803 Szold, quoted in Rowley, *Job*, 291.
2804 Rowley, *Job*, 291.
2805 Ibn Ezra, *Job*, 254; Freehof, *Book of Job*, 223.
2806 Freehof, *Book of Job*, 223.
2807 Tur-Sinai, quoted in Rowley, *Job*, 291.
2808 Szold, quoted in Rowley, *Job*, 291.
2809 Duhm, quoted in Rowley, *Job*, 291.
2810 Beer and Strahan, quoted in Rowley, *Job*, 291.
2811 Gray, quoted in Rowley, *Job*, 291.
2812 Steinmann, quoted in Rowley, *Job*, 292.
2813 Fohrer, quoted in Rowley, *Job*, 291.

2814 Dhorme, *Le Livre de Job*, 539; Pope, *Job*, 268.
2815 Kissane, quoted in Rowley, *Job*, 292.
2816 Rowley, *Job*, 293.
2817 Rowley, *Job*, 293.
2818 Mezudat David, in Rosenberg, *Job*, 256.
2819 Freehof, *Book of Job*, 224.
2820 Bickell, quoted in Rowley, *Job*, 293.
2821 All quoted in Rowley, *Job*, 293.
2822 Rowley, *Job*, 293.
2823 Dhorme, *Le Livre de Job*, 541.
2824 Rowley, *Job*, 293.
2825 Rashi, in Rosenberg, *Job*, 257.
2826 Freehof, *Book of Job*, 224.
2827 Mezudat David, in Rosenberg, *Job*, 256.
2828 Rowley, *Job*, 293.
2829 Rowley, *Job*, 293.
2830 Masoretic Text, 36:13; and Rowley, *Job*, 293.
2831 Freehof, *Book of Job*, 224–25.
2832 Driver, quoted in Rowley, *Job*, 293.
2833 Duhm, quoted in Rowley, *Job*, 293.
2834 Rowley, *Job*, 293. And Dhorme, *Le Livre de Job*, 542.
2835 Rowley, *Job*, 294.
2836 Freehof, *Book of Job*, 225.
2837 Rowley, *Job*, 294.
2838 Dhorme, *Le Livre de Job*, 547.
2839 Gray, quoted in Rowley, *Job*, 294.
2840 Budde, quoted in Rowley, *Job*, 294.
2841 Peshitta, 36:21; Wright, quoted in Rowley, *Job*, 294; Dhorme, *Le Livre de Job*, 547.
2842 Rowley, *Job*, 297.
2843 Freehof, *Book of Job*, 226; Szold, quoted in Rowley, *Job*, 297.
2844 Rowley, *Job*, 297; Freehof, *Book of Job*, 226–27.
2845 Rashi, in Rosenberg, *Job*, 259.
2846 Mezudat David, in Rosenberg, *Job*, 258.
2847 Mezudat David, in Rosenberg, *Job*, 258.
2848 Rashi, in Rosenberg, *Job*, 259.
2849 Rowley, *Job*, 298.
2850 Rashi, in Rosenberg, *Job*, 259.
2851 Duhm, quoted in Rowley, *Job*, 298.
2852 Gersonides, *On the Book of Job*, 220.
2853 Driver, quoted in Rowley, *Job*, 299.
2854 Tur-Sinai, quoted in Rowley, *Job*, 299.

2855 Author's analysis.
2856 Pope, *Job*, 74.
2857 Rosemuller, quoted in Rowley, *Job*, 299.
2858 Freehof, *Book of Job*, 226.
2859 Freehof, *Book of Job*, 226; Peake, quoted in Rowley, *Job*, 299.
2860 Driver, quoted in Rowley, *Job*, 299.
2861 Henry, *Commentary on the Holy Bible*, 458.
2862 Newsom, "Job and His Friends," 590.
2863 Rowley, *Job*, 301.
2864 Bickell, Duhm, and Budde, all quoted in Rowley, *Job*, 301.
2865 Duhm, quoted in Rowley, *Job*, 301.
2866 Duhm, quoted in Rowley, *Job*, 301.
2867 All quoted in Rowley, *Job*, 301.
2868 Budde, quoted in Rowley, *Job*, 301.
2869 Dhorme, *Le Livre de Job*, 561.
2870 KJV, RSV, and the Masoretic Text, 37:6.
2871 Hitzig, quoted in Rowley, *Job*, 310.
2872 Rashi, in Rosenberg, *Job*, 260.
2873 Mezudat David, in Rosenberg, *Job*, 259.
2874 Newsom, "Job and His Friends," 590.
2875 Newsom, "Job and His Friends," 590.
2876 Newsom, "Job and His Friends," 590.
2877 Newsom, "Job and His Friends," 590.
2878 Pope, *Job*, 90.
2879 Newsom, "Job and His Friends," 590–91.
2880 Rowley, *Job*, 305.
2881 Duhm, quoted in Rowley, *Job*, 305; Dhorme, *Le Livre de Job*, 565.
2882 Freehof, *Book of Job*, 229.
2883 Newsom, "Job and His Friends," 591.
2884 Rashi, in Rosenberg, *Job*, 262.
2885 Rashi, in Rosenberg, *Job*, 262.
2886 Newsom, "Job and His Friends," 591.
2887 Newsom, "Job and His Friends," 591.
2888 Mezudat David, in Rosenberg, *Job*, 261.
2889 Kimhi, *Commentary on the Prophets*, 222.
2890 Ibn Ezra, *Job*, 256.
2891 Rowley, *Job*, 305.
2892 Gray, quoted in Rowley, *Job*, 305.
2893 Duhm, quoted in Rowley, *Job*, 305.
2894 Author's analysis.
2895 Freehof, *Book of Job*, 229.

2896 Rowley, *Job*, 306.
2897 Rowley, *Job*, 306.
2898 Gersonides, *On the Book of Job*, 221.
2899 Rowley, *Job*, 305.
2900 Newsom, "Job and His Friends," 591.
2901 Dhorme, *Le Livre de Job*, 570.
2902 Fohrer, quoted in Rowley, *Job*, 306.
2903 Rashi, in Rosenberg, *Job*, 265.
2904 Mezudat David, in Rosenberg, *Job*, 264.
2905 Targum of Job, 37:20.
2906 Driver, quoted in Rowley, *Job*, 306.
2907 Newsom, "Job and His Friends," 591–92.
2908 Newsom, "Job and His Friends," 591–92.
2909 Rowley, *Job*, 306–7.
2910 Kissane, quoted in Rowley, *Job*, 307.
2911 Pope, *Job*, 286.
2912 Rashi, in Rosenberg, *Job*, 265.
2913 Newsom, "Job and His Friends," 591–92.
2914 Rashi, in Rosenberg, *Job*, 265.
2915 Szold, quoted in Rowley, *Job*, 307.
2916 Rowley, *Job*, 307.
2917 RSV, 37:24b.
2918 RSV, 37:24b.
2919 Watson, *Job*, 393.
2920 Peake and Strahan, quoted in Rowley, *Job*, 309.
2921 Dhorme, *Le Livre de Job*, 575.
2922 Dhorme, *Le Livre de Job*, 575.
2923 Stevenson, quoted in Rowley, *Job*, 309.
2924 Dhorme, *Le Livre de Job*, 575.
2925 Rowley, *Job*, 307.
2926 All quoted in Rowley, *Job*, 307.
2927 Gray, quoted in Rowley, *Job*, 307.
2928 Author's analysis.
2929 Dhorme, *Le Livre de Job*, 575.
2930 Fohrer, quoted in Rowley, *Job*, 307.
2931 Dillmann and Duhm, quoted in Rowley, *Job*, 310.
2932 LXX, 38:11.
2933 Driver, quoted in Rowley, *Job*, 310.
2934 Driver, quoted in Rowley, *Job*, 310.
2935 Guillaume, quoted in Rowley, *Job*, 310.
2936 Rowley, *Job*, 310.

2937 Targum of Job, 38:19.

2938 Ibn Ezra, *Job*, 260.

2939 Mezudat David, in Rosenberg, *Job*, 266.

2940 Hoffmann, *Hiob*, 253.

2941 Dhorme, *Le Livre de Job*, 584.

2942 Dhorme, *Le Livre de Job*, 584.

2943 Ibn Ezra, *Job*, 260.

2944 Mezudat David, in Rosenberg, *Job*, 266.

2945 Mezudat David, in Rosenberg, *Job*, 266.

2946 Rowley, *Job*, 313.

2947 Rowley, *Job*, 313.

2948 Guillaume, quoted in Rowley, *Job*, 313.

2949 Dhorme, *Le Livre de Job*, 585.

2950 Hoffmann, quoted in Rowley, *Job*, 313.

2951 Merx, quoted in Rowley, *Job*, 313.

2952 Siegfried and Driver, quoted in Rowley, *Job*, 313.

2953 Tur-Sinai, quoted in Rowley, *Job*, 313.

2954 Peshitta and Targum of Job, 38:25.

2955 Dhorme, *Le Livre de Job*, 587.

2956 Rowley, *Job*, 311.

2957 Peake, *Job*.

2958 Dhorme, *Le Livre de Job*, 587.

2959 Dhorme, *Le Livre de Job*, 587.

2960 Rowley, *Job*, 311.

2961 Bickell and Duhm, quoted in Rowley, *Job*, 314–15.

2962 Gray, quoted in Rowley, *Job*, 315.

2963 Mezudat David, in Rosenberg, *Job*, 267.

2964 Mezudat David, in Rosenberg, *Job*, 267.

2965 RSV, 38:30.

2966 Driver, quoted in Rowley, *Job*, 315.

2967 Rowley, *Job*, 315.

2968 Dhorme, *Le Livre de Job*, 590.

2969 Freehof, *Book of Job*, 243.

2970 Erhlich, quoted in Rowley, *Job*, 315.

2971 Driver, quoted in Rowley, *Job*, 315.

2972 Rowley, *Job*, 316–17.

2973 Peake, *Job*, 292; or Rashi, in Rosenberg, *Job*, in Rosenberg, *Job*, 223.

2974 Watson, 381–82.

2975 Rowley, *Job*, 317.

2976 Leubisch, *Das Buch Hiob*, 229.

2977 Rashi, in Rosenberg, *Job*, in Rosenberg, *Job*, 216.

2978 Rowley, *Job*, 31.
2979 Duhm and Beer, quoted in Rowley, *Job*, 317.
2980 Rowley, *Job*, 317.
2981 Rashi, in Rosenberg, *Job*, 270.
2982 Rashi, in Rosenberg, *Job*, 270.
2983 Rowley, *Job*, 318.
2984 Duhm, quoted in Rowley, *Job*, 318.
2985 Mezudat David, in Rosenberg, *Job*, 269.
2986 Rowley, *Job*, 318.
2987 Mezudat David, in Rosenberg, *Job*, 269.
2988 Rashi, in Rosenberg, *Job*, 270.
2989 Ibn Ezra, *Job*, 263.
2990 Rowley, *Job*, 319.
2991 Gersonides, *On the Book of Job*, 239–40.
2992 Duran, *Ohev Mishpat*, 202.
2993 Mezudat David, in Rosenberg, *Job*, 269.
2994 Leibusch, 207.
2995 Rashi, in Rosenberg, *Job*, 270; Mezudat David, in Rosenberg, *Job*, 269; Targum of Job, 39:8.
2996 Rowley, *Job*, 319.
2997 Davidson, quoted in Rowley, *Job*, 319.
2998 Gersonides, *On the Book of Job*, 240.
2999 Rowley, *Job*, 319.
3000 Rashi, in Rosenberg, *Job*, 271.
3001 Leubisch, *Das Buch Hiob*, 207.
3002 Leubisch, *Das Buch Hiob*, 207.
3003 Ibn Ezra, *Job*, 264.
3004 Rowley, *Job*, 319.
3005 Mezudat David, in Rosenberg, *Job*, 270.
3006 Leibusch, 207; Terrien, *Job*, 1014.
3007 Terrien, *Job*, 1014.
3008 Stevenson, quoted in Rowley, *Job*, 319.
3009 Rowley, *Job*, 320.
3010 Mezudat David, in Rosenberg, *Job*, 270.
3011 Freehof, *Book of Job*, 247.
3012 Buttenwieser, quoted in Rowley, *Job*, 320.
3013 Ibn Ezra, *Job*, 222.
3014 Mezudat David, in Rosenberg, *Job*, 270.
3015 Mezudat David, in Rosenberg, *Job*, 270.
3016 Rashi, in Rosenberg, *Job*, 271.
3017 Rashi, in Rosenberg, *Job*, 271.
3018 Mezudat David, in Rosenberg, *Job*, 270.

3019 Dahood, quoted in Rowley, *Job*, 320.

3020 Mezudat David, in Rosenberg, *Job*, 270.

3021 Rowley, *Job*, 321.

3022 Dhorme, *Le Livre de Job*, 612.

3023 Gray, quoted in Rowley, *Job*, 321.

3024 Terrien, *Job*, 1015.

3025 Mezudat David, in Rosenberg, *Job*, 271.

3026 Mezudat David, in Rosenberg, *Job*, 271.

3027 Dahood, quoted in Rowley, *Job*, 321.

3028 Rashi, in Rosenberg, *Job*, 272.

3029 Ibn Ezra, *Job*, 265.

3030 Rashi, in Rosenberg, *Job*, 273.

3031 Rowley, *Job*, 324.

3032 Rowley, *Job*, 324.

3033 Gray, quoted in Rowley, *Job*, 324.

3034 Mezudat David, in Rosenberg, *Job*, 271.

3035 Mezudat David, in Rosenberg, *Job*, 271.

3036 Mezudat David, in Rosenberg, *Job*, 271.

3037 Rowley, *Job*, 324.

3038 Rashi, in Rosenberg, *Job*, 272.

3039 RSV, 39:27.

3040 Stevenson, quoted in Rowley, *Job*, 324.

3041 Author's analysis.

3042 Author's analysis.

3043 Rashi, in Rosenberg, *Job*, 272.

3044 Terrien, *Job*, 1017.

3045 Terrien, *Job*, 1017.

3046 Mezudat David, in Rosenberg, *Job*, 271.

3047 Mezudat David, in Rosenberg, *Job*, 271.

3048 Rowley, *Job*, 325.

3049 Rowley, *Job*, 325.

3050 Dhorme, *Le Livre de Job*, 614.

3051 KJV, 40:4.

3052 RSV, 40:4.

3053 NIV, 40:4.

3054 NRSV, 40:4.

3055 2 Sam 6:22 RSV.

3056 Newsom, "Job and His Friends," 613.

3057 Hitzig, quoted in Rowley, *Job*, 325.

3058 Rashi, in Rosenberg, *Job*, 273.

3059 Mezudat David, in Rosenberg, *Job*, 272.

3060 Leibusch, 209.
3061 Freehof, *Book of Job*, 251.
3062 Freehof, *Book of Job*, 251.
3063 Rowley, *Job*, 326–27.
3064 Rowley, *Job*, 326.
3065 Freehof, *Book of Job*, 251.
3066 Rowley, *Job*, 327.
3067 Mezudat David, in Rosenberg, *Job*, 272.
3068 Mezudat David, in Rosenberg, *Job*, 272.
3069 Rowley, *Job*, 327.
3070 Mezudat David, in Rosenberg, *Job*, 272.
3071 Mezudat David, in Rosenberg, *Job*, 272.
3072 Leibusch, 210.
3073 Rowley, *Job*, 327.
3074 Duhm, quoted in Rowley, *Job*, 327.
3075 Kissane, quoted in Rowley, *Job*, 327; Dhorme, *Le Livre de Job*, 617.
3076 Rashi, in Rosenberg, *Job*, 271.
3077 Rashi, in Rosenberg, *Job*, 271.
3078 Mezudat David, in Rosenberg, *Job*, 272.
3079 Gersonides, *On the Book of Job*, 253–54.
3080 Rowley, *Job*, 327.
3081 Rowley, *Job*, 328.
3082 Rowley, *Job*, 328.
3083 Mezudat David, in Rosenberg, *Job*, 272.
3084 Ps 73:22 RSV.
3085 All quoted in Rowley, *Job*, 328.
3086 *Apocalypse of Enoch*; see Pope, *Job*, 320–23.
3087 *Fourth Esdras*, 6:47–52.
3088 Pope, *Job*, 320–23.
3089 Pope, *Job*, 320–23.
3090 Rashi, in Rosenberg, *Job*, 275.
3091 Rashi, in Rosenberg, *Job*, 275.
3092 Ibn Ezra, *Job*, 270.
3093 Mezudat David, in Rosenberg, *Job*, 274.
3094 Rashi, in Rosenberg, *Job*, 275.
3095 Rashi, in Rosenberg, *Job*, 275.
3096 Rashi, in Rosenberg, *Job*, 275.
3097 Ps 50:10 RSV.
3098 Mezudat David, in Rosenberg, *Job*, 274.
3099 Ibn Ezra, *Job*, 270.
3100 Gersonides, *On the Book of Job*, 255.

3101 Gersonides, *On the Book of Job*, 255.
3102 Author's translation.
3103 Saadiah, *Book of Theodicy*, 188.
3104 Maimonides, *Guide to the Perplexed*, 204.
3105 Freehof, *Book of Job*, 251–52.
3106 Gordis, *Book of God and Man*, 301–2.
3107 Pelaia, "What Is Behemoth," 1–3.
3108 Quoted in Simonetti and Conti, *Ancient Christian Commentary*, 209–10.
3109 Quoted in Simonetti and Conti, *Ancient Christian Commentary*, 209–10.
3110 Quoted in Simonetti and Conti, *Ancient Christian Commentary*, 209–10.
3111 Quoted in Simonetti and Conti, *Ancient Christian Commentary*, 209–10.
3112 Quoted in Simonetti and Conti, *Ancient Christian Commentary*, 209–10.
3113 Quoted in Simonetti and Conti, *Ancient Christian Commentary*, 209–10.
3114 Quoted in Simonetti and Conti, *Ancient Christian Commentary*, 209–10.
3115 Aquinas, quoted in Vicchio, 2:143–44.
3116 Brandier, quoted in Vicchio, 3:224.
3117 Milton, in Vicchio, 3:224.
3118 Collin de Plancy, *Infernal Dictionary*, 39.
3119 Rashi, in Rosenberg, *Job*, in Rosenberg, *Job*, 224.
3120 Peake, quoted in Rowley, *Job*, 328–29.
3121 Noyes, *Book of Job*, 221.
3122 Ewald, *Commentary on the Book of Job*, xx.
3123 Hutchinson, *Commentary on the Book of Job*, 236.
3124 Driver and Gray, quoted in Rowley, *Job*, 329.
3125 Fredericton, *Book of Job*, 243–44.
3126 Garland, *Book of Job*, 224.
3127 Fielding, *Book of Job*, 204.
3128 Quoted in Vicchio, 3:221–24.
3129 Jennings, *Commentary on the Book of Job*, 297.
3130 Davidson, quoted in Rowley, *Job*, 329.
3131 Vicchio, 3:221–24.
3132 Vicchio, 3:221–24.
3133 Vicchio, 3:221–24.
3134 Vicchio, 3:221–24.
3135 Vicchio, 3:221–24.
3136 Vicchio, 3:221–24.
3137 Vicchio, 3:221–24.
3138 Steinmann, quoted in Rowley, *Job*, 329.
3139 Rowley, *Job*, 328–29.
3140 Driver, quoted in Rowley, *Job*, 328.
3141 "Liber Floridus" (ca. 1090–1120), Ghent Museum. https://www.liberfloridus.be.

3142 "Behemoth and Leviathan" (1825, reprinted 1874), Tate Museum, UK.
3143 Newsom, "Job and His Friends," 623–24.
3144 Newsom, "Job and His Friends," 624.
3145 See Ps 74:14 RSV.
3146 Henry, *Commentary on the Holy Bible*, 470; Newsom, "Job and His Friends," 623–24.
3147 Rowley, *Job*, 332–33.
3148 Rowley, *Job*, 333.
3149 Dhorme, *Le Livre de Job*, 630.
3150 Peake, quoted in Rowley, *Job*, 333.
3151 Dhorme, *Le Livre de Job*, 630.
3152 Thomas, *Book of Job*, 277.
3153 Gordis, *Book of God and Man*, 304–5.
3154 Driver, quoted in Rowley, *Job*, 333.
3155 Driver, quoted in Rowley, *Job*, 333.
3156 Duhm, quoted in Rowley, *Job*, 333–34.
3157 Rowley, *Job*, 334.
3158 Budde and Kissane, quoted in Rowley, *Job*, 333.
3159 Dhorme, *Le Livre de Job*, 635.
3160 Rowley, *Job*, 333.
3161 Budde, quoted in Rowley, *Job*, 334.
3162 Kissane, quoted in Rowley, *Job*, 334.
3163 Gunkel, quoted in Pope, *Job*, 336–37.
3164 Pope, *Job*, 336–37.
3165 Pope, *Job*, 22–23.
3166 Gray, quoted in Rowley, *Job*, 334.
3167 Dhorme, *Le Livre de Job*, 635.
3168 Kissane, quoted in Rowley, *Job*, 335.
3169 Steinmann, quoted in Rowley, *Job*, 335; Pope, *Job*, 337.
3170 LXX, 41:11.
3171 Merx, quoted in Rowley, *Job*, 335.
3172 Rashi, in Rosenberg, *Job*, 282.
3173 Mezudat David, in Rosenberg, *Job*, 281.
3174 Rashi, in Rosenberg, *Job*, 282.
3175 RSV, 41:12.
3176 RSV, 41:12.
3177 Dhorme, *Le Livre de Job*, 636.
3178 Pope, *Job*, 338.
3179 Dhorme, *Le Livre de Job*, 636.
3180 LXX, 41:13.
3181 LXX, 41:13.
3182 Rowley, *Job*, 336–37.

3183 Peshitta, 41:14.
3184 Septuagint, Vulgate, and Aquila, 41:15.
3185 Newsom, "Job and His Friends," 623–24.
3186 Pope, *Job*, 338.
3187 Newsom, "Job and His Friends," 624.
3188 Newsom, "Job and His Friends," 624.
3189 Rowley, *Job*, 337.
3190 Peake, quoted in Rowley, *Job*, 337.
3191 Pope, *Job*, 340–41.
3192 Bickell, quoted in Rowley, *Job*, 337.
3193 Peshitta and Vulgate, 41:20.
3194 Strahan, quoted in Rowley, *Job*, 337; Pope, *Job*, 341.
3195 Newsom, "Job and His Friends," 624–25.
3196 Cross, quoted in Newsom, "Job and His Friends," 625.
3197 Rashi, in Rosenberg, *Job*, 284.
3198 Rowley, *Job*, 339.
3199 Duhm, quoted in Rowley, *Job*, 339.
3200 Duhm, quoted in Rowley, *Job*, 339.
3201 Kissane, quoted in Rowley, *Job*, 339.
3202 Dhorme, *Le Livre de Job*, 643–44.
3203 Peshitta and Targum of Job, 41:25.
3204 Pope, *Job*, 343–34.
3205 Newsom, "Job and His Friends," 624–25.
3206 Newsom, "Job and His Friends," 625.
3207 Rowley, *Job*, 339–40.
3208 Newsom, "Job and His Friends," 625.
3209 Aelian [X, 24].
3210 Rowley, *Job*, 340.
3211 Habel, *Book of Job*, 573–74.
3212 Newsom, "Job and His Friends," 625.
3213 Newsom, "Job and His Friends," 625.
3214 Perdue, *Voice from the Whirlwind*, 137.
3215 Rashi, in Rosenberg, *Job*, 284.
3216 Mezudat David, in Rosenberg, *Job*, 283.
3217 Frankfurt (1955), image no. 478. Iraq National Library, Museum no. 1M15618.
3218 Bousset, *Kyrios Christos*, 319.
3219 *Investigations at Beth Shean*, 63.
3220 Wood bean painting of Behemoth and Leviathan. See, Lois Drewer, "Leviathan, Behemoth, and Ziz," *Journal of Warburg and Courtauld Institutes* 44.1 (1981) 148–56.
3221 "Hellmouth," by Marion Simon; Tondal Museum (1475).
3222 "Hellmouth" Westchester Psalter (ca. 1150). See Lubbock, "Anonymous: Hellmouth, from the

Westchester Psalter."

3223   Wall painting, Wenhaston, Suffolk, St. Peter's Church (1520).

3224   Abbey of Conques-en-Rouergue (11th c.); Lincoln Cathedral (mid-12th c.); Paris National Library (Ms. Fr. 403, fol. 40r); Fitzwaren Psalter (Paris National Library, MS. Lat. 765, fol. 15v); Pierpont Morgan Library (MS. 945. Fol. 158 v).

3225   *Qisas al-Anbiyah* (Chester Beatty Library, MS. 231, fol. 156r).

3226   Bosse, illustration of Hobbes's *Leviathan* (1651).

3227   Blake, "Behemoth and Leviathan" (1825).

3228   Doré, "Destruction of Leviathan" (1865).

3229   Julian Levi, "Leviathan" (Smithsonian, 1960); Seymour Lipton, "Leviathan" (Philadelphia Public Art Display, 1963); Salvador Dali, "Leviathan" (1969).

3230   "Head of Leviathan" (Kazuya Akimoto Museum, Tokyo, 2005).

3231   Zanakan, "Rage of Leviathan" (2012).

3232   *Avoda Zara*, 3b.

3233   *Moed Katan*, 25b.

3234   *Pirke de Rabbi Eliezer*.

3235   Archeological Dig at Bet Zavit. See "Lying about Leviathan," *Haaretz*, August 2, 2019.

3236   Orel, *Handbook of Germanic Etymology*, 462. Also see *Codex Parisinus* Gr. 2327, National Library of France.

3237   Orel, *Handbook of Germanic Etymology*, 462. Also see *Codex Parisinus* Gr. 2327, National Library of France.

3238   "Leviathan," *Paradise Lost*; in *Oxford English Dictionary* (Oxford University Press, 1971).

3239   Hobbes, *Leviathan*.

3240   Melville, *Moby Dick*.

3241   *Leviathan*, a ship at the Battle of Trafalgar, October 21, 1805. The British ships battled against the French and Spanish Navies.

3242   Lord Byron, "An Oak Leviathan," *Childe Harold*, canto IV.

3243   Burke, quoted in Pardes, "Job's Leviathan," 241.

3244   "The Leviathan, Shor Habar and 'Reserved Wine,'" *Chabad House* magazine, August 2, 2019.

3245   George Oppen, "Leviathan," from *Collected Poems* (New York: New Directions, 1965).

3246   Robert Shea, *Illuminatus Trilogy* (New York: Dell, 1983).

3247   Karl Shukar, *In Search of Prehistoric Survivors* (London: Brandford, 1996).

3248   Newsom, "Job and His Friends," 627–28.

3249   Wycliffe Bible, 42:1–6.

3250   Rowley, *Job*, 341–42.

3251   Driver, quoted in Rowley, *Job*, 342.

3252   Delitzsch, *Biblical Commentary on the Book of Job*, 2:379–81; Zockler, and Kissane, quoted in Rowley, *Job*, 342.

3253   Rashi, in Rosenberg, *Job*, 288.

3254   Ibn Ezra, *Job*, 299.

3255   Rowley, *Job*, 342.

3256   Peake, quoted in Rowley, *Job*, 342.

3257 Rowley, *Job*, 342–43.
3258 Rashi, in Rosenberg, *Job*, 288.
3259 Driver, quoted in Rowley, *Job*, 3423.
3260 Fredericton, *Book of Job*, 160–61.
3261 Saadiah, *Book of Theodicy*, 292.
3262 KJV, 42:6.
3263 Chalice, 42:6. (Dead Sea Scrolls Q11).
3264 Curtis, "On Job's Response to Yahweh," 503–4.
3265 Newell, "Job: Repentant or Rebellious?," 157.
3266 Greenstein, *Job*, 185.
3267 Shaw, Vicchio, 2:219–20.
3268 Wiesel, Vicchio, 2:220.
3269 Curtis, "On Job's Response to Yahweh," 505–6.
3270 Jung, quoted in Curtis, "On Job's Response to Yahweh," 505–6.
3271 Jung, quoted in Curtis, "On Job's Response to Yahweh," 505–6.
3272 Curtis, "On Job's Response to Yahweh," 506.
3273 Rowley, *Job*, 345.
3274 Rowley, *Job*, 345.
3275 All quoted in Rowley, *Job*, 345.
3276 Peake, quoted in Rowley, *Job*, 345–46.
3277 Mezudat David, in Rosenberg, *Job*, 285.

Index of Foreign Words and Expressions

Akkadian/West Semitic/Ugaritic

Aib (Ugaritic name).

Aiab (Babylonian name).

Ayab (Name in Akkadian).

Alily "name for god."

Anat (Ugaritic goddess of war).

Asah "Maker."

Asharites (Islamic School of Philosophy).

Baal (Canaanite god of fertility; from Akkadian, *Belu*, or "Master.")

Banu "a limb" (Babylonian).

Bedad (Idumean King).

Bir "name of a weather god" (Babylonian).

Bita kima bita "house for house" (Ugaritic).

Bir-Daddan "name of Semitic King."

Gew "community" (Phoenician).

Hayyin (a Ugaritic god).

Kinsu "bridle" (Akkadian).

Lotan (brother of Anat) (Ugaritic).

Mot (Canaanite god of Death).

Resheph (Canaanite god).

Sipparu "bronze" or "copper" (Assyrian).

Arabic

Akzar "cruel."

'akzaru "my people failed."

Al-Lawh Al-Mafooz "the Preserved Tablet" (the Book of Deeds in Islam).

'awab "one who turns to God."

Ayyub "Job."

Gabab "to answer."

Gabbim "backs."

Hafadh "to protect."

Halak "to perish."

Iblis "the Demonic"

Jannah "Heaven."

Mayahum "without luck."

Mutazalites (Islamic School of Philosophy).

Nafs "soul"

Ragab "pebbles."

Rahab (Chaos Monster).

Ra's bira's "one head for another."

Shaytan "Satan."

'yb "root 'to repent.'"

Tiamat (Mesopotamian Chaos Monster).

Wahihan "express plainly."

Aramaic/Syriac

Gawab "defenses" (Syriac).

GBS "root meaning 'hail storm.'"

GWB "root for 'protection.'"

SWP "root 'to dislodge.'"

URL "root meaning 'urchins.'"

French

Fils d'Elohim "sons of God."

La Fin de Satan "The End of Satan."

Le Grande Seduto "The Grand Seduction."

Le Livre de Job "the Book of Job."

Mal de Job "Syphilis."

German

Beglucken "bless."

Darum spreche ich mich schuldig und Busse und Asche "Thus I am guilty myself and repent in dust and ashes."

Erheben "to lift up."

Fromme "pious."

Der geist "the ghost."

Hemd sitzi naher als der Rock "The shirt is closer than the coat."

Hiob "Job."

Der letzte "the last."

Die Seele "the soul."

Morgenrot "the red of morning."

Sage Gott und stirb "say God and die."

Schadenftreuden "restoration of fortune."

Wettersstrum "Tempest."

Greek

Apollon (Greek name of Abadon).

Apollymi "destruction."

Diazannumi "to gird."

Elysian (mythological field).

Gehenna "Hell."

Lepra "leprosy."

Perizanummi "to gird."

Phomikos "Phoenix."

Resen "bridle."

Siryon "armor."

Sor "stone."

Stelekos phonikox "like the Phoenix."

Tapeinosis "to be humble."

Zonnumi "to gird"

INDEX OF FOREIGN WORDS AND EXPRESSIONS

Latin

Bacullus Jacobi "Jacob's ladder."

Bemo "fire."

Carneum alienam pro carne sua "the skin of one for your own."

Diabo aduitrix "handmaid of the Devil."

Dolens "grieving."

Et involent peded ejus "And thy will be afraid at their feet."

Glebae "clods."

Imitation Christi "imitation of Christ."

Iob "Job."

Jobus Christi "Job as Christ-figure."

Lepra "leprosy."

Liber Jobi "book of Job."

Magnitudinus suae male "Will contend with power."

Moralia in Jobi "Gregory's commentary."

Morbus Jobi "Job's disease."

Mysteria "mystical."

'ogem "pot."

Peccatum originale "original sin."

Pety Job "poor Job."

Puritas innocentis "purity of the innocent"

Puritas poenitensis "purity of the repentant."

Redemptor Meus "My Redeemer."

Si lyra non lyrasset "If Lyrah ad not piped."

simplex and rectus "simple and upright."

Lutherus non satasset "Luther would not dance."

Tractatus Theologica-Philosophicus "work of Spinoza."

Hebrew

Abad "destroy."

Abeh "desire."

Abhadh "maker."

Ad "even."

Adonai "Lord."

Afar va efer "dust and ashes."

'ak "Surely."

'aksar "to shut" or "to close."

'ala' "sucks up."

Alah "oath" or "promise."

Alaw "torrent."

'alily "god."

Almah "young woman."

Alah "about him."

Alemo "to him."

am "people."

Amal "trouble."

Aph Beri (angel who rules the clouds).

Aphad "gird."

Aphar "dust."

Arak "long-suffering."

Araki-mishpat "to be found innocent or just."

Araphel "darkness."

Hebrew (continued)

Asah "maker."
Ashtoth "thought" or "cogitation."
'at "secret."
Attem "you."
Atiyn "bowels."
'atsar "withhold."
Aviyl "little ones."
Azar "gird."
Baklalah "blooming girl."
Bala "swallow."
Barach "bless" or "curse."
Baruch "bless" or "curse."
Baruch Elohim ve mos "bless or course God and die."
Basar "flesh."
Be'ad "of"
Beheqi "my bosom."
Belima "without anything."
Ben "sons" or "family."
Bene ha Elohim "sons of God."
Berith "covenant."
Besar "distress."
Beser "gold."
Bethulah "virgin"
Betoke "among."
Binah "understanding."
Binate "members."
Cathar "secret."
Chabar "to join."
Chagar "to gird."
Chaneeth "spear."
Ce'arah "whirlwind."
Chamets "marked."
Chaphar "paws."
Chasak "darkness."
Charcah "Sun."
Chashub "gold."
Chazah "to see."
Chemah "Sun."
Cherec "Sun."
Chol "sand" or "Phoenix," or "palm tree."
Cowd "secret."
Cuwp "tempest."
Cupawh "tempest."
Daka "crush."
Dam or *dammo* "blood."
De'abah" "dismay" or "sorrow."
Derash "allegory."
Devar/devarim "word/words."
Eben "stone."
'ed "mist," or "vapor."
Edh "witness."
Edo "lightning."
El "God."
Elohim "God."
Eloah "God."
El Olam "God of the universe."
Elohi "God."
Emeq "valley."
Emas "despise" or "reject."
'emer "speech" or "utterance."

INDEX OF FOREIGN WORDS AND EXPRESSIONS

Esah "plan."

Emas "despise."

Erek "patient."

Eyphal "darkness."

Gabbim "backs."

Gaddiys "tomb."

Gal "rock pile."

Gan "garden."

Gaylel "dung," or "turd."

Geburah "wisdom"

Gelel "to spoil."

Gewa "pride" or "courage."

Gilgul "reincarnation."

Gobah "lofty one."

Goel "Redeemer."

Gome "papyrus."

Halaila li "far be it from me."

Haphak "to overturn."

Hasak "darkness."

Hemma "these things."

Ha-Shem "God."

Hatap "seize."

Hema "yogurt."

Hen! "Behold!"

Hinne or *hinneh* "defective for 'Behold.'"

Hirhiq "he alienates."

Hokmah "wisdom."

Hoq hoq "without limit" or "he encircles."

Hug "vault of Heaven."

'im "if."

Iyyov "Job."

Ka "like."

Ka'as "vexation."

Kabed "heavy."

Kachol "like sand."

Kenaim "priests" or "princes."

Kesse "full moon."

Kesita "coin or money"

Kethem "gold."

Kethuvim "Writings."

Kabbir "big" or "powerful."

Kedown "spear."

Kidon "bow."

kiplayim "double."

kipla'Im "wonders."

Ki ruah hayyah "my life is empty."

Kisse "throne."

Kittor "smoke."

Kophar "ransom."

Lappid "lamp" or "torch."

Le "be strong."

Lehem "bread" or "heat."

Li hu "is mine."

Lis "Mediator."

Lo "not."

Lo "to him."

Lo ehad "there is no one."

lo hu "is mine."

Lotan "chaos monster"

Luah "tablet."

Luwts "mediator."

Ma "how."

Hebrew (continued)

Ma'al "false."

Mah "what"

Malakim "angels."

Masal "proverb."

Mappal "flakes" or "folds."

Masos "joy."

Mazzalot "constellation."

Mazzatot "girding stars."

Me'appar "from dust."

Mehuqqi "more than my law."

Mekukki "for my bosom."

Melek "King."

Melis "to scorn."

Melisay re'ay "My scorners are friends."

Merora "gall."

Me'zummah "purpose" or "thought."

Mi hi "who indeed."

Milleh/millin "word/words."

Min "from."

Mishpat "justice."

Missopeti "from my Judge."

Mishpati "justice."

Mishtar "rule" or "dominion."

Miskam "habitation."

Mithappek "flaming sword."

Mittahat "beneath."

Mokiah "Arbiter."

Moso "mine."

Mot (Canaanite god of Death).

Mots "chaff."

Nagah "to acquit."

Nahal "palm tree."

Nathan "maker."

Nazal "drop" or "drops."

Nefesh "soul," "self" or "appetite."

Nezam "ring."

Niham "comfort" or "repent."

Nihamti al "to repent in" or "to repent about."

Ohev "tent."

Ophel "darkness."

'orbo "his ambush."

Orehu "his light."

oro

Osh, *Kesil*, and *Chimah* "Constellations."

'owr "light" or "Sun."

Oyev "enemy."

Pa'al "maker."

Padah "ransom"

Paynim "Gentiles."

Paz "gold."

Perah "literal-historical interpretation."

Pid "misfortune."

Pidyom "ransom."

Qalal "light."

Qamat "wrinkles."

Qasar "impatient."

Qeber "grave."

Qes "end" or "extremity."

Qeset "bow."

Qillil "curse."

Qinrah "grave."

INDEX OF FOREIGN WORDS AND EXPRESSIONS

Qimanu "enemies."
Qoheleth "Ecclesiastes."
Pid "misfortune."
Ra'am "thunder."
Ratab "watered plant."
RBS "root for 'four-legged.'"
Raqam "small stones."
Ratab "a well-watered plant."
Re'em "unicorn" or "wild goat."
Rehi "my smell."
Rephaim "shades."
Renaim "large bird."
Ribot "pleading."
Rimmah "worm."
Rimmon "worm."
Riyb "case."
Ruah "spirit," "breathe," or "wind."
Ruhi "my wind"
Sadap or *sazap* "blighted."
Saddin (*cadiyn*) "to envelop."
Samek "sin," or "withers away."
Sar "closely."
Sawah "directed."
Sazap "scorched."
Sebu'oth "oath."
Sebu'ah "oath."
Schechin "sore" or "boil."
Sefer "book."
Seter "mask" or "veil."
Shaddai "Almighty."
Shanac "girding up."
Shapat "Judge."

Shawar "marked."
Shemesh "Sun."
Sheqer "false."
Sheteph "twice seven."
Sillem "replacement."
Shiyr "behold."
Siryah "armor."
Soa "rich" or "wealthy."
Sur "rock."
SWB (Hebrew root, "to disgorge.")
Ta'amulah "secrets."
Tachli rekeb "nether millstone."
Tahumot "warning."
Taklit "limit."
Tam/tamim "blameless
Taman "secret."
Taphon "North."
Taswit "bed."
Teben "stubble."
Tebo'ateka "will come to him."
Tebura "wisdom."
Telleth "aware of."
Te'su'ot "a scraping tool."
Timmale "cast down."
Tipla "unseemly."
Tiqwah "hope" or "thread."
Tohuwabohu "without form and void."
To'apa "horn" or "peak."
Topet "to spit."
Towla "worm" or "grub."
Towthach "darts" or "clubs."
Tsaphan "secret."

Hebrew (continued)

Tsel "shadow," or "shade."

Tusiyyah "success."

Torecha "speaks to the Earth," or "vermin."

Ulum "But!"

Wa'a'babber "and I will tell."

Wa'a'sallem "who will confront me?"

Wayisalam "what has given me."

Yahweh "the Lord."

Ya'ahil "shine."

Yahel "shine."

Yahmos "shall scatter."

Yam "the Sea."

Yirah "fear."

Yar'em "thunder."

Yar'enu "shows us."

Yaser "he confesses."

Yashar "upright."

Yasur "turn aside."

Yatsagh "maker."

Yahtop "chambers of south" or "store houses," or "strikes suddenly."

Yetzer ha ra "evil imagination."

Yerak "becomes tender."

Yetzer tov "good imagination."

YHL root that means "be quiet."

Yirah "fear."

Yirtob "becomes flesh."

Yishar "fresh product."

Zahab "gold."

Zaham "loathes."

There are also countless other Aramaisms (Syriac, Aramaic, and Arabic) words that we have not listed in this index.

Appendix A: The Theological Views of the Characters in the Book of Job.

EACH OF THE PRINCIPAL characters in the biblical book of Job have individual, theological understandings of the nature of Job's suffering. In this appendix, we will look at these theological positions of each of those characters, beginning with Eliphaz, Bildad, Zophar, and Elihu.

Eliphaz

The first of Job's friends, Eliphaz, mentions the Divine nineteen times: ten *El*; three *Shaddai*; one *Eloah*; one "Maker"; and one *Elohim*. Among the theological themes mentioned by Eliphaz are the Dome or Firmament of Heaven, at 22:14; the Wisdom of the Fathers motif, at 15:18; the *Qodesim*, or "Heavenly Beings," at 15:15; and a variety of precious metals, at 22:24–25.

Among the theological responses about the nature of Job's suffering, Eliphaz employs retributive justice theory at 4:7–8; 15:5–6; and 15:20, among a number of other places in his three speeches. Some critics suggest that Eliphaz alludes to the original sin perspective at 4:17; 5:7; 15:14; and 22:2. Others suggest that Eliphaz endorses the moral qualities view at 5:17; 5:19–20; 22:4; and 22:29–30.

Bildad

Bildad, Job's second friend, in his speeches at chs. 8, 18, and 25, mentions God nine times. Four of those are *El*; three are *Eloah*; and three are *Shaddai*. Bildadhas a variety of words for "net," "trap," etc. Bildad reveals a version of social immortality, at 18:17. He has two different words for "worm" *rimmah* (used five times) and *temeni*, employed twice by Bildad.

In terms of theological explanations for Job's suffering, Bildad uses retributive justice at: 8:4; 8:10; 8:13; 8:19; 8:20; and 18:5. What appears to be a version of the contrast perspective can be found at 18:5–6 and 18:18. And some critics suggest that Bildad endorses original sin theory at 25:4.

APPENDIX A: THE THEOLOGICAL VIEWS OF THE CHARACTERS IN THE BOOK OF JOB.

Zophar

Job's third friend, Zophar, mentions the Divine twelve times: two *Elohim*; six *El*; two *Eloah*; and two *Shaddai*. Zophar mentions *Sheol* twice, at 11:8 and 24:19; at times he is preoccupied with various body parts: "eyes" at 11:4; "lips" at 11:5; "mouth and tongue" at 20:12–15; "belly and tongue" at 20:15; and simply "flesh" at 20:23. Zophar refers to social immortality at 24:20; and he employs "if, then" constructions at 11:10, 13, and 14.

Theologically, like Eliphaz and Bildad, Zophar's primary approach is retributive justice, that can be found at 11:20; 20:5; 20:29; and 27:17–19. A version of divine plan theory seems to be the view expressed at 11:7; and Zophar also endorses the contrast perspective at 24:13–14 and 24:17.

Elihu

Earlier, in the commentary, we have suggested that the fourth friend of Job, Elihu, has a much wider theological vocabulary than the other three friends, particularly in regards to moral terms, hapaxes, thirty-three in the Elihu speeches, and names for God, where he employs: ten *El*; three *Elohim*; fifteen *Eloah*; five *Shaddai*; five *Asah*; and three others.

In terms of theological responses to the cause of Job's suffering, the fourth friend, Elihu, also uses a much more variegated approach than the other three friends. Elihu employs retributive justice, at 33:26; 34:12; 34:21–22; 34:24–26; 34:36–37; 35:5–6; 36:6, 10, 14, and 21. The moral qualities view can be found at 36:15 and 37:13, as we have suggested in the commentary.

Elihu employs the test perspective at: 33:1–6; 33:19; 34:3 and 36; and 36:21. Elihu also suggests a version of the divine plan theory at 33:12; 34:31–32; 36:22; 36:26–33; 37:14–21; and 37:22–24. Indeed, he uses the word *esah*, or "plan," at 37:17, and the term *derek*, or "ways," at 34:11, 21, and 27.

Yahweh and *Satan*

Although Yahweh and the Satan are also principal characters of the book, the latter's comments are mostly to be understood in terms of retributive justice theory, while the former, in his various names in the book, primarily resorts to divine plan theory, in his two speeches from the whirlwind. The opening of ch. 38, is a prime example of this perspective, as are the descriptions of Behemoth and Leviathan.

Appendix B: Job as a Law Case

A NUMBER OF CRITICS and interpreters of the book of Job have suggested that the primary understanding for making sense of the book is the language and the law and the courts of Ancient Israel. In an article for the *Biblical Archeological Review*, for example, Edward L. Greenstein entitled his essay "When Job Sued God." Greenstein suggests that the author of Job was fully aware of the ancient legal system of Israel. He knows he cannot call witnesses against God, so lacking witnesses, he makes an exculpatory oath, as was standard in legal cases.

Indeed, Greenstein suggests that oath may be found in ch. 31 of the book, where the patriarch from Uz swears to his innocence, and lists numerous wrongs and crimes he dud not commit. He also challenges God, Greenstein argues, to provide evidence against him that proves his guilt.

Finally, God does respond; but in legal terms, he throws out Job's case on a technicality in his oath. Job had claimed to know everything about God and how the universe works. So Yahweh reprimands Job. Where was Job when Yahweh established the foundations of the Earth? To this, Job had no reply.

A host of other scholars also have agreed that the book of Job is primarily a law suit of some kind. Richter understands the book as a secular law suit of Job against God, whereby the friends serve as witnesses, who attempt to develop a counter-suit against Job. In his view, Richter, believes that chs. 4–14 are an attempt at reconciliation out of court, and chs. 15–31 are seen as the formal, court proceedings between Job and his friends.

Whether or not this is the most fundamental metaphor for understanding the book of Job is not clear. What is clear, however, is that the language of the book contains far more words about the ancient Jewish court system than any other book of the Bible. This is particularly clear in chs. 9, 10, 13, 16, 19, 24, and 31.

See, for examples, the following verses:

- 9:2–3.
- 9:27–28.
- 9:32–35.
- 10:1–7.
- 13:18–23.
- 16:18–19.

- 19:23–27.
- 24:2–12.
- all of chapter 31.

Among the words related to the court system in Ancient Israel—words to be found in the book of Job—are the following:

- *Mishpat* "just" (twenty-eight times in book of Job).
- *Hug* "statute" (not in Job).
- *Dat* "law" (Aramaic word) (not in Job).
- *Sedeq* "righteousness" (eight times in Job).
- *Saddiq* "justice" (three times in Job).
- *Sadaq* "righteous" or "just" (three times in Job).
- *Sedaqah* "goodness" (four times in Job).
- *Miswa* "law" (not in Job).
- *Shofet* "Judge" (three times in Job).
- *Torah* "law" or "instruction" (one time in Job).
- *Diyn* "to judge" or "judgment" (two times in Job).
- *Chaph* "innocent" (once in Job).
- *Naqiy* "blameless" or "clean" (twice in Job).
- *Tam* "blameless" or "innocent" (eight times in Job).
- *Yashar* "upright" (seven times in Job).
- *Shaphat* "judge," or "judged" (five times in Job).
- *Peliyli* "to judge" (twice in Job).
- *Shaphat* "to judge" (seven times in Job).
- *Mokiah* "arbiter" (used once in Job).
- *Edh* "witness" (used twice in Job).
- *Goel* "redeemer" or "blood avenger" (used once in Job).

In total, these twenty-one legal terms are employed eighty-eight times in the book of Job, far more than any other book of the Bible of a comparable size. For this reason, many scholars have argued that the legal suit is the most fundamental way of understanding the biblical book of Job Perhaps the earliest and most original thinker who has held the Job as law suit view is former California philosopher, Herbert Fingarette. His essay, "The Meaning of Law in the Book of Job," was the first lengthy treatment of the theme. Two of the most original ideas in Fingarette's essay are first, that the classical Hebrew term, *naqam*, that means "revenge" or "retribution" does not appear in the book of Job. Fingarette's other important observation about the Job as Law Suit View is that the most important term to describe Job's relationship to Yahweh is the word "obedience." In Fingarette's view, Job's obedience to the "Law of Yahweh" is the most relevant characteristic of the Man from Uz's relationship to God.

Bibliography

Bible Sources

The Bible: King James Version [KJV]. Christian Art Publishers, 2016.
The Bible: New International Version [NIV]. Zondervan, 2018.
The Bible: Revised Standard Version [RSV]. Saint Benedict Press, 2009.
English Revised Version. Oxford University Press, 1991.
Geneva Bible. Hendrickson, 2007.
The Hebrew Bible: Masoretic Text [HB]. Zondervan, 2008.
New English Bible. Oxford University Press, 1980.
The Peshitta. B&H, 2017.
The Septuagint [LXX]. Edited by Lancelot Brenton. Hendrickson, 1986.
Tanakh: The Holy Scriptures [JPS]. Chapel Hill: University of North Carolina Press, 1985.
Vermes, Géza. *The Complete Dead Sea Scrolls*. 4th ed. New York: Penguin, 2011.
The Vulgate. Edited by Robert Weber. Deutsche Bibelgesellchaaft, 1983.
The Wycliffe Bible. Moody Publishers, 1990.

Ancient Texts

Book of Sirach. Edited by Jeremy Corley. Collegeville: Liturgical, 2016.
Book of Tobit. Edited by Adolf Neubauer. Eugene, OR: Wipf and Stock, 2005.
Divrei Iyyov. New York: Alshich Tanach Series, 1996.
Egyptian Execration Texts. Edited by EAW Budge. London: Hopkinson, 1924.
The Genesis Rabbah. Edited by Jacob Neusner. Tampa: University of South Florida, 1985.
The Holy Qur'an. Edited by Ahmed Ali. Princeton: Princeton University Press, 1993.
The Life of Job. By Aristeas. In Migne's *PG*, vol. 21, col. 728 a and b. Also see: Gifford, E. H. "Aristeas' Life of Job." In *Preparations for the Gospels*. Oxford: Clarendon, 1903.
The Mishnah Torah. Tel Aviv: Moznaim, 1998.
New Edition of the Babylonian Talmud. Tel Aviv: Aersire, 2015.
Midrash Rabbah. Edited by H. Freedman and Maurice Simon. New York: Socino, 1961.
The Targum of Job. Jerusalem: Ha Va'ad le-hosta, 1972.
The Targum on Numbers.
Tell Armana Letters. Edited by William Moran. Baltimore: Johns Hopkins University Press, 2002.
The Testament of Job. Edited by Maria Haralambakis and Lester Grabbe. Edinburgh: T. & T. Clark, 2014.

Bibliography

Abraham, Euchel Isaac. *The Book of Job*. Berlin, 1780.

Abraham, Israel ben. *Sefer Iyyov*. Berlin, 1809.

Abravnel, Isaac. *Six Lectures*. Cambridge: Cambridge University Press, 2015.

Abufelda. *Les Annales musalmanes*. Leipzig, 1834.

Akdamut ha-Shem. New York: Karmel, 1994.

Aked, Charles. *The Divine Drama of Job*. New York: Scribner, 1913.

Albo, Joseph. *Sefer Ha-'Ikkarim*. New York: Jewish Publications Society, 1946.

Al-Baydawi. *The Light of Revelation*. Boston: Beacon, 2016.

Albright, William F. "The Name of Bildad, the Shuite." *American Journal of Semitic Languages and Literature* 49 (1927) 31–36.

Al-Maqdisi. *Mukhtasar Minhaj*. Karachi: Dar Al-Manarah, 2010.

Al-Tabari. *The History of al-Tabari*. New York: State University of New York Press, 1989.

Alter, Robert. *The Wisdom Books*. New York: Norton, 2010.

Al-Thabani. *The Stories of the Prophets*. Charles Cutler Torrey published a translation with the Society of Biblical Literature in 1946.

———. *Tafsir al-Qur'an*. Cairo, 1450.

Al-Zamakhshari. *Kitab Al-Jibal wa al-Ambina*. Karachi: Dar Sader, 1860.

Andersen, Francis. *The Book of Job*. New York: IVP Academic, 2008.

Angioletti, Giovanni. *Giobbe*. Milan, 1955.

Anonymous. *Investigations at Beth Shean*. Jerusalem: Jerusalem Institute of Archeology, 1986.

Anonymous. *La Patience de Job*. Paris: Klincksieck, 1971.

Anonymous. "Morbus Jobi." *Urologic and Cutaneous Review* 40 (1936) 296–99.

Aquinas, Thomas. *Commentary on the Book of Job*. Steubenville, OH: Emmaus Academics, 2016.

Aristotle. *Generations of the Animals*. Cambridge: Harvard University Press, 1942.

Aufrecht, Walter, ed. *Studies in the Book of Job*. Toronto: Canadian Corporation for Studies in Religion, 1985.

Augustine. *The City of God*. Edited by Marcus Dods. New York: Penguin, 2017.

———. *Forgiveness of Sins and Baptism*. New York: Create Space, 2018.

Balchin, Frank. "Medicine." In *Dictionary of the Bible*, edited by James Hastings, 637–41. New York: Scribner, 1946.

Ball, C. J. *The Book of Job*. London, 1922.

Barnes, Albert. *The Book of Job: A Commentary*. London, 1847.

Barr, James. "The Book of Job and Its Modern Interpreters." Lecture delivered at John Rylands Library, Manchester, UK, February 10, 1971.

Barton, G. A. *Commentary on the Book of Job*. London, 1750. Reprinted by Forgotten Books, 2015.

Baskin, Judith. *Pharaoh's Counsellors: Job, Jethro, and Balaam in Rabbinic and Patristic Tradition*. Brown Judaic Studies 47. Chico, CA: Scholars, 1983.

Baumann, Emile. *The Book of Job*. Anne Arbor: University of Michigan Press, 1922.

Bede, the Venerable. *The Codex Amiatinus*. Leiden: Brill, 2019.

Beer, G. *Das Buch Hiob*. 2 vols. Berlin: 1895–1897.

Beeston, A. F. I. *The Book of Job and the Septuagint*. London, 1954.

Beirler, Jaime. "Though He Slay Me." In *Though He Slay Me*, edited by Jamie Freeman, 100–102. New York: Christian Focus, 2014.

Berg, P. S., ed. *The Essential Zohar*. New York: Harmony, 2011.
Bergant, Dianne. *Israel's Wisdom Literature*. Minneapolis: Fortress, 2005.
Berger, Alan. *Children of God*. New York: State University of New York Press, 1997.
Berkholz, C. A. *Das Buch Hiob*. Berlin, 1859.
Bernard, H. H. *Le Livre de Job*. Paris: Champion, 1959. Reissued 1988.
Bernard of Clairvaux. *Steps of Humility*. Collegeville: Cistercian, 1989.
Besserman, Lawrence. *The Legend of Job in the Middle Ages*. Cambridge: Harvard University Press, 1979.
Beza, Theodore. *Job Expounded*. London: Forgotten, 2018.
Bickel, G. *The Book of Job*. London, 1894.
Bigot, M. "Job." In *Catholic Dictionary*, edited by John Hardon, 219–20. New York: Image, 1980.
Blackmore, Richard. *A Paraphrase of the Book of Job*. London: EEDBO Editions, 2010.
Blake, William. *Illustrations of the Book of Job*. London, 1825.
Bloch, Ernest. *Atheism and Christianity*. London: Verso, 2009.
Blois, Peter. *L'Hystore Job*. New Haven: Yale University Press, 1937.
Blommerde, Anton. *Northwest Semitic Grammar*. Biblica Et Orientalia 22. Rome: Gregorian, 1969.
Bode, William. *The Book of Job*. London, 1848.
Bodin, Jean. "Behemoth." In *On the Demon-Mania of Witches*, 46–47. Toronto: Centre for Reformation and Renaissance Studies, 1995.
Bouquillon, Thomas. "Job's Disease." In *Book of Job*. Baltimore, 1888.
Bousset, Wilhelm. *Kyrios Christos*. Nashville: Abingdon, 1970.
Boye, Karin Maria. *The Seven Deadly Sins*. Stockholm, 1941.
Brandier, Urbain. *Arrest and Condemnation*. Paris, 1634.
Brodsky, Beverly. *The Story of Job*. New York: Braziller, 1986.
Browning, Robert. "The Bishop Orders His Tomb at Saint Praxed's Church." In *English Victorian Poetry*, edited by Paul Negri, 293–95. London: Dover, 1998.
Bruin, H. de. *Job*. Epic poem. 1944.
Buber, Martin. "A God Who Hides His Face." In Glatzer, *Dimensions of Job*, 56–65.
Budde, K. *Das Buch Hiob*. Berlin, 1913.
Burr, J. K. *A Commentary of the Book of Job*. London: Wentworth, 2016.
Burrell, David. *Deconstructing Theodicy: Why Job Has Nothing to Say to the Problem of Suffering*. Ada, MI: Brazos, 2008.
Buttenwieser, Moses. *The Book of Job*. London, 1922.
Byrd, William. *Anthems, Motets, and Services*. Griffin Records, 2010.
Calmet, A. *Commentary on the Book of Job*. Paris, 1722.
Calvin, John. *Sermons from Job*. Translated by Leroy Nixon. Grand Rapids: Eerdmans, 1952.
Cartensen, Roger. *Job: Defense of Honor*. Nashville: Abingdon, 1963.
Caryl, Joseph. *A Directory of the Afflicted*. London: The Classics, 2013.
Cassel, David. *Iyyov*. London, 1849.
Cauley, Kevin. "Job's Affliction." *British Numismatic Journal* (2006) 1102–7.
Chalice, Leander. *The Dead Sea Scrolls of Job from Cave 4 and Cave 11*. Manchester: Manchester University Press, 2013.
Chateaubriand, Francois-Rene. *The Genius of Christianity*. London: Forgotten Books, 2019.
Cheyne, T. K. *Job*. London, 1877 and 1901.
Chesterton, G. K. *Book of Job*. London: Forgotten Books, 2018.

Clarke, Adam. *Commentary on Job*. London: Macmillan, 2015. Kindle edition.
Clines, David J. A. *The Book of Job*. Nashville: Nelson, 2015.
———. *Job 1–20*. Nashville: Zondervan, 2017.
Collin de Plancy, Jacques-Albin-Simon. *Infernal Dictionary*. Paris, 1818.
Conder, C. R. "The Old Testament and Ancient Monuments." *Peshitta Enquiries for Quarterly Semitics* (1905) 155–58.
Coverdale, Miles. *Writings and Translations of Coverdale*. London: Parker Society, 2006.
Cowles, Henry. *The Book of Job with Notes*. New York: BiblioBazaar, 2009.
Cox, Samuel. *Commentary on the Book of Job*. London, 1880.
Crenshaw, James L. *Reading Job: A Literary and Theological Commentary*. Macon, GA: Smyth & Helwys, 2011.
Cross, Frank M. *Canaanite Myth and Hebrew Epic*. Cambridge: Harvard University Press, 1973.
Curtis, J. B. "On Job's Response to Yahweh." *Journal of Biblical Literature* 98 (1979) 268–82.
Dahood, Michael. "The Bible in Current Catholic Thought." *Biblia* (1962).
———. "Northwest Semitic Philology and Job." In *The Bible in Current Catholic Thought*, edited by John L. McKenzie, 55–74. New York: Herder, 1962.
———. "Some Rare Parallel Words in Job and Ugaritic." *Biblia* 38 (1957) 306–20.
Dallapiccola, Luigi. "Giobbe." On *Six Sonatas*. Musical album. Staple Bound, 1955.
Davidson, A. B. *The Book of Job*. London, 1884.
Delebecque, Edmee. *Le Livre de Job*. Paris: Leroux, 1914.
Dell, Katherine. *Reading Job Intertextually*. London: Bloomsbury, 2012.
Delitzsch, Franz. *Biblical Commentary on the Book of Job*. 2 vols. Edinburgh, 1876.
Devine, Minos. *The Problem of Pain*. London, 1927.
Dhorme, E. *Le Livre de Job*. Paris, 1926.
Dhorme, P. "Le Pays de Job." *Revue Biblique* 8 (1911) 102–7.
Di Lasso, Orlando. *The Complete Motets*. DVD. A. R. Editions, 2001.
Dillmann, A. *Hiob*. 4th ed. Berlin, 1891.
Dostoyevski, Fyodor. *The Brothers Karamazov*. New York: Dover Thrift, 2019.
Drewer, Lois. "Leviathan Behemoth, and Ziz." *Journal of Warburg and Courtauld Institutes* 44 (1981) 148–56.
Drexelius, Jeremiah. "Job's Disease." In Vicchio, *Job in the Medieval World*, 248.
Driver, G. R. *Canaanite Myth and Legend*. Edinburgh: T. & T. Clark, 1956.
Driver, S. R. *The Book of Job in the Revised Version*. London, 1906.
Driver, S. R., and G. B. Gray. *The Book of Job*. London: Scribner, 1921.
Duhm, B. *Das Buch Hiob*. Berlin, 1897.
Dumas, Alexandre. *The Count of Monte Cristo*. New York: Penguin, 2003.
Duran, Simeon. *Ohev Mishpat*. Oxford: Oxford University Press, 1930.
Ehrlich, Arnold B. *Das Buch Hiob*. Leipzig: Schiff, 1908.
Ehrlich, Leonard. *Karl Jaspers: Philosophy of Faith*. Boston: University of Massachusetts Press, 1975.
Eisemann, Moshe. *Iyov*. New York: Artscroll, 1994.
Eisen, Robert. *The Book of Job in Medieval Jewish Philosophy*. Oxford: Oxford University Press, 2004.
Eitan, I. "Job Thirteen." *American Journal of Semitic Languages and Literatures* 45 (1928–1929) 2–3.

Eknoyan, Garibed. "The Kidneys in the Bible." *Journal of the American Society of Nephrology* 16 (2005) 3464–71.

Emmerich, Anne Catherine. *The Life of the Blessed Virgin*. Springfield, IL: Templegate, 1954.

Evans, Jean M. "The Square Temple at Tell Asmar." *American Journal of Archeology* 11 (2007) 597–607.

Ewald, Georg. *Commentary on the Book of Job*. Berlin, 1852. Reprinted by Wipf and Stock, 2004.

Farissol, Abraham. *Sefer Iyyov*. New York: Hebrew Union College, 1981.

Fielding, G. H. *The Book of Job*. London: Macmillan, 1898.

Finkelstein, Louis. "Insight into Our Deep Need." Review of *J.B.*, play by Archibald MacLeish. *Life*, May 15, 1959.

Fishbane, Michael. *Midrashin Imagination*. New York: State University of New York Press, 1993.

Fohrer, G. *Studien zum Das Buch Hiob*. Berlin: Mohn, 1963.

Frankfurt, Henri. *Animal Remains from Tell Asmar*. Chicago: University of Chicago Press, 1941. Republished in 1955.

Fredericton, John. *The Book of Job*. London: Macmillan, 1879.

Freedman, David Noel. "The Structure of Job Three." *Biblica* 49 (1968) 503–8.

Freehof, Solomon. *The Book of Job: A Commentary*. New York: Union of American Hebrew Communications, 1963.

Frost, Robert. *Masque of Reason*. New York: Holt, 1945.

Froude, James Anthony. "The Book of Job." In *Short Studies on Great Subjects*. London, 1868. Reprinted by Wentworth, 2016.

Fullerton, Kemper. "Double Entendre in the First Speech of Eliphaz." *Journal of Biblical Literature* 49 (1934) 320–74.

Gammie, John. "The Angelology and Demonology in the Septuagint of the Book of Job." *HUCA* 56 (1985) 1–19.

Ganneau, Charles Clermont. *Etudes d'archeologie orientale*. Paris, 1880.

Garland, G. V. *The Book of Job*. London: Longmans, Green, 1891.

Garrett, Duane. *Shepherd's Notes: Job*. Nashville: Zondervan, 1998.

Geiger, Abraham. *Hiob*. Berlin, 1866.

Gensius, Wilhelm. *Hebrew Grammar*. 17th ed. London: Nabu, 2011.

Gersonides. *On the Book of Job*. Edited by Abraham Lassen. New York: Bloch, 1946.

Gibbs, Paul T. *Job and the Mysteries of Wisdom*. Nashville: Southern Publishing, 1967.

Gibson, E. C. S. *The Book of Job*. London: Methuen, 1918.

Gibson, John C. L. *Job*. Edinburgh: Saint Andrews Press, 1985.

Gilbert, George. *The Poetry of Job*. Chicago: McClurg, 1889.

Gilkey, Langdon. "Power, Order, Justice, and Redemption: Theological Comments on Job." Chapter 10 in *The Voice from the Whirlwind*, edited by Leo G. Perdue and W. Clark Gilpin. Nashville: Abingdon, 1992.

Girard, Rene. *The Scapegoat*. Baltimore: Johns Hopkins University Press, 1989.

Glatzer, Nahum. *The Dimensions of Job*. New York: Schoken, 1968.

Godinez, Felipe. *Los Trabajos de Job*. Seville: University of Seville Press, 1991.

Goethe, J. W. *Faust*. New Haven: Yale University Press, 2014.

Goldsmith, Robert Hillis. "The Healing Scourge: A Study of Suffering and Meaning." *Interpretation* 17 (1963) 1–27.

Good, Edwin. *In Turns of Tempest*. Palo Alto, CA: Stanford University Press, 1990.

Good, G. M. *Commentary on the Book of Job*. Edinburgh, 1812.
Gordis, Robert. *The Book of God and Man*. Chicago: University of Chicago Press, 1965.
———. *The Book of Job: A Commentary*. New York: Jewish Theological Seminary, 1978.
Gray, John. *The Book of Job*. Sheffield, UK: Sheffield Academic, 2010.
Greenberg, Hayim. *The Inner Eye*. New York: Jewish Frontier Association, 1964.
Greenberg, Irving. "Theology after the Shoah." *Modern Judaism* 26 (2006) 213–39.
Greenstein, Edward L. *Job: A New Translation*. New Haven: Yale University Press, 2019.
Gregory. *Moral Reflections on the Book of Job*. 5 vols. Collegeville: Cistercian, 2014.
Guillaume, A. "The Arabic Background of the Book of Job." In *Promise and Fulfillment*, edited by F. F. Bruce. Edinburgh: T. & T. Clark, 1953.
———. "Job." In *New Commentary on Holy Scripture*, edited by Charles Gore et al. Leiden: Brill, 1968.
Gunkel, Hermann. *Creation and Chaos*. Berlin, 1895.
Gutiérrez, Gustavo. *On Job*. New York: Orbis, 1970.
Guy, William. "Job's Disease." *Archives of Dermatology* 71 (1955) 355–56.
Habel, Norman. *The Book of Job*. Philadelphia: Westminster, 1985.
Hahn, H. A. *Commentar uber das Buch Hiob*. Berlin, 1850.
Halle-Wolfssohn, Aaron. *Commentary on Iyyov*. Prague, 1791; Vienna, 1806.
Hanawi, Jakut El. *Dictionary of Countries*. Istanbul, 1228.
Hanbeli, Mugir ed Din. *Tafsir*. Musul, 1495.
Handel, Georg F. *Der messias*. 1741.
Harper, Lisa. *Job: Bible Study Book*. Nashville: Lifeway, 2018.
Harper, W. R. *The Book of Job*. London, 1908.
Hartley, John. *The Book of Job*. 2nd ed. Nashville: Eerdmans, 1988.
Hastings, James. *Dictionary of the Bible*. Edinburgh: T. & T. Clark, 1909. Available online at https://www.studylight.org/dictionaries/hdb/u/uz.html.
Hegel, Georg. *Lectures on the Philosophy of Religion*. Bristol, UK: Thoemmes, 1895.
Hen, Zerahiah. *Sefer Iyyov*. Madrid, 1254.
Henry, Matthew. *Commentary on the Holy Bible*. 3 vols. London: Logos International, 1975.
Herder, J. G. *The Spirit of Hebrew Poetry*. London: Forgotten Books, 2012.
Heschel, Abraham. *The Prophets*. London: Harper, 1955.
Hirzel, L. *Hiob*. Berlin, 1839.
Hitchcock, R. D. *Bible Names Dictionary*. Benediction Classics, 2010.
Hitzig, F. *Das Buch Hiob*. Berlin, 1871.
Hobbes, Thomas. *Leviathan*. New York: Penguin Classics, 1982.
Hoffman, Yair. *Blemished Perfection*. Tel Aviv: Library of Hebrew Bible, 1996.
———. "The Relation between the Prologue and the Speech Cycle in Job." *Vetus Testamentum* 31 (1981) 160–70.
Hoffmann, G. *Hiob*. Berlin, 1891.
Holscher, G. *Das Buch Hiob*. Tubingen: Mohr, 1937.
Homer. *The Odyssey*. New York: Penguin, 1999.
Hone, Ralph. *Voice from the Whirlwind*. New York: Chandler, 1972.
Horst, F. *Hiob*. Berlin, 1902.
Hugo, Victor. *Hunchback of Notre Dame*. New York: Dover, 2006.
———. *La Fin de Satan*. London: Wentworth, 2016.
Hupfeld, B. *Das Buch Hiob*. Berlin, 1853.
Hutchinson, R. F. *A Commentary on the Book of Job*. London, 1873.

Ibn Ezra, Abraham. *Job*. Amsterdam, 1728, 1853.
Ibn Kathir. *The Stories of the Prophets*. New York: Create Space, 2014.
Israel, Manasseh ben. *The Conciliator of Rabbi Manasseh ben Israel: The Prophets and Hagiography*. London: Nabu, 2011.
Jacobs, Joseph. *Commentary on the Book of Job*. London, 1896.
Jahiel, Meir Loeb. *Buch Iyyov*. Vilnius, 1872. Reissued by KTAV of Jersey City, 2003.
James, William. *The Varieties of Religious Experiences*. New York: Collier, 1968.
Jantzen, J. Gerald. *Job*. Interpretation. Louisville: Westminster John Knox, 1997.
Jastrow, Morris. *The Book of Job*. London: Lippincott, 1920.
Jennings, William. *A Commentary on the Book of Job*. London: Macmillan, 1926.
Jerome. *Collected Works*. Edited by Philip Schaff. Amazon Digital Services, 2015.
———. *The Vulgate*. Tel Aviv: Leeway Infotech, 2016.
Jordan, W. G. *Commentary on the Book of Job*. London: Macmillan, 1929.
Josephus. *Antiquities of the Jews*. New York: Create Space, 2013.
Jung, Carl. *Answer to Job*. Collected Works 11. Princeton: Princeton University Press, 2014.
Kafka, Franz. *The Trial*. New York: Dover Thrift, 2009.
Kahana, Rabbi Abba ben. *Derushim*. Los Angeles: University of California Press, 2012.
Kallen, Horace. *The Book of Job as a Greek Tragedy*. London: Forgotten Books, 2012.
Kara, Joseph. *Sefer Iyyov*. Paris: Gerstenberg, 1978.
Kauztsch, K. *Das Buch Hiob*. Berlin, 1876.
Keil, C. F., and Franz Delitzsch. *Commentary on the Old Testament*. Nashville: Hendrickson, 2006.
Kelly, William. *The Book of Job: A Commentary*. London: Macmillan, 1879.
Kempis, Thomas à. *The Imitation of Christ*. New York: Create Space, 2015.
Kierkegaard, Søren. *Fear of Trembling and Repetition*. Princeton: Princeton University Press, 1983.
Kimhi, David. *Commentary on the Prophets*. Berlin, 1770. Reprinted by Kessinger, 2010.
Kissane, E. J. *The Book of Job*. London: Brown and Nolan, 1939.
Kivistö, Sari, and Sami Pihlström. "Kantian Anti-Theodicy and Job's Sincerity." *Philosophy and Literature* 40 (2016) 347–65.
Klostermann, A. *Job*. London, 1900.
Konig, E. *Das Buch Hiob*. Berlin, 1881.
Kraeling, Emil. *The Book of the Ways of God*. London, 1938. Reprinted by Kessinger, 2010.
Kuenen, Abraham. *Lectures on National Religions*. Berlin, 1888.
Kutz, Ilan. "Job and His Doctors." *British Medical Journal* 321 (2000) 1613–16.
Laato, Antti. *Theodicy in the World of the Bible*. Leiden: Brill, 2003.
Lamartine, Alphonse. *Cours familiar de Litterature*. New York: HardPress, 2016.
Lancre, Pierre de. *On the Inconstancy of Witches*. Tempe: Arizona Center for Medieval and Renaissance Art, 2006. Originally published 1612.
Larramore, Mark. *The Book of Job: A Biography*. Princeton: Princeton University Press, 2013.
Lebensohn, M. J. *Three Vintage Hebrew Books*. Berlin, 1869.
Le Hir, Arthur Marie. *Le Livre de Job*. Paris, 1873.
Leivick, H. *Iyov*. The Complete Writings of H. Leivick. New York: Posy Shoulson, 1940.
Lesetre, Abbe H. *Le Livre de Job*. Paris: Lethielleux, 1886; reprinted 1903.
Leubisch, M. W. Z. *Das Buch Hiob*. Krakow, 1736. Reprinted 1936.
Leveque, Jean. *Job et Son Dieu*. Paris: Etudes Bibliques, 1970.
Lewis, Marshall. *Viktor Frankl and the Book of Job*. Eugene, OR: Pickwick, 2019.

Limentani, Giovanni. *Le Grande Seduto*. Rome: Giacoma, 1979.
Loisy, A. F. *Le Livre de Job*. Paris: Wentworth, 2011.
Lowth, Robert. *Lectures on Sacred Poetry of the Hebrews*. London: Adamant, 2001.
Lubbock, Tom. "Anonymous: Hellmouth, from the Westchester Psalter." *Independent*, January 13, 2006.
Lucretius. "On Life and Death." Book 3 of *De Rarum Natura*. New York: Penguin Classics, 2003.
Luther, Martin. "Preface to the Old Testament." In *Luther's Works* 35, edited by E. Theodore Bachmann, 235–51. Philadelphia: Muhlenberg, 1960.
MacLeish, Archibald. *J.B.* New York: Houghton Mifflin, 1958.
Maimonides, Moses. *Guide to the Perplexed*. London: Friedlander, 1904.
Marshall, J. T. *Job and His Comforters*. London: Clarke, 1905.
Mason, Mike. *The Gospel according to Job*. New York: Crossways, 1994.
McFadyen, Edgar. *The Problem of Pain*. London: Macmillan, 1917.
Meir, Samuel ben. *Sefer Iyyov*. Tell Aviv: Institute for Publication of the Writings of Rabbi Meir Kahane, 1994.
Melville, Herman. *Moby Dick*. New York: Dover Thrift, 2009.
Mendelssohn, Fanny. *Hiob Cantata*. 1831.
Mendelssohn, Moses. *Philosophical Writings*. Cambridge: Cambridge University Press, 1997.
Merx, A. *Das Gedicht von Hiob*. Berlin, 1871.
Meyouchas, Rabeneau. *Sefer Iyyov*. Jerusalem: Chaval, 1969.
Michael, Meir Loeb. *Iyyov*. Halle, 1870.
Michaelis, J. H. *Das Buch Hiob*. Halle, 1720.
Mitchell, Stephen. *The Book of Job*. New York: HarperCollins, 1992.
Moffat, James. *New Translation of the Bible*. Chicago: University of Chicago Press, 1935.
Morgenstern, Julian. "The Mythological Background of Psalm 82." *Hebrew Union College Association* 56 (1985) 1–19.
Moritz, B. *Das Buch Hiob*. Berlin, 1889.
———. "Edomitsche Genealogien." *ZAW* 44 (1926) 81–92.
Mowinckel, S. *Diktet om Ijobog hans tre vennar*. Kristiania [Oslo], Norway, 1924.
———. "Hiob's Goel und Zeugeim Himmel." *BZAW* 41 (1925) 207–22.
Mumford, A. H. *The Book of Job*. London: Macmillan, 1922.
Murphy, Roland. *The Book of Job: A Short Reading*. New York: Paulist, 1999.
Murray, Gilbert. "Beyond Good and Evil." In Glatzer, *Dimensions of Job*, 194–97.
Nachmanides. *Sefer Iyyov*. New York: ArtScroll, 2010.
Ned, Edouard. *Job le Glorieux*. Brussells, 1933.
Newell, B. Lynn. "Job: Repentant or Rebellious?" In Zuck, *Sitting with Job*, 441–56.
Newman, John Henry. *Parochial and Plain Sermons*. London: Rivingtons, 1875.
Newsom, Carol A. *The Book of Job: A Contest of Moral Imaginations*. Oxford: Oxford University Press, 2009.
———. "Job and His Friends." *Interpretation* 53 (1999) 235–53.
Nichols, H. H. "The Composition of the Elihu Speeches." *AJSLL* 27 (1910–1922) 97–186.
Noyes, G. R. *The Book of Job*. London, 1848.
O'Connor, Kathleen. *Job*. New Collegeville Bible Commentary. Collegeville: Liturical, 2012.
Orel, Vladimir. *A Handbook of Germanic Etymology*. Leiden: Brill, 2003.
Orr, James, ed. *International Standard Bible Encyclopedia*. New York: Zondervan Academic, 2011.

Ortlund, Eric. *Job: A 12-Week Study*. Nashville: Crossway, 2017.
Ottendosser, David. *Commentary on Iyyov*. Halle, 1808.
Ottenhosser, Abraham. *Das Buch Hiob*. Berlin, 1906.
Otto, Rudolf. "The Numinous in the Old Testament." In Glatzer, *Dimensions of Job*, 225–28.
Owen, Frederick. "The Land of Uz." *Zondervan Pictorial Encyclopedia of the Bible*. Nashville: Zondervan, 1975.
Pardes, Ilana. "Job's Leviathan." *Prooftexts* 27 (2007) 233–53.
Parente, Pascal. "The Book of Job: Reflections on the Mystic Value of Human Suffering." *Catholic Biblical Quarterly* 8 (1946) 213–19.
Peake, Arthur. *Job*. London: Macmillan, 1905. Reprint, Forgotten Books, 2018.
Pelaila, Ariela, "What Is Behemoth." *Learn Religions*, February 11, 2020. https://www.learnreligions.com/what-is-the-behemoth-2076679.
Peloubet, Francis. *The Book of Job*. London, 1906. Reprint, Wentworth, 2016.
Perdue, Leo. *The Voice from the Whirlwind*. Nashville: Abingdon, 1992.
Phillips, Elaine. "Speaking Truthfully: Job's Friends and Job." *Bulletin for Biblical Research* 18 (2008) 31–43.
Pliny, the Elder. *Natural History*. New York: Abracax, 1991.
Polloch, Seton. "God and a Heretic." In Glatzer, *Dimensions of Job*, 268–72.
Pope, Marvin. *Job*. Anchor Bible Commentary. New York: Doubleday, 1965.
Prat, Frederick. *The Book of Job*. London, 1903.
Quarles, Francis. *The Complete Works in Prose and Verse*. London: Palala, 2018.
Quiller-Couch, Arthur. *Adventures in Criticism*. New York: CreateSpace, 2012.
Rawlinson, George. *Job*. London: Funk and Wagnalls, 1906.
Reichert, Victor. *Job*. New York: Socino, 1965.
Reider, J. "The Book of Job." *JBL* 39 (1920) 60–65.
Renan, Ernest. *Le Livre de Job*. Paris, 1859. Reprint, Wentworth, 2019.
Resende, Luis Antonio. "Solving the Conundrum of Job." *Arwuivosde euro-Psiquiatria* 67 (2009) 1613–16.
Richards, I. A. *Job's Comforting*. London, 1970.
Robinson, H. Wheeler. *The Religious Ideas of the Old Testament*. London: Duckworth, 1913.
Rodd, C. S. *The Book of Job*. Philadelphia: Trinity, 1990.
Rohr, Richard. *Job and the Mystery of Suffering*. New York: Crossroad, 1998.
Rosenberg, A. J., ed. *Job: A New Translation*. Translation of text, Rashi, and commentary by A. J. Rosenberg. New York: Judaica, 1995.
Rosenmuller, M. H. *Scholia in Vetus Testamentum*. Berlin, 1896.
Roth, Joseph. *Job: The Story of a Simple Man*. New York: Viking, 1931.
Roth, Leo. "Job and Jonah." In Glatzer, *Dimensions of Job*, 71–74.
Row, C. A. *Future Retribution*. London: Ibister, 1883.
Rowley, H. H. *Job*. Nashville: Nelson, 1970.
Royce, Josiah. "The Problem of Job." Chapter 9 in *Religion from Tolstoy to Camus*, edited by Walter Kaufmann. New York: World, 1996.
———. *Studies in Good and Evil*. New York: Appleton, 1898.
Royds, T. F. *Job and the Problem of Suffering*. London: Wells Gardner, 1911.
Saadiah Gaon. *The Book of Theodicy*. Edited by L. E. Goodman. New Haven: Yale University Press, 1988.
Sale, George. *The Holy Qur'an*. London, 1801.
Sanders, Paul S. *The Book of Job*. Englewood Cliffs, NJ: Prentice Hall, 1968.

Scharer, J. R. *Das Buch Hiob*. Leipzig, 1810.
Scheindlin, Raymond. *The Book of Job*. New York: Norton, 1999.
Schottmann, K. *Das Buch Hiob*. Leipzig, 1851.
Shultens, Albert. *Das Buch Hiob*. Berlin, 1736.
———. *Liber Jobi*. 2 vols. Tubingen, 1737.
Schutz, Heinrich. *Geistliche chormusik*. 1648.
Schwarz, Israel. *Tikwat Enosh*. Berlin, 1860.
Scott, Thomas. *The Book of Job in English Verse*. Cincinnati: Christian Book Concern, 1848.
Seow, C. L. *Job 1–21*. Grand Rapids: Eerdmans, 2013.
Sermisy, Claudin de. *Motets*. DVD. Noel Akchote, 2016.
Sforno, Obadiah ben Jacob. *Commentary on the Torah*. New York: Art Scroll, 1987.
———. *Mishpat Zedek*. Venice, 1589.
———. *Sefer Iyyov*. Jerusalem: Mosad Ha Rav Kok, 1996.
Shakespeare, William. *Sonnets*. Edited by Helen Vendler. Cambridge: Harvard University Press, 1990.
Shaw, Jean. *Job's Wife*. Nashville: Wogelmuth and Hyatt, 1990.
Siegfrid, C. *The Book of Job*. London, 1893.
Simonetti, Manlio, and Marco Conti. *Ancient Christian Commentary on Scripture: Job*. Downers Grove: InterVarsity, 2006.
Simundson, Daniel. *The Message of Job: A Theological Commentary*. New York: CSS, 2001.
Snaith, N. H. *The Book of Job: Its Origins and Purpose*. New York, 1968.
Sokoloff, Michael. *The Targum to Job from Qumran Cave XI*. Jerusalem: Bar Ilan University, 1974.
Sommi, Leone Judah de'. *The Performing Arts*. Tel Aviv: Katz, 1997.
Sophocles. *Electra*. Edited by Michael Shaw. Oxford: Oxford University Press, 2001.
Spanheim, Frederick. *Das Buch Hiob*. Berlin, 1670.
Spark, Muriel. *The Only Problem*. New York: Penguin, 1995.
Spinoza, Baruch. *Theological Political Treatise*. Cambridge: Cambridge University Press, 2007.
Spitzer, Victor. *Iyyov*. London, 1935.
Stedman, Ray C. *Let God Be God*. Grand Rapids: Discovery House, 2007.
Steinmann, J. *Le Livre de Job*. Paris: Editions du Cerf, 1955.
Steuernagel, C. *Das Buch Hiob*. Berlin, 1923.
Stevenson, W. B. *Critical Notes on the Hebrew Text of Job*. London: Aberdeen University Press, 1951.
———. *The Poem of Job*. London: Oxford University Press, 1947.
Strahan, R. H. *The Book of Job Interpreted*. New York: Macmillan, 1913.
Strigel, V. *Das Buch Hiob*. Berlin, 1571.
Strong, James. *Exhaustive Concordance to the Bible*. Nashville: Nelson, 1995.
Stuhlmann, M. H. *Das Buch Hiob*. Berlin, 1804.
Susman, Margarrete. *The Book of Job and the History of the Jewish People*. Halle, Germany: Juedischer Verlag, 2019. First published 1946.
Szold, Benjamin. *Sefer Iyyov*. Baltimore: Siemers, 1866.
Tam, Jacob ben Meir. *Sefer Iyyov*. Berlin, 1149.
Telemann, Georg. *Four Motets*. DVD. Breitkopf & Hartel, 2000.
Terrien, Samuel. *The Book of Job*. Interpreter's Bible. New York, 1954.
———. *Job: Poet of Existence*. Eugene, OR: Wipf and Stock, 2004.

Tibbon, Samuel Ibn. "Commentary on Iyyov." In *Philosophy and Exegesis on Samuel Ibn Tibbon*, 79–110. New York: Paul, 2010.
Tsevat, Matitiahu. "The Meaning of the Book of Job." *Hebrew Union College Association* 37 (1966) 73–106.
Terrien, Samuel. *Job: Poet of Existence*. Eugene, OR: Wipf and Stock, 2004.
Thomas, David. *The Book of Job*. London: Kregel, 1982.
Tillich, Paul. *Christianity and Existentialism*. New York: Columbia University Press, 1959.
Tollerton, David. *The Book of Job in Post-Holocaust Thought*. Sheffield: Sheffield Phoenix, 2012.
Trani, Isaiah di. *Sefer Iyyov*. Commentary on the Bible. Venice, 1551.
Tur-Sinai, N. H. *The Book of Job*. Jerusalem, 1957.
Tyndale, John. *Old Testament Commentaries: Job*. Edited by Francis Anderson. Perth: IVP Academic, 2008.
Umbreit, F. W. C. *The Book of Job with Expository Notes*. Berlin, 1860.
Van Heck. "From Conversation about God to Conversation with God." In *Risking Truth*, edited by Scott Ellington, 119–20. Eugene, OR: Wipf and Stock, 2008.
Vicchio, Stephen J. *Biblical Figures in the Islamic Faith*. Eugene, OR: Wipf and Stock, 2008.
———. "The Image of Ayyub (Job) in the Qu'ran and Later Islam." *Bible and Interpretation* (August 2005) 1–8.
———. *Job in the Ancient World*. Eugene, OR: Wipf and Stick, 2006. (Vol. 1).
———. *Job in the Medieval World*. Eugene, OR: Wipf and Stock, 2006. (Vol. 2).
———. *Job in the Modern World*. Eugene, OR: Wipf and Stock, 2006. (Vol. 3).
———. *The Sweet Uses of Adversity: Images of the Biblical Job*. Baltimore: Institute for Public Policy Press, 2002.
———. *The Voice from the Whirlwind: The Problem of Evil in the Modern World*. Eugene, OR: Wipf and Stock, 2001.
Vigouroux, F. G. *Le Livre de Job*. Paris, 1915.
Volck, W. *Das Buch Hiob*. Berlin, 1899.
Walkley, Charles Thomas. *Commentary on the Book of Job*. London: Revell, 1917.
The War Scroll. Jerusalem: Fifth Estate, 2014.
Watson, Robert. *The Book of Job*. London: Hodder and Stoughton, 1942.
———. *Job*. Expositor's Bible. New York: Armstrong, 1892.
Weiser, Meir Lubish [Malbim]. *Sefer Iyyov*. Vilnius, 1842.
Weitzstein, Johan G. "La Pays du Job." In *Biblical Commentary on the Book of Job*, edited by Franz Delitzsch, 2:395–410. Edinburgh: T. & T. Clark, 1876.
Wells, H. G. *The Undying Fire*. London: B and A, 1919.
Welte, B. *Das Buch Hiob*. Berlin, 1849.
Wesley, John. *Explanatory Notes on the Old Testament*. Amazon Digital Services, 2011.
———. *Wesley Study Bible*. Nashville: Abingdon, 2017.
Westermann, Claus. *The Structure of the Book of Job*. Nashville: Fortress, 1981.
Whedbee, William. "The Comedy of Job." *Semeia* (1977) 1–39.
Wiernikowsky, Isaac. *Das Buch Hiob*. Breslau, 1897.
Wilcox, John. *The Bitterness of Job*. Anne Arbor: University of Michigan Press, 1994.
Wilder, Thorton. *Hast Thou Considered My Servant Job?* In *Short Plays of Thorton Wilder*. London: Theatre Communications Group, 1998.
Williams, Stephen. *The Quest for Theodosius*. New Haven: Yale University Pres, 1998.
Wolf, Bertold. *Hiob*. Leipzig: de Gruyter, 1934.

Wolfskehl, Karl. *Hiob*. Berlin: Spiegel, 1950.
Wolfssohn, Aaron Hale. *Silliness and Sanctimony*. New York: University Press, 2000.
Wood, James. *Job and the Human Situation*. London: Bles, 1966.
Wray, Newton. *The Book of Job*. London: Hamilton, 1929.
Wright, G. H. B. *The Book of Job*. London, 1883.
Yagel, Abraham. *Valley of Vision*. Philadelphia: University of Pennsylvania Press, 1990.
Yalom, Marilyn. *The History of the Wife*. New York: Harper, 2002.
Zalman, Elijah ben Solomon [Rabbi Gra]. *Rav Pe'alim*. Vilnius, 1874.
Zapffe, Peter Wessel. *Om det tragiske*. Oslo: Gyldendal Norsk Forlag, 1941, 1983.
Zimmermann, F. "Note on Job 9:23." *JTS* 2 (1951) 165–66.
The Zohar. Edited by Daniel C. Matt. Palo Alto: Stanford University Press, 2003.
Zolckler, O. *The Book of Job*. Berlin, 1875. Translated into English by L. J. Evans, 1875.
Zuck, Roy B., ed. *Sitting with Job: Selected Studies on the Book of Job*. Eugene, OR: Wipf and Stock, 1992.
Zuckerman, Bruce. *Job the Silent*. Oxford: Oxford University Press, 1998.

Index

Abel, 126
Abraham, 8, 106
Abraham, Euchel Isaac, 38
Abravanel, Isaac, 27
absoluteness, of divine omnipotence, 238–39
Abufelda, associated Damascus with the biblical Land of Uz, 37
acquittal, Job's certainty of, 174
Adam and Eve, xiii, 59
Adonai, referring to God as, 194
adultery, 179, 206
adversity, dealing with, 22
affliction
    God as the author of Job's, 69, 142–45
    God sending for good, 229–32
    purpose of, 221, 247
    traced to iniquity, 249
agony, swift death preferable to a life in, 73
agricultural pursuits, suspension of, 253
Akdamut Jewish hymn, on Leviathan and Behemoth, 275
Akkadian words, in the Book of Job, 304–7, 389
Al-Ahbar, Ka'b, 23
Al-Baydawi, 24
Albert of Metz, 20
Albertus Magnus, 277
Albo, Joseph, 26–27
Albright, William F. (Bill), xi, 46, 75
Ali, Mohammad, 25
"all living," as all animals and people, 193
Allah, 5
allegory, 12, 277
alliteration, 200
all-seeing eye, of God, 238
Al-Maqdisi, 24
Al-Tabari, 24
Al-Thabani, 24
Altschuler, David. *See* Mezudat David
Al-Zamakhshari, 24
Ambrose, Bishop of Milan, 17
Anatomy of Melancholy (Burton), 30
ancients
    Bildad wanting us to learn from, 78
    Job questioning the judgment of, 100
    wisdom of, 169

Andersen, Francis, 139, 221–22
angel(s)
    Adversary as, 52
    appointed as guardian, 231
    as both good and bad, 21, 50
    Elihu on the intercession of, 218
    God sending to reclaim Job, 230
    heavenly bodies associated with, 185
    imperfect in God's sight, 183
    scattering the Omnipresent's storm clouds, 253
Angel Jibril, 35, 61
"Angel Mediator," spoken of by Elihu, 219
"Angel of Reconciliation," 12
angel-mediator, mediating man to God, 230
Angry or Iconoclastic Job, xiv
animals
    order of presented to Job, 270
    verses on, 263
    vignettes on, 269
animals, sheep, camel, oxen, and asses, double the original number of restored, 296
annihilation, 69, 138, 140
Anti-Christ, reference to, 139
anti-Semitism, 19, 20
Apocalypse of Enoch, oldest Jewish reference to Behemoth, 275
"Apocalypse of Paul," mentioning Job, 4
Aquinas, Thomas
    on Behemoth as the elephant, 277
    on Bildad, 78, 134
    commentary by, 20–22
    on the dissipation of Job's members, 126
    distinguishing good and bad angels, 21, 50, 52
    on divine wisdom, 94
    on Elihu, 219
    on Eliphaz, 67, 117–18, 119
    on the frailty of the human condition, 119
    on Job accusing Eliphaz of unfitting consolation, 123
    on Job describing his innocence, 126
    on Job knowing his Redeemer lives, 149
    on Job reproving his friends, 117–18
    on Job showing his humiliation, 125

Aquinas, Thomas *(continued)*
    on Job's lament, 64
    on Job's words destroying themselves, 118
    on man living for a short time, 127
    method of exegesis, 21
    on no hope for recovery by the proud, 121
    on pain producing harm unjustly afflicted, 122
    on Satan and the Devil as one and the same, 52
    on Satan sparing Job's wife, 59
    on skin for skin, 56
    on those throwing themselves into sinning, 136
    on the ultimate end of the impious, 139
    on "wise of heart and strong of might," 83
    on Zophar, 97
Arabic words, in the Book of Job, 304–7, 389
Aramaic, replacing Classical Hebrew as the vernacular, 215
Aramaic words
    in the Book of Job, 304–7, 390
    of Elihu, 233
Aramaisms
    in the Book of Job, 304–7
    in the Elihu speeches, 214, 246
"arbiter" (*mokiah*), Job calling for, 147
Aristeas's "Life of Job," 2–3
Aristotle, *Generations of the Animals*, 6
"arm of God," 273
arrogance
    Elihu as an emblem of, 219
    of Eliphaz, 120
    Mezudat David on, 121
    none in Job, 196
    Philip the Priest on, 80
"arrows of the Almighty," parallels for, 69
art, Leviathan in, 287–89
astrological Determinism, argument against, 254
"Astronomer's View," of human life, 26–27
Atheism and Christianity (Bloch), 39
attention, Job entreating, 160
Augustine, 17, 59
author of Job, as a supreme poet of nature, 257
Ayab, mentioned in the fourteenth-century BCE, 46
Ayyub. *See also* Job
    age of at his demise, 35
    Arabic name for Job, 5
    conclusions about in medieval Islam, 25
    from Damascus by tradition, 24
    medieval Muslim sources on, 23
    modern views of, 35–37
    as a "Muhammad figure," 25
    physical description of, 23–24
    wife of, 24, 61

Babylonian Talmud, 3. *See also* Talmud
    banquet story at the end of time, 275
    on Elihu as "one of the seven prophets of the Gentiles," 216
    identifying *ha Satan* with the evil imagination of human beings, 51
    on Job denying the resurrection of the dead, 148
Babylonians, on the netherworld, 74
Barnes, Albert, 54, 79, 220
bartering view, on "skin for skin," 55
Barton, G. A., 90, 109
battle, war horse smelling from afar, 269
battle horse, description of, 263
beast(s)
    Behemah translated as, 274
    Behemoth as a huge, 277, 278
    descriptions of two great, 256
    Elihu appearing as a Satanic, 216
    Leviathan as king of, 287
    lion as king of, 263
    as natural creatures or mythological, 277, 278, 280
    wild taking prey in its teeth, 107
Behemoth, 272, 274, 275
Behemoth narrative, analysis of, 275–79
Beirler, Jaime, 107
bene ha Elohim, translations for, 50–51
Bernard of Clairvaux, 59
Besserman, Lawrence, 18
Beza, Theodore, 32, 34–35
biblical commentaries. *See also* commentaries
    of Gersonides, 14
    by Thomas Aquinas, 20
biblical text, three-level approach to, 14
bibliographies, on the book of Job, 45
Bildad
    believing in the retributive justice theory, 12
    confining himself to the third part of Job's statement, 77
    as a descendant from Shuah, sixth son of Abraham and Keturah, 76
    first speech of (chapter 8), 75–81
    on God's just dealings with Job, 80–81
    on the happiness found in the material goods, 78
    Job's responses to, 81–92, 187–89
    origins of the name of, 75–76
    preoccupied with externals, 139
    repeating ideas expressed earlier, 186–87
    reproving Job, 76–79, 134–36

INDEX

second speech of (chapter 18), 133–40
sinning of Job's sons, 77
on suffering as punishment, 79
theological orientation of, 76–77
theological positions of, 397
third speech of (chapter 25), 182–87
Bildad, Eliphaz, and Zophar, as forms of twentieth-century Determinism, 42
birds, verses on, 263
birth, awareness of the equality of, 207
"The Bishop Orders His Tomb," poem by Browning, 73
Biskra Button, as Job's disease, 58
bitter things, writing, 110
bitterness
    of Job, 85
    passing the night in, 129
"Black Leprosy," as Job's disease, 58
Blake, William, 39, 222, 279, 288
blameless and upright, as one translation for *tam va yashar*, 49–50
Blemished Perfection (Hoffman), 45
blessing, lamp and light as symbols of, 195
Bloch, Ernest, 39
blood
    in Old Testament and Book of Job, 127–28
    oozing from Job's wounds, 126
"blood avenger" (*Goel*). See Goel ("blood avenger")
"Blood Covenant," God making with humans, 128
Bode, William, 79, 87
Bodin, Jean, 278
body, rotting away, 111
body parts, Zophar preoccupied with, 398
boldness, of Job, 109
Book of Deeds
    Hebrew Bible's, 28
    idea of much stronger in Islam, 29
    Job referring to the Hebrew tradition of, 146
    motif in ancient Judaism, 126
    references to, 100, 260
Book of Job
    in the 21st century, 44–45
    Aramaisms in, 304–7
    commentary by Gersonides, 14
    in contemporary times (20th century to the present), 40–44
    early modern readings (1500 to 1800), 25–37
    "East Wind" (*kedem ruwach*) in, 122
    Gregory laying open the deep mysteries in, 18
    hapax legomena in, 298–303
    as a law case, 124, 173, 175, 399–401
    modern readings of (1800 to present), 37–40
    paraphrases of in the sixteenth and seventeenth centuries, 35
    premodern views of to 1500, 1–6
    theological views of the characters in, 397–98
    translated into Hebrew out of another language, 30
    words about the ancient Jewish court system, 399–400
The Book of Job and the History of the Jewish People (Susman), 41
The Book of Job as a Greek Tragedy (Kallenin), 34
The Book of Job in Post-Holocaust Thought (Tollerton), 44
The Book of Theodicy (Saadiah), 7
Book of Tobit, 2
bow, as a symbol of strength, 197–98
bowels, as the seat of emotions, 99, 203
Brandier, Urbain, 277
breath of God, animating human beings, 187
breathe, being loathsome for, 144
brevity of life, images of, 112
Buber, Martin, 63
building, Earth likened to, 258
Burrell, David, 68, 71
Burton, Robert, 30
Buttenwieser, Moses, 71, 72–73, 95
Buz, as a brother of Uz, 223

calamity from God, feared by Job, 208
Calmet, Dom, 87
Calvin, John
    on Bildad, 78
    on a doleful representation of Job's grievances, 124
    on Elihu, 219
    on God as a power that is matched with rightfulness, 228
    on God's transcendence and imminence, 170
    on Job as insisting on defending the doctrine of resurrection, 33
    on Job cursing the day of his birth, 64
    on Job's condition as very deplorable, 125
    on Job's wife as "Satan's tool," 59
    preaching on the Man from Uz and his book, 33–34
    refusing to grant that Job is "blameless and upright," 34
    sermons on the book of Job, 32
    on Zophar's words, 94
Canaanite men, well-to-do having the name Job, 46
Cansdale, George Soper, 278

Canterbury Tales (Chaucer), references to the Man from Uz, 31
Cato the Younger, Augustine comparing Job to, 17
challenges, to Job, 257
"chambers of the south," as "rooms where storms are kept," 84
charity, Job turning to sins against, 207
chastity, duty of, 205
Chateaubriand, Francois-Rene, 39
Chesterton, Gilbert, 42
child in the womb, formation of, 90
children
    of God, 50
    of Job. *see* Job, children of
"Children of the East," Job being of, 48
child's toy, making Leviathan into, 281
"choral interlude," 28:28 as, 194
Christ, Old Testament precursor of, 147
Christian commentaries on the book of Job, produced by nineteenth-century Christian churches, 40
Christian Gnostics, on Behemoth and Leviathan, 277
Christian iconography, Job's wife depicted as a shrew, or an agent of the Devil, 61
Christian images, of the book of Job in the eighteenth and nineteenth centuries, 39–40
Christian interpretations, of the book of Job in the fifteenth to seventeenth centuries, 31
Christian Middle Ages, commentators on the book of Job, 16
Christian scholars, writing about Job in the fourth century, 4–5
Christian sources, on the book of Job, 3–5
Chrysostom, John
    on Behemoth, 277
    on Bildad, 78, 134
    on Eliphaz, 118
    finding original sin, 112
    on Job knowing the doctrine of the resurrection, 74, 149
    on Job's wife, 59
    on memories as dead, 86
    on "no stranger marching against them," 120
    on the "passion of Christ as foreshadowed," 100
    "The Power of Man to Resist the Devil," 16
    on time needed to understand things, 101
church fathers, 51, 216
city and its gate, as the place for political speech and debate, 196
City of God (Augustine), 17

Clarke, Adam, 126
classic tragic hero, Job as, 41
Clement of Rome, 4, 148
Pope Clement VI, 13
Clermont-Ganneau, Charles, 36
Clines, David J. A.
    on Bildad, 78–79
    comprehensive bibliography on the Book of Job, 43
    on death as God's victory over human hope for life, 116
    on Eliphaz, 66–67
    "Feminist Readings" regarding Job's wife, 63
    giving parallel passages combining hearing and seeing, 104
    on Job expanding his request to the friends from "be silent" to "listen," 108
    on Job uncovering of divine cruelty, 104
    on Job urging God to leave him alone, 113
    on Job's *mokiah, edh,* and *Goel,* 147
    on Job's wife as parallel with Eve, 59
    on lack of theological content in Job's lament, 65
    on "one skin for another skin," 55
    on the retributivist theory, 80–81
clothes, personification of, 87
cloud image, for ending life, 74
clouds, 250, 261
collective retributive justice. *See also* retributive justice
    arguing against the idea of, 128
    beneath Eliphaz's first speech, 79
    endorsement of, 130
    version of, 120, 139
collective sin, Saadiah refusing to assent to, 7–8
Collin de Plancy, Jacques-Albin-Simon, on Behemoth ruling over the domain of gluttony, 277
commentaries
    by Aaron Halle-Wolfssohn, 38
    by Abraham Yagel, 29
    on the book of Job in both the Eastern and the Western Churches, 4
    Christian Middle Ages, 16
    by David Ottensosser, 38
    by Duran, 25–26
    English in the early twentieth century, 41–42
    French in the nineteenth-century, 40
    French in the twentieth century, 41
    by Gersonides, 14
    by Gregory, 17–19, 20
    Jewish, 6, 25, 37–39
    by Nicholas of Lyra, 22–23
    by nineteenth-century Christian churches, 40

by non-Muslim European scholars, 36
by Odo of Cluny, 20
by Saadiah Gaon, 6–8
by Thomas Aquinas, 20–22
by Venerable Bede, 20
Commentary of Universal Holy Scripture (Nicholas of Lyra), 23
compass, determining the four points of, 174
compound name, Bildad as, 75
constellations, translated in myriad ways, 84
consumption, of the flesh of a sick person, 230
contempt, Job showing to outcasts, 200
contention, kinds of, 83
contrast perspective, xiii, 397, 398
contrast theodicy, 167
controversy, surrounding the meaning of 42:6, 293–95
corruption, sin making man subject to, 114–17
cosmic struggle, of God with Behemoth and Leviathan, 275
"counting steps," interpretations of, 114–15
courage, as the central attribute of Job, 3
court, Job speaking of an oath to, 188
court system in Ancient Israel, words related to, 400–401
Cowles, Henry, 52
Cox, Samuel, 58–59
Creator, 88, 90, 126
crocodile
    Behemoth as, 278
    Leviathan as, 283, 284, 287
crown, of Job's prosperity, 197
cruelty, of God, 202–3
cry of the oppressed, God hearing, 239
culture, Leviathan in, 289–91
"curse," words in Job designating, 206
cursing God, Job refraining from, 65
Curtis, J. B., 295
cylinder seal, showing a seven-headed monster, 287
Cyprian, "God and Patience," 16

"dark," associated with evil, xiii
"dark" and "darkness," words related to, 92
darkness
    banished with the coming of the day, 259
    as major symbol of doom, 169
    only in the grave, 91
    personified, 260
daughters, of Job, 296
Davidson, A. B., 135, 278
Davidson, Samuel, 150
dawn, representing death rather than life, 179
days, as swifter than the weaver's shuttle, 73

dead, no longer having knowledge of Earth concerns, 116
dead man, as sharing in his own funeral, 166
Dead Sea Scrolls, Jewish views of the figure of Job, 3
dealings, of God's providence, 162–64
death
    confirmation of survival of, 106–7
    dawn representing, 179
    descendants cut off after, 164
    exalting in pain hastening, 70
    gates of, 260
    as the gathering place of all living things, 192
    graphic and pathetic description of, 116
    hope of Job in, 131–33
    Job anticipating, 129
    Job longing for, 69–70
    Job regarding as imminent, 152
    Job talking about, 114
    like a hireling, 113
    on looking beyond physical, 150
    meaning gloom in Sheol, 91
    Mezudat David on saving from, 232
    preferable to a life in agony, 73
    preserving protestation of innocence after, 146
    Rashi on sudden, 238
    resurrection and, 259
    survival after, 23
    terrors of the shadow of, 179
    underworld and, 137
    wicked man not caring about his house after, 164
Decamps, Alexander G., 39
deceit, preparing, 122
Dedad, nephew of Shuah, 76
"the deep," as the primeval abyss, 192
"deep darkness," as the darkness of Sheol, 260
deference, paid to Job by young and old, 196
Delitzsch, Franz
    on God as Almighty, 101
    on the identity of *Bir-Daddan* as Bildad, 75
    on Job, 205, 209
    on words of Job, 131
    on Zophar, 93, 96–97
demonic force, Satan as, 15
demonic forces, influence of, xii–xiii
demonic forces view, 22, 53, 59, 101–2, 277
deontological approach to ethics (retributive justice), 214
deprivation of the good theory, xiii–xiv
Derash, allegorical and symbolic meanings of a text, 8, 14
dereliction, misery and, 203–4

INDEX

dermatitis, as Job's disease, 57
descendants
    dread of having no, 139
    oaths might also bind, 211
    of a sinner are punished, 159
desires of Job's heart, destroyed, 131
Devil. *See also* Satan
    appeared to Ayyub's wife, 36
    Behemoth as a representation of, 277
    as the source of Ayyub's suffering, 5
    trying to upset Job through his wife and through his friends, 21
Devine, Milos, on Job's wife imposing an additional strain on his faith, 62
Devine, Minos
    arguing against the demonic view of *ha Satan*, 53
    on Elihu meeting Job's necessity, 221
Dhorme, E.
    on adopting the language of the cunning, 118
    on being stripped of glory, 142
    on Bildad, 135
    on crying for help, 142
    on double meaning of "secret" and "secret counsel," 118
    on Elihu, 225–26
    on Eliphaz, 66, 118, 119, 120
    on the godless man, 121
    on hope and happiness not following a dying man, 133
    on the human spirit rising to moral grandeur, 131
    on Job being recorded for future generations, 146
    on Job ceasing to regard God as the cause of his ills, 130
    on Job explaining his days have not seen happiness, 132
    on Job giving free rein to his complaints and bitterness, 89
    on lifting up one's face, 225
    making a number of form-critical and historical-critical remarks, 41
    on man as so vile and wretched, 89
    on the name "Job," 46
    on nothing as so ephemeral as the flower, 112
    on passing the night in bitterness, 129
    on the pledge which Job offers to God, 129
    on proposing to rebel against God, 83
    on the role of the wife in temptation, 59
    on servants not condescending to answer, 143–44
    on songs in the night as "the crashes of thunder," 244
    on state of mind of the wicked man, 120
    translating 32:22, 226
    on the tyrant settling in the rooms of others, 121
    on the wicked man relishing his sin, 156
    on wisdom going back to previous generations, 119
    on Zophar, 94
dialectical philosophers, giving dialectical philosophical accounts, 40–41
Didymus the Blind, 78, 79, 113, 114
Dinah, as Job's second wife, 59, 60
disaster, striking those sated with sin, 157
disease of Job, 56–58, 73, 203
"dismay," Leviathan inspiring, 285
disputation, Job using the rhetorical device of, 89
the Divine
    Eliphaz mentioning nineteen times, 397
    Zophar mentioning twelve times, 398
divine act, causing a person's death, 116
divine equity in government, 221
divine justice, defense of, 236–38
divine omnipotence, as absolute, 238–39
divine plan, 258, 291–92
divine plan view, 7
    ascribing to, 292
    assenting to, 194
    blending of, 254
    clear reference to, 205
    consistency with, 95–96
    Elihu arguing for, 33
    Elihu assenting to, 219
    Elihu continuing his use of, 251
    Elihu employing, 398
    Elihu suggesting, 212, 213–14
    on evil and suffering making sense, xiii
    in the God speeches, 258
    indication of, 126
    Job ascribing to, 292
    of Job's suffering, 94
    Mezudat David on, 185, 250
    Rashi on, 9, 233
    reference to, 260
    regarding Job's suffering, 234
    Rowley endorsing, 256
    suggesting, 153
    Terrien assenting to, 243
    of Yahweh, 398
    Zophar expressing, 398
divine Providence, wicked denying, 170
divine silence, meaning of, 240–41
divine terrors, 175–76
Divrei Iyyov, speaking of Job having two wives, 59

Dome or Firmament of Heaven, mentioned by Eliphaz, 397
Doré, Gustave, *Destruction of Leviathan*, 288
Dostoyevsky, Fyodor, 39
Dragon, Behemoth as, 277
dramas, in the first half of the twentieth century, 43
driver, of animals, 265
Driver
    on eyes dimming as a reason of vexation, 131
    translating 30:24-25, 203
    translating 34:20, 238
    on Zophar claiming to speak out of his understanding, 154
Driver, G. R.
    on being counted a liar, 235
    identifying Behemoth with the crocodile, 278
Driver, S. R.
    on Eliphaz's first discourse, 66
    on God's omniscience, 239
    on Job turning pathetically to God, 73
    on Job's complaints, 69
    on Job's condition, 72
    on Job's friends, 70, 71
    on the methods of God's Providence, 189
    on sinners enjoying a long life, 181
    translation of 26:14, 186
    translation of 35:14, 245
dualism, of light and darkness, 189
Duran, Simeon, 25-26
Dürer, Albrecht, *Job and His Wife*, 61
dust, fusing into mud, 263
dust and ashes, 293-94, 295

eagle, building its nest, 269
earliest Christian sources
    on Behemoth, 277
    on Bildad's first discourse, 77-78
early Christian thinkers, on Job and his book, 15-16
Earth, 26, 186, 258
East Wind, 122-23, 261
Eclanum, Julian, 78, 102
eczema leprosy, as Job's disease, 57
Ehrlich, on giving back your soul to God, 119
Eisen, Robert, 218
El, "as the decisive punitive power," 156
elephant, Behemoth as, 277, 278
elephantiasis, 57, 73
El-Hamawi, Jakut, 37
Elihu
    appropriating thoughts of his friends, 243
    Augustine's understanding of, 17
    blaming Job for reflecting on God, 228
    bragging about own ability, 227
    calling Job by name, 212, 227, 232, 254
    on the cause of Job's suffering, 15
    chiding Job's three friends, 256
    containing his anger on account of his youth, 223
    continuing his discourse (chapter 36), 246-51
    continuing teleological explanations of Job's suffering, 251
    counseling Job, 249-50
    dealing with the general concept of his theology, 234
    denying that wisdom is reserved for the aged, 223
    desiring Job's attention, 232-33, 237, 246-47
    on God as indifferent to suffering, 245
    on God destroying the wicked, 247
    on God having the case of the unfortunate in His mind, 244
    on God not needing to go through the process of the court, 238-39
    on God's providence according to Maimonides, 12
    on government guaranteeing justice, 237
    Hebrew terms to designate the Divine, 252
    on Job becoming a blasphemer, 243
    more closely related to Job than the other three friends, 223
    as the most controversial figure in the book of Job, 217
    name meaning "My Gog is He," or "He is My God," 223
    name meaning "Whose God is He," 220
    new idea of, 12
    not among the friends of Job as introduced, 212
    observing the power of God, 252-54
    offering to reason with Job, 227-28
    on pedagogic purposes of God, 254
    poetic images of the wind, 253
    as a Prelude to the Theophany, 242
    quoting Job word for word, 212
    reminding Job on scornful speeches, 234
    reproving Job and his friends, 224
    on "scoffing for iniquity," 235
    second discourse (chapter 33), 226-33
    speaking in behalf of God, 223
    speaking of the intercession of an angel, 218
    speaking without partiality, 224-26
    as a stranger to impartiality, 225
    as a stranger to modesty, 246
    on suffering, 212, 229-30, 250
    suggesting that God is not affected by human sin, 244

Elihu *(continued)*
   theological positions of, 398
   theological views of, 12
   various descriptions of, 217
   vocabulary of, 233, 252
   on why Job must expose his errors, 241
   words for God, 226
   as a young, brash bystander, 218
   youthfulness of emphasized, 223
Elihu speeches
   adjustments to, 33
   Aramaisms found in, 249
   Calvin on, 34
   chapters 32-37, 211–56
   close of (chapter 37), 251–56
   continuation of (chapter 34), 233–41
   continuing (chapter 35-36), 242–51
   employing a broad range of terms for the divine, 214–15
   first six verses written in prose, 212
   Hebrew of, 218, 298–99
   as later additions to the Book of Job, 211–12, 215–16, 220, 307
   mimicking the style of the divine speeches, 254
   as a precursor for the God speeches that follow, 28
   providing theological responses not introduced earlier, 212
Eliphaz
   answering Job on behalf of the Almighty, 167–68
   beginning his first speech by praising Job, 66
   believing in the retributive justice theory, 12
   continuing Job's first response to, 71
   described fears bred evil in the wicked, 133
   first speech (chapters 4-5), 66–68
   indicating an over-abundant flowing arrogance, 120
   invoking tradition, 120
   Job continuing his third response to, 176–81
   Job's second response to, 123–33
   as the oldest and wisest of the three friends, 66
   representing Job's discourse as without profit, 123
   saying to Job to amend his profession of faith, 119
   second speech of, 117–22
   telling Job to speak less before the presence of God, 117
   theological positions of, 397
   thinking of himself as the mouthpiece of God, 171
   third speech (chapter 22), 166–72
   urging Job to return to God, 172
   visions in the night, 67
"Elysian Fields," 86
Emmerich, Anne Catherine, 60
emotion or feeling, seated in the kidneys, 152
English commentaries, in the early twentieth century, 41–42
English dramas, inspired by the book of Job, 43
English literary works, late medieval with Job's motifs, 31
English novels, twentieth-century employing themes in the book of Job, 43
English Puritans, adopted the name Job, 47
English Romantic uses, of Job in scholarly work, 39
English translation, of 25:1-6, 182–83
ephemeral nature of life, verses about, 111
Ephrem the Syrian
   on Behemoth as a Dragon, 277
   on Bildad's first discourse, 77–78
   on Job predicting manifestations of Emmanuel, 149
   on a prophecy of baptism, 113
   on punishment, 138
   on the wicked defeated by distress, 120
errant person, not placing his trust in truth, 122
erysipelas, as Job's disease, 57
erythema, as Job's disease, 57
Esau and Adah, on Eliphaz as the first son of, 66
essays and articles, on Job, 44–45
essays and collections of essays, in the twentieth century, 43
Ethics (Spinoza), 29
ethics and morality, vocabulary of words of Elihu, 215
evil, xii–xiv, 156
evil actions, retribution for, 157
evil and suffering, teleological understandings of, 9
evil imagination, 7, 12, 51
evil-doers, taking the path of, 236
Ewald, Georg, 66, 134, 135, 150, 219–20
exegetical problems, with chapter 10, 88
exegetical rules, of Spinoza, 30
existentialist Job motif, xv, 29, 41, 44
exploitation, in the ancient world, 177
eyes, 127, 131
Ezra, 121

the faint, giving no water to drink, 168
fairness, Job asking about God's, 89
faith, of Job remaining unswerving, 107
family members, restored double to Ayyub, 5

familys of the wicked, will perish, 138
Farissol, Abraham, 27–28
"Father of Modal Logic," Gersonides as, 14
favoritism, Job's friends showing, 105
fear, 194, 287
fears, of Job, 112
female personification, of Wisdom, 96
feminist thought, Job's wife in the context of, 63
fertility, in herds and flocks as a mark of divine blessing, 161
Fingarette, Herbert, 400–401
finitude, Job as content with his, 293–94
Finkelstein, Louis, 219
flying serpent, defeat of, 186
"forced conversion," Gregory against, 19
foreign words and expressions, index of, 389–96
former comforts, of Job, 195–96
formula, introducing an oath, 188
foundation of the world, accompanied by music and song, 259
Fourth Esdras, mentioning both Behemoth and Leviathan, 275
Frankl, Viktor, 44
Fredericton, John, 221
free will defense, xiii, 7, 27, 118, 153
freedom, of God from man, 243–44
Freehof, Solomon
    on Behemoth, 276
    on Bildad, 77, 133
    on Elihu, 218
    on everyone listening to Job, 198
    on God as omniscient, 238
    on God asking Job if he can manage the affairs of men, 272
    on God not needing to hold a court hearing with man, 239
    on God testifying to the truth of Elihu's statements, 246
    on the great blessing of God to man, 245
    on Job reacting to the effect of the speeches of both friends, 87
    on Job speaking out in the bitterness of his heart, 75
    on Job wishing that God would make clear wherewith he has sinned, 210
    on Job's description of God's attack, 143
    on Job's present misery, 199
    on man accommodating to all the changes of the wind, 255
    on man proving himself in a discussion with God, 82
    on the old having no monopoly on wisdom, 224
    on the power of God, 237
    on prosperity tempting us to pride and evil, 249
    on the real tragedy for Elihu, 248
    rendering 34:3, 234
    on Satan, 53
    on sucking the poison of asps, 156
    on those who suffer and do not turn to God, 248
    on truth in the inward parts, 262
    on wickedness tasting sweet, 156
French commentaries
    in the nineteenth-century, 40
    in the twentieth century, 41
French dramas, in the first half of the twentieth century, 43
French words, in the Book of Job, 390
friendship, violating the rules of, 124
Froude, James Anthony, 220
Fullerton, Kemper, 66
Future Retribution (Row), 42

garden of Eden, 60
Garland, G. V., 135, 220
"gates of death," as the entrance of Sheol, 260
Gemara, illuminated the Talmud, 3
genealogy, of Job not mentioned, 46
Generations of the Animals (Aristotle), 6
Genesis Rabbah, on *ha Satan*, 51
Gensenius, on feeling taking the place of sight, 103
German words, in the Book of Job, 390
Gersonides
    on Behemoth, 276
    on Bildad, 134
    on "the depths of the underworld," 133
    on the Elihu passages, 218
    on the end of Zophar's first discourse, 97
    on idoltry, 99
    on Job not believing in the resurrection, 148
    on mental darkness of men, 255
    on salt land, 265
    on the speeches of Elihu, 15
    summing up Zophar's first discourse, 93
    on two kinds of ignorance, 96
    on unjust taking of property of the poor, 197
    wrote extensively on the book of Job, 13–15
giant human, Leviathan depicted as, 288
Gibbs, Paul T., 67
Gibson, E. C. S., 95, 96, 135–36
Gibson, John C. L., 53, 123, 278
gift, of God to man, 244–45
gifts of nature, Job required to explain, 254–55
"girding of the loins," 258
Glatzer, Nahum, 105, 110

INDEX

"glory," to which Job refers, 142
gluttony, 157
God
    abasing the proud, 171
    above the petty feelings of Job, 228
    administering the emetic, 156
    allowing participation through anger, 113
    allowing the wicked to feel secure, 180
    as the Archer shooting arrows, 125
    associated with "Light," 92
    as the author of Job's affliction, 142–45
    bestowing His Providence upon man, 270
    Bildad mentioning nine times, 397
    blinded the faith of Job's friends, 129
    bringing evil and suffering to develop moral characteristics, 7
    brushing any examination or investigation aside, 239
    calling men to repentance, 228–29
    caused the ostrich to forget wisdom, 267
    commanding the moon not to shine, 184
    comparison to a potter, 90
    controlling all of his created beings, 100, 279
    cruelty of, 202–3
    destroying the wicked, 247
    different names for in the Elihu speeches, 216
    directing the hawk and the eagle, 269
    on the eagle "sucking up the blood of its young," 128
    Elihu employing multiple names for, 251
    Elihu observing the power of, 252–54
    enclosed in Heauen, 170
    endowed human beings to acquire and test knowledge, 101
    enraged against Job, 125
    exalting as Creator of all, 100
    first speech of (chapter 38-39), 256–70
    founding the Earth and the Heavens before everything else, 258
    freedom of from man, 243–44
    gave Job peace in his sufferings before giving him relief, 109
    gift of to man, 244–45
    as the "Good One," 170
    as great and to be feared, 256
    guiding the happenings of the world, 205
    having the righteous forever in his watchful gaze, 247
    as hidden, 28
    Job professing his confidence in, 106–9
    Job questioning, 109
    as Job's adversary at law, 174
    Job's complaint against, 160
    Job's final word to, 291–95
    as the judge of all, 164
    knowing all and All-Powerful, 250
    knowing more about the meaning of Job's suffering than human beings do, 213
    knowing what humans do not, 95
    limitations of, 89
    making all visible, 102
    making Job a target for His arrows, 125
    methods of for dealing with men, 247–49
    names for used by Elihu, 233, 398
    not addressing Elihu, 212
    not favoring one man over another, 237
    not needing man's righteousness, 244
    not responding to Elihu, 217–18
    as our great Guide and Teacher, 245
    penetrating all secrets and darkness, 102
    power of, 82, 84, 101, 180
    praising Job, 122
    Providence of, 261
    punishing subsequent generations, 163
    raising up the humble, 250
    rebuking Job, 29, 237
    responses from the whirlwind, 214
    rights of man before, 242–43
    second speech of, 256
    sending affliction for good, 229–32
    separate names for in chapter 40, 270
    showing His revelation by hiding His face, 109
    similarities of the two speeches of, 257
    sparing the wicked to the day of doom, 159
    speaking to Eliphaz, Bildad, and Zophar, 295
    speeches a response to a mortal Job, 258
    spreading the lightning with His hands, 251
    as supreme and subject to no one, 250
    as supreme Lord of the universe, 183
    treasuring up Job's sins, 115
    two different views of, 74
    understanding the way to wisdom, 193
    using evil and suffering, 212, 213
    variety of nouns signifying, 140
    walking on the *Hug*, or "vault," of heaven, 26
    wisdom belonging to, 101
    withdrawal of, 173–74
    as the witness, 127
    as Yahweh in the epilogue, 295
godless in heart, not realizing the value of chastisement, 248
godless man, as a bloated egoist, 121
Goel ("blood avenger")
    as a human being seeking revenge for some wrong, 128, 147
    Job's proclamation of, 140
    John Wesley on, 149

INDEX

John Wycliffe on, 152
Robert Gordis on, 151
Saadiah Gaon on, 148
Goethe, J. W., 39
"gold," words for, 192, 194
Goldsmith, Oliver, 35
Goldsmith, Robert Hillis, 93–94
Good, Edwin, 56, 151
"good die young" adage, 248–49
good imagination, 7, 12
good things, about Job not being written down, 110
Gordis, Robert
    on arguments cited by the friends, 159
    on Behemoth as a natural creature, 276–77
    on Bildad, 77, 135, 139
    on Elihu, 218
    on a five step development of procreation, 90
    on the *Goel* passage, 151
    on Job reaching the apex of his bitterness, 88
    on mining, 190
    on Zophar, 93
granulomatosis, as "Job's Disease," 58
grass, growing in a desert place, 261
the grave, 128, 129, 165
Gray, G. B., 69, 70, 71, 72, 73
"great wind," coming across the wilderness, 122
Greek mythology, many-headed dragon named Typhon, 289
Greek Septuagint LXX version, of Job, 1
Greek tragedy, book of Job modeled on, 34
Greek words, in the Book of Job, 390
Greenberg, Hayim, 42
Greenstein, Edward L., 45, 399
Gregory the Great
    on alms after sin, 121
    on arrows, 69
    on Behemoth, 277
    on the body's house, 74
    commentary on Job, 17–19
    on Elihu, 216, 219
    on Eliphaz's pride, 120
    finding proof for resurrection of the body, 18
    on a fore-shadowing of the resurrection, 114
    on the Heavens declaring the glory of God, 83
    on hypocrisy, 80, 139
    on Job as a proof text for original sin, 18
    on "Job coming to the realization of his own limits," 87
    on Job considering who would come into judgment and who would judge, 112
    on the light of the wicked as put out, 136
    on losing the eye of the mind, 84
    on presenting our bodies ready to be wounded, 55
    on recourse for hope, 71
    on Satan and the Devil as one and the same, 52
    on strength and wisdom from God, 101–2
Guide for the Perplexed (Maimonides), 11
guilt, God establishing, 239
guilty, Job knowing himself to be, 104
guilty conscience, despairing of deliverance, 120
gums, escaping complete affliction only by, 144

ha Satan, identification of, 51–53
Habel, Norman
    on daily toil of the destitute, 178
    on eating with relish leading to food poisoning, 156
    on finding a mortal innocent before God, 188
    on the friends as disloyal by deferring to God, 166
    on God as Job's adversary at law, 174
    on Job acknowledging that he is guilty, 90
    on Job proceeding with litigation, 104
    on Job's claim to knowledge and wisdom, 104
    on Job's impossible questions, 89
    on Job's wife as a realist, 62
    personifying death as "the Hungry One," 137
    on sins of exploitation, 179
    on the wicked, 154, 157, 163, 180–81
hail, 261
Halle-Wolfssohn, Aaron, 38
Hanbeli, Mugir ed Din, 24, 36–37
hand of God, Job's instruction concerning, 190
"hand on my mouth," indicative of being silent, 271
Handel's *Messiah*, "I Know That My Redeemer Liveth," 149
hapax legomena
    atiyn as giving interpreters trouble, 164
    in the Book of Job, 208, 231, 281, 285, 286, 298–303
    in chapter 21, 158
    in chapter 37, 252
    "destruction" in v. 20 as, 163
    "drops," 262
    in the Elihu speeches, 214, 224, 398
    "glass" or "crystal," 192
    "grieve" as, 203
    Mazzaroth constellation as, 262
    noun "pressure" as, 228
    pirhah as the word for a plant, 200
    related to a verb connected to "try" or "test," 233
    "rule" or "dominion" (*mishtar*), 262

hapax legomena (continued)
  "suck up" as another, 270
  the verb for "They make oil," 178
  of the word for "adversaries," *qimanu*, 170
  yahtop as one, 84
happiness for the wicked, standard doctrine on the brevity of, 154
Hartley, John
  on Behemoth, 278
  on Bildad, 134, 137
  on Elihu, 222
  on God speaking to Job, 95
  on Job, 100, 110, 111
  on wisdom residing in God, 101
  on Zophar, 93, 97
hawk, description of, 269–70
"healers of worthlessness," Job's friends as, 105
healing stream, curing Ayyub, 35, 61
"heart," as the seat of the intellect, 99
heavenly bodies, linked in thought with angels, 185
"Heavens," declaring the glory of God, 83
Hebrew Bible
  derash, or allegorical understanding of, 8
  name Uz mentioned several times in, 47–48
  words used to designate an "oath" or "promise to God," 211
Hebrew of the Book of Job, as difficult, 32
Hebrew words, in the Book of Job, 391–96
Hegel, George, 39
Hellmouth, Leviathan as, 287–88
"helpers of Rahab," as "the proud of Egypt," 84
Hen, Zerahiah, 60
Henry, Matthew
  on Eliphaz's vision, 67
  on God making desolate all Job's company, 124
  on Job as a type of Christ, 124
  on Job justifying himself, 68–69
  on Job's expectations of his friends, 70, 124
  on Job's lament, 64
  on the parts of chapter 18, 133
  on the parts of chapter 24, 176
  on the parts of chapter 29, 195
  on the parts of chapter 31, 204
  on the parts of chapter 32, 217
  on the parts of chapter 33, 226
  on the parts of chapter 34, 233
  on the parts of chapter 37, 251–52
  on the parts of chapter 41, 280
  seeing Job as a type of Christ, 125
  on "windy words" as "words of air," 123
Herder, J. G., 219
Heschel, Abraham, 60

Hesychius of Jerusalem
  on Bildad, 134
  on Job questioning his friends, 98
  on Job rebutting Bildad on the suffering of the righteous, 86
  on Job's wife as in league with the Devil, 59
  on the lion image, 90
  on original sin, 112
  on the passion of the Devil, 51
  preserving the fruit of virtue, 79–80
"hidden places," as the dark recesses of Sheol, 274
hiding the face, as a sign of anger or unfriendliness, 109
"*Hiob Cantata*," cantata on Job, 38
hippopotamus, Behemoth as, 276–77, 278, 279, 288
historical-critical method, Nicholas of Lyra as the father of, 23
history, of interpreting the book of Job, 1–45
Hobbes, Thomas, *Leviathan*, 289
Hoffman, Yair, *Blemished Perfection*, 45
hol, rendering as "sand" or "Phoenix," 197
Homer, in the *Odyssey*, 138
"honey and curd," 156
honor, paid to Job, 196–97
hope, of Job in death instead of Life, 131–33
"hope" and "thread," word-play on the term *tiqwah* rendered as both, 73
hopes, of man destroyed little by little, 116
horse. *See* battle horse; riverhorse; war horse
hospitality, yogurt-like food associated with gestures of, 196
host of ailments, as Job's disease, 58
hostility, of society, 201–2
"Hosts of Heaven," equivalent with sons of God, 50
house
  of the prosperous sinner, 159
  of the wicked man, 138
Hubris, as the tragic flaw of Job, 34
the *Hug*, or "vault," upon the Earth, 26
Hugo, Victor, 39
human beings
  as children of God, 50
  not capable of ascertaining all that God knows, 95
human existence, Job contemplating the ephemerality of, 111
human intelligence, not fathoming the depths of wisdom, 194
human life, 26–27, 72, 164
human lifespan, power of God over, 112
human prisoner, speaking of Leviathan as, 281
human wisdom, God outwitting, 102

humility, Job lacking, 12
Hunchback of Notre Dame (Hugo), 39
the Hungry One, as death, 137
hunting, as a motif in the Leviathan section, 279
Hutchinson, R. F., 62–63, 278
Hymn to Wisdom, 192–93
    extensive vocabulary of, 194
    as a later addition to the Book of Job, 182, 216, 307
    Simeon Duran on, 26
hypocrites, 79–80, 82

"ibex," found in the high mountains, 264–65
Ibn Asakir, on prophet Ayyub, 24
Ibn Ezra, Abraham
    on the Adversary as an angel, 52
    on the angel appointed as guardian, 231
    on Behemoth, 276
    on "the belly representing hidden thoughts," 122
    on error hidden deep within, 141
    on Job not prophesying, 292
    on perishing forever like dung, 154
    on the power of Creator, 90
    on respect paid to Job, 198
    Spinoza referring to, 30
    on the throne representing the heavens, 185
    on understanding all that has been done, 260
    on when terrors turned upon Job, 202
Ibn Ishaaq, on prophet Ayyub, 24
Ibn Munabbih, Wahb, 23–24
Iconoclastic Job, xiv
Idea of the Holy (Otto), 42
if-then constructions, 211, 398
ignorance, kinds of, 96
ill health, of Gregory, 18
Illustrations of the Book of Job (Blake), 39
imaginations
    evil, 7, 12, 51
    failing as a shadow, 130
    good, 7, 12
Imitatio Christi (Thomas à Kempis), 22
immortality, 27, 150
"in the dust," 273
inclinations or imaginations, in the souls of human beings, 7
infected sores, as Job's disease, 57
Influences of Demonic Forces view, 52
iniquities, of Job's youth, 110
injustices, of the world, 172
The Inner Eye (Greenberg), 42
innocence, 174, 189, 204–11
insignificance, of Job compared to God, 110

integrity, of Job, 174–75, 188–89, 206–7, 210, 272–73
"intellectual humility," Job lacking, 21
intellectual virtues, Job lacking, 96
irreligion, of Job, 235–36
irreverence, of worthless men, 199–201
Isaiah di Trani, 119
Ishodad of Merv, 19, 20, 52, 120, 277
"Ishtar's Descent" Babylonian text, 91
Islamic tradition, on Prophet Ayyub, 37
Iyyov, derivation of, 46

jackals and ostriches, 203, 204
Jacob, talked Eliphaz out of killing him, 66
Saint James, on the steadfastness of Job, 3–4
Jastrow, Morris, 95, 187, 201–2, 204
J.B. (play by MacLeish), 42, 61, 94
Jennings, William, 221, 278
Jerome
    agreeing with the opinion of the Talmudists, 216
    on "catch by the heel" reminding of the birth of Jacob, 137
    on Elihu, 219
    on Job believing in resurrection, 16
    Latin translation of Job, 16–17
    pointed out parallels of book of Tobit to Job, 2
    preferring the Septuagint, 16
Jewish Apocrypha, references to Job in, 2
Jewish commentaries, 6, 25, 37–39
Jewish community of Amsterdam, excommunicated Spinoza, 29
Jews (ancient)
    prohibition against the eating of blood, 128
    treatment of slaves, 207
Job. *See also* Ayyub
    answering as wicked men do, 241
    appealing to God to take His attention off of him, 91
    appeals from Man to God, 128–31
    Arabic name for as "Ayyub," 5
    arguments, vanity of, 245–46
    asking for the Almighty to appear, 212
    blaming God for his misfortunes, 203
    boldness of, 109
    bringing two charges against El, 89
    certain of the outcome of his case, 108
    challenged God's moral right to be in charge of the world, 273
    challenged to display his knowledge, 260
    challenging God to appear and defend His actions, 108

Job *(continued)*
  changing his mind on contending with God, 85
  children of, 295–96
    as the cause of his suffering, xii, 77
    Job making sacrifices for, 77
    Job referring to the loss of, 195
  complaining
    of social injustice, 244
    that God has withdrawn, 173–74
    of unkind usage, 141–42
  completion of his final speech, 204–11
  continuing his final response (chapter 30), 199–204
  continuing the assault, 68–69
  crown of his prosperity, 197
  cursing the day of his birth, 63–65
  declining to answer Yahweh, 271
  defending his own wisdom and dignity, 99
  denying the resurrection of the dead, 73
  described as a king of Egypt in Tobit, 2
  described as "blameless and upright" by Saadiah, 8
  desiring that he might meet God, 173
  desiring to weigh his pleas in the balance with those of God, 68
  developing his uprightness, 205–6
  disease of, 56–58, 73
  "dying old and full of days," 296
  entreating attention, 160
  entreating to know his sins, 109–11
  as an example of *puritas innocentis*, 21
  exercising his own critical judgment, 100
  expecting a few years of life more, 127
  expressing conviction of his imminent end, 74
  fearing that God would bring him calamity, 208
  feeling that death is near, 131
  final discourse (chapters 29–31), 194–211
  final lament of, 210–11
  final words to God, 291–95
  as the first drama written in the world according to Sommi, 29
  as the "first of the Existentialists," 41
  as a flawed man lacking intellectual capacity, 8–9
  former comforts of, 195–96
  fortunes of, 295
  friends of
    Abravanel on the first three, 27
    accusing of heartlessness, 71
    air of superiority of, 104
    answer to Bildad (chapter 26:2-4 and 27), 187–89
    answering Bildad's second speech (chapter 19), 140–52
    arguments cited by, 159
    arguments of, 159, 166
    Bildad castigated by Job, 186
    Bildad reproving, 134–36
    Bildad reproving Job, 76–79
    developing a counter-suit against Job, 399
    Elihu counseling, 249–50
    Elihu desiring his attention, 246–47
    Eliphaz's indictment of, 167
    failed to understand the situation of Job, 130
    false comfort of, 132
    first response to Bildad (chapters 9 and 10), 81–92
    first response to Eliphaz (chapter 6-7), 68–75
    first response to Zophar (chapter 12), 98–117
    guilt, Eliphaz fully convinced of speaking like a friend, 66
    Job ceasing to address, 109
    Job dismissing the value of the speech of, 187
    Job lashing out at, 98
    Job not offering a rebuttal to Elihu, 217
    Job not responding to Elihu, 212
    Job pleading for them to stop giving traditional arguments, 145
    Job rebutting Bildad on the suffering of the righteous, 86
    Job recognizing his image in the descriptions of, 165
    Job reproving, 104–6, 117–18
    misery of being mocked by one's, 99
    motivation for volunteering to defend God, 105
    not desiring to meet God, 173
    picking up key words from Eliphaz's first speech, 68
    representing the general opinion of mankind, 98
    scorning Job, 127
    second reply to Zophar (chapter 21), 158–66
    second response to Eliphaz (chapter 16 and 17), 123–33
    third answer to Eliphaz (chapter 23), 172–76
    third response to Eliphaz (chapter 24), 176–81

as too God-like, 145
usefulness of, 70–71
violating justice by showing favoritism, 105
as wrong and Job as right, 295
frightened by God's ways, 176
genealogy of, 23
as a Gentile or a Jew, 18
going far beyond mere charity to the needy, 208
on his error remaining with him, 141
honor paid to, 196–97
impatience of, 67
incapable of understanding the overall plan of God, 292
insisting on the soundness of his moral judgments, 71
integrity of, 174–75, 188–89, 206–7, 210, 272–73
interpreting God's silence, 174
irreligion of, 235–36
issuing a challenge on who will prove him a liar, 181
as a *Jobus Christi*, or Christ figure for Gregory, 18
justified himself rather than God, 223
lacking "intellectual virtues" for Gersonides, 14
laments of, 63–65, 195
law case of, 124, 173, 399–401
longing for death, 69–70
making his own vow or promise to God, 188
marshaling his arguments, 108
meaning of in Hebrew, 46–47
mentioning God as a source for his afflictions, 69
needing to repent and put away his sins, 96
needing to show that his power is equal to the purposes he would impose upon God, 274
never in his heart wished his enemies harm, 209
never suggesting sin as the cause of his suffering, 243
not abandoning his belief that goodness should be rewarded, 204
not abandoning his faith that God will be his salvation, 107
not claiming that he is sinless, 110
not disregarding God's commandments, 70
picturing the wicked man, 159
pleading that God grant him some relief in his few remaining days, 91
professing his confidence in God, 106–9
as pronounced in various languages, 46–47
as a public menace, scoffing at religion, 235
questioning God, 109
questioning why he was born, 91
reaching the apex of his bitterness, 88
ready to hear any counter-charges God might bring against him, 173
realizing his own limits, 87
regarding death as imminent, 152
remaining helpless in the hands of his Creator, 90
reorganizing social space, 196
replies to God, 257
representing his case as deplorable, 118–20
required to explain the gifts of nature, 254–55
respectfulness of, 207–9
responding to God after each speech, 256
responding to theological explanations for his suffering, 158
response to Yahweh's first speech from the whirlwind, 270
as responsible for the treatment of his slaves, 207
returning to his lament, 130
returning to his morbid desire for death, 132
as "riddled with corruption" according to Zophar, 157
rises and youngsters jeer at him, 144
saying many times "[if] I have sinned," 75
saying the wicked live to old age, 161
second response to God, 257
second response to Yahweh, 291–97
seeking to fathom the mysteries causing God's cruel treatment of him, 89
self-righteousness of, 223
as a shepherd who would risk his own life to rescue a sheep, 197
shown standing in a spring flowing around his feet, 35–36
as of small account or unworthy, 271
speaking
  on the demands of friendship, 70
  directly to God, 68, 72
  of man's death, 113–14
  of man's life, 111–17
  to Paul in the "Apocalypse of Paul," 4
  in the plain language of the desprate, 106
  at the risk of his life, 107
  of the world of the shades, 185
suffering of. *see* suffering
on the suggestion of hidden sin as false, 87
swearing to his innocence, 399

Job *(continued)*
    taking an oath that he never worshipped Idols, 209
    turning to address the Omnipresent, 129
    unshakable certainty of the righteousness of his case, 108
    unwavering loyalty to the law of God, 175
    voicing a hope that his Redeemer lives, 146–47
    weakness in regard to humility, 21
    wife of
        as an agent of the Devil, 17
        ascribing the best intentions to, 60
        causing Job to curse God so that he will die, 60
        as a *diablo aduitrix*, or a "helper of the Devil," 18
        as the mother of ten children suddenly reduced from affluence and happiness, 63
        named Sitidos in Tobit, 2
        not seen as a "hand-main of the Devil" by Saadiah, 8
        opinions on, 58–63
        rendered a number of times in drama and fiction, 61
        says *Baruch Elohim ve mos*, usually translated as "curse God and die," 58
        Thomas Aquinas on, 21
        as a "witness to his own iniquity," 124
        yielding himself in active reverence to find peace, 292
Job and David (Ambrose), 17
Job and His Wife (oil painting), 39
Job and the Dead Christ, wood painting by Carpaccio, 149
"Job as Warrior or Wrestler," helping the cause of God, xiv
"Job of the Resurrection," xiv
Job of the Resurrection, in "Apocalypse of Paul," 4
Job penitent motif, 67, 93
Job repentant motif, version of, 46
Job Visited by His Wife, painting by Georges de la Tour, 62
Jobab, Job identified with in the LXX version, 1–2
Jobina, as the female form of the name, 47
Jobs, kinds of, xiv–xv
Jobus Christ motif
    allusion to, 101
    applications of, 150
    employed by Goldsmith, 35
    Pope Gregory employing, 70
    Henry ascribing to, 124
    instance of, 125
    Jerome assenting to, 148
    reference to, 100
    Thomas assenting to, 149
    version of, 102, 125
Jobus Christi figure, Job as, 20
Jobus Christi image, xiv, 31, 149
"Jobus Christi" understanding, of text, 150
John, Bishop of Fredericton, 65, 87
John, the Abbot, 20
John of Damascus (650-750), 19, 20
Jordan, W. G., 65, 67, 221
Joy, restored man singing for, 231
judgment, of the wicked, 165–66, 180–81
Julian of Eclanum
    on Behemoth, 277
    on Bildad, 78, 134
    on humans driving away the greatest losses, 55
    on Job suffering under the scourge of God, 138
    on Job's response to Bildad, 86
    on the power of the Devil, 52
Jung, Carl, 53
justice, government guaranteeing, 237
justice and righteousness, God's power coordinated with, 256

Kallen, Horace, 34, 42
Kant, Immanuel, 105
Kara, Joseph, 10–11
Kelly, William, 87, 220
Kempis, Thomas à, 22
"kidney ailment," as Job's disease, 58
Kierkegaard, Søren, 39, 62
Kissane, Edward J.
    on Elihu, 221
    on Eliphaz, 124
    on Job contrasting months with the day of the hireling, 72
    on Job's call for redress, 125–26
    on no one resisting God, 83
    on Zophar, 95
kohanim, translated as princes or priests, 102
Kokoschka, three-act drama called *Job*, 39
Kraeling, Emil, 222

La Fin de Satan (Hugo), 87
Laato, Antti, 13
Lamartine, Alphonse de, 39
laments, of Job, 63–65, 72, 130, 194, 195, 210–11
lamp, as a symbol, 136

Lancre, Pierre de, 278
land, testifying for Job, 210–11
land of Uz, information regarding, 47–49
landmarks (*gebulah*), necessary to preserve one's inheritance, 177
lappid, meanings of, 99
Lassen, Abraham, 14
late medieval Christian works, portraying the saintly, patient Job, 31
Lathcen (d. 661.), 19, 20
Latin words, in the Book of Job, 391
law case
    book of Job as, 124, 173, 175, 399–401
    Job proceeding with, 104
    Job ready to pursue, 188
"Law of Yahweh," Job's obedience to, 401
laws
    of God, 194
    of inheritance for children, 296
lawsuit with God, notion of, 82
Le Hir, Arthur Marie, 133, 220
lead tablet, on which an inscription is made, 146
legal vocabulary, in chapter 23, 173
leprosy, 57, 58
Levi Ben Gershom. *See* Gersonides
Leviathan
    in art, 287–89
    consequences of getting close to, 281
    crushing the heads of, 279
    as dangerous, 282
    defeat of, 186
    description of as an addition, 272
    dwelling in the abyss of the ocean, 275
    eating a whale a day, 289
    in the Hebrew Bible, 279
    Islamic depiction of, 288
    as the king of beasts and feared by all, 287
    in literature and culture, 289–91
    majesty of, 285
    meaning of as a word, 279
    minute details of, 282–83
    motion in the water, 286
    narrative on, 279–87
    no one facing can survive, 282
    as no threat to God, 286
    physical description of, 286
    possibility of domesticating, 281
    set of symbolic associations, 279
    as unvulnerable to any weapon, 285
    as "without fear," 286
"Leviathan" poem, by George Oppen, 289
Lewis, Marshall H., 44
Liber Job (Riga), 20
life
    blood as equivalent to, 127
    as fleeting, 112
    as nothing more than a passing breath, 74
    as very brief, 91
light
    being as darkness, 91
    versus darkness, xiii
    God associated with, 92
    in parallel with the "east wind," 261
    of the wicked being in "darkness," 259
light and darkness, 136, 260
lightning, Elihu developing the themes of, 252
lion, 90, 263
literal-historical understanding, of text, 23
literary figures, incorporating passages of the book of Job, 39
literary techniques, used by Elihu, 215
literary works, patterned on the book of Job, 31, 35
literature, Leviathan in, 289–91
locations, proposed for Uz, 47–48
"loins," nouns for, 258
longing for death, Job seeking God's final act of annihilation, 69
Lowth, Robert, 76, 219
Lucretius, "On Life and Death," 75
Luther, Martin
    agreed with Nicholas, 23
    concluding that God alone is righteous, 33
    on the difficulties of translating the Book of Job, 32
    on Job's wife, 32
    on the speeches of Elihu, 33
    suggesting a body-soul dualism, 32
    suggesting *Der Satan* has a lower status than the other angels, 32
    translated the book of Job from the original Hebrew to German, 32–33

MacLeish, Archibald, play *J.B.*, 42, 61, 94
Maimonides, Moses
    on the banquet at the end of time, 276
    on Bildad, 76
    on Elihu, 216, 218
    glosses on the comments of, 26
    on God as a Righteous Judge, 108
    on God dooming the hope of hypocrites, 82
    indebted to Aristotle, 13
    on Job, 72, 144
    remarks on the book of Job in his *Guide for the Perplexed*, 11–12
    on "signs of the zodiac," 84
    on Zophar, 93, 94
"Maker," words for in Job, 226

mal'akim, Hebrew plural of angel, 50
Malbim, 84, 196, 271–72, 273
Malbin, on providence for lions, 263–64
man
    cannot be just before God, 82
    ceasing to strive for wisdom independently, 194
    as constantly deteriorating, 112
    death of, Job speaking of, 113–14
    life of, Job speaking of, 111–17
    not doing a favor to God by being righteous, 244
    as puny in contrast to superhuman monsters, 85
    reaping what he has sown, 195
    as a worm or grub, 184
marvels, as the slightest whisper of God's power, 186
Masoretic Text, 23, 28, 141
masos, meaning of, 80
"The Mass of Separation," as a celebration for lepers, 57
McFadyen, John Edgar, 74, 82
medieval Christian painters, renderings of Behemoth and Leviathan, 287
medieval Islamic sources, referring to Job's wife as Rahmah, 60
medieval Jewish accounts, of Elihu as more positive, 216
Medieval Jewish tradition, on Behemoth, 275
Medieval Period, image of Job in, 6–25
Meditation on the Passion, wood painting by Vittore Carpaccio, 149
Melchizedek, references to Job and, 102
Melville, Herman, 39, 289
Mendelssohn, employing the historical-critical understanding, 37–38
Mendelssohn, Fanny, 38
Mendelssohn, Felix, 38
Mendelssohn, Moses, 37
Mendelssohn family, 38
methods, of God dealing with men, 247–49
Mezudat David
    on becoming as repulsive as dung, 154
    on Behemoth, 276
    on the bitterness of Job, 85
    on blaming God for allowing the constellations to determine his life, 85
    on the body rotting away into a decayed object, 111
    on bringing back the soul from the grave, 232
    on bringing down much wisdom, 118
    on choosing judgment, 234–35
    on clothing stripped of the naked, 168
    on comprehending Divine Providence, 187
    on delivering the innocent from woe, 171–72
    on the depths of wisdom, 194
    on Elihu, 225, 233
    on Eliphaz, 67
    on evil inclination teaching Job's mouth to speak, 118
    on "the fear of retribution," 123
    on fears of Job, 112
    on flying away like a dream, 155
    on food becoming like snake venom, 156
    on Gehinnom, the place of the dead, 185
    on "the generation of the flood," 162
    on God attacking Job, 143
    on God bringing man to the point of being crushed, 151
    on God destroying the wicked, 239
    on God illustrating to Job His Providence, 269–70
    on God increasing the water, 101
    on God knowing Job's innocence, 205
    on God making Job a target for His arrows, 125
    on God preparing wisdom for the creation, 193
    on God sealing the knowledge of the rain, 253
    on God's works of creation, 250
    on the heart preparing deceit, 122
    on helping our enemies, 209
    on hiding hearts from understanding, 129
    on the hope of Job, 132
    on indulging until flesh became fat, 121
    on Job asking for his friends "to have pity on him," 145
    on Job delivering the poor man and the orphan, 196
    on Job depicting God as commanding that Job be castigated, 109
    on Job lamenting his own wretched lot, 72
    on Job not yearning to live any longer, 297
    on Job openly accusing God, 69
    on Job praying that his wounds remain exposed, 126
    on Job refuting arguments of the friends, 224–25
    on Job seeking forgiveness, 75
    on knowing you would be born, 261
    on lacking knowledge of understanding, 248
    on Leviathan, 282, 287
    on man's disobedience as a grave transgression, 184
    on "men of an understanding heart," 236

on murderers and thieves avoiding the light, 179
on no son or grandson remaining, 139
on not becoming wealthy because of arrogance, 121
on not setting up words before God, 255
on one suffering pain as angry with himself, 130
on people not understanding the ways of God, 239
on the poor man's gratitude to Job, 208
on the power of a man compared to God, 273
on preserving script for posterity, 146
on the questions of Job, 271
recalling Noah and the flood, 170
on remaining silent because of invalid arguments, 108
on returning to God, 171
on a righteous man wrangling with God, 83
on righteous men being rewarded with spiritual pleasures, 131
on the righteousness of Job, 189
on saving from death, 232
on sending widows away, 169
on speculation concerning God's judgment, 240–41
telling thoughts of flattery, 130
on terrors turned upon Job, 202
on the Torah as given from His mouth, 170
translating 34:12 as God not perverting justice, 236
on who gave the horse its strength, 268
on a witness on Job's behalf, 126
on words striking Job on the cheek, 125
Michaelis, J. H., 78, 219
Midian, brother of Shuah, 76
Midrash Rabbah on Genesis, contrasting Job with Adam, 59
Milhamot (Gersonides), 14
Milton, John, 277, 289
miners and mining, describing, 190–92
mining and the Hymn to Wisdom (chapter 28), 189–94
miracles, as natural events, 30
misery, dereliction and, 203–4
modern Jewish scholars, observations about Behemoth, 276
modern scholars, on Behemoth and Leviathan, 280
Mokiah, translating as "Judge" or "Arbiter," 87
"monster of the deep," 75
months, for Job instead of days, 72
moral character
    of God, 292
    of Job, 4
moral content of Scripture, as the most important aspect, 30
moral education, continuing for Job, 11
moral qualities theodicy, 78, 250
moral qualities view
    in chapter 22, 167
    in Elihu speeches, 33, 212, 219, 248, 249–50, 251, 398
    Eliphaz endorsing, 397
    on evil and suffering, 7
    Julian assenting to, 79
    Kraeling assenting to, 222
    Rashi endorsing, 9
    Rawlinson suggesting, 221
    reference to, 218, 247, 249
    Roth ascribing, 218
    by Thomas à Kempis, 22
moral virtues, developing by experiencing evil, xiii
Moralia in Job, as Gregory's Job commentary, 18, 20
Moses, 7, 29
motets, with Jobean themes, 32
mountain goat, description of, 264
mourners, Job comforting, 198
murdered man, blood of calling down the vengeance of Heaven, 126
Murray, Gilbert, 42, 222
musical compositions, on the book of Job in the sixteenth century, 31–32
Mutazilites, as Bildad's theological orientation, 76
"my autumn days," meaning of, 195
"My Redeemer lives," affirmation of, 151
mysteries, 95
mythological creatures, 277, 278, 280

Naaman, provenance of the name, 92–93
Nachmanides, 60
Nahman, location of, 92
nations, making and destroying of, 102–3
nauseous food, parallels to Job's sickness, 69
"Navigator's Line," of stars, 260
the neck, seen as a seat of strength, 284
Nermeylen, Francois, sculpture entitled *Job Dejected*, 39
netherworld, earth as, 100
Newsom, Carol A.
    on Behemoth as "first in rank," 286
    on Bildad, 135
    on the "bounds that humans cannot pass," 113–14
    on dark clouds associated with theophanies, 169

Newsom, Carol A. *(continued)*
    descendants being cut off in death, 164
    on Elihu, 252, 255, 256
    on the "human inability to comprehend the ways of God," 254
    on images of chaos before creation, 91–92
    on the introduction to chapter 21, 158–59
    on Job as like a shepherd, 197
    on Job parodying God's knowledge of the individual," 90
    on Job recounting his sense of God's protective presence, 195
    on Job talking about resurrection and death, 114
    on Job's speech to Bildad, 82
    on Leviathan, 279, 283, 284, 285
    on the moral purposes of natural phenomena, 253
    on the parts of chapter 41, 280
    on people staying indoors to avoid winter storms, 253
    on the power of God over human lifespan, 112
    on Rahab as the name of a Chaos monster, 84–85
    on Zophar, 94, 95
Nicholas of Lyra, 22–23
night and day, description of the succession of, 259
nights
    as the saddest time for sick people, 69
    turning into days for Job, 132
Noah and his sons, 170
non-Muslim European scholars, commentating on prophet Ayyub, 36
"Northern View," for the location of Uz, 48–49
nostrils, of Leviathan, 282, 284
"novella," book of Job as, 29
Noyes, George R., 135, 150, 220, 278

oath(s)
    in the book of Job, 203
    chapter 31 of Job as an extended, 211
    Job making exculpatory, 399
    in Job's final speech, 204
    in the Old Testament and the book of Job, 211
    reference to, 187
    second mention of, 188
"obedience," describing Job's relationship to Yahweh, 401
Odo of Cluny, commentary on Gregory's *Moralia*, 20

Ohev Mishpat treatise, Duran's commentary of the book of Job, 25–26
Old Testament, East Wind in, 122–23
Olympiodorus
    on the absolute solitude of the impious, 121
    on Bildad, 78, 136
    on the impious suffering, 80
    on a prophecy of Christ's advent, 102
Olympiodorus of Thebes, on Eliphaz, 119
omnibenevolence, of God, 292
omnipotence, Job acknowledging God's, 85
omniscience of God, reference to, 102
On the Forgiveness of Sins and Baptism (Augustine), 17
"On Valid Syllogisms" (Gersonides), 14
original sin
    doctrine of for Calvin, 34
    early Christian exegetes finding, 111
    finding, 112
    Job believing in, 22
    Luther finding in the book of Job, 33
    on passages having nothing to do with the Christian understanding of, 28
    proof text for, 4
original sin theory
    Bildad endorsing, 397
    Eliphaz alluding to, 397
    nod in the direction of, 121
    on the problem of evil, xiii
ostrich, description of, 267–68
Ottensosser, David, 38
Otto, Rudolf, 42
outcasts, taunting Job, 200
outer frame, of Leviathan, 283
Owen, G. Frederick, 48
ox, Behemoth as, 278–79, 287

pain, exalting in if it hastens death, 70
paintings
    Job and His Wife, 39
    Job and the Dead Christ on wood by Carpaccio, 149
    Job Visited by His Wife by Georges de la Tour, 62
    with Leviathan as the subject matter, 288–89
    wood beam, at Saint Catherine's Monastery in the Sinai, 287
    "Zophar Condemns Job," 94
Palestinian Talmud, 3
Paradise Lost (Milton), 91
paraphrase genre, 35
Parente, Pascal, 222
pasturage, for the wild ass in the desert, 265

patience and steadfastness, Job seen as a man of, 4
"The Patience of Job," anonymous fifteenth-century Middle French poem, 31
"the patience of Job," describing the patriarch's character, 47
Patience of Job, calling Bildad Baldach, 76
Patient Job
    described, xiv–xv
    emphasis of Riga's poem on, 20
    indications of, 4
pawing of the earth, 268
"peacock," 266–67
Peake, Arthur
    on Behemoth, 277
    on the conflict of feelings in Job, 105–6
    on Elihu, 227–28
    the image of the weaver's shuttle, 73
    on Job challenging God, 108
    on Job's narrow outlook, 261
    quoting Mallock's paraphrase of Lucretius's "On Life and Death," 75
    on showing Job will be vindicated, 150
"pedagogical purpose," of suffering, 222
Pelaia, Ariela, 277
pellagra, as Job's disease, 57
Peloubet, Francis, 55, 221, 278
pen of iron on lead, probable meaning of, 146
Penitent Job motif, 96
Perdue, Leo, 98, 102, 181–82
"perfect and upright," Job as for Gersonides, 15
Pety Job: Lessons of the Dirge, 31
Philip the Priest
    on an allusion to Christ's power, 101
    on arrogance, 80
    on Behemoth, 277
    on Bildad, 79
    on Eliphaz, 122
    on Job's friends, 99
    on mentioning the fatness of the neck, 120
Philips, Elaine, 67
philosophers, nineteenth-century on the book of Job, 39
"Philosopher's View," of human life, 26–27
philosophical essays, in the early twentieth century, 42
philosophical exegesis, of Gersonides, 14
philosophy, using to answer questions about the Bible, 30
The "Phoenix," 19, 20
"Phoenix" theory, opinions on, 197
physical brightness, linking with ethical purity, 185
physical things, all coming to an end, 192

physical weakness, as the result of hunger, 200
"pillars of the Heavens," 186, 258–59
Pit
    going down into the, 232
    the innermost part of, 133
"place of all places," Job as a resident of, 49
Plan of Yahweh, following, 259
plant metaphors, common in Wisdom Literature, 79–80
"plasterer of lies," similar idiom in Akkadian, 104
The Poem of Job (Stevenson), 68
poetry, luxurious display of, 118
Pollock, Seton, 222
poor, robbery of, 178
Pope, Marvin
    on Behemoth and Leviathan as mythological creatures, 280
    on Elihu as flatulent with words, 222
    on the parallel of Job's wife to Tobit's wife, Hannah, 63
    rendering *bene ha Elohim* as "sons of the gods," 50
    on the role of the Satan, 53
    support for this book, xi
portion, of the wicked, 157–58
potter, comparing God to, 90
power
    Bildad expressing himself with, 135
    of Christ, 101
    of the Devil, 52
    Job invited to exercise, 273
    Job needing to show, 274
power of God, 82
    controlling the billows of the sea, 84
    coordinated with justice and righteousness, 256
    as Creator, 90
    Elihu observing, 252–54
    H. H. Rowley on, 175, 239
    John Calvin on, 228
    marvels as the slightest whisper of, 186
    over human lifespan, 112
    over the mighty, 180
    over the moon and the stars, 184
    over water, 101
    Solomon Freehof on, 237
prayer, value of intercessory, 295
preachers, notes for on the book of Job, 45
"Preserved Tablet" (*Al-Lawh Al-Mafooz*), in Islam, 29
pride, swelling up like a mountain, 116
priests, 102, 127–28
"Prince of Ashtartu in Bashan," 46
princes of the Earth, groping in darkness, 103

problem of evil. *See* evil
property rights, given to Job's daughters, 296
prose
    epilogue written in, 295–97
    first five verses of chapter 32 written in, 223–24
prosperity, 161–62, 163
prosperity and prestige, bred no arrogance in Job, 196
prosperous sinner, Job's portrait of, 159
prostitute, beginning her operations at dusk, 179
Providence
    dealings of God's, 162–64
    everything in life is subject to, 79
    forgetting about God's, 245
Prudentius, poem the "Psychomachia," 16
psychogenic causes, for Job's disease, 58
"Psychomachia" (Prudentius), 16
psychosomatic origins, for Job's disease, 58
pure of heart, God despising not, 247
puritas innocentis, 21
puritas poenitentis, 21
purity, Thomas distinguishing two kinds of, 21
purpose, of the divine plan, 291–92

the *Qodesim*, or "Heavenly Beings," mentioned by Eliphaz, 397
quiver of arrows, rattling of, 268
Qur'an, 5, 6

rabbis in the Talmud, believing Job was not a Jew, 2
Rahab, 84–85, 186
Rahmah, the daughter of Ephraim as Job's wife, 24, 60
Ralbag. *See* Gersonides
Rambam. *See* Maimonides, Moses
ransom, 231
Rashbam, grandson of Rashi, 10
Rashi
    on the Adversary as an angel, 52
    on Behemoth, 275, 276
    on being despised in the eyes of children, 144
    on Bildad's theory of retributive justice, 81
    on a blossom not lasting long, 112
    on the calamity which God sends to the wicked, 209
    on calling God a "scoundrel!" and "wicked!" 240
    on "chambers of the south," 84
    comparing Job to Abraham, 8
    on conceiving trouble and bearing iniquity, 122
    on contending with God, 83
    on the counsel of Eliphaz, 67–68
    on descending to the grave, 133
    on dying suddenly with strength, 155
    on the Earth coming to an end, 191
    on Elihu, 218, 224, 248
    on Eliphaz, 66, 67, 167–68
    on encircling a boundary, 185–86
    examples of the instruction of Job, 9
    on "fatness" referring to "plenty," 119
    on fear of familiarity with Job, 198
    on food turning into snake venom, 156
    on the forgiveness of God, 232
    on "gazing at the Heavens," 243
    on God completing retribution, 176
    on God delivering Job to be a fool, 125
    on God letting rain fall on mountains and hills, 254
    on God's power over the moon and the stars, 184
    on happiness for the wicked, 154
    on haughty people building ruins for a name, 121
    on "helpers of Rahab," 84
    on the hireling completing his day, 113
    identified with the School of Mainz, 8
    on an inlaid inscription, 146
    on Job as a "witness to his own iniquity," 124
    on Job asking about God's fairness, 89
    on Job denying resurrection of the dead, 73
    on Job fearing to raise his voice before God, 85
    on Job grieving for the needy, 203
    on Job not finding moral basis of the universe, 160
    on Job not giving up his innocence, 188
    on Job referring to his sickness, 109
    on Job speaking to God and not to a man, 160
    on Job's bones being cleaved, 144
    on Job's friends comparing themselves to Abraham, 106
    on Job's Redeemer enduring, 148–49
    on the "latter people," 139
    on Leviathan, 282, 285, 287
    on mining, 190
    on the mountain goat hating its young, 264
    on naked people having no refuge, 178
    on no stranger passing in their midst, 120
    on the noble spirit that rested upon Job, 202
    on not boasting to God about knowledge, 118
    on one casting evil showing no compassion, 189

on ordering the eagle to fly high, 269
against the original sin response, 113
on the ostrich not caring for her young, 267
on pain Job is suffering, 110
on people not understanding the ways of God, 239
on "the people of Sodom and Gemorrah and their destruction," 191
on "people of the age of the Flood," 179
on perishing forever like dung, 154
on Persians putting poison on the tips of their arrows, 69
on physical success as of no value, 192
on physicians of no value, 105
on the rain sealing a person in his house, 253
on the raven as black, 264
on reasoning, 71
on respect paid to Job, 198
on the rivers of Paradise, 156
on rope as a trap, 136
on a servant seeking the cool shade of the evening, 72
on "sons of ignoble people," 201
on sudden death, 238
on sweetness referring to the custom of the wicked man, 156
on terrors of the shadow of death, 179
on thick clouds as concealment, 169
on tolerating judgments of God, 240
toning down vitriolic speeches, 10
translations by, 9–10, 202, 244
on the uprightness of Job, 196, 208
on the wicked man vomiting up wealth, 156
on wickedness or righteousness bringing benefit, 244
on "the Wisdom of Divine Providence," 233
on wise men confessing transgressions, 120
on "your mouth teaching others your iniquitous beliefs," 118
on Zophar, 93, 153
Rabbi Rav, 68
Rabbi Rava, 64
raven, as black, 264
Rawlinson, George, 221
reason, Job appealing to God's, 104
reconciliation, between man and the Providence of God, 257
Redeemer as Christ view, 149
Redeemer passage, neutral approaches to, 150
Reformation, literature on Job, 32
Reichert, Victor, 93
reincarnation, Job rejecting the idea of, 27
The Religious Ideas of the Old Testament (Robinson), 42
religious techniques, futile of themselves, 193
"renal failure," as Job's disease, 58
renewal, waiting for, 120–22
repentance, 228–29, 293
Reshef (Canaanite god), firing arrows of poison, 158
"resistance to temptation," Job as a model for, 22
respectfulness, of Job, 207–9
Resurrected Job motif
    advocates of, 149
    employed by Calvin, 33–34
    Gregory assenting to, 114
    Jerome assenting to, 148
    Thomas assenting to, 149
resurrection
    belief in, xiv
    Job as a champion of, 1, 2
    Job sharing in according to the LXX, 297
    Job talking about, 114
    Job's belief in, 145–52
    as a possibility for human beings, 15
    reference to, 259
retribution
    as a criticism of the ways of God, 162
    fear of, 123
    not appearing in the book of Job, 401
    propounded by Bildad, 77
    reaffirming the dogma of, 136
retributive justice. *See also* collective retributive justice
    Bildad giving his general theory of, 80
    Bildad using, 397
    Bildad's love of, 78
    in chapter 22, 167
    collective form of, 163
    Elihu employing, 398
    Eliphaz employing, 79
    employed by Eliphaz, Bildad, and Zophar, 17
    indicating in Job's mind, 89
    Saadiah assenting to a version of, 119
    version of, 7, 55
    as Zophar's primary approach, 398
retributive justice response, to the problem of evil, xii
retributive justice theory
    application of, 67
    assent to, 236
    blending of, 254
    as the cause of Job's suffering, 94
    collective form of, 67
    David Thomas assenting, 139
    Dhorme finding, 121
    in the Elihu discourses, 214
    Eliphaz employing, 397

retributive justice theory *(continued)*
    endorsement of, 271
    of the first three friends, 214
    Freehof seeing an example of, 272
    indication of, 123
    Julian endorsing a collective form of, 78
    Mezudat David consenting to, 243
    nod in the direction of, 136
    other friends putting much more emphasis on, 249
    Rashi assenting to, 168, 180
    regarding Job's suffering, 234
    of Satan, 398
    suggesting, 153
    Tur-Sinai endorsing, 77
    versions of, 93, 138
"revenge," not appearing in the book of Job, 401
ribot, as a term for "pleading," 105
Richter, 399
Riga, Peter, 20
righteous man, 90, 170, 171
righteousness, 145, 189, 204, 231
rights of man, before God, 242–43
"rings of gold," 296
riverhorse, Behemoth as, 278
rivers of sweet prosperity, wicked will not behold, 156
robbery, of the poor, 178
Robinson, H. Wheeler, 42
"rock pile," turning into a spring or a pile of water, 80
Rodd, C. D., 71–72, 202
Rodd, C. S., 135, 136, 199
Romantic movement, employing the book of Job, 39
Roth, Leon, 218
Row, C. A., 42, 222
Rowley, H. H.
    on the arguments of the friends, 166
    on autumn as the season of maturity, 195
    on the beginning of chapter 41, 280
    on being repulsive, 144
    on the boldness of Job, 109
    on choosing what is right, 235
    on coined currency, 296
    on comparison of the wicked with vegetative life, 138
    on the darkness that God conceals from us, 255
    on death in its most terrible form, 137
    on "the deep" as the primeval abyss, 192
    on deference paid to Job, 196
    on deliverance for those who profit by discipline, 249
    description of chapter 23, 172
    on dying prematurely full of the sins of youth, 155
    on Elihu, 224, 225, 227, 233, 234, 235, 236, 243, 246, 250, 254, 255
    on the fortunate kicking the unfortunate down, 99
    on God administering the emetic, 156
    on God as great and good, 256
    on God as indifferent in moral issues, 238
    on God as supreme Lord of the universe, 183
    on God doing no wrong, 236–37
    on God hiding His face from Job, 171
    on God listening to Job complain against Him, 245
    on God putting brethren far from Job, 143
    on God seeking again to reclaim Job, 230
    on God's actions as beneficent, 229
    on God's impartiality, 237–38
    on honor as a garment, 142
    introducing chapter 24, 176–77
    on the jaws of the crocodile, 283
    on Job arguing his righteousness face to face with God, 107
    on Job as confident that God will give him a fair hearing, 173–74
    on Job as now scorned and condemned, 201
    on Job as willing to speak at the risk of his own life, 107
    on Job being invited to adorn himself with the attributes of power, 273
    on Job confessing that he is reduced to silence, 270
    on Job continuing his sarcasm, 105
    on Job exercising government of the world, 274
    on Job going beyond defending his own integrity, 272–73
    on Job invoking a curse upon himself, 206
    on Job lashing out at his friends, 98
    on Job lifted to a new plane of peace, 292
    on Job ministering to the poor, the widow, and the fatherless, 207
    on Job not repudiating his integrity, 188–89
    on Job questioning the ancients, 100
    on Job speaking out fearlessly, 106
    on Job swearing an oath by the God who has harmed him, 187
    on Job trying to appeal to God's reason, 104
    on Job's certainty of righteousness of his case, 108
    on Job's complaint against God, 160
    on Job's integrity, 210
    on Job's misery, 199–200

on Job's reply to Bildad, 81–82
on Job's slaves ignoring his wishes, 143
on the littleness of man, 184
on man escaping destruction, 116
on man not seeing the works of God close at hand, 250
on a man's righteousness or wickedness, 244
on the migration of the hawk, 269
on not learning from discipline, 248
on "opening the ear," 229
parallels given by, 111
on the "pillars of the Heavens," 186
on the poor prospect Job seeing before him, 132
on the position of the raven between the lion and other wild animals, 264
on the power of God, 175, 239
on preserving the protestation of innocence after death, 146
on the purpose of affliction, 247
on the Redeemer passages, 151
on retributive justice, 79
on the righteous suffering, 247
on the rights of slaves, 206
on the second divine speech, 272
on the sick man restored to life, 231
on "teach me what I do not see," 240
on when the crocodile issues from the water, 284
on wickedness and the fate of the wicked, 140
on the wild ass, 265
on the wild ox following the wild ass, 266
on wisdom which only God can refute, 224
on Zophar's second speech, 153
Royce, Josiah, 222
Royds, T. F., 135
ruah or "wind," as transient and unsubstantial, 73
ruin, of the wicked, 136–40, 155–57

Saadiah Gaon
    on Behemoth, 276
    on Bildad's first speech, 76
    on clothing stripped off, 168
    commentary on the book of Job, 6–8
    on Elihu, 217
    on Eliphaz, 119
    on God knowing that Job is in the right, 174
    on *Goel* referring to a human being, 148
    on holding up one's hands to avoid a blow, 55
    on man as a worm or grub, 184
    on man as like an army at a halt, 72
    not finding a belief in resurrection of the body in Job, 8
    on pretending to have experiences, 122
    references to Midrashic understandings of Job, 8
    relied on Aristotle, 6
    on Satan as a human being, 52
    on "sun threads," 80
    on tradition being continuous each generation, 120
    translating 32:22, 226
    on trouble encompassing the unjust, 120
    on the wise man offering a love of wind, 117
    on words trusting not in fairness, 122
sacrifice, blood employed in, 127–28
Saint Catherine's Monastery in the Sinai, wood beam painting, 287
Sale, George, 36, 60–61
"salty soil," as land that is infertile, 265
Samuel Ben Meir. *See* Rashbam
sarcasm, of Job, 105
Satan. *See also* Devil
    absent after the prologue, 52–53
    Calvin seeing as a demonic figure, 34
    causing deviation from the path and will of God, 15
    church fathers on, 51
    as a demonic figure in Tobit, 2
    as a demonic influence on Job, 12
    described by Saadiah as a "human being," 7
    leading Job to impatience and blasphemy, 21
    Martin Luther on, 32
    on protective barriers raised by God around Job, 142
    saying let me touch his soul, 56
    as the source of Job's suffering, xii–xiii
    theological positions of, 398
    Thomas Aquinas on, 52, 59
scales, on the back of Leviathan, 283
schadenfreuden, described, 81
schechin, as sickness that cannot be healed, 56–57
Scheindlin, Raymond P., 77
Schreiner, Susan, 34
Schultens, Albert, 78
scientific achievements, futile of themselves, 193
scorners, as friends, 127
Scott, Thomas, 52, 79, 135, 277
Scripture, Spinoza's rules for reading and understanding, 30
scurvy, as Job's disease, 57
sea, wrapped in clouds like swaddling clothes, 259
sea monster, Leviathan as, 279
Sea Serpent, depicting Leviathan as, 288
"secret" and "secrets," vocabulary for, 119
seeing and hearing, linking to understand, 104

INDEX

Sefer Ne'emanah Firyah, comments on Job from Jewish scholars, 38
self-righteousness, of Job, 223
Semitic inscriptions, the name Job appearing in ancient, 46
Septuagint, expanding Job's wife's speech for several lines, 59
Septuagint text, differences from the Masoretic Text, 1–2
"servants," nothing more about Job's original, 296
Sforno, Obadiah ben Jacob, 112
"shade" or "shadow," words indicating, 92
Shaw, George Bernard, mocking Job, 294
Shebah, nephew of Shuah, 76
shehin, describing Job's disease, 56
Sheol
   darkness of, 191
   description of existence in, 117
   employed as a synonym for the "grave," 165
   gates of, 133
   Job intensifying traditional ways of describing, 91–92
   Job on the pain and suffering of, 97
   as a land from which there is no return, 74
   reference to the entrance of, 260
   time in as a pressed service, 114
   Zophar mentioning, 398
shining of the Sun, as a symbol of propriety, 209
Shlomo Yitahaqi. *See* Rashi
Shreiner, Susan, 33
Shuah, 76
silence
   of God, 41, 240–41
   Job reduced to, 270
"simple and upright," Job as, 17
Simundson, Daniel, 65, 67, 81
sin(s)
   Job wanting the particulars of his, 109
   making man subject to corruption, 114–17
   relationship with subsequent retribution, 165
   represented by tally stones placed in a bag, 115
sincerity and uprightness, of Job, 9
Sirach, 2
Sitidos, as Job's wife, 2
skin, afflicted with boils and worms, 144
"skin for skin," views on the meaning of, 54–56
skin of his teeth, 145
slaves, 206, 207
sleep, Job lacking, 132
small pox, as Job's disease, 57, 58
snares and traps, terms related to, 137
snow, kept in store by God, 261
social immortality, 397, 398

social isolation, of Job, 201
society, hostility of, 201–2
Sodom, people of stingy with travelers, 157
Sommi, Leone Judah de, 29
sons of God, 50–51
"Sophar." *See* Zophar
sores, descriptions of those of Job, 73
soul, 114, 116
South Wind, in the Old Testament, 123
"Southern View," for the location of Uz, 48–49
sovereignty of God, Calvin's overriding principle of, 34
Spalatin, George, friend of Luther, 32
Spanheim, Frederick, 78
Spark, Muriel, 62
Spinoza, Baruch, 13, 29–31
"spit," as a hapax in Job, 130
spitting in the face, as "a grievous insult," 130
springs of the sea, as subterranean depths, 260
stars, fading before the oncoming light of the day, 260
status in society, of Job, 198
Stevenson, W. B., 66, 68, 164, 176, 184
STN, Semitic root meaning "Adversary," "Opponent," or "Accuser," 51
"stocks," as a *hapax* of the book, 110
Stories of the Prophets (Al-Thabani), 24
storms, accompanying appearances of Yahweh, 258
Strahan, R. H., 153
Strigel, V., 219
stubborn of heart, God despising, 247
Stuhlmann, M. H., 216
suffering
   being humble and patient in the face of, 4
   coming to those who have sinned, 7
   demonic forces view explaining Job's, 52, 53, 59
   developing moral character, 7, 248
   Devil as the source of Ayyub's, 5
   divine plan view of, xiii, 94, 234
   Elihu on, 15, 212, 229–30, 245, 250, 251
   God gave peace to Job in his, 109
   God understanding Job's, 213
   God using evil and, 212, 213
   of the impious, 80
   of Job, 129, 138, 158, 199
   Job describing his, 72
   Job's children as the cause of, xii, 77
   moral qualities view on, 7
   original sin response to Job's, 113
   "pedagogical purpose" of, 222
   in the present time, 199–204
   as punishment, 78–79

Rashi on the pain of Job's, 110
retributive justice theory causing Job's, 94, 234
   of the righteous, 86, 247
Satan as the source of Job's, xii–xiii
sent by God for the wholesome discipline of his children, 221
in Sheol, 97
sin not the cause of Job's, 243
sources of, xii–xiv
Talmud on the origins of, 3
teleological understandings of, 9
test perspective on, xiii
test theodicy of Job's, 234
testing character, 6
suffering and providence, confronting the issue of, 18, 34
"sulphur," for "disinfectant purposes," 138
Summa Contra Gentiles (Thomas Aquinas), 20
Summa Theologica (Thomas Aquinas), 20
sun, words signifying in the Book of Job, 83
superiority, air of from Job's friends, 104
Susman, Margarete, 40, 41
sympathy, having no place in the heart of Elihu, 235
syphilis, diagnosis of Job's disease being, 57
Syriac words, in the Book of Job, 304–7, 390
Szana, Jim, 45

Talmud. *See also* Babylonian Talmud
   central questions about Job, 2, 3
   earliest references to Leviathan, 289
   negative view of Elihu, 217
tam, signifying the opposite of "guilty," 49
tam va yashar, various understandings of, 49
Targum, 158, 296
Targum of Job, 59, 68, 116
teeth, of Leviathan, 283
teleological view of ethics (divine plan), 214
tenuousness of life, motivating Job's direct appeal to God, 74
Terrien, Samuel
   on the angel-mediator, 230
   on chapter 31, 204
   on a dead man as unaware of the fate of his progeny, 116
   on death coming indiscriminately to all men alike, 164
   describing the opening of the psalm to wisdom, 192
   on Elihu, 224, 225, 241
   on God chastening man by physical pain, 229–30
   on God destroying the wicked, 163
   on God refusing to go to trial with Job, 238
   on Job addressing his divine tormentor, 202
   on Job as wrong in thinking that God is deaf to his appeals, 229
   on Job's first response to Zophar, 98
   on Job's theme of his own social isolation, 201
   on the parts of chapter 30, 199
   on the parts of chapter 35, 242
   on the parts of chapter 36, 246
   on textual corruption, 148
   on wisdom as the supreme possession of God, 193
terrors, turning upon Job, 202
Tertullian, "On Patience," 16
test perspective
   Elihu and, 212, 213, 249–50, 398
   on evil and suffering testing moral character, xiii
   Freehof endorsing, 234
test theodicy
   in chapter 22, 167
   Devine as an advocate of, 53
   Rashi endorsing, 9
   regarding Job's suffering, 234
   Thomas à Kempis reference to, 22
   using evil and suffering to "test" character, 6
   version of, 7, 175
Testament of Job
   on Bildad (Baldas), 134
   closer to the Septuagint version of Job, 2
   on Elihu, 216, 217
   on Job's disease as leprosy, 57
testimony, of Job's conscience, 125
testing, words needing, 234–35
textual difficulties, Christian interpreters pointing to, 152
theodicy, 7, 292
Theodore of Mopsuestia, 16, 34, 216
theological views, of the characters in the Book of Job, 397–98
theology, as the primary aspect of Bildad's first speech, 77
theophanies, use of hail in, 261
theophany, preparing the way for, 256
third round of speeches, organization of (chapter 22-27), 181–82
Thomas, David, 54–55, 136, 139
"Though He Slay Me, Yet I Will Hope in Him" (Beirler), 107
throne of the universe, Job invited to assume, 272
thunder, as the voice of God, 252
thunder storm, transition to the winter frost, 253
Tibbon, Samuel Ibn, 76
"time of service," meaning warfare, 72

443

Tissot, James, 94
Tobit. *See* Book of Tobit
Tollerton, David C., 44
Tophet, where human sacrifices were made to Moloch, 130
Torah
    Book of Job having the authority of, 26, 29
    could not have been written by Moses according to Spinoza, 30
Tractatus Theologico-Philosophicus (Spinoza), 29–31
The Tragic Life (Zapffe), 41
transgressions, God forgiving, 232
treatment of Job, harmonizing with divine omniscience and exultation, 88
tree, representing hope for new growth, 114
The Trial (Kafka), parallel structure and plot with the book of Job, 42
troops, of God, 183
trouble, encompassing the unjust, 120
truisms, series of, 132
truth, placing trust in, 122
Tsevat, Matitiahu, 65
Tur-Sinai, N. H., 56, 76, 77, 110, 155
twentieth century, staggering number of literary depictions and adaptations, 42–43
Tyndale, John, 69–70

Ugaritic god Mot, god of death, 137
Ugaritic words, in the Book of Job, 304-7, 389
Umbreit, F. W. C., 52, 69, 135
understanding, shunning evil as the introduction to, 194
undeserved punishment, Job's idea of, 172
unrighteousness of God's conduct, Job attacking, 105–6
"uplifted arm," as the "Navigator's Line," 260
uprightness, Job developing his, 205–6

valleys, near-east armies often formed in, 268
Van Heck, 111
vanity, of Job arguments, 245–46
Venerable Bede, 20, 219
venom of the cobra, food turning into, 156
"vexation," as the sense of undeserved treatment, 68
Vicar of Wakefield (Goldsmith), 35
victims, plight of, 178
Vilna Gaon, on great deeds, 84
violence, 110, 209–10, 279
virtue, Job clinging to, 236
vocabulary
    in chapter 36, 251
    designating "secret" and "secrets," 119
    of Elihu, 214, 215, 216, 233, 252
    of Hymn to Wisdom, 194
    legal, 173
    of words related to "dark" and "darkness," 92
Vulgate, spelling Bildad's name as "Baldad," 134
vulnerability, symbols of, 178
"vulture," word for, 269

Walafred of Strabo (808-849), 19, 20
Walkley, Charles Thomas, 53, 150
Wall Scroll, on the location of Uz, 48
war horse, description of, 268–69
warning, not to rouse Leviathan, 282
water, not given to the fainting, 168
waters of creation, controlling the primeval, 186
Watson, Robert
    on Job's wife, 62
    on a man being just, 86
    on the meaning for God's first speech, 257
    on the ordering of beasts, 263
    on skin for skin as hide for skin, 54
"way of the righteous," leading to "the light," 180
weapons, useless to bring against Leviathan, 285
weaver's shuttle, image of, 73
Weiser, A., 66
Weiss, Paul, 222
Weitzstein, Johan G., 36
Wesley, John
    on the corruption of the grave, 132
    on crying out but not being heard, 141
    on Eliphaz, 67, 118, 123
    on falsehood, 166
    on fat meaning to pamper himself, 121
    on fears, 120
    on God watching over holy men, 120
    on the *Goel* passage, 149
    on hope, 133
    on the number ten as "many times," 141
    on the shadow of a man, 130
    on sinning against God with a high hand, 120–21
    on wicked men, 162
    on a wise man uttering vain knowledge, 117
West Semitic words, in the Book of Job, 389
"When Job Sued God" (Greenstein), 399
whirlwind, 214, 252, 257, 270
the wicked
    annihilation of, 140
    cutting off, 180, 273–74
    denying divine Providence, 170
    despairing of deliverance, 120
    of the flood, 160
    God separating from the humble poor, 247

having no reason to reject God, 162
having no stability, 181
Job and Christ delivered into the hands of, 125
judgment of, 165–66, 180–81
left the poor to their fate, 157
like "a well watered plant," 80
living long and prosperous lives, 161
meeting with a terrible end, 139
memory of shall be lost, 139
portion of, 157–58
power to crush, 273
prosperity of, 161–62
ruin of, 136–40, 155–57
short joy of, 153–55
shunning the light, 179–80
theme of punishment of, 121
transfixed by a spear or a bow, 158
way of as like darkness, 180
words and actions of under the cover of darkness, 259
wicked man
    exploiting and oppressing the weak and the unfortunate, 180
    fate of, 139
    given an elaborate funeral, 159
    memory of vanishing from the Earth, 138
    not caring about his house after his death, 164
    scared in the day of his calamity, 165
    as torn away from his home, 138
wickedness, 140, 177–78
widows and orphans, stealing of the goods of, 178
Wiesel, Eli, 294
wild ass, 265–66
wild beast, taking its prey in its teeth, 107
"wild goats," found in the high mountains, 264–65
wild ox, great strength of, 266
wind, 117, 253, 261
"Wind of the wilderness," East Wind as, 122
wineskins, meanings of, 225
wisdom
    of the ancients, 169
    contrasting with things in the world, 191
    due to "the spirit in man," 224
    female personification of, 96
    with God alone, 101
    God outwitting human, 102
    Job boasting of, 117
    Job not having a monopoly on, 119
    Job raising questions about divine, 159
    leading to successes, 102

man not finding true, 190
in the minds of the living, 262
poem on the inaccessibility of, 192
preciousness of, 193
receptiveness to, 224
as superior to everything in the world, 194
Wisdom Literature
    comparisons of a lifetime to a shadow in, 79
    images of light and darkness, 136
    plant metaphors in, 79–80
    tam and *yashar* used throughout, 49
    techniques in employed by Bildad, 77
    words often seen in, 251
wisdom of the ages, 104
"wisdom of the Fathers" approach, 78
wisdom of the fathers motif
    instance of, 193
    mentioned by Eliphaz, 397
    Rashi alluding to, 169
    used by Chrysostom, 118
    Zophar appealing to, 154
wisdom of the sages motif, use of, 120
the wise, enjoying peace, 120
"without guile and upright," Job as, 21
witness(es), 90–91, 127, 147
wonders of God, 250–51, 254
"word" and "words," terms used for by Elihu, 215
words
    disdainful striking Job on the cheek, 125
    of Job as once authoritative and final, 198
    of knowledge, 227
    need to test, 234–35
    without knowledge, 258
works
    of creation, 88, 250–51
    literary, 31, 35
    of nature, 83
world, spreading over empty space, 185
worms, words used for, 184
worship, after the angel's successful mediation, 231
worthless men, irreverence of, 199–201
wrath, 69, 152, 249
the wretched, clinging to a rock, 178
Wycliffe, John, 127, 152, 159, 166, 179, 190

Yagel, Abraham, 29
yahtop, disagreement about, 84
Yahweh
    accompanied by storms, 258
    following the Plan of, 259
    as God in the epilogue, 295
    Job declining to answer, 271
    Job's obedience to the Law of, 401

INDEX

Yahweh *(continued)*
    Job's response to the first speech of, 270
    Job's second response to, 291–97
    reprimanding Job, 399
    shown as a master of sarcasm, 260
    speaking from the whirlwind, 257
    theological positions of, 398
    use of the word, 100
Yalom, Marilyn, feminist account of Job's spouse, 63
yashar, moral understanding, comparable to "going straight," 49
Yaws, as Job's disease, 58
Yemeni Jews, as the earliest medieval Muslim sources on Prophet Ayyub, 23–24

Zapffe, Peter Wessel, 40, 41
Ziz, large monstrous bird, 275, 287
Zophar
    appealing to Job to restore hope and security, 96
    appealing to the wisdom of the fathers motif, 154
    bearing the least status of the friends, 93
    as a conservative, born-again preacher in *J.B.*, 94
    demanding that Job humble himself, 97
    desiring to reply, 154
    on the Divine Will, 12
    on the fate of the wicked, 97
    first speech (chapter 11), 92–97
    on his thoughts as artificial, 153
    ironic barbs of, 155
    Job first response to, 98–117
    lack of a third speech of, 187
    origins of his name, 92
    passionate and intemperate speech of, 153
    on retribution theory, 93
    second speech (chapter 20), 152–58
    sermon against pride, 154
    theological positions of, 398
    on the unlikeliness of an empty-headed person getting understanding, 96
    on the wicked dying prematurely, 161
"Zophar Condemns Job" (painting), 94
Zoroastrianism, 209

www.ingramcontent.com/pod-product-compliance
Lightning Source LLC
Chambersburg PA
CBHW081145290426
44108CB00018B/2445